THE CRIME AND THE SILENCE

T0057991

FARRAR, STRAUS AND GIROUX   NEW YORK

THE
CRIME
AND THE
SILENCE

CONFRONTING THE MASSACRE OF
JEWS IN WARTIME JEDWABNE

ANNA BIKONT

TRANSLATED FROM THE POLISH BY ALISSA VALLES

Farrar, Straus and Giroux
18 West 18th Street, New York 10011

Originally published in Polish in 2004 by Wydawnictwo Prószyński i Ska,
Poland, as *My z Jedwabnego*
English translation published in the United States by Farrar, Straus and Giroux
First American edition, 2015

Frontispiece map copyright © Magdalena Korotyńska.

Grateful acknowledgment is made for permission to reprint "Mr. Cogito Seeks Advice," from
The Collected Poems: 1956–1998, by Zbigniew Herbert. Translated and edited by Alissa Valles.
Copyright © 2007 by the Estate of Zbigniew Herbert. Translation copyright © 2007 by
HarperCollins Publishers LLC. Reprinted by permission of HarperCollins Publishers.

Library of Congress Cataloging-in-Publication Data
Bikont, Anna.
[My z Jedwabnego. English]
The crime and the silence : confronting the massacre of Jews in wartime Jedwabne / Anna
Bikont ; translated from the Polish by Alissa Valles. — First American edition.
pages   cm
"Originally published in Polish in 2004 by Wydawnictwo Prószyński i Ska, Poland,
as My z Jedwabnego"—Title page verso.
ISBN 978-0-374-53637-4 — ISBN 978-0-374-71032-3 (e-book)
1. Holocaust, Jewish (1939–1945)—Poland—Jedwabne.   2. Jews—Poland—
Jedwabne—History—20th century.   3. Bikont, Anna—Diaries.   4. Jedwabne (Poland)—
Ethnic relations—History—20th century.   5. Jedwabne (Poland)—Biography.
6. Collective memory—Poland—Jedwabne.   I. Title.

DS134.66.J43 B4513 2015
940.53'1844—dc23

2014046631

Designed by Abby Kagan

Farrar, Straus and Giroux books may be purchased for educational, business, or
promotional use. For information on bulk purchases, please contact the Macmillan
Corporate and Premium Sales Department at 1-800-221-7945, extension 5442,
or write to specialmarkets@macmillan.com.

www.fsgbooks.com
www.twitter.com/fsgbooks • www.facebook.com/fsgbooks

P1

This publication has been subsidized by Instytut Książki—the ©POLAND Translation Program.

Contents

THE CRIME AND THE SILENCE

Journal

AUGUST 28, 2000

"It's a lie that Poles killed the Jews in Jedwabne," says Tadeusz Ś., a retired doctor from Warsaw and an eyewitness to the events of July 10, 1941.

My boss, Adam Michnik, the editor in chief of the *Gazeta Wyborcza*, receives this visitor in his office. When Adam informed me that according to Tadeusz Ś., who was referred to him by a friend, the crime committed in Jedwabne could not be blamed on the Poles, I heard in his voice both excitement and relief. I knew he hadn't been able to come to terms with the facts revealed by Jan Tomasz Gross in *Neighbors*. We'd talked about it many times. Before Gross's book appeared in May 2000, I'd said in a *Gazeta* editorial meeting that we should report on the little town confronting the crime from its wartime past.

Gross reconstructs events on the basis of three different sources: postwar testimony given by Szmul Wasersztejn, court papers from the postwar trial in which the defendants were charged with collaborating with the occupation forces, and the *Jedwabne Book of Memory*, recollections of Jewish emigrants from Jedwabne recorded in the United States. He draws tough conclusions and formulates even tougher hypotheses. In Jedwabne, Poles burned all the town's Jews in a barn, a total of sixteen hundred people. "It was a collective murder in both senses of the word," writes Gross, "in terms of the number of victims and of their persecutors."

Adam rejected all my proposals to go to Jedwabne. Nor did he want to publish excerpts from Gross's book before it was released. Now he wants me to hear for myself what really happened. He has insisted that I be present at this meeting, although Tadeusz Ś. wanted to meet with him alone. Our visitor doesn't allow us to record the conversation or print his surname. Reluctantly he agrees to let me take notes. In 1941 he was fifteen. He happened to be in Jedwabne on July 10. He says he was on his way to the dentist.

"In the morning two Germans in black Gestapo uniforms rode into the market square on motorcycles. From a balcony I watched them ordering the Jews to assemble. They put the rabbi's black hat on a stick to mock him. I followed the Jews all the way to the barn."

"How many Germans did you see at the barn?" asked Adam.

"Three. Germans like to do things properly, so they had the barn owner brought out to open it with a key, though they could have just lifted the doors out."

"And that was all done by three Germans?"

"There were probably more of them in plainclothes. There were three in uniform, with handguns. I saw the Jews go into the barn of their own accord, as if they were under hypnosis."

"And they didn't try to escape when it was on fire?"

"No, they didn't. It's horrible."

"Did any Poles take part in this crime?"

"No, none."

"In every society there's some criminal element. Pick up any newspaper, you'll find plenty of reports on rapes, murders. During the occupation there were *szmalcowniks*, people who blackmailed Jews in hiding."

"Only in big cities. You don't know the provinces. It's native-born Poles, the impoverished gentry, who live there. They wouldn't think to take revenge on the Jews for betraying Poles to the Soviets. At the barn they were shouting: 'Get yourselves out of there, Yids!' There were just three Germans standing there with sawed-off shotguns, not even rifles. The older people who were there thought it was wrong. They talked about it at church the week after."

"They thought they themselves had been wrong?"

"No, the Jews. Not one of them had it in him to turn on the Germans."

"The Poles thought the victims were in the wrong?"

"For not defending themselves."

"But if someone is being murdered in front of me, I should come to his aid, right? And if I don't, because I'm scared, or stunned, because the situation is too much for me, I'd blame myself, not the victims."

"Poles would have helped them if they'd fought back against the Germans. When the Jews grabbed rifles and went around town under the Soviets, they were real tough guys, but when the Germans took them to the barn, what did they do? Folks get offended if you get them caught up in something like that. The Jews should have defended themselves. People called them cowards because they waited for the Poles to defend them and didn't do anything for themselves. But saying that there were sixteen hundred people in there is a lie and a joke."

"And how many of them do you think there were?" I interject.

"A thousand, no more," Tadeusz Ś. replies. I look at Adam and see his face go pale.

At the end Ś. warns us again: "Please don't mention my name. I don't want those Jewish vultures to lie in wait for me at my house."

SEPTEMBER 1, 2000

The Institute of National Remembrance announces it is launching an investigation into the Jedwabne massacre. When I run into Adam Michnik in the hallway at the *Gazeta Wyborcza*, he tells me that the conversation with Tadeusz Ś. haunts him. He suggests I use it as the basis for a short story set in the town of J. during the war. But I don't write fiction.

I decide to put in a request for a year's unpaid leave and go to Jedwabne for myself, if I can't do it for the *Gazeta*. There must be a memory of the atrocity in the town, there must be some witnesses. I will try to reconstruct the facts, but also what happened to the memory of those events over the last sixty years.

SEPTEMBER 5, 2000

The Jewish Historical Institute in Warsaw. I hold five little pages written in a sprawling hand, with certain words crossed out. It's Szmul Wasersztejn's Jedwabne testimony, translated from the Yiddish. "Infants were murdered at their mothers' breasts, people were brutally beaten and forced to sing and dance. Bloodied and maimed, they were all herded into the barn. Then gas was poured on the barn and it was set afire. Afterward thugs went by Jewish homes, looking for the sick and the children left behind. The sick they carried to the barn themselves, children they hung in pairs by their little legs and dragged them there on their backs, then lifted them with pitchforks and heaved them into the hot furnace of the barn."

SEPTEMBER 6, 2000

The *Jedwabne Book of Memory* was edited by two rabbis, the brothers Julius and Jacob Baker, who emigrated from Jedwabne to America before the war; for twenty years only a hundred copies existed. Today I read it on the Internet. In the book I find testimonies about 15 Tamuz 5701—or July 10, 1941—recorded by Rivka Vogel ("Goys cut off the head of Gitele, Judka Nadolnik's daughter, and kicked it around like a soccer ball"), Itzchok Newmark ("With a song on their lips, the Poles poured gas on the barn crammed with Jews"), Awigdor Kochaw ("A gang of boys beat me mercilessly and dragged me into the market square; they hounded and savagely beat the tortured, hungry, and thirsty people who were fainting from standing all day in the burning sun"), and Herschel, the third Baker brother from Goniądz, about forty kilometers northeast of Jedwabne ("Completely exhausted, my mother reached Goniądz on July 14; fleeing from the massacre, she ran from Jedwabne through the fields and forests . . . She was beside herself after what she'd seen, Poles destroying all the Jews.")

SEPTEMBER 28, 2000

On a trip to Wilno with a group of friends, Irena Grudzińska Gross among them. She says that a few years ago Jan Gross wanted to include Szmul Wasersztejn's testimony in a Polish edition of his essay collection *The Ghostly Decade*. Irena read it and advised him to leave it out. How can you believe something as monstrous as that on the basis of a single testimony?

NOVEMBER 17, 2000

An interview with the historian Tomasz Szarota in the *Gazeta Wyborcza*. He accuses Gross of not even attempting to explain why "fifteen hundred persons in the prime of life, led to their deaths by fewer than a hundred men armed only with sticks, didn't try to defend themselves or at the very least to escape."

It's hard to understand how Szarota, author of an excellent book on pogroms in Nazi-occupied Europe, could bring himself to utter those words. There were elderly people in that crowd, women with infants, toddlers holding on to their mothers' skirts (Jewish families were often large), whereas young men were scarce—from Wasersztejn's testimony it emerges that they had been killed earlier that day. How many examples does Szarota know of a crowd of people led to slaughter rebelling and attacking its executioners?

In the investigation conducted in the late sixties and early seventies, prosecutor Waldemar Monkiewicz of the Main Commission for the Investigation of Nazi Crimes claimed a unit of 232 Germans led by Wolfgang Birkner had arrived in Jedwabne that day, July 10. Referring to this claim, Szarota reproaches Gross for not having studied the role of the Germans in the atrocity: "I doubt that the prosecutor plucked those 232 Germans out of the air, or the trucks for that matter, or the figure of Wolfgang Birkner. In any case it can't be right that the name Birkner isn't mentioned once in Gross's book."

Personally, I would approach any investigation conducted in the late 1960s, at the time of an anti-Semitic campaign orchestrated by the state, with extreme caution. Gross had testimonies from the 1949 trial at hand. How is it that not one of the witnesses noticed a convoy of trucks? I don't know how many Germans were there by the barn in Jedwabne, but Tadeusz Ś., who was trying to convince Adam Michnik that the Poles were innocent, saw three of them.

NOVEMBER 21, 2000

I'm told a man phoned the *Gazeta* saying he was prepared to talk about Radziłów. I call him back. Jan Skrodzki now lives in Gdańsk, but is originally from Radziłów, eighteen kilometers from Jedwabne. Three days before the massacre in Jedwabne, the whole Jewish population of Radziłów was rounded up and burned.

On July 7, 1941, he was a small boy and watched from behind the curtains as Jews were driven to their deaths. He saw no Germans. He tells me, "I feel responsible for Jedwabne, for Radziłów, for everything that may still come out." We agree I'll go to see him in Gdańsk.

NOVEMBER 23, 2000

At the Jewish Historical Institute I read Menachem Finkelsztejn's testimony on the burning of the Jewish community in Radziłów. And there—he testifies—the perpetrators were Poles. I struggle through horrific scenes of rape, beatings, children thrown into the burning barn, a Jewish girl's head hacked off with a saw, and I want to believe that the horror itself made survivors exaggerate and overstate the facts.

In an attempt to understand the outburst of barbarity, Finkelsztejn writes, "The grain of hatred fell on fertile soil, expertly primed by the clergy over many years. The desire to get hold of Jewish business and Jewish riches further whetted the locals' appetites."

NOVEMBER 24, 2000

A colloquium of historians discusses Gross's book at the Polish Academy of Sciences. From the threshold one feels an emotional charge rare at scholarly gatherings in Poland.

Tomasz Szarota presents the current state of knowledge on Jedwabne. He cites a number of publications authenticating the claim that the Białystok commando unit led by Birkner was operating in Jedwabne. But there is just one source, namely prosecutor Monkiewicz, who repeated this over and over, at every opportunity, as he did at the celebration of the 250th anniversary of Jedwabne's town charter.

Gross introduces a different tone. He speaks sharply, frankly, ironically. He reminds Szarota of a meeting in May, at which Monkiewicz declared that Poles had not killed Jews in the Białystok district in July 1941, nor aided in their killing, and that there had been just one instance in which Germans forced Poles to join hands, and that was to form a chain to prevent Jews from escaping.

"I realized we could dismiss the prosecutor," says Gross. "It's a sad state of affairs when an academic authority like Tomasz Szarota lends credence to a muddled version of the tragedy in Jedwabne by bringing Monkiewicz's views into wide circulation. We talked about this, Tomasz," he addresses Szarota directly, "and I told you Birkner being in Jedwabne was an invention and you should forget about Monkiewicz."

After several people have drawn attention to the scholarly shortcomings of Gross's book, Marek Edelman steps up to the microphone. "Everybody here would like to find some proof that Gross is a shoddy historian, that he made a mistake and Mr. So-and-So was killed earlier and Mrs. Such-and-Such later. But that's not what this is about," says the last living leader of the Warsaw Ghetto Uprising. "Jedwabne was not the first case, nor was it an isolated one. In Poland at that time the mood was ripe for killing Jews. And it wasn't all about looting. There's something in man that makes him like killing."

Professor Jerzy Jedlicki, who is moderating the discussion, speaks: "Hatred toward Jews, contempt and mockery of Jews, are part of twentieth-century Central European culture, and that includes Poland. By that I don't mean to say everybody would have been prepared to commit atrocities. But the destruction of the Jews was watched with amusement by a significant part of the local Polish population. That amusement, the laughter that accompanied the Holocaust—I remember it, because at that time I was on the other, Aryan side of the wall. Until today, our stance, and I include myself in this, has been a flight from the subject, a cowardly fear of the darkness lurking in our collective history. With his books, Gross rouses us from our torpor. And that's the most important thing."

The colloquium lasts almost five hours, and at times it's like a group therapy session. A young Polish staff member of the Holocaust Museum in Washington, D.C., speaking of the tide of hatred toward Jews that she's encountered during the year she's been in Poland reading archival materials, bursts into tears.

NOVEMBER 25, 2000
There wouldn't have been so many people in Jedwabne prepared to kill if they hadn't felt the support of like-minded others and of the authorities. A psychology professor writing this in the *Gazeta* refers to studies showing that Poles treat their own national suffering as a kind of special contribution or investment for which the world is more in debt to them than it is to others. "We see ourselves as exceptional, ascribe to ourselves moral achievements, a unique contribution to world history. Studies show that people who think this way more readily accept the killing of innocents."

At Jacek Kuroń's. I tell him about the conference of historians. Jacek's memory accords with Edelman's: a social climate permitting harassment of Jews. In Lvov he saw with his own eyes how young people threw stones into the ghetto. It didn't shock anyone, and he heard the same refrain all around him: "Hitler's doing the job for us."

"Even the Holocaust didn't change that," says Jacek. And he tells me about living in Kraków in the summer of 1945 with his parents, grand-parents, and younger brother, Felek. One day on a walk his grandfather tugged Felek's hand and the child began to cry. Right away a crowd started to gather, yanking the elderly man back and challenging him. They thought he was a Jew and the boy a Polish child who was going to be turned into matzo. Just because Felek was blond and his grandfather wore a cap. Not long after there was a pogrom in Kraków.

"Hatred," Jacek goes on, "comes from a person having a subconscious feeling of guilt. At some level he knows a whole people was destroyed here, and he benefited from it, because he's got a house or at least a pillow that belonged to a Jew. He won't face up to it and hatred takes root in him."

He quotes a passage from a text published in the *Gazeta* by Jacek Ża-kowski, a prominent political commentator: "Jan Gross speaks for himself, and I for myself. None of us has the right to reproach another for what happened to his compatriots or ancestors." "Nothing good ever came of people not feeling responsible," Jacek comments.

DECEMBER 5, 2000

A letter to Adam Michnik from Kazimierz Laudański. The older brother of Jerzy and Zygmunt Laudański, who were sentenced to fifteen and twelve years in prison respectively, for the killing of Jews in Jedwabne, presents his version of events. In it, the Germans are the main protago-nists, actors, whereas the Jewish Communists "together with the NKVD drew up lists of Polish families for deportation to Siberia."

One can't help asking: if we accept that the crime was committed by the Germans, what can it have to do with Jews denouncing Poles to the NKVD?

Protesting the vilification of his brothers, Kazimierz Laudański praises his family's patriotism.

Jan Gross, who read the documents in the case conducted against the Jedwabne murderers after the war, found among them a letter from Zyg-munt Laudański to the Communist authorities, describing how he had been an NKVD informant during the Soviet occupation and had joined the Polish Workers Party after the war. "It is on shoulders like these that our labor system can be built," he wrote. Gross was struck by "the relent-less conformism of a man who tries to anticipate the expectations of each successive regime in an age of gas ovens and engages himself to the hilt each time—first as an NKVD informant, then as a Jew-killer, finally by joining the Polish Workers Party."

Kazimierz concludes his letter to Michnik with the words "We were and are always prepared to serve our country *pro publico bono*." This is apparently too much for Adam. The embargo is lifted. I phone Laudański to arrange an interview for the *Gazeta*.

DECEMBER 9, 2000

Pisz, a hundred kilometers north of Jedwabne. Kazimierz Laudański is waiting for me at the turnoff to the little road leading to his house. Before we even reach the house he has asked me where my parents are from and what my mother's surname was. There was nothing wrong with my mother's maiden name, and her first name was also just as it should be. At least after a Pole who was in love with her got her Aryan papers and a baptism certificate, and married her. That's how Lea Horowicz disappeared in Lvov in 1942. She disappeared so completely that I only learned of my origins as an adult by accident, standing in the street.

My mother didn't keep in touch with her family; no uncle or cousin ever visited our house. I accepted that my mother, an independent-minded, rebellious person, found family ties and gatherings a boring, middle-class obligation that she didn't feel like fulfilling. Only when I was fully grown and graduated from college did I meet a man in his fifties at our dacha outside Warsaw, whom my mother introduced as the son of her beloved sister murdered in the Soviet Union in 1937, at the time of the Great Purge. I was with friends, so I just said hello to him and ran on to the river. A few years passed before I saw him again. I told him he was the only relative I knew on my mother's side—perhaps he knew something about our family? "Our grandfather Hirsz Horowicz . . . ," my cousin Oleś Wołyński began.

I systematically called all the friends and acquaintances in my address book from *A* to *Z*. "I'm Jewish," I announced. Somehow the fact didn't make much of an impression on anyone but me, though a Solidarity advisor I knew suggested we not take any more people of Jewish origin on at the editorial office of the *Tygodnik Masowsze* (Masowsze Weekly), Solidarity's underground paper, which I had cofounded. ("There are so many of you already, and if you get caught, it might hurt the cause," he said—but in good faith and with genuine concern, not hostility.) The biggest surprise was that most of my friends already "knew." If only because the mother of one of them had been in the same class as my mother at a renowned Jewish gymnasium, or high school, before the war.

"Why did no one tell me?" I asked them. One of them was convinced I knew but had decided to pass for a hundred percent Polish (I'd often asked him what it was like being Jewish). Another friend thought it was up to my mother to reveal my origins (he apparently accepted the supposition—to him self-evident—that Jewishness was something shameful that had to be "revealed"). A third concluded that if I didn't know, I was better off.

Kazimierz Laudański invites me into the house. A well-kept villa in the center of town, elegant china on the table. He's prepared for me a map of the town as it was in 1941, drawn on graph paper. The street names, churches, cemeteries are marked in blue pen, the synagogue and barn in red. Of the massacre in Jedwabne, he says it resulted from German orders. When I ask how many Germans were there, I'm told there was a uniformed German on every corner. I ask him to point out on the map where they stood. He draws four little crosses. Four Germans.

"The Jews in Jedwabne, whether they were burned that day or not, their fate was sealed," Kazimierz Laudański says. "The Germans would have killed them sooner or later. Such a small thing and they slap it on the Poles, on my brothers of all people. We forgave the Gestapo, we forgave the NKVD, and here we have a little quarrel between Jews and Poles and no one can forgive?" Laudański goes on: "It's not about defending my brothers. They were tried, rightly or wrongly, and you can't convict them again for the same thing. I'm meeting you so you can tell Mr. Michnik that we shouldn't be reopening old wounds. It's not right to make our people out to be criminals. It's wicked to accuse Poles of such things. And it's not the time to launch a campaign to teach the Poles what's right, when Jewish finance is attacking Poland."

I persuade Kazimierz Laudański that to write a piece for the paper I need to meet his brothers, too. We agree that I'll come back.

DECEMBER 10, 2000

Kazimierz Mocarski, a retired school director who before the war lived in Nadbory, a village ten kilometers from Jedwabne, wrote a letter to the editor of the *Gazeta*. I visit him in his little town on the Baltic Sea.

In his letter he described prewar Jedwabne: "Times were hard, we counted every penny. The richer Jewish shops could afford lower prices. The Poles reacted by knocking down stalls and smashing windows. Poisonous anti-Semitism, myths about Jews killing Christ, drove some of the people crazy with hatred."

He was fourteen at the time. He remembers that two days before the massacre a group of Jews passed by his house. "My mother was baking rye bread and gave them two loaves. She warned them, 'Run as far away as you can,' because we already knew the Jews had been burned in Radziłów the day before."

He knows from his mother that some of the peasants in their village saddled their horses and went to Jedwabne in the hope of looting Jewish stores and workshops, while a few people who didn't want to take part in the pogrom fled from Jedwabne to relatives in the surrounding villages. A few days after the burning he was invited by a friend bragging about having moved with his family into a house that had belonged to Jews. He heard about the Jews having been beaten, rounded up, forced to say Christian prayers.

"I go to Jedwabne sometimes," he continues, "it's an unhappy place, backward, without infrastructure. There are no jobs, people are crushed, they feel they're victims. One of the slogans of the National Party before the war was that Jews were the cause of poverty. Now there are no Jews, but the poverty is the same."

I return to Warsaw by a circuitous route—via Jedwabne. I want to visit Leon Dziedzic, a farmer from near Jedwabne who has given several press interviews. This is rare in Jedwabne; generally the residents refuse to talk to journalists. From Dziedzic's account it emerges that Poles not only carried out but also initiated the killing. "They say that the next day the German police station commandant flew into a rage at the Poles who'd led the pogrom: 'You said you'd clean up the Jews, but you don't know how to clean up a damn thing.' He meant they hadn't buried the remains and he was afraid of infection spreading, because it was hot and the dogs were already getting to them," Dziedzic explained.

But Leon Dziedzic has left Poland. From the time an article about him appeared, for which he'd allowed himself to be photographed, whenever he rode his bike to a store, someone would puncture his tires. He went to the States, where his wife and four sons had lived for many years.

I find Leszek Dziedzic, the fifth son, who stayed on the farm. This fall he was visiting his family in the States while his wife stayed in Poland with their children, ten-year-old Tomek and fourteen-year-old Piotrek. "I came back earlier than I'd planned because I was worried for my wife and children after what my dad had said. And on the street people were saying: 'Don't think you can get away, we're ready for you.' We fear for our kids. We take them to school and pick them up."

I go to see Janina Biedrzycka, the daughter of Śleszynski, the man who owned the barn in which the Jews were burned. I already know how she's received previous uninvited guests. First she refused to let a film director in, and the next time she told her, "I thought you were a Jewess but the priest told me you were Evangelical. There were decent Evangelicals among the Germans." She met a local reporter with the words "Do you have any ID? You don't have a Polish name. I don't care either way because they all listen to the Jews anyway, nobody wants to know the truth."

"There are houses that belonged to the Jews in Jedwabne, but I live in my own," she begins the conversation with me. "I didn't get anything out of it. I know how vengeful the Yids are."

She can't say the word "Jew" in anything under a shriek. Of the atrocity, she says it was the work of the Germans.

DECEMBER 15, 2000

I visit my cousin Oleś Wołyński. Gross's book didn't shock Oleś. The idea of Jews being murdered by their neighbors was a plausible scenario.

Before the war, Oleś's mother and father were active in the Communist International and Oleś spent the first years of his life in Moscow. When his parents fell victim to the Great Purge—both were shot in 1937—he was put in an orphanage, and from there he went to the Lubyanka prison and then to the Gulag.

"In Siberia I didn't encounter any anti-Semitism," he says. "I first heard anti-Semitic talk in 1954 in Mińsk, still in the Soviet Union. In the hospital where I wound up, the nurses were talking over my head about a friend of theirs who was marrying a Jew. 'I would throw up if I had to go to bed with a Jew,' I heard one of them say. After repatriation to Poland in 1958, I went to a holiday guesthouse for police in Zakopane, in the mountains, for my TB. There I found the same primal, passionate, visceral anti-Semitism. People repeated an idiotic story about the head of the Polish

Radio Orchestra, who had emigrated from Poland: he had wanted to smuggle valuables out of the country, so he had a pan cast of gold, but it was too shiny, so he fried an egg in it and packed it unwashed. The customs officer found the filthy pan suspect. That story had everything: Jews have gold, are arrogant and slovenly."

Oleś, who has a habit of carrying on conversations by means of books, fishes out of his vast library Zygmunt Klukowski's *Diary of the Occupation*. The author, a doctor and social activist who headed a hospital in Szczebrzeszyn, took daily notes during the war. He described the behavior of Poles during a liquidation raid on Jews on November 22, 1942: "They took part eagerly, hunted down Jews, drove them to the magistrate or police station, beat them, kicked them. Boys chased little Jewish kids, who were killed by policemen right in front of everyone. I still see before me Jews beaten up, groups of Jews led off to their deaths and corpses thrown any which way onto wagons, bruised and bloodied. Many of the city dwellers looted and stole what they could, without the least shame."

DECEMBER 16, 2000

I drive to Pisz, this time to meet all three brothers Laudański. I take a slightly longer route, via Łomża, to pass through Jedwabne by daylight for the first time. Great stretches of open space, here and there scant clumps of trees. The flat Mazowsze landscape makes me realize how small the hope would have been that you could hide from persecutors here. But it's winter now, while then it was July, and there were unharvested crops in the fields.

When you enter the town from the Łomża side, you see the remains of the Jewish shtetl. Its atmosphere can best be felt in an alley off the Old Market, with its narrow passageway between houses, its broken cobblestones. Little wooden houses huddled to the ground, low windows, everything is tiny but the large puddles of melting snow. You'd only have to hang mezuzahs on doorways with excerpts from Deuteronomy to ward off the powers of evil, and you could shoot a film here about the events of sixty years ago.

I walk across the market square, now John Paul II Square, where the Jews were driven together that July day. With the map I was given by Kazimierz Laudański I drive to the site of the crime. A fenced-off plot of ground with a stone inscribed: *Place of Execution of Jewish Population.*

Gestapo and Hitler's Police Burned 1,600 People Alive. July 10, 1941. Thick shrubbery on the far side, but my map says those are the grounds of the Jewish cemetery. I go in deeper and see broken gravestones protruding from the snow.

In Pisz the Laudański brothers are waiting for me. We sit across from each other, drinking tea, eating homemade gingerbread. Kazimierz Laudański and his brothers are well-known as beekeepers in the area, and customers come all the way from Germany for their honey. The brothers—poised, calm—present well, they speak their parts like a well-learned lesson.

We've been talking for more than three hours and I'm on something like my third piece of gingerbread before we come to the events of July 1941.

The youngest of the brothers, Jerzy, is the least talkative. A smile plays around the corners of his mouth.

From Szmul Wasersztejn's testimony: "The Germans gave the order to destroy all the Jews, but Polish thugs took it and carried it out in the most horrible ways. At the time of the first pogroms and during the slaughter the following scum distinguished themselves by their cruelty: . . ." Jerzy Laudański is among the few dozen names given here.

"I was at the barn," says Jerzy Laudański, "but at a distance of about thirty meters. There were a lot of people in front of me."

I wonder how many such people there could have been near the barn. And how many of them limited themselves to watching.

Toward the end Jerzy Laudański tells a story. How Karol Bardoń (one of the men charged in the postwar trial with killing Jews in Jedwabne) went to the prison authorities, saying he wanted to give testimony about who took part in burning the Jews. "I heard it from a prison orderly," says Laudański. "Bardoń threatened to put a hundred men behind bars, but when they gave him paper to make a list, his hands were paralyzed and he couldn't speak, and that's how he died in prison. 'A miracle happened,' was the orderly's comment." Does that mean, I wonder, that Bardoń could have given the names and surnames of a hundred perpetrators? But I ask no provocative questions.

"We don't have any problem with Jews, but you've got to stop reopening the wounds," Kazimierz Laudański warns me in parting. "What were

Jews doing in the secret police after the war? What can I say? It's a disgrace, so why should we reproach each other?"

I listen to them and can't avoid the impression that scenes from 1941 are being replayed under their eyelids. I have a hotel booked in Pisz, but I decide to make my way home by night. I drive on a road completely deserted and covered with ice, just to get as far away from the Laudańskis as I can.

DECEMBER 17, 2000

Gdańsk. Jan Skrodzki, who was born in Radziłów, meets me at the station and takes me to a tidy apartment in a block on an embankment at the edge of a wood, where I'm greeted by a shaggy dog called Cha-Cha and given homemade brandy.

"It wasn't the Germans who did it, it was our people," he starts.

I give him the testimony of Menachem Finkelsztejn, which I photocopied at the Jewish Historical Institute. The scenes described in it are so horrifying it is hard to imagine Polish memory finding a place for them. But to Skrodzki nothing comes as a surprise—on the contrary, he adds specifics, fills in the details. I read him a description of Poles from the start joining in German operations brutalizing Jews. People bound to wagons were driven to the muddy river near the town. "Germans beat them, Poles beat them. The Jews cry in anguish, but they, the Germans and Poles, rejoice."

"He's talking about the Matlak, a narrow, shallow stream," he explains. "There was a meadow alongside the Matlak where farmers kept geese and ducks, and between the stream and the buildings on Nadstawna Street there was peat land and ditches where peat was cut. That's where they drove the Jews."

He's prepared to talk about the massacre and to be quoted in the Gazeta. We talk for nine hours, but I don't dare ask him the obvious question: Where was your father on July 7, 1941?

DECEMBER 19, 2000

Pisz. I have a meeting at the local museum with its retired director, Mieczysław Kulęgowski. I was led to him by a chain of people, each referring me on. He is supposed to tell me about the Laudański brothers—apparently he could say a lot about them, he's from Jedwabne himself—but when we meet he is so frightened it's hard for me to get anything out of him. I'm not surprised. At the museum, a granddaughter of one of the Laudańskis is waiting for us, as if by coincidence. How did she find out about this meeting? It's obvious one of the people in my chain of communication informed the brothers. Mieczysław Kulęgowski explains why he doesn't want to talk to me: "Maybe I carried the fear with me from there, but today friends warned me about talking to you: 'You'd better not get involved.'"

He only recalls that in the summer of 1941 he went by Jewish homes with his pals: "They were all occupied and looted, but I was looking for the plates that hung on the doorposts. I liked unrolling what was inside, there were Hebrew words written on hide, sheep's hide I think. After the war, when they founded a museum in Pisz, I gave those mezuzahs to the museum."

DECEMBER 20, 2000

In the evening I'm back in Pisz. Unannounced, I knock on the door of the little house on the edge of town where Mieczysław Kulęgowski lives. Maybe I'll get something out of him now? Finally, after three cups of tea, he reluctantly begins to talk: "In 1941 I was twelve years old. Some mothers didn't let their children outside that day, July 10, but I was always sticking my nose into everything. When Poles were going from house to house chasing Jews into the market square, you heard screams and weeping everywhere because they were taking the children and elders, too. Poles used clubs to force the Jews into rows, and they didn't put up any resistance. There weren't sixteen hundred of them, a thousand at most. I was at the barn. There wasn't a big crowd outside, just some men, maybe fifty of them. I was standing a little off to the side with my friends. The fear was that they'd take you for a Jewish child and throw you into the flames. It was a hot summer, it took only a little gas and some matches. When they set the barn on fire, the screaming went on until the roof caved in. Józef Kobrzyniecki threw children into the burning barn. I saw it with my own eyes. I heard that Kobrzyniecki led the mob and that he beat them the worst, and that he even went by the houses to stab people hiding in attics with a bayonet. Other murderers were named, too: Karolak, the Laudański brothers, Zejer. When I grew up I left the town right away and since that time I haven't wanted anything to do with it."

He cautions me, "Please don't mention my name, the Laudański brothers are still alive, I buy my groceries in Pisz, I met one of them in the street once and it sent a shiver down my spine. I really don't need that."

DECEMBER 21, 2000

Mieczysław Kulęgowski told me he had an uncle in Zanklewo, not far from Jedwabne, a wealthy farmer who sheltered a Jewish family from the neighboring town of Wizna, in return for which his farm was set on fire by Polish neighbors after the war. He gave me the name: the uncle is no longer alive, but his children are, and they were old enough at the time to remember. I drive there.

Zanklewo, a backwoods village on the road from Jedwabne to Wizna. A well-kept, prosperous farm, a warm welcome. Yes, that's right, says the uncle's son, his parents hid a tailor from Wizna, Izrael Lewin, with his wife and two children. He was a teenager at the time and remembers it well.

"They were hidden under the floor, near the stove. No one knew about it, it only got out after the war." He speaks of the postwar anti-Communist partisans: "In 1945 partisans took our clothes, cattle, pigs, and burned the farm buildings. We were left with nothing. That was the time when if someone was a little better off, gangs stole from him, so they must have thought we had Jewish gold. Those were impoverished times. Under the Polish partisans there was just as much fear as under the Russians or Germans, or worse."

That fear must persist, because as we say goodbye my interlocutor asks me never to mention his name.

DECEMBER 22, 2000

I decide to begin work on my book with Radziłów, before the atrocity committed there becomes as widely known as the one in Jedwabne. It will be easier to talk to people there.

I drive to Kramarzewo near Radziłów to look up Marianna Ramotowska, née Finkelsztejn, who was rescued by Stanisław Ramotowski. I reach a wooden cottage hunched over a stream. On the threshold Ramotowski announces he's not going to talk, but I somehow manage to get inside.

It's bone cold in the house. His wife sits wrapped in several sweaters. She's slight, frail, and wears thick glasses. She's even less willing to talk than her husband. She's hard of hearing, unable to walk. It's Ramotowski who makes me a cup of tea. We begin to talk, but he keeps drawing back.

"The Jews were driven out by Poles. Even if I knew who, I wouldn't tell you for the world. I can't. We have to live here."

Or: "I won't tell you how I arranged with the priest to get married in wartime, when I wanted to marry a Jewish girl. A thousand horses couldn't drag it out of me, those are religious matters."

"Don't say anything, Stasinek, God forbid," his wife pleads, holding his arm. She calls him by his tender diminutive, Stasinek for Stanisław.

I tell her that at the Jewish Historical Institute I read the testimony of Menachem Finkelsztejn, and I ask if he was a relative of hers. Though they have the same surname, Mrs. Ramotowski claims she has no idea who he is. It doesn't sound convincing; I have the impression she's terrified of everything that reminds her of her Jewish origins.

Ramotowski, too, stubbornly refuses to answer my questions, "because I live here among these people and they might come for me." But when I tell them I'll come back to see them in the New Year, he's clearly pleased. He seems to feel isolated. When I ask him directly, he says he had friends in Wąsosz, sixteen kilometers from Jedwabne, a Jewish woman and her Polish husband, they married during the war but they have since died. He mentions in passing that in Wąsosz the Poles did the same with the Jews as they did in Radziłów and Jedwabne.

DECEMBER 28, 2000

In the library I read the *Sprawa Katolicka* (The Catholic Cause), a regional diocesan weekly of the thirties. The subject of Jews as the greatest threat to Poland is raised obsessively. The contempt, and the deep satisfaction in the fact that Jews were starving in some village because of the economic boycott—it's astonishing. I knew the prewar Catholic Church was in large part anti-Semitic, but it's another thing entirely to read these hateful texts in the context of the atrocity to come.

1

Lord, Rid Poland of the Jews

or, On Polish-Jewish Relations
in Jedwabne in the Thirties

It is the tenth of Tishri 5699, or, according to the Gregorian calendar, October 5, 1938: Yom Kippur, the Day of Atonement, the most important Jewish holiday. On that day, all Jews go to the synagogue. Crowds of people flock across the market square. The next day no Jewish child in Jedwabne or Radziłów will go to school, and Jewish shops will be closed until sunset. There are no Catholic townspeople to be seen, only Yiddish can be heard that evening. In Jedwabne the mayor's mother, Mrs. Grądzki, who's not particularly fond of Jews, stands leaning against the wall of the synagogue on Szkolna Street as she does every year; she is moved by their songs. She has come to hear her favorite, the Kol Nidre, the prayer for absolution of oaths forgotten, or taken rashly or under duress.

The older children go to synagogue and participate in the daylong fast, but the young ones—many households have up to seven or eight children—are entrusted to Polish neighbors that day. They are given a hard-boiled egg or milk straight from the cow, which they drink from their own cups—the neighbors respect that the children are to keep kosher. They understand each other well enough—Yiddish is a language they hear every day: in shops, on the street, working with Jews. Some Poles speak it fluently. Among those in Jedwabne who speak good Yiddish is Bronisław Śleszyński, the man who will give his barn to burn the Jews.

It is May 3, 1939: a big Eucharistic procession on a national Polish

Seventh-grade graduation ceremony. Jedwabne, 1936. Meir Ronen from Israel (formerly Meir Grajewski from Jedwabne) told me: "My sister Fajga Grajewska, who was in the class, took this photograph with her to Palestine. There are several Jewish children here, although most Jewish kids had been taken out of school by their parents after being harassed by teachers and classmates. We had been friends with Polish children, but by the end of the thirties they stopped treating us as friends." (Courtesy of Meir Ronen)

holiday. In church the choir sings, "We raise our plea before your altar / Lord, rid Poland of the Jews." In their Sunday best the faithful come out after Mass to participate in a celebration organized by the church in collaboration with local members of the National Party, a party founded by Roman Dmowski, whose obsession was the eternal Jewish conspiracy against Poland.

The procession moves through the streets around the market square, on either side a file of girls in white carrying bouquets of flowers, and in between them, little boys in surplices, with bells. They are followed by older kids belonging to the Association of Young Catholic Men and Women, and adults bring up the rear of the procession, which fills the street from end to end. They are accompanied by an orchestra and flag-bearers on bicycles. On the steps of the church on the square a National Party member invited over from the larger town of Łomża, gives a speech. He speaks of Poland today, dominated by the foreign element, and Poland tomorrow, when the nation will liberate itself from its enslavement to international Jewish finance, and Poles will buy only from Poles. At the visitor's side stands the parish priest, also a National Party member. The people gathered unfurl banners: *Peasants and workers into trade—Jews to Palestine or Madagascar*; *A penny to a stranger harms the nation*; *Rid Poland of Jews*. They shout slogans and sing:

Ah, beloved Poland,
you've people in the millions
and on top of all that
you're filled up with Jews.
Rise up, white eagle,
smite Jews with your claws,
so that they will never
play the master over us.

That day the Jewish inhabitants of the town don't leave their houses, don't allow their children to go out. The next day they will say with relief that it wasn't too bad: a gang of National Party members getting drunker and drunker, singing patriotic songs to the accompaniment of an accordion, and yelling "Beat the Jew," until deep into the night, but only a few windows were broken in Jewish homes.

1.

Although the Jewish and Christian inhabitants of Radziłów and Jedwabne did not ordinarily look very different (in these parts Hasidim were rare and Jews most often dressed like regular townspeople; the elders wore hats), although their children generally went to the same schools (Jedwabne had no separate Jewish school; Radziłów did, but it was private and few parents could afford the fees), although Jews and Christians often lived side by side in the same apartment buildings, and there were friendly ties among children, neighbors, and business partners—they lived separate lives and spoke different languages. Jews, especially the young, got along fine in Polish, but at home they spoke Yiddish. The keeping of kosher kitchens ruled out reciprocal invitations to visit. Jewish children often studied Hebrew and Jewish history after school, and they also helped their parents in their shops or workshops. Polish children went to help on the farms (even the Poles who lived in small towns usually had farmland, cows, and pigs), and often for that reason left school after a few grades.

Social and cultural life ran on separate tracks. Immediately after World War I there had still been a few things Poles and Jews did together—picnics, festivities initiated by the volunteer fire brigade, the riflemen, or the reservists—but Jews often met with an unfriendly response from Poles, and in the latter half of the thirties they were simply thrown out of these organizations. The lives of Catholics revolved around the parish and the world of churchgoers, as well as events organized by the National Party, which was blatant in its exclusion of Jews.

In this region 90 percent of both communities were poor or destitute. Remembering the thirties in his diary, Mosze Rozenbaum of Radziłów, who emigrated to Australia in April 1939, wrote that hunger would wake him at night and he wasn't able to concentrate in class. In winter he would go out into the courtyard and eat a handful of snow to fool his stomach out of its pangs.

However, the Jews were not as poor as the Poles whom they employed—women in the household, men in the workshops. The Sabbath *czulent* was often the most nutritious dish the Polish neighbors' children had a chance to eat all week, when they brought their school notebooks over to a Jewish friend's house on Saturday night. When the

Catholic neighbors were told that the Jews were the cause of their poverty, many had no trouble believing it.

Morris Atlas, formerly Mosze Atłasowicz, who left Radziłów before World War I, asked his father in a letter from across the ocean in the latter half of the twenties whether he should come back to Poland to help him in his old age. His father's answer was brief: "Better stay where you are. This isn't a good country for Jews."

2.

The stories told by Catholics and Jews about how good relations were before the war can be explained by a need on the part of Catholics to erase their guilt and a nostalgic idealization of youth by Jews. When a wave of anti-Semitism swept across Europe in the thirties, the people of Jedwabne were up to the European standard. You could even say they were in the avant-garde. The Łomża area in which Jedwabne was located had been a bastion of right-wing National Party support for more than a century. The National Party was the most powerful political force in the region; its leitmotif was the battle against Jews, and it turned shtetls in the impoverished and backward part of Poland into places pulsing with political activity. The summons to "Beat the Jew" mobilized youth in the National Party, organized as the Youth Movement of the Greater Poland Bloc, which had fascist tendencies.

"The rabbi's yard was right next to the yard of the school head, whose daughters were friends of mine," said Halina Zalewska from Radziłów. "We would watch the rabbi from the roof when he went to the outhouse, we'd keep the door open and call him names, not letting him catch us. He was like a rat, his eyes were black, and his wife came out and said: 'Oy, young lady, that's not nice of you, I'm going to pay a visit to your daddy and tell him what you're up to.' We liked pestering the rabbi. The same with the Jewess Psachtowa. She kept a shop, and since she had bad eyesight, children buying seeds or fruit drops would give her buttons instead of change."

Jan Cytrynowicz, who lived in Wizna before the war and had been baptized, remembered how, before the Jewish holiday of Sukkoth, when one room in the house has to have an open roof, boys plotted at a meeting of the church youth group to let cats into Jewish homes. Jan Skrodzki recalls his older friends catching ravens and releasing them in the synagogue in the middle of prayers. There was no electric light then, Jews prayed by candlelight, and the ravens flew toward the light, extinguishing the candles. Stanisław Przechodzki, born in Jedwabne after the war, heard his mother relate with distaste how groups of young people would go by Jewish homes on Shabbat with a concertina and disrupt their contemplative day, how Jews' yarmulkes were yanked off their heads and Jews were made to pay a zloty or two to get them back. She said the Laudański brothers were instigators of this sort of thing.

There wouldn't be anything so terrible in these stupid pranks—kids getting up to no good as they do all over the world—if they hadn't taught contempt and hostility toward Jews, feelings that were reinforced in the course of their upbringing.

"I remember Kazimierz Laudański standing in front of a Jewish shop telling people not to buy there," Jaków Geva, then Jakub Pecynowicz—who lived in Jedwabne before the war—told me.

"At a Polish shop you could get two doughnuts made of lesser-quality flour for five groszy, whereas at a Jewish shop they'd only ask three," remembered Leon Dziedzic of Przestrzele, on the outskirts of Jedwabne. "But when I went by the Jewish shop there were two guys standing there with sticks, pointing and saying: 'The Polish shop is over there.'"

Chaja Finkelsztejn of Radziłów described in her memoir how, toward the end of the thirties, customers would come into Jewish shops by the back door, as they were too afraid to be seen coming through the front entrance.

Jan Cytrynowicz remembers an acquaintance of his father telling a story with great hilarity about a Jew who came to his native village selling things door-to-door, and the local peasants forcing a nonkosher sausage into his mouth, while he fought so hard blood was spilled.

Professor Adam Dobroński, a historian specializing in the Białystok region, of which the Łomża area (including Jedwabne and Radziłów) was a part, cited an anecdote to me about the National Party announcing a contest in one of the villages in the area: a sheep for the brave fellow who kicked a Jew.

Szmul Wasersztejn, in the memoirs he dictated in Costa Rica not long before his death, said how hard it was for him to live in a country where "half of the population thinks you're a poor Jew, a rat, and tells you to bugger off to Palestine, insults you and throws rocks through your windows," a country where "gangs of thugs give Jewish children a thrashing under any pretext, make them kneel and take off their caps." And he told how humiliated he was to be taught by his father that, as a Jew, he should always step down from the sidewalk when a priest or a soldier was passing by.

When I asked him about Polish-Jewish relations before the war, Jan Sokołowski of Jedwabne offered me his point of view: "Well, what do you think it was like, when the Jews made Poles do all the heavy jobs, like carpentry and bricklaying, and they themselves only made hats or ran mills or were in some kind of trade? A bun cost five groszy at a Pole's and two groszy at a Jew's, so how can you talk about competition here? You took your horse whip into church on a Sunday because it might get stolen, that's how poor people were. And when you were poor, you went to a Jew. You could get money on credit, the Jew would write it into his book and then he had the Pole in his power. A farmer would have to sell a cow sometimes to give the Jew his money back."

3.

Several people I interviewed used the word "revolution" in connection with a pogrom that took place in Radziłów on March 23, 1933; they all used the word with a positive connotation, with the notion that it was a revolution of nationalists, a prelude to their takeover of power.

Halina Zalewska remembered the event that swept up the whole town: "'A revolution,' they said. Shooting, windows broken, shutters closed, women shrieking, running home."

Another person told me, "A cousin of my father's driving earthenware pots to market was injured in that revolution. He was lying on the foldout bed, that was what we had for a sofa bed in those days: by day it was a bench, at night you folded it out and there was a straw mattress inside. The medic Jan Mazurek tried to help him, but he died anyway."

"In the market square, windows were broken and tubs of herring knocked over," another witness recalled. "Four peasants were shot, and a lot of people went to jail. They were held in the Czerwoniak in Łomża, the old tsarist prison, then they were taken to the bishop to do unpaid work."

Only Stanisław Ramotowski, a Pole who saved a Jewish family during the war, unambiguously called it a pogrom: "I saw a gang out breaking

Jews' windows. And policemen killing a man who'd knocked down a Jew's tub of herring. The nationalists weren't boys, they were grown men, the same ones standing in the marketplace with crowbars, in front of Jewish shops. I saw a few of them again later on in the attacks."

These were members of the Camp for a Greater Poland, the outgrowth of an alliance between peasants and the middle class that had its own action squads. Peasants from small villages led by middle-class Łomża youths drove from town to town in trucks instigating anti-Jewish brawls. The height of the camp's activity fell in March 1933. Hitler's accession to power in January of that year opened up new perspectives: it turned out that anti-Jewish slogans, which until then had been bandied around in Germany and Poland by a single group—the Nazis—had a chance of becoming the basis for an official state ideology. The camp organized campaigns in different parts of Poland, but the worst pogrom in this area took place in Radziłów.

Years afterward, Mosze Rozenbaum also remembered this pogrom. First he described the weekly market, which took place on Thursdays. The Jewish merchants of the surrounding villages brought in sheepskin coats, knee boots, pickled herring. Polish peasants sold wheat, rye, buckwheat, and oats. Small Jewish merchants bought up all the grain and sold it on to Germany. That day, when school had let out, Mosze saw the devastated marketplace, after the "peasants from the nearby villages had invaded Radziłów armed with iron crowbars and wooden cudgels, attacking Jews." Chaja Finkelsztejn remembered carts headed for the market just as they did every week. But that time they weren't loaded with produce. There were peasants sitting on them armed with poles and clubs. Not one window was left intact in any Jewish home after the pogrom.

The *Przegląd Łomżyński* (Łomża Record), the official weekly of the ruling party, which engaged the nationalists in a heated debate, reported on the incidents and informed its readers in the next issue that "Chana Sosnowska has died, a victim of crimes committed by the Camp for a Greater Poland."

She was the wife of a shoemaker from Jedwabne who lived next door to the Wasersztejn family, a friend of Szmul's mother. Meir Ronen, then Meir Grajewski, who lived in Jedwabne before the war, remembers her: "On the way home from school, I saw a truck with a woman lying on it, covered in blood. It was Chana Sosnowska from Przytulska Street, who went to market in Radziłów every Thursday to sell shoes." Rabbi Jacob Baker of Jedwabne also remembers her. He ordered shoes from her several times, and after the pogrom he visited her in the hospital. He was a yeshiva student in Łomża at the time, so he was asked to visit her. He remembers fanning her in the hospital that exceptionally hot April. Soon after he took part in her funeral. He also recalled an earlier victim of anti-Semitism in Jedwabne: "This was in 1932. We heard a cry, and we found Mosze Lasko in a ditch. They found the people who did it, and they admitted they'd done it for a laugh. Mosze was going somewhere on business and instead of a business deal he got his own funeral."

The exact course of the Radziłów pogrom is known to us from a report drawn up by the Interior Ministry branch in Białystok. The police put members of the Camp for a Greater Poland in jail in Radziłów as a preventive measure. But a mob broke into the jail and set them free. As a result, Jewish stalls were demolished, Jews were beaten up. Shots were fired from within the mob, and the police, under attack, used its weapons. Two participants in the pogrom died on the spot and two more died later from injuries sustained.*

Seventeen participants received suspended sentences from three months to two and a half years. Józef Przybyszewski, the editor in chief of the attack squad's paper *Camp for a Greater Poland Youth*, published in Łomża, was designated the moral instigator of the Radziłów pogrom and sentenced to two years in prison, but the appeals court in Warsaw overturned the verdict and declared him not guilty.

The Białystok office of the Interior Ministry reported to Warsaw, commenting on events in Radziłów (with an emphatic "confidential and very urgent"): "The Camp for a Greater Poland is an extreme threat to

---

* According to reports by the Interior Ministry in Białystok, after the events of March 20, when Camp for a Greater Poland members broke fifty-three windows of Jewish properties in Grajewo and the same, though on a smaller scale, took place in Szczuczyn and Rajgrod, nine CGP members were arrested in Radziłów on March 23 as a preventive measure. In the morning, special CGP couriers went on horseback from Radziłów to the directors of CGP offices in villages nearby to round up as many men as possible to break them out. An organized crowd protested to the police, demanding the immediate release of the arrested men. Rocks and crowbars began to rain down on the policemen. A group of people demolished the jail and freed the arrested men. The mob scattered across the market and started to smash the windows of Jewish shops and loot all the stalls. Nine Jews were beaten up.

public order and safety. It enjoys the wholehearted support of the clergy. In the Białystok area the Camp for a Greater Poland is an integral part of the National Party, carrying National Party ID cards, etc., and is the ideological avant-garde of the National Party."

The minister of the interior dissolved the organization. But it didn't help much. Administrative decisions in faraway Warsaw could at most thwart the nationalists' movements a little; in the region, they held sway. The youth activists of the Camp for a Greater Poland strengthened the ranks of the National Party, turning their officially dissolved cells into sections of the National Party Youth and causing a further radicalization of the National Party in the sphere of "a solution to the Jewish question."*

It was the youth section of the National Party that inspired the so-called school strikes in many towns in the environs of Łomża in the autumn of 1934, according to regional historian Henryk Majewski. These were a boycott by children of classes taught by Jewish teachers, combined with protest meetings by parents in front of school buildings.

In the following years words increasingly led to actions. Other towns repeated the scenario that was played out in Wysokie Mazowieckie, sixty-five kilometers north of Jedwabne, in September 1936: "At the local market, Jewish merchants were beaten and slashed with knives. Many fled, leaving their wares unsupervised, and wares were looted."

In Radziłów every Thursday, on market day, attack squads knocked down stalls and beat up Jews.

Here are some typical Interior Ministry reports from the Białystok area in 1936: "At a fair in Długosiodła 51 windows were broken, 15 stalls knocked down, five Jews beaten up"; "In Wyszonki-Kościelne 474 windows were broken at night, 17 doors hacked with axes, two shops destroyed, wares ransacked, and two persons lightly injured with stones"; "At a National Party meeting in Łomża, a delegate from Warsaw ordered the creation of special squads that, after special training, would be used exclusively for fighting Jews."

* The effectiveness of the disbanded Camp for a Greater Poland merged into the National Party is illustrated by a National Party convention in Łomża at which—as we read in a Interior Ministry report for September 1936—2,500 people sang the Greater Poland anthem in closing: "We bring rebirth to Poland / We stamp out baseness, lies, and filth," standing to attention with one hand raised in imitation of the Hitler salute.

"The village youth," a report ran, "whipped up by the slogan 'Beat the Jew' propagated everywhere and at every step by the National Party as well as from the pulpit, have fallen into a dangerous psychosis that threatens public safety. More and more frequently we see spontaneous and autonomous actions against Jews."

Every month the Interior Ministry office in Białystok put together this kind of report, called a "report on Polish political movements and the sociopolitical life of national minorities"—they can be found in the state archive in Białystok. These reports are worthy of any sociologist, offering an excellent picture of the changing moods in the region. They show the state authorities' hostile attitude not only toward the Camp for a Greater Poland but toward the nationalist movement as a whole. The state was bothered not only by nationalists' attitude toward their Jewish fellow citizens but also by the opposition party's sharp criticism of every move by the government, every resolution of parliament. The reports prove incontrovertibly that the Polish state felt responsible for its Jewish citizens, that it tried to protect them, and that it arrested and sentenced members of the attack squads. The reports emphasize that the Jews tried to show their loyalty to the Polish state.

4.

One can gain a sense of the depth and scope of anti-Semitism in the region from reading the local press, especially the Łomża diocese weekly *Życie i Praca* (Life and Work), which was aimed at farmers. Its editor in chief was Father Antoni Roszkowski. When the weekly was closed by the authorities in 1935, it reappeared almost immediately under the same church banner and with the same editor in chief, only under a new title: *The Catholic Cause*. The paper was printed by the diocesan press, under the bishop's wing, which for the most part protected it from confiscation. Along with advice on battling weeds and vermin, an important theme was "unceasingly reminding our brothers of the Jewish menace."

Here are some front-page headlines: "Jews Take Liberties," "Take Land from the Jews," "Polish Youth Suffers for Jewish Wrongs," "How Poland Became Jewified." "The Polish people have matured and come to see that they have to break off relations with the Jews, not in a year or two, but now," we read in an editorial titled "Let's Break with the Jews." "No people would suffer what we have suffered from the Jews for many years. Jews have grabbed control of our trades and crafts. The horrible specter of a Jewish Poland hovers before our eyes. We do not wish to repay evil with evil, our response must be worthy of a Christian and cultured people. We will break off relations with the Jews. Jews are not suitable friends for young Poles, friendly relations with Jews do not befit a Christian and must be broken off. We should sound the alarm. The Jews are obstructing the Poles' path to greatness. Reason and conscience demand that we cease to consort with Jews."

The Germans are held up as an example. They have found "a good way to deal with the excess of Jews." "The National Socialist plan to throw the Jews out of Germany would truly be a heavy blow to Jewry," runs a commentary on the Nazi program. A text called "A Warning to Jews" reads: "The Jews have it too easy in Poland if they dare to criticize Poles." They write: "Such a massive Jewish population no country can stomach or sustain." "No delaying," urges an editorial, arguing that there should be no Jews in Poland.

Jews are told to be reasonable: "Poland is the way it is, but it's for us to put things in order, and I'd like Jews to get that into their heads!" "Jews should make every effort not to pester our people needlessly. It will be good when Jews understand that it is for their own benefit to curb their appetite for Polish land, for buildings, business, and work in our cities." But no great faith is put in Jews' reasonableness or curbing of appetites, and more in action by local Poles. The appeal goes out: "When a little child goes out for a bun or a candy, a pencil or a notebook, or the head of the household goes to buy goods, the path should lead only to a Polish shop. Poles buy from Poles!" They paint the vision of a "Jewish Poland" where "Yids squeezed out of trade" buy up land and "the Polish people, immemorial custodians of that land, are condemned to a life of misery and wandering among strangers," for "every Jewish farm is a thorn in the side of the Polish farmer." "It seems the time has come for Jews to understand that Poles are the boss in Poland."

Even priests were exposed to the danger: "Two Jewish agents who have material for priests' cassocks have appeared in the area of the Łomża diocese. They show the visiting cards of various priests in our diocese, which makes it easier for them to persuade people to buy from them. Honorable Priests are therefore warned not to give their visiting cards to these Jews, for in so doing they support Jewish trade without any good reason, contrary to the slogan 'Our people buy from their own, and only their own.'"*

Parenthetically, people were told not to believe too readily in popular sayings about Jews: "Until recently many have spoken disparagingly about Jews, one often heard things like: 'A Jew's a dope, he'll buy old rope,' 'You work like a Jewish farmer,' 'You look like a Jew on a horse.' None of this made any sense and it detracted from our caution and vigilance against Jews . . . Folks laughed at Jews, and all the while those incompetent, simple, ordinary Yids took over all of our trade, took control of crafts, became landowners, factory owners, doctors, lawyers."

Life and Work and later *The Catholic Cause* played an active role in the boycott of Jewish shops. "Whoever buys from Jews or uses the services of Jewish doctors, lawyers, craftsmen, will answer to God and the people for the growth of poverty and crime in Poland, for the rise of Communism, godlessness, and socialism." People were encouraged to fight Jewish competition by devious means: "In Stawiski, the Polish bakery wasn't doing very well, but someone put the word out that typhus fever was going around among the Jews and they were using loaves of bread to beat each other, and business at the Polish bakery picked up."

Examples of successful boycotts were cited without any mention of the beatings and destruction of market stalls that accompanied them. Violence was not yet openly encouraged, but it was made clear that various tactics were permissible. The grandiose defense speeches at the trials of nationalist attack squad members were reported by the newspapers, even when the charges involved beatings and lootings.

After the pogrom in Radziłów in 1933, the censors confiscated a

---

* Jews sewing cassocks and selling Catholic devotional objects must have been a particular outrage to the anti-Semites among the clergy. Father Trzeciak, a famous anti-Semitic priest, postulated the introduction of a ban on buying devotional objects from Jews and those peddlers who got their products from Jews: "This can be most effectively achieved by announcing that no religious cult objects deriving directly or indirectly from Jews will be blessed and no indulgences will be granted" (from *Dejudaizing the Manufacture and Sale of Devotional Items*, a brochure quoted by Anna Landau-Czajka in "They Stood in the Same House: Ideas for Solving the Jewish Question in the Polish Press, 1933–1939," Neriton, Institute of History, Polish Academy of Sciences, Warsaw, 1998).

whole edition of *Life and Work*. The next issue of the paper already carried an ironic appreciation of the pogrom in the note, "A Fine Example of Helping One's Neighbor," about the arrests, in connection with the Radziłów pogrom, of two brothers who had left their farm unattended and their mother alone at home. "However, the old woman and the farm have been looked after by friends of the men under arrest, former members of the Camp for a Greater Poland, who worked together to plough and sow the farmland."

According to the National Party's ideology, Poles were supposed to not only weed Jews out of retail trade and crafts, but also refuse to sell them land or allow them into schools or state offices.

The diocesan press repeated: "No Christian family will give its child into Jewish hands." "Protesting against letting Jews into Polish schools, we Catholics are only doing what our faith commands . . . Our Catholic conscience and national pride command us to get rid of Jewish teachers." When a state office employed a Polish citizen of Jewish origin, there was outrage under the headline "A Jew Instead of a Pole": "The rumor we once gave voice to has proved true, for a Jew has become head physician at the Łomża Health Fund. The fact that the most prominent positions in Poland are occupied by persons of an alien race pains the Polish population." Or "Just such an impossibility that has nevertheless become a reality, is a Jew, a certain Turek, being the representative of the Union of Farm Workers. Is it not extraordinary that a person who by race, religion, and nationality is alien to the Polish spirit should decide the fate of a purely Polish union?"

The diocesan press was the local population's window on the world. The column "National News" reported on "Jewish usury," "Łódź's de-Jewification," "Gold Stolen from Churches Bought by Two Lvov Jews," "Jewish Teacher in Nowo-Święcane Spreads Communism," and "the Jewification of the Boy Scouts." Under the heading "World News": "Rumors of Ritual Murder," "Jews Whipped for Opening Shops on Sunday" (in Tripoli), and so forth. Most energy was devoted to spreading modern, economic anti-Semitism, although traditional, religious anti-Semitism also had its place in these publications. Recommending reading materials to their parishioners, they praised a brochure by Father J. Unszlicht, *An Outline of the Life and Teachings of Jesus Christ*, which dealt with the "perversity of Jews in relation to Jesus."

5.

One can argue about the immediate influence the press had in an area where one-third of the residents were illiterate and another third finished two grades of school at most. Reading documents from the postwar trials of participants in the massacre, one notices some of the witnesses and defendants sign with a cross. (Jan Cytrynowicz told me that peasants in Wizna buying three-quarters of a liter of oil would take three quarts paying for each separately, because they couldn't do addition.) But the town elites, including the priests, read the local press. And it was they who set the tone.

In its approach to the Jewish question the diocesan press was no different from the press in other parts of Poland, and sometimes things got much worse elsewhere. Toward the end of the 1930s, brutal anti-Semitism was an obsession in the press.* A firm majority of Catholic papers argued that the battle with the Jews was a virtue in the eyes of God, not a vice, and they called for people to work to rid the country of Jews.

What was fundamentally different about the Łomża area, as the historian Dariusz Libionka has shown, was the high degree to which priests were involved in the activity of the National Party. The Łomża area was quite a phenomenon in that regard.†

The National Party already enjoyed the support of a majority of parish priests in the Łomża diocese, and the highest percentage fell in Łomża County (twenty-three of twenty-eight parish priests). Local bishop Stanisław Łukomski, a friend and collaborator of National Party

---

* This is shown very well in the writings of Dariusz Libionka, who cites the Poznań weekly, *Culture*, in 1936: "It is no accident that the idea has become common that Jews are parasites. In fact, our emotional relationship with them resembles the attitudes we have toward fleas or lice. Killing them, destroying them, getting rid of them. The point is that the Jew is quite different from a flea. The Jewish problem can exist even when there is no longer any Jew left." Libionka shows that anti-Semitism was to the Catholic press a convenient tool for describing reality, battling liberalism in social mores, socialism, the Communist movement, everything that—to use the terminology of "Clerical News"—exposed "the fresh Slavonic soul to the moral influence of the over-sophisticated Semitic spirit."

† Dariusz Libionka, "The Clergy of the Łomża Diocese in the Face of Anti-Semitism and the Holocaust" (in *Wokół Jedwabnego* [Regarding Jedwabne], Institute of National Remembrance, Warsaw, 2002).

leader Roman Dmowski, conducted a strong campaign against "introducing teachers and pupils of other faiths, particularly Jews, into Polish schools." At the Congregation of Deans in 1929, he had already ordered parish priests to report on the number of Jewish teachers and pupils and offered as a model Father Rogiński of Wysokie Mazowieckie, who had "achieved the removal of a Jewish teacher." Libionka also makes the point that Bishop Łukomski was exceptionally effective among higher church authorities in popularizing the notion of "ridding trade of Jews"—in a 1935 address to the clergy in his diocese he urged them to follow the example of a priest who had made his parishioners swear not to buy anything in a Jewish shop.

From the reports of the Interior Ministry it clearly emerges that it was priests who propagated the National Party ideology from the pulpit and in addresses on national holidays. Activities on the party's behalf were mainly organized by branches of the church-based groups of Catholic Action, which in the Łomża area were de facto appendages of the National Party, active in the greater part of the parish. Priests pressured their parishioners with threats and entreaties to participate in party activity. The curate Jan Rogowski of Piątnica, a village located between Jedwabne and Łomża, would ask residents when he went Christmas caroling if they were members of the National Party, and if they weren't he threatened not to hear their Easter confessions or bless their Easter dishes. Father Marian Wądołowski urged the population in the nearby village of Mosty to join the Catholic Action club, "because it is a second pulpit—what can't be said from the pulpit can be freely said there."

Any pretext sufficed to prompt an anti-Jewish statement: the building of a Christian bakery or a Catholic house, Easter or the harvest festival, the Feast of the Assumption or the blessing of National Party pennants.

A notice in *The Catholic Cause*: "After the service on May 3, 1936, a procession took place in the town of Jedwabne with the participation of about 1,500 members and sympathizers of the National Party, accompanied by an orchestra and bicyclists carrying flags. There were two speeches, and during the procession there were cries of 'Long live the Great Polish Nation,' 'Long live Polish national trade,' 'Down with Jewish Communism.' Said procession was a success and made a great impression in Jedwabne and its environs."

The alarm was sounded: "Reports are growing of religious celebrations at which parish priests call on people to 'rid the country's trade and industry of Jews,' and which end with cries of 'Beat the Jews,' 'Jews out.'"* A Father Cyprian Łozowski of Jasionówka in the Białystok region, who "propagates anti-Jewish acts at a May 3 Academy and has his church choir sing 'Lord, Rid Poland of the Jews,'"† appears in one Interior Ministry report.

The Church taught Poles hostility and contempt for Jews from childhood. Younger children participated in the Eucharistic Crusade called the Knighthood of Jesus; the elder children joined the Young Men's and Young Women's Catholic Associations, where they performed plays—the title "The Jewish Matchmaker" leaves little to the imagination; the adults attended lectures such as "On the Urgency and Means of Battling Jewish Communism." When a school hired a Jewish teacher, protest signatures were collected in the parish. In the *Parish Chronicle* of Łapy near Białystok a priest proudly describes a successful 1934 campaign to remove a Jewish teacher from a school.

Jan Cytrynowicz said: "In church it was constantly emphasized that Jews had killed Christ, there could be no sermon without that theme. Father Rogalski of Wizna was forever calling on people not to buy from

---

* The authorities, who had no doubt as to who had power over souls, conducted conversations with the clergy aimed at warning them. "At almost every market or fair anti-Jewish excesses have taken place," they reported. "After conversations with the clergy they decreased. The number of towns where there are boycotts has increased, but they take a form which does not require police intervention. Bishop Łukomski has indicated to the clergy under his authority that there should not be active campaigns against Jews. However, members of the National Party apply the boycott with great determination. Christian tradesmen reward picketers. But picketing in groups of four wearing National Party sashes has been eliminated. The clergy have also intervened to get National Party members to stop carrying canes and clubs." The clergy taught not so much that violent attacks were reprehensible as that they were ineffective. The report quotes one of the priests saying at a Christmas gathering: "Your fighting stance and hot temperament are known to all, but now is not the time for exploits whose victims are usually nationalists themselves."

† After the Soviets left in June 1941 and peasants from the surrounding villages met in Jasionówka to loot Jewish homes, the same Father Łozowski "shouted and lectured at people and didn't allow them to do it" and also "threatened them with Hell if they went on doing such an injustice," as described after the war by the survivor Pesia Szuster-Rozenblum. He was probably a supporter of the economic boycott, which was supposed to force Jews out of Poland, but didn't support violence and looting. However, he wasn't able to prevent the pogrom.

Jews, not to visit Jews. He held it against my father, who had converted, that he did business with Jews, and as a punishment he kicked me out of religion class. That's why my education stopped after elementary school. With an F for religion you couldn't pass to the next grade."

Judging by the amount of space the Interior Ministry reports devoted to the priests of Wąsosz and Radziłów, the towns where Catholics murdered almost all Jews in 1941, they were particularly active supporters of anti-Jewish campaigns.

Father Piotr Krysiak of Wąsosz was an important figure in the National Party not only on the local level; he often visited Drozdowo, where the founder of the National Party, Roman Dmowski, moved toward the end of his life. It was under the intellectual leadership of Father Krysiak, the Interior Ministry reports stress, that a circle of National Party supporters came into existence, and it was the priest himself who organized National Party member meetings and called for picketing Jewish shops. Even on his way out, in September 1937, at a ceremonial farewell to the priest, who was retiring, he urged his parishioners to organize a picket in neighboring Szczuczyn as well.

Mosze Rozenbaum had Polish acquaintances who remembered Father Aleksander Dołęgowski, the Radziłów parish priest, proclaiming at the funeral of the National Party attack squad members in 1933: "If the blood of Jews does not flow to all four corners of the world, Christianity will perish." Perhaps the words were not quite that brutal. In any case, we know from the Interior Ministry reports that Father Dołęgowski dedicated a Mass to the memory of the squad members on the first anniversary of the pogrom, and gave an address to five thousand people crowded into the marketplace.

By the Polish residents of the town, Father Dołęgowski was remembered above all as an exceptionally miserly priest. He kept gardens where he had the faithful work for meager wages, which as a rule he neglected to pay them. His curates were outspoken anti-Jewish activists—and it was they who led the boycotts.

First, the curate Władysław Kamiński. I was told that "he hated Jews so much that when he was drunk he shot at the windows of the tailor Monkowski, who lived across the street." Stanisław Ramotowski recalled, "I saw with my own eyes how he went with boys from the National Party to break the windows of Jewish shops." We know from the Interior Ministry reports that he gathered together kids from the senior classes and urged them to combat Jewish trade. As an official at the Interior Ministry department elegantly phrased it, "He put forward the argument that Jewish bakers mixed dough with their dirty feet and spat in it. He stressed that a student who dared to buy a product from a Jew would fail religion class." On another occasion, Father Kamiński said in class that during the war between Poland and Soviet Russia in 1920, Jews had scalded General Rydz-Śmigły's head with boiling water, leaving him bald. For that reason the general harbors hatred toward Jews and plans to drive them out of Poland. It's unknown to what extent the curate was conveying Rydz-Śmigły's sentiments, but this was doubtless a way to express his own. At a National Party county convention in Grajewo in 1936, which brought together twenty-five hundred participants, the curate, appealing for a battle against Jews and Communism, thundered that it was for their own purposes that Jews permitted their women to marry Poles, and there were ministers who had Jewish wives.

The name of another curate of the Radziłów parish appears even more frequently in the Interior Ministry reports: Father Józef Choromański. In March 1937, the curate personally organized pickets of Jewish shops. In his religion classes he sneered at children whose parents shopped with Jews, and "the schoolchildren, remaining under the influence of the curate, were guilty of anti-Jewish speech and behavior." On July 18 in Wąsosz, at the Catholic ceremony blessing the National Party flags, the curate spoke to a group of seven hundred people and organized picketing campaigns. On July 29, he intervened at a police station in Radziłów on behalf of arrested picketers. In Radziłów on August 12, he sent people out picketing (and after being transferred to nearby Kolno in 1938, he organized campaigns at the beginning of the school year in which Polish children blocked their Jewish fellow students from entering the schoolhouse).

Jedwabne appears only episodically in the reports, although there, too, like everywhere, anti-Jewish excesses are noted: "On August 25, 1937, in Jedwabne picketers would not let Jews put up their stalls. One of the Jews put up his stall with hats despite being told not to, and the picketers overturned it." In the same year, Father Marian Szumowski wrote in the Jedwabne parish book, "All the tradesmen in the marketplace are now Polish. No one has dared to enter a Jewish shop, and the one woman who defied the warning to go to a Jewish baker was thrashed (with a stick)."

As the nationalists were increasingly subjected to trials and other restrictions, like the suspension of some groups' activity, the Church shielded them more and more closely. From August 1938, Father Antoni Kochański was the executive director of the Łomża district branch of the National Party, which—as Professor Szymon Rudnicki, an expert on the nationalist parties of the interbellum, told me—is a testament to the extremely close ties between the local church hierarchy and the party.

The Polish-Jewish conflict, or rather the conflict between nationalists and Jews, did not determine the entire network of neighborly ties. Conflicts among Poles also inflamed great passions. The Church in the Łomża district forbade the dedication of Masses on the occasion of the name day or memorial celebrations of Marshal Piłsudski, the head of state in independent Poland, a politician favorably disposed to national minorities and therefore hated by nationalists.* Piłsudski's followers, among them a large part of the local intelligentsia, teachers, and officials, were politically closer to the educated Jewish elite than to fellow Poles who joined the National Party.

6.

Reading the reports of the Interior Ministry, one could easily think that the life of the Jedwabne or Radziłów Jews was one long succession of humiliations and persecution. But it is worth remembering that the reports of security services usually create a distorted image of reality.

Although it was not easy for Jews to live in a hostile environment, and though they often suffered from poverty, they nevertheless lived a life that was often sorely missed by those who managed to escape across the ocean. Relations with their Polish neighbors were only the backdrop to the life of a Jewish community bound by strong ties and equally strong

---

* The Jedwabne parish chronicle notes in 1937: "From the time when regent Romuald Rogowski, in collaboration with Mayor Walenty Grądzki, hired firemen for twenty zlotys to ring the bell all day for the funeral of Marshal Piłsudski against the parish priest's will, which was condemned by the whole parish population, the church authorities have issued an interdiction against the Jedwabne fire brigade, banning it from participating in church celebrations." In the parish chronicle of nearby Łapy we read: "The year 1938 is a period of the greatest development ever of the Catholic spirit in Łapy. It is a period of full bloom for Catholic Action. True, the godless Union of Rail Workers, with its close ties to the Polish Socialist Party, going hand in hand with Jews, is still active, but the range of their activity is shrinking more and more."

antagonisms, absorbed in its own dreams and quarrels. The Jews in the region constituted a strong, separate modern society. Even in the smallest towns there were Jewish institutions, parties, mutual-aid groups, banks, and associations.*

The reports of the Interior Ministry, which monitored the Yiddish press, give a good sense of just how much Jews led a life of their own, how remote the issues at the heart of the Jewish community were from the things that occupied their Polish neighbors.

Let us take the time of the pogrom in Radziłów. In March 1933, on the premises of the Union of Jewish Butchers on Zamenhof Street in Białystok, at the conference of delegates of Jewish butchers' guilds of the Białystok region, Icchak Wałach and Lejb Szlapak gave speeches protesting a law intended to restrict ritual slaughter. In May in Białystok, there was a strike by Jewish textile workers, and the Zionist Orthodox organization Mizrachi created a consortium of artisans and businessmen committed to establishing a textile factory in Tel Aviv. Thanks to the daily press these kinds of events were on everybody's tongue in no time.

In Warsaw, Lvov, or Białystok, assimilated Jews often treated both Jewish tradition and the activity of Jewish organizations as a kind of alien folklore. But in Radziłów or Jedwabne, every Jew—even ones who preferred speaking Polish rather than Yiddish and were proud of service in the 1920 Polish war of independence—went to the synagogue and belonged to some Jewish organization.

The growing influence of the National Party was met among the Jewish population with the reactive growth of Zionism, which involved Zionist groups competing with one another. None of them had any liking

---

* Parties and associations that had branches or affiliates in the towns and villages of the Łomża area included Zionist parties of various stripes: General Zionists, Poale Zion-Right, the religious Mizrachi, the Revisionist Zionists, the socialist Bund; educational, cultural, and sports associations: the Zionist Tarbut, the Association of Evening Classes, the Education Association, the Jewish Association for Athletics and Sports Makabi, the Bundist League of Cultures; youth organizations: the leftist Zionist scouting organization Ha-Szomer ha-Cair, He-Chaluc, which prepared young people for life in Palestine, and Brit Trumpeldor, a revisionist Zionist youth organization; mutual-aid organizations: Jewish Guilds of Butchers, the Central Union of Jewish Artisans, Gemilut Chesed, a savings and loan bank, the Jewish Shareholders Bank, the Jewish Cooperative Bank of Real Estate Owners, Keren Kajemet, or the Jewish National Fund, which collected funds for the purchase of land in Palestine, the League of Aid for Workers in Palestine, and others.

for Jewish Communists, or vice versa for that matter. Agudat Israel, the organization of Orthodox Jews, fought with equal passion against both Zionists and Communists.*

7.

"The nationalists broke down their stalls until the police had to intervene," remembered Kazimierz Mocarski, "and the Jews at those stalls were so polite: 'Good day,' they said to Mother, 'what a fine little boy you have there,' and they gave me a candy. It was enough for Mother to say: 'Hey, that other Jew has that fabric for 2.10, and you're asking 2.20?' and the man bowed right away, saying: 'I'll give you a bit extra, Mrs. Mocarski, and you can have it for 2.05.' "

Jews can't only have been polite to the nice Mrs. Mocarski. They replaced the shop windows that had been broken and went on doing business on credit with the National Party activists who'd broken them. They made an effort to behave properly, even ingratiatingly, toward Poles, trying to win their favor.

According to the stories I heard from Polish and Jewish interlocutors, good neighborly relations were usually based on Jews performing some service to Poles; it could be writing a letter or keeping peelings for the pigs. Probably apart from ordinary neighborliness a role was played by the centuries-old tradition that taught them they had to pay their way into the societies they lived in, and the Jews saw nothing odd in it. But what did their Polish neighbors feel, raised on anti-Semitic propaganda, when they experienced such courtesies? Many of them must have experienced them as a humiliation.

The majority of Polish residents felt distrust for and distance from

---

* An Interior Ministry official has preserved for us an image of these conflicts. On the occasion of a visit to Białystok on July 2, 1933, by Włodzimierz Jabotyński, an advocate of the armed struggle for a Jewish state in Palestine, two thousand supporters of the Revisionist Zionist Party gathered, and when they set off to the synagogue carrying banners, a group of Bundists and the right-wing Poale Zion-Right members threw rotten eggs at them. Jabotyński also came to lecture in Łomża, where Jews from Jedwabne and Radziłów probably had a chance to hear him. He was very popular in the area. Szmul Wasersztejn describes in his diary that when he got to the police station in Jedwabne on July 10, 1941, the Germans interrogated him about whether he or his father belonged to Jabotyński's organization and whether it had helped him hide during the pogrom.

Jews, and also a sense of superiority because of the fact that they belonged to "the true faith." In turn, Jews felt scorn for "goys" (even when they tried not to show it) because they were illiterate, or because they drank and beat their wives, or didn't make sure their children got an education.

"My father was a tailor, he sewed cassocks for the priest, he had a lot of Polish acquaintances, but we children weren't allowed to play with Polish children," I was told by Izaak Lewin. "We saw them in school, which was mixed, or in the courtyard, but at home it was drummed into us: 'The only good things are Jewish.' "

8.

In 1936 the parliament passed a law restricting *shehita*, or ritual slaughter, violating the Treatise on Minorities, which forbade the state from interfering with the religious customs of minorities. Edicts followed on both the state and local level that reduced Jews to the status of second-class citizens. State schools that taught Yiddish lost their funding, and Polish schools were forbidden to skip the Sabbath. The Interior Ministry reports in those years show—probably without meaning to—how the state's attitude toward the Jewish question changed after Piłsudski's followers adopted a moderate form of the National Party's anti-Jewish ideology to shore up their own power. From 1936 onward, one notices a certain change of tone in the officials' reports. The National Party was gaining strength and assertiveness, and at the same time the nationalists are described in more positive terms, with some blame being placed on their victims. "The National Party's unruly supporters have permitted themselves minor anti-Jewish excesses. The Jews were partly responsible for bringing this on themselves by their arrogant and provocative behavior" (report of May 1936).

In March 1936, *The Catholic Cause* was still furious—in an article titled "A Jewish Master of Ceremonies' Brazenness at a Rifle Meeting in Ostrołęka"—that reformist circles had allowed a Jew to be master of ceremonies. Before long the Riflemen would not only refuse to entrust a Jew with that position but would also refuse to let him participate in its meetings.

Local ties binding the community, which developed at least in part from the citizens meeting at town council sessions, were already under pressure, and now they were often severed for good. A report from January 1938 discloses that in Białystok, after funding for Jewish schooling had been cut, the Jewish council members had left the meeting and withdrawn from the council's work. After 1936, many Jewish organizations were established, a majority of which were efforts by a threatened community to protect itself. And so it was that in Białystok in September 1936, an aid committee was set up to collect funds on behalf of the owners of boycotted shops. We know from Interior Ministry reports that it helped Jews in Radziłów and Jedwabne.

On March 23, 1937, a delegation from Ciechanowiec in the Białystok region set out for the capital with a petition to Jewish parliamentarians: "On market days two to three hundred people come into town from the countryside and groups of five or six of them picket a shop, not letting a single customer in, hurling insults like 'swine,' 'Jewish lackeys,' dragging customers out by force, and it sometimes happens that a customer who resists is picked up, thrown out, and even beaten. Within two or three months new Christian merchants have built themselves shops along the whole length of the marketplace and they egg the hooligans on. We turn to you, representatives. Save our town from annihilation."

An August 15, 1937, proclamation of the Białystok district conference of Jewish small-business owners, in which optimism masked despair, stated, "In the conviction that the present manifestation of racial terror is transitory, we call on all Jews not to yield to despair or apathy, but to hold fast their threatened positions in trade with good humor." At the same time it appealed to the Joint Distribution Committee, a Jewish relief organization in the United States, to enlarge its credit to small-business owners.

Things only got worse.

In August 1937, sixty-five violent anti-Jewish incidents were noted in the Białystok region. And so, "on August 19 during a market in the hamlet of Śniadowo a crowd shouting 'Jews to Palestine!' and 'There's no room for you in Poland!' drove away tradesmen. The fleeing Jews were thrashed with whips and one of them was hit on the head with a post. At the same time a basket of apples belonging to Jews was tipped over, 8 sacks of grain were slashed, and a horse's harness was cut up." A report of September 1937: "Although the number of violent incidents has dropped (62 compared to 65 in August), one feels a significant deepening of hatred toward Jews in the village as a whole."

Mosze Rozenbaum noted that Jewish boys had stopped going to swim in the river near Radziłów because they were immediately attacked by

Polish boys of their age. He himself was gravely beaten when he was thirteen, and his eleven-year-old cousin, Dawid Sawicki, was trapped in a stable by a gang of boys and roughed up so badly that he died two days later.

In February 1937, *The Catholic Cause* wrote enthusiastically: "The mood of excitement has turned into a systematic campaign in which the whole county population takes part. Farmers refuse to sell food to Jews, and entering villages, one sees signs that read 'No Jews.' Jewish shops are empty, water mills and windmills stand still, for no one gives them grain to grind." In August 1938, the diocesan paper praised the situation in Zaręby Kościelne: "Jewish stalls are watched so carefully that no peasant can go near them and 250 Jewish families are doomed to go hungry."

That hunger increasingly stared Jews in the face. But one should also remember that these were the times immediately following the Great Depression and the boycott only added to dramatically worsening economic conditions.

Toward the end of the 1930s, National Party activists changed their tactics. The state would intervene when they launched anti-Jewish campaigns, so nationalists started to fight against Communists, which was in keeping with government policy. When the National Party leaders euphemistically called for an "anti-Communist" vigil, it was code for an anti-Jewish vigil, but the authorities took them at face value and didn't intervene.

Zionists, who were staunch opponents of Communist Jews, were abused in exactly the same way as Jews with Communist leanings. Every manifestation of Communist activity was scrupulously recorded in the reports of the Interior Ministry. Those notes reveal how weak the activity of the Polish Communist Party was in the area.*

* In Radziłów, 1932 saw the peak of Polish Communist Party activity. Here are its activities: In March, a banner was hung out—*Down with the bloody Fascist dictatorship, long live the Polish Republic of councils, long live the Polish Communist Party.* In April, Chona Zeligson and Zajdel Rozenbaum were picked up while distributing Communist appeals. During a church fair in July, Chona Moruszewski and Zajdel Rozenbaum let loose in a crowd two pigeons painted red, with antistate slogans on ribbons. In September, Abram Moszek Bursztyn delivered sixty-six Communist appeals to a confidant for distribution, and a hundred appeals to "Comrade peasants" were scattered in a pasture. It is hard to know how many Communist Party members there were in Radziłów itself; the existing data relate to the whole district committee, which covered various areas, sometimes including Grajewo, sometimes Szczuczyn as well, and mention is made of dozens of people. After: Józef Kowalczyk, *The Polish Communist Party in the Łomża District, 1919–1938*, Warsaw: PWN, 1978.

In Radziłów on October 3, 1937, an anti-Communist vigil, prefaced by a church prayer service and the laying of a wreath on the grave of a fallen Camp for a Greater Poland member (who must have been one of the men shot by the police during the 1933 pogrom), gathered a thousand people in the marketplace. At that time Radziłów was a town of fifteen hundred inhabitants, including about six hundred Jews, so the "anti-Communist" vigil attracted almost the entire non-Jewish population, plus people who had come from neighboring villages. The next time there was such a large flock of people in the Radziłów marketplace was July 7, 1941.

In an Interior Ministry report of February 3, 1939, we read, "Anti-Semitism is spreading uncontrollably." In a climate where windows being smashed in Jewish homes, stalls being overturned, and Jews being beaten were daily occurrences, one case from Jedwabne that came to trial in 1939 concerned an accusation made against a Jewish woman. The district court in Łomża sentenced Etka Serwetarz to six months in prison for profaning the cross. *The Catholic Cause* revealed that "despite having it pointed out to her several times, she hung her underwear to dry near the cross and poured out slop and dirty water." Petty gripes among neighbors; by then, Jews and Poles lived in bitter hostility but still had common courtyards.

A Polish government official who had started the thirties thinking of Jews as full citizens, by the end of the decade treated Jewish citizens as aliens. This is clearly demonstrated by the reports of the Białystok Interior Ministry for 1939: "Jewry in these parts will always seek its own advantage and interests. This is due to its exile's psychology, links to world Jewry and extremely materialistic tendencies." Or: "The Jewish question, particularly how to resolve it in a way that is good for us, is one of the more emotionally charged and urgent subjects among wide swathes of the population" (the phrase "for us" connects the aims of nationalist thugs with the state's interests). And when Jews demonstrated civic virtue, they were given a condescending pat on the shoulder: "The subscription campaign on behalf of the Anti-Aircraft Defense Loan is being intensively and energetically conducted by the Jewish community, which has performed its duties as it ought, declaring a sum of six and a quarter million zlotys."

Besides the increasing anti-Semitic disturbances, the Jewish community was also worried about the coming war. Whereas previously, Zionist activists had had to campaign vigorously among young people to get them to leave for Palestine, there were now many more eager to go than had been foreseen when the quota was imposed by the British Mandate. Almost every Jew in the region dreamed of emigrating or at least sending his or her children to Palestine—or even better, to America. Not many made it.

Journal

JANUARY 2, 2001

I call to wish Stanisław Ramotowski a Happy New Year. He's just been discharged from the hospital with a prescription for some kind of salve, but his leg is still so painful that he can't sleep. I call the doctors I know; despite the vague description they all agree that if this patient doesn't get real medical help soon he may develop gangrene, leading to amputation or a painful death. I have to find him a hospital in Warsaw.

JANUARY 4, 2001

Białystok, seat of the regional branch of the Institute of National Remembrance. I've come to read documents from the Jedwabne trials. In the first trial in 1949, when twenty-two persons were charged with perpetrating the crime, eleven received prison sentences from eight to fifteen years; Karol Bardoń was sentenced to death but the sentence was subsequently commuted to a fifteen-year prison term.

Hundreds of pages of court reports in an awkward hand, with spelling errors. The years in which the interrogations were conducted make me regard them skeptically. I got my first impression of a Stalinist investigation from reading testimonies in Soviet trials and from Arthur Koestler's *Darkness at Noon*. But here no one is trying to link the accused to any subversive organization.

Gross wrote that the investigation was extraordinarily slipshod and that the whole thing bore little resemblance to a political trial. True, yet the testimonies sound authentic.

The suspect Władysław Miciura named these men as having taken part in the Jew-hunting: Eugeniusz Śliwecki, Franciszek Łojewski, Józef Sobuta, Franciszek Lusiński. "And there were also a lot of peasants from the countryside whom I didn't know. Most of them were young, they enjoyed the hunt and were cruel to the Jewish population."

The suspect Antoni Niebrzydowski: "There were a lot of people standing guard. I stress that when we stood guard over the Jews so they couldn't escape, they wept bitterly."

In the discussion in the press about Jedwabne one keeps hearing the argument that we can't believe the testimony of the accused men because it was extracted under duress. They spoke of beatings during the investigation and there's no reason not to believe them. The suspects may well have been beaten, people in police custody were "routinely" beaten at that time. It's strange that no use was made of the "forced" testimonies, in fact they were openly made light of. No attempt was made to reconstruct events, only routine questions were asked, and when the accused gave the names of additional killers, nothing—at least in the court documents—indicates that anyone took the trouble to locate them.

What's more, the witnesses said the same things as the suspects.

Roman Zawadzki: "Józef Żyluk came with a truncheon and took away a Jew who was hiding in the mill before the killings, but Józef Żyluk found him and took him away, another Jew was also taken . . . and Józef Żyluk herded the aforementioned Jews into the marketplace and later all the Jews were burned."

Julia Sokołowska: "Marian Karolak was the leader of the action I mentioned, he had a truncheon and he was whipping up all the Poles to kill Jews. I saw with my own eyes how Karolak brutalized Jews in the market square with his truncheon and drove Jews from their homes into the square and beat them so badly with his truncheon it was a terrible sight, all that killing."

Aleksandra Karwowska: "Józef Kubrzyniecki, residing in Jedwabne, stabbed eighteen Jews with a knife, he told me this at my house when he was putting in our stove."

Józef Grądowski, who escaped the pogrom but who was in the square that day, saw two Gestapo officers dragging Jews into the square, and only Poles apart from that: "I was sitting in the middle of the square, weeding grass . . . Many people were standing guard at that time, for each Jew there must have been five people standing guard. There weren't any people who were just onlookers; those who were there were helping round up the Jews. Polish children were wandering around the square. I heard two Polish women walking along the street, saying: 'Got to make sure there aren't any witnesses left.' "

In none of these trials did the investigating officers or the court take the slightest interest in establishing the personal details of the victims. The surnames of the victims appear only incidentally. And so Wincenty Gościcki, a suspect, testifies on the subject of individual murders that took place on July 10, before the Jews had been driven into the barn: "My wife got me up early, saying: 'I feel terrible, they're beating Jews with sticks right by our house.' I went outside. I was called outside by Urbanowski, who said: 'Look what's going on,' showing me the bodies of four Jews. They were, one, Fiszman; two, two of the Stryjakowskis; and Blubert."

JANUARY 5, 2001

Still poring over documents at the Białystok Institute of National Remembrance.

At the trial both suspects and witnesses contradicted the statements they had made during the investigation. From the new versions of events— as well as from the applications for early release made by families—you could reconstruct an ordinary day in Jedwabne. Sadly, July 10, 1941, was not that kind of day. But in the statements, the residents are wholly absorbed in their daily routines. Karol Bardoń (death penalty) repairs his car all day. Władysław Miciura (twelve years in prison), employed by the police as a carpenter, spends it wielding a carpenter's plane. Stanisław Zejer (ten years) is cutting clover in a field, on the mayor's orders. Antoni Niebrzydowski was weeding potato beds, and Czesław Lipiński also "spent time in the potatoes." Józef Żyluk was working in his garden, Feliks Tarnacki was riding his bicycle, Zygmunt Laudański was doing repairs in the kitchen, and Bolesław Ramotowski was just standing around.

Every other minute I have to break off reading the documents, because I'm trying to find a better hospital for Stanisław Ramotowski (the Bolesław Ramotowski who was convicted is no relative, he tells me).

The Białystok Institute of National Remembrance has only just been set up, which means it's squeezed into three rooms in an office building. I sit facing prosecutor Radosław Ignatiew, who is conducting the investigation into Jedwabne. A small man with round metal-rimmed glasses, a stiff collar, a tight necktie. His posture and manner are stiff. He lives in Łapy, just outside Białystok.

"I wasn't sure if I should come to the institute. I worked on murder cases, I was very engaged in what I did, I'd sit up late into the night. Formulating charges so that a murderer can't wiggle out of punishment, I tell you, it's better than an orgy," he tells me in a dry, dispassionate voice.

Sitting with Ignatiew is useful to me in that I constantly engage him in small talk by commenting on what I'm reading. The letters written by townspeople made a big impression on me: "I attach an affidavit of loyalty," and then you read that citizen So-and-So "was a good person, a good citizen of the Polish State, and of good reputation." Dozens of signatures at the bottom. The investigation doesn't leave much doubt as to what these good people were doing on July 10, 1941. "Can loyalty between local Poles really have kicked in to this degree when it came to the killing of Jews?" I venture. "In the first interrogations the suspects and the witnesses both knew a lot about the massacre, but by the time of the trial they've forgotten. Mustn't witnesses have retracted their testimony because the families of the suspects asked them to and because they were neighbors among whom they were going to live out their lives?" I wonder out loud. "It's appalling how sloppy this investigation was," I keep saying.

Ignatiew isn't entirely sure an informal conversation with a journalist doesn't violate some professional rule, and it's probably only old-fashioned courtesy to a woman that keeps him from cutting me off. But I have no doubt we read the case documents in the same way. It's hard for me to imagine that the current investigation isn't monitored and influenced by "political elements," but the prosecutor doesn't give the impression of a man who can be steered, particularly when it comes to the truth in a legal case.

JANUARY 6, 2001
I drive Stanisław Ramotowski from his miserable provincial hospital to Warsaw for a consultation.

JANUARY 7, 2001

An e-mail from my friend the poet Ewa Lipska in Vienna, who asked me if anything more could be written about Jedwabne after Gross's book. I replied that this was a strange question coming from a poet, and I told her about my research so far. "My dear, you're right," she replied. "I wasn't taking into account that life can't be reduced to a string of historical facts. A few months ago, before the whole discussion about Jedwabne, a woman from Łomża wrote to the Simon Wiesenthal Center. She'd read Wiesenthal's book *Justice Not Vengeance*, and described to him the history of her family, her town, the neighbors who stoned a Jew in 1941. At the end she asked him for a photograph. I replied to that letter in his name, I was deeply moved. It's a good thing people in Poland are beginning to talk about all this."

JANUARY 10, 2001

Visit to Ramotowski in the Warsaw hospital where, miraculously, he was admitted. We don't talk about Radziłów, because whenever I ask him any question about the killing of Jews he looks nervously down the hallway in case someone is listening.

JANUARY 12, 2001

Conversation with the theater director Erwin Axer at a dinner. He's skeptical about publicizing the Jedwabne affair. He tells me his late cousin Otto Axer, a graphic artist (and a friend of my father's), heard what happened to his father in the war only a few years before he died. I know what he's talking about. I read the beautiful story in the press. On the day Jews were told to report for "transport to the labor camps," Paul Axer, an elderly music teacher from Przemyśl, took off his yellow armband, gathered up his cat and fold-up chair, and set out on foot, ultimately reaching the banks of the San River. There he unfolded his chair and sat until dark, gazing at the river's depths. He was found by a couple of shepherds, brother and sister, who took him home, where they had room for him after their grandfather's recent death. He didn't make it till the end of the war, but he died among people who took him into their family. Erwin Axer corrects me: it wasn't a chair and a cat, it was a stool and a balalaika.

"His whole life, Otto loathed the peasants for their anti-Semitism. He was always saying they denounced Jews during the war. And then it turned out it was peasants who'd saved his father and the whole village knew about it. Besides, Jews denounced Jews, too," Erwin Axer concludes pointedly.

JANUARY 13, 2001

I visit Stanisław Ramotowski in the hospital as I've been doing every day. This time only briefly. "I'm in a rush," I explain, "because I have to take my daughter Ola to the synagogue. Ola is preparing for her bat mitzvah, a ceremony for a girl turning thirteen. A ceremony your wife wouldn't have had because in her time they only held bar mitzvahs, for boys. Ola has Hebrew lessons and meets with a rabbi to work on her own commentary on an excerpt from the Torah, which she has to present during the ceremony at the synagogue."

"You really are a brave woman to tell me these things," Ramotowski comments. "Because you really don't look Jewish at all."

JANUARY 15, 2001

In the hospital, a talk with the attending doctor. They can't amputate Ramotowski's leg on account of his age, eighty-seven, and his heart condition. He'll have to undergo many months of treatment.

Meanwhile his wife, whose osteoporosis makes her unable to walk and who is almost completely blind, has remained behind in Radziłów, in the cottage where the cold seeps in through cracks in the beams and the privy's out in the yard. Every day I call Stanisław's niece to pass on greetings to his wife. I hear that Marianna isn't getting out of bed and has stopped eating. The only thing to do is to bring her to the same hospital as Ramotowski. She really needs a checkup, too.

JANUARY 17, 2001

I arrange a date for Marianna to be admitted to the hospital and bring the news to Stanisław like a precious gift. She has already been prepared for the journey by his niece. But he stiffens, saying it's out of the question. He is furious. It takes a lot to get out of him what's the matter. There are four old resistance fighters on his ward (he's in a military hospital because he was in the Home Army during the war) who giggle constantly at jokes about Jews. When his wife appears they'll see she's Jewish and give him a hard time.

"How will they know?" I ask.

He answers my question with a question: "Does she look and talk like a woman from Radziłów?"

JANUARY 18, 2001

In the Jewish Historical Institute archive I take microfiche from wooden boxes from Jedwabne and surrounding towns: Kolno, Radziłów, Stawiski, Szczuczyn, Wizna, Tykocin, Wąsosz. Dozens of testimonies of Holocaust survivors that, besides giving descriptions of German atrocities, also describe pogroms carried out by Polish neighbors. An appalling picture emerges from them of what was going on all across eastern Poland after the Soviets left. Germans ordered Jews to weed squares and conduct "funerals" for Lenin or Stalin, that is, smash statues with a song on their lips. They were humiliated and beaten with the help and to the applause of locals. Jews were taken out of town and shot or killed in the road in broad daylight, and Poles helped hunt Jews down. In three cases, villages were almost entirely annihilated, and this was done—so write Holocaust survivors—by Polish inhabitants with the permission or even at the urging of the Germans. Not just on July 7 in Radziłów and July 10 in Jedwabne, but earlier, on July 5, in Wąsosz.

Szymon Datner, a renowned historian who worked at the Jewish Historical Institute and with the Main Commission for the Investigation of Nazi Crimes, took down witness statements and edited some of the testimonies for the Jewish Historical Commission in the Białystok district after the war. He wrote about Wąsosz: "This quiet little town was the first to fall victim to bloodthirsty instincts. The police and local hooligans went to the houses of Jews in town and carried out a "sacred task" after the example of the slaughter in Kishinev, he wrote, referring to the most famous Russian pogrom, which took place at the beginning of the twentieth century. There was killing in homes and on the street. Women were raped and had their breasts cut off. If children were found with their parents at home the children were killed first. They were smashed against the walls."

I should add the massacre in Wąsosz to my book.

From Radziłów there is a series of testimonies, one by Menachem Finkelsztejn, one by Chana Finkelsztejn, and a collective testimony edited by Datner, about one family that got away in Radziłów: the Finkelsztejns, husband, wife, and four children. Menachem and Chana must be siblings. Chana describes not only the massacre but their time in hiding. "The peasants, supported by the village head, wanted to tie us up and take us to the Gestapo. We escaped, each in a different direction, I with my younger brother . . . We suffered hunger, cold, filthy conditions. Death stared us in the eye every day. During this time we changed hiding places fifty-two times."

Datner writes that in 1945, right after the liberation, peasants murdered two Jews from Radziłów, Mosze Dorogoj and his son Akiwa, immediately after they came out of hiding, because they were inconvenient witnesses to the massacre. At that news the Finkelsztejns fled to Białystok, which was their salvation. What became of them later? Can they still be alive? How can I find them?

JANUARY 19, 2001

My thoughts keep returning to the marketplace in Jedwabne. Did the Jews know they were going to their deaths? Or did they delude themselves into thinking they would survive, up until the moment when the flames erupted?

In Menachem Turek's testimony, which I read at the Jewish Historical Institute, there is a story about Jews from Tykocin, a little town in the Białystok region, who were taken out of town and killed by Germans on August 25. This came after a whole series of killings, both German and Polish, but the Jews did not give up hope. "It was announced that all Jews were to assemble in the marketplace the next day at 6:00 a.m., men, women, and children, with the exception of invalids. Many of the women were in hysterics. There was weeping and confusion, they began running to visit each other. Wringing their hands, raising their eyes to heaven, they asked: What's happening, what are we to do? There was a spontaneous gathering at the rabbi's. Some thought they should run away, others maintained nothing terrible would happen, and if part of the community fled, firstly they would be caught, because the whole area was hostile to Jews, and secondly, the Jews who stayed behind might suffer because of the ones who fled. They tried to get some information, but the Poles kept quiet. After a long discussion they decided they would all go to the marketplace together. It was a long night, nobody got any sleep."

JANUARY 20, 2001

In today's *Gazeta*, an interview with the chairman of the Institute of National Remembrance Council, Sławomir Radoń. He comes to one conclusion: Gross is damaging Poland. At a press conference in December he was already saying *Neighbors* was a dishonest, unreliable book, that the pogrom was organized by the German authorities, and that the Germans provided the fuel to set the barn on fire. Is this going to be the Institute of National Remembrance's official position?

In his 1946 study, historian Szymon Datner writes, "For virtually the entire population of the Łomża and Szczuczyn districts, who were under the spell of the ultranationalist, anti-Semitic ideology of the National Party movement, the occasion arose to rid themselves—under the highest German protection—of their centuries-old neighbors and competitors, those alien and accursed Jews."

Menachem Turek remembers, "To the sounds of savage threats, cries of revenge, and curses, a mob drunk on looting, led by nationalists who were experienced in boycotting Jewish shops, dragged everything that fell into their hands from Jewish homes. This was a heavy blow not only because family possessions gathered and preserved for generations disappeared overnight and the next day not a single pot was left for a family to cook its dinner in, but because it was all done by inhabitants of the same town."

Basia Kacper of Szczuczyn testifies that the pogroms were organized by "decent Polish youth and hooligans." She mentions "Jonkajtys the school head" as their organizer.

I look through a later text by Datner from the Jewish Historical Institute newsletter of 1967, *The Destruction of the Jewish Population in the Białystok Region*. It was cited at the session at the History Institute of the Polish Academy of Sciences as proof that the July 1941 pogroms were the work of the Germans.

"The invasion of German troops was accompanied by the cruel and bloody slaughter of the Jewish population," Datner wrote. The town of Wąsosz "fell victim first"; in Radziłów "people were burned alive"; in Jedwabne they "perished in cruel conditions." Only an attentive reader will notice the impersonal construction, mentioning no perpetrators, and the subsequent sentence: "However, the greater part of the slaughter in these first months of occupation the Germans carried out on their own."

JANUARY 21, 2001

A conversation with Helena Datner-Śpiewak, Szymon Datner's daughter. We've been friends for years; I visited her while her father was still alive and living with her.

Helena tells me she has known about Jedwabne for a long time, from her father, but only now has she realized the scale of the crime. I ask her why her father wrote a piece in 1967 that refused to say straight out that the pogroms were the work of the local populations, which he knew because he had taken the testimonies of survivors. In 1946 he wrote about pogroms carried out by locals. Was it that this book, which he wrote in Yiddish, wasn't destined for a Polish readership? And if not, what happened during those twenty years to make him reluctant or unable to repeat the truth he revealed right after the war? Did he think only a text that airbrushed the truth could pass the censors? Did he fear a wave of Communist Party–orchestrated anti-Semitism would destroy the Jewish Historical Institute and that its archive would end up in the trash? Perhaps he was terrified, in a state of mind not unknown to many Jewish Historical Institute employees, and not without reason.

Helena says that the existence of the institute was indeed under threat at that time, but her father only became its director in 1969, and remained so only briefly. He was not a timid man, it seems to her. At the height of Stalinism he was fired from the institute because he protested when some insult to the Joint Distribution Committee was added to a text of his—in accordance with the mandatory party line. Until 1956 he did various jobs, was a mason's assistant, taught literacy classes. "In the Stalinist period it was much more dangerous to behave decently," says Helena, "and my father paid a high price for it. But later, during the anti-Semitic campaign, he joined Kazimierz Kąkol, the editor in chief of the then disgraceful weekly *Prawo i Życie* (Law and Life) and the author of vile texts, and in 1968 my father's book *A Forest of Righteous Men* appeared, about Poles who rescued Jews." Datner's joining with Kąkol makes one realize what fear must have been caused by the renewed hatred toward Jews. Publishing a book like that at that time meant taking the official line— one of the leitmotifs of the anti-Semitic campaign was the theme of ingratitude: Jews slander Poland, though so many Poles risked their lives for them. The book, as Datner wrote in the introduction, was to "illustrate the stance taken by the Polish people in the face of the Jewish people being cut off at the root in full view of the world."

"My father always stressed that he hadn't written a single word in the book that was untrue," says Helena. "And whenever anyone started speaking badly of the Poles he would say he wouldn't have survived without the help of Polish peasants after his escape from the ghetto." Datner described how his hosts in the village of Dworzysko near Sokółka in the Białystok region provided the partisan division he had joined with food and once warned them against the Germans. Once, he told Helena they were Belorussians, not Polish peasants.

In a chapter on Poles in the Białystok region who had saved Jews I find the name of Antonina Wyrzykowska of Janczewko near Jedwabne and the names of those she sheltered: Izrael (Srul) Grądowski (he must be the same man whose trial testimony I read); Jankiel Kubrzański (later he will become Jack Kubran); Berek, Elke, and Mojżesz (Mosze) Olszewicz; Lea Sosnowska (later, Lea Kubrzańska or Kubran), Szmul Wasersztejn.

JANUARY 25, 2001

Marianna Ramotowska in the hospital on Szaserów. Ramotowski spends hours sitting in her room. He tells me that his wife testified in some trials (I *must* find information on the trials and her testimony), and he was interrogated many years later by the prosecutor and asked how he'd saved his wife. He told the prosecutor that the Poles had committed the atrocity. "He started screaming at me that it was the Germans. I got upset, grabbed my cap, and said: 'If you know better, there's nothing for us to talk about,' and left."

Was the prosecutor who interrogated him Waldemar Monkiewicz? And did he see trucks full of Germans in Radziłów as well?

JANUARY 27, 2001

In the *Rzeczpospolita* (Republic), a piece by a well-known historian, Professor Tomasz Strzembosz, "Collaboration Passed Over in Silence." The author cites stories about Jews in the Jedwabne area who killed Poles and also collaborated with and made denunciations to the Soviet authorities, and concludes: "The Jewish population, and especially the youth and urban poor, took part en masse in welcoming Soviet troops. Weapons in hand."

Where are those masses of Jews supposed to have gotten their arms from? It's ridiculous.

The professor, as he wrote in 1991 in the journal *Karta*, researched the anti-Soviet partisan groups in the Białystok district, concentrating on the Kobielno wilderness area, the marshes along the banks of the Biebrza river that are almost inaccessible for the greater part of the year. Several dozen partisans were in hiding there, at times several hundred camped out, mainly those who were in hiding from the Soviets. Now Strzembosz refers to people he interviewed years ago and with whom he carried on a correspondence regarding Kobielno. As proof of the Jews' collaboration, Strzembosz quotes a letter by a local resident, Kazimierz Odyniec, who wrote that "the corpses of Polish partisans who had fought in Kobielno were carted off by a neighbor of my uncle Władek Łojewski, the Jew Całko." But what does that prove? Polish peasants were regularly forced to transport Jews to the ghettos and sites of execution, but it would be nonsense to treat this as collaboration.

Strzembosz cites several witnesses from Jedwabne. One of them was Łucja Chojnowska, a relative of the Laudańskis': "In Jedwabne, where the majority of the population was Jewish, there were only three homes that didn't fly the red flag when the Russians came. Our house was among the three." But Jedwabne was only about 40 percent Jewish. The statement that only three houses didn't fly a flag means that almost all Polish homes welcomed the Russians with red flags.

Another local, Jerzy Tarnacki of Jedwabne, described how they came to arrest him: "A patrol made up of the Polish citizen Kurpiewski and a Jew named Czapnik came for me and my brother Antek." So: one Pole and one Jew.

After citing testimonies like this, Strzembosz takes the moral high ground: "Even if the Jews didn't see Poland as their fatherland, they didn't have to treat it like the occupying forces did and work with Poland's mortal enemy to kill Polish soldiers and murder Polish civilians fleeing eastward. Nor did they have to take part in selecting their neighbors for deportation, those terrible acts of collective responsibility."

"Deportation" is a word with an overwhelming emotional charge; whole families, mothers, children, elderly people fell victim to deportations, and the truth about them was suppressed for years. Just like the murder of Jews in Jedwabne. But the professor must know what most read-ers don't know: that along with all the Poles, thousands of Jews were also deported from Poland (according to the historical estimates, Poles made up 50 percent of deportees, Jews 20 to 30 percent, though they consti-tuted no more than 10 percent of the population). The special role of de-portations in Polish martyrology is a separate matter. Compared to the gas chambers of Auschwitz, the deportation of Jews into the interior of Russia, even to Siberia, offered what later turned out to be the greatest chance of survival.

Strzembosz reproaches Gross for basing his work on "security police materials gathered from the brutal investigations of 1949 and 1953, at a time when Polish bishops were condemned for treason against the Polish nation and spying for 'imperialists.'" Had he cast an eye over the trial documents he would have noticed that although the Jedwabne killers were tried at a time when there were show trials of priests and bishops, the trial on Jedwabne was an ordinary criminal trial. Writing about collaboration and treason by Jews who welcomed the Red Army, the author seems un-aware that the alternative to the Soviets wasn't a free Poland but a Nazi regime. Use of the term "treason" has another built-in trap. The same terms should be used for the Polish population that welcomed the German troops to the area with flowers and triumphal gates in June 1941. After all, they did so for analogous reasons—they weren't glad that Poland was under foreign occupation, they were glad the hated Soviets had gone.

Ten or fifteen years ago, when Strzembosz was doing his research in the area, many more perpetrators and witnesses of the Jedwabne massacre were still alive than are today. How many of them did he interview? Just think of the invaluable material he had at hand. It seems unlikely to me that he never came across the subject of the killings of Jews in the course of his research. On the other hand, it's possible he wasn't paying atten-tion. He was studying the fate of the partisans of Kobielno, denounced and killed on the spot by the NKVD or deported to Russia, so he didn't want to hear anything else. To the question of why he never touched on the theme of the crime committed against the Jews before, Strzembosz replies that Polish-Jewish relations was never his field. Which doesn't prevent him from suddenly becoming an expert on the subject after the publication of Gross's book.

FEBRUARY 2, 2001

In the *Republic*, Adam Cyra, an employee of the Auschwitz-Birkenau State Museum, delivers a homily to Jerzy Laudański, a prisoner of Auschwitz and Sachsenhausen. Regarding the crime in Jedwabne, Cyra has nothing more to say than that his hero was tortured and tried in a Stalinist court for participation in the crime. "Kazimierz, Jerzy Laudański's eldest brother, defends him with zeal, believing in the just verdict of history," Cyra says, bemoaning the Laudańskis' fate.

The *Republic* published this piece without a word of commentary. Or rather, with a visual commentary: camp photographs of Jerzy Laudański. The connotation is obvious: the striped prisoner's uniform of Auschwitz is probably the clearest symbol of victimhood in twentieth-century Europe. Photographs like that also play a polemical role: Jews reserve to themselves the right to be the worst victims of Auschwitz, and here you have a Pole, and one slandered by Jews, to boot. The text leaves no doubt: a righteous man, a hero, is being attacked. As if only decent people were deported to Auschwitz.

In the hospital with the Ramotowskis. Marianna doesn't get out of bed, but Stanisław has made himself at home in the hospital; he knows everyone around him and has a lively social life (the chief doctor complains to me that he spends the whole day on his feet). When I arrive, he pulls me out of the ward, we find a spot where he can smoke, and sitting on hard chairs we talk for hours.

Stanisław went drinking with the killers many times, to get from them details of the crime. He had no children. He had no one he could tell the truth. But he wanted to know. Now I am getting that knowledge out of him.

FEBRUARY 4, 2001

In Radziłów with Jan Skrodzki. We begin by visiting a childhood friend of his, Marysia Korycińska, and find her sister, brother-in-law, and husband. Jan Skrodzki recalls the Jewish cemetery, some two kilometers from town, where after the war he saw only a tombstone here and there.

"They took those stones away for sharpening axes," Marysia's husband, Józef Koryciński, says, taking up the subject. "I don't think there was a farmer in Radziłów who didn't have whetstones made of burial stones. They cut down all the tall pines that grew there for firewood. I remember them, because during the war we went there to gather crows' eggs, and a crow isn't like a raven, it doesn't build its nest on a low branch."

"When people started rebuilding, they took gravel in wheelbarrows and plastered their walls with Jews," Marysia's brother-in-law Józef K. chortles. "And the new authorities used whatever the country folk hadn't stolen in the night to build some road. Sorrel grew wild on the graves, it stood tall, and you always earned those few extra zlotys."

"What are you going on about?" his wife interrupts. "Sorrel like that would be foamy, there was a lot of fat in that ground. Who would eat sorrel like that from a cemetery?"

"But it fetched a good price."

Jan and I are staying with his family in Radziłów. We talk with his cousin Piotr Kosmaczewski. After the war Piotr drove people who were being interrogated "about the Jews" to the railway station, and waited all day at a farm near the station to pick them up and take them home. He drove Jan's father, Zygmunt Skrodzki. He also remembers another trial that involved charges "about the Jews." In his view it was no more than a pretext for interrogating people connected to the anti-Communist underground, but still, this means there was more than one trial on Jedwabne. This is a big discovery.

FEBRUARY 5, 2001

We visit Jan Skrodzki's old friends one by one. One of the people we talk to pulls out a book about Home Army operations in the region by Jan Orzechowski, whose underground name was "Strzała" (Arrow). It has photographs of Home Army members from Radziłów. I know three of their names from Menachem Finkelsztejn's testimony. From the pages of a book on Polish patriots the faces of three murderers gaze out at me.

FEBRUARY 6, 2001

Back in Warsaw, where Adam Michnik has arranged for me to talk to the film director Jerzy Skolimowski. Adam is urging him to make a film about Jedwabne. He thinks there is bound to be a film and, fearing it will be anti-Polish, he wants to get ahead of the curve. I'm supposed to supply heroic figures. A friend of mine who's helping me take care of the Ramotowskis thinks they are the perfect heroes for a movie: a Jewish woman and a Pole, a great peril, a great love that lasted sixty years: in other words, all the ingredients of a good screenplay. However, I dampen Skolimowski's enthusiasm, which in any case is only moderate. I explain to him that Jedwabne doesn't provide the best material for a pro-Polish film.

2

I Wanted to Save Her Life— Love Came Later

or, The Story of Rachela Finkelsztejn and Stanisław Ramotowski

Stanisław Ramotowski was on his way from Kramarzewo to Radziłów when he saw the first German tank on the road. It must have been June 23, 1941, because he remembers the Russians had fled Radziłów the day before. Antoni Kosmaczewski was sitting on the tank, and as soon as he saw Ramotowski he yelled, "Take your hands out of your pockets!" Ramotowski thought, He's already feeling like a big shot, in a position to lecture people on how to behave toward the new authorities. He couldn't have known that two weeks later Kosmaczewski would participate in the murder of Radziłów's Jews.

"In the Kramarzewo I knew," Ramotowski tells me, "people lived quietly, nobody looted or went around killing Jews. Until one day I met my friend Malinowski from Czerwonki and he says to me: some people are getting together from the villages in the area to do the same job they did the day before in Wąsosz. And what had they done in Wąsosz? The farmers drove by Jewish houses in wagons and murdered the men, women, and children with axes. The streets were drenched in blood. I ran to warn the Finkelsztejn family right away."

The Finkelsztejns had a mill in Dziewięcin, right next to Kramarzewo; their garden bordered the Ramotowskis'. One of their daughters was already married; their other daughter—Rachela—had long been a favorite of Ramotowski's.

Marianna Ramotowska,
formerly Rachela Finkelsztejn,
and her husband, Stanisław.
Dziewięcin, near Radziłów,
1950s. (Author's private
collection)

Marianna and Stanisław Ramotowski in an Evangelical
nursing home near Warsaw toward the end of their lives,
2001. (Photograph © Krzysztof Miller / Agencja Gazeta)

"She was delicate, with two little braids. She'd worn glasses since she was a child," he says, looking at his wife with tenderness and pride.

Sixty years after Rachela first stole shy glances at him, Ramotowski himself is still a handsome man, tall and fair with a noble profile and big blue eyes with a perpetual twinkle. And Rachela? I look at old pictures of her and see a modest girl, skinny, alert, and bespectacled.

"What did your parents say?" I ask.

"They weren't crazy about the idea. Before the war, my wife's mother once pursued us so hotly when we were going to hide in the corn that Marianna lost a shoe."

"But back then you called her Rachela. Do you still sometimes call her that?"

"As soon as we had her baptized, I switched to Marianna."

"Why Marianna, exactly?" I asked Mrs. Ramotowski later.

"I took the name they gave me."

"They thought they were safe," Ramotowski goes on. "They didn't believe me and I had to spend quite a while persuading them before they agreed to come onto our land. It was still night when people started to drive to Radziłów in wagons to settle scores with the Jews. Dziewięcin was on their way, so they stopped to smash the windows at the mill and loot what they could. Not much, because that evening I had gone with my brother-in-law and packed up the Finkelsztejns' things in sacks and thrown them up in the attic. There were some supplies there; a crate of vodka, a crate of soap."

"Where were they coming from?"

"From Wąsosz, from Żebry. All of Orlikowo must have been there. The same with the folks from Słucz. I don't think any one of us in Kramarzewo or from Czerwonki nearby took part. I promised the Finkelsztejns I'd go and see what was going on in town . . . They were dragging Jews out of their homes and driving them into the square. I saw little Jewish kids hugging one another and bowing their heads. I didn't see the barn burning, I wanted to get back and find a good way to hide the Finkelsztejns, but I had a good look around. Poles were guarding the streets so that Jews couldn't get away. They were already looting Jewish homes when the Jews were on the way to the barn."

"Did you see Germans?"

"One policeman. He was standing on a balcony taking pictures. There were about four policemen for all of Radziłów at that time. No German joined in the killing, either in Wąsosz or in Radziłów, or in Jedwabne. Poles were the ones hunting down and rounding up the Jews. And right away they went to Jewish homes to take what they could find. Had they lost all sense of decency? People went crazy, they went into homes, ripped open quilts, feathers were flying around, the wind blew them in all directions, and they went home with a bundle on their backs, only to come straight back with an empty sack."

"Men?"

"Mostly, but I saw women, too, only fewer of them."

"What about children?"

"Those who could carry things were eager enough. There were crowds of people lining up for it, I just don't know where God was at that moment."

When I ask Stanisław Ramotowski why he thinks it all ended in an atrocity, his wife breaks in: "That's not for us to know."

From our first encounters, Marianna Ramotowska has kept a distance, hiding behind feigned memory loss, trying to keep us from talking about the atrocity or about anything Jewish. When I wished her a happy Hanukkah or Rosh Hashanah, she would start to say a rosary. Asked what she remembered of Hanukkah in her parents' home, she answered with a question: "Hanukkah is the Festival of the Harvest, right?" How can she not remember? Hanukkah is a holiday virtually invented for children: they get presents, the table is covered with sweets.

But Ramotowski takes up the subject: "Some people probably did it for the killing itself, we had such backward Christians here that for them the life of a Jew wasn't worth anything. But most of them did it for the looting and because the Germans gave permission."

"Did you have the feeling you were the only just man in Radziłów?"

"Oh no, there were plenty of decent folk in Radziłów! The problem is, there were more of the other kind."

"And where did you get the idea to help Jews?"

"My whole family were decent people. Stealing or killing, my God, it was unthinkable. I was well brought up. And I was smart enough, I suppose, I wasn't afraid of anything, a scared man probably wouldn't have done it. But also, for as long as I can remember, I played with Jewish girls and boys, went to their dances, listened to their fiddles."

"Were you alone in this?"

"It was probably just me. I always liked being around them."

Izaak Finkelsztejn's family had been settled in the area for centuries. Besides the mill they had eight hectares of farmland; they kept cattle, horses, chickens, ducks, and turkeys.

"At our mill," Marianna Ramotowska explains to me, "we had modern machines we bought for dollars. A Francis water turbine, Hungarian Ganz rollers, shorter and longer ones for rye, a German Seck press for wheat. After the war, when they were looting everything, they couldn't drag the turbine out of the water, and that's how we managed to rebuild the mill."

The family of her mother, Sara Jankielewska, was from Kielce in central Poland. Her mother knew German and Russian as well as Yiddish and Hebrew. And her Polish was so good the neighbors came to dictate letters to her. Rachela remembered her mother always bent over the same heading: "Praised be the Lord Jesus Christ."

"Grandfather Jankielewski always said that he would never let a daughter of his marry in the village, as he could afford a better dowry," she says. "Mama had brothers who had office jobs. One was the director of a steel mine in Kądzielnia, another lived in Kielce and was managing director of mines that belonged to the Warsaw branch of the family, another built bridges, my mother's sister married a doctor. There was also a professor in our family who lived in Berlin."

Her father died when Rachela was a small child, and her oldest brother became the head of the household. In 1930 she finished school in Radziłów and was sent to her uncle in Kielce, in whose household—in contrast with her own—Polish was spoken. There she got a junior high school certificate and went to work as a cashier at a German company that sold Chevrolet cars. Whenever she went home to Radziłów, she sent a Polish farmhand with a note to Ramotowski telling him she was home—a sign of affection to her neighbor across the way.

Ramotowski went to see the wedding of Rachela's sister, Matylda. Rachela had told him about it, but she didn't dare go up to him or invite him as a wedding guest.

"The wedding took place in front of their house. A rabbi came, the couple stood under a canopy, the groom broke a glass. I was the only Pole there. I stood off to one side. Though Marianna's cousin invited me inside I didn't go in the house because I knew Rachela's sister wasn't expecting any Poles."

"If there hadn't been a war, Rachela's mother probably wouldn't have let her daughter marry you?"

"Never."

"And if she'd agreed on the condition that you convert to Judaism?"

"I would have said yes, without even asking for time to think it over. I never had any Polish girlfriend I can remember."

The war ended Rachela's career in the city. In September 1939, she was on holiday at her mother's in Radziłów and didn't go back to Kielce.

She: "As soon as the Soviets came they took over our mill."

A Pole was appointed by the new authorities as manager of the Finkelsztejns' mill, but they, the Finkelsztejn family, were permitted to live and work in the mill as hired labor.

He: "Under the Soviets our life here in Kramarzewo went on as normal. There were twenty-six households and not one family was deported. Only a farmer who got up at a meeting and made a critical comment about poverty in the Soviet Union—'There are more pigs at our fair than in that whole Russia of yours.' They came and took him away the next day."

I ask Ramotowski if he remembers how Rachela's family behaved at that time.

"God forbid they'd ever take a liking to the Communists!"

"But the people in Radziłów say it was Jews who supported the new regime."

"The poorest Poles went to work in some capacity for the Soviets right away, but I didn't see any Jews do that. At least not in Radziłów."

To say that Stanisław has no prejudices against Jews is an understatement. When I remind him that someone from Rachela's family was said to have collaborated with the Soviet authorities, he breaks out: "What are you talking about? It's true Rachela's brother-in-law Lejbko Czerwiński was a Communist, and under the Russians he strutted around with a machine gun, but he was a black sheep in the family, they didn't like him, no, not one bit."

Ramotowski doesn't remember the Soviet occupation changing anything in relations between Jews and Poles. No one had any particular complaints about Jews in Kramarzewo, and Rachela's mother looked askance at him, the same as before.

Until the Germans and July 7 arrived. After making sure that the Finkelsztejns were safely hidden in the grain and bringing them food, Stanisław went to see what was going on at their mill. It was already late in the evening.

"There were looters there, behaving as if they owned the place. We all drank four bottles of vodka that I'd brought from upstairs. When they had all drunk a bit, my brother-in-law and I threw the Finkelsztejns' things, the things we'd hidden the day before, on our horse-drawn cart. It would give them something to live on later."

"Where did you hide them?"

"In the rye."

She: "We heard screaming and saw smoke from there. We were four kilometers from Radziłów."

He: "They lay in the grain for two days and two nights. They were thirsty, it was very hot. In the morning I chased the geese around with a bucket in my hand to show it was water for the geese. I was afraid of the neighbors. At my mother's house I walled off a hiding place for Rachela with planks between the stove and the wall, and another hiding place nearby for her family—her mother, Sara; her brother, Szabsa; her sister, Matylda, and her two children: Icchak, who had a paralyzed leg, and Hewel, the younger boy. I moved them in at night. Mama didn't say anything to the neighbors, but she went to Mazurek for advice—he was a friend, a paramedic, respected in the village. His idea was to baptize Marianna—then Rachela—and to have us marry. Mazurek, a good man, a little boorish, was very religious, you could call him a pietist. He wanted to bring Rachela into the faith. He persuaded me that as soon as she was baptized, we would be left in peace. 'You get married,' he said, 'and she will be registered with you.' And so it was. I didn't marry for love, that came later. I just liked her. I wanted to save a life."

She: "On All Saints' Day I always brought a candle to Mazurek's grave."

Kramarzewo belonged to the parish of Wąsosz, so Ramotowski went there to arrange the baptism and the wedding.

He: "I went to the presbytery—a big table, five stove burners, each with a goose prepared for roasting. The priest asked, 'How are you going to pay me? Cash isn't worth anything these days.' I said, 'We don't have anything, Father.' He replied, 'It can be rings, earrings, any gold.' I told him the Finkelsztejns' house in Dziewięcin had been completely plundered, there was nothing there, just broken windows and gaping holes. The priest said, 'I'll give you an example. We had Chaim around here, a poor Jew with a bundle, but when they laid a scythe to his throat, it turned out he had dollars *and* gold.' I started to shake, as if a flame was shooting from my head to my heels.

"He told me to go out to the entrance hall and wait. He didn't ask me back in, he just handed a piece of paper to me over the threshold and told me to take it to the priest in Radziłów, to get married there. On the way back I opened the message, and it said not to marry us at any cost. I crumpled it up and threw it away.

"That priest must have been given Jewish gold by the Wąsosz killers. He probably said he'd grant them absolution and some dumb farmer went to get him something for his trouble.

"After the war when my mother died, my brother went to him, and the priest told him he would bury my mother for less, just as long as I didn't come. And fool that I was, I didn't go to my own mother's funeral.

"I went to Radziłów; I had to talk to Father Dołęgowski fast, before he got together with the Wąsosz priest. I found him playing cards with his neighbor. He was a good man, only for starters he wanted six meters of rye. I said that the Germans took less than that for forged papers and in the end he came down to three. When I went with my brother-in-law to unload it in his barn, I saw the presbytery, it was long and wide, and there was grain stored there that no one would get any use from, it was eaten away by weevils. A store that would keep us going until spring would last weevils three hours."

Earlier, when Ramotowski was a boy and his father died, the former priest in Wąsosz demanded three hundred zlotys from his mother for the funeral.

"All my mother's savings came to one hundred fifty zlotys, our neighbor stood us the other one hundred fifty. Later my mother couldn't pay it off and we were hounded by a collector. If a priest in these parts had no mercy on a Christian woman, why would he take pity on Jews?" Stanisław muses.

The Radziłów parish chronicle shows that Rachela was baptized on July 17, 1941, in the presence of two witnesses: Józefa Burgrafowa, seventy-seven years of age, and Jan Mazurek, fifty-five years of age.

Ramotowski remembers taking her to the baptism.

"I drove her to the church, and we had to cross a little bridge near the Finkelsztejns' mill. The thugs who had occupied the mill were standing there, but they only watched us, they didn't do anything. I didn't see the baptism; Rachela went into the church with Mazurek and Burgrafowa, his close friend whom he'd asked to be Rachela's godmother. I waited outside. Feliks Mordasiewicz came up to me then and yelled, 'I know you have a Jewess living with you.' I said, 'Now she's been baptized, just you try to hurt her.' And he said, 'If it wasn't you I sure would.'"

The wedding took place two months later, on September 9, 1941, at eight in the morning, in the presence of two Polish witnesses.

He: "We were married by the curate—it was a quiet, modest wedding. There were maybe ten people present. My mom was still against it, but she wasn't saying anything anymore. At the wedding reception there was a lot of moonshine vodka. One of my friends, Feliks Godlewski, got drunk and shot at the windows. He was very warm toward us throughout; it's hard for me to believe that he had a hand in the killing, too."

"Were the bride's family at the wedding?"

"Her mother sat at a separate table, not at the main table, because the food wasn't kosher. In the beginning my Marianna hardly ate anything; she couldn't. I argued with her: 'You'll die of hunger, kiddo, is that what your God wants?'"

She: "When we got back from the church, my mother took off her ring, put it on my finger, and said, 'You're the only one who will survive.'"

He: "It was her fate to survive, and I was sent to make sure."

Ramotowski goes on: "I didn't know what I was getting into with that wedding. I was deluded; I was clever enough for any situation, but in this case I listened to people stupider than me. Somebody reported on the wedding, and they started to look for me, too. From that time on I was marked, and we both had to go into hiding. A couple of times policemen came to the house, but we took turns watching the farmyard through a gap in the beams and we'd duck right behind the stove. Once I saw Henryk Dziekoński asking my brother's little children about us, with a German policeman standing nearby. He didn't get anywhere on that occasion. But in the end a spy turned up who sent Marianna's family to their deaths. The Finkelsztejns were taken away and later Dziekoński came for Marianna, saying her family had been taken and that he knew

Marianna was with us. There was nothing we could do. Marianna came out of the hiding place. She knelt down in front of him, but it wasn't any use. I could have killed him, but my family would have died."

"Who was the spy?"

"I have my idea who it was, but I'm not sure. There was only one person in our neighborhood who looked for Jews everywhere, sniffed them out. Stanisław Żelechowski from Czerwonki. He informed on a grain trader in Wąsosz who had managed to escape from the roundup in the square and run to farmers he knew. Żelechowski tracked him down there, locked him in the pigsty, made him drink a whole bucket of water in one go, just to make him suffer, and then he handed him over to the police. Later he told the story himself with laughter. They gave him two kilos of sugar for it. The Germans weren't that generous but it was enough for some."

"How did you save Marianna?"

"The Germans were keeping several families in the shul who had escaped on the day of the massacre. I followed Marianna and Dziekoński and realized that's where she was being taken. I waited until it was evening, and the moment a policeman turned away, I ran inside. I lit a lantern, saw Marianna hunched up in a corner, gave her a hand up, and we ran out. I couldn't get the whole family out, but at least I got her out."

She: "The militia officer guarding us was Łasiewicz. He knew I was Stasinek's wife and he brought me a pillow that night."

It was too risky at home behind the shelf, so they found a hiding place at one of the neighbors'. In 1942 they had a child.

"The woman who delivered the child said it died right away," says Marianna, in tears. "Why was that? It was healthy when it was born."

"It died within a few hours, and it was for the best," Stanisław explains gently. "The three of us would never have been able to stay hidden."

She often returned to this, crying, and once she said to me that she was sure the child had been smothered with a pillow. A little while later she got pregnant again.

"My wife was pregnant, pretty far on, but she began to miscarry and she needed a doctor or she wouldn't survive. I took her all the way to Jedwabne, it was winter, I carried her in from the sled. The doctor was a *Volksdeutscher*, not from here."

"Did your wife look Jewish?"

"Not really. She spoke good Polish. But he got some help from a woman from near Jedwabne who recognized us. I carried my wife back to the sled, went back in to thank the doctor, and heard her saying, 'You just had a Jewess in here.' I left without saying thank you and drove the sled as fast as it would go. I always carried a gun. If they caught us, they wouldn't make us suffer; first I would slug them and then I would kill us both."

Ramotowski joined the Home Army. He was invited by a son of Mazurek's, the man who had told Rachela she should be baptized.

"In this area most people joined the NSZ, or National Armed Forces, the underground army that hated Jews,"* he recounts. "Dominik Grabowski and I were the ones from Kramarzewo who were in the Home Army. Sometimes I got an order to distribute arms somewhere. Once I got a pile of machine guns, all beat-up fossils. I had to drive down the road between Szczuczyn and Białystok, where I saw one German car after another. I thought, Risk a human life for a load of junk? But orders were orders. I made it. Later there was an operation near Czerwony Bór, where a lot of Germans were shot, so maybe one of those guns did the job. Marianna came with me on operations; she said she didn't want to live without me anyway."

Three times they encountered someone from Rachela's family. The first time Ramotowski ran into his wife's brother-in-law, the one who was the black sheep of the family.

"We were near the village, at the Laskowskis', and once they asked me to cross the river and help them mow on the other side. Over there, two men came out of the rye, in German uniforms, holding guns. I almost died, because it was Lejbko, her brother-in-law, with a friend—they'd recognized me by my voice. The friend was the son of Zandler, who had a dry-goods store in Radziłów before the war. After the massacre one of the killers, Aleksander Godlewski, moved into Zandler's house. They

---

* NSZ: Narodowe Siły Zbrojne, or National Armed Forces, a Polish underground armed formation at odds with the Polish Home Army over what the National Armed Forces considered the excessively conciliatory stance of the Home Army toward the Soviet Union and Red Army; the National Armed Forces, which were blatantly anti-Semitic, took the view that the Nazis were a lesser threat than the Soviets, and they continued anti-Soviet partisan operations after the war ended.

had killed two Germans. They said,. 'Today we're crossing over to the Soviet side. If we live through the night, we'll survive.' They wanted to find the Russian partisans."

One day Rachela's sister appeared at Ramotowski's mother's house. She had been in the synagogue in Radziłów, but had been taken with other Jews who'd survived the pogrom to the Milewo estate near Grajewo. A German was in charge there, but no one really guarded them closely.

"They were so terribly hungry there. She would come all the way over to us at night, by narrow lanes, about twenty kilometers, to ask for something to eat for her children. She was completely different from Marianna, strong as an ox and so proud she had never even spoken to me before. It was only when she came to us so horribly poor that she said, 'Stanisław, help me.' I scraped some food together, lard, bread, butter. But I had to bring her back, too. Dominik Grabowski, with whom we were hiding then, gave me his cart. I loaded some peat on the cart, hid her and the food underneath, and drove off. There was a militiaman on guard at the little bridge in Kramarzewo, but he didn't stop us."

Another time when Ramotowski was working in the fields of some farmers who were hiding them, a voice called out to him from the grain. "I looked and I saw a guy with a big head of hair, unshaven, and it was her cousin, Lejbko Finkelsztejn; he'd escaped from a transport to Treblinka. He was jumping with fleas, his whole body was crawling with them. I gave him some clothes, came back with a razor, and shaved him. He got involved with some thief from the town, they went out at night and stole geese. I tried to talk some sense into him but couldn't get him to listen. Somebody told the police about him and they came to get him; they caught him and killed him."

I ask him how many people helped them, how many knew about them.

He: "In the beginning, four households in Kramarzewo knew. They weren't helping us, but they knew. When Marianna's family had been taken away we took more trouble to hide properly, I didn't trust anybody then. The devil could get into anyone. We stayed with good friends from before the war, the Laskowskis from Kramarzewo and the Karpińskis from Czerwonki. I had an aunt in Konopki, and when we went by she called me 'darling, dearest,' but the first night already she told us to go, she couldn't stand being so scared. She didn't even give us a piece of bread for the road. Another uncle was prepared to hide us, but his son was the village head and gave him a terrible time about it. We stayed with a sister of my father's in Pieńki. It was all right there, and Rogowski lived in that village, too; we spent the night at his house sometimes. In Glinki there were two brothers, Franciszek and Józef Mrozicki, who were hiding from the Germans. They had a hiding place under the floorboards and we could go there to get some sleep. Friends from the Home Army knew how to contact me. In the daytime I worked in the fields for farmers I knew; in the evening I brought Marianna something to eat."

She: "So many nights we had to sleep in the woods, in gorges, in bunkers with the rats."

A critical time for Jews in hiding came with the evacuation of those territories by the Germans in 1944, when the front line shifted.

"But we stayed. I dug out a hole in a field and concealed it with a stone slab. German soldiers were coming from Kramarzewo and cutting a path through the rye right where our hiding place was. One shoved the slab aside with his foot and we were face-to-face. Marianna spoke to him in German. He told us the misery he'd suffered in the war and walked on."

In the evening a car came with another German and took them to a safe place beyond the front line.

"Toward the end of the war the Germans themselves felt shaken up," he goes on. "They were coming from Stalingrad, poor guys, all beat up, that's how we could tell it was almost over. Once the Czerwonki village head happened to come by the Karpiński settlement; he noticed us and went to find a German to tell him there was a Jewish woman staying with the Karpińskis. A German came by, asked if it were true, but he didn't insist, he didn't search the house."

As soon as the war ended they moved into the ruins of what was once the Finkelsztejns' house.

She: "Stasinek's mother was against me at first, but after the war she came from Kramarzewo to see us every day. I suppose she realized I was worth something."

They rebuilt the mill. He was the miller, she did the accounts.

"That should be said—they let us rebuild," says Mrs. Ramotowski, nodding.

At first, I think she means the Communist authorities, who could have taken the mill from them, but she means the neighbors.

I ask whether there was talk of the killings in town.

He: "In whispers or when people were drinking. Father Dołęgowski once came to carol with us; he was so fat you could barely pull him out of the sled. I asked him, 'Doesn't it bother you when a murderer comes to church wearing a Jew's fur coat?' Everybody knew that Dziekoński killed Jews and went around in Wolf Szlapak's coat. He didn't reply. Marianna was scared, she was tugging my sleeve."

I ask whether anyone survived from her extended family.

She: "They all died in Treblinka. Only my brother-in-law survived. He made it over to the Soviet side, he ended up in a camp, but got out in the end. After the war, he went to Sweden. He wrote to me from there asking whether his wife and children were alive. I didn't answer."

"Why not?"

She: "I didn't want to and you couldn't. The Dorogojs, a Jewish father and son from Radziłów who survived in hiding, were killed right after the war ended. Kosmaczewski and his brother had someone ask them to come drink half a liter of vodka and make peace with them, but in the hallway they came down on the Jews with axes. So there wouldn't be any witnesses. We lived in fear and they stole from us. All kinds of things happened."

He: "A few of them forced their way into the mill we'd just rebuilt, ordered me to lie on the floor, held a gun to my head. Earlier they'd left a note signed 'Tiger,' demanding twenty sacks of flour. They threw grain around and threatened the next time they'd blow up the mill. That time it wasn't for hiding Jews, it was pure robbery. But the next time, two years after the war had ended, Marianna wanted to buy back an oak cupboard that belonged to the family. It was in Rydzewo, at Chrostowski's—he'd even dug up trees from the Finkelsztejns' garden and taken them home. Somebody didn't like her wanting it back."

She: "They hung a note with a death sentence on our door. Because I wanted to pay for my own cupboard. I could have had a better one for the money, but it was a family keepsake. It was dark wood, in three sections, little doors on the side, two shelves inside."

He: "Two guys from Rydzewo hung that note on our door, Nietupski and Skrodzki. The National Armed Forces issued a lot of those sentences in our parts. They stole, beat people up, killed people. I went to my own people, who were in the Home Army. They got our sentence retracted. Somehow we survived. But there was pressure all the time."

"And did you get the cupboard back later?"

"Oh no, later I didn't want it anymore."

Marianna had a miscarriage soon after the note was nailed to their door. She couldn't have children after that.

"Did you have anything left from your family home?"

"We had a whole set of dishes made of Ćmielów porcelain. One of the neighbors gave us back two soup plates. Another neighbor gave us back a laundry basin, also of his own will. Good people."

Ramotowski interrupts her: "You're being ridiculous. Fat lot of goodness, giving back what doesn't belong to you. They would come by later: 'Lend me this, lend me that.' Not just them, others, too."

"They thought you had to pay for the fact that you had a Jewish wife?"

"That's what it came down to."

I ask Stanisław if his marrying a Jew was held against him.

"You can't really say that—she was respected."

Marianna chimes in: "They respected me for having been baptized, and they nodded to me when I passed."

He: "Once the carpenter Wiśniewski, one of the killers, was drinking beer at the bar at the inn. He was chattering on about my wife being Jewish. I went back at him: 'Haven't you killed enough of them already?' and slugged him. He hushed up and left and didn't jibe at me after that. I was with a couple of friends then, and one of them said, 'You're brave, all right, Stanisław.' I said I was just speaking the truth. Fabian Mordasiewicz came up to our table and threatened me: 'Maybe you should keep your truth to yourself.'"

I ask Marianna Ramotowska if it ever happened after the war that someone came up to her and said they were ashamed of what the Poles had done.

"No, but they weren't that bad to us, either; they knew we wouldn't accuse them. On the contrary, when there were suspicions in any case, we went to testify on their behalf. I testified for Władysław Łasiewicz, who was in the militia and in the Home Army. Once when he met Stasinek on the road he yelled at him: 'Get into the potato field!' Moments later, a whole army patrol passed by."

I read the testimony of Marianna Ramotowska at the trial of Feliks Godlewski, who was charged with killing Jews: "I am a baptized Jew ... I heard from Jews that they had an exceptionally good opinion of Godlewski. He always helped them, before and after the incident."

Despite the incriminating testimonies of other witnesses, the Ełk court decided to exonerate Godlewski. In the justification of the verdict it says: "We must emphasize the significance to the case of the testimony of Marianna Ramotowska—Jewish by origin—who presented the defendant Godlewski as someone who enjoyed an exceptional sympathy and good reputation among Jews. If the defendant Godlewski therefore had taken any part in the destruction of the Jews or had been hostile toward them, he would certainly not have earned this sympathy among them."

"And I also testified in the trial of a man who later came to me, kneeled down, threw his arms around my legs, and kissed me," she adds, in tears.

Every time I try to find out who this third man was, Marianna bursts into suppressed sobs. In the end she confesses to me that it was Leon Kosmaczewski.

I say: "Kosmaczewski is said to be among the worst murderers. Did you know what they all did, Godlewski, Łasiewicz, and Kosmaczewski?"

"I didn't know what the first two had done that day, and later they truly helped us. Everyone knew about Kosmaczewski. We would have helped any of the killers, otherwise we wouldn't survive."

He: "For them, killing a human being was like killing a fly. We lived here like sparrows in a bush. That's why there were no guilty verdicts. We had to defend them."

She: "Once, Henryk Dziekoński came to the mill, the one who had taken me to the ghetto back then. 'I can't take this, I'm going to kill him,' said Stanisław. And I said, 'Pour him out a bit more flour. Evil must be answered with good. Show him how to live in the world.'" (This was one of the stories Marianna Ramotowska told me many times, always in tears.)

In 1955 the secret police installed surveillance bugs around Ramotowski's farm, with his consent. They were keeping tabs on a neighbor, Jadwiga Dąbrowska, a relative of the partisan Stanisław Marchewko, a.k.a. "Fish," who died two years later, in 1957, betrayed to the secret police by his fellow partisans.

"In the evening we went to Ramotowski's house," a major in the secret police reported back on his business trip, "and after discussing with him the subject of introducing a working group to his farm, he presented the proposal to his wife, noting that since they couldn't very well do otherwise, they should agree and keep it secret, to which she expressed her assent, stressing that she understood the importance of keeping it quiet. Ramotowski's brother accepted our proposal in the same way. After they had committed to keeping the secret, Ramotowski showed us a place in the pigsty where our staff might set themselves up, and he went home to take his rest."

I never spoke about this with Stanisław. Nor did he tell me about it himself, and these papers only came to light after his death.

In the course of our dozens of conversations, Ramotowski remembered more and more killers.

"Aleksander Godlewski, oh, he was a killer, but he never went on trial. When I was walking around in Radziłów, he would duck into a side street. Once I said to him, 'Come on, let's go get a pint; why are you avoiding me?' It was such a relief to him; he didn't even let me pay for the beer.

"Mieczysław Strzelecki was one of the killers, he was a thug and a swine; Leon Paszkowski, Wincenty Piotrowski. I saw Jan Szymanowski and Jan Kreska driving their wagons from Żebry to go killing in Radziłów. Szymanowski was one of the first to kill in Wąsosz, but it still wasn't enough for him. And from Wąsosz there was also Karwowski who came; he later became their boss in the National Armed Forces. From Konopki there was Jagódko, he was terrible, and then Wiśniewski from Mściski, who had married a girl in Radziłów. I think of each of them from time to time.

"There were a lot of people like Felek Siedlecki, who didn't exactly join in but who watched and egged on the others. Or Bolek Siedlecki—you couldn't say he rounded people up, though he was in the square at the time. But there were plenty of people who were doing the killing. God forbid you ever meet any of them"—he looks at me anxiously, speaking of murderers who have been dead for years.

"Feliks and Mietek were real butchers," he says of the Mordasiewiczes. "There was a third brother, Jan, no better than they were. Professional thugs. But those who killed didn't have an easy death themselves later. A friend of mine who was in the hospital next to Feliks Mordasiewicz told me he was calling out the names of the Jews he'd killed. Death was nearing and it was all coming back to haunt him. The family tried to shut him up, but he was shouting in his hospital bed, 'There are a lot of them in the grain, out with them.'"

I brought Ramotowski all the newspaper articles I had on Jedwabne and Radziłów. He started reading them on the spot, before I left. (Marianna told me he had borrowed every book in the Radziłów public library five times.) One time we were looking at a Radziłów paper from the sixties, at pictures of an orchestra at a funeral.

"Lovely shot," he commented. "Look, he's a killer, and there's another killer. That guy's son once asked me if my wife would forgive him for his father's behavior. Another time Jan Chrostowski was sick in bed. He and his wife sold moonshine vodka. I went to get some vodka. He ordered a chair to be brought for me and confessed to me what he had done to the Jews. 'If you would only take a tiny part of the burden off me, you and your wife,' he said. I said to him, 'Man, we don't have anything against you, but for forgiveness you'll have to look somewhere else.'"

In the sixties, the villagers stopped bringing grain to the mill, and the Ramotowskis had to live off their farm. It is located in an impoverished area, the earth is miserable there, but I've rarely seen the kind of poverty and desolation that I did on their farm. The house was sunk on its dilapidated foundation, wind howled in gaps between the beams, the toilet was in the yard, its doors fallen off and never put back on their hinges. I don't know why it was so bad. Was it because Marianna spent most of her life perched nervously on a stool and didn't know how to make a home? Stanisław told me that she didn't like cleaning and cooking and wasn't good at it, and so he did it. Not perfectly, I suppose. Was it because Stanisław was a drinker? He had half-destroyed hands with frostbitten fingers; they'd had to be thawed once after he fell asleep in the snow on his cart. The horse brought him home, saving his life.

But it seemed to me the main reason for their poverty was Marianna's belief that she had to keep paying off Stanisław's family in order to be accepted by them. When I met them, they were supporting two families— couples of working age with children—on the modest sum Stanisław received from Yad Vashem after he was recognized in Israel as one of the

Righteous Among the Nations: a Gentile who had helped to save Jewish lives. Once I told Ramotowski my hypothesis.

"That you see these things." He looked at me in admiration. "I thought of so many hiding places in the house, but no matter how well I hid the money, my wife would always find it in time for the next family visit."

No one from Radziłów ever made the slightest effort to help these two ailing old people. But as soon as the Jedwabne affair flared up, the name Ramotowski was on everybody's lips.

"He got himself a short little Jewish girl. Pretty, though. He was after the mill."

"When the Germans were hunting Jews, people in Radziłów wanted to help. Like that Ramotowski, who married a Jewish woman. She converted to our faith. She wasn't shunned; everyone talked to her."

You heard this all the time. That she was beautiful and rich. Whereas it was Stanisław who was the looker in that marriage, and the Finkelsztejn home was pretty well cleaned out, plundered, the mill reduced to its foundation, and the locals must have known that. Evidently they somehow had to explain to themselves why one of them took a Jewish woman as a wife.

"When the war was over," says Ramotowski, "I said to my wife: 'Now, my sweetheart, you're free; go where you will.' She said she wasn't going anywhere. 'Well,' I said, 'if that's the way it is, we'll be together ever after.' And that's how it has been."

For the next sixty years they didn't part, even for a split second. When I saw them the first time, they looked as if they were posing for a portrait. He was sitting near her, holding her hand. Later I saw that this was how they spent most of the day. "Stasinek," the nearsighted Marianna called whenever he moved away for a moment. "I'm coming, Marianna," he answered with no sign of impatience.

"Didn't you ever think of leaving Poland?" I ask.

He: "I was ready to go to America, her cousins were always inviting us, but Marianna wouldn't go for the world. I told her again and again: 'Kiddo, let's leave this rotten place.'"

She: "I was attached to the place where I was born, my ancestors lived here for three centuries."

He: "She was afraid I'd be attracted to other women over there. But even if I had been, I would never leave her, not for long anyway. I was always lucky with the ladies, but I liked the one I had and I wasn't such a bad guy. If ever I came home late, I kissed her, showed her some affection, and somehow it passed. There isn't and there could never be anyone like her in Radziłów. The others couldn't hold a candle to her."

Journal

FEBRUARY 7, 2001

I set off for Jedwabne at dawn to attend a meeting of residents who are to be informed by prosecutor Ignatiew of the principles on which his investigation will be conducted. A vandalized manor house where in Communist times there was a cultural center and movie theater. At the entrance I introduce myself to a small group of men as a journalist from the *Gazeta Wyborcza*. A chorus of voices responds:

"Heard about the deportations? And you know who was behind all that?"

"Your people, the Jews. When the Soviets were here, the Jews wanted to put a movie theater and toilets in our church."

I try to interject that synagogues were turned into movie theaters and storehouses, too.

"Sixteen hundred people in one barn? You must be kidding."

I ask why no one questioned the inscription on the monument earlier— it gave precisely that number as having been burned by the Gestapo.

"You spat on us and our children. We're not going to talk to you."

Father Edward Orłowski, the parish priest, enters the hall with Janina Biedrzycka (the woman whose father gave his barn for the burning of the Jews) and sits down at the table on the stage. There are maybe two hundred people in the hall, the majority men between thirty and fifty years old. When the prosecutor counters anti-Semitic remarks, he is met with a menacing growl. Voices speaking of Jews denouncing people to the NKVD are rewarded with applause.

"It's lies they're writing. Even if you packed them in like herrings in a barrel you couldn't get sixteen hundred Jews in there."

"We're not anti-Semites. I played with Jewish kids. But it has to be said: when Poles were taken off to Siberia, there were two Jews standing guard at the door."

"Who's accusing the people of Jedwabne? We don't even have to ask: we know that money rules."

"Let the institute put Gross on trial for his lies."

One of the men in the hall tells me later, without giving his name, "That guy on the right who was yelling loudest that the Jews got Polish patriots deported, he knows very well that his father denounced my father, and even joined the NKVD when they came to arrest him. Later he got down on his knees, pleading with my father to keep it a secret."

For the first time I see Father Orłowski in action. Jovial, sturdy, energetic, with a powerful voice and a round face made even rounder by his bald head. After the meeting he steps off the stage, stands before the camera—Channel 2 is shooting a report on Jedwabne—straightens his cassock, and declaims: "They want to make us believe we're murderers. The peaceful coexistence of Poles and Jews was violated by the Jews during the Soviet occupation. When Poland was conquered in 1939, no town was as quick to organize a resistance movement as Jedwabne. Poles died in Auschwitz. What they're saying is not just slander against Jedwabne, but against the Polish people. We have to defend ourselves."

I go with the prosecutor to the town hall, and introduce myself to Mayor Krzysztof Godlewski, who invites us to tea.

"It's beneath human dignity to be a bean counter in a matter like this," the mayor says. "Maybe there weren't sixteen hundred victims, but thirteen hundred or fewer. What does it matter? We have to come to terms with the fact of this crime—with Christian humility. The Jewish citizens of Jedwabne were cruelly murdered. It's good that this has been brought to light. The whole thing about Jews collaborating with the NKVD is just a red herring—we should be talking about changing the inscription on the monument."

I ask how he intends to do this in a town where the priest is calling on parishioners to defend themselves against the truth.

"A handful of people took part in the crime. The townspeople are outraged that the condemnation has fallen on the whole community. Many of them are convinced the Germans carried out the atrocity. That's what they used to hear and it's hard to change their minds. Perhaps it could be shown that in 1949 some innocent man was convicted, that would show people that the Institute of National Remembrance wants to get to the truth. The townspeople have been put in an extraordinarily difficult situation. They need time to digest it. It's natural to choose the easier truth. But I see from the town council how the more difficult truth is gradually sinking in."

At this moment one of the councilmen comes in.

"Even if you quartered sixteen hundred Jews, you couldn't fit them in that barn. I was born in 1950, but I know from my parents and neighbors that the Jews were destroyed by Hitler. Whoever says it was Poles was paid to say that. Poles rounded them up, for fun or under duress, I don't know, but a German was standing there with a gun."

I interrupt him to ask what he thinks the monument's inscription should say.

"*Sixteen hundred Jews were not burned here.* That lie has to be rectified."

Godlewski—a tall man with a handlebar mustache, a talented actor—stands behind him and makes desperate faces at me, covers his eyes, his ears, lifts his hands to the heavens.

I visit the priest at the presbytery, and open the conversation politely: "A lot of your parishioners came to the meeting with the prosecutor, which I know you organized."

"I announced it in church. I told people to go and they responded to my call," he says with satisfaction. "Everyone agrees that the Polish and Jewish communities lived in perfect concord, like a loving family. It went wrong with the Russians' invasion of Poland, when many Jews joined the NKVD and friendships with Poles were broken off. We have to look at Gross closely. Jedwabne is the tip of the iceberg."

"What are you saying?"

"If the Jedwabne affair is dealt with in the way Gross would like, it'll be like knocking a hole in the hull of a ship and waiting for it to sink. The truth is that the Germans did the killing, not the Poles. But Jews do things that way."

"What do you mean by that?"

"When we had Bible class the priest told us, 'A Jew will put a cap on a stick and tell you: "Watch out, there are two of us."'' That's what the Jewish character is like. In New York I met a Jewish multimillionaire who bragged about the huge factory he sold to the Germans during the war: 'They gave us a lot of gold and drove us to Hamburg, and from there we sailed to America.' Here his whole people was perishing and he did that—the ultimate swindle."

"Do you ever hear anti-Semitic remarks in your parish?"

"We don't have the problem of anti-Semitism here."

"What do you think the inscription on the monument should say?"

"*Here the Jews were destroyed by the Nazis.* That's a compromise that should placate both the Jews and the Poles. Otherwise the town will have to defend itself."

"How do you see that?"

"Maybe we'll have to get organized, we have a lot of patriots here. I'm considering setting up a committee to defend the town's good name."

I'd looked for Leszek Dziedzic in vain at the meeting with the prosecutor, so I go by his house in Przestrzele, about three kilometers from Jedwabne.

"I don't go to the priest's parties," he says, "but you tell me what happened."

He listens to my account without moving from his chair, and comments, "Same priest, same people. Their only problem is, there aren't any Jews left to kill."

FEBRUARY 8, 2001

From articles on Jedwabne, of which there have been several in the press, I found a few names and got the addresses from the phone book.

Above all, I want to meet a Jewish woman who lives here, identified in the press as Helena Ch. She was baptized during the war and married a Pole. I read about her: "Black bushy eyebrows, lively blue eyes, hair covered with a flowery scarf. The *Tygodnik Katolicki Niedziela* [Sunday Catholic Weekly] lay open on the kitchen table. 'Don't give my name, why would you? That name is gone, those people are gone. It was God's will they should all perish in the barn. I don't bear any grudge. Poles gave me life. It's been quiet for so many years, why revisit it all? Don't give my name. I'm not worried about myself but about my children. When my son was studying in Białystok he let his beard grow. I had to ask him to shave it off or people might have a bad association. Later he wanted to name my grandson David, but I explained to him people might get angry. I don't want to hurt anyone. I want to die in peace. Quietly, peacefully.'"

I go by her house, but Helena Chrzanowska, as I have learned her full name is, asks me in a low voice not to disturb her and her husband. He is very sick; they need peace and quiet.

Another Jedwabne resident, Henryka Adamczykowa, told a journalist, "I can still hear the screaming of people being led to their deaths. I can smell the burning."

She lives in an apartment building; I talk to her through the door. After the unpleasantness that followed the publication of the article I read, she doesn't want to talk to any more journalists. The next name I try is Halina Popiołek. She remembered that her father, Józef Bukowski, said on July 9, 1941, that the townspeople were plotting against the Jews. She saw Jews being herded and beaten with sticks. She saw "our folks" making young Jews carry a statue of Lenin.

She lets me in but is reluctant to talk about the atrocity.

"For years I went to light a candle on the anniversary of the massacre, and on All Saints'," she explains. "This year, when I turned up with candles on July 10, there were journalists there, photographers, some TV cameras, and my picture was in the local paper. The priest bawled me out, my neighbors turned their backs on me. I hear everywhere that I was paid off by the Jews. I won't ever say anything again."

I express my regret that Helena Chrzanowska won't talk to me, either.

"You have to understand her. How many times have people insulted her for being Jewish. I would never call a person names like that," she assures me.

I visit Alina Żukowska; I know from Zygmunt Laudański, one of the killers, that she was in Jedwabne on that day, July 10, 1941. I find her chopping wood. She lives in a crumbling communal apartment without central heating. For twenty-eight years she darned stockings. She doesn't stop working for a minute during the whole two hours of our conversation. The cold is so biting it's hard to take notes because my hands are freezing.

"Did Zygmunt Laudański tell you then that he fled into the fields because he didn't want to participate in hounding Jews?"

"Nothing of the sort," says Alina Żukowska, who seems to have forgotten she testified on behalf of several of the accused, including Zygmunt Laudański, at the trial in 1949. "I've already given testimony to prosecutor Ignatiew. He didn't get in touch with me before, so what does he want from me now? I was in Pisz last year, they had already started writing about Jedwabne then. I met Jerzy Laudański, asked him, 'Have you read it?' And he said he hadn't. He was lying. Everybody's lying."

Żukowska ridicules what Gross quoted from the trial of Karol Bardoń, one of the men convicted, who died in prison. "I read in Gross that Bardoń told the court he didn't round up Jews, because he was a mechanic at the police station and he was repairing cars all day. What cars? They didn't have as much as a motorcycle, or even a bicycle. When they wanted to go somewhere they had a local hitch up a cart. Bardoń was sentenced to death, then pardoned, and he ate our Polish bread in prison. Even though he was from Silesia, he was a German stooge, not a mechanic. And there's a Jew in Gross's book who's lying, Icek Neumark, who says he escaped from the barn, but he wasn't even there. I saw him go into hiding the day before. That rotten Jew Wasersztejn left the country and passed sentence on Jedwabne.

"That night, after the burning of the Jews, I met the Laudańskis' neighbor, Genek Kalinowski. He said the mayor had ordered everyone to stand guard at the cottages overnight because the Jews might take revenge. I sat with the Laudańskis in front of our sheds. Now the Laudańskis are playing grandees, their pictures in the paper, they want to whitewash themselves, make out they're so clean. So why were they convicted? I didn't see them at it. But you could hear the screaming two kilometers away."

"Did you ever hear someone say afterward, 'It's a pity they're gone'?"

"Until the Gross book came out, no one mentioned the Jews."

One of the people I talked to yesterday has introduced me to a woman who witnessed the atrocity. She agrees to talk to me, but won't allow me to print her initials. She was ten years old at the time.

"I saw the Smułek family being driven out. It was all people they knew doing it, Poles. There weren't any Germans there. The Choneks, for whom my mother had worked before the war, said to her when they were on their way to the market square: 'Our hour has come.' That's how indifferent they were, how resigned, their children weren't even crying. Bielecki, on horseback, chased a young Jewish woman, Miss Kiwajkowa. When he was in prison under the Soviets, she'd taken care of his children."

I check the name on my laptop. There it is. Władysław Bielecki, who chased Jews on horseback, is mentioned by Antoni Niebrzydowski, one of the suspects in the trial of 1949.

"It was scorching hot," the woman continues. "A Jew, well on in years, wanted to go to the well in the market square to draw water, and a boy who couldn't have been more than twelve hit him and pushed him away. The Poles were holding sticks, pieces of tire, and they were furious. They must have cut up those tires earlier, right? I followed the Jews when they were put into rows. There were young girls and women, such pretty ones, some pregnant and some with children in baby blankets. I saw boys of twelve hounding Jews; a lot of those taking part were in their late teens. Some were herding their own schoolmates. How could they look them in the eye, killing them? I was afraid to go near the barn in case they forced me in, too. They poured gasoline from a can at the barn's four corners. It caught fire immediately. I can't sleep at night. I see it as if it were yesterday. There were many more participants in the crime than were later convicted. It was an inferno of hatred. That terrifying scream that probably didn't last for more than two minutes, it's still inside me. This morning I woke up at four again because it came back to me. Why I went there, a little girl, I don't know. Maybe so that I could be a witness to the truth now."

Before the war her parents worked for Jews, and her mother always spoke well of them. She remembers the names of her Jewish neighbors: the Powroźniks, who had a grocery, the Prawdziweks had a granary, the Kiwajeks had a farm, the Fiszmans a sawmill.

At the Dziedzices' home in the evening, Leszek tells me about Helena Chrzanowska.

"You can't talk to her about what she went through; she can't bear to remember it. She keeps saying, 'May God forgive them, it's not for me to judge.' Once a woman from the neighborhood told her to get her son Józek to run for town council. She replied, 'God forbid, he can't run, if anything goes wrong, they'll say it's the Jew's fault.' When I tried to persuade her that it probably wouldn't be that bad, she confessed that a neighbor of hers, an older man, had threatened her across the fence: 'We're not done yet, we can still finish what we started.' I know him, his family took part in the killing. He can barely stand, but he could still manage to do someone in. And recently, I went to the pharmacy. Miss Helena was just buying something. A neighbor comes in, sees her, and starts yammering about Jews, just like that, on purpose."

In the midst of the conversation, Dziedzic interjects: "Because in your religion . . ." It was clear to the participants in yesterday's meeting with Ignatiew that I must be Jewish, since I work for the "Kosher Times," as they call the *Gazeta Wyborcza* here, and don't yet use their code phrases "Soviet collaboration," "Jewish conspiracy," and "Gross's lies." But why does Leszek Dziedzic decide I'm Jewish? He probably can't imagine that someone who's not herself a Jew would wish to discover the truth or feel for those who were murdered. Experience tells him it doesn't happen. He has always been completely isolated in his compassion for the victims.

FEBRUARY 9, 2001

Łomża. In the state archive I look for minutes of prewar meetings of the town council, which had to be made up of a mixture of Poles and Jews. The archivist explains that the documents could just as well have made their way east with the Red Army, in which case they might be in Mińsk or Grodno, as west with the German army, in which case they might be in Gdańsk, for example. Or they could have wound up elsewhere by accident. Probably they were destroyed. It transpires that the archivist herself is from Jedwabne. I ask if she knows what's being said in the town.

"This week I was at my mother's. The priest warned people in his sermon not to reveal to strangers anything that might damage Poland."

She pulls out an invaluable item: "List of Post-German and Post-Jewish Real Estate Abandoned in the Jedwabne Area," drawn up on September 3, 1946. It includes dozens of names of former Jewish owners of houses and lands.

I drive to Jedwabne to find my next subject, but he won't let me print his name, either. "In the sixties, when I was no more than ten, I overheard drunken neighbors quarreling about it. Who got the most gold, who raped a Jewish woman. One guy screamed, 'You asshole, I know where you got that fur-lined coat.' And another replied: 'And you thrashed that Jewish girl behind the mill and cut her throat.' I remember who it was, but I don't want to give any names, I'm just telling *you*. Another time I heard adults talking about a couple of thugs who went into a Jewish home, and one of them hit a child with an iron rod—so his brain splattered the man's clothes, and he made the mother clean it up. Another time, a friend's mother told a story in my presence, not seeing me there, about locals going to Polish homes to rustle up a gang to 'get the Jews.' This woman wrapped her husband's head in bandages to make it look like he was sick and couldn't get up. Sure, the Germans incited the Poles, but some of the locals were already on the same page with the Germans. It wasn't all imposed. All the older people in town know that. No Pole was ever harassed by Germans for *not* burning Jews. On the other hand, Poles went from house to house, made others join them, and sometimes they really came down on someone if he wouldn't go with them."

Back to Łomża for a visit with Jan Cytrynowicz. He was baptized before the war, and after it ended he lived in Jedwabne, where he ran a leather workshop until his retirement. He lives in a tidy little house in the center of Łomża. He, his wife, and a small dog on the ground floor, their son on the floor above them.

I read him my notes from the 1949 trial documents. Cytrynowicz demonstrates extensive knowledge of the subject. His wife, Pelagia, keeps raising her voice: "What is all this nonsense he's telling you? We are always arguing about it. Would a Pole have done such a thing if a German wasn't standing behind him with a rifle?"

I ask Cytrynowicz, who survived the war in Russia, when he first heard about the atrocity.

"Right after the war. I tanned sheepskins for coats, and they paid me in grain and salt pork. I was a bachelor, I liked to drink. My drinking buddies didn't know about my background at first, I wasn't from Jedwabne, after all, so after a few glasses of vodka they would boast: 'I chased him all over town,' 'I stabbed him hard.' They were happy they'd killed a couple of Jews. But sober, they didn't say anything. Just that the Jews had gone to the burning of their own accord, because their religion told them to. Peasants wore spencers, those short homemade jackets. If someone went to church in a fur-lined coat, you knew it had belonged to a Jew."

"And when your friends found out you were Jewish, did their attitude change?"

"I was baptized as a boy, and so as a Catholic I was considered a Pole. Girls cuddled me, none of them called me a Jew-boy. But I felt a strangeness. If I'd met any Jew at that time I would have left Poland, as did many Jews after the war, but I didn't have any contact at all. Where were you going to find a Jew after the war? Even if there was one he'd be afraid to admit it."

Once in Przasnysz a man came up to Jan and whispered, "You a Jew by any chance?" He denied it, but the man didn't believe him and said if he went to such and such a place, he could arrange to emigrate. That was after 1956, when for a short time Jews were legally permitted to emigrate. But by then he had a Catholic wife.

I return to Jedwabne on an ice-covered road. Krzysztof Godlewski invited me for the evening. A nice big villa, his sweet wife (a teacher), three children. He was born in 1955. He's not from Jedwabne itself but from the area. He became mayor in 1992, he's in his third term. Immediately after reading Gross's *Neighbors*, he laid a wreath at the monument on July 10 with the chairman of the town council, Stanisław Michałowski. At the next council meeting, the councilman Stanisław Janczyk proposed buying yarmulkes for Mayor Godlewski and Chairman Michałowski to portray them as "serving Jewish interests."

FEBRUARY 10, 2001
I start the day in Łomża, where I ferret around in local libraries. I look in on the reading rooms of the Wagów Society, the public library, and the Northern Mazovia District Museum. I read issues of *Wolna Łomża* (Free Łomża), a paper from the time of the Soviet occupation. "Everyone should unmask the lordly minions who—in wholesale and speciality stores—sold out the interests of the masses in Poland before the war." In the same issue there's a piece by Chaim Katz, a shoemaker: "The liberation has come for me, I'll be able to work in a co-op, I won't have to live in poverty anymore. I would have been able to accept that penniless existence if it weren't for the Poles' attitude toward me." Texts like this in an occupation paper couldn't have aroused sympathy for Jews.

Following the trail of names mentioned in the 1949 court trial documents, and also deciphering initials that have already been published in the press, I look for witnesses in Jedwabne and its environs.

I've found a strategy for talking to people. The chief principle: don't ask about the massacre. Those questions send people into a panic. Instead, I open my laptop. I say, "Were you at the meeting with the prosecutor? That was quite a drama. Shall I read you my notes?" Or, "I found testimonies from the 1949 investigation in the archive. Do you remember that both the Laudańskis were convicted? I'll read you what they said."

Discreetly I note down the commentaries. For example: "Just look at that, Eugeniusz Śliwecki was accused of doing Jews! He was a mailman, always quiet and friendly. Well, he messed 'around with his own daughters, you think he wouldn't with a Jewish woman?" "Czesław Strzelczyk was in on it. Bloody sadist, he took a pitchfork to his own wife. He was active politically, on the Russian side when they were here, on the German side under the Germans, and when People's Poland came in he built podiums and gave speeches." "There were three Kubrzyniecki brothers, all thugs. Even before the war they had a bad reputation. When people from around the area came to the parish fair, the Kubrzynieckis stood in the road and robbed them. They'd go to bars and get loaded on vodka, they lived off thieving. Józef Kubrzyniecki was a stove fitter, but he had a taste for robbing and brawling, and his wife was his equal in every way."

It's clear that among Jedwabne's older generation it's universal knowledge who did the killing and who got rich off the Jews—I hear the same names over and over: Jerzy Laudański, Feliks Tarnacki, Eugeniusz Kalinowski, Józef Kubrzyniecki, Czesław Mierzejewski, Stanisław Sielawa, Józef Sobuta, Michał Trzaska.

I ask each one of my interlocutors if they remember themselves or from family stories the surnames of any Jedwabne Jews. "With Jews, you just knew their first names, really," they told me.

I drive to Janczewko, a few kilometers past Jedwabne, to have a look at the Wyrzykowskis' farm buildings, where Szmul Wasersztejn was in hiding, and to inquire after the former residents of the farm—I already know the Wyrzykowski family doesn't live here anymore. One of the locals points out the house to me but doesn't want to talk. Walking across the abandoned farmyard, I am met by a man who turns out to be Wyrzykowska's nephew Franciszek Karwowski, who lives in Jedwabne but whose son owns a field here.

"In the country only my family knew about the Jews in hiding here, nobody else. Once, four policemen on horseback came looking for them. They tore up the floorboards with bayonets but they didn't find them. After the war, Home Army soldiers beat my aunt unconscious because they thought she had gold from Jews. When I heard one of them, Wądołowski, had got himself veterans' papers, it was like someone stuck a knife in my heart."

Strangely enough, however, since *Neighbors* has come out he doesn't feel the greatest anger toward the men who brutalized his aunt.

"And how did Wasersztejn show his gratitude to my aunt? How could he write that Poles killed Jews since he was saved by Poles himself? With that one testimony he ruined all the good she had done him. None of those seven Jews came out with that kind of nonsense, just him. There was a burning in Radziłów, killings in Szczuczyn, but whatever you say, we helped Jews and made enemies by it. When I was supposed to go to the States, friends warned me: 'Don't go: when Jews find out you're from Jedwabne they'll kill you.'"

When I was checking in the *Gazeta*'s web archive to see if we had published anything on Jedwabne before Jan Gross's book was published, I found one piece in the Białystok supplement from April 1999 titled "Let's Have Some Fun: We'll Burn Rysiek." It was about a court case in which people were tried for setting a Jedwabne man on fire. The killers testified they'd done it as a joke. When I go by Przestrzele to see Leszek Dziedzic, whose father helped hide Szmul Wasersztejn, Dziedzic tells me, "That Rysiek was a loner, a bit of an eccentric, but a cultured man. His drunken pals dragged him out of the house, poured gas on him, set him afire. They were repeating exactly what was done to Jews two generations ago."

On the way back to Warsaw I drop by the Cytrynowiczes—Jan, the baptized Jew from Jedwabne, and his Gentile wife, Pelagia—for coffee. The lady of the house gives me a warm welcome but makes it clear from the threshold that although she was not at Jedwabne in that time, she knew for sure that her husband was talking nonsense when he said Poles burned the Jews. I ask her about her native town.

"I lived in Grajewo. There was a wooden storage container in the marketplace, no bigger than the table we're drinking tea at. They caught Jews, forced them down onto the container, and beat them up."

"Who beat them?"

"I have to say I saw Poles from Grajewo doing it with my own eyes. One of them hit a Jew on the head with a hammer. I was watching from the kitchen window, shaking. A Jew came by to hide in our cellar; Mama hid him there. She was afraid he'd stay on.

"Another time I was walking by the synagogue when the Jews had been forced to leap from an upper floor. They were lying there with broken legs. Sad to say, it was Poles, but on orders from the Germans, who were standing there with guns."

"Did you see those Germans?"

"They must have been standing nearby giving orders. Polish people coming up with it themselves? Being so heartless?"

"Miss Pelagia," I ask, recognizing in her the dangerous sort of person who wouldn't hurt a fly, "if a German with a gun had told you to beat up a girl your own age at that time, and then he'd gone off somewhere else, what would you have done?"

She doesn't reply. Nor does she interrupt my conversation with her husband, even when I read out notes from the 1949 investigation, which I had avoided doing before. In them their daughter's father-in-law appears as one of the suspects.

I stay with them too long and once again drive back to Warsaw after dark, on an icy highway.

FEBRUARY 11, 2001

Maria K. of Jedwabne (from a piece published in a local weekly in the eighties): "So many people took their wagons and went out looting! . . . I'm not afraid to speak of it because I didn't profit by the burning. Just one down quilt, two pillows, and a cupboard my mother brought me. And how complicated to get it all home!"

In the *General Weekly*, Jan Gross reminds us in his article "The Pillow of Mrs. Marx" that the first reaction to his book *Neighbors* was a piece by the prominent anti-Semitic journalist Jerzy Robert Nowak in the largest Catholic paper, *Nasz Dziennik* (Our Daily), which said the whole thing was about finagling compensation for lost Jewish property. Gross says: "That argument didn't surprise me, because among people ideologically close to the *Our Daily* writer, associating Jews with money is a common reflex." And he goes on to describe—following the Holocaust scholar Saul Friedlander—a scene that took place on Kristallnacht, when all over

Germany and Austria thousands of Jewish shop and house windows were broken, sometimes along with lootings and beatings. Mrs. Marx, wife of a kosher butcher in the town of Wittlich, went out to meet her German neighbors, saying: "What have we ever done to harm you?" And years later the grandson of Mrs. Marx's neighbor turns up at a lecture to say that his grandmother, tormented by pangs of conscience, still keeps the pillow she got that night at the back of her closet.

Gross writes that a church collection in the Łomża diocese to fund maintenance of the Jewish cemetery in Jedwabne could be a significant gesture. He also points to something that has been bothering me: the general concern with what will be thought of Poles abroad. After all, for half a year after *Neighbors* appeared, a relative quiet reigned. Up to the moment people realized the book was about to appear in the United States. Anxiously looking for our reflection in the eyes of others won't help, writes Gross. It's about the work of coming to terms with our own history.

FEBRUARY 12, 2001
The president of the Institute of National Remembrance, Leon Kieres, at a meeting with American Jews in New York: "It is certain that in Jedwabne, Jews died at the hands of Poles. The truth, even if it is hard, must be accepted with humility."

I read World War II memoirs that I bought at the Wagów Society in Łomża.

In the reminiscences of Henryk Milewski, who was deported to Siberia, and from 1989 onward served as the president of the Association of Siberian Deportees in Łomża, one Jew appears: Aaron Szwalbe of Zambrów. This fellow passenger on the transport became an object of scorn to the author, who calls him a "speculator." Szwalbe was a wholesaler, played all kinds of tricks dealing in tanned hides. Naturally, the Polish patriot could not abide the con games of the Soviet workplace. "A Jew sees fraud as a positive act," he commented. "And he was above all a Jew. The word speaks for itself."

Stanisław Gawrychowski, the son of a prewar village head and author of *On Patrol with the Home Army 1939–1945*, also has his views. "The Poles' attitude toward Jews—there were 500 of them in Wizna—was fair and square. You can't say that of the Jews." And later he writes about the Soviet occupation as a paradise for Jews and a hell for Poles: "After the

Russian invasion in 1939, the majority of Jews showed their hostility to all things Polish. They came to believe they were the lords of these lands, and Poles felt it very painfully and intimately. The Jews shouted 'Bravo' and the scorned and powerless Poles watched the traitors and occupying forces with tears and hatred in their eyes." Next to the statement that before the war the Poles' attitude toward Jews was fair and square, this doesn't sound convincing. When a Pole collaborates, he's a renegade, but when a Jew collaborates, it's proof of what Jews are really like.

Both books confirm what has emerged from my conversations with people in Jedwabne. In this region, anti-Semitism is the default position, nothing to be ashamed of.

Jerzy Smurzyński, author of the book *Black Years in the Łomża Lands: Nazi Mass Murders in 1941–1945 in the Light of Documents*, reconstructs the dates and names of victims of the Nazis. Only the ethnic Poles. In that period, almost all Jews in this area who were Polish citizens were killed. Weren't they worth mentioning, just once?

FEBRUARY 14, 2001

A visit to the Ramotowskis near Warsaw, where they found a place in a nursing home run by the Evangelical Church. It's a joy to see Marianna, who has revived in the stylish two-room apartment with a balcony and a view of birch trees. She's transformed from a granny swaddled in four sweaters into an elegant lady. I've brought her a green-checked skirt and a brown turtleneck. She steers her wheelchair toward the window and peers at the colors through her thick glasses. "Good thing the sweater's brown; if it were bordeaux, I couldn't wear it with a green skirt."

I've prepared a selection of press clippings for Ramotowski. I read him the historian Jerzy Jedlicki's essay in *Polityka* (Politics) arguing against the idea, which I hear again and again, that the fuss caused by Gross's book only provokes an anti-Semitic response: "We won't cure ourselves with fantasies, either. Virtually unnoticed the younger generation in Poland has been infected with anti-Semitism; they have no knowledge or experience of it, but some of them already react to the usual signals and slogans. They should at least know what they're talking about and what they think they believe. It's time to call things by their proper names."

Stanisław nods his head in acknowledgment but can barely believe that any periodical in Poland would publish such things.

I visit the Karta Center for the documentation of contemporary history, which provides me with interviews conducted by a historian in the nineties with partisans who participated in the postwar struggle against Communism in the Białystok region.

"With us, hostility to Jews derived from prewar times," he was told by Józef Stankiewicz of Długołęka, code name "Kmicic," who was imprisoned in the Stalinist period. "For the local population, religious questions were very important, and the crucifixion of Christ. National Party members appeared in our village and spread their propaganda. It got to the youth, especially in that time of high unemployment. I wrote on the door of my house: *No entry for Jews, Gypsies, or devils.* One Jewish woman told my mother: 'Ludwika, you're a good person, but your son is a devil.' After the German invasion a friend urged me to join the National Armed Forces. 'Józek, do you want to fight for a free Poland?' 'I do,' I replied. 'Look, the Home Army is with the government. They want to fight for that free Poland—together with the Jews. Jew or Pole, it's all the same to them.'"

FEBRUARY 16, 2001

A lunch with the great Polish writer Tadeusz Konwicki. The subject of Jedwabne comes up, though it is not raised by me—I watch myself, because common sense tells me it isn't the *only* topic of conversation.

"In the Vilnius area we didn't have anything like that," says Konwicki. "Jews were killed by the Germans with the help of Lithuanians. If someone had asked me before if anything like this could happen, I would have said with a clear conscience: no, Poles wouldn't be capable of such a crime. Not that I had such a high opinion of Polish society. I concerned myself professionally with its weaknesses and failings, but I was convinced that we had been spared the mark of cruelty. I thought things like that could happen only in the Balkans. It shocked me, hurt me, it was devastating."

In reaction to the anti-Semitic campaign in 1968, Konwicki invented a Jewish grandfather who had a romance with his grandmother, and made the romance the background of one of his novels. In it, he wrote: "What a strange word, Jew. There's always an instant of fear before you say it."

Another letter from Kazimierz, one of the three Laudański brothers implicated in the massacre, awaits me back at the *Gazeta* offices. It's dated February 12. Laudański is emboldened by success; his tone is getting more strident. "Poles are acccused of anti-Semitism, but it's hard to demand of us that we love our neighbors when they are traitors. The fact that Professor Gross dares to put out such nonsense freely is its own testimony to our tolerance. In Iran he probably wouldn't have the nerve. Mr. Gross demands that Poles build a monument to victims in Jedwabne, confess to the crime in the epitaph, and have the entire Polish elite including the clergy at the monument's unveiling. But who will put up hundreds of monuments on the trail through the Urals to Kołyma for our Poles, the Siberian exiles? Because there are different kinds of neighbors. Wouldn't it be better to shut up? Do we have to hold up the Egyptian, Spanish, or German exile before the people of Israel? The prescription is simple: change your attitude to your neighbors and to . . . money."

In the *Republic* there's a reply to the historian Strzembosz's article from Józef Lewandowski, a historian in Uppsala. He takes issue with the thesis that no one killed Jews in Poland between the wars. He reminds readers that in the months immediately following Polish independence, pogroms took place: in Lvov a total of forty to two hundred victims is given, in Vilnius there's mention of fifty-five dead. In Pińsk, Major Łuczyński ordered the shooting of thirty-five Jews (as Communists, though it turned out later they'd been a Zionist group gathered to distribute food aid rations). He recalls a conversation he had in Israel with an old painter from the Pińsk area who had greeted Polish independence enthusiastically and who told him how that enthusiam had died at the news of the events in Pińsk.

I remember a conversation I had with my elderly aunt (she was born in the nineteenth century) when I visited her in a kibbutz outside Haifa. She spoke Russian with me even though she knew Polish; she refused to use the language. She told me how the Polish army invaded her little town in 1918, the year Poland achieved independence, and drunken soldiers suggested to Jewish boys hanging around the market that they go to the bakery and take as much bread as they could carry. And when the children came out with loaves of bread under their coats they shot at them like ducks.

A phone conversation with Ignatiew. I tell him that when I'm in Jedwabne a tide of anti-Semitism engulfs me, that I've never encountered anything like it before, and it hurts. Ignatiew, who typically keeps his distance, unexpectedly starts on something personal. He'd never given much thought before to the fact that there were Jews in Poland; nor could he remember hearing any anti-Semitic remarks. Now he's not sure whether he might have simply missed them, because he now hears them at every turn. "To the point where I began to wonder," he jokes, "if Poles hadn't imbibed it all with their mother's milk. But my background is White Russian, my great-grandfather and grandfather fled the revolution and stayed in Poland."

In the evening a visit to my friend Jacek Kuroń in the hospital—a place he can't stand but where he returns now with increasing frequency. We talk about nonremembrance. I tell him that after July 10 there were still a few dozen Jews who'd survived by some miracle living in the so-called ghetto in Jedwabne—two designated houses. I haven't found anyone who can remember when the last Jews disappeared from the town—according to the testimonies at the Jewish Historical Institute it was in November 1942—as if not only the memory of the massacre had been wiped out but also the memory of the Holocaust.

During the war, everyone was a witness to the Holocaust, says Jacek, who was then in Lvov. He keeps breaking off his story to inhale a little oxygen from a tank (on top of every possible organ failure he is now battling chronic pneumonia). He remembers Jews with shaved heads in striped uniforms crossing the city in groups of four on the way to work in the Janowska concentration camp. They were made to sing (Jacek croaks: "Marshal Śmigły Rydz didn't teach us a thing / but glorious Hitler came and set us all working"). He remembers hearing a shot while playing in a courtyard and seeing the body of a Jewish boy in a pool of blood. He remembers images from the ghetto, children starving to death on the streets—he saw them when traversing the ghetto on the tram to go to the swimming pool. When he talks to friends who were children or teenagers during the war, he most often hears that no, they didn't notice the Holocaust, because the Jews were behind the ghetto walls.

"We lived in a vortex of death, but they didn't see a damn thing," Jacek marvels.

FEBRUARY 18, 2001
I've set aside a bunch of books on Polish-Jewish relations for Ignatiew. But the prosecutor is also gaining knowledge on his own, because when I call him he says, "I've been reading about the pogroms in Odessa, in Kishinev. I tell you, *that* was real anti-Semitism! That whole thing about imbibing it with a Polish mother's milk here is no explanation. It's not only in Poland."

FEBRUARY 19, 2001

I'm looking for someone to lead dancing and provide entertainment at my daughter Ola's bat mitzvah party. Her bat mitzvah falls on Shushan Purim, the day after Purim, which is the merriest Jewish holiday. According to tradition people should be joyful, dance, and drink. But classmates of Ola's start calling to say they won't be able to come if there's dancing: this year Purim falls in the period of Lent. Because I associate everything with Jedwabne—I know it borders on an obsession—I immediately imagine towns where Catholics were fasting, remembering the crucifixion of Christ, at the same time that ordinarily quiet Jews were whistling and stamping in the synagogue, and their children were making a ruckus with groggers and clappers.

FEBRUARY 23, 2001

Back in Jedwabne. I've made a list of Jedwabne-born residents who were at least ten years old in 1941. On the way, in Łomża, I drop by to see Mr. Zejer, the retired plumber whose father went to prison for the atrocity in Jedwabne and died in prison. The son was by then old enough to remember something. His family doesn't let me in.

Antonina Narewska appears in an article on Jedwabne in a local monthly. She recalls her prewar friendships with Jewish girls and how she missed her Jewish classmate Dwercia Łojewska, who emigrated to Palestine. "Later, when 'it' happened in our town," she says, "I thanked God for saving her life." She doesn't say a word about who did "it." But I hear Miss Narewska is under house arrest—her family won't let her out.

I knock on her door. "My mother-in-law isn't going to talk to you," says a furious voice.

I knock on the door of a villa that belongs to an older gentleman who I heard had seen Jews being herded into the marketplace when he was a little boy. A man who looks about forty opens the door.

"You're not sticking your nose in here, lady!"

He slams the door in my face with such force that I barely manage to jump away.

At least the older residents who live alone are prepared to talk to me, although the conversations are not very fruitful. It's worse when the younger generation lives in the same house. It's hard to get across the threshold. At the next stop the conversation is just as brief:

"Father's not here."

"And when might he be back?"

"Not today, I'm sure of that."

"I'll come by tomorrow, then."

"He won't be here tomorrow, either."

At the Cytrynowiczes' in Łomża. As soon as I come in Miss Pelagia starts up in an excited voice: "I was just in Jedwabne. All they're talking about is how many Poles the Jews denounced to the Soviets. It's the only topic. Jedwabne has no business defending itself like that! What are they trying to say? That genocide is allowed if it's payback for something else? I told my grandson what his grandfather on his father's side did on July 10, 1941! It's right that he should know!"

FEBRUARY 24, 2001

Jedwabne. Not for the first time I meet with an older lady, an eyewitness to the abuse and killing of Jews. Every time we meet, new details come back to her. "Right after the Soviets left I was passing by the bakery and saw a boy lying there who'd been stoned; he was tall and fat, he could have weighed more than a hundred kilos. He was still breathing."

It's probably this boy who is mentioned in a letter from prison by Karol Bardoń. On the day the Germans entered the town, Bardoń was summoned by Jedwabne resident Wiśniewski. "Pointing at a young man of Jewish origin named Lewin, about 22 years old, lying there murdered, he said to me: 'We killed that son of a bitch with stones.'"

Later, Wiśniewski showed him a stone weighing about twelve to fourteen kilos and said, "We bashed him with that stone. I don't think he's getting up."

The lady I'm talking to also remembers that the day before the burning, a lot of young people came in from the surrounding countryside and chased Jews to the synagogue, where they forced them to sing and destroy their holy books.

FEBRUARY 27, 2001

Warsaw. The courthouse on Leszno Street, Criminal Justice Department VIII. I'm looking for prewar court cases concerning the crime in Radziłów. But there's no central case registry; I have to look in the archives of regional courts. To get to a particular trial you have to know the names of the accused. I know from Skrodzki that in the Radziłów trials the accused were Leon Kosmaczewski, Władysław Łasiewicz, and Aleksander Godlewski, and that they stood trial in Ełk.

I phone the regional court in Ełk and discover that the documents may be at the regional prosecutor's office. From there I'm referred to the state archive in Ełk. There I hear that it may have been an out-of-town court session, I'd have to look in Białystok or Olsztyn, not to mention that the documents might have been destroyed.

After a few phone calls to Ełk I realize that without prosecutor Ignatiew's help, finding the documents of the Radziłów investigation could take me months. But I also know the press should keep its distance from the judiciary. When I worked on economic affairs for the *Gazeta* it wouldn't have occurred to me to work with a prosecutor. After a consultation with the paper, I call Ignatiew and give him a list of Radziłów murderers I drew up with Skrodzki, specifying those whom I know were the subjects of investigation. He warns me that if he finds the documents, he won't be able to give me access to them without permission from his superiors.

FEBRUARY 28, 2001

At Marianna Ramotowska's birthday party. She is eighty-six. Both Ramotowskis are very taken with their new priest in Warsaw, Father Sikora. "A priest who's so friendly to us?" Stanisław marvels. "Maybe it's because he's Evangelical."

I phone Father Michał Czajkowski. I heard him on television talking about the teachings of the Church before the war: "It was teaching people contempt. And then we're surprised that people lost their sense of conscience. That contempt paved the way. The murderers are a great moral and religious problem for me but so are the Christians who didn't help, even though they could have, the ones who were indifferent. For that kind of passivity we answer to God." I don't know him personally, but I want to thank him. He has just had an indignant call from Father Orłowski in Jedwabne, who sought him out at Cardinal Stefan Wyszyński University, where Czajkowski is a professor. There, someone high up in the university assured him that Father Czajkowski does not represent the views of the Catholic university.

MARCH 1, 2001

In the Karta Center's Eastern Archive I read copies of testimonies held at the Hoover Institution at Stanford University, stories of people from the Białystok region deported to the USSR. The historian Tomasz Strzembosz has read these testimonies before me (I find recent entries by him in the files) and he uses them to demonstrate that Jews collaborated and informed during the Soviet occupation.

These recollections, recorded during the war, have a special weight. When I talk to contemporary residents of Jedwabne, I can believe they're reacting to the revelation of the crime by trying to cast guilt upon the victims. But there's no reason to think that people who left Poland before the massacre was committed and who couldn't even have known about it (no one from Jedwabne would have written to relatives about killing Jews) gave testimony with the intention of bearing false witness.

I read questionnaires from the Łomża district, which included Jedwabne, and the Szczuczyn district, which included Radziłów. It might appear that Strzembosz and I read the same files. But two people can read the same thing very differently. Indeed, the testimonies do mention Jews bossing people around, but one finds the greatest concentration of Jews collaborating with the NKVD in general statements. When concrete situations are described, their number falls drastically. It's the very nature of prejudice.

It would be useful to compare these testimonies with data relating to the participation of Jews in various official bodies. Only then could we assess the degree to which they reflect reality, and how much they reflect the subjective feelings of the witnesses. At the very start of the discussion about Jedwabne, Krzysztof Jasiewicz, a historian of the Borderlands (the lands on the border of eastern Poland and the USSR), wrote about this problem in the *Gazeta*, saying that the "conviction that Jews collaborated with the NKVD was quite widespread and may have contributed to the crime in Jedwabne. Even if the sources indicate that the basis for the conviction was very weak." On the basis of Soviet documents with statistics on nationalities, he showed that there was no mass collaboration with the Soviet occupying authorities by Jews. In the Jedwabne area, the *vydvizhentsy*, or local careerists, openly collaborating with the Soviets included 126 Poles (70 percent) and 45 Jews (or 25 percent). Jewish *vydvizhentsy* made up 3.2 percent of the Jewish population of the area;

among Poles, *vydvizhentsy* were 0.34 percent. It's true that Jews collaborated in greater numbers than Poles in proportion to their population, but Jews still constituted only a small portion of the national population.

Strzembosz extensively cites the testimonies in which Jews appear in an unfavorable light as a counter to Gross's book. Somehow nobody seems to remember that these very testimonies were discovered, brought into the light of day, and used as the basis for a book by Irena Grudzińska Gross and Jan Gross: *In Nineteen-Forty, Holy Mother of God, They Sent Us to Siberia.* What I'm reading in the Eastern Archive at Karta are copies—the Grosses read the originals. Irena told me how they were deposited at the Hoover Institution in the seventies and how she and Jan took the manuscripts out of the boxes. Many of them had whole sections redacted, but they could occasionally manage to read fragments underneath that seethed with anti-Semitism. The testimonies of Polish citizens deported to the interior of the Soviet Union were collected and edited at the Documentation Bureau of the Polish Army in the East for the authorities in emigration, in case of talks with the Allies on the future borders of Poland. They were intended to document Soviet repressions, deportations, election fraud, and so forth. Apparently someone thought they should black out the things that didn't show Poles in the best light, such as the anti-Semitism of the deported Poles.

Despite this kind of censorship, anti-Semitism comes through in most of the testimonies. When Tadeusz Nitkiewicz, a pharmacist from Wizna, describes how Jews "welcomed the arriving Red Army by brutalizing our soldiers and population mercilessly," one must take his nonsense with a grain of salt.

In the *Gazeta* archive I read the *Catholic News Agency Bulletin*: "Gross based his whole book and the verdict it contains on the testimony of Szmul Wasersztejn, an employee of the Security Service; this was what Professor Tomasz Strzembosz—who has long studied this period of Polish history—concluded on the basis of testimonies by two reliable witnesses interrogated by Wasersztejn in the postwar period."

I know from the Dziedzices that Wasersztejn left Poland immediately after the war.

As reconstructed by the Catholic News Agency, the massacre looks like this: "German policemen surrounded Jedwabne. They used dogs to force Poles to take part in the massacre. The Jews did not try to defend themselves or escape, but passively obeyed orders." The *Bulletin* refers to the words of John Paul II, who calls for the truth to be fully uncovered. The Catholic News Agency is seconded by Kazimierz Laudański. He has sent me a copy of a letter he sent to Adam Cyra at the Auschwitz Museum (dated February 24): "Szmul Wasersztejn was an able officer of the Security Services up to 1968, which is why Professor Gross, as a sophisticated and experienced historian, put his trust in him. He went everywhere, he saw and heard everything. Another Sherlock Holmes in an invisibility cape. He saw the Jewess Ibram raped and killed, beards burned, infants murdered at their mothers' breasts to the strains of an orchestra. Didn't he see and hear a little too much for one little boy?"

I think the Laudański brothers could indeed provide much more reliable information than a hunted man, whose perspective was necessarily limited. How frustrating it must be for them: knowing details from their own observation that would undermine Wasersztejn's testimony, but not being able to put facts straight without giving themselves away.

MARCH 2, 2001
My article on the Laudańskis is to run next Saturday. I'm making some additions. Adam Michnik, returning the latest version of the article to me, has urged me to try to grasp the mentality of the townspeople in that particular area at that time by talking to regional historians and sociologists. I've had several such conversations, but I didn't get much out of them. The subject of Jedwabne sets people on edge. Today a well-known sociology professor simply hung up on me.

In the evening, a meeting with the playwright Tadeusz Słobodzianek, who plans to write a play, a novel, maybe a story; in any case it will be set in Jedwabne. In his view the situation is falsified by the dichotomy "Jews vs. Poles." We should instead talk about Jews and Catholics, because both are fully legitimate Polish citizens, differing only in religion. There's something to be said for that view.

MARCH 3, 2001
An evening phone call to Jedwabne. Consternation in the town after President Aleksander Kwaśniewski's statement in the Israeli newspaper the *Yediot Akhronoth*: "It was a genocide carried out by the Poles of Jedwabne against their Jewish neighbors. We must therefore bow our heads

and ask forgiveness. After this, Poles may become better as a people." The president has announced that on the sixtieth anniversary of the Jedwabne massacre he will apologize to the Jewish people in the name of all Poles.

Jacek Kuroń's birthday party. I spend it talking to Marek Edelman. I say I hadn't fully realized the scope and intensity of anti-Semitism in the years before the war broke out.

"Before the war," Edelman remembers, "I was beaten up more often than under the Germans; right before September 1939 it was easy to run into nationalist paramilitary squads—hunting Jews. I also remember the feeling of fear mixed with shame when I went in the first months after the war to register at some office with dozens of people standing there and I had to say my surname aloud."

I tell him about the shoemaker from Radziłów named Dorogoj, who managed to survive the war with his son. Both of them were butchered with axes when they came out of hiding in 1945.

"I went to Kielce immediately after the pogrom there and at every station I saw a few corpses; they were Jews dragged off the trains and killed. There is information collected by the Jewish Committee after the war showing that fifteen hundred Jews were killed in the 'railroad operation.'"

I tell him about Stanisław Ramotowski, who saved a whole Jewish family on the day of the massacre and hid them with his mother, who received no payment.

"What does it matter?" Edelman counters. "In Warsaw probably about a hundred thousand Poles took part in rescuing Jews; they did it for various reasons—to spite the Germans, but for money, too. It's true it was hard to go into hiding without money. I know examples of people who took money, and how! They asked more every time, but when the ghetto was cut off, and later when the ghetto was gone and they saw they wouldn't get anything out of it, they went on hiding Jews with complete devotion."

I go on to tell him that of the Finkelsztejn family, only one person survived the war: Rachela, now Marianna Ramotowska. There's another Jewish woman who lives in Jedwabne, who survived the slaughter and also married a Pole. The two women never visited each other; they wanted to blend into the local population, no doubt hoping their sin of being Jewish would be forgotten.

Edelman tells me about the mother of Krzysztof Kamil Baczyński, the great Polish poet who was killed in the Warsaw Uprising of 1944. Edelman found her in Warsaw after the war; she was living in poverty and he had money for her from the Joint Distribution Committee. She wouldn't take it. "That's nothing to do with me," she said. She was afraid her Jewish background would tarnish her son's posthumous glory as a Home Army soldier who fell in an uprising of Poles.

MARCH 4, 2001

In the liberal Catholic monthly *Więź* (Bond), an article by Archbishop Józef Życiński: "It would be insane to suggest there could be any justification for a mass burning of human beings in a barn. Therefore, let us not look for imaginary historical documents that might turn the Jedwabne tragedy into a trivial episode. There can be no such documents, because you can't reduce the deaths of innocent people to an episode. Today we need to pray for the victims of the massacre, showing the solidarity of spirit that was lacking at the hour they passed away from the land of their fathers where they lived."

Meanwhile, a representative of the Popular Christian Alliance of Łomża arrived to meet with Jedwabne residents. He read them an open letter he'd brought them: "In response to the vicious worldwide campaign to slander Poland itself, the undersigned state that the atrocity in their town was committed by Germans." A Committee to Defend the Good Name of Jedwabne has been set up, with Mayor Krzysztof Godlewski at its head.

Of course, some politicians were bound to take advantage of the mood in Jedwabne. I wasn't surprised that a committee had been formed. But why was the mayor heading it and not the priest? I happen to be in the editorial offices when our correspondent sends in a short interview with Godlewski. I read it and can't believe my eyes. He speaks the language, albeit somewhat tempered, of the anti-Semitic sector of the local population, using the expression "Jewish interests." This is now the main tendency of the Jedwabne deniers, to say that the whole story was dreamed up by Jews who want to demand billions of dollars in damages from Poland. In the course of several visits to Jedwabne, I've come to know and like him, though I suspected he might have a problem standing firmly on one side or the other. He didn't fit the part of the lonely sheriff. On the contrary, he's a cheerful, sympathetic fellow, the kind of person who doesn't want to offend anybody. Not because he's timid, but because he's convinced something can always be done to make everyone happy.

I call him. He tells me how someone stood up in the town hall and said in a menacing tone, "The mayor has a chance to rehabilitate himself; he should head the committee." He talks to me by turns in two different discourses. First he explains that if he hadn't joined the committee, they would have collected signatures for a letter written in hateful language, which would have compromised both the town and the country. Then he explains that the residents of Jedwabne rightly feel indignant, because only a handful participated in the massacre—the dregs of society—and now all local Poles are being accused, which might become a basis for financial claims. Then he is furious with the president for having no doubt about who is guilty of the crime, and at the press for reaching a verdict while the investigation is still under way. I repeat that he knows as well as I do that the committee's aim is to airbrush the truth. After a conversation of almost an hour, Godlewski asks me to read back to him what he said to the *Gazeta*, so he can cut the unfortunate phrases.

MARCH 5, 2001

I call Godlewski. His voice is somber. The members of the committee are demanding that the letter be tougher. I quote him what Primate Glemp said yesterday on the Catholic radio station Józef: "The massacre, perpetrated by burning alive the Jewish population after forcing them into a barn, cannot be denied . . . To recognize our generational responsibility is to ask God for forgiveness for the sins of our ancestors and ask forgiveness from the descendants of those who were wronged." Finally, a proposal for Poles and Jews to join together in prayer.

Godlewski's voice changes at once: "After what the primate said, I'll convince the committee to formulate its letter differently."

In fact, I read Godlewski only the fragments of Glemp's interview that offered a glimmer of hope. The piece as a whole doesn't sound promising. The primate disassociated himself from the idea that the Church should participate in the ceremony of July 10 in Jedwabne: "This is not about any rash, hysterical atonement." He hinted at some kind of Jewish conspiracy: "Brothers and Sisters! A year ago an important Jew informed me that the matter of Jedwabne would soon be given publicity." In other words, the Jews had a plan ready for Jedwabne.

The primate, referring to a letter about the Jedwabne commemoration from the rabbi of Poland, Michael Schudrich, with an invitation to communal prayer, recalled that the rabbi invoked a text from scripture. The *Gazeta* editors ask me to check from which book of the Bible the quotation is taken. I call Schudrich on his cell phone. He happens to be in New York. I hear his inimitable Polish: "Jedwabne is important, but other things are very, very important. I was just going to call you." It turns out he has his daughter Arianna on his other cell phone: she's calling from a store in Brooklyn to say they only have napkins with the words "bar mitzvah," not "bat mitzvah." But they are lovely napkins with a golden Star of David. What kind should they bring to Ola's party? Before I hang up I remind him of the quotation and note down the reference: Deuteronomy 21:1–9.

Ola's bat mitzvah is such a huge, emotionally charged project for our family that I talk about it nonstop. Before long I realize how confused people in Jedwabne are by my decision not to keep my Jewishness a secret. One of them assured me, "I give you my word of honor. I won't tell anyone about your background." It wasn't until someone at the Institute of National Remembrance swore not to breathe a word about it at work, that I was really dumbstruck. I knew many people with a Jewish background were afraid their origins would come to light, but I had seen in that more a sign of trauma, their own or one inherited from their parents, which made them see a threat where none existed. Only now do I realize how many Poles see something intrinsically wrong with being Jewish.

MARCH 6, 2001
In the morning a conversation with Krzysztof Godlewski (his tone is determined): "I'm going to propose my own version of the letter, in accordance with the primate's message. We must accept the truth, even the most painful truth. I'm considering a spectacular gesture, getting a group of people to pray at the site of the massacre, kneeling there together."

This sounds like an exercise in positive thinking. I ask if it wouldn't be better to give up on the committee and form a new one, in support of the ceremony on the sixtieth anniversary of the crime. This seems to bring him back to reality. He sighs. "For now I can't see anyone volunteering for that."

In the evening another talk with Godlewski (his tone now downcast): "I'm hearing a completely different interpretation of the primate's sermon in town: we should stand up against the Jews' persecution of Poland. Either the committee accepts a statement in accordance with my understanding of the primate's message, or I resign. I can only hope the bishop will come out with an unambiguous sermon."

The bishop of Łomża is to deliver a homily in Jedwabne on Sunday, March 11. Members of the Committee to Defend the Good Name of Jedwabne, like Godlewski, are expecting a sermon providing moral clarity. It's just that each side expects something different.

MARCH 7, 2001

I call Godlewski, who has resigned from the committee.

"I went into it in the hope that we could work out a consensus," he says. "I wanted to temper those who, instead of covering their head with ashes during Lent, have perpetuated the town's bad reputation. You can defend its good name by admitting guilt. I didn't want to abandon people here and leave them to the mercy of hysterics. But I can't fight them all by myself."

At the same time, the Jedwabne affair is obviously accelerating; not a day goes by without an article or pronouncement of some kind in the press. Prime Minister Buzek declared that "the participation of Poles in the crime in Jedwabne is beyond any doubt." Edward Moskal, the president of the American Polish Congress, who lives in Chicago and enjoys great popularity in Jedwabne, denounced the accusations leveled at Poles, explaining that "the Jews decided that Poland should not be Poland but a suburb of Israel," and the president of the Institute of National Remembrance, Leon Kieres, is working for "lackeys with a strange sympathy for Jewish demands... All they want is to quell their own insatiable appetites."

Baffled by contradictory statements, the residents of Jedwabne are waiting tensely for their bishop to speak. Meanwhile the town has adopted a catchphrase for the ceremony announced by the president: "Jew is coming to apologize to Jew."

In Warsaw, there's already a rumor going around about why the primate first disassociated himself from the ceremony and shortly afterward announced he would participate in the Mass given for the victims. People are saying he was admonished by the pope.

MARCH 8, 2001

A visit to the Ramotowskis. At times Marianna speaks fluent Polish, carrying on a conversation with me about the latest skirmishes in the government, then she falls into dialect: "I gone," "I throws." She must have spoken that way with the locals in order to fit in. I ask her for the names of relatives, but she doesn't hear my questions. She doesn't hear well generally, but her hearing is also highly selective. When we talk about what's going on in politics and the world, Marianna, who listens to the radio all day, hears me pretty well, but when I ask about the crime in Radziłów, her hearing worsens dramatically. When in turn I speak of the crime with Stanisław, Marianna's hearing comes back and she reminds her husband not to say too much.

MARCH 9, 2001

My friend Nawojka is bringing agar from Munich to replace nonkosher gelatin for gefilte fish. Her plane is delayed and Shabbat, when we are not allowed to cook, is about to begin. By this time the fish is done, it just has to be covered with aspic. I should call around to find out if anyone can lend me some emergency agar. But I'm at the editorial offices of the *Gazeta*, where my four-column article on the Laudański brothers, "We of Jedwabne," is being set. It contains some passages on contemporary Jedwabne. Because more has gone on there this week than in the last sixty years, I'm constantly adding and authorizing things. Now I have to choose: either I look for gelatin, or I phone Godlewski to find out if the Committee to Defend the Good Name of Jedwabne has announced its members. Luckily, it turns out the paper's first edition closes twenty minutes after Shabbat begins. I manage to call Jedwabne and check all the facts.

MARCH 10, 2001

Ola's bat mitzvah. The synagogue is full. Among our guests, Bożena and Jan Skrodzki, who came from Gdańsk, and Stanisław Ramotowski. Several hundred people, including almost all of Ola's class, and many children came with their parents, no doubt participating in synagogue services for the first time.

Ola presents her commentary on the Torah and tells us why she has chosen Lea, my mother's name before the war, as her Jewish name: "In choosing it, I wasn't thinking of the biblical Leah but of my grandmother.

My grandmother, who died three years ago, wished to hide from us the fact she was Jewish. She was afraid that it might make our lives as difficult as hers had been. In fact, this was a great sacrifice on my grandmother's part: breaking off with her family, starting a new life. I loved my grandmother and I still love her very much, and this time not flowers or stories about her will perpetuate her memory, but my new name, Lea."

In accordance with tradition, candy—kosher candy, of course—is thrown at Ola.

Now it's my turn to speak. I talk about a Passover Seder at my friends Małgosia and Kostek Gebert's house. As the youngest child, Ola, then four years old, asked the questions, "Why was that night different from all other nights?" "Why do we eat bitter herbs tonight?" The Geberts' daughter, Zosia, then eleven and the oldest child at the table, answered, "We eat bitter herbs to remember the bitterness of our life in Egyptian servitude for forty years." Falling asleep later that night, Ola whispered, "Remember, Mama, when we were walking forty years in the desert in Egypt and I was crying so terribly, terribly hard?" I remember the feeling of relief that Ola would be able to draw strength from some tradition, whereas I, whose mother never told me about my origins, about her life before the war, but who also never had me baptized, had always felt somehow without an anchor.

Stanisław Ramotowski is delighted with the ceremony, the synagogue, Rabbi Schudrich.

3

We Suffered Under the Soviets, the Germans, and People's Poland

or, The Story of the Three Brothers Laudański

Of the ten men convicted in the 1949 trial for the murder of the Jews of Jedwabne, Zygmunt and Jerzy Laudański are the only ones still alive. They live in Pisz, eighty kilometers north of Jedwabne, as does their older brother, Kazimierz Laudański, the unquestioned head of the family. Whether he was in Jedwabne on that July day in 1941, we don't know; the accounts are contradictory. He himself claims that he arrived three days later to find out what happened to his brothers. But there is a witness who insists that Kazimierz Laudański went to Jedwabne with him the day before the massacre and remembers details of their trip together. In any case, it was Kazimierz who got his brothers out of Jedwabne after the atrocity, and after the war he found them jobs and places to live. "They're always with me," he says. "I give them advice, and they listen to me."

In the case files from 1949, one can find basic information about the accused on a yellowed form where the blanks have been filled out in an uncertain hand, under the heading "Dossier on Suspects of a Crime Against the State," furnished by the county security service in Łomża:

Name and Surname: Zygmunt Laudański
Date of Birth: January 12, 1919
Relatives Employed in State Institutions: Brother Kazimierz
  Laudański, County Council Secretary for Pisz

Etka Rochla Prawda (née Sztabińska) and her husband,
Chaim Józef Prawda. They were killed by Poles on
July 10, 1941, in Jedwabne with their children, Welwel
and Bari. (Courtesy of Jose Gutstein, www.radzilow.com)

Daughters of Abraham Aaron Ibram, owner of a
fancy-goods shop in the New Market in Jedwabne.
Left to right: Rywka, Loczke, and Judes. Jedwabne,
1930s. Judes managed to survive on July 10, 1941, but
after the liquidation of the ghetto in 1942, Poles found
her hiding place, raped her, and killed her. (Courtesy of
Rabbi Jacob Baker)

Professional Schooling: Mason
Education and Knowledge of Languages: Five grades elementary
  school
Habits and Addictions: Doesn't smoke
Suspected of: Killing Jews in the Town of Jedwabne, Łomża County
Membership: Polish Communist Party (PZPR) in Pisz
Posture: Straight
Eyes: Blue
Teeth: All healthy
Speech: Pure Polish

The 1949 case files also have a dossier on his brother Jerzy, who was born three years later and completed seven grades of school. Under "profession" is given "shoemaker." He has "particularly important contacts" with the "German Police in Jedwabne"; his speech, besides being "pure Polish," is also "loud."

Despite their years, the brothers still have erect postures and loud voices.

From Zygmunt's testimony of January 16, 1949: "Yes, I took part in the murder of Jews in Jedwabne . . . Some guy from Jedwabne came and told me the mayor of Jedwabne was calling on me to go and round up the Jews in the marketplace. When I got there, the Polish population had already rounded up about a thousand five hundred persons of Jewish nationality in the marketplace. Then Mayor Karolak told me to make sure no Jews escaped from the marketplace. The Jews were carrying the Lenin statue around the market. Later, we herded all the Jews with the statue out of town to Bronisław Śleszyński's barn, where they were burned."

From Jerzy's testimony of January 16, 1949: "At that time I took part in driving the Jews into the marketplace. Eugeniusz Kalinowski and I . . . made about eight persons of Jewish nationality go into the marketplace. When we got back there from driving them all out of their houses, Jews were already carrying the Lenin statue around the market singing a song, 'The war's our fault.' Who ordered them to sing it I don't know, but we Poles made sure the Jews didn't run away. I stress that there were Germans around, too. Later Marian Karolak, the mayor of Jedwabne, gave us the command to herd all the Jews in the market to Bronisław Śleszyński's barn, which we did. We drove the Jews to the barn and told them to go in, and they were forced to go in, and after they were all in there, the barn was locked and set alight. Who set the fire I don't know. After the fire I went home and the Jews were burned. There were more than a thousand of them."

Not only the Laudańskis' own testimonies were incriminating; there was also the testimony of other witnesses and fellow suspects.

Czesław Lipiński, suspect: "Eugeniusz Kalinowski, Jerzy Laudański, and a German came to me and we took a Jew and two little Jewish women to the marketplace. When we were rounding up the aforementioned Jews with the Germans, I found a stick on the way and I picked it up."

Julia Sokołowska, witness: "Jerzy Laudański participated in the murder of Jews with a rubber truncheon. He chased them into the marketplace; he beat them and drove them to the barn, where the previously mentioned Jews were burned. I stress that Laudański was the head *Schutzmann* [policeman] in Jedwabne. I saw the aforementioned beating a Jewish woman in a pigsty."

Bronisława Kalinowska, witness: "The townspeople started killing Jews. The way they tortured Jews, you couldn't bear to look. I was standing on Przytulska Street and Jerzy Laudański, who lived in Jedwabne, came running down the street and said he'd already killed two or three Jews. He was very worked up and he went on running."

Stanisław Sielawa, witness: "Jerzy Laudański, Jerzy Kalinowski, and a Russian beat the Jew Eluń after the burning. They threw him down, beat him with sticks, and when I started questioning them they told me it's coming to you, too, just like the Jews. I stress that after the beating the previously mentioned Jew couldn't get up for two weeks. I saw the previously mentioned fact with my own eyes."

Zygmunt Laudański was sentenced to twelve years in prison, of which he served six; Jerzy Laudański was sentenced to fifteen, and he served eight.

In the accounts, both direct and secondhand, that I heard from present or former residents of Jedwabne, the name Laudański was almost always mentioned among examples of particularly active participants in the crime.

They were even mentioned by those who insistently denied that the Poles had committed the atrocity. Like Jadwiga Kordas, an eyewitness: "Maybe that Jerzy Laudański was getting his revenge," she said to Father

Eugeniusz Marciniak in the book *Jedwabne in the Eyes of Witnesses*. "Professor Strzembosz asked me about him and I said: 'Because his father was arrested, and they came to take his mother to Siberia, but she escaped.' And the professor says: 'An eye for an eye, a tooth for a tooth. And probably that's the way it could have happened.'" She added that Jerzy Laudański "had a whip, but he didn't use it on anyone. I didn't see him thrashing anyone. He just drove them out of their houses and kept the order."

Kazimierz Laudański, outraged: "The court case came seven and a half years after the crime. The secret police roughed people up, but no one talked then about little Yids, small kids being thrown into the burning barn. And now after sixty years people are saying these things. When none of us are alive anymore, people will say the Jews had their eyes put out."

Zygmunt Laudański: "There was nothing as horrible as all that. People are making it up now in revenge. It's nonsense that my brother and I killed over a thousand Jews. Our family was and is honest. Our honesty can't be drowned out by this tragedy."

Kazimierz lashes out at him: "It's me who's talking now. You shut up, Zygmunt. You'll talk when I tell you." He goes on: "We're from a truly patriotic Polish family. Our family has suffered enormous losses, fallen and martyred. It's no accident all three of us are alive. We don't smoke, we don't drink vodka. How can they call my brothers thugs? What we did, we did out of patriotism: from time immemorial not one of us ever associated with an enemy of the nation."

In a letter to Adam Michnik, Kazimierz wrote about himself and his brothers: "Like all of the Polish people, we suffered under the Soviets, under the Germans, and under People's Poland."

"Our people organized the roundup of Jews, but didn't take part in the burning. They behaved as peaceful people," says Kazimierz Laudański, who supposedly wasn't in Jedwabne that day. "There was fear, there was compassion, and there was a terrible stench within a radius of three hundred meters. The shocked Poles kept saying, 'It's God's punishment.' It was a diabolical stunt organized by the Germans. The Germans directed it, and used the Poles like actors in the theater. But Poles wanting to burn Jews, there was nothing like that."

We talk about prewar times. Jews leased garden plots from peasants in the summer, so Kazimierz Laudański says he decided to get in their way by doing the same thing. The chemist Michał Jałoszewski, a local National Party activist, gave him five hundred zlotys to start his business.

"I invested in apples and in the traveling cloth trade. Poles always bought from Jews because they sold cheaper. Why? Because Jews had capital. They had mines, warehouses, they controlled everything. And I was getting annoyed that I didn't have work."

In his letter to Michnik, Laudański went on to say, "President Mościcki personally recommended me to the Łomża district head for employment in the administration of independent Poland." When I ask him how Ignacy Mościcki, president of Poland between the wars, knew of his existence, he tells me he'd written him a letter because he was afraid that as a nationalist in Piłsudski's time he would have trouble finding a government job. "I opened with: 'You, Father, are the safekeeper of the Polish nation . . .' And later: 'Despite the fact that we're nationalists and our forefathers fell fighting for Poland in the uprisings, we are now at a disadvantage . . .' I was always lucky, but you have to give luck a hand. I left trade to my brothers and parents, and thanks to President Mościcki I became a clerk's aid. When the war broke out I was making 176 zlotys—more than a schoolteacher."

Kazimierz Laudański tells me about his father: "He was active on the church construction committee; he was close to the priests, which made him hated by the Communist cell."

The Laudańskis' father, Czesław, a local National Party activist, led a boycott against a Jewish teacher in Jedwabne. People I talked to remember that children walked out of class when Miss Hackerowa came in, until the board of directors finally succumbed and fired her.

The Laudańskis' favorite subject is the Soviet occupation.

Kazimierz Laudański: "The Soviets came and threw Father in prison. My mother and my two brothers fled into the woods to hide. Everyone knew who was the indirect cause of the deportations: Jewish Communists. When they came to take away families at night there would be one NKVD officer, one Polish Communist, and two Jews. The NKVD didn't know us, but the Jews were our neighbors."

"And who came for your father?"

Zygmunt butts in: "I wasn't home at the time, but Granny said it was two Russians and a Pole."

"To prove to you it was the work of Jewish Communists," Kazimierz cuts in, no doubt realizing the Jew is missing from the account, "I'll tell you that there were a lot of rich Jews in Jedwabne; none of them were deported or had their shops taken away. Only the Jew Jakub Cytrynowicz was deported; the Jews got back at him for having converted to Catholicism."

However, the truth—of which Kazimierz cannot be ignorant—is that shops *were* taken from everyone, and that Cytrynowicz was not even remotely the only deported Jew.

I ask what hiding during the Soviet occupation was like.

"You moved from place to place in the area, and five months went by that way," says Zygmunt Laudański. "I was a stonemason and I would sleep where I was working. I had a girl in a village where I'd worked, and in another place I'd know someone else. My cousins would put me up, and my uncle did, too. He had a big wooden house, and he built a double-layered roof, where my mother would sometimes sleep with me and my brother. But it wasn't a very nice place to hide: my uncle believed in dreams and he'd wake me at midnight, saying, 'Go jump on your bike! I had a dream about a black dog being run over!' It was a dog's life. I preferred to write to Stalin. If it had been the other way around, I'd have written to Hitler and praised Hitler. That much is clear. With the letter it was like this: While I was still in hiding, I found out the Russians were organizing meetings where they would explain their purpose was to liberate us, and they handed out the Stalinist constitution. I borrowed a copy, examined it, and I saw the fourth paragraph said that in the Soviet Union no one is responsible for anyone else, neither the father for the son, nor the son for the father. At night I went to the priest to get writing paper and I wrote to Stalin. I wrote straight out that Stalin had liberated us from the capitalists and the Fascists, and I was taking up not arms but the pen, standing on the ground of the constitution. I started like this: 'The Polish people are very grateful to the Red Army for liberating them from Fascism and capitalism, and for wealth which will be communal . . .' You don't write to the devil with a holy pencil, miss. And I went on to say that I had to hide because my father had been arrested and they could come for me to punish me in his place. 'If that happened,' I declared bravely, 'half the population will take to the woods.'"

Zygmunt Laudański wrote about this letter in July 1949 from Ostrołęka prison in an application to the interior minister:

"At that time I did not join the gangs then being formed in our parts, but sent a request to Generalissimus Stalin that was forwarded by the Moscow procurator's office at 15 Pushkin Street to the NKVD in Jedwabne with the order to study it carefully. After they questioned me and carried out a local investigation, they found I had been unjustly damaged and I was freed from hiding from deportation, and given compensation. After studying my views, the Jedwabne NKVD allowed me to join the work of liquidating anti-Soviet evil. At that time I made contact with the NKVD in Jedwabne (I will not give my code name in writing). At the time of the contact my superiors ordered me to take an anti-Soviet position to make me more effective and not betray me to the reactionaries."

"They sent my letter from Moscow to the NKVD in Jedwabne," Zygmunt Laudański tells me. "A month went by and they told my cousin to tell me that if I reported in I'd be vindicated or declared innocent. I wrote an application in my father's name to the chairman of the Presidium of the Supreme Soviet of the USSR, Mikhail Kalinin. I had taken a Russian language course for army conscripts, and the next letter I wrote to Stalin, on my father's behalf, was in Russian. There was a Russian officer quartered with us, and he corrected it for me. In May 1941, I reported to the NKVD to get them to pass on the letter for my father's signature. I get there and the boss says, 'Bandits killed a good man of ours.' They had just killed the deputy head of the NKVD in Jedwabne, Shevelyov. I say, 'Zhalka' [Too bad]. And he says, 'If you want you can help us find the bandit.' I ask him, 'How?' He says, 'You know people. When you see new faces around town, let us know.' 'How?' I ask. He says, 'We have a mailbox at the station. Leave a note there and sign it, but not with your surname, sign yourself Popov.' I say, 'Kharasho'—Russian for 'fine'—'I'm sure I'll be in touch.' He just asked, it wasn't a commitment. That trick came off well for me. I got a reply from Stalin that my father should be freed or tried, because they couldn't keep him so long under investigation, and that I would be informed. But then the war broke out. The partisans came and knocked down the wooden monument erected where Shevelyov had been buried, and I think they dragged him out of his grave, too."

Kazimierz Laudański wrote about Shevelyov's killing in a letter to Adam Michnik—but not to explain how his brother became an NKVD agent. On the contrary, killing Shevelyov was an act in line with the patriotic traditions of the Laudański family and other Jedwabnians: "Now, patriotism . . . The very existence of the partisans, the death of our aunt in the fight against the Soviets and the death of so many other Poles speaks for itself. Just as in Warsaw Poles killed Kutschera, so they killed Shevelyov, who was the same kind of torturer, in Jedwabne."

The German-Soviet war found Kazimierz Laudański about eighty kilometers south of Jedwabne, in Ostrów Mazowiecka: "When the Germans came in," he says, "they burned down the Jewish quarter, rounded up Jews, chased them down the road, made them dig a hole, and killed them there. A friend of mine was there and he had to watch the Germans shoot them. He came back pale as a sheet, trembling. That was a Pole's fate."

"You said Jews joyfully greeted the invading Red Army," I say. "But when the Germans arrived, didn't some locals ever go out to greet them?"

"Before war broke out between Germany and Russia, the Poles were in a terrible situation—constant arrests, deportations to Siberia. The population prayed to God: 'May Lucifer come, if only this devil goes.'"

"So Poles were glad when the Germans arrived?"

"When the Germans attacked the Russians, the prison doors opened. There was euphoria. Thousands of people who'd been hiding out in the forest came home. Everyone was happy: that the head of the school had come back, or a neighbor, a son who'd been hiding in the forest. How could my brothers not be glad that Father came home from prison and Mother from the forest?"

From the joy prompted by the German invasion we proceed to the heart of the matter.

"Why," I ask each Laudański, "were the Jews of Jedwabne burned in the barn?"

"It was the Germans' revenge," each brother answers in turn.

They refer to an event that took place in the winter of 1940 to 1941.

Before the war there were about fifteen German families living in Jedwabne, of whom the majority moved to the Reich in the period of the Soviet occupation, in accordance with the Stalin-Hitler pact of 1939, which divided future control over Polish territory between Soviet Russia and Germany. At that time a commission came from Germany to evaluate the value of the property left behind in order to make restitution.

"Officers in shining coats stepped out of two black cars," Jerzy Laudański tells me, "and Jews crowded around those cars, throwing wet snow into them and being so provocative that the Germans had to call the Soviet militia to their aid."

Jerzy Laudański heard about this in the prison yard from Karol Bardoń, who had been sentenced in the same trial as he had. Bardoń supposedly told him that one of the Germans who came to Jedwabne in July 1941 was from that team and that he had threatened: "They gave us a hard time, we'll teach them a lesson."

"That's probably why," Zygmunt Laudański comments. "The Jews were wrong to do it, why throw snow?"

Kazimierz Laudański admits that right after the Soviets left, Jews were punished by mobs.

"There was a lot of revenge," says Kazimierz. "But who did they kill? It was the Communists and snitches who were tried by mobs and lynched. They were the ones who got it. The Jewish community is one thing, Communist gangs another. Our guys acted in self-defense, just like in all the other uprisings, which we're not ashamed of. But when you make an omelette you've got to break some eggs. And since there were some uneducated people there, they might have caused the deaths of a lot of innocent people. But Polish and Jewish Communists were wrong to collaborate with the NKVD. Traitors get their throats cut." He makes a throat-cutting gesture.

Karol Bardoń, the man who got the heaviest sentence for the massacre in Jedwabne, described in his testimony this settling of scores on the first day after the entry of the German army: "There were some people in civilian clothes holding poles as thick as tow bars standing in front of the Germans, and the Germans were yelling at them: 'Don't kill them right away!' 'Give it to them slowly, let them suffer.' Of the six people beaten and later shot by the Germans in the woods nearby, three were Polish and three Jewish. Bardoń named Jerzy Laudański as one of the participants in the beatings.

On July 9, 1941, word spread in town and in the surrounding area that the next day they were going to get rid of the Jews in Jedwabne. This is repeated in many accounts. Peasants in the area got their tools ready for the day: stanchions, sticks, poles; they cut themselves what were called truncheons, or lengths of thick electric cable. On the morning of July 10, a group of uniformed Germans appeared in Jedwabne in one or two cars. The mayor sent messengers to Polish houses to tell the men to report to the magistrate's office. There they were given the order to drive the Jews out into the marketplace, and they were probably told which houses or neighborhoods to go to.

Stanisław Danowski, witness in the 1953 trial, an offshoot of the first Jedwabne trial in 1949: "Karolak summoned people, gave them vodka, and then he got those who were willing—and there were plenty of them— to rout the Jewish population from their homes."

They were driven out under the pretext that they had to pull up the weeds from between the cobblestones in the marketplace, to clean it up. The Germans who had come to town were there when the Jews were driven into the marketplace. Stanisław Zejer, a suspect, testified that Jerzy Laudański and Bolesław Rogalski, a postal worker, "having got themselves poles . . . went to drive six families into the market square, they were Kosacki Mendel (family of four); Szymborski Abram (family of six); Gutko Josel (family of four)—I, Zejer, don't remember the names of the other families."

A crowd of people from Jedwabne and the surrounding area stood around the throng of Jews. This is repeated in almost all the testimonies, that "the rounded-up Jews were surrounded by a mob of people." There were also a few Germans, in uniform, with weapons. Among those who organized the chasing of Jews from their homes, the names return again and again: Bardoń, Wasilewski, Sobuta, Eugeniusz Kalinowski, and Jerzy Laudański.

The locals split off a group of a few dozen men and led them to a little square fewer than a hundred meters from the market, where there was a statue of Lenin. They forced the Jews to smash it, and then they were made to carry pieces of Lenin's torso on wooden poles and to sing. A rabbi, the elderly Awigdor Białostocki, was put at the head of the procession. They made him carry a red flag in one hand, and in the other a pole with his hat on it. Noon was approaching as the group carrying Lenin circled the marketplace. They were humiliated in various ways, beaten, ordered to sing and do squats ("I saw Wasilewski and Sobuta picking out a few dozen Jews there and making them do a funny kind of gymnastics," said Roman Górski, a suspect in the investigation of 1949).

The marketplace was loud with cries and weeping. First a large group of men was led out of the marketplace, and in the next stage the women, young people, and children were driven into the barn.

Testimonies from 1949 and 1953: "They were driving out Jews. I didn't see any Germans in the crowd" (Wincenty Gościcki, suspect). "We Poles stood on one side and the Jews on the other, grouped in fours, so they wouldn't run away. I had no order from the Germans to chase Jews" (Józef Chrzanowski, suspect). "The police helped hunt down the Jews in town, but at the barn there were mostly Poles" (Stanisław Sokołowski, witness). "I was ordered to go and get gas to pour on the barn for Eugeniusz Kalinowski and Józef Niebrzydowski. They took the gas, eight liters of it, and poured it on the barn when the barn was filled with Jews" (Antoni Niebrzydowski, suspect).

All three brothers maintain that no one in town really expected the Jews to be burned. Is it possible, I ask, that news of the burning of Jews in nearby Radziłów three days previously didn't reach Jedwabne? "I didn't hear anything of the kind back then," says Jerzy Laudański.

Kazimierz Laudański presents his version: "When I got to Jedwabne you could still smell the hideous stench of burned flesh. I worked out what had happened. The Germans found a barn beyond the bridge, on the Łomża side. They wanted to requisition it from Józef Chrzanowski, who was serving in the German army, and he begged them in German not to. They found another barn near the Jewish cemetery. 'We'll burn down the barn,' said the Germans, 'and build a new one in its place.'"

Zygmunt Laudański: "On the critical day we were crossing the marketplace. We looked and there were Jews weeding it with spoons. It was overgrown with grass. They were doing it quietly, as if it was nothing. Poles were watching. Karolak, whose house was on the market square, told me to come and do repairs on his kitchen. His wife said, 'Mr. Laudański, I'm sorry to ask you on a day like this'—because it was the day the Jews were rounded up, maybe she knew what was going to happen to them, and she was a decent woman—'but my husband the mayor has to receive some Germans, and we can't make tea here because the stove isn't working.' I cleaned the stove, carried out the ashes, covered the ashes with clay. When I had finished I headed toward Przytulska Street, but there was a German on guard saying, 'Zurück' [Back]. I went toward Łomża, but there was a German there, too, telling me the same thing; I went toward Wizna—same thing. So I went through a backyard in the direction of November 11 Street, where my friend Borawski lived. We had a chat. No one had any idea of the horror going on. I went on, went to sit in a cornfield, and when I got back to my own yard I saw smoke."

Zygmunt Laudański gave this version of events in 1949, when he appealed his guilty verdict from prison. However, at that time he added a detail that testified to the fact that someone was aware of the horror. With a Gestapo officer, Mayor Karolak was leading a Jew from a courtyard: "a tailor, whom I had given some trousers to alter a few days earlier while the Soviets were still in power; when he saw me he called me over and gave them back to me, unfinished, explaining he didn't know if he'd be back."

It's hard to imagine a Jewish tailor, driven out of his home by the Gestapo and conscious that he might not return, taking a piece of unfinished work with him on his last journey. Nor is it clear why Laudański went to "sit in a cornfield" in a situation where "no one had any idea of the horror going on."

Jerzy Laudański: "The mayor gave directions, but the initiative was German. I was standing near the bakery and mixed with the crowd."

"How did you come to be there?"

"Curiosity. When your car crashes, you know how many people are going to stand around gawking. Something was going on, the Germans were rounding up Jews, making them carry the statue of Lenin. No Pole was sorry they were carrying Lenin, unless they were fans of his."

"Were the Poles beating up Jews at that time?"

"There were Poles in the marketplace, but I didn't see any Jews beaten up. The Jews were talking quietly, quietly weeding the earth between the stones. Germans like order, so the Jews were made to weed the marketplace. And then they all went on their own steam, it looked spontaneous."

"What do you mean, 'spontaneous'?"

"The Jews obeyed and went spontaneously, the Poles followed them spontaneously, because nobody expected a tragedy like that. If people say it was the Poles who killed them, it would be a disgrace for Poland. It's not true."

"How did the Poles react?" I ask Jerzy Laudański.

"Some liked what was going on. Others didn't, but everyone was curious. People joked that not long before, under the Soviets, Jews wouldn't have been cleaning up the marketplace."

"And you?"

"I was near the barn, but about thirty meters away. There were a lot of people in front of me."

"And what were you doing there?"

"I was talking to friends."

"Did no one try to help the Jews?"

"Who could have helped them?"

Jerzy Laudański invokes the figure of Maksymilian Kolbe, a Polish Catholic saint, who as a prisoner in Auschwitz chose to starve himself to death in the place of a condemned fellow prisoner, also a Pole. "There was one great hero, Father Kolbe, but he knew he had TB and wasn't going to get out of the camp alive. But he was a hero anyway, because many a man might know the end was near but wouldn't give his life for another."

"And the Germans?"

"I think the Germans were at the back taking pictures."

In the course of a few hours of conversation I hear the same thing from Jerzy: the Jews went in front, then the Poles, then the Germans.

"What were their uniforms like?" I ask.

"I couldn't tell you."

Zygmunt Laudański changes the subject from German uniforms to German guilt.

"The Germans did it on purpose using Polish hands."

"But what did those Polish hands do?"

But he doesn't respond to that question. Instead he spins me a yarn about many Jews escaping and ending up in the Łomża ghetto. He suddenly becomes more animated, remembering the business he did there, buying up clothes and shoes.

I ask Zygmunt Laudański what he knows of the looting and by what principle Jewish homes were occupied by Poles.

"People took over homes because some of them lived in basements. They spontaneously moved into the homes and the magistrate didn't throw them out. Some people say things were looted. Where the police didn't manage to take everything away, maybe someone would drag something out, bedsheets or clothes. But it was the Germans who sold things at auction: they'd hold up the rags and say such and such a price—in rubles, because at the beginning of the war there weren't any deutsche marks."

"A German sold Jewish clothing for rubles?"

"He wanted to make enough for a beer."

"Do you remember the screaming?" I ask Jerzy Laudański.

"When they were locked into the barn, they yelled something in Yiddish. I don't know what. It was a spontaneous shout, maybe to open the doors, or maybe that's how they prayed. Then they were stifled by the smoke. When they fell silent, it was till the end of the world."

"Did the memory of that screaming ever wake you up in the middle of the night?" I ask Zygmunt Laudański.

"A young person doesn't react that way. It never kept me awake at night."

"And what did you think about it all?"

"What could I think? It happened, that's all."

"Do you regret anything in your life?"

"Ask anybody: I don't have a single enemy, and nobody ever said anything bad about me at work, either."

"I understand you fulfilled your obligations, but do you regret anything you ever did?"

"Nothing whatsoever."

A moment later Zygmunt Laudański adds that he couldn't hear the screaming anyway, because he was more than two hundred meters away.

. After the Germans arrived and a German police station was set up, Jerzy Laudański went to work there. At the trial in 1949, he admitted this and charged his brother Zygmunt with having told him to work there. Jerzy Laudański now says that he never worked at the police station; he only went by a few times because the mayor had him take the policemen's shoes to his brother-in-law, who was a shoemaker. In Jedwabne I was told that Jerzy was in the first auxiliary police force, and then he became a guard. In any case, the police did not use messengers or runners at first but had Jews do the jobs required.

"I came to get my brother Jerzy, to tell him to run away," Kazimierz Laudański explains to me.

"Why was he supposed to run away?"

"Because the Germans needed young men like him for the police. We'd already run away from the Russians; now he had to run away from the Germans."

It's not clear why Kazimierz Laudański thought at that time that there was anything wrong in working at the German police station, considering that he also worked for the Germans. He was a clerk working in the administrative machine designed for the destruction of the Jews in Poręba nad Bugiem, which was part of the General Government.

Frequently in my later conversations with the inhabitants of Jedwabne, I encountered eruptions of hatred toward Jews. The Laudański brothers display no such emotion. They are calm and self-assured. After a monotonous recitation of their own version of the events of July 1941, the brothers energetically move on to other subjects.

Kazimierz Laudański claims that in Poręba he belonged to the Home Army and distributed underground publications. But at the same time he tells me without embarrassment that he was an official in the German administration working inside the Holocaust machine, and that he was interrogated after the war "about Jews from Poręba on the Bug River." (Unfortunately I couldn't find the court records for this case to determine what the charges were.) He himself tells me of the order that arrived in Poręba on February 10, 1942, saying the Jews were to be sent to Treblinka. (Given the early date this was probably the labor camp Treblinka I, not the death camp, which was established later.) He was told to make a list of all Jews, and the ones who didn't leave within the set time period were to pay a fifty-zloty fine. This is his account of the Holocaust: "In May another order came and then all of them went to Treblinka. Well, not all, because one of them survived and became the secret police chief in Ostrów."

He also tells me about his brother's life during the occupation: "I think Jerzy was a hero. He spent three years in German camps and never betrayed anyone. Here's a photograph of him in the camp. Jurek, show the lady."

Holding out a camp picture of himself, Jerzy Laudański says: "I was a member of the Home Army. They entrusted me with the distribution of underground newsletters. There was a massive manhunt across the county of Ostrów, and a few dozen of us were picked up in the woods. I was held for four months for interrogation in the Pawiak prison in Warsaw. Twice they took me off to the Gestapo headquarters on Szucha Avenue. I was a concentration camp prisoner."

When I ask Jerzy Laudański if he could give me the name of any person in the Home Army he worked with, he tells me he didn't know any names, they all used pseudonyms. Which is odd, because when I talked to other Home Army members from the region they said it was a small community where everybody knew everybody else. In Jedwabne I had also heard Jerzy Laudański was caught smuggling Jewish gold. Not that I'm inclined to believe that right away, since the theme of enriching oneself with "Jewish gold" is one of the constant themes in local conversation and mythology.

I called the Auschwitz Museum. They referred me to Warsaw, to the Pawiak Prison Museum. If Jerzy Laudański had been transported from there, that's where his documents should be. But the files from that period were burned. The only thing we have to go on is Laudański's own testimony—given in the nineties—that he was picked up in a raid while in the woods with a Home Army detachment. There is no evidence to confirm this.

After the war, the brothers set out to help build the new order of the Communist Party with great zeal. Kazimierz was active in various wings of the party. Zygmunt Laudański: "We had two partisan groups in Jedwabne, the Home Army and the National Armed Forces. Some thought I was in the Home Army, others that I was in the National Armed Forces, but I never belonged to either. After the war they were tried in military court in Jedwabne and the new authorities announced we had to go to the trial. A peasant told them how his last cow had been taken away and beaten so that its ear bled, to that day it had an abcess and it was deaf. And I left Jedwabne right then in 1947 to stay out of that whole mess. After People's Poland was established and my brother became secretary for the municipality in Biała Piska, he got me a job in a shop there. That was the shop where they later came to arrest me."

Many times, in prison, he gave an account of his life after the war: "I went to the remote town of Biała in order to work for the good of the state and support my family, free from the reactionary gangs operating in our area." He wrote to the Office of Public Security in Warsaw on July 4, 1949, proposing himself as an informant: "As a former member of the Polish United Workers' Party and party cell supervisor until my last days in my former place of residence, one who at meetings sounded the call for social justice such as we enjoy today, I now seek that justice for myself and I would like to experience it and to open the eyes of reactionaries who are glad whenever a worker cooperates with the system and is thrown in jail" (sentence review application to the Supreme Court in Warsaw, November 8, 1949).

Jerzy Laudański's brother got him a job as controller of material benefits in the office of the district authorities. "The farmers had to deliver grain quota and we went to check how much each municipality delivered. We made sure they gave the right amount, because they were resistant. There was a rumor the Russians were taking grain to Russia by plane." In the documents there is mention of Jerzy Laudański being sentenced in 1947 to nine months of camp labor in Mielęcin.

"How shall I put it? In trade, you could be off by a certain percentage, and I took that permissible margin," he explains to me. "Then I worked for National Agricultural Properties; then for a collective farm in Kaliszki, in the storehouse. They removed me from that job. They arrested me at work."

Kazimierz Laudański's professional and political careers were not affected by his brother's arrest. He went on working as municipal secretary and was politically active.

"On the anniversary of Stalin's death a crowd gathered in Biała. And I get up and praise the great Stalin."

He gets up from his chair and his voice sounds younger and stronger as he repeats the speech from all those years ago:

"'Great Stalin was a leader. The victorious Polish people will never forget it. He did not die without heirs. He urged us to be critical and self-critical. If Stalin asked you today what you did for the Polish nation, how would you look him in the eye?' And I pointed: this is a mess and that is a mess. I showed my fist. The secret police and the party applauded me, but the crowd was with me, too, because they saw I was putting on a parody. I always had guts."

Zygmunt Laudański also offered his services to the authorities: "I wish to testify to the secret police about very important evidence that remains. I urgently request this, and it will clear up the case" (letter sent to the president from Ostrołęka prison, June 4, 1949). But the authorities did not respond.

The Laudańskis tell me about being beaten during their interrogation. They had spoken of it at their trial, retracting their testimony, and they wrote about it from prison, appealing their sentence. They say they confessed because they were beaten. Their father, Czesław Laudański, was also arrested, but he didn't confess and was released.

"Why did they let your father go?" I ask.

"Well, they found no proof against him."

"And why were you found guilty?"

"We were suspect, because we had been in hiding during the Soviet occupation."

The suggestion that their father, who was imprisoned during the Soviet occupation, was not an easy target for the new Polish Communist regime, but Zygmunt, who collaborated with the NKVD, was, makes little sense. But generally the brothers Laudański are impressively prepared for their conversations with me. They have a ready answer to every question.

Zygmunt Laudański got out of prison in 1955.

"How did people treat you after you got out?" I ask.

"Very well. The director of the dairy in Biała came to me and said, 'Come work for us.' They knew they could rely on me."

In 1956, Jerzy Laudański wrote to the minister of justice from Sieradz prison, four pages of graph paper covered in even, controlled writing: "I fell victim to the legacy of prewar politics at such a young age, because at that time, young people were educated solely in a nationalist spirit. All the more so as I came of age and was shaped as a citizen of the Fatherland at a time when the most ferocious anti-Jewish battles were raging. People, young people, were raised on all sorts of anti-Jewish slogans . . . After our Liberation by the Soviet Army in 1945, I did not go the way of those who despised their ruined Fatherland and indulged in a luxurious existence in the West, only to return later as spies or subversives. Without a moment's hesitation, I returned to my ravaged Homeland, to the People for whom I had sacrificed my youth before I was twenty years of age . . . I am a laborer and the son and grandson of laborers, and I have met with nothing good in my life; I am broken by fate. Presently, having learned this much from life, I have perfect proof of who made me, a young man, suffer so terribly: it was Fascism, capitalism, the prewar government ideology, these are what condemned me to languish so long in prison."

A last opinion on "holding the prisoner Laudański" was put forward at Sieradz prison in 1956: "General observation and interviews have not revealed hostility to People's Poland. He considers his sentence just, but excessively harsh."

Jerzy Laudański was set free in 1957.

These days the brothers meet often, talk politics, share the same preoccupations. "We brothers are nationalists, we're on the right," says Kazimierz Laudański. "As they say: there must be order, *Ordnung muss sein.*"

Journal

MARCH 11, 2001

I was still sleeping after the bat mitzvah reception when Bishop Stefanek of Łomża addressed a crowd of the Jedwabne faithful: "My friends in Warsaw told me long ago in the privacy of their high state offices: 'There's going be an attack on Jedwabne, and it's all about money.'" In this I hear an echo of Primate Glemp, who said he'd been warned of the attack by "an important Jew." And what can you expect from the residents of an impoverished town when the tabloid tone pervades even bishops' palaces?

"The people behind the attack want to provoke a new spiral of hatred," the bishop went on. "The same hatred made Nero burn Rome and blame the Christians for it." Bringing to light the truth about Jedwabne is, in his words, part of the "Shoah business."

I call a few people in Jedwabne in the evening to ask them about the bishop's visit. They tell me:

"There was a lunch at the presbytery, and then the priest and the bishop went to the site of the massacre. They didn't even light candles. They stood there, chatted about the Germans having done it."

"The bishop met with the Committee to Defend the Good Name of Jedwabne and said, 'What do they want from you, dear people? What do they want from your priest, who is fighting with such dignity against unjust claims?'"

"Leszek Bubel, whose anti-Semitic rags are popular in Jedwabne, was distributing copies of the Protocols of the Elders of Zion outside the church, and people reached out for them. As the host, our priest should have kicked him out, but what can you expect? In his sermon he called the Laudański a family of Polish patriots. It's typical of small towns that the priest lords it over everyone. And now his voice has been strengthened by the bishop's."

"When the bishop was coming down the church steps, surrounded by people from the Good Name committee, one of them shouted to the reporters, 'Here on the market square lives a Jewish woman who converted. She survived the war. Ask her how it was.' But she won't say anything, she's terrified."

I've heard before that Helena Chrzanowska, who still refuses to talk to me, is the town's hostage. The priest forbade her to speak to anyone, whereas he uses her himself as an excuse for the town: here we have our own Jew who was saved by Poles.

"It's getting worse and worse. Jedwabne has become a training ground for extremist nationalist groups," the town council chairman Stanisław Michałowski tells me. "They swamp us with the products of their sick minds. What will happen when they form a united front with some of our colleagues?"

MARCH 12, 2001
On the front page of the *Gazeta*, a photograph of the church steps in Jedwabne after Mass. The bishop is standing a little toward the back; in front of him, representatives of the Committee to Defend the Good Name of Jedwabne; the figure of a stocky man in his prime stands out. It's Stanisław Janczyk, head of the committee.

Earlier I checked out the key people chosen for the committee by Father Orłowski. One of them beat his wife so badly she ran away. "If he didn't apologize to his wife and children, you think he's going to apologize to the Jews?" my source said. Another works as a teacher and catechism tutor, but has an extra job at an insurance company for the clergy. When the priest asked him, he couldn't refuse. A third went to prison for participating in a particularly cruel gang rape. They left the woman with a wine bottle in her vagina.

The man convicted of rape is Councilman Janczyk, the man in the photograph with the bishop. The same man who, at a council meeting, told off the mayor and council chairman for visiting the monument on July 10 last year. I phone him and ask, "When is the committee going to assemble formally and announce its members?"

"I'm certainly going to be on the committee. I talked about it with the deacon. He's even getting calls from Warsaw professors who want to join," says Janczyk.

"The president, the primate, and the prime minister have all spoken of the participation of Poles in the massacre and the need for an apology," I reply.

"When they talk nonsense, I can't accept it. That's pronouncing a verdict on oneself. On me and on you, if you feel Polish. Bishop Stefanek says rightly: 'Let them speak the truth about how it was.' The president swore an oath to defend his fatherland, and now he's coming out with this idiocy. Primate Glemp should wait for the investigation to be over."

"But the parish priest is also pronouncing a verdict before the end of the investigation, saying the Germans did it."

"The father is saying what really happened. They're trying to blacken our name. The ones who are telling lies, they're not our Jedwabne youth. The mayor's not from here. If we change the inscription on the monument, we'll have to leave Poland, because every child from Jedwabne, wherever he goes to school, will flee. Wasersztejn wants the inscription to be changed because he wants compensation from Poland."

"People say you were convicted of a particularly cruel rape."

"I was thrown into the case because my dad was village head before the war."

"But were you sentenced?"

"That woman died a month later; she got an infection because she was pregnant and hadn't been taking the right medication."

"What was your sentence?"

"Ten years. I did seven years, me, an innocent man. More than twenty years have passed, so my record is clean now."

"But don't you agree you may not be the most suitable person to defend Jedwabne's good name?"

"I wanted to act for the good of Poland, not just for the good of Jedwabne, but if some jerk digs that stupid stuff up, I'll step down."

I leave a transcript of my conversation with Janczyk at the editorial offices of the *Gazeta*. I'm going to Jedwabne tomorrow. The *Gazeta* lawyer confirms that the term of his sentence has expired, so Janczyk's record really *is* "clean now." The *Gazeta* editors decide to publish the conversation. A public person's life must be transparent; it shouldn't be veiled by the statute of limitations.

MARCH 13, 2001

I've come to Jedwabne for a longer stay, to experience what goes on in a place confronted with the memory of an atrocity. I walk down Przytulska Street holding a list from 1945 that I found in the Łomża archive, with the prewar addresses of Jedwabne residents. The handmade tables on big sheaves of office paper show that on Przytulska, a street leading to the market, almost all the houses belonged to Jews.

I read off the names of the owners of the houses, squares, and gardens like an elegy to the vanished Jewish town: Całka Wasersztejn, Mejer Grądowski, Jankiel Piekarski, Symcha Grajewski, Jankiel Blumert, Mosiek Kamionowski, Alter Marchewko, Daniel Szklarkiewicz, Mosiek Lasko, Josle Cynowicz, B. Gorfinkiel, Abram Zaborowski, Auhhter Blumert, Osier Krzywonos, Fajba Drejarski, Jutke and Wolf Zimny, Brauszejn Gutman, Kiwi, Szmul Wajsztejn, Abram Zajdensztat, Eli Pecynowicz, Icek Stolarski, Jankiel Semborski, Berek Szmuił, Meszek Zaborowski, Mojsze Białoszewski, Ici Kapuśniak, Jankiel Josel, Berek Jedwabiński.

At number 3 there's a wooden house; at number 5, a brick house; and at number 7, a wooden one, just as it says on the old list. A man of about forty rides past on his bike.

"I noticed you've been sniffing around here since yesterday."

I show him the list of homes and ask if he ever heard anything about the people who lived here before the war.

"You're Jewish, right? I could tell by your accent. There's nothing for you here. These homes belonged to Germans."

The man, once a truck driver, now says he lives off nothing, doesn't get any social support.

"Maybe somebody was mad at the Jews, so he had to do something to them. Anyway it wasn't just Jedwabne, there was Stawiski, Wąsosz, Wizna, Radziłów." He reels them off to me, so he must know something of what happened here sixty years ago. "Why are *they* being left in peace? Because our mayor let the Jews in, and in Radziłów the village head wouldn't let them in. My mother spoke well of Jews, she said they gave her work."

I go from door to door. Maybe someone who lives here played with one of the Jewish kids on Przytulska Street as a child?

A house on the even-numbered side. In a yard strewn with junk, by a dilapidated shed, an older woman is chopping wood. I ask if she perhaps remembers the names of Jewish friends from before the war.

"Don't you try to scare me. Whoever's got what doesn't belong to them may tremble in fear, but this house was left behind after the war. I don't know who lived here before. It doesn't concern me who killed whom. Why should it concern me if I'm not from here? Now people come here, buy you a vodka, give you money, they'll always find someone to tell them what they want to hear. And then they accuse the Poles."

"So why did the primate say that Polish participation in the crime in Jedwabne is beyond question?"

"He said no such thing, it would be a lie."

I try my luck with the houses on the odd-numbered side.

The brick house at number 1 Przytulska Street is empty, garbage piling up in the yard. Once, there was a boarding school here. At number 3 an older lady comes to the door. I am told the house used to belong to Germans, and she came here from Wizna in the sixties: "Once, Father went to Wąsosz for grain, it was 1941 but the Germans hadn't come yet, and he met two little Jews. They showed him cherry leaves, and that summer they were brown and twisted, a sign that the Lord Jesus had decreed that 'blood will flow onto you and onto your children.' They read it in the Talmud that God had decreed that they would perish, and they accepted it."

In a friendly tone, without any of the anger I usually encounter, she tells me how it really was. Listening to anti-Semitic ravings from seemingly sweet elderly ladies is probably even more disturbing than listening to an openly anti-Semitic and unsympathetic priest.

At number 5, a man: "I was born in 1931, but I came here after the war. Gross writes a pack of lies. When I came here a lot of people were still alive who told me how the Germans rounded up the Jews."

At number 7, a well-dressed man in his thirties, the owner of a business, speaks to me across a fence: "Jews have positions in government and the Church. Why are you digging it all up? Because it's a gold mine. Now the Jews want to get money out of us. Those journalists who come here, they're Jewish citizens. Gross looks like a bum. The Jews behave as if this were their home, but when I'm in a foreign country I can't do whatever I like. It was wrong of the Jedwabne authorities to let journalists in to dig up Jewish truth. It's not our truth."

Polish truth, Jewish truth. It's obvious to many residents that there are two separate truths here.

At number 9, a leather workshop. A man in his forties leans out. Like the previous man, he talks to me without opening the gate. "I don't comment on political matters," he says coldly, and closes the house door behind him. So that's what the Cytrynowiczes' son-in-law (and son of one of the participants in the massacre) looks like.

I go no farther. Janina Biedrzycka lives in the next house. I'm already acquainted with her nasty views.

Perhaps going around Jedwabne with maps showing what used to be Jewish property wasn't the greatest idea. I put the papers in my backpack. I stop residents in the former Old Market to ask them where the temple stood before the war, and they tell me quite politely they don't know, though you might expect them to be tired of the hundreds of questions put to them by journalists visiting the town recently. Radio reporters run around the market, sticking out microphones to anyone they meet, cameras shoot footage, Western TV crews park their cars outside city hall.

In the evening, after returning to the hotel, I read in the *Gazeta* about the electoral convention of the SLD (Union of the Democratic Left) in Łódź on Sunday. "In the matter of Jedwabne we can never express our pain sufficiently or use the word 'sorry' often enough," the party leader Leszek Miller said. Asked at the press conference how he knew what had really happened in Jedwabne, he replied that he recommended that everyone read Anna Bikont's piece in the *Gazeta*.

MARCH 14, 2001

At the hotel I read the morning papers. Father Stanisław Musiał, a Kraków Jesuit, comments on Bishop Stefanek's sermon for the *Gazeta*. He says he read it "with sadness and astonishment." "It's hard to find a more despicable or cruel crime in human history," he says. "Jedwabne reveals to us and to the world a new truth about our people (after all, the Jedwabne killers were members of our Church). I would expect priests of the Catholic Church not to waste time looking for circumstances that mitigate the scale and significance of the crime in Jedwabne, but to help Polish Catholics whose compatriots soaked their hands in the blood of innocent Jews to find a path to God, to civil society, and to peace with themselves. Unfortunately the Church in Poland didn't undertake this pastoral task immediately after the war, nor did it do so later."

No one points to anti-Semitism as a sin of the Polish Church as clearly as Father Musiał. I know he has suffered various kinds of trouble and chicanery from Church authorities because of it. I talked to him once and thanked him for what he wrote. He asked me if I knew of a derelict synagogue that, if rebuilt, would be used for prayer by Polish Jews. He wanted to hold a collection among his parishioners for such a reconstruction. Later I heard how much hostility he encountered among his parishioners for his stance in the Jedwabne affair. I doubt that he could raise that money.

Jedwabne. A shop on Przytulska Street with a sign saying WESTERN CLOTHES and a sign on the door reading 50% DISCOUNT. It was closed yesterday.

"I'm not from here," the nice older saleswoman tells me. "But I heard the house was built after the war."

I ask how sales are going.

"Badly. Only people with money come in."

I am witness to the purchase of a necktie—before, it cost one zloty, with the discount it's fifty groszy.

A traveling salesman comes into the grocery store on the market square—once upon a time he would have been Jewish—and displays a little dressing case: a measuring tape, scissors, a sewing kit, twelve colors, eight zlotys for the lot. The woman shopkeeper turns the box around, interested. "If you come back tomorrow I'll have the money ready and buy it off you."

A visit to city hall.

"We had our budget cut this year," say the social security center workers. "The money we had last year for temporary benefits would have been our salvation. We could have helped the neediest clear their debts."

From their stories a picture emerges of a town in decay, one that hasn't managed to find its place in the new reality. Once, there was a knitwear factory where ladies' panties and bras were assembled, but it collapsed at the beginning of the post-Communist period. There used to be an agricultural co-op, but only the building is left. You can look for jobs with the Cooperative Bank, the city, in schools. There are shops, doctor's offices, a veterinarian's practice, two hair salons, a post office, and that's it. There are a few private firms, but they don't employ many people: Kruszywa supplies gravel, Polbruk produces paving blocks, Sonarol fits windows, Viga is a company trading in anything and everything. Last year the furniture manufacturer Ital-Polfin closed down after being in business only two years.

"People probably go on living here from pure habit," say my interlocutors. "And also if you wanted to leave, it's hard to sell your home, a lot of houses stand empty."

My *Gazeta* piece on the Laudańskis has an unexpected effect. One of the women at the municipal offices says: "Everybody knows that Laudański scum did it all, and afterward got out as fast as they could. Is the town to blame for that?"

I look in on the mayor.

"We have about forty percent unemployment in this town," says Godlewski. "Add to that the hidden unemployment in the countryside, where several adults work a few hectares. People feel they're worse off than before 1989. Poverty is spreading. Under the Communists you couldn't squeeze into the morning bus to Łomża; the cotton factories employed three and a half thousand people. There was a lot of fake employment, too, like at the state stores where there was never anything for sale, but you could always make a living. Maybe that's why part of the population in Jedwabne reacts aggressively. They're down on their luck, and it's hard to expect noble feelings from people to whom life is brutal."

A visit to the next office. "Only God forbid you tell anybody who you talked to"; "It's best if you put your notebook away, we'll be honest with you."

"Are you ladies from here?"

"I am, unfortunately."

"My parents came here after the war, in 1951, or as they'd say now, on the tenth anniversary of the burning of the Jews."

"I came here in 1974, so my parents couldn't have rounded up any Jews."

"If only Adam Małysz, the ski jumper, came from Jedwabne!" the first lady says, and sighs.

"My friend and I were trying to work out how to change the birth records here, because you're ashamed to admit you're from here. I might ask to have Kossaki put down as my birthplace, that's where I grew up. It's part of the Jedwabne municipality, but you wouldn't see that right away."

"My daughter defended her master's thesis," another lady responds. "They lowered her grade after asking her if she was from Jedwabne. People in town are already talking about new troubles with getting a visa."

"Our children are embarrassed," says a third. "My son had a pen with the company name *Sonarol—Jedwabne* on it. I called him in Białystok and he told me he'd hidden it. He's twenty-four, a student, and he's ashamed of his pen because it says 'Jedwabne.' Nowadays no one would get it into their head to kill a neighbor for having a different religion."

The husband of one of the women comes in: "Gross heard from three drunks in a bar what was supposed to have happened here, and the more beers he bought them, the more had happened."

"Are you sure that's how it went?" I ask. "Gross met with a bunch of drunks, and then the prime minister, the president, and the primate came out and spoke about the participation of Poles in the massacre?"

"Did the Jews apologize for denouncing Poles to the NKVD?"

"Franek, you'd better go." His wife soothes him.

I wanted to bring Halina Popiołek—the one person in Jedwabne who for years has been going to the place where the Jews were burned to light a candle on the anniversary of the atrocity—a copy of the *Gazeta* with my piece on the Laudańskis. Her niece opens the door.

When she sees me she starts shrieking: "She's not here. Do you know how old my aunt is? And the lies she tells? Please don't come back here!"

I try to protest politely that I'm not there to get any information, just to give her my piece.

"Leave at once, please. I'm not letting journalists onto my property, I'll have to deal with the consequences later."

A man in his thirties calls to me from the other side of the street and invites me in.

As it turns out he's a relative of Ms. Popiołek, Henryk Bagiński. It is he who drives her to the site of the massacre.

"My wife is unemployed, I'm unemployed, but around here they say we get paid well for lighting a candle from time to time, that we're living on Jewish money. People call my aunt to say they're going to burn her.

Now, would it be so hard to pour gasoline in the window at night, and who would ever trace the person who did it?"

I'm in the habit of driving to Przestrzele to see the Dziedzic family between visits to Jedwabne, even though it's quite a long drive. I know several people in Jedwabne who have the same sensitivity as Leszek Dziedzic, but I don't know anyone whose voice sounds as clear: Yes is yes, no is no, regardless of whether he's talking to me or his own neighbor. As a result, he doesn't have an easy life. He tells me how people are constantly sniping at him.

"I don't know what they have in store for us. I don't think they'd burn our house down, but they can make our lives miserable, it's enough for a neighbor to put something in a container of milk so it won't meet requirements—and what will we live on then?"

I ask him if he hasn't considered emigrating to America for good, since his whole family is already there.

"My brothers and my mother, all of them can manage, but I'm not one for living anywhere but on my own piece of land. I'm crazy about farming. Whatever I earn in America I put into my land, and every year I hope the land gives it back, though for that I'll have to wait for the economy to pick up. My land is here and no one's going to chase me away or forbid me to say whatever I want to say."

Late evening at Mayor Krzysztof Godlewski's house. Delightedly he quotes me excerpts from an interview given to a Polish journalist by Rabbi Jacob Baker, who emigrated from Jedwabne to America as a young boy: "I could give many examples of Jews and Poles living peacefully together in Jedwabne. We trusted each other." "I grew up with Poles, had them as friends, we were like one family." "You are decent as a people. But unfortunately some Poles succumbed to Hitler's propaganda." Particularly important in Godlewski's view are Rabbi Baker's words to the effect that the majority of residents of Jedwabne did not participate in the atrocity, just "a group of degenerates and thugs from surrounding villages, driven by an urge to loot Jewish property."

"What a fine person, how I'd like to shake his hand," says Godlewski. "Now people will understand that the Jews aren't accusing everybody, just a few criminals. A couple of no-goods joined with the Germans and we have to bow our heads for them, but it wasn't the community that did it. I respect Gross, but in this case he exaggerated.

"But is there any hope at all," he asks me anxiously after a moment, "that on July 10 Rabbi Baker, of a massacred people, and our bishop, who speaks of the 'Shoah business,' will stand side by side?"

I have with me a printout of the Internet text of the *Jedwabne Book of Memory*, edited by two rabbis, Jacob Baker and his brother, Julius, but I don't dare quote it to Godlewski, in case it dashes his illusions. In it, Rabbi Jacob Baker expresses himself quite differently: "After a series of shameful cruelties on the part of their Christian neighbors, who acted with the permission of the Nazi authorities, the brutalized Jewish community of Jedwabne, 1,440 persons in total, were burned alive. It's obvious to us that the Jews of Jedwabne must have lived for centuries among similarly cruel and inhuman neighbors. And here the question arises: how did they survive so long?"

The vision of Polish-Jewish relations in Jedwabne as a centuries-long nightmare amid cruel neighbors may be exaggerated, though it's easy to imagine a man most of whose family was murdered by Poles seeing it that way. In the whole book there are only a few episodes indicating relations were sometimes good, like the description that Gross cites of a priest walking arm in arm with a rabbi.

Now Rabbi Baker has changed his point of view nearly 180 degrees, in favor of idyllic remembrances. Was he moved so deeply by Poland's preparedness to face up to the crime's legacy? Perhaps he thought that by speaking what Godlewski called "an easier truth," he would touch people's hearts in Poland? Or that it would be better for the Jews that way? I must ask him these questions at some point.

I return to the hotel after midnight and stay up late reading the *Jedwabne Book of Memory*. In 1660 the first group of Jews moved to Jedwabne from Tykocin. The oldest records on the Jedwabne synagogue are from 1771, but they speak of its expansion, so it must have been built earlier. It burned to the ground in September 1913. The fire was blamed on a peasant woman who was milking a cow by gaslight and knocked the lamp over. When the straw caught fire the woman ran for water, instead of putting out the fire with the milk. The fire, which consumed the synagogue and three-quarters of the buildings attached to it, seemed to the following generations of Jedwabne Jews the worst imaginable misfortune that could befall their God-fearing town.

The book is full of nostalgic recollections, most of them written in

Yiddish. "Although fifteen years ago Yiddish was the dominant language at meetings of the Jedwabne community in New York," the Baker brothers write mournfully, "today almost 70 percent of our community do not understand the language. So we were obliged to copy, translate, and redact the main parts of this book into English and Hebrew."

Hersz Cynowicz's recollections go back farthest into the past. His grandmother Malke told her grandchildren of Napoleon's armies marching on Moscow and soldiers quartered in Jewish homes in Jedwabne. A few authors remembered life at the turn of the nineteenth to the twentieth century. They described village tailors darning, mending, and altering clothes; away from home for months, they carried kitchen dishes with them to keep kosher. Children were taught their prayers and reading and writing Yiddish by the *melamed*, who used tried-and-true methods—the instruments of persuasion were the strap and the ruler, with which knowledge was rammed into kids' heads. These little schools were usually set up in the kitchen of the house where the teacher and his family lived. There were also better-equipped schools in Jedwabne, with desks and inkpots, run by better-educated teachers, but not everyone could afford them.

Tzipora Rothchild remembers that when Jedwabne, before World War I a quiet place on the fringes of the Russian Empire, received news of workers' protests, it precipitated a one-man strike: "Nachum Mosze Piątkowski's son Arie rebelled against his father. Nachum Mosze beat him with an iron ring and Arie screamed with pain and shouted, 'I'm a socialist, I'm not going to work at night, after hours!' His father had to send him to America to prevent other workers from being infected by socialism."

Posterity has also preserved a story about Józef Szymon Markusz, the only person who dared to criticize the community's spiritual leader, Rabbi Józef Chower. It happened around 1850, during the Kol Nidre service. The rabbi raised the question of Jews engaged in smuggling goods across the Prussian border and thereby avoiding paying taxes to the government. Markusz, who was sitting among the wealthiest members of the community, got up and interrupted the rabbi: "If that's the case, kindly tell me why you accepted the position of rabbi in a border town?" At that time Jedwabne, like other border towns, owed its prosperity—in large part—to smuggling.

MARCH 15, 2001

In Łomża I go by the editorial offices of *Tygodnik Kontakty* (Contacts Weekly*)*, which was the first periodical to publish reportage on the atrocity back in the eighties. I have an appointment with the editor in chief, Władysław Tocki.

"I heard of it first twenty years ago," Tocki tells me. "I was writing an article on looters, and that's how I found myself in the cemetery in Jedwabne. There, I bumped into a history teacher, Jerzy Ramotowski, and he started talking, unexpectedly. After a few sentences he broke off: 'You're not getting any more out of me, and if you write this I'll deny it. You don't understand. There were two hundred Jewish homes abandoned here. They disappeared and their property was left behind. Almost everybody had a hand in it. That's why no one in town will tell you what happened here.' I tried to talk to the locals but hit a wall of silence. If it had been the work of the Germans, I'm sure they would have talked about it. They confirmed the fact of the crime in every aspect of their behavior. The key evidence was the silence."

In 1993, *Contacts Weekly* published an article on the massacre in Radziłów; in 1995, one on the Wąsosz massacre; in May 2000, another one, on the massacre in Jedwabne. There was no response. Nothing, total silence. "The only reaction I got," Tocki says, "was in the summer of 2000, when guests who visited our website wrote, 'Tocki, the editor, must be a Jew.'

"My research shows that the scale of local collaboration with the Soviets was significant. Activists in the prewar nationalist movement were captured by the Russians, who said, 'Either you collaborate, or we'll deport your whole family.' When a Jew collaborated, he boasted about it. He dreamed of parading around in a uniform with a gun. You only found out about a Pole collaborating when he was exposed."

I'm in Jedwabne around noon. I learn that an excavator drove up to the monument in the morning and removed the stone with the inscription saying the Jews were murdered by the Gestapo and the Nazi police. The operation was lightning-fast, and no one was informed, "in order to prevent any incidents."

It's almost impossible to drive to the site of the crime. The furrows left by the tractors traveling back and forth are a big deterrent. At the place where the barn stood, the earth is trampled. There are fields all around, and across from the site stands a forest of hazel trees, which hides the broken Jewish gravestones sticking up here and there—you have to look carefully to notice them.

I look in on Henryk Bagiński and his wife, Elżbieta, and find Ms. Popiołek with them. She has been forbidden by her niece to receive anybody at home.

"People didn't see a thing, but they go on screaming, 'It's all lies,'" she says. "If they saw what I saw . . ."

"Do you think there are many people in this town who feel sympathy for the victims?"

"Not a lot. Because the priest keeps screaming, 'It's not true.' The thing that I mind most is the hostility in my own house, such pain and humiliation. If it turns violent again I'll go to the police. At first I was glad everything had come out. I prayed, 'Lord, let good triumph over evil.' And now I can only cry. If they mean to kill me, too bad, let them kill me."

"Nobody defends my aunt, they're all too scared," says Bagiński. "The journalists listened to her, recorded her, and then they left her in the deep end without asking if she could swim. Someone should go on TV finally and say there will be consequences for anyone obstructing the investigation."

Like everyone else around here the Bagińskis flip from channel to channel to find something about Jedwabne. Cable news—because cameras with their logo were seen in town. Channel 1—because they've announced a studio discussion. The news programs *Wiadomości*, *Panorama*, and Białystok TV—because they've scheduled reports. I look at the smiling face of the Bagińskis' beautiful daughter, Sylvia, who was taken out of school years ago and now studies at home because she suffers from a degenerative disease—she's thrilled that Białystok TV caught her on camera for a split second.

We watch the report together. A journalist reads a letter: "We protest against the slander of our town." My hosts comment nervously. "Why didn't they bring us that letter?" Bagiński wonders. "They knew we wouldn't sign it? How could they know?"

"Wait a minute, wait a minute," says Elżbieta. "They came by with a letter yesterday about construction work on Kościuszko Street. They said: 'We need your signature so they'll let us build this road instead of a road for the Jews.' They had three copies. Maybe the third was that letter?"

But it wasn't the letter. The world of the screen was getting mixed up with the real world. Białystok TV was showing a report filmed a few weeks ago, on a matter that was already old news—the letter by the Committee to Defend the Good Name of Jedwabne, then being formed, protesting against "the worldwide campaign that is using outrageous methods to slander the committee and all of Poland." There were rumors going around town that some letter from townspeople was sent to the parliament, but without signatures. And indeed—the signatories remained anonymous.

On the other hand, the letter my hosts received yesterday was an initiative of the councilwoman Zenona Kurkowska. She came up with the idea that when the money comes in for restoration of the market square and the roads leading to the barn, the town should instead use it for roads that would benefit the residents, or replace the cobblestones on Kościuszko Street in the town center with asphalt, to improve the town. And she's started gathering signatures in support of this plan.

I'm already familiar enough at city hall that I go by even when the mayor's out, sit at his desk, am given tea with lemon, and type up conversations I've just had. Having my own spot like this is invaluable. Unfortunately the offices are only open till 4:00 p.m. There's no place in Jedwabne or in Radziłów where I can get a cup of tea, apart from a bar where I'd be the only woman in a company of boozy men. If I hear in Radziłów that the person I want to talk to will be back in two hours, I drive to Jedwabne and back to Radziłów, because there's absolutely nowhere else to go. The weather is better now, but in February I sometimes drove two hundred kilometers a day on roads not properly cleared of snow between Łomża, Radziłów, and Jedwabne.

I knock on the door of one of Jedwabne's rental apartment buildings and chat with a series of locals about a proposal to name a school here after Antonina Wyrzykowska. To those who haven't heard of her I explain that Wyrzykowska sheltered seven Jews during the war. Their response is not fit to print. One of the residents gives me a card with the poem "The Truth About Jedwabne," signed Jan Gietek of Porędy.

> *The Germans did it, learnèd Mister Gross,*
> *It's time you kissed us Poles upon the nose.*
> *It was the Jews who helped, you pseudo-Neighbor,*
> *Deport Poles Eastward to do hard labor.*

> By that time the Jews had already forgot
> How Judas was with silver bought.
> So if there's a fashion for apology,
> Let the Jews apologize for Calvary.

Photocopies of this nasty doggerel are passed from hand to hand in Jedwabne like a Solidarity pamphlet during martial law.

An unexpected conversation with a woman of about forty who lives in Jedwabne, Krystyna N.: "Ever since I was a child I knew Poles had burned Jews in the barn. In my family no one went around hunting Jews. I remember Mother talking about how people hid Jews in their cellars until their money and property was gone and then killed them. About two years ago my sister and I went to look at the monument for the Jews. There was a swastika painted on it. I read your piece on the Laudańskis, murderers walking around with their heads held high. It's hard living in this town. It's split into two camps. If you could look into our hearts there are more who feel compassion for the victims, but all you see on the outside are the ones who are against the ceremony, because they make the most noise.

"My sister, who lives a hundred kilometers away, called me as soon as she heard about the ceremony to say she'd come to it, but when I told her what had been going on here in town, she was scared off."

I ask her if people who see things the way she does might not come forward, and form a committee for the ceremony.

"Why should I join anything? It's the loudmouths who form committees. Whenever I think about it, I start crying."

At the Cytrynowiczes' in Łomża. I ask more questions of Jan and Pelagia for insight into how they could bear to live among killers for so many years. But apparently I'm the only one to whom the question occurs. In Jedwabne there's no separation between those who participated in the killing and looting, and those who didn't accept it.

Jan recounts, "As soon as I moved to Jedwabne after the war I hired Stanisław Sielawa to put a door in at my workshop. If I'd known then what he'd done maybe I wouldn't have taken him on. But I'm from Wizna, I was a stranger to Jedwabne, and I knew him because he'd been the vet's driver before the war when the vet had to go to the slaughterhouse in Wizna. You were young so it didn't bother you so much. Water under the bridge, you know—the war."

When Cytrynowicz was arrested for some administrative offense, he shared a cell with Roman Górski, one of the men convicted in the 1949 trial. "He didn't show any anti-Semitism to me, didn't talk about Jews," his cell mate praises him, "and when he got out he bought part of a horse's harness from me."

In the evening, at the hotel, I read a text distributed to trusted workers at one of the government offices in Łomża. The handsomely printed brochure "What Happened in Jedwabne and How," sent across the Atlantic by the Polish American Congress, begins with the statement "there's no crime in the history of Poland that the Jews hadn't already commited." The list of crimes begins with the murder of Abel and the crucifixion of Christ, and ends with the "Moscow-Jewish-Communist provocation of the Kielce pogrom in 1946."

Tocki, the editor, gave me copies of all the articles in *Contacts* concerning the massacre. I read the Wroniszewskis' 1988 *Contacts* article again closely, through the prism of the knowledge I had recently acquired. They mentioned Wasersztejn's testimony but found it unreliable. They accepted on faith the findings of prosecutor Monkiewicz, that there had been "over two hundred German thugs" there. Nonetheless, it is an invaluable source, because the Wroniszewskis talked to many witnesses still living at that time. Two of their interviewees are people who I've heard took part in the killings. They quote one of them, Eugeniusz Śliwecki, as stating that the Nazis were the animating force behind the crime and had just used a few local hooligans to help them. What a conspiracy of silence there must have been, since no one ever told the Wroniszewskis about him being a participant in the killings.

Gabriela Szczęsna's *Contacts* article on the atrocity in nearby Wąsosz, "Conscience in the Trenches," leaves no doubt about who did the killing. "It's to our eternal shame," say people from Wąsosz. "Blood ran in the streets, poured from haycarts, marking the final journey of Jews to a trench outside the village. They were thrown in there at random: the living on top of the dead, the dead on top of the living. Earth was packed on top of them all and stamped down by the killers, who finished people off with sticks, spades, axes. Two days after the atrocity, on Sunday, the killers came to church. Many wearing clothes the others instantly recognized. Nor did they try to hide their newly acquired watches. Years passed. Once, the priest declared: 'Whoever has anything taken from Jews must buy something for the church.' And that's what they did."

MARCH 16, 2001

Jedwabne. A pile of newspapers on the first pew by the entrance to the church. The fat headline jumps out: "Szmul Winterszajs, Jew, Secret Police Rat, Polish Workers Party–Führer der Waffen Secret Police, Falsely Accuses Poles of Jedwabne Massacre!" That's from the paper the *Najjaśniejsza Rzeczpospolita* (Most Serene Polish Commonwealth). I also find it at the kiosk across from the church, displayed by Maria Mazurczyk, an activist with the Committee to Defend the Good Name of Jedwabne.

Szmul Wasersztejn is public enemy number one in Jedwabne. The line of attack is simple: Wasersztejn was in the NKVD during the Soviet occupation, and in the UB after the war. Tomasz Strzembosz, who as Jan Gross's main adversary has made himself the best-known historian in Poland, said in a March 3 interview for the weekly the *Głos* (Voice) titled "They Were Secret Police Memoirs": "I know Wasersztejn acted as investigator with the rank of lieutenant in specific cases. This information is confirmed by all, that Całko, also known as Całka, was Wasersztejn and that he was an officer of the Łomża secret police after the war." And why is this information confirmed by all? Because the residents of Jedwabne, feeling supported by Strzembosz's authority, are eager to slander Wasersztejn.

Public enemy number two is Gross. How dare he tell such lies and give sixteen hundred as the number of victims? It doesn't matter that Gross didn't come up with the number, and got it from some archive no one had previously studied. Right after the war the new mayor of Jedwabne reported to the Commission of Magistrates' Courts that 1,642 Jews had been killed, of whom 1,600 died in the barn and 42 by shooting. That number was given by Polish witnesses and participants in the massacre ("I took part in guarding the Jews in the square," said suspect Władysław Dąbrowski in the investigation of 1949. "There were over fifteen hundred of them, rounded up by the local Poles"). That number was actually confirmed by the Main Commission for the Investigation of Nazi Crimes in Poland. Why would the Main Commission exaggerate the number of Jewish victims? Until yesterday you could see the figure on the monument. The residents had forty years to suggest it be changed. And besides, if the Germans perpetrated the crime, why do people suddenly want to lessen the measure of German guilt?

I've arranged to meet Janusz O., a teacher who moonlights selling insurance to priests, and who joined the Committee to Defend the Good Name of Jedwabne. Now it appears he's left it, although the membership list is still secret, so it's not easy to figure out. People say he changed his mind because his wife is related to one of the killers. I ring the buzzer at the gate and hear the familiar sound of a door being slammed shut.

"My husband isn't here, I don't know when he'll be back."

I insist I had arranged by phone to meet him. I wait in the car.

"Please don't park in front of our house," Janusz O.'s wife calls out to me after about an hour.

When discussing the people involved in setting up the Committee to Defend the Good Name of Jedwabne, I heard it said more than once of two men, a certain Goszczyński and Śleszyński (from a different family than Bolesław Śleszyński, the owner of the barn), that they were "from pure families." In other words, families in which no one participated in the massacre. So in spite of all the denials, a memory of the truth persists. It's passed on, however, in linguistic codes comprehensible only to the initiated. On the one hand there are those "from pure families"; on the other, those who "made a fortune in Jewish gold." Some of my younger interlocutors remembered these things being said of some of their neighbors. Before Gross's book came out they didn't give much thought to what it might mean.

Talk of "God's punishment" is also widespread. The two teenage daughters of mailman Eugeniusz Śliwecki got food poisoning from sausage at a wedding and died. At the funeral people whispered that the daughters had answered for the sins of the father. Two sons of another participant in the massacre drank themselves to death. Yet another had a disabled son.

"You can often find him in the square where people park in Łomża," Leszek Dziedzic told me. Dziedzic, a farmer from Przestrzele near Jedwabne, is becoming a closer and closer friend. "He waits for someone to give him a zloty to watch their car. He has deformed arms and crooked legs and sometimes he says to me, 'Daddy did this to the Jews,' and makes the gesture of cutting a throat, 'and God in Heaven did this to me,' and he shows his crooked arms."

Several of those I phoned to arrange a meeting asked me not to park in front of their house. So I cross the darkening little town on foot to find the spot where I parked. As I am turning the key in the door, a man of about sixty comes up to me.

"I looked out from time to time to make sure your car was all right," he says, and goes on without any questioning: "I was a year old at that time, so I don't remember much myself. I spent my adult life in a mine in Silesia, but when I was in school I heard stories about our people killing, and finishing the wounded off in the rye fields nearby. If we don't all go to the monument together, it'll bring shame on the town."

On my way back to Warsaw I wonder how many people like that there are in Jedwabne.

MARCH 17, 2001

I'm off to the Ramotowskis in a minute. I'm bringing Stanisław one of the Hoover Institution testimonies, that of Stanisław Mroczkowski, a farmer from the village of Czerwonki. In Kramarzewo, where Ramotowski lived, there was a candidate for local office in Soviet times, one Zitkowski from the village Zakrzewo, "a poor farmer, a thief, who killed the farmer Antoni Gliński of Zakrzewo a few days after the elections, for which he was not punished." Ramotowski not only doesn't remember if he voted for Zitkowski, but he can barely remember if he voted in Soviet elections at all. For over a year and a half he was a citizen of another country, and now I have to convince him that he must have taken Soviet citizenship and, when he was given his new ID papers, that he must have taken the oath "not to strive for the restoration of an independent Polish state." We are good enough friends by now that I know he wasn't trying to hide this information from me. He simply obliterated it from memory. Wartime experiences of all kinds must have been pushed so far into oblivion that they never entered public consciousness. Whereas others are seemingly etched in stone. It's hard to find anyone of the older generation in Jedwabne or Radziłów who doesn't vividly remember a Jew pointing a rifle, jumping off a truck to oversee the deportation of a Polish family, as if it were yesterday. But it's a phantom of their imagination. The Soviets arrested people at night or at dawn. In the dark it's hard to tell from behind curtains who exactly is standing on a truck or what his nose looks like. The names of these Jews are rarely mentioned, though they would have been familiar neighbors. Apparently the Soviet occupation is subject to mystification, and a thick layer of stereotypes has obscured individual experience.

I'm worried about Stanisław. I consult with Marek Edelman on Ramotowski's state of health or, rather, illness. Edelman promises he'll look in on him.

Every few days I call prosecutor Ignatiew, who seems used to it by now. Especially as I don't ask him anything much; I just share my observations with him. We once talked about Jakub Kac, one of the first victims in Jedwabne, beaten to death by locals right after the Russians left. Kac was by then an elderly man, around seventy. What could the killers have wanted? Under the Soviets he had worked as a guard at the youth club that had replaced the Catholic club; was that enough to get him killed? I heard more than once in Jedwabne that "Kac pissed against the church." I told Ignatiew this sounded to me like an old anti-Semitic fable, a bit like Halina Zalewska, Jan Skrodzki's cousin, saying Dora Dorogoj was killed because she "stood at the cross and blasphemed." Ignatiew asked me if I could point him toward some source that could show that relieving oneself against a church belonged to the repertoire of anti-Semitic imaginings.

So I leafed through Alina Cała's book *The Image of the Jew in Polish Folk Culture*. In the seventies, Alina set off into the Polish provinces to carry out a study. She thought it would be a difficult subject, but people talked to her eagerly and colorfully. She understood that the image of the Jew didn't function at the margins of folk culture but was an integral part of it. "The Jew is necessary to the dichotomous separation of the world into 'us' and 'them.'" One of the respondents quotes a prewar song from the Białystok area: "Don't buy from Jews, only from your own / Take a knotted stick / Chase them out of Poland / Why let Jews lord it over us? / Let them be the Arabs' horses in Palestine!" But there are no examples that corroborate my thesis. I phone Alina.

"A Jew relieving himself against the church?" She ponders the question. "No, I've never heard that one."

MARCH 18, 2001
"Writing these words, I feel schizophrenic: I am a Pole, and my shame about the Jedwabne murder is a Polish shame. At the same time, I know

that if I had been there in Jedwabne at the time, I would have been killed as a Jew." Adam Michnik's piece "The Shock of Jedwabne" appeared today in the *Gazeta* and *The New York Times*. "I do not feel guilty for the murdered, but I do feel responsible . . . that after they died they were murdered again, denied a decent burial, denied tears, denied truth about this hideous crime, and that for decades a lie was repeated . . . Why then did I not look for the truth about the murdered Jews of Jedwabne? Perhaps because I subconsciously feared the cruel truth about the fate of the Jews during that time."

Adam reminds people how courageously Poles behaved during the war, how they fought, how they died, how many Righteous Gentiles there were. "For these people who lost their lives saving Jews, I feel responsible, too. I feel guilty when I read so often in Polish and foreign newspapers about the murderers who killed Jews, and note the deep silence about those who rescued Jews."

What deep silence is Adam talking about? The trees planted at Yad Vashem for the Righteous Among the Nations and the inscription *Whoever saves one life, saves the whole world* are the most resounding universal symbol that even in the worst of times, times of evil and contempt, there are people who do good.

MARCH 19, 2001

I'm trying to find Jan Skrodzki some descendant of the Jew Konopka, who once warned Skrodzki's parents of an imminent deportation to the Gulag. Skrodzki knows only that he was a grain merchant. When we went to Radziłów he insistently asked about him, but no one remembered his first name. Skrodzki keeps saying: "I owe that Jew who saved us some kind of compensation. If they put up a truthful inscription commemorating the massacre, I'd like to put up a little memorial stone next to it: *The Jew Konopka lived here. He saved my life.*"

I search genealogical lists of Radziłów Jews on the Internet. After going onto the website jewishgen.org and clicking on "Jewishgen Family Finder," a site where people from the same town or with common ancestors can meet, and after searching the keyword "Radziłów," I find twenty e-mail addresses, among them Jose Gutstein and his website radzilow.com. I soon find myself looking at photographs, recollections, a "virtual shtetl" of Radziłów—a whole world resurrected by an American in Miami.

There's an extraordinary testimony on the site: an interview with Chaja and Izrael Finkelsztejn conducted for Yad Vashem. They are the parents of Chana and Menachem, whose accounts I read at the Jewish Historical Institute and whom I've dreamed of finding ever since. On July 7 the whole Finkelsztejn family was driven into the market square in Radziłów. "I witnessed the Germans organizing the local Poles," Chaja Finkelsztejn testified. "However, the Poles carried out the whole operation." Three of her brothers perished in the barn in Radziłów. Chaja keeps saying she can't talk about it, that it's all in her 360-page memoir, written in 1946, which she gave to Yad Vashem. I must go to Israel to read it. Chaja was born toward the end of the nineteenth century, so she is no longer alive, but maybe I can find her children. The Finkelsztejns lived at 32 Yotam Street in Haifa. True, that was forty years ago, but it gives me something to work with.

MARCH 21, 2001

I drop by the *Gazeta* to read articles kept in our archive under the file name "Jews in Poland/History/General Materials. Kielce Pogrom. Ejszyszki. Jedwabne." There's such a deluge of texts that a separate file has been created for "Jews in Poland/History/Jedwabne." In the week I haven't looked at the file, an impressive pile of interviews, statements, and articles has collected—mainly attacking Gross.

Lech Wałęsa talking to journalist Monika Olejnik on Radio ZET: "There's no point making such a fuss because somebody wrote a book and made some money. How many Jews worked for the security services after the war and murdered Poles? Not one Jew has apologized to us for that."

The chairman of the World Association of Polish Home Army Soldiers: "The call for a nationwide apology to the Jews for the massacre in Jedwabne is, to say the least, premature and wildly exaggerated."

The Parliament of Student Self-Government of the Catholic University in Warsaw in an open letter to Bishop Stefanek: "We express our support for his Excellency's position regarding the massacre in Jedwabne." And they go on about the profits the Jews are after by slandering the Polish people.

The National Board of the SLD (Union of the Democratic Left)—the post-Communist party: "Almost the whole Jewish population of the town perished at the hands of their Polish neighbors. The Jedwabne massacre is cause for pain and shame."

It's cause for pain and shame that only the post-Communists can bring themselves to say these words.

MARCH 24, 2001

Jedwabne. I've heard that the main power player in town besides the priest is Wojciech Kubrak, a doctor by profession, and at present district head of Łomża. He published "A Declaration by the Łomża District Board on the Jewish Pogrom in Jedwabne," in which the board distances itself from the ceremony: "Although the Institute of National Remembrance investigation is still in progress, the verdict has already been pronounced."

Jedwabne lives a mirrored life. Journalists and politicians feed on statements made by the town's residents, but the reverse process is far more powerful. The residents speak of what happened in their town in the language of journalists, historians, and politicians. And so from the time Tomasz Szarota gave his interview to the *Gazeta*, people in Jedwabne speak of the "Białystok Commando" as an obvious and irrefutable part of the story. Similarly, the phrase "truckloads of Germans" has entered into general currency.

When I was conducting my first interviews, several members of the younger generation were surprised to discover that there had been an investigation into the Jedwabne affair in 1949, and that there were convictions. They told me, "They were tried for being in the partisan underground, not for the Jews." Forgotten facts can easily reenter the current of memory. Now the Stalinist investigation belongs to the body of information known to everyone. "We know there was a trial, they found the guilty ones and convicted them. Since they were already tried once, why do it a second time?" It must mean the Jews want money.

Crossing the market square, I suddenly make a simple connection: the same people who say that Jews deported Polish patriots to Siberia also say they saw—or their families saw—lots of Germans on July 10. Others just saw lone Germans in the market square, a policeman taking pictures, but only in the square, not on the road to the barn. I call Ignatiew to share this observation with him. He offers no comment. I know he won't reveal to me the results of his investigation, but if I were mistaken he'd probably contradict me, saying my attitude to the case is too emotional. I've heard this response from him several times already and it was hard to deny it.

I visit Leszek Dziedzic.

"What they're most afraid of," he says, "is that the Jews will take away what was stolen from them. People keep saying, angrily, 'The Jews will come to get their things.' Not 'our things,' but 'their things.' If things are 'theirs,' they should be returned."

I explain to him that connecting the recovery of memory to the recovery of former Jewish property only serves to spread fear among the townspeople, and I'm sure no descendant of Jews from Jedwabne will turn up to get some ramshackle cottage back.

"But they should come and get them back," he insists.

The truth is that Jews left their property here, and Poles of Jedwabne, Radziłów, and the surrounding areas took advantage of it. There are testimonies to this effect from surviving Jews from nearby towns in the Białystok region. "The Poles' slogan was 'Wasilków without Jews.'" Paintings and photographs were slashed, down quilts were ripped up. During the pogrom the leaders shouted: "Don't break anything, don't tear anything up. It all belongs to us anyway" (testimony of Mendel Mielnicki, 1945).

"Poles from Zaręby Kościelne, wishing to take over Jewish property, sent requests to the German authorities in Łomża to liquidate the Zaręby Jews as well. Prominent residents signed these requests, Dr. Jan Gauze among them" (testimony of Rachela Olszak and Mindel Olszak, 1945).

"Someone in hiding heard Christians talking after Jews had been taken away. One guy was saying what he'd seen was terrible, one woman told him: 'Don't worry, we'll get used to it, we'll be better off without them.' Then she looked at the buildings nearby, which she'd long dreamed of owning. Every Pole furnished his home with stuff they took from Jews. They felt they were the bosses now, their hour had struck" (testimony of Pesia Szuster-Rozenblum on the liquidation of the Jasionówka ghetto, 1945).

Dziedzic speaks calmly, determinedly, but as soon as his children disappear from his field of vision he gets up, looks for them in the yard, calls after them. I read him back what he has said, which I would like to insert in my *Gazeta* piece on Jedwabne today—making sure he wouldn't prefer to remain anonymous, but he agrees to the publication of everything he's said under his own name. He is the only such example among the people I talk to.

For the situation in town is deteriorating. People who just a few weeks ago talked to me without withholding their names (talking not about the crime, but about the current situation in Jedwabne) now say when I ask them to authorize quotes, "We already have so much trouble. I'm sorry, but I'd like you to leave my name out." The part of the Jedwabne population that shouts the loudest that the Jews are to blame for everything, though they form a minority, is nevertheless in ascendance in this town. They feel powerful. They have Father Orłowski's support. They have their own scholarly authority—even the least sober-minded of my interlocutors, whom no one would suspect of reading history books, has invoked Professor Strzembosz.

Before, they were frustrated people, living in a town without prospects or hope. Now, prominent people—politicians, MPs, senators—devote their time to them. They are also visited by personalities such as the film director Bohdan Poręba. The fact that he is known not only from films but also for belonging to an anti-Semitic Communist organization in the eighties called Grunwald doesn't bother anybody here. They don't like Communists unless they're anti-Semites. And when people from this area emigrate to America—remittances from relatives who work in the United States are one of the main sources of income in these parts—they are sure of being embraced by the Chicago Polish community as Polish victims unjustly accused by Jews, and of being helped to find work.

Thinking of all this, I have the absurd sense that history is repeating itself. Before the war, too, the local parish priest organized the community around hatred toward Jews. National Party activists from the greater world—Łomża, even Warsaw—began visiting settlements far from the main roads, and small-town life took on a new glamour.

The most aggressive deniers of the Poles' responsibility for the massacre are among people in their forties, usually from families who lived here during the war. Now a second generation stands guard over a falsified memory.

In the evening I read the Catholic paper *Our Daily* at the hotel; it includes a report from Jedwabne—people were talking about it in town today—involving an event with the historian Tomasz Strzembosz. It was held in the parish house. Janina Biedrzycka, whose father gave his barn for the burning of the Jews, treated the gathering as her own throne room. She recalled the German atrocities in Łomża: "They killed the only true Poles." She hasn't noticed that the Germans wiped out all Jews there, one-third of the city population. And she summed up: "Because we Poles have no one to remember us. This is not our country anymore."

MARCH 25, 2001

Leszek Bubel, publisher of a whole array of anti-Semitic periodicals and books along the line of "Know Your Jews," has convinced some of the town council members that Edward Moskal should be made an honorary citizen of Jedwabne. Moskal is president of the Polish American Congress and has just published a statement expressing outrage at the accusation that Poles committed the Jedwabne massacre.

Bubel, a completely marginal figure in Poland, has already grown to be a local hero and a permanent fixture in Jedwabne. He participates in council sessions, has dinner with the parish priest, visits council members.

"He called me about that honorary citizenship," Godlewski tells me when I visit him at home. "He said: 'If you say what people want to hear, you can make a career. You have a chance to be somebody, to shine, make history.'"

Bubel's initiative would probably have been carried through if it hadn't been for Stanisław Michałowski, as council chairman, asking Bubel to leave the session.

I keep having the same conversation with Godlewski. I recount to him the anti-Semitic views voiced by one of his council members, and he says that it's hard to talk to me because for me everything is black-and-white.

"The residents of Jedwabne have come under attack. They are accused of crimes, although the people who live here now didn't commit them. That's why it's hard for them to accept that the killers were from here. They have to mature to be able to carry the burden. That takes time, but I see a gradual transformation."

But it is hard to see any transformation. The council doesn't like anything that's going on, least of all the mayor receiving Western journalists and film crews—Jews, in other words—in his office. Godlewski tried to persuade the council members to place a marker where the synagogue once stood, and perhaps to sell that parcel of land back to the Jewish community. He didn't dare suggest it be given to the community as a gift. Nevertheless, he was told he was trying to give all of Jedwabne back to the Jews. The vice chairman of the council, Piotr Narewski, said, "The mayor is educated, that's why he thinks differently from us."

I look through letters the mayor has received recently. On top, a letter from one Andrzej Kamieński of Warsaw, who proposes that Jedwabne institute a stipend for study in Poland for a high school senior from Israel orphaned by a terrorist attack. Other letters are written in a completely different tone. "Idiot Mayor, get that Jewish scum out of town. You have no Honor or National Pride. You were paid off by Jews, you're an enemy of Poland." Letters of support come from people who still associate him with the Committee to Defend the Good Name of Jedwabne: "We stand with you. The Jedwabne affair is a case of Goebbels propaganda, Jewish-style." "Don't let any kind of cemetery be established here. Even the Gospels say the Jews are a tribe of serpents. Make sure the minority doesn't become the majority. Group for the Open Integration of Polish Patriotic Organizations."

I drop by to see a man who has been very nice to me but who refuses to appear under his own name. "I get calls: 'You son of a bitch, you Jewish lackey, we know how to deal with you.'"

The close-knit, aggressive group of the killers' families and people who live in formerly Jewish homes dominate everyone else. Those whose families participated in the massacre and the looting feel they have to defend themselves. The killers' families are the ones who intimidate others, for fear the truth about the crime will be revealed. The war brutalized people, and when there were no more Jews to kill, Poles started killing one another.

Even Leszek Dziedzic has lost the optimism he showed in our first meetings, when he believed the confrontation with truth would bring about a catharsis, at least for some of the locals.

"Most of all people are outraged that the president announced he will come here and apologize. They'd like to bar him from entering the town. No one here plans to attend the ceremony. They keep saying no local should dare show his face, and that curtains should be shut in every window. But I'm certainly going to be there with my family. The word 'sorry' must be spoken. And if those who did the killing don't want to apologize, I'm prepared to apologize for them, for the fact that the land on which I was born produced such bloodthirsty monsters."

MARCH 26, 2001

A press conference at the state archive in Warsaw called by director Dr. Daria Nałęcz. Files from the municipal court of Łomża are presented. They are documents from 1947 civil cases in which Jewish heirs of houses in Jedwabne sought a declaration of the deaths of the prewar owners, so that they could sell the houses. The heirs testified that the Jews died at the hands of the Germans. It seems obvious they couldn't have said anything else if they wanted to live in peace in the town. Why hasn't this person, who is surely trained to read documents critically, understood that? I don't suspect her of any bad faith beyond a desire for media attention, but I can already imagine how much empty fuss will be made over this.

MARCH 27, 2001

For two days Stanisław Ramotowski has been coughing up blood and feeling too weak to get out of bed. Through the writer Tadeusz Konwicki, who is friendly with a prominent vascular surgeon, Dr. Wojciech Noszczyk, I've arranged a personal consultation with the doctor, to whose hospital I have brought Ramotowski. It turns out his condition was very bad, and he survived only because Noszczyk intervened immediately.

The newspaper headlines after Daria Nałęcz's press conference show it got results: "Germans Did the Burning . . ." (Życie, Life), "Witnesses Accused the Germans" (Życie Warszawy, Warsaw Life), "No Part Played by Poles" (Our Daily).

I call acquaintances in Jedwabne and Łomża. Town council chairman Stanisław Michałowski tells me that after the war, intermediaries went around previously Jewish towns looking for Poles living in Jewish homes and offering them legalization of any sales transaction for a small fee. They found citizens of Jewish origin who, to make a little money promised to them by the intermediaries, declared their families had lived in Jedwabne, on Przytulska Street number such-and-such, and that they were the only heirs.

Another person I talk to: "I thought what a different perspective you have if you're from Jedwabne and you know what we know. Those were all civil suits, they were about recognizing the homeowners as deceased so their real estate could be sold. And who was it sold to? Poles. So the transaction was already agreed on and it was just a matter of rubber-stamping it. Polish citizens of Jewish origin testified that the Germans had been the killers. If people are still receiving threats now, after sixty years, what must the atmosphere have been like a few years after the war, when gangs roamed the countryside, when not a month went by without a murder? No one in their right mind would have said the Poles had done the killing. Why would they? Poland hadn't even come out of the shock of the war, there wasn't a single family that hadn't lost someone. The atmosphere was anti-German, the Fascists were blamed for all the evil perpetrated. Neither the authorities at the time nor the people cared about revealing the truth. And now those lies are coming back like a boomerang."

I remember that in one of the issues of *Karta*, in a collection of documents on secret police activity in those Borderland territories, there was a description of houses being sold under false pretenses with the involvement of secret policemen from Białystok. The procedure is described by Eliasz Grądowski of Jedwabne, who survived because he was deported during the Soviet occupation, and after he came back, he got into shady dealings in formerly Jewish homes. Papers were sold to people who already had the property. Some of them must have taken part in the massacre, hence they had the loot. In court they said the Germans did the killing, and now their version is becoming objective truth, confirmed and buttressed by real documents.

I learn from my calls to Jedwabne that councilman Janczyk, the man who participated in the gang rape, since my interview with him has not wanted to make statements in the name of the Committee to Defend the Good Name of Jedwabne, but has filed a suit against the *Gazeta* for a million dollars in damages. At least that is what he says. I reminded one of the people I talked to that to file a suit, Janczyk would have had to pay a deposit of about a hundred thousand dollars.

MARCH 28, 2001

Jan Skrodzki has come from Gdańsk; we're driving to Radziłów tomorrow. In the evening I take Jan to a Ministry of Justice training center near Serock. I want to introduce him to Ignatiew, who is there on a professional training course. In the middle of Skrodzki's tale about the massacre in Radziłów, Ignatiew suddenly turns to me: "This was your people being killed. It must be hard for you to hear these things."

Ignatiew's concern is particularly touching because he doesn't seem the type of person who readily comes out from under the shell of his official persona.

I try to understand what really happened during the Soviet occupation.

The historian Dariusz Stola brought to my notice how the fact that the Germans were present in this area in the first weeks of September 1939 permits us to compare the behavior of the locals toward Jews in 1939 and 1941. (In 1939 the Germans appeared in a gentler guise, but the differences were not dramatic enough to explain the events of late June and early July 1941.) In September 1939, when Jews were returning to the homes they had left empty for the time it took the German army to pass through, they found them looted by their Polish neighbors. In June 1941, even before the German troops arrived, pogroms, lootings, and killings took place. In September 1939, a large part of the population felt alienated from and hostile to Jews. In June 1941, an explosion of hatred followed. Alternative: the hostility erupted into violence. What happened in those two years of Soviet occupation to make neighbors hate each other so much?

There aren't many good witnesses on the subject here. Although I would bridle when people started bringing up Jewish collaboration with the Soviets in the context of Jedwabne (absolving oneself of guilt by blaming the victims is a dirty tactic), in the end I became convinced that, beyond prewar anti-Semitism, the key to figuring out what happened on July 10 was the Soviet occupation. That was the fuse.

4

You Didn't See
That Grief in Jews

or, Polish and Jewish Memory
of the Soviet Occupation

It is New Year's Eve 1940, a Saturday, and a dance is about to start in the former Catholic House, which has been turned into a House of Culture. More than a year has passed since the Red Army invaded the town. The town is no longer in Poland but in western Belorussia. The inhabitants themselves voted for this and took Soviet passports. What else could they do, since refusing to vote could mean deportation? Besides fear and forced taxes, the Soviet authorities also brought some lures with them: Saturday dances, film screenings, various festivities that may have been tedious but sometimes involved free beer. Besides, it gave them something to do. Russian women brought to town by representatives of the new political order dress up to go out. Their Polish neighbors, watching from a next-door window, laugh at them for putting on nightgowns and mistaking them for ball gowns. Jewish girls dress up while their mothers chide them that it's still Shabbat. Many young people are going to tonight's party, most of them Jewish, but not all. It is not until later that Poles will say only Jews went to these events.

Nowadays the residents of Radziłów and Jedwabne like to say that it was the Jews above all who joined the NKVD, who informed on others and pointed guns at Poles being deported to Siberia. From their stories you might think that in reality it was the local Jews who established the Soviet

Jewish Tarbut School. Radziłów, 1930s. The school was closed during the Soviet occupation. (Courtesy of Jose Gutstein)

Halutz youth organization. Jedwabne, 1930. Approximately fifteen of them managed to get to Palestine before the war. The organization was disbanded during the Soviet occupation. (Courtesy of Rabbi Jacob Baker)

occupation. They recall how Jews jeered: "You wanted Poland without Jews, now you have Jews without Poland."

This is seen differently by Jews. They count on the fingers of one hand the Jewish collaborators they knew, and explain that the clear majority of the religious community of merchants and craftsmen could not possibly be happy with the Soviet system, which was atheistic and deprived them of their private property. And in fact, although the Holocaust came later, the Soviet occupation had already destroyed the entire fabric of social life built up over centuries: the Jewish municipal government was liquidated, Hebrew schools were closed, Yom Kippur became a normal workday, political parties were dissolved, and Zionist activists and Bundists were put on deportation lists.

1.

"In September 1939 many Jewish homes were looted," Menachem Turek testified about the town of Tykocin to the District Jewish Historical Commission in Białystok in 1945. "It soon felt as if everything had become ownerless, not just the material property people had accumulated but even human life. The day before Yom Kippur, when the Kol Nidre was being said, when the Jews gathered in the synagogue and asked God for mercy, five trucks drove into town carrying German soldiers from the nearby main road who were retreating in accordance with the treaty with Soviet Russia, and they hacked open the locked doors of Jewish shops with axes, loaded everything onto cars, and left town, happy with the loot they'd managed to grab."

"The Germans didn't have time to commit many murders," Chaja Finkelsztejn wrote in her memoir, having loaded her family and possessions on a wagon upon hearing news of the war. They set off in the direction of the nineteenth-century fort town Osowiec in the hope that Polish forces would stop the German army there. When she returned to Radziłów on September 16, she found her house looted by neighbors. "On Yom Kippur the Germans went to the synagogue, threw out the men praying there, ordered them to take off their coats and give them to Poles." The date was September 23, 1939.

2.

The Jews and the Poles of Jedwabne and its environs did not share the same fate and do not share the same memory.

For Jews the invasion of Poland by the German army on September 1, 1939, was a nightmare scenario made real. Terrifying reports had already reached them from the Reich, and these were confirmed by the conduct of the Wehrmacht, which deliberately humiliated Jews and egged on the local populations to do the same. For most Jews the Soviet occupation also meant hard times, but it offered some hope of survival, and also a certain thinly disguised satisfaction that the Poles were now as badly off as they were themselves.

For the Poles, the Soviet occupation meant the loss of independence. It's true that the German army marched eastward in early September 1939, but there was a powerful belief that the Germans would soon be defeated, as had been proclaimed by prewar propaganda. People had been told to be more afraid of Soviet Russia than of Hitler. It was only with the Stalin-Hitler pact that the inhabitants of the area realized they were captives. Added to this were fear of deportation and the inevitable deterioration of living conditions caused by the taxes imposed by the Soviets.

The Red Army entered the Jedwabne area on September 29, following the agreement on the withdrawal of German troops. The NKVD was the army's advance guard, giving the local Communists their instructions; hence the identical scenario for all places of welcome: in a marketplace decorated with posters and red flags, the Soviets were greeted with flowers presented by delegations of local residents waiting, in accordance with ancient Polish custom, with bread and salt, at tables covered with red cloth.

The barn owner's daughter, Janina Biedrzycka, remembers that the Soviets were welcomed to Jedwabne by two Jewish couples, Socher Lewinowicz and his wife, and the Chilewskis. But when I question her further, it turns out she also remembers two Polish Communists and a word of welcome pronounced by a Pole. But besides the "official" hosts of the welcome ceremony a sizable group of rubbernecks, children, and young people gathered. Many of the testimonies of Poles deported to the USSR preserved at the Hoover Institution repeat that Jews were in the majority. A locksmith from Grajewo described "individual Jews and a paltry number of Communist sympathizers welcoming the Red Army with bread and salt and a red banner reading: 'With Stalin into France and Great Britain.' Because these imperialist states provoked the war and Comrade Stalin would liberate us without war."

It's hard to say if the majority of those welcoming the Russians were really Jews. The event was momentous enough for many residents of the town to want to have a look (after all, Janina Biedrzycka remembers the welcoming of the Red Army because she was there, too). But among the cheering crowd, apart from a few Polish Communists—the Communist movement was weak in these parts—Jews were no doubt in the majority, because they had reason to feel a sense of relief. In Jewish accounts it looks like this:

"The Jews breathed a little more freely, but not entirely, because various marauders turned up in town, as well as some reactionary elements who sympathized with the Germans fleeing the approaching Red Army," said Menachem Turek of the situation in Tykocin. "Those people spread crazy rumors, such as we were already familiar with, for example that Jews in Grodno and other towns had poured boiling water on the heads of Polish soldiers, and they said all Jews should be killed. This inflammatory behavior had no effect, because on the first day of Yom Kippur, Soviet tanks thundered into town and for quite a while their noise silenced or muffled the voice of poisonous anti-Semitism—the anti-Semitism nourished by the right-wing nationalist regime dominant here in the last few years before the war. The Jews of Tykocin received and saluted the Red Army with special sympathy, they felt free, breathed fresh air, and gratefully and respectfully offered their services to the Soviet authorities, who began to introduce an order based on the principles of love for humanity and nations, equal rights, freedom and equality."

In a book of memory at the Israeli kibbutz named after the Ghetto Fighters, Meir Paparle remembered, "When the Russians came we were very happy, my brother Wolf Ber was simply beyond himself with joy. Russian soldiers came and asked him for something and he wouldn't even take money from them, he was so happy. The whole town was delighted with the Russian troops." In 1941, Paparle was fifteen years old, lived in Jedwabne, and was called Jedwabiński.

Turek, a graduate of Batory University in Vilnius, already had Communist sympathies before the war. Meir Jedwabiński's three older brothers were also Communists (in Jedwabne there was another such family, where four of five sons were Communists—the Catholic Krystowczyk family). But even Jews who felt very remote from Communism felt relief at the entry of the Red Army. Like Chaja Finkelsztejn, wife of a Zionist activist, from one of the wealthiest families in Radziłów, and whose memoir shows that she had no love for Communists at all. "We heard on the radio that our area was passing into Soviet hands, and we thought maybe we would survive," she wrote. "Many hoped that when the Soviets arrived they'd make the Poles return the things they'd looted from us."

3.

Before Soviet administration was established, many towns organized civilian guards. The Soviets renamed them auxiliary militia divisions. Polish accounts repeated that they were made up of Jews. The Jews themselves talk about Jews who made themselves of service to the Soviets in this first period, but they emphasize that they were the exception rather than the rule.

Meir Ronen of Jedwabne, who was deported to Kazakhstan and left for Palestine after the war, told me, "There were five Jews, ruffians, lording it around Jedwabne. They ran the town in the first weeks before the Soviet authorities got set up. And a Pole, Krystowczyk, a Communist."

"In Radziłów, Jewish Communists put themselves at their disposal, there were some bootlickers, plenty of them, and they provoked all the misfortune," remembered Chaja Finkelsztejn, who complained many times of the "Jewish devils," or those who eagerly collaborated with the new authorities. The hostility between Zionists and Communists before the war now found an outlet: Jewish collaborators were only looking for ways to cheat her family.

"In Wizna maybe five Jews followed the Communists," Izaak Lewin told me in Israel, remembering what his father had told him, "among them one old tailor, who said, 'I've been going to the synagogue for twenty years to pray for the Communists to come.' Everyone laughed at him. The other one was Awigdor Czapnicki. When he emigrated to Israel he tried to meet up with my father, who said, 'I don't want to know him.' How few Wizna Jews survived, and yet my father didn't want to know him. That must say something about how Jewish Communists were disliked among Jews."

One Pole deported by the Soviets, Lucjan Grabowski, wrote of such zealots in recollections preserved by the Hoover Institution: "Three Jews armed with rifles and red armbands came to Kapice from Tykocin. They no longer said *dobry dzien* ["good day" in Polish] in greeting, but *zdrastvuyte* [Russian]. When I took a good look at them I recognized one of them, it was Fiska, the ragman's son. His father often came to Kapice to buy rags. During the National Party's boycott of Jews we more than once drove him out of the village with stones."

It's easy to imagine those young Jews who only dreamed of getting back at their recent persecutors. The humiliated, when they can take revenge, rarely show their most sympathetic face. Swaggering around town with rifles must have seemed pretty impressive to them. They wouldn't have hesitated to give the Soviet authorities names of National Party activists, who were both enemies of Communists and persecutors of Jews.

In those earliest days Jews turned to the new authorities for help recovering their lost property, looted from Jewish houses and shops by their Polish neighbors right after the Germans had arrived. "A number of house searches were carried out, as a result of Jewish merchants accusing Poles of stealing various goods from them while they were away. There were a lot of arrests of people against whom local Jewish Communists had claims," said Marian Łojewski, a locksmith from Jedwabne, in an account preserved by the Hoover Institution.

"When the Soviets marched in, there was an outbreak of joy among Jews," remembered Mieczysław K., a former resident of Jedwabne. "Some of the youth started wearing red armbands and joined the police. It didn't last very long, the Soviets kicked them out; they preferred to deal with things themselves. The poorer Jews went on swaggering around a bit: from their point of view the Soviets were bringing liberation. The slightly wealthier ones felt just as much under threat of deportation as the Poles."

4.

In the fall of 1939, Soviet authorities began to organize a referendum on adding the territory they had occupied in eastern Poland to western Belorussia, and elections of parliamentary representatives.

Their propaganda machine was excellent. A witness from Downary, about fifty kilometers from Jedwabne, described the preelection campaign: "They made a little boy brought in by his father say, 'God, give me candy.' Then he had to say, 'Comrade Stalin, give me candy,' and a soldier went over to him and handed the boy a fistful of candy." A farmer from the village of Słucz near Radziłów remembered that after voting, you were allowed to buy two hundred grams of candy, two packets of cigarettes, and two boxes of matches.

The candidates for the western Belorussian parliament chosen were Czesław Krystowczyk, the Polish Communist from Jedwabne, and, as Tadeusz Kiełczewski of Jedwabne put it, "an illiterate floozy from the village of Pieńki-Borowe."

The Soviet authorities didn't appoint Jews to local office in greater numbers than others, least of all in the municipal administration, probably thinking Jews were already more sympathetic to them than Poles, and Polish candidates would command more respect. Evidence of this is the case of Chaim Wołek, examined at a session of the Regional Party Committee in Jedwabne. Wołek was selected to represent the nearby village of Łoje-Awissa at the Regional Council of Delegates, but at a preelection meeting in the village he was "mocked as a Jew," and withdrew his candidacy.

Karwowski of Jedwabne remembers a story told about a local Jew who came with his rifle to arrest a certain Polkowski. "Polkowski asked him to let him go, but the Jew says: 'Do you know who you're talking to? I'm the government.' Polkowski gave him a punch and ran away. Later everyone joked that Polkowski had overthrown the government."

"Jews only acted as militiamen at the very beginning," Kazimierz Mocarski from near Jedwabne related. "The Soviet authorities understood they'd made a mistake, because they weren't suited for the role. The village environment was anti-Semitic and Jews couldn't get people to obey them. Once, three Jewish policemen turned up in my village, Nadbory, because someone had informed them that one inhabitant (unrelated to the above-mentioned witness) owned a gun, and they were ordered to take it away from him. His brother hid the double-barrel shotgun under his coat. They searched the house but didn't have the nerve to do a body search and left empty-handed."

From October 1939, when western Belorussia was created, the provisional militia was replaced by the Workers and Peasants Militia. Not many locals, neither Poles nor Jews, were given jobs in the Soviet militia or administration. The Soviets brought their own cadres from eastern

Belorussia—the so-called *vostochniks* (easterners). This is confirmed unanimously by Soviet sources and by archives in the Hoover Institution, which cover a longer period than the first few months.

5.

What did an ordinary day under Soviet occupation look like? In the testimonials at the Hoover Institution, the Soviet occupation is portrayed as an invasion of barbarians. The new authorities carried out a census and an inventory, to be used as instruments of pillage. They appropriated household equipment and livestock; they felled forests. A visit in the night could mean deportation, but also the looting of jewelry and clothing. Apart from the pillaging and deportations, the people I talked to emphasized another theme: the poverty and coarseness of the occupying forces. They like to recount how the Soviet officers picked rotten cabbage left in the fields, how they slaughtered pigs and cooked the meat right there in the marketplace.

Chaja Finkelsztejn described daily life under the Soviets in her memoir: "The Soviet Army arrived in our town with its whole propaganda machine. They said they wouldn't let workers go on foot, they'd drive cars. There were lines everywhere for bread and everything else. They formed in front of shops even before anyone knew what was going to be for sale. We took everything they gave us. That's what it was called: *dayoot* [Russian for "they're giving"]. When the Soviets came, at first Christians kept their distance and didn't participate in the holidays we were told to celebrate. But they soon accepted the situation and joined in everything. The Soviets formed a *sielsowiet*, a village council with both Jews and Poles. They were much easier on the Christians than on the Jews. The life of a modest Jewish merchant was impossible, and that meant most Jews. Christians could have two and a half acres of land and sell produce on the street, and even meat, while Jews were forbidden to. So Jews entered into partnerships with Christians and sold things through them." She described how even the workshops of poor Jews were requisitioned and turned into cooperatives, how cheders and Hebrew schools were shut down, how children had to go to school on Saturdays.

Herschel Baker, who lives in Florida but is originally from Jedwabne, told me, "Communism literally invaded our house: a few Russians broke in and took our shoes. Those may have been the good times, but only for a person who had nothing to lose and didn't want to buy anything. We had to work for them, not for ourselves, and we barely had enough money for bread. But we felt safer, because the local hooligans were scared. I have to admit the Russians treated everyone the same, and that was a good thing; but they took away everything you had, and of course that was bad. I already lived with my own family in Goniądz. There were a few Jews in the police force there, and they probably liked it. I remember we Jews were unhappy with the Soviets, and the Poles were unhappy, too. Everyone was impoverished, including the rich Jews, so we were all on the same level as the Poles, who had been poorer before the war. It's hard to say Jews rose higher, it was more like we were all reduced to the same level of poverty. I myself had to hide because I was an 'exploiter'—I had employed thirty people before the war—and they were about to deport me."

6.

"I can do without that kind of liberation, I hope it was the last one." These words of Mendel Srul, a milkman from Łuck, are quoted by Irena Grudzińska Gross and Jan Gross in the book *In Nineteen-Forty, Sweet Mother of God, They Sent Us to Siberia.* Many of the older generation must have thought the same thing, at least those who had managed to build something for themselves. It was different for the young.

They were not as fed up by the worsening living conditions, nor was keeping the Sabbath their greatest worry. It seemed to them that in western Belorussia they'd finally be able to feel at home, that a Jew was no worse off than anyone else, and they often remarked that among the Soviets, Jews even got to be generals. Soviet teachers didn't distinguish between Jewish pupils and others, and didn't make Jewish children sit in the back rows. Not long ago Jews had had no chance of continuing their education beyond grade school, and now they were encouraged to go back to school, and more than that, they were invited to continue their studies in the many schools attached to factories in Soviet Russia. This was the dream of a large part of Zionist youth, because that kind of education would come in handy when they were building a new state in Palestine.

Meir Paparle's father, who was a shoemaker in Jedwabne, became night watchman in a hospital under the Soviets. He would probably have preferred to have his own workshop, even if it kept him in poverty, so as not to be forced to work on Shabbat. But for his sons, the Soviet occupation was the chance of a lifetime to move up in society. "My brother Wolf Ber went to the Russian forces," Paparle wrote. "He served in Jedwabne, patrolled the streets there. My other brother Ruwen also joined the Russian forces. I signed up with some other Jewish and Polish boys to go to Sverdlovsk in the Urals and work in a factory."

Age was an important determinant of attitudes toward the Soviet occupation, and not only in the case of Jews. Film screenings and dancing were also attractive to some of the local Polish youth. Jan Cytrynowicz, the Jedwabne Jew who was baptized before the war, remembered that in Wizna, Poles ran the beer and wine taverns, where there was cheap wine and beer in pints, so the youth, both Polish and Jewish, liked gathering there.

"When the Russians came," a former resident of Radziłów told me, "the film screen was set up in the marketplace, for everyone, and who had ever seen any movies in Radziłów? I remember films about the revolution, with Orlova, a famous actress. And events organized at the ice house."

I asked how relations between Polish and Jewish children at school changed with the arrival of the Soviets. "The Jews were confident in class, they liked to show off," I heard from a man who had grown up in Radziłów. "They felt confident because as they liked to say, Stalin's wife was 'one of theirs.' Oh, they were no saints. They made fun of us in front of the Soviets. There were Polish boys who carried red flags, too, but not as many. Of all the members of the Communist youth organization Komsomol there was one Jewish girl who had the most arrogant attitude toward the Poles; we called her Fat Sara. She called the Poles 'Polack dogs,' and Polish kids for her were 'Polack puppies.' I had a Russian teacher named Marusya who made me sit in the first row next to that Jewish girl. She moved away, saying she wouldn't sit next to a 'Polack puppy.' At school and on the street you had to make way for the Jews."

"Make way how?"

"A Jewish kid would be standing there, taunting, 'Your government is gone, your government is done.'"

"We got along fine with them," another man from Radziłów remembered. "Right after the Russians arrived they proudly said, 'Our comrades are here,' but they sobered up pretty quickly. A teacher tried to get them to join the Soviet scout group, the pioneers, but they didn't want to join, at least not the ones I remember."

"Soviet education ruined kids," Chaja Finkelsztejn recounted. "There were holidays, posters with thundering slogans, dancing, singing; it all drew kids like a magnet. For the older kids there was the Komsomol; the younger ones had the pioneers. They got red scarves, so they were happy. My kids said thanks but didn't wear the scarves, although the Polish teachers made it clear this might get them into trouble. I didn't want my kids to go on those field trips, but the teachers found us and dragged them off to the Soviet authorities in Jedwabne. My older son suffered a lot, he was called a Jewish nationalist because he didn't join the Komsomol. At school somebody wrote an illicit slogan on the wall: 'If I forget thee, O Jerusalem, may my right hand forget its cunning,' and the Jewish director sent from the Białystok NKVD suspected Menachem Finkelsztejn of having done it."

7.

So Jews welcomed the Soviets more often and more warmly, but the Soviets made their lives a misery anyway. Jews may have collaborated with the Soviets more frequently, but do we know that for a fact? Though Jews did not play a dominant role in the Soviet power structure or the Soviet system of repression, Poles were convinced that the Jews were responsible for the persecution of Poles. What made the idea of Jews being solely responsible for all evil endure in the memory of so many of their neighbors?

Chaja Finkelsztejn: "Quarrels and fights often broke out between Jews and Christians in queues. There were plenty of Jews who said, 'Your two decades of being the boss are over.' The Poles remembered that."

In fact, it wasn't so much about those few Jews in every small town who showed special zeal in their service to the Soviet authorities, who informed on others and intimidated them. There were Poles doing the same thing, and everyone knew it, even if they later erased it from their collective memory. It was about the remarks like "Your time is over," which Jews hurled at their recent nationalist persecutors with relish.

In the underground archive of the Warsaw Ghetto, called the Ringelblum Archive, there is a description of a school in Rutki where Polish teachers had taught for a long time; two Jewish teachers arrived, refugees from the General Government (or German-occupied zone). The local doctor and veterinarian also employed Jewish refugees in their practices.

The refugees were in a difficult predicament, sleeping in strangers' houses, unsure whether the next day would bring new decrees as to where they could or could not reside. From their point of view they were vulnerable, uncertain of their future; from the point of view of the Polish residents, the new Jewish teachers, doctor, and vet were in an excellent position—they had usurped the place of Polish locals deported to Siberia.

A large portion of school time was dedicated to propaganda, anniversaries, and poems about friendship with the USSR. Polish and Jewish teachers did the same things in class. But according to Chaja Finkelsztejn, Polish teachers "organized splendid festivities to mask their true sympathies and play the part of loyal subjects of the new authorities." Polish teachers who prepared celebrations in honor of the October Revolution at school may well have packed lunches after school for anti-Soviet partisans hiding in the marshes by the Biebrza river.

Bolesław Juszkowski remembered that when he had to go vote, he found Soviet soldiers in the election hall "dancing with Jewish girls" to the sound of a band (Hoover Institution testimony).

It caused bad blood, the Jewish girls dancing with Russian soldiers when Poles were obliged to turn up to vote for the loss of their fatherland.

Another Ringelblum Archive testimony tells of how things were in Wasilków: "It was quiet and cheerful; there were movies and a Jewish theater that had frequent concerts and plays; there was a wind orchestra, a mandolin orchestra. Jews felt good, very free. They could walk down any street, even the ones where they had formerly been pelted with stones. You didn't hear anyone say 'dirty Jew.'"

Poles were irritated by the happy Jewish boys unafraid to go out on the street.

"The Poles were grief-stricken after losing to the invaders, and you didn't see that grief in Jews," wrote Chaja Finkelsztejn. "You could even see most Jews were glad. 'Jews are in charge,' said the Poles. Most young Jews were living it up, there were a lot of weddings, under the Soviets you could get married for three rubles. You saw a lot of freshly minted married couples, feeling content and happy, and a lot of babies were being born, couples sat with their prams in parks where until then only the Polish intelligentsia spent time."

The Soviet occupation imposed on almost everyone—except those in hiding and in armed resistance units—the necessity of some degree of collaboration. If they wanted to avoid arrest or deportation, residents of Radziłów or Jedwabne had to participate in numerous meetings, decorate their barns with portraits of Lenin and Stalin and red flags, take part in the electoral farce, and accept Soviet citizenship. It must have been a humiliation of the kind that afterward is consigned to the most profound oblivion. How much easier to replace reality with a stereotype like "the Jews collaborated," all the more so if you know those who might have corrected this misconception had perished. And the cognitive dissonance must have been particularly hard to bear for the nationalists, who by definition considered themselves exceptionally patriotic. The strange new situation in which the "kikes" were given relative equality in civil law must have been a provocation to those neighbors raised on prewar anti-Semitism.

"If the Jews had kept quiet under the Soviets like they did before the war, things wouldn't have ended the way they did," claims Janina Biedrzycka, the Jedwabne barn owner's daughter. To prove this she tells me of neighbors who greeted her family courteously before the war but stopped doing so under the Soviets. Biedrzycka's father had organized anti-Jewish actions before the war, but even so his Jewish neighbors had been afraid not to greet him politely. Now they were no longer afraid. And suddenly here are all these Jewish officials, Jewish policemen, Jewish teachers. It must have been a shock to most of the Radziłów and Jedwabne population, and one that exacerbated their sense of vulnerability and frustration.

8.

When the current residents of Jedwabne say—as many do—that Jews were the ones who determined who was deported from Polish territory to the Soviet Union, they are wrong. It wasn't local Jews who dictated repression tactics to Soviet Russia. In the first great deportation, on the night from February 9 to 10, 1940, it was military and civilian *osadniks** and foresters who were taken away. No Jewish denunciations were required for that.

* *Osadnik* (Polish; settler, colonist) was the word used in the Soviet Union for a veteran of the Polish Army given land in the Kresy, or Borderland territories (current western Belarus and western Ukraine), ceded to Poland by the Polish-Soviet Riga Peace Treaty of 1921 (and occupied by the Soviet Union in 1939).

"The Russians wanted to deport the tailor Lewin and my dad just for having fought for Polish independence toward the end of the First World War," Tadeusz Dobkowski of Zanklewo, a village between Jedwabne and Wizna, told me.

"At first they deported people who belonged to some category designated for deportation, like foresters or teachers, or because they'd committed some act of hooliganism," Jan Cytrynowicz explains to me. "A friend of mine from Wizna was deported for getting drunk at a Communist meeting and pissing in a jug."

"Young Jews were happy. They went around smiling, I saw that," says his wife, Pelagia, who spent the occupation in Grajewo. "They felt an aversion to Poles. They felt they'd been oppressed, and now under the Russians they'd cast off their chains. But we don't know that someone who was happy that way really went and put in a complaint against Poles."

The second wave of deportations, in April 1940, targeted the families of those previously arrested: police officers, senior officials, leaders of political parties, the local intelligentsia. The third wave, in June 1940, involved "refugees"—persons who had fled from the General Government. Jews formed over 80 percent of this wave of deportation (and a substantial number of them expressed a desire to return to the General Government, so not all Jews were so thrilled with the Soviets).

Zionist activists were also deported. The head of the NKVD reported (on September 16, 1940): "The region is known for being riddled with insurrectionary elements as well as various Polish and Jewish parties and anti-Soviet organizations: the National Party, the Jewish Bund, Zionists."

For Jews, June 1940 went down in history as the time of great deportations, while Poles remember it as the time of the NKVD raid on the Kobielno wilderness area on the Biebrza river, where partisans and people evading imprisonment or selection for deportation were hiding in inaccessible swampy terrain. The raid was accompanied by many arrests. Some of those arrested were sent to Jedwabne, which under the Soviets was promoted to the regional capital; a temporary jail had been set up in a basement under a pharmacy.*

* "An especially large number of Russians came to Jedwabne. It was the headquarters of the Regional Committee of the Communist Party of Belorussia, the Regional Executive Committee of Delegates of the Working People, the Regional Department of the NKVD, and others. All the highest positions were occupied by new arrivals (per

But the jails and prisons in the region were also crowded with Jews who had tried to conduct some kind of economic activity, in other words, to buy or sell something outside the official state economy; they were put behind bars as speculators.*

The last wave of deportations, in June 1941, was intended to cut off at the root the partisan independence movement, which was strong in this region. Polish Catholic informers were a hundred times more useful than Polish Jews for this purpose. Since Jews were never accepted into Polish underground organizations in the Jedwabne region, it would be hard to count on them for intelligence.

In the early morning of June 22, 1941, a Sunday, trucks pulled up to many homes in Jedwabne and the surrounding villages, and the NKVD rounded up the relatives of earlier deportees. "Poles railed against Jews and clearly showed their hostility," Chaja Finkelsztejn wrote, describing the mood created by that last June deportation. "I saw with my own eyes how very early in the morning several trucks stopped by a large group of arrestees and NKVD officers. A few older Jews happened to be walking to the synagogue for morning prayers. They stopped to see what was

---

Michał Gnatowski, "Dokumenty radzieckie o postawach ludności i polskim podziemiu niepodległościowym w rejonie jedwabieńskim w latach 1939–1941" [Soviet documents on popular attitudes and the underground Polish independence movement in the Jedwabne region in 1939–1941], in Wokół Jedwabnego [About Jedwabne], vol. 2, eds. Paweł Machcewicz and Krzysztof Persak, Warsaw: Institute of National Remembrance, 2002).

* Mark Timofiejewicz Rydaczenko, secretary of the Regional Committee of the Communist Party of Belorussia in Jedwabne, writing on June 19, 1940, to his counterpart in Białystok, described "the attempts of hostile elements to penetrate trade and cooperative institutions to raise prices and sell products to speculators, arousing the discontent of the working masses." Many Jews were jailed or deported on such charges. The fact itself that Jews were employed in shops they used to own made them suspect individuals. From Informacje o sytuacji polityczno-ekonomicznej w rejonie jedwabieńskim (Information on the political-economic situation in the Jedwabne region), September 16, 1940: "Labor collectives, points of sale, regional cooperatives of grocers and groceries are inundated with former tradesmen and speculators—for example the salesman Hersz Dembowicz used to be a speculative tradesman, the saleswoman Dwojra Kon used to own a glove shop, Chilewska Chana used to be a speculator . . ." (in Michał Gnatowski, Niepokorna Białostocczyzna. Opór społeczny i polskie podziemie niepodległościowe w regionie białostockim w latach 1939–1941 w radzieckich źródłach [Insubordinate Białystok: Popular resistance and the underground Polish independence movement in the Białystok region, 1939–1941, in Soviet sources], Białystok: Białystok University, 2001).

happening. Suddenly we heard the bitter cry of a Polish woman: 'Jews, you see them sending our people to Siberia! A curse on you!' But what had the Jews done wrong? Didn't the Soviets send Jews off to Siberia by the thousands? But we heard this all the time and more and more often. We felt storm clouds gathering."

The Soviets had evacuation plans ready in the event of war against the Germans. Those prisoners kept in Łomża were to be transported to the Gulag. But they didn't manage to move them. When troops entered the town on the first day of the Soviet–German war, June 22, more than two thousand freed prisoners returned to their homes. Meanwhile, trains had left for the east with their wives, parents, and children, who had all been arrested.

Pogroms took place in dozens of villages in the region at the end of June and beginning of July 1941. Most testimonies say that the newly freed prisoners—activists of the prewar National Party—took part in them.

Journal

MARCH 29, 2001

Jan Skrodzki and I set off for Radziłów. Entering the town, I no longer notice the flaking plaster and crooked pavement—I begin to see the beauty of the simple wooden architecture of the old squat Jewish homes. It wasn't until I had seen them on Gutstein's website that I could appreciate them in real life.

Jan and I are going back to see the childhood friend of his whom we visited last time. This time Jan tells her straight out that we've come to find out the truth about the massacre. "It was the Poles who did the killing," he announces, and Eugenia K., who has not left the town in seventy years, expresses polite surprise: "Not the Germans? Lordy me!" And changes the subject.

I become aware in Radziłów, where Jan Skrodzki introduces me as his cousin, that when we speak to people without a direct connection to the crime, their emotions remain tepid. This indifference is usually shaded one way or another, friendly or hostile, but it is indifference more than anything else. Only in Jedwabne, which is under fire from the media and where my role is that of a journalist, does the community seem split between those who have carried the hatred of that time across sixty years into today's world, and those who, in their sleep, can still hear the victims screaming.

The topic that raises the residents' tempers is the postwar period. They can spend hours going over old ground: who was killed, when and why, and on whose orders. There was practically a civil war in these parts. Not only representatives of the new Communist order were killed. Many people lost their lives around here in fratricidal battles between various offshoots of the underground. The partisans fought each other, and in the course of those battles, women and children were sometimes killed. In the surrounding villages, the residents kept night watches so as not to be taken by surprise.

This is the special painful history of the Polish inhabitants of these lands, their very own remembered fear. The story of the burning barn is someone else's history.

Two heroic tales stand out.

One is about the partisans' takeover of Grajewo, when on May 8, 1945, two hundred underground soldiers came into town, let prisoners out of jail, destroyed local documents in the possession of the secret police, and occupied the treasury and the district administration building.

The second was when Jedwabne freed itself from Communist power for one day, four years later, on September 23, 1949. An underground group took over the municipal offices and then summoned the residents to a gathering where they were urged to fight the Communists.

Cytrynowicz remembers it well: "They took a car from butchers going to market. They drove it into the marketplace. Twelve of them, in English uniforms. They announced that the British army was in Poland, Warsaw was in revolution, and the Communist government had fallen. People stormed the co-ops, mainly grabbing vodka."

In the journal *Karta* I read the story of "Wiarus," also known as Crazy Staszek, a.k.a. Stanisław Grabowski, commander of the National Armed Forces unit that led the operation. Grabowski's group smashed up two shops and the municipality offices, then they convened a meeting and called for a fight against the Communists. Terrified police didn't intervene and the unit left town quietly after the meeting. In 1951 partisans attacked a bus to Jedwabne on which a cashier was traveling with money. They ordered the passenger to read out a flyer saying that Stalin "wants hunger and cold."

Everyone in the area knows the pseudonyms of the last partisans. "July" fought up to 1952, "Groove" to 1954, "Fish" to 1957. They were killed when their fellow partisans betrayed them, and often by a brother's bullet.

"By day you were scared of the secret police, who came to arrest you for real or alleged help to the underground, and at night you were scared of the partisans," Jan Skrodzki and I were told by Skrodzki's relative Edward Borawski when we visited him in Trzaski.

"The guys from the National Armed Forces mainly went in for looting," Stanisław Ramotowski told me. "A lot of men around here were in the National Armed Forces, not from Kramarzewo and Kiliany, those were always decent towns, but from Żebry and Kownatki, sure."

Several more times in conversations I came across that mention of "decent" villages where people joined the Home Army, and bad ones where the National Armed Forces held sway.

A resident of Radziłów told me, "The National Armed Forces were active here, but I never heard of them carrying out any operation against the Germans. They were called a 'gang of thieves.'"

These two narratives, of the heroes and the villains, are not entirely independent of each other. It was often units led by underground heroes who looted and robbed; their leaders were not able to discipline those under their command, and in time they joined in.

The day after tomorrow my article on present-day Jedwabne, "Please Don't Come Back," is to appear in the *Gazeta*. From early morning I'm traveling between Radziłów, where I leave Jan Skrodzki for the moment, and Jedwabne, where I'm still fact-checking and getting authorization for quotes. Later I drive up on a hill outside of Radziłów, where there's a cell phone signal and I can dictate corrections over the phone.

On the road from Radziłów to Jedwabne I receive a message from Dr. Noszczyk, saying Ramotowski is being quite impossible, demanding he be discharged from the hospital despite the severity of his condition. I point out to the doctor that if Ramotowski hadn't been so unbearably stubborn, he would never have rescued his Jewish wife to spite the whole town.

MARCH 30, 2001
Jan Skrodzki and I drive to Grajewo, about thirty kilometers from Radziłów, to see Jan J., the older brother of a school friend of Jan's. His wife, furious, spews anti-Semitic jokes. We hear that Leon Kosmaczewski is most certainly still alive, and we are given his address in Ełk.

"He keeps bees, a peaceful man, never hurt a fly," Jan J. says of Kosmaczewski. Jan J. can't be unaware that he is speaking of one of the chief murderers of July 7, 1941. Another beekeeper, like the Laudański brothers.

We set off for Ełk at once, it's very near Grajewo. But we discover that Kosmaczewski died two years ago; we find only his daughter.

We go on looking for Klimaszewski, the man who set the barn in Radziłów on fire. We've heard he later joined the Home Army and was active in the veterans association in Ełk. We got his address from the phone book. We drive there: dilapidated apartment blocks, no one opens the door. Skrodzki learns from the neighbors that the tenant died two years ago. But he gets into a long conversation, as always, from which we learn that the Klimaszewski who lived there was in the Home Army and veterans association but he couldn't have been the one we're looking for because he was much older. We'll keep looking. We know one of the people we talked to met him not so long ago at a sanatorium, so we're counting on him being alive. Luckily Skrodzki shows no sign of being bored with our search. He is used to the large number of dead-end roads you go down before you find witnesses.

Tomorrow the *Gazeta* is printing my piece on "Jedwabne Today," with extensive quotes from Stanisław P. He told me his story about the massacre while expressing a wish to remain anonymous, like others I've talked to. He is from a family that has lived on the market square in Jedwabne since the mid-nineteenth century.

"On July 10," he told me, "Father hid in the garden and then in the attic at my grandmother's house on November 11 Street, which is now Sadowa Street. I have to make it clear he was hiding from Poles, so they wouldn't force him to go and kill Jews. My parents didn't know the Jews would be herded right by where they were hiding. My mother, when she saw the march of death, took my older sister and fled in the direction of Łomża. Mother remembered that screaming up to a few days before she died, and when she heard it, she was already far from the barn. If my parents, who lived in the eye of the cyclone, were able to get away from the market unhindered, it means it was possible for people not to take part in the massacre. It's not true that the Poles were held at gunpoint by the Germans. No one forced anyone. Maybe some German was standing on the sidelines somewhere, but Mother didn't see any. She passed freely through Jedwabne with her child. There may have been a dozen policemen watching what was going on, but no big military force came to town. It was the Laudańskis who did it, among others. On the day of the massacre they went by Polish homes, saying, 'Come with us. You're either for us or against us.' The whole town knew the part they played. My family didn't tell me about violent scenes. Once Mother, showing me a photo of her seventh-grade class, pointed out her Jewish friends: 'She was burned, and she was burned, and this girl had her throat cut.' I came to this knowledge gradually, and I didn't learn about many events until the seventies, when I started asking the witnesses myself. In 1980, I started working at the Łomża governor's office and one of the employees there, who had been a teacher in Jedwabne, told me about the burning of the barn and the murders committed elsewhere. He gave names and details. He told me about Kubrzyniecki—how he chose his victims from the Jews rounded up. Later I heard from another witness who said he had gone to his privy and found a Jew there with his throat cut, still alive and gasping for breath. Discussions about how many people fitted into the barn are ridiculous. There was killing on almost every street and in many yards. And what happened by the pond? Corn grew thick there and people combed through it and if they found a Jew they'd drown him. Jews were drowned in wells, too. It's known who killed whom, they weren't quiet murders, everything took place in broad daylight. 'When a Yid was caught in the fields he was buried on the spot': that's what the people of Jedwabne tell you themselves. The barn was still burning when some of the locals started grabbing Jewish property. What conscience does a woman have who stole a feather quilt when it was still warm, or dragged out a poor neighbor's clothes? They say now that the Germans took the stuff and carted it off. Those rags and ruins? The Germans took antiques and furs from the Warsaw residences of lawyers and industrialists."

I decided I'd try to convince him to appear under his full name. In Jedwabne itself I don't encourage anyone to reveal their personal details, but with Stanisław P. it's different. He left the town in the eighties. He's one of the few who achieved something substantial, finished their education, have a high status in their profession. His voice must mean something to the townspeople. But I can't get through to him anymore. Just before I send my piece to the printer, between the first and second proofs, I call the paper to tell them to cut all his statements from the piece. I'll ask him for a separate interview for the *Gazeta*. Maybe an interview like that will give someone in Jedwabne something to think about.

Stanisław P. had pointed out to me that it makes no sense to get worked up about the fact that an atrocity like this didn't become public knowledge for sixty years. "After 1945, even talk about the Russians deporting people to Siberia was taboo, not just officially, but in family circles. I remember the disbelief of my fellow students when I told them that where I came from, near Łomża, we were under Soviet occupation in the years 1939 to 1941. Sure, they knew Stalin occupied Lvov and Vilnius, but that he got as far as Białystok or Łomża, that they wouldn't believe. The Soviets distorted all that history, not just Jedwabne."

Today the papers write that four Mauser rifle cartridges have been found on the grounds of the barn.

"This confirms those people were shot," Minister Przewoźnik declares.

None of the people I talked to, who say there were a lot of Germans, ever mentioned shooting. I call Ignatiew and tell him this. He doesn't contradict me, so apparently his witnesses hadn't mentioned shooting, either.

APRIL 1, 2001

Back to Warsaw in the morning. I'm turning the key in the apartment door when the phone rings. Yet another person full of noble intentions explains to me that putting Jedwabne in the spotlight is causing a trauma the locals don't deserve, especially those whose families took part in the massacre. Something simply must be done to help—therapists, priests. I feel how reluctantly the caller listens to what I have to say: that the people whose families took part in the massacre feel just fine, better at any rate than those whose families helped Jews, and maybe it is the latter who are more in need of support.

Father Czesław Bartnik in the largest Polish Catholic newspaper, *Our Daily*: "In Poland national minorities are still causing wounds to fester, especially Jews. The Polish ship is going down."

APRIL 2, 2001

The Institute of National Remembrance has initiated an investigation into the massacre in Radziłów. "Finally!" Jose Gutstein, the author of the Radziłów website, e-mails me from Miami. "And so—may I put a request to you? Will you help them? I wrote to Director Kieres of the Institute of National Remembrance, offering my help. I asked them to include Radziłów in the ceremony. It was probably the Radziłów massacre that 'inspired' the people of Jedwabne. It would be a shame if Radziłów were excluded from the program of commemoration."

The *Gazeta* is printing "More of the Bad Kind," my interview with Stanisław Ramotowski. It begins with my asking him if he thinks it's a good thing the institute opened the investigation. Ramotowski sighs. "Oh my God, it's so good." But he still won't yield to my urgings and give testimony to prosecutor Ignatiew. I can't understand why he tried to resurrect the truth his whole life if he doesn't want to report it in testimony for the Institute of National Remembrance, which will have greater historical weight than my reports. He in turn can't grasp why I'm giving him such a hard time about it. He's never told anyone what he learned— never, no one. I have the feeling with other interviewees that I am freeing them from the burden of carrying the truth alone. Stanisław claims he's telling me all of what he knows just because he's come to like me.

The historian Tomasz Strzembosz wrote a letter to the *Gazeta* saying that I accused him of trying to use Jewish collaboration with the Soviets as an explanation for the Jedwabne masscre. He called it an insinuation.

I sit down to reply to him: "I am very sorry if what I wrote upset you. It didn't enter my mind that to write that a historian explaining something is an insinuation. On the contrary, I thought the explanation of phenomena was one of the fundamental responsibilities of a scholar. If the main theme you touch on in the context of Jedwabne is Jewish collaboration with the NKVD, I take it that you are trying in that way to explain the crime to your readers. Just as I, writing about Jedwabne, quote extensively from the prewar anti-Semitic diocesan press, and not at random. I am trying to find some partial explanation of the massacre."

In *Our Daily*, recollections of wartime Jedwabne from Leokadia Błaszczak, who now lives in Warsaw. She writes about the Soviet occupation, when "Jews supplied the Soviets with lists of names of Polish 'enemies of the people'—prewar policemen, military men—and later took over their homes and belongings." I have never heard of such a case in Jedwabne. Here you have Freudian projection in its purest form. It was Poles who took over Jewish property in Jedwabne.

According to her version, on July 10, 1941, paddy wagons appeared in the market square and uniformed Germans soldiers jumped out of them.

She then went with her younger brother to watch what was happening. She saw Polish boys rounded up by Germans with birch whips in their hands, "defenseless, terrified little boys, forced to stand guard by Germans armed with rifles." She walked along with the Jews to the barn, where the Germans who escorted them chased the non-Jewish children away.

She thinks the vilest thing about the whole story is the fact that "Szmul Wasersztejn, a longtime secret police investigator, quietly left for Israel in March 1968 like the worst Judas without suffering any consequences for having tortured Polish patriots, handed over innocent Poles to the secret police on the charge of having 'participated in the slaughter of Jews.' But the 19-year-old Jerzy Laudański, a fine man and fierce patriot, a soldier with the Home Army, prisoner of the Pawiak prison, Auschwitz, Sachsenhausen, who under torture betrayed no one, was arrested after he returned to his fatherland and subjected to horrific torture in secret police dungeons . . . Jan Gross, who isn't fit to lick the boots of this hero of the struggle against Hitler, of a concentration camp martyr like Jerzy Laudański, permits himself—in a miserable little book worthy of the gutter press—to slander the name of Laudański and that of other noble Poles of Jedwabne."

Leokadia Błaszczak is the daughter of Franciszek Lusiński, named among participants in the massacre—his name appeared in testimonies in 1949 (which also mention her brother, then sixteen years old and sharing his father's name, Franciszek, as being one of those who took part in driving Jews into the marketplace). I myself have heard the name Lusiński several times in interviews:

"Lusiński dragged a Jew from the group being marched to the barn and killed him in front of his own smithy."

"Franciszek Lusiński boasted that when he struck the Jew hard with a hammer or die, the man flew a meter into the air before he fell down dead."

APRIL 3, 2001

At a scholarly conference on "The Other in Literature and Culture," I hear a talk by cultural anthropologist Joanna Tokarska-Bakir: "The Jew as Witch, the Witch as Jew, or How to Read Interrogation Transcripts." Tokarska-Bakir describes the demonization of Jews and the Judaization of witches on the basis of trials conducted in the sixteenth, seventeenth, and eighteenth centuries in what is now Lower Silesia. She analyzes how the two categories were confused at that time, witches accused of profaning the Host and abducting Christian infants (to use their blood in making ointments, *maści*, instead of matzo, *maca*), and Jews accused of conducting clandestine rituals as well as engaging in sodomy, cannibalism, and metamorphoses into cats.

Wherever I go, the subject I've chosen offers me new paths of inquiry. Especially since a bizarre confusion of mind on the subject of Jews and their customs reigns in Jedwabne and its environs, and after many centuries people still seem to think it obvious that Jews use Christian children to make matzo.

In the afternoon, Stanisław Ramotowski and I set off for Kramarzewo—he wants to sit on his porch and watch the brook rushing by his cottage.

APRIL 4, 2001

At seven in the morning I'm woken by the phone. It's Ramotowski telling me we've got to return to Warsaw immediately. I get in my car and drive over to see him. He's heard from his nephew what's being said about him in town and that the priest has been looking for him, probably in order to shut him up. He's had enough. I remind him we still have his bank and insurance affairs to sort out.

I begin the day with a visit to Łomża. I've managed to persuade Stanisław P. to let me publish an interview with him under his own name. Stanisław Przechodzki is the director of the Podlasie District Public Health Center. I sent him the text earlier, and am due to get his authorization at 9:00 a.m. The text will appear in the *Gazeta* tomorrow. But now we have a deadlock. In his conversation with me, Przechodzki pronounced on various general topics, like the necessity of respecting other peoples and faiths. Now he has rewritten the interview, keeping these general views in but cutting out both the emotional content and the factual description of the crime. The new version of the piece makes no sense at all. In the end we return to my version.

I look in on Ramotowski in Kramarzewo and drag him out of the house so he can show me where the Jewish cemetery used to be. Skrodzki and I couldn't find it. Pointing to a field outside the town, he says disapprovingly: "Sowing crops in a cemetery doesn't bother them, either."

In the evening I'm in Jedwabne at the Godlewskis'. I learn that there was a closed meeting of the town council with the governor today on the matter of financing an access road to the massacre site. The governor said that according to public finance regulations, a donation from the highest level of government could not exceed 75 percent of the projected cost, so Jedwabne has to pay 25 percent. Krzysztof Godlewski explains to me that this is a big opportunity: after the ceremony the guests will leave, but the asphalt roads will stay, and the town will be able to pave the marketplace in the bargain and modernize the sewage system. But proposing to the council members that they lay out 25 percent "for the Jews" is like waving a red cloth in front of a bull.

APRIL 5, 2001

Driving to get Ramotowski I stop by a school in Radziłów on the way. I ask whether in connection with all the recent media attention, they have figured out how to discuss Jedwabne with the schoolchildren.

"Neither the pupils nor the teachers have given me any sign that we should talk about the whole business at school," says the nice young headmistress, who seems taken aback by my question. The school has a website; you can tell the school webmaster has put a lot into it. I click on "The History of Radziłów" and read that "a group of killers from the Grajewo unit of the Einsatzkommando 8, led by Karl Strohammer, came one day in trucks, chased the Jews into a barn, and set it on fire." There's not even a date.

I drive to Kramarzewo. Today I'm taking Stanisław Ramotowski back to Warsaw. At the moment, he's hiding in his nephew's room off the kitchen. Yesterday Agnieszka Arnold's documentary on Jedwabne and Radziłów (which included my interview with him) was shown on TV, and by early morning two cars had appeared in the courtyard—the local radio and a foreign TV crew. His nephew told them his uncle wasn't home. We drive through Jedwabne and visit the Dziedzices in Przestrzele. Leszek's wife, Ewa, whose husband also appeared in the documentary, has spent the last two nights crying for fear their house will be burned down. Sixty years after the fact, Ramotowski, Righteous Among the Nations, and Leszek Dziedzic, whose grandmother sheltered Szmul Wasersztejn, feel compelled to hide from their neighbors after showing their faces on television.

Back in Warsaw, before going to sleep, I read my interview with Stanisław Przechodzki, published in today's *Gazeta*. Seeing it in print I'm even more impressed by his courage.

"First, the Germans gave permission for it. Second, before the war there were powerful National Party influences, and numerous anti-Jewish excesses took place. Third, there was an active group of people led by Mayor Karolak ready for a pogrom, and they hatched a plan and incited the rest of the townspeople by saying, 'Look, it turned out well in Radziłów, they're rid of the problem.' And finally, fourth, Satan got into the town. It's probably just the way human nature works, when a man sees a lot of bloodshed, pain, and suffering around him, it makes him an even worse person. Today the problem of the victims has vanished. Leon Dziedzic, who was ordered to bury bodies, told how they were intertwined with each other like roots, you couldn't separate them. It was mothers who died there, with their children clasped to their chests! And no one's conscience is bothered by it, because those weren't human beings but Jews. And Jewish traitors, to boot, who'd denounced people to the NKVD. I never heard that before," Przechodzki stresses, "the deportations to Siberia being blamed on the Jews. In Jedwabne it was Poles who did most of the denouncing.

"There's no use pretending, we still have anti-Semitism here. I always hoped the atrocity would be brought to light. But I never suspected the case would take on the proportions it has, that it would turn into a political game, a driving force for nationalist groups."

Przechodzki comments on statements by the witnesses that typically appear in right-wing publications (and are quoted by the historian Tomasz Strzembosz as well): "In *Our Daily*, Ryszard Malczyński tells us he saw from the church tower Germans rounding up Jews. What was Mr. Malczyński doing in that tower? He says the priest had told him to fix a roof tile. It's 10 a.m. on July 10, 1941, and the priest tells him to mend the roof? Franciszek Karwowski claims in the same article: 'On the morning of July 10 my father heard that the Germans were to destroy the Jews in Jedwabne that day. So he harnessed a horse, because he wanted to retrieve a scale he'd lent to [the Jew] Kosacki.' So Karwowski's father knew in a village several kilometers from Jedwabne that they were going to kill the Jews, and the priest didn't know and decided it was the right day for fixing the roof? Jadwiga Kordasowa, née Wąsowska, a teenager at the time, went to the site of the massacre three days after the burning, to the threshing floor. She remembers: 'At the northwest apex, a pyramid of bodies, almost up to the ceiling.' She, a young girl, went to the barn after they perished? What psychic resilience it would have taken to go there of one's own will. Leon Dziedzic, who was forced to go there, says that when they were removing the bodies, each one of them vomited dozens of times. Why did she go there? We know some of the people in Jedwabne went to the barn to loot."

Przechodzki goes on: "I've been reminded of the 1949 trial and how witnesses were intimidated. They were threatened that if they didn't withdraw their testimonies they would see their own bodies in coffins. The secret police was in Łomża, far away, and neighbors were right next door. They were afraid of no one as much as their neighbors. A witness was going to go home after he gave evidence and wanted to wake up the next morning. And what was going on after the war? A great many assassinations, families settling scores, and some were about Jewish property. Today the same atmosphere of intimidation prevails in Jedwabne. Doesn't that show you the scale of the crime, if there's still intimidation sixty years on? It means some of the witnesses don't pass on information to the Institute of National Remembrance or they give false testimony. I think that people who try to intimidate witnesses should be aware of the legal consequences. To my mind the role of a priest in a town like Jedwabne should be telling people, 'It wasn't you who did this, but the generation of your fathers. They didn't make a reckoning, so it falls to you to do so. If you lie, how will you stand before God?' Defending murderers and falsifying facts now makes you an accomplice to the crime. Participating in a lie, I would feel as if I'd taken part in that massacre, because the dead can't rise again to tell us how they were murdered."

APRIL 6, 2001

Yesterday the newspapers carried as their main news story that the crime in Jedwadne was carried out by the Germans. Today it's in all the headlines. All because Professor Edmund Dmitrów of the Białystok Institute of National Remembrance said that he found in the German archives that the crime in Jedwabne could have been led by Hermann Schaper, commando leader from Ciechanów, because he was in Radziłów.

I read about Schaper in Chaja Finkelsztejn's Yad Vashem testimony. Her testimony was the basis for the initiation of proceedings against Schaper. Chaja saw him that day in the marketplace, and she recognized him twenty years later from a photograph. But she states clearly that two cars with Germans, Schaper among them, arrived in the morning and left soon after, leaving the residents to deal with the Jews themselves. Without that knowledge I could easily believe it was all the work of some Schaper. I think bitterly that no one will believe Przechodzki, now that there's a more palatable truth being offered.

APRIL 7, 2001

An event dedicated to Jedwabne in the crypt of a Warsaw church on Chłodna Street. "This is about the martyrology of the Polish people," says historian Andrzej Leszek Szcześniak. "They are trying to take that martyrology away from us. It's a theft of suffering. The hysteria around Jedwabne is aimed at shocking Poles and extracting sixty-five billion dollars from our people in the framework of the Holocaust business."

I know Szcześniak well. The author of history textbooks, on which he had a monopoly in Communist times, he has deftly opened a path for himself from Communist times to the Poland of today under the guise of nationalism, changing only the adjectives in his textbooks (for example, the word "thriving," which in People's Poland belonged to the "revolutionary movement," has come to describe "independence movements," and instead of a "diligent and modest" Lenin we now have a "ruthless and cunning" Stalin). I've done battle with him in the pages of the *Gazeta* with my sister, Marysia Kruczkowska, pointing out, among other things, the anti-Semitism that suffuses his books. After our piece was published, more than two hundred scholars, artists, and writers protested to the Education Ministry against teaching the young from his textbooks. But an equally large group immediately stepped forward with a letter defending the textbook and the "Polish values" contained in it.

Bohdan Poręba, a film director known for his anti-Semitic views, introduces himself as a friend of Father Orłowski of Jedwabne: "The lady who hid seven Jews says she was beaten. Most of those seven went to work for the Communist secret police. She was thrashed for being on the side of the secret police [*applause in the hall*]. It was slaughter all around at that time. Let's count the corpses frozen in Siberia and people tortured by the Jewish secret police. Reconciliation is possible, but not by our licking their boots. Let's talk about Jewish crimes [*applause*]. We're not discussing what happened sixty years ago. We're discussing whether we're going to be able to breathe. The people have been humiliated. The idea of a Polish state without Poles is back."

For Bohdan Poręba the actions of world Jewry constitute a coherent course whose aim is "to crush the Polish people." That's why the publicizing of Jedwabne and the publication of the "famous anti-Polish comic book *Maus*, where Poles are pigs," were planned to coincide.

In the early 1990s my then husband, Piotr Bikont, was encouraged by Lawrence Weschler to translate *Maus: Story of a Survivor*, Art Spiegelman's graphic account of his father's experiences during the Holocaust. Weschler, then a writer for *The New Yorker*, had introduced us to Spiegelman. A major Polish publisher acquired the rights to the book, and then for ten years couldn't decide whether to publish it or not. Apparently several respected individuals, called in for expert advice, criticized the book for its "anti-Polishness." *Maus*, whose main story takes place in Poland, had already been translated into many languages, when unexpectedly two young people who founded the publishing house POST in Krakow contacted Piotr, saying they wanted to publish it. And so by a complete coincidence *Maus* was published at the same time that the discussions about Jedwabne were raging.

"There's no point in debating Anna Bikont's vile insinuations," one of the panelists cries out. "Nothing happened in Jedwabne to justify one of Adam Michnik's hacks leveling base accusations at the National Party. We'll defend ourselves and unmask the lies of Jewish chauvinists."

The assembled decided to convene a Committee to Defend the Honor and Dignity of the Polish Nation, and wound up the gathering by singing the patriotic song "Rota" (Oath).

APRIL 9, 2001
In the Washington-based weekly *The New Republic*, Leon Wieseltier's response to an article by Adam Michnik: "My friend has produced a contorted moral calculation . . . Michnik begins by reminding his readers that the Poles were also victims . . . And Michnik repairs also to the Poles who rescued Jews during the war . . . 'Do the murderers deserve more recognition than the righteous?' Michnik asks. Well, yes, they do, because

there were many more of them (I write this as the grateful son of a Jewish woman who was saved by Poles) . . . I am puzzled by the haggling tone of his reckoning with Jedwabne."

APRIL 10, 2001

In the *Gazeta* editorial offices I read letters sent to me after my piece today on Jedwabne: "Woman, what's keeping you in Poland? May you be consumed by hellfire for your perversity and lies. Poland for the Poles"; "Miss Bikont, Jewess possessed by crazy anti-Polonism, we'll be meeting soon. A kamikaze has already been assigned to you"; "You've managed to ignite a Polish-Jewish war in your newspaper. A few more such stories in your pages, and I'll become an anti-Semite, I already associate Jews with lying and swindling."

One letter is written in a radically different tone, and it is the only one signed: "After your report I howl and cry. Enough hatred toward other nationalities. When I was five years old I lost my mother, and I was the fifth child in our family. It wasn't the priest who came to our aid in that difficult situation but Icek Borensztajn—that's a name I'll never forget. I'm letting you know that I'll be in Jedwabne on July 10. Anna Mazurkiewicz, Wrocław."

APRIL 12, 2001

Father Henryk Jankowski of the Church of St. Brigid—where in the time of Solidarity and martial law, the Lord's Tomb was used to convey bold political statements—has joined in the discussion on Jedwabne, not for the first time, and given full rein to his anti-Semitism, presenting a partially burned miniature barn as the Lord's Tomb with a skeleton rising from it and the inscriptions: *The Jews killed Jesus and the prophets and persecuted us, too* and *Poles, rescue Poland.*

APRIL 13, 2001

I'm on my way to Gdańsk, where Jan Skrodzki and I have arranged to meet Antoni Olszewski from Radziłów. He knows a lot. Olszewski keeps saying as we talk, "This wickedness happened in a Christian country." We find out from him that Klimaszewski, the man who set fire to the Radziłów barn and whom we looked for in Ełk, is dead.

APRIL 18, 2001

Jedwabne. A little right-wing publication left in the church prints letters sent to Father Orłowski: "During the two years of Soviet-Jewish power the Jews of Jedwabne systematically deported hundreds of Polish families, and not one Jewish family. The lists were drawn up in the temple under supervision of the rabbi." The witness goes on to write that his family hid a Jew on July 10.

This is classic. It's almost impossible to find an anti-Semite in Jedwabne who doesn't maintain that his family hid a Jew. The people who really hid Jews at that time are still too scared to speak about it.

I've tried to meet with Jerzy Ramotowski several times since I read his remarks in the weekly *Contacts*: "From July 10, 1941, on, the names of the perpetrators were an open secret." It's from him that Tocki, the chief editor of *Contacts*, heard of the grim secret of Jedwabne back in the eighties.

This local history teacher, now retired, is the one person who was always interested in the crime committed so many years ago and who collected accounts. He met with Gross. From then on he sometimes came home from the Relax bar roughed up. Because Jerzy Ramotowski knows a lot and drinks a lot. I've heard that after he was beaten up by his bar buddies, he started speaking with the voice of the Jedwabne deniers. I'm still determined to meet with him. I've made several appointments to see him, waited in the agreed-upon place, but he never shows up. He doesn't this time, either.

I drop by Godlewski, who is very tense. For some time negotiations have been going on with Henryk Biedrzycki, the heir of Bronisław Śleszyński, owner of the barn and the surrounding land. In the sixties, when the authorities came to build a monument, the parcel of land was purchased by the treasury. Surveys have shown that the Jews' mass grave extends beyond the terrain indicated at that time, and an additional piece of land must be acquired. The provincial governor's office has assessed the land to be worth thirty thousand zlotys. Meanwhile, the anti-Semitic publisher Leszek Bubel has offered a hundred thousand dollars. Obviously Biedrzycki preferred Bubel, both in terms of the price and the political views they share. However, he has proposed to the government that he'll sell them the land for a hundred thousand, naturally, because why would he sell at a loss? And he will do it under the condition that in a year's time, the groundskeeping be handed over to the Committee to Defend the Good Name of Jedwabne. The plan is to erect an adjacent monument to the memory of Poles killed by Jews. Bubel has no doubt this plan will be readily accepted by the town council.

The same things are constantly repeated in Jedwabne: it's all about money; Gross and journalists, false witnesses and world Jewry are enriching themselves at the expense of the townspeople. Meanwhile, it seems that the only person who has a chance of getting rich is the grandson of the farmer who made his barn available for the burning of Jews.

I manage to cross Janina Biedrzycka's threshold to ask her about the Germans rebuilding her father's barn. But I get nowhere.

"That's nonsense. The Germans did the burning, and the Jews denounced Poles to the Soviets. I saw it with my own eyes. I'm so upset about all this, because I simply hate lies."

Not only did Biedrzycka see Jews writing nonexistent denunciations with her own eyes, she also heard nonexistent Germans addressing the Jews through a megaphone in the market square on the morning of July 10, 1941. She was told what they were saying by a Jewish friend whom she'd taken into hiding in her attic: that the Jews were to be put on a labor transport and should form groups of four. She saw them obediently forming groups.

I learn that my interview with Przechodzki is having an entirely different effect than I'd hoped. Slander has been spreading about his father, how he took part in looting and got rich on Jewish gold. Exactly the same as the Dziedzices. When it got around that Leszek was talking to journalists about the massacre, people started to say that his father had dug up gold teeth out of the ashes. As soon as anyone lifts the veil of secrecy an inch, he or his family is immediately accused of participating in the crime.

An acquaintance tells me about a conversation with Krystyna N., who said no one was going to go to the ceremony because the whole thing was just about money. When I spoke to her in March she claimed the town was split into two camps, but there were more who felt sorry for the murder victims. It looks like she's stopped feeling sorry.

On the way back to Warsaw I stop off at Przestrzele.

"We've finally decided to leave Poland," says Leszek Dziedzic. "We'll stay to go to the ceremony. It's not just about the attacks on us, but the whole atmosphere."

I'm not surprised. The other target of the smear campaign is the mayor, who is also thinking more and more of emigrating.

APRIL 19, 2001

With my daughters Ola and Maniucha and some friends I've set off for a few days in the Tatra Mountains, in the Five Lakes Valley. We're just coming up to the last stretch before the shelter when my cell phone, which isn't even supposed to have reception here, rings. It's Stanisław Ramotowski, who's feeling very poorly. I don't know by what miracle I manage to get my sister, Marysia Kruczkowska, on the phone, but she promises to go to see him immediately.

APRIL 22, 2001

Back in Warsaw. At the hospital where my sister has brought Ramotowski, I hear Stanisław has had a heart attack. Even worse, his X-ray showed a spot indicating lung cancer. Two months ago the film showed nothing.

APRIL 24, 2001

In the room at the Jewish Historical Institute that houses the files on the Righteous Among the Nations, I search for documents on the Wyrzykowskis of Janczewko, who sheltered seven Jews. I find a 1963 letter from Mosze Olszewicz about awarding the Wyrzykowskis the medal of the Righteous Among the Nations. There is also a letter from Antonina Wyrzykowska: "I hid seven people for 28 months under the manure in our pigsty. I emphasize they didn't have a penny. For me it wasn't about money, but about saving human lives, it wasn't about religion, just about people. After the liberation I was beaten more than once and they, too, were under threat, so I had to leave the area where I was born."

There's correspondence from the Lewins of Wizna related to the recognition of the Dobkowskis of Zanklewo. The whole family is registered at Yad Vashem, the Dobkowskis' parents and their three sons, among them the Zanklewo farmer I visited in December last year and his brothers. They received medals; their parents had already died. There's a letter from the brothers: "In May 1945, our family was subject to an act of revenge carried out by unidentified partisan units for having sheltered the Lewin family. The action consisted of beating and abusing our father and taking away all our possessions and leaving the family without means to live."

I found the address of one of the brothers, Wincenty Dobkowski, in the correspondence. In the evening I call him in Ełk. "Such filth, such lies are being spouted now. And why?" Dobkowski says nervously. "So there were some thugs in Jedwabne. They put twelve men on trial, the ones the Germans sent out and forced to stand guard over the Jews. I respect Israelis, but then you also have to say what the Jews did under the Soviet occupation. How can they say the Polish people did it? Our peoples should be reconciled, anti-Semitism shouldn't be stirred up again."

I tell him I'm going to Israel, where I'm visiting the Lewin siblings, whose address I got from his brother in Zanklewo. As soon as he starts to speak of Izaak and Ida—or Janek and Tereska, as they were called when they were in hiding—Wincenty Dobkowski's voice softens.

"You have to meet each of them separately, because they don't speak to each other. They quarreled over their mother's inheritance. Such a pity, there's just the two of them in the world and they went through such hard times together."

APRIL 25, 2001

In an anti-Semitic rag with the telling name *Nasza Polska* (Our Poland), I read an interview with a woman from Jedwabne who now lives in Toronto. "My brothers and sisters and I were lying on the floor at home, throwing up," she says of the time right after the burning of the Jews. "There was a nauseating smoke spreading across all of Jedwabne, carried by the wind, penetrating into houses, poisoning everything." She was ten years old at the time, living on Przytulska Street. At 3:00 p.m. she had gone out with her mother to visit an aunt who lived on Cmentarna Street, and they saw the procession of Jews with the rabbi at the front, carrying his hat on a stick.

Why did they go out at precisely that moment to see the aunt who lived on the route of the Jews' march? Evidently they wanted to get a look. This is the umpteenth time I hear of parents letting their children watch the scene of the Jews being rounded up in the market square. This is the ludic dimension of the massacre.

MAY 4, 2001

"For Our Sins and Yours"—the front-page headline of the *Gazeta* conveys perfectly the meaning of the primate's speech at Jasna Góra. Józef Glemp announced that a formal apology for Jedwabne will be made in Warsaw on May 27. At the ceremony, the Episcopal Convention will pray—he stressed—not only for the Jewish victims in Jedwabne but also "for the evil visited upon Polish citizens of the Catholic faith, in which Poles of the Jewish faith took part . . . The Poles," the primate continued, "were also wronged . . . suffered from evil perpetrated by Jews, including during the period when Communism was introduced in Poland. I expect the Jewish side to make a reckoning with its conscience and bring itself to apologize to the Poles for those crimes."

MAY 9, 2001

At Jacek Kuroń's. When I last visited him in the hospital we talked about the interview given to the *Gazeta* by the éminence grise of the National Party movement in the new Poland, the current justice minister, Wiesław Chrzanowski. To the question of whether the deaths of Jews who lived in Jedwabne should weigh on the conscience of the interwar nationalist movement, Chrzanowski replied, "Why that again? Why would it weigh on our conscience? There weren't even any National Party members there." This part of the conversation enraged Jacek. He showed me a passage where Chrzanowski says the bastion of the nationalist movement before World War I and between the wars was the Podlasie region.

"But that's exactly where Jedwabne and Radziłów are," Jacek fumes. "He says it was there that the activities of educational institutions created by the National Party had their greatest results. And he doesn't see what those results were!" He reads me the article he has prepared for the *Gazeta* against Chrzanowski's theses "on the beneficial influence of the educational work of the National Party": "The Institute of National Remembrance is currently conducting an investigation into the massacre in Jedwabne and trying to determine what role the German occupying forces played in it. They certainly had a role, but that is a marginal factor in the face of the century-long educational campaign of Polish national hatred."

I've given Jacek a running account of my reading in the regional prewar diocesan press and told him about the processions dominated by the National Party, which culminated in the demolition of Jewish shops.

Jacek carefully notes down the names of the towns where such violent excesses occurred: Wąsosz, Radziłów, Jedwabne, Szczuczyn, Grajewo, Tykocin, Kolno, Suchowola, Wizna, Zaręby Kościelne. He wants to add them to his text. Jacek, who for years furnished the Western media with detailed information on the Communist state repression of the Committee in Defense of the Workers (KOR), well knows that general statements sound stronger when they are grounded in fact.

MAY 10, 2001

I read documents in the court case against the Radziłów killer Henryk Dziekoński obtained by the Białystok Institute of National Remembrance. I try to decipher the clumsy handwriting of the person taking down testimony.

"We received an order from the Gestapo to round up the Jews in the market and torment them," the accused begins. "We responded very eagerly and compliantly to the order." His detailed account of the eager and compliant execution of the order must have surprised the court in Białystok: they sent him for psychiatric testing.

MAY 12, 2001

With Jan Skrodzki, whose main occupation for several months now has been helping me find witnesses to the Radziłów massacre, I drive to Reda, on the sea, to see a witness he has tracked down. Jan has a bulldog's grip. He read a piece in a Gdańsk newspaper in which an anonymous witness from Radziłów appeared, and tracked him down by methods known only to himself.

Andrzej R. is an extraordinary witness. He was thirteen at the time and ran from place to place taking notes on what was going on because he dreamed of being a reporter. He saw Jews being tortured in the first days after the Soviets entered the town and he actually saw the massacre being perpetrated.

"At the end of each day when everything was over, I rushed home to make notes by candlelight."

The journal was lost, Andrzej R. did not become a reporter, but he preserved in his memory dozens of scenes, including who killed and when and how. He recognized friends of his, boys and girls, among the crowd being rounded up. And what he saw he remembered. Hour by hour.

He speaks of it without emotion. Now he is trying to describe it anew. He shows me his efforts. Carefully recorded in a lined notebook, circular sentences without any of the concrete detail we got out of him. He'd like to publish his account under a pseudonym.

The massacre was taboo in most houses, that's easy to understand. But it's harder to see why the same taboo applied to—and still applies to—those who helped Jews. Andrzej R., who gave the names of murderers, hesitated before telling me whose field it was where father and son Dorogoj hid in a mud hut: "That farmer's daughters are still alive. I'd have to ask their permission."

5

I'll Tell You Who Did It: My Father

or, The Private Investigation
of Jan Skrodzki

Jan Skrodzki, an engineer retired from the Gdańsk shipyard, was a little boy when, from a window of his parents' house in Radziłów, he saw Jews driven to their place of execution by Poles. When he left the town as a teenager he vowed never to return. At gatherings with family and friends he always said openly that it was locals who had burned the Jews in Radziłów. It always ended in a quarrel, but Skrodzki stubbornly went on saying that no German had held a gun to anyone's head, and that anti-Semitism and a lust for pillage were the causes of the atrocity.

He has an astonishing memory; he talks about things that happened in his childhood as if they were still before his eyes. He describes the image he saw from behind a curtain as if looking at a photograph:

"I was six years, seven months, and fourteen days old at the time. First I saw how Jews were forced to pull up weeds in the marketplace; it was paved and weeds grew up between the stones. Then from another window I saw the column of people on Piękna Street. Later I saw plenty of film showing Jews being rounded up elsewhere. SS men, guns, dogs: there was nothing like that here. It was our people from Radziłów and the surrounding villages. They must have plotted it earlier—on such and such a day we'll kill them—how else would they have all met up like that? It wasn't any underclass doing it. There were a lot of young people, not with little sticks but with heavy clubs.

Jan Skrodzki with his dog, Czacza, at home in Gdańsk, 2002. (Courtesy of Jan Skrodzki)

Szyma, Bencyjon, and Fruma, children of Szejna and Mosze Dorogoj. Radziłów, 1922. Bencyjon emigrated to Palestine before the war. Fruma fled as soon as the Germans entered Radziłów and survived the war in Soviet Russia. Szyma, also called Dora, was brutally murdered by Poles in July 1941. Jan Skrodzki's father, Zygmunt, was one of the perpetrators. (Courtesy of Jose Gutstein, www.radzilow.com)

"I often hear there's no anti-Semitism in Poland now. I always say, 'There are a lot of anti-Semites in my family, and of the people I know, every other one, or maybe every third, is anti-Semitic, and I could easily have been, too.' And where did we get our anti-Semitism? The priest preached it from the pulpit, that fat Father Dołęgowski. And Poles in Radziłów lapped it up because they were uneducated or completely illiterate. Envious of Jews because they were better off. While Jews were working harder, organizing their work better, supporting each other."

Skrodzki speaks of his father with pain and respect: "He was a sought-after tailor, and he employed several skilled artisans. How is it possible that such a wise, honest man, an outstanding tailor too, could be such an anti-Semite?"

He knew that to compete with the Jews, his father opened a bakery and got an excellent baker in from nearby Tykocin, Mr. Odyniec, also a National Party member. As if that weren't enough, he had a sign painted to say: CHRISTIAN BAKERY.

"Why *Christian* bakery?" Jan asks, and replies to his own question: "Just to annoy the Jews. He must have really been a good tailor, because after the war when we moved to Milanówek near Warsaw he was taken on at the Industrial Design Works, the best design institute in Poland. He was courageous, too; during the war he joined the Home Army, and he had a radio in a hiding place he'd made between the stove and the floor.

"When the amnesty was proclaimed my father appeared with his division. The guys then brought all their arms in to the station on trucks. They were naive. Two months later the authorities came for my father, they threw him in jail, and he spent nine months there before the trial took place—it was at the court in Ełk. My mother was left to take care of all the kids. I was in eighth grade at school in Łomża and I had to drop out for a year to help at home. In the meantime they started to prosecute the criminals who had killed Jews. My father was put in jail a second time. They didn't manage to convict him for the Home Army, maybe they could get him convicted for the pogrom? Nothing was proved against him."

It's Skrodzki who proposed to go with me to Radziłów. He knows best who to talk to and how. He's prepared to help me get something out of people who won't want to talk to me, a stranger and a journalist in the bargain. And he can do his own investigating while we're at it. He wants to find out what the people whom he remembers fondly from childhood were doing that day.

The first time we went was in February 2001. Jan was thoroughly prepared. He had a list of people who were in town in 1941, and who live in Radziłów today. And a separate list of people who participated in the murders, reconstructed from things he himself had heard as well as from Menachem Finkelsztejn's testimony. Next to the names of people about whom there was no doubt he had put a plus, and where he wasn't sure, a question mark.

We went by his cousins' house. An affluent farm, well maintained, with an old Mercedes in the driveway. On the front steps, when we were already at the door, Skrodzki suddenly switched from addressing me formally as *pani* (Miss) to the informal *ty* (you): "I told them you were my cousin," he explained. "Otherwise they won't talk to you."

Somehow the conversation with his cousins wouldn't get going. The chatty Skrodzki reminisced about his childhood. How under the Soviets his father stopped sleeping at home for fear of being deported. He went into hiding, and when the news got around that families would be deported, his mother gave Jan to relatives to hide, and she found a hiding place somewhere nearby with her two youngest children.

Then our hostess spoke up: "When there's talk about the Soviet times I always think of what used to be said around here about the Jews sending people to Siberia."

Skrodzki protested, "With us, it was a Jew who saved our lives, because he told my mother what night the Soviets were coming for us. I was taken to the Borawski family in Trzaski on a truck. When anyone came by they hid me in the closet or the annex. There were no Jews living there, and to be quite clear, my hosts were hiding me from the Polish neighbors. If that Jew hadn't told Mother about the deportation we wouldn't be talking right now. Mama would have died on the way to Siberia with her three children."

"That's true," his cousin admitted. "The Jews knew everything in advance because they pointed out who to deport."

Skrodzki explained that there are bad apples among every people, and a decent Jew wouldn't collaborate with the Soviets any more than a decent Pole.

"You're right," said the cousin's wife. "When I was a cleaning lady in

America, once I worked for Jews, and another time for Germans who had family pictures with people wearing swastikas. Both were decent people."

Skrodzki tried to turn the conversation to the subject of the massacre. He started by recalling Zalewski, their uncle and an eminently decent fellow. He said he'd heard from his daughter Halina that a Jewish woman who had been beaten up by one of the Mordasiewiczes had run to the Zalewski house for help.

"That's right," his cousin chimed in, "because the Mordasiewiczes' mother was deported to Siberia, with a small child. If someone's family hadn't been deported they wouldn't have been there that day. Anyway, why are we talking about it, none of them is even alive anymore."

"If you know none of the killers is alive, does that mean you know who they were?" I blurted.

"I'm not going to speak ill of the dead, especially since they'd suffered injustice."

And that was the end of it.

We visited a number of Jan's childhood friends. Accustomed to steering conversations myself, I had to be patient, because I was only Jan's cousin on his wife's side who had come along almost by accident. To visit everyone on Jan's list would have taken many days. All the conversations went on for hours. Jan took the lead and I fidgeted restlessly, waiting for him to start asking about the massacre. After all, I thought, they must guess what brings us here. A lot was already being said and written about nearby Jedwabne.

"Do you remember," Skrodzki asked one friend from childhood, "that my father owned the most powerful Pfaff sewing machine, and he was one of the first in Radziłów to have a Diamant bicycle?"

"Your uncle Zalewski had a Pfaff, and a Singer, too, the kind where you moved the treadle with your knee. I was a journeyman working for him then, but only your uncle used a Pfaff, and only the ablest, Antoni Mordasiewicz, was allowed to sit at it."

I had already heard from Stanisław Ramotowski that this Mordasiewicz was not only an able journeyman but also a murderer. Yet there I was listening to them going on about sewing machines, about Henio's sister who had her eye on Jan, and Henio who in his turn liked Władzia. They could also talk without end about postwar partisan groups, how "Groove" was killed, how Marchewka was killed. Only after exhausting these topics did

Jan reveal why he had come: "I have to find out about everything, because the Institute of National Remembrance is examining the Jedwabne affair, they're sure to come to Radziłów, and they'll ask me about Father, so I have to be prepared. Cousin Anna, you take notes," he tossed off in my direction, which allowed me to do so without raising suspicion.

I soon understood this tactic would get us invaluable information that I would never have gotten by myself. It was exactly this kind of conversation, this small talk about old times, that gave us that chance.

"You remember there was a guy, his nickname was Dupek [Ass]," Józef K. related. "You know, the guy who set the barn on fire, the widow's son, Józef Klimas."

When we talked to anyone over seventy it was hard not to wonder if he or she had taken part in the atrocity. And so when we visited Franciszek Ekstowicz, a tailor trained by Jan's father, and I looked into this quiet man's noble, chiseled face, I thought: No, not him, I'm sure.

Franciszek Ekstowicz had been herding cows that day and only got back to town in the early evening. I asked him if his friends who were looting abandoned houses hadn't called on him to join them.

"I went into one house; Kozioł, the son-in-law of the Jewish woman who lived there, was an educated man and he had a lot of books. My friends took out the chairs, the table, but I took the Jew's books. They laughed at me later: 'Stupid guy, he took the paper.'"

When I asked him what the books were, he was quick to withdraw, as if I'd demanded restitution. A minute later, perhaps not by accident, he quoted the poets Adam Mickiewicz and Adam Asnyk. But I didn't dare to ask him directly if those were the "post-Jewish books" that he took from Kozioł's house.

The second day of our visit we realized Jan's cousin must have looked in the rooms where we had slept. Remarks she made to Jan showed she had read his notes, where under the heading "probable murderers of July 7, 1941," he had written her uncle's name in his clear handwriting, if with a question mark. From the looks she cast in my direction I inferred she had also familiarized herself with my appointment book, in which I'd written "Call Mr. Skrodzki" several times.

We left Radziłów in the late afternoon, it was already dark, and it would have been more sensible to leave early the next day, but the atmosphere where we were staying was tense—to put it mildly. I drove on icy roads with snowdrifts. The drive to Warsaw, which usually took me three hours, this time took seven and a half.

Not long after our expedition to Radziłów, Skrodzki received a letter from his family commenting on his bringing me there: "The devil must have gotten into you, Jan."

He sent back the copy I had given him of the historian Szymon Datner's text "The Holocaust in Radziłów" with corrections, giving the proper spelling of names often extremely distorted in the article. There were a few ambiguous fragments in the text. The following sentence, for instance: "The first victim fell, a tailor named Skondzki, and Antoni Kostaszewski committed the bestial murder of a seventeen-year-old girl and Komsomol member, Fruma Dorogoj, saying she wasn't worth a bullet. They cut her head off in the forest near the Kopańska settlement and threw her body in the swamp." Reading this again, it occurred to me that the text was badly edited, that the tailor wasn't the first victim but a perpetrator of the atrocity, along with Kosmaczewski (I already knew that was the real name. I also knew the murdered girl was in fact called Szyma, not Fruma). When Skrodzki told me his father was a tailor I wondered if there hadn't been another confusion of names; it's not hard to turn Skrodzki into Skondzki.

Janek must have had the same thought, because when he returned Finkelsztejn's testimony to me with corrections, he had crossed out Skondzki and written in Skrodzki in pencil, with a question mark. Then I proposed that if he was worried about that tailor being his father, I would take him to see Stanisław Ramotowski, who is the walking memory of the massacre.

Earlier when I told Ramotowski I had visited Zygmunt Skrodzki's son in Gdańsk and that we were planning to go to Radziłów together, he protested vehemently: "Miss Ania, you don't want that kind of friends." But when I came back from Radziłów and asked him directly if Skrodzki's father was one of the killers, he clammed up. He said he hadn't been at the barn, and how was he to know who had been there? He only knew what he saw with his own eyes, that before the war when the vicar Kamiński headed a nationalist attack squad that broke Jews' windows, Zygmunt Skrodzki was right behind him.

"He was the best man in town for those things." And he added: "He was an enemy of Jews."

But when I visited him with Jan Skrodzki, he didn't want to remember any of it.

"No, no, we're not talking about your father, it might have been Eugeniusz Skomski, a tailor who lived across the street from the depot, he was involved," he explained, and changed the subject to the beautifully tailored black leather jacket he still wears, and which was made for him half a century ago by Zygmunt Skrodzki.

After we left, Jan took back my copy of Finkelsztejn's testimony with his corrections for a moment and with relief changed Skondzki to Skomski, in pen this time.

In Warsaw we visited a cousin of his, a retired seamstress living in the Praga district. The fragile seventy-three-year-old Halina Zalewska, tottering around the house, elicited sympathy from the first glance. It didn't last, unfortunately. She knows a thing or two about Jews; she listens to the anti-Semitic ultra-right-wing Catholic Radio Maryja all day long.

She saw her Polish friends driving her Jewish friends, some pushing prams, to their deaths. She pitied the victims and railed against the killers, but at the same time she spiked her account with phrases like "dirty Jews," "that damn parade of Soviet flunkies," "those Jewish beggars, now they want their property back," and blithely laid blame for the atrocity on the victims.

"Eight hundred head from Radziłów were burned. There were so many because Jews multiplied like rabbits. The Jew lorded it over us. They spread out, supported their own. Jews stopped at nothing in their efforts to impoverish Poland and keep it from developing. We put up with it for many years. There wasn't any prejudice against Jews, Poles were just angry about what the Jews had done under Soviet rule. Jews joined the NKVD, drew up deportation lists. I remember under the Soviets how they stood at the bed at night, pointing guns: 'Ublyudok [motherfucker], tell me where your father is hiding.'"

"Local Jews swore in Russian?" I asked to make sure.

"No, no, those were the ones who'd come from Russia. But there were plenty of locals in the police force, routine Communists and traitors to the Polish nation, the Jews Lejzor Gryngas, Nagórka, Piechota, and there was our maid Halinka's brother-in-law, no matter what his name was— he was a Pole, not a Jew. Holy Scripture tells us the Jews are a tribe of vipers, perverts, they're untrustworthy and faithless. They played tricks on the Lord himself, and He had to send down plagues on them. He made them wander in the wilderness for thirty years. It's no accident He punished them the way He did. I've known about that from before the war, from religious studies. I remember everything, I'm seventy-three and I've still no sclerosis at all, though I don't eat margarine, only butter, because it's Jewish companies that make margarine."

Skrodzki tried to intervene: "The Old Testament, the source of our faith, we share with the Jews, and Jesus was a Jew."

"What are you saying, he was God's son, that tribe has nothing to do with him. He didn't speak much Hebrew and no Yiddish at all."

Janek quoted her Finkelsztejn's testimony on the tailor Skondzki, who, with Kosmaczewski, committed the bestial murder of a young girl.

"Ah, that was the daughter of the shoemaker Dorogoj, who lived near the depot. Dark hair, she wore it short," Zalewska immediately remembered. "She threw a rock at the cross and blasphemed. I don't say I approve of them killing her in the swamp and cutting her head off, but it should be said she was a member of the Komsomol."

Janek asked her if his father might have been involved.

"I want to know the truth, even the worst," he prodded. "As his son I have a right to know if my father took part in an atrocity."

"It was a shock, but on the memory of your mother and mine, I swear no one knows what really happened. Your father was a young man and game for a fight," his cousin said nervously. "Your father was a nationalist, it's an honor to remind you of it. Strong young men would knock over the Jews' barrels of herring, knock down their stalls, tell Poles not to buy from Jews. The Yids remembered your dad was an activist, that's why they put him down for deportation."

During our visit with Halina Zalewska I whispered for him to question her about each of the people we'd talked to in Radziłów.

"Waldek K. wasn't involved, was he, just his brother?" Jan asked. Waldek K. was father-in-law to Jan's cousin, the one who welcomed us on our first visit and later. "Oh, no, how could you say that, he had God in his heart. He might have done some looting, whoever was strong and happened to be around took advantage. In the marketplace that day, Father met an artisan he employed who'd come to town to take a bed from a Jewish house, because his family were so poor they slept on the floor. The only Polish people who took part in the killing all had seen members of their family deported by the Soviets."

"So Józef K. didn't join in?" I wanted to make sure about the brother-in-law of the friend of Jan's we'd met in Radziłów, none of whose family had been deported; I knew that for a certainty. He was an open, sympathetic person, but I had grown suspicious when he broke into a nervous giggle a third time; each time he'd done it we had been talking about killing and raping.

"Józef took part in those pogroms of Jews, they went by houses at night. His family hadn't been deported, he just did it for the company."

In Otwock, just outside Warsaw, we went to see Bolesław Ciszewski, who had been Jan's father's tailoring assistant. He was fifteen at the time. He saw Jews driven into the marketplace and infants thrown into the burning barn. He spoke of it without compassion. Jan asked him directly whether his father had taken part.

"Your father was a tough guy and let's not forget what the Jews had done. How many Polish families did they send to Siberia? People had reason to bear a grudge against the Jews, and now I don't know what the Jews bear a grudge about."

When we went back to Radziłów, we didn't go to see Jan's cousins again. Jan understood from their letter that relations had been severed. Instead, we headed for his childhood friend Eugenia K. and her husband. When we had been with his family the situation had been tense, but now we were met with warmth, implored to stay the night, beds had already been made up for us. And then our host started to talk: "I met your cousin in the market. He said you'd come to see him with a Jewish girl. I just shrugged and said, 'I don't believe Jan would soil his own nest.' And turned my back on him."

When we got back to the hotel I gave Jan documents to read from the 1945 trial of one of the Radziłów killers, Leon Kosmaczewski. I'd only just received them and hadn't yet managed to look them over. My favorite detective series, *Columbo*, was on TV. During the commercials, Jan read me excerpts from the investigation.

Columbo said, "Now I can tell you who's the killer." Commercial break. Jan started reading the record of Menachem's father Izrael Finkelsztejn's interrogation on December 3, 1945: "Kosmaczewski got several people together in a gang and started demolishing Jewish homes. They dragged people out of their homes and beat them until they lost consciousness. They also raped a lot of young girls, special note should be taken of their rape of the Borozowieckis, mother and daughter, whom they later killed. Those night rampages went on for two weeks, until July 7, 1941." He listed the gang members: "Skrodzki, tailor, was also one of the leaders."

"Somehow I knew that," Jan said. His voice was calm, but his fingers were nervously paging through the records.

With this new and bitter knowledge, he continued the search with me.

"This was a decent family," said Jan, leading me to another house in Radziłów. "They lived on Piękna Street. Aleksander is still alive, he must have seen a lot."

Aleksander Bargłowski was not happy to see us. He didn't know what happened during the war, and he didn't remember the period before the war. But when Jan began to talk about the National Party's activities, he involuntarily began humming a song he remembered from his child-hood, sung to the tune of a Kościuszko-era peasant recruits' song:

> Onward, boys, make haste,
> A harvest now awaits us.
> Let's take back all trade,
> Seize the Jews' big gains.

I didn't manage to get the second verse, he was singing it softly under his breath. When I asked him to repeat it, he seemed to realize how in-appropriate it was in the context of what had happened later. He grew flustered, fell silent, and no longer remembered anything at all. Jan put a blunt question to him: "Who did it?"

"I didn't see anything. I know it was the Germans."

"I'll tell you who did it: my father was one of them. Poles did it."

A silence fell, but our interlocutor couldn't bear it in the end. Softly, under his breath, he swore: "Fuck, you're right, it was a foul thing that happened."

And he started to talk.

"The day before, Jews had already hidden in the grain. They found them there and dragged them off to the barn. That day I was digging peat near Okrasin. I heard the screams, saw the smoke. The wife of the Jew Lejzor, the ragman, whose son had a big family, hid in our chicken coop. I saw her and said, 'You just sit tight, woman.' But later she got herself together and left. That day the postman came by, Adam Kamiński, who was in Russia during the revolution. He said, 'Don't go there, don't go looting.' Nobody from our family went, none of us laid hands on anything that didn't belong to us. People were running over there out of curiosity. I would have been ashamed to go there, or take anything. I'd gone to school with Szlapak's boy, his dad had a shop. And I was supposed to steal from them, from my friends? Anyway, Mother made me clothes on her loom, my aunt in America sent me things, I didn't have to pounce on their old stuff. It was those shits from the villages, from Wąsosz and Lisy, who arrived in droves. That scum did it, and they gave all of Poland a bad name."

When back in Warsaw, I brought Stanisław Ramotowski the documents from the trial against Leon Kosmaczewski; Ramotowski admitted seeing Zygmunt Skrodzki on the day of the massacre, standing in front of his house, and said he had to have taken part. Ramotowski hadn't wanted to say it when he was talking to me and Jan Skrodzki, because he didn't want to make me uncomfortable.

The next time Jan and I went to Radziłów, we tried to find Antoni O., who was mentioned in the *Dziennik Bałtycki* (Baltic Daily). He had witnessed Polish residents armed with sticks and clubs rounding up Jews. It turns out there is such a person, the initials fit; he lived in Radziłów throughout the war. Jan Skrodzki even remembers him a little from old times. We spoke to him in the courtyard, because even though it was cold, he didn't ask us in. He emphatically denied he had told any journalist anything.

Evidently we were looking for a different Antoni O. This man told us, "Jews denounced Poles to the NKVD en masse. I wouldn't say that if I hadn't heard it with my own ears just a few days ago on the radio."

His father-in-law hid a Jewish woman in Wąsosz (this checked out—I heard about Władysław Ładziński from Stanisław Ramotowski), and "when later [their] daughter Sabina worked for Jews in America and revealed this to them, they just worshipped her." When I asked for further details as someone happened to be walking down the little street, Antoni instantly changed the subject.

Soon we managed to find the right Antoni O.

He was Antoni Olszewski of Gdańsk; Olszewski's mother, Aleksandra, hid two Jewish children on the day of the massacre. She quickly moved them on, fearing retribution from her neighbors, but in the 1980s the children she saved found her and invited her to Israel with her son.

"After the war kids were sometimes told, 'Go get some sand from the grave,' because there was good yellow sand there for plastering. I took it from there, too," he continued, adding that there were stones from the burned barn in the foundation of their house. "Everybody took them. Once I found a bone and threw it out in a rage, and a friend of mine threw a skull into the river. It's so shameful when I think about it now, but then we didn't have the imagination to realize."

He remembered going from village to village with the volunteer firefighters orchestra to give concerts. Sometimes they heard, "You're from Radziłów, where you burned the Jews." No one talked about it back in Radziłów.

"Though when you bought a half liter of vodka from Strzelecka or from Bronia Pachucka, who sold vodka back then, tongues would wag. Later I knew a lot about it, because in our house it was spoken of freely. Jews had been driven into the swamps near the mill and drowned, and Mother always said, 'Don't go there, people were drowned there.' When women from the neighborhood came over Mama brewed them beer, and they always ended up talking about that same thing. I remember my mother raging about one of the killers: 'I don't know how that shameless son of a bitch has the gall to carry the canopy in the procession.' The mothers of those killers were hardest hit. Olek Drozdowski's mother would come by to have a cry: 'My dears, what could I do? He was a grown man, he once threatened to split my chest open, too.'"

Whether due to fear, complicity, or a need to forget, the killers melted back into the community.

Antoni Olszewski's mother didn't hesitate to send him to apprentice with one of them, Feliks Mordasiewicz.

"He taught me blacksmithing—he was a good craftsman and my dad had to sell a cow to afford to pay him," Olszewski recalled. "A group of thugs would gather at his place to reminisce. They'd chase me away: 'Get lost, you little shit.' My aunt had let something slip once, I hadn't realized what it was about at the time, so I repeated what she'd said: 'Master, don't those Jews ever come to you in your sleep?' He said, 'You son of a bitch,' and threw a hammer at me."

I remembered Ramotowski telling me that he went to Mordasiewicz because there wasn't another smith who shod horses as well as he did. "But I wouldn't look at him, or he at me; he kept his head down," said Stanisław. It turned out Olszewski remembered those occasions: "Mordasiewicz made him blades for his mill. Ramotowski's wife always came to town with him, but she refused to set foot in the smithy. Whenever she passed by she would stiffen and quicken her step."

In the course of our research Skrodzki and I went back to Radziłów and its environs more than once, as well as visiting the Mazury, Kaszuby, Pomorze, and Mazowsze regions—anywhere Jan managed to find a lead. He never failed to astonish me with his skill in conducting interviews. He patiently waited for the moment when his subject had said everything he could get out of him, and then, all of a sudden, he would confront him with the truth: "Poles did it. There weren't any Germans there."

"But they could have been there in plainclothes!" they'd protest.

"There were none," Skrodzki countered. "The Germans came and went. They figured out they could trust the Poles to do their work for them."

"So that's what happened," said his cousin Piotr Kosmaczewski, who thought the Jews themselves were to blame.

In Grajewo we went to see Jan Jabłoński, the brother of one of Skrodzki's childhood friends. He was ten years old in 1941, and remembered pasturing cows on the other side of the Matlak river that day. He seemed wary about speaking with us.

"The Germans did it," he claimed.

"Did you see them?" I asked.

"It had to have been the Germans, it was during their time."

Toward the end of our visit, in the heat of conversation, Jan Jabłoński remembered that he had been at the barn after all. There were Germans there, in blue uniforms, helmets, SS insignia. Dozens of machine guns were pointed at the barn. The Germans had blocked the gates with wheels so no one could open them, and they ordered Józef Klimaszewski at gunpoint to set fire to the barn. Then they brought chlorine or quicklime and sprinkled it around to prevent infection.

Skrodzki interrupted him: "You should tell the truth, not spout this kind of crap. If we don't get to the truth, it will go on until it falls on the generation of our children and grandchildren."

Jan Jabłoński admitted there were several killers. He also remembered the Poles looting. "When they came from Wąsosz, our people said,

'*Pashol von*,' Russian for 'get out of here'—'you're not going to steal from our Jews.' It's twenty-five kilometers from Radziłów to Wąsosz. But if looters came from five miles away, they weren't turned back."

Jan and I tried to build a picture of what life was like in the town after the massacre. The people we talked to told us:

"They said the Germans would show their gratitude for our welcoming them and doing away with the Jews by leaving us in peace."

"But later it was even worse than under the Soviets," said Andrzej R.

And after the war?

"After the war everything was normal. As if there had never been any Jews," said Jan C.

"In church there was never any mention of the massacre of the Jews. It happened and that was that," said Bolesław Ciszewski.

"The brothers Dominik and Aleksander Drozdowski, who had both been very active in the killings, went out in the marketplace right after the liberation and set out the goods they'd looted. It was a big event, and everybody bought from them," said Andrzej R.

We asked why nobody pointed a finger at the killers after the war.

"They were scared."

"Why do you think, to keep the peace."

"I'm telling you, they were scared," Marysia Korycińska said, supporting the first speaker. "When Feliks Godlewski was drunk once, he got up and made a gesture of cutting someone's head off with a scythe, saying, 'A man to me is nothing more than a whistling of the air.'"

"I have to get at the truth to atone for what my father did," Jan Skrodzki said the next time we set out in search of witnesses, this time in Pomorze and Kaszuby. He found no understanding. One subject, Andrzej R., brought a form for a contribution to the High Divinity Seminary. "Why spend all that money driving around Poland? Pay for a Mass to be said for your father and your conscience will be clear."

In Ełk we found Leon Kosmaczewski's family. A spacious villa on a slope right on the lake where Kosmaczewski's daughter and twenty-year-old granddaughter live; he himself died two years before, at the age of eighty-eight. He was in good health to the end. They had no intention of talking to us, but Skrodzki gave them no chance to throw us out, saying his mother's maiden name was Kosmaczewska, so that as a child he had called all Kosmaczewskis "Uncle."

"They accused him of raping a Jewish woman in the marketplace, but he saved a Jewish woman," his daughter shrieked. "A German asked him, pointing at the woman, 'Jude?' and he said no, and allowed her to escape. A few years later a Jewish woman turned up in town asking about him, I'm sure it was the one he saved, wanting to thank him. We know Father stood trial, but that trial was started by a vicious rumor. He had been denounced because of a deal gone wrong, a woman from the neighborhood had a feud with Father."

The granddaughter chimed in, "Granny said Grandfather saved a Jewish woman from Kramarzewo, and now they just write anything. There's one historian you can take seriously, Professor Strzembosz. We're not going to listen to any nonsense from anybody else."

Skrodzki and I both knew the Jewish woman from Kramarzewo could only have been Marianna Ramotowska. We also knew she had given false evidence in his defense in court because she feared for her life.

Skrodzki tried to cut her off, but he is a mild man, and the woman kept raising her angry voice. Finally, he got up from his chair.

"I'm not going to listen to this. The responsibility falls on us, their children. If you can't acknowledge it, so much the worse for you. Anna, let's go!"

And we left.

Janek seems like a content person. He has made a success of his life, was the only one of six siblings to get a higher education. He became a recognized professional engineer. He sent his two daughters to medical school. When he had to join the Communist Party in the sixties, he joined, and as soon as he could leave after 1980, he left. He greeted Solidarity with relief, as did many party members. He sang in the Solidarity choir at the Church of St. Brigid in Gdańsk. He values order and discipline. He likes getting to the train station early and planning his time so that he never has to rush. He thinks punishment is a necessary part of raising children. He loves talking about his dog, about sailing. He likes to tell jokes. I would like to understand why he of all people, an "ordinary Pole," decided to carry the burden of memory throughout his life.

Journal

MAY 13, 2001

I'm off to Israel in a week. I want to talk to the witness to the massacre whom Gross cited in *Neighbors*. I've already called Awigdor Kochaw several times, trying to arrange a meeting, but I always get the same reply: he's not well, he doesn't feel like talking. I felt he was hostile toward me. I was afraid seeing someone from Poland might be traumatic for him. So I sent my uncle Szmul Horowitz to see him—Szmul is the founder and director emeritus of a home for the elderly in Tel Aviv, and one of the warmest people I've ever met. It helped. Szmul is supposed to call him again when I'm in town. Kochaw promised him he would receive us.

A long piece by Tomasz Strzembosz in the newspaper the *Republic*: "Satan's Entry or Arrival of the Gestapo?" (a reference to my *Gazeta* interview with Stanisław Przechodzki, which had as its title a quote from Przechodzki: "Satan Entered into Jedwabne"). Adopting the ironic style of the brothers Laudański, killers of Jedwabne (who mocked Wasersztejn: "Didn't he see and hear a little too much for a teenager?"), the respected history professor comments on the testimony of Awigdor Kochaw, who fled from outside the barn where his family perished: "Would he go back to the barn to listen in on murderers' conversations?"

Strzembosz refers to two witnesses to prove the Germans committed the crime in Jedwabne. The first is Stefan Boczkowski, who lived in Grądy

Małe in 1941; he wrote the professor a letter: "We both walked along with many other locals at some distance behind the tail end of the column of Jews. When they had all been forced into the barn a military truck carrying troops drove up at great speed, and some of the soldiers jumped off the truck while the remaining soldiers quickly started handing the ones on the ground canisters of gasoline, and they started pouring the gasoline in the corners of the barn, also at lightning speed." An army truck, soldiers jumping off, an operation at lightning speed, these are the images that I see, too, after watching so many movies about the war.

Strzembosz doesn't go into why "many other locals" followed the column of Jews and what Stefan Boczkowski, a fifteen-year-old boy from Grądy Małe, was doing in Jedwabne that day. Grądy Małe is four kilometers from Jedwabne; it's one of the villages from which wagons with peasants armed with clubs and sticks set off on the morning of July 10.

The second witness is Apolinary Domitrz from the village Rostki, quoted in an interview for *Życie Warszawy* (Warsaw Life). Domitrz now resides in Greenpoint, the Polish neighborhood in Brooklyn, New York. He says he was grazing cows with two friends in the meadows between Rostki and Jedwabne, about half a kilometer from the barn. When the flames blazed up, they ran to Jedwabne right away. "We rushed across the marketplace. It was quiet, everything was shut down, no one was on the street. And the barn was on fire. So we headed to Cmentarna Street. The Germans were retreating from the heat."

"And the others?"

"What others? There were only Germans. We didn't see a single Pole there. Just us."

Of Gross's book he says: "All one big lie, sir. How could he make all of that up? When a friend and I read it we couldn't believe how anyone could tell lies like that."

The *Warsaw Life* journalist who interviewed Domitrz counters that President Kwaśniewski does not question the guilt of the Poles.

"So was Kwaśniewski there or what? I was there, not him, and I saw what happened."

Strzembosz finds all of this very believable, ignoring the fact that the two accounts contradict each other. If, as Domitrz says, there were "only Germans" at the barn while the Jews were being burned—which in his view, by the way, was their punishment for giving Christ to be put to death, and the only Poles were Apolinary himself with his two friends, then Stefan Boczkowski couldn't have seen what he saw, because he wouldn't have been there. Not to mention that you only have to look at the map to see that Domitrz's tale is topographically implausible. Rostki is two kilometers south of Jedwabne, and the barn was situated on the northeast side of town, about half a kilometer from the market as the crow flies. By now, the accumulated idiocy and unjust accusations flung at Gross have overrun all bounds.

Professor Tomasz Strzembosz is a recognized historian, whose books on the armed underground in Warsaw during World War II are very popular, and he is a social activist. He feels compelled to defend the Poland of the Home Army and the Polish people. "The Jedwabne affair awoke a demon in this traditional Polish patriot," a historian friend of his explains.

That is precisely why all Strzembosz's absurd statements pain me so much. Jerzy Robert Nowak, the prolific anti-Semite who is now writing a book on the "lies of Gross," doesn't bother me as much—I'm prepared to accept that in any case like this there will be a lunatic fringe. Anyway, according to the probability theory of Gauss (who invented the bell curve), without Jerzy Robert Nowak, we wouldn't have on the opposite side of the curve those Polish Catholics who from a profound need of their own, undertook to clean up Jewish graves in the seventies. Still, historians who know Strzembosz say he is not an anti-Semite, and his life's achievements inspire respect and recognition. He is to me the embodiment of what a decent Pole is capable of saying about Jews when the image of his fatherland and his compatriots is at stake.

MAY 14, 2001
Konstancin. Stanisław Ramotowski's birthday. He keeps saying, "God forbid anybody finds out where we are." But at the same time he's a sociable person and he's glad when I bring guests along. He particularly likes my sister, Marysia. This time I've brought my friend Helena Datner-Śpiewak, which turns out to have been a great idea. After a few minutes they're talking like old friends. Helena tells Ramotowski about her father, Szymon Datner. How he fled from the Białystok ghetto to fight the Germans. He managed to join a Russian Jewish partisan group, but had to run away after he and a friend shot two guards. To the end of his life it pained him that he had killed. Soon after the liberation of Białystok, he

became chairman of the District Jewish Committee, as well as, briefly, a member of the Communist town council. He put forward a bill to ban the teaching of German in schools permanently, and the council passed it. But he didn't intend to stay in Poland. He left for Palestine. He came back because he was in love and Helena's future mother didn't want to leave Poland. "Just like my wife—she wouldn't leave, either," Stanisław says, nodding in sympathy.

MAY 15, 2001

A shocking interview with Primate Glemp for the Catholic Information Agency. The primate says that for a long time now the Church has been subjected to a smear campaign aimed at making it apologize for crimes against Jews; Gross's book was clearly written on commission and the massacre in Jedwabne had no religious subtext whatsoever. After which he pulls out a full array of anti-Semitic clichés, including pearls like this: "The Jews were smarter and knew how to exploit the Poles," and "Jews were disliked for their strange folklore." And of course: "Shouldn't the Jews admit that they're guilty toward the Poles, especially for the period of collaboration with the Bolsheviks, their collaboration in the deportations to Siberia, the way they sent Poles to prison?" At the end, the primate says anti-Semitism doesn't exist; however, anti-Polishness does. A commentary the *Gazeta* added to the interview reminds the primate that the Church's anti-Semitism isn't an invention of Gross's, since the pope has previously apologized to Jews for it.

MAY 17, 2001

A phone call from Leszek Dziedzic asking me if I can stop by, because his father, Leon, has come from America for the memorial ceremony. I jump in the car and three hours later I'm in Jedwabne.

Leon Dziedzic—small, slight, shy—sits in the kitchen in a peaked army cap turned back to front. He was fourteen when he was selected to bury the remains of Jews burned in the barn. He knows a great deal about the crime, but it's not easy to talk to him about it. His voice breaks, he tries to hide his tears. I ask him how he explains the crime to himself.

"They needed underwear so they took it from Jews."

Leszek interrupts: "Tell her, Dad, like you told me: they went out killing for a shitty Jewish nightshirt."

Leon Dziedzic says the lust for pillage compounded the anti-Semitism instilled in them in religion class at school: "There were those who were pillars of the church, who carried the banners in religious processions, and then went and ripped open the bellies of Jews. I reminded a neighbor who, no matter what the topic is, always sticks in something nasty about the Jews: 'You yourself pray to a Jew and his Jewish mother.' The neighbor replied, 'Leon, you're an idiot.' And his brother, a priest who happened to be visiting, backed him up. Don't I know Jesus wasn't baptized till he was thirty, and the apostles were Jews? But people around here don't know any religion at all. Before the war I'd eat the matzos my friends brought with them to school. People said there was Christian blood in that matzo, and after the war I got up the nerve to ask Helena Chrzanowska about it. And she said it was all a lot of nonsense."

Leon Dziedzic continues: "Miss Helena had a difficult life here after the war even though she'd been baptized and married a Pole. And yet she never complained, though she did burst into tears once, and said that if she'd known how strong the prejudices were she would never have married, so she wouldn't have children."

I wonder how I might get back in touch with Helena Chrzanowska. Leszek Dziedzic suggests he pay her a visit and try to persuade her to talk to me. If she agrees he'll come back for me.

I ask Leon Dziedzic how he was chosen to remove the bodies after July 10.

"A few days after the massacre they ordered one person from each street in town and from the outskirts to report for duty. They picked young people like me. We tried to figure out who was who, the charred bodies were on top, and toward the bottom they were only slightly singed. When the murderers set the barn on fire, people had all rushed to one air shaft on the east side. They were all piled up. It was impossible to say how many there were, because we'd take out an arm and then a head separately, with pitchforks. We buried them in pieces. Three policemen stood guard over us. There was a lightly singed shoe box, someone picked it up and gold coins fell out. A lot of people started gathering them, but a policeman ordered the money be returned; only one guy, who stuck a coin in his boot, kept it. I picked up a watch and threw it into the grave, because it wasn't mine."

Leon Dziedzic saw freshly shoveled earth across the road from the barn, on the grounds of the Jewish cemetery—a sign that Jews had been buried there, the ones who had been killed separately, not in the group.

He had helped Szmul Wasersztejn twice, the first time toward the end of June 1941, before the massacre: "The Russians had left, the Germans hadn't taken over yet, and the thugs were already gearing up for pogroms. Jews were getting their belongings out and burying them somewhere or leaving them for safekeeping with farmers they knew. Szmul hid his things in a field, in a potato cellar. After a few days it looked as if the situation was calming down and he'd be able to go bring them home safely. I knew Szmul well, so he asked me for help. We went in a wagon and were stopped by three guys in the market square. They hit Szmul, started looking through the clothes, unharnessed the horse and lashed it with the whip, and I got a few lashes, too. Those three later took part in herding the Jews into the marketplace."

Leszek, with some difficulty, gets his father to give me their names: Bolesław Ramotowski, Napoleon Piechocki, and Jerzy Tarnacki.

The second time the Dziedzices helped Szmul was after the massacre.

"I went to the barn to put down straw for the horses and almost stuck him with the pitchfork. I heard a voice: 'Leon, forgive me, it's me, Szmul.' I said, 'Quiet!' because the walls had ears. The lady next door lived with a German and would come over to steal our chickens . . . When dusk fell my mother put on an extra layer of clothes over her regular clothes, to bring to Szmul without anyone noticing, he didn't have anything warm to wear. She said she was going out to feed the dogs; there were eight kids and one of us might let something slip. Later Uncle Klemens brought him to Janczewko, to the Wyrzykowskis."

When Szmul Wasersztejn moved to Białystok immediately after the war, he sent a letter to Leon's mother, asking her to visit him there. He gave her shoe leather for her five sons, and cloth to make dresses for her daughters.

As Leon Dziedzic remembers it, they hid Szmul Wasersztejn right after July 10, 1941, but as I reconstructed his life it became clear to me that Szmul hid with them after the hunt for Jews that took place in the autumn of 1942, and thus a whole year later. Ramotowski in turn insists that Rachela's family were taken to the Radziłów ghetto in 1943, whereas it must have happened much earlier, because by 1943 there was no longer any ghetto in Radziłów. As far as dates and numbers go, you can't rely on anyone.

Leon is hurt because his sister-in-law, wife of the late Klemens, greeted him on this visit with the words "Got a lot of those teeth you took from the Jews?" She knew very well the locals made a practice of searching the bodies of murdered Jews for gold teeth. It's always the same: whenever someone felt compassion for Jews, immediately others sniped that he or she loved Jews because of their riches.

"I gave it to her straight about what my brother-in-law Klemens did back then, because I saw it with my own eyes," continues Leon Dziedzic. "He didn't kill anybody, but he did do some looting. Just before the Germans came, a Jewish family was fleeing on a cart with everything they owned, and he and a friend forced them to get down and they took it all away from them. The Jews continued on foot, in tears."

Leon Dziedzic tells me that some were troubled by the crime committed by their compatriots: "Janek Kalinowski, who had a smithy near the cemetery, was keeping an anvil and tongs there for Szmuił, a smith from Przestrzelska Street. Janek had nothing to do with the Kalinowski who killed Jews. Janek was told by the local killers to take over the workshop equipment. They came to Kalinowski to run a smithy, because the Germans had said the Poles could kill all the Jews as long as all the workshops were manned afterward. I was a guard across the street at a meat co-op, and Janek Kalinowski brought up the story of that equipment many times."

Leszek comes back empty-handed. Miss Helena is sorry but she's very ill.

"She's scared, you've got to understand that," says Leszek. "My dad, too, since they showed him on TV, he's worried they'll burn our house down. I reassured him: 'Dad, if someone's stupid enough to throw money at me, let them go ahead, I'm insured.' I'm not sorry for anything, at least I don't have any illusions about where I live."

MAY 18, 2001
News from Jedwabne. After long negotiations, Biedrzycki agreed to sell the land under the monument back to the government for half the price offered him by Bubel. For fifty thousand zlotys, that is.

A call to Ignatiew. I look through my notes from the Jedwabne trial proceedings again and am unable to figure out why some are convicted and others cleared, though everything points to them all being guilty. Did some of them agree to collaborate with the secret police—there was still a kind of civil war going on in these parts—and so their murder of Jews was swept under the carpet? Ignatiew replies that a journalist can posit any hypothesis, whereas a prosecutor has to have proof. But I hear a note of acknowledgment in his voice.

MAY 22, 2001

Tel Aviv. I ask Uncle Szmulek to help me find the Finkelsztejns of Haifa in the phone book. They lived there in the seventies, when someone was sent by Yad Vashem to record their testimony. Chaja and Izrael were by then already elderly, but perhaps their children are still living? There are several dozen Finkelsztejns in the phone book. Szmulek patiently phones them one by one, engages them in some kind of conversation, but each time he indicates that it is not them. Eventually, after about seven calls, we give up.

MAY 23, 2001

Jerusalem. I cross an empty city from which tourists have vanished because of terrorist attacks. I'm going to see Meir Ronen, who lived in Jedwabne before the war. I got Ronen's contact information from Morgan Ty Rogers, a young New York lawyer who prepared the Internet version of the *Jedwabne Book of Memory*. Ronen is a distant relative of his.

Meir is a delicate, frail man of great elegance, startled by my visit. He hasn't spoken Polish in the last sixty years; he suggests that his son-in-law, who lives nearby, translate from Hebrew to English for him. But it took only a quarter of an hour for him to return to the language that had seemed buried irretrievably in the remotest corners of his memory. I never heard such beautiful Polish spoken in Jedwabne. He has preserved in his memory the names of all the Polish kings and of all the children in his class. And many bitter recollections, such as how toward the end of the thirties, the teacher made Jewish children move to the back rows of the classroom and Polish children stopped speaking to them. I don't have to ask him many questions. For many hours he tells me about his Jedwabne. I listen and see the shtetl that survives only in his memory. He remembers being quite small and his still-living great-grandfather, Nachum Radzik (who is the ancestor he shares with Ty Rogers), telling him his own great-great-grandfather was in the delegation that set out to

Catherine the Great with a petition to grant Jedwabne the status of a city. (In fact, the rights of the city were granted in 1736, but maybe this great-great-grandfather had been in some other delegation to the tsarist court and family legend preserved the story of him helping to found the city with the participation of Catherine the Great herself. In parting he says: "Good night, madam."

MAY 24, 2001

I look on the Internet in the morning and read an article in the *Gazeta* about the preparations for the exhumation.

I remember Ignatiew asking my opinion before I left about whether exhumation was permissible for Jews. I said it wasn't really, but that there are exceptions to the rule. And that if he sought a rabbi who would support an exhumation and be prepared to participate in it, he would surely find one, because in this matter as in most, rabbis have differing views.

Yad Vashem. In the archives I find the memoir of Chaja Finkelsztejn of Radziłów, and also testimonies from nearby Wizna about what happened in Jedwabne, by Izrael Lewin and Awigdor Kochaw. Unfortunately there's nothing from Wąsosz, the village where Poles killed all their Jewish neighbors five days earlier than in Jedwabne.

I spend all day searching for material and making photocopies. Using the archive is expensive, but the worst thing is having to do it myself. Technical tasks were always the bane of my life. And here the photocopier gets stuck every thirty pages or so. It's stuffy, I get pages from different files mixed up, and they're often unnumbered. I try to ask in Russian—the language the young women working in the archive speak with one another—what is written in the last line of one page and the first line of another, to check if they correspond. But they can't help me—they don't know Yiddish.

Chaja Finkelsztejn's testimony and the memoir she deposited have been lying unread in the Yad Vashem archive in Jerusalem, just like her son Menachem's testimony at the Jewish Historical Institute in Warsaw. Not many Polish historians know Yiddish, and perhaps not many contemporary Israeli historians know Yiddish, either. The testimonies of the Holocaust are written in a language that also perished in the Holocaust.

In the evening Uncle Szmulek translates the testimony of Izrael Lewin of Wizna for me; Lewin survived the war in hiding with his wife and two children. In December of last year I was in Zanklewo to look at the buildings where they hid. In Ełk I visited Witek Dobkowski, the son of the farmer who hid them. I've arranged to meet Izrael's children here in Israel; he is no longer alive.

Lewin describes the first days in Wizna after the Soviets left. Józef Gawrychowski, brother of the Wizna village head, who had heard about the pogrom being planned, came to them with the intention of taking them home with him. "He was a good friend of mine," Izrael Lewin wrote. "The Soviets were going to send him to the polar bears in Siberia unless he paid sixty thousand rubles. He came to us in the middle of the night, weeping. I was the kind of Jew who always had money. I went to the cupboard, took out the money, didn't ask for a receipt."

When the Germans came, Wizna was bombed and people slept out on the street. "The village head ordered the Jews of Wizna to move to Jedwabne," Lewin wrote. "The Poles knew that Jews from the small towns were gathering in Jedwabne. One day, on a Wednesday in Tamuz, the day before the massacre, goyim came to Wizna from Jedwabne carrying sticks and went from house to house saying: 'You have two children, send one to Jedwabne with a good stick.'" But Gawrychowski warned the Lewins not to go to Jedwabne and drove them to Łomża. When the Lewin family had moved into the ghetto there, they heard stories about Jews, including many from Wizna, Radziłów, and Stawiski, being burned in the barn in Jedwabne.

"Some got away," he continued, "among them a woman from our town, Rywka Leja Suraski, who went to the doctor's house in Jedwabne and begged the doctor's wife: 'Save me.' The doctor's wife hid her in the stable, threw a pile of straw over her, and covered it with a rag, and Rywka lay there till morning. Her husband was burned with their children. One day Rywka showed up in the ghetto where we were. 'I have my children here,' she said, taking out white bones from her blouse. 'This is Jankiel and Mosze.' Risking her life, she'd gone to the barn and taken the little bones. She was in hiding somewhere, but she would come to the ghetto and show everybody the bones."

The Lewins ended up in the ghetto and before it was liquidated they tried to find a hiding place. Izrael Lewin knocked on the doors of Poles he knew before the war. One of the houses belonged to the Dobkowskis.

"'If you can't do it,' I told Dobkowski, 'I won't blame you. And I'll give you all my property, because the end is coming for us, and I don't want the Germans to get it all.' I gave him several gold rings, a few gems, a gold needle, a gold watch, a couple of lengths of fabric. I kissed his hand. The goy made us a shelter in the cellar, disguised it. That goy was taking a big risk, because this was right in the center of town. After a few weeks he thought we should get some air, and he introduced us to the dogs—they were frightening dogs, but they learned not to bark at us . . . He wouldn't keep Jews for free. He exploited us terribly. My wife looked after the child that had just been born to them, I sewed, they made us do all the kitchen work, including preparing slop for the pigs. We did it all at night."

Once, they were almost thrown out after the Germans came after Sunday Mass to scare the local population.

"They said: 'We came to your country to rid you of Jews. When you needed a quart of gasoline, they took one of your chickens. Things are beginning to change now. But there are still a lot of Jews in the parish. You're sheltering your own enemies. When we find a Jew, we will burn the property and shoot everybody, so any farmer who hides Jews will rot in a grave with them.' The lady who was sheltering us came back and yelled at her husband: 'You bastard, as soon as we laid eyes on them I said, Shut the door and put the chain on it!' and she hit him. We heard every word. The children understood everything and cried. Then his mother came in, saying: 'It was settled when you took them in.' She said there was hope because the front was coming closer. She always acted as our advocate. She'd say: 'If you let them go, the Germans will catch them and they'll have to say where they were hiding, and we'll all be lost.' If there's a life after death, may his mother be held in reverence there."

In 1944 the front line moved closer to Wizna and the village was evacuated. Each member of the family set off alone to look for some work on a farm in the area, pretending not to be Jewish. Izrael grew a handlebar mustache and went to farms offering his services as a tailor. The Russians were already on the far banks of the Narew and Lewin knew it was a matter of a week—if he could last that long, he knew he'd get through it. He was taken on at another farm. "The woman brought out her fabric. I told her I'd cut everything first and then start sewing. I was thinking: if she starts to suspect I'm Jewish but all the cloth is already cut, she might think it'd be a pity to throw me out. There was enough sewing for a month. And when I finished and she had a shirt for her husband and a vest for herself, she didn't think about whether I was Jewish, but about what a good job I'd done."

Izrael's wife, Chaszka Fejga, also took part in the interview at Yad Vashem. She recounted how they returned to their home when the war had ended. "I went by to see a non-Jewish woman I knew, to ask her for a frying pan. Her husband was in the Home Army. She said to me: 'If you want to live, run away, they're coming for you.' My husband wanted to stay in Wizna, but I said: 'No way. We've been through so much, we kept ourselves alive, and now we're going to let a Home Army soldier come and take it all away from us?' So we left."

MAY 25, 2001

I read on the Internet that the grounds surrounding the barn site in Jedwabne have been covered with green netting and put under police guard. It is forbidden to go near or take pictures. Archaeologists, prosecutor Ignatiew, and Rabbi Schudrich are on the spot. The rabbi's comments are quoted: "Exhumation is forbidden in Judaism, but I understand this decision." His openness is impressive; I know he is among the opponents of the exhumation.

In the section for the Righteous Among the Nations, I look for testimonies from Jedwabne, Radziłów, Wąsosz. Once again there is nothing from Wąsosz.

An afternoon in Tel Aviv, where I arranged to meet Izrael Lewin's daughter, formerly Tereska. Ida Sarna is now a retired bank director.

She tells me about her escape from the ghetto. "Father didn't want to go. He said, 'May what comes to everyone come to me, too.' Mother thought you couldn't go off into the unknown with a sick child (I suffered from chronic arthritis). But I tugged my parents' sleeves, begged them, swore I'd be strong enough. I was the one in our family who wanted to live. I don't remember thinking even once during the war that I was going to die."

She tells me about her time in hiding: "As soon as we crossed the threshold at Bolesław Dobkowski's house you could tell right away it was a decent house, because there weren't any things stolen from Jews in it. I doubt I'd have the courage he had to hide us. Their children didn't know we were Jewish, they thought we were American cousins, and they couldn't let anyone find out about us because America had declared war on

Germany. Lent came and from the attic I heard people from the whole village gathering near the Dobkowski house, singing, 'Jesus crucified by the Jews, Jesus sold for thirty silver pieces, Jesus betrayed by the traitor Judas.' You heard it everywhere before the war: 'They killed God and then made sure they lived better than the Poles.' Father kept track of when Pesach was, and Yom Kippur, and observed the holidays. I didn't want to. I was furious that I was Jewish."

Ida Sarna Lewin goes on: "In 1944 the front line came close, the village was evacuated, and from then on we had to manage on our own, without a hiding place. I went to work for the Germans. I wore a shawl on my head like a Polish peasant woman, because my hair was red. But at least my eyes were blue. The Germans didn't think there were any Jews left, so they weren't suspicious, and we didn't know about Auschwitz or Treblinka, so we weren't so terribly afraid."

Of the period after the war: "Father went on working as a tailor in Łódź, at 27 Wschodnia Street. We left in 1950. We were scared to live in Poland under Soviet occupation. We already knew what the Russians were like from spending two years with them in Wizna at the start of the war."

Ida Sarna Lewin has never gone back to visit Poland, because she was always afraid of what might happen to her there.

"I go to an exercise class for stress reduction, and when we are instructed to imagine something very pleasant, I imagine the view from the attic at Dobkowski's, where we were sometimes allowed to climb and breathe fresh air—the fields, greenery, lake, sky. I'd like so much to see that view again, but I'm still scared. My grandma was killed in a pogrom in Wizna. There was no Gestapo or SS there, just a few Wehrmacht soldiers and Poles who'd been given vodka by the Germans. And how many Jews did the Poles kill after the war?"

Members of my own family, from Skryhiczyn, a village situated on the Bug in southeastern Poland, have told me many times of the affection and longing they feel for the Polish landscape.

My uncle Monio, or Mosze Anaf, who right before the war spent four years in kibbutzes in Kielce and Warsaw preparing to emigrate to Palestine, visited Skryhiczyn many times and encouraged his cousins to emigrate.

They kept telling him: Look at our Bug River, look at our forests, in

Palestine there's nothing but sand, swamps, and mountains. "If it hadn't been for their fondness for Skryhiczyn, they would have survived," Monio said to me sadly, years later. When he settled in Rosh Pina, a little town in the Galilee hills, he brought raspberry shoots, wild strawberries, and lilies of the valley back from Poland for his garden, where the branches of fig, mandarin, orange, avocado, and every kind of olive intertwined.

Uncle Avinoa Hadasz from the Kinneret kibbutz once took me to the bank of the Jordan, a place where pilgrims poured out of buses pulled up to the side of the road and washed their feet under three-hundred-meter-tall eucalyptus trees. "This land belongs to the kibbutz," Avinoa told me. "Here we sell bottles of Jordan water, because the Christians believe Christ was baptized here. Father always took me here when I was little. We came to swim, catch fish, have important conversations. My father planted these trees, and I helped him. Father chose this river bend because it reminded him of a bend in the Bug near Skryhiczyn."

MAY 26, 2001
I've arranged to meet Ida Sarna Lewin's brother Izaak Lewin, a retired army driver.

He tells me Witek Dobkowski, son of the farmer who hid him, is now his best friend. "He spends several months a year here with me. I visit them. In Israel, Witek sometimes comes to the synagogue with me, and when I'm in Poland, I go to church with him."

I ask Izaak how he can bear hearing his close friend saying Germans killed the Jews in Jedwabne, and that Jews denounced Poles to the Soviets.

"I'm ashamed to tell him it was the Poles who did it. It would hurt him, and after all, without his parents, I wouldn't be talking to you now."

He tells me how he stumbled on a meeting in Jedwabne on February 17, 1945.

"I was headed for Wizna on foot. People were gathering for a meeting, because they were about to elect a village head. They were shouting at each other, 'Not him, he collaborated with the Germans!'; 'Not him, he collaborated with the Soviets!' They were at each other's throats. No one stood up, no one said a terrible tragedy had taken place here. I thought, Not my cart, not my horse, and took off as fast as I could go."

After the war the Lewin family moved to Łódź. On a tram Izaak heard someone say: "Damn, there are still so many Jews around." The next day a military Jeep pulled up next to him; they were questioning the passersby about something. He suddenly realized these Polish-speaking soldiers in British uniform must be Jews from the Palestine brigades. He ran up to them. They were organizing the Bricha—the underground effort that facilitated the illegal emigration of Jews from Eastern Europe to Palestine. By 1946 he made it there.

Like most survivors, he didn't talk about what he'd been through in Poland. "We were happy being in this country. I didn't tell my children anything, so they would be healthy and normal. Until Witek came to visit I didn't know I could still speak Polish. It was only when I took the children to Poland, and by that time they were grown up, that I told them how I'd survived."

For six years he has come to Jedwabne every July 10.

"When I went back to Wizna for the first time, I stood on the spot where the old temple had been. There's a house there now. Its owner came out: 'I bought it, I can show you the papers.' He thought I wasn't there to look but to take it away from him. When I go to Jedwabne I remove the weeds at the monument, I bring paint and repaint the fence in the colors of the State of Israel—blue and white—and I say a prayer, though I'm not religious."

The way the Lewin siblings tell the story of their time in hiding differs in essential details.

Izaak says he was friends with Witek and played with him. Ida says they didn't play with anyone, just sat quietly in the dark with their legs pulled up. When they went into any of the rooms, it was only to do some kind of housework, not to play, and it was always at night, when the Dobkowski children were asleep.

In Izaak's version, the priest knew where they were hiding. He knew their father, who had sewn him his cassock before the war. When Bolesław Dobkowski went to confession, the priest told him: "Those people must survive," and each time he passed on his greetings to them. In Ida's version the priest reminded his flock in his sermons not to hide Jews, because the Germans would not only kill the whole family in retribution but burn down the village, too. Dobkowski's wife returned from church in tears and shaken.

Ida claims Izaak, who is several years her junior, was too young, he doesn't have his own memories, he erased everything from his memory when he came to Israel. He's spent a lot of time with Witek and only knows what Witek told him. It seems that Ida preserves Jewish memory and Izaak acquired Polish memory.

In the afternoon Szmulek and I drive to Yehud to meet Awigdor Kochaw. He greets us with a rant against my boss for his article in *The New York Times* (the same one that appeared in the *Gazeta*). He speaks pretty good Polish, sometimes interjecting English words.

"I read on the Internet that Mr. Michnik called Poland a heroic nation and praised the Poles for how they helped the Jews. Is that all he has to say about Jedwabne?"

I try to protest that that is not the only thing Michnik or the *Gazeta* have to say about Jedwabne, but Kochaw doesn't let me finish.

"I wouldn't have agreed to see you. We're only talking because I didn't want to offend your uncle."

After two hours Kochaw's gracious wife asks us firmly to stop. Kochaw has throat cancer and is undergoing chemotherapy, he's between the first and second sessions of radiation. To the pain of remembering is added the physical pain of speech.

MAY 27, 2001

Back to see Kochaw in Yehud. This time I went alone. Szmulek gave me directions for a shortcut and told me to follow the signs. However, at one fork in the road the place names were only in Hebrew and Arabic. I was late, which is something I really can't stand.

Kochaw returns several times to a story about Chonek Kubrzański, who stood up against his tormenters in the marketplace on July 10. He refused to carry the statue of Lenin and they beat him with sticks until he collapsed.

"Not everybody went like sheep, as people say," he comments. He tells me of his wartime life with pride and spirit, but also as if he were answering some kind of unspoken reproach, as if the victims should be ashamed of their defenselessness. This is a problem many Jews struggled with after the Holocaust. I myself remember discussions with my Haifa uncle, Pinio, or Pinchas Rottenberg, who left for Palestine before the war. I was furious that he could consider it unworthy that people go to their deaths without resisting, holding their mother or child in an embrace.

I tell him that exhumations are under way in Jedwabne, but that when I called there I heard they may be called off as a result of rabbis protesting. "Why would those *Moshki* decide about the exhumation?" Kochaw rages. "I call rabbis *Moshki* because of the Zionist upbringing I received in Poland, at a secular Zionist school in Wizna. *Moshki* was a derogatory word Poles used for Jews, and I use it for the rabbis."

In the evening, Szmulek and I start calling the next Finkelsztejns in the phone book. Again in vain.

"Here the 'blacks' are always protesting against exhumations," I'm told by Szmulek, who like Kochaw does not attempt to hide his dislike of Orthodox Jews. "We couldn't build a single highway in this country if we listened to them."

MAY 28, 2001

Five-thirty in the morning. I'm leaving with Izaak Lewin to celebrate Shavuot at a farm cooperative with which he has friendly relations.

"Look." He proudly points out the Bank Leumi building we pass on the way. "My mother, when she went to synagogue in Radziłów, put a kopeck into the blue tin for the purchase of land in Palestine. That money built this bank."

He tells me about his mother. From the time the Germans took his two brothers from the Łomża ghetto to be shot, she kept saying there was no God, but she still kept kosher. When they fled the ghetto, they went to see a friendly farmer in Kramkowo. The farmer didn't want to keep them there, but he changed his mind when his mother showed him a gold ring. Just one night; the next morning he told them to move on. "What, a fat ring like that for one night?" his mother raged. When he refused to give it back, she smacked him in the face and took it away from him. In November 1944, when the front shifted, she was commandeered as a Pole to cook for the frontline troops. A Ukrainian realized she was Jewish. She warned him, "If you denounce me I'll tell them we know each other because you had a Jewish woman as a lover, and they'll kill us both." After that he stayed well away from her. At the very end of 1944, she made it to Królewiec with the retreating German army. She got her hands on a sled, loaded it with clothes, down quilts, and food, and made her way to Wizna on foot, pulling the sled for more than a hundred kilometers through the snow.

We pass Haifa and soon reach our destination, a *moshav*, or farm cooperative. The loudspeakers blast Israeli disco music. Everybody is dressed up, even the tractors are decorated: they do a "dance of the tractors" in front of the stage. "In the course of the past year," we hear over the ne, "our *moshav* delivered eleven million liters of milk from ndred cows, and one million four hundred and fifty thousand

: "Our agriculture holds first place in the world for productivity re, and we have a space program, too. Many people in Poland gine how well we live here. Look at how healthy our young e! Jewish children never looked like that before the war. Before vhat were we? Nobody. And now we're creating a healthy, pure- le."

muster much enthusiasm for any form of nationalism, but Lewin ch optimism and warmth that I can't bring myself to object. e way back I tell Izaak about my meetings with Kochaw.
dor doesn't like Poland," Izaak comments. "When I talk about say some critical things, so people here won't take me for a trai- ostly I say good things. My friends wonder why I go there. I them that I love the river there, the forest, the river path, the houses where Jews used to live. I tell them about the symbolic monument in the forest at Giełczyn dedicated to the memory of three thousand murdered Jews from the Łomża ghetto, two of my elder brothers among them, and the sixteen thousand Poles who perished in wartime in that area. They don't believe it. 'But the Poles helped the Germans kill Jews, what did the Germans have against the Poles?' they ask me. My heart is torn. I feel for Poland, she hurts me and yet I long for her. We lived alongside Poles, my childhood was spent there. I knew some good Poles: Gawrychowski, the village head before the war, to him my dad was a citizen just like any other. If there had been more like him, a few more Jewish children would have lived, and look how many children came from those children! I have *seventeen* children and grandchildren. But I also saw what the Poles did. I grew up playing with Poles, but in 1941 our good neighbor Parnas came looking for our father to kill him and take over the other half of the house. When a Jew was wandering in the forest, Poles would catch him and take him to the Gestapo or kill him themselves. Papa gave lengths of cloth to his best Polish acquaintance, you could say friend,

for safekeeping. One day when we were in hiding we got on Dobkowski's cart to go get those linens and bring them back with us. Instinct saved us—he was taking a bit too long to get the stuff so we drove the horse off at the last minute, when we were already being surrounded by people trying to catch us."

Izaak tells me about his visit to Wizna a few years ago.

"Every single person there says to me, 'We hid Jews,' 'We helped,' 'We gave food,' and I just think to myself, But no one survived, so where are those people you saved? I don't want to think about it and people shouldn't write about it."

In the afternoon, Ruta, my cousin Igal Bursztyn's wife, takes me along for a meeting with a friend, an older lady from New York. Ann Kellerman remembers the school she attended in Vienna in the thirties. One day they made the Jewish girls move to the back rows. At first their friends kept turning around to them from the front rows. They were reprimanded severely. When that didn't help, the teachers rapped their knuckles with a ruler, and they left a row of empty desks between the Jewish and Austrian girls. After three days the Austrian girls stopped noticing their Jewish friends. When they knocked into one of the Jewish girls running during recess, they didn't say sorry; they didn't speak to them when they ran into them on the street.

"We ceased to exist for them."

I tell her that I heard a similar story a few days ago in Jerusalem, about being moved to the back rows and a feeling of alienation from former friends. It was about a school in Jedwabne.

MAY 29, 2001

Off to Jerusalem to meet Meir Ronen.

"After your visit I couldn't sleep for three nights, because everything came back to me," he says in greeting. He spent those days at the computer, where he tried to make an Excel sheet for me of who died in Jedwabne and where they lived. It is titled "List of Jewish Families Burned by Neighbors in Jedwabne." The list starts in the New Market with Abram Ibram, who lived on the front side with his daughter and son-in-law. On Łomżyńska Street there was Chawa Alenberg, on Przytulska, Szolem Atłasowicz. Altogether there are more than a hundred names preserved in Ronen's memory.

"You're surprised I remember so many people?" Ronen says. "I remember every stone in Jedwabne."

MAY 30, 2001

I phone Stanisław Ramotowski in the morning to hear how he is feeling. He tells me about a kaddish said for the Jews of Jedwabne on Sunday, three days ago, in the Warsaw Church of All Saints on Grzybowski Square. He watched the reports on TV and must have been moved, because he complains that if I'd been in Poland, we would have gone there together. When I proposed to him before my departure that a friend of mine could take him, he snorted that he'd been in enough churches in his life.

I only saw a report on the Internet, but I can easily imagine the impression made by the sight of fifty bishops, led by Primate Glemp, clad in penitential purple. And the words spoken by Bishop Gądecki, as an introduction to the liturgy of penance: "As pastors of the Church in Poland we wish to stand in truth before God and His people, and especially before our Jewish brothers and sisters, regarding with sorrow and remorse the crime that took place in July 1941 in Jedwabne and elsewhere. Its victims were Jews, and among the perpetrators were Poles and Catholics, persons who had been baptized. In Jedwabne, and wherever any man inflicted cruel violence on another, it was God who was most grievously wronged."

Back at Yad Vashem. In the corridors I meet Professor Szewach Weiss, the current Israeli ambassador to Poland, for many years chairman of the board of the Yad Vashem museum. We talk about the inscription on the monument in Jedwabne, which has just been made public: *In memory of the Jews of Jedwabne and surroundings, men, women, children, fellow stewards of this land, murdered and burned alive in this place on July 10, 1941. A warning to posterity that the sin of hatred incited by German Nazism should never again turn the residents of this land against one another.*

Weiss expresses his opposition to the inscription sharply: "What does that mean, 'against one another'? It means the victim is guilty, too. I'm also appalled by the content of the inscription—it leaves out who committed the atrocity, which may make sense, given that the Institute of

National Remembrance hasn't yet completed its investigation, but the second sentence sounds extremely evasive."

I look in on Professor Izrael Gutman, who heads the International Institute for Holocaust Research at Yad Vashem. I tell him about my conversation with Kochaw, and how tormented he seemed by memories.

"I saw a picture of him in the newspaper," he tells me, "in his living room, with an old photo of a synagogue somewhere in eastern Poland on the wall. I would never hang a photograph like that in my house. For some Israelis the shadow of the past presses on every moment of their lives. For others, working to build the country was therapeutic, and they manage to be happy despite their memories. I am a good example of this. For twenty years I was a member of a kibbutz and felt and lived the life of my country to the hilt. That gives me strength."

I ask him if he knew before Gross's book who committed the massacre in Jedwabne.

"I didn't know. We treat the testimonies of survivors with reserve; usually they could only have seen part of the events they describe, the rest they add from hearsay. I relied on Szymon Datner's article of 1966, where I read that the Germans committed the crime on those lands in the summer of 1941, with the collaboration of local thugs. When I read the same text again recently, I saw you could easily read the truth between the lines. We made a mistake, and I feel guilty. I didn't believe the people of a small town could be capable of a crime like that. I thought the indifference, the willingness to denounce Jews, was specific to larger cities," continues Gutman, who during the war was in the Warsaw Ghetto and then in Auschwitz. "I thought none of that applied to little towns where Jankiel and Mosze were neighbors you knew well. It turns out it was precisely in little towns like that that the anti-Semitism instilled before the war reached its most extreme form."

In the Yad Vashem café I meet with Professor Aron Wein, chief editor of *Pinkas Hakehillot*, a commemorative book of Jewish communities in many volumes. I ask Wein why his encyclopedia doesn't say what really happened in Jedwabne and other towns.

"From the testimonies I read it was clear that the local population had a part in killing Jews in June and July 1941. When I was editing I wrote 'mob,' because I didn't know exactly if there were also Belorussians or Lithuanians in that part of Poland, and I didn't want to insult the Polish people."

I hear there's a former resident of Jedwabne, who left during the Soviet occupation, now living in the kibbutz named Kibbutz of the Ghetto Fighters, near Haifa.

Szmulek phones the kibbutz. Sadly, Meir Paparle died two years ago, and his daughter knows nothing of her father's native town. But Szmulek has a four-volume book of recollections of the founders of the kibbutz and promises to find me Paparle's story.

MAY 31, 2001

In Yehud I visit first Kochaw and then Jakow Cofen vel Geva, who lives one street away in a lovely house with a garden. His name was Jakub Pecynowicz, but like many Polish Jews he changed it to a Hebrew name after arriving in Israel. The Pecynowiczes owned a mill in Jedwabne, and it was they who hosted Kochaw's family after they had been thrown out of Wizna. He speaks Polish hesitantly, searching for words.

On September 1, 1939, the Pecynowiczes fled town before the advancing German army. They had made it to Zawady in the direction of Tykocin when the Germans crossed the Narew River and surrounded the town. They drove the refugees—among them many Poles from Jedwabne as well as from Wizna, Radziłów, Szczyczyn, Grajewo—into the church. The Germans abused the Jews, pulled their beards, made them clean up excrement with their hands, threw chocolate into the rubbish and then made them eat it under threat of being shot. They chased all of them out into a fenced field. The Jews were to build a shelter, but only the Poles were allowed to stand under it. The Jews stood all night—they weren't allowed to sit, it was raining. Toward morning the Germans ordered the Poles to carry out a pogrom. Pecynowicz, frozen to the bone, went up to some Poles he knew for a moment, to warm up. He heard one of them arguing they should hold back from the pogrom, with others still undecided gathering around him.

"But some other Poles went to work, grabbing our arms, legs, stripping off our shoes and pants, and then the undecided ones joined in, too. One Jew resisted his coat being taken off, and a German helped a Pole undress him, jabbing the Jew with a knife."

When he got home, the neighbors had already managed to carry off all his belongings.

"That crippled guy Stanisław Sielawa took most of what we had. My brother went to him: 'Just give me back two pots so we can make ourselves something to eat.' And then the Soviets came."

In the first weeks before the mill was taken from them they paid the representatives of the new authorities in millet, barley, and buckwheat. Jakow Geva thinks that's why they weren't put on the deportation list. But how could they imagine it could save all their lives?

"I was the only one who survived, and I had a sister who had ten children. They took me into the army and that's how I stayed alive. In Russia I got a letter from home saying everything was fine with them. I went with the Soviet army as far as Georgia, Azerbaijan. There were nineteen Poles in the company apart from me. They got packages and shared them among themselves, but they never treated me."

When he returned to Poland in 1945 on a Russian repatriation train, there were Jews at the stations warning him not to go home because Poles would kill him. And telling him they had to stick together, because when anyone found a Jew on his own, they'd throw him off the train and shoot him.

"I was afraid to look around in Jedwabne. I was afraid to separate from my friends. We arrived at the seaside, in Szczecin. When we got off the train, stones were thrown at us, but a delegation from a kibbutz showed up right away and told us we could join them and emigrate to Palestine."

He made his way by a circuitous route across half of Europe and was almost in Palestine when the British caught him just off the coast. He was sent to a camp on Cyprus, where he spent two years. While there he heard what had happened in Jedwabne. He worked maintaining the gardens. Eventually he moved to the settlement where he lives to this day: Kiryat Białystok. The settlement was built for Jews from the Białystok region who arrived after the Holocaust, by Jews from the Białystok region who emigrated before the war.

JUNE 1, 2001
Yehud. My last meeting with Kochaw. Every meeting takes the same course. Kochaw talks until his wife interrupts us. Again and again, always

with slightly different details, he tells me about the Jews of Wizna, how they were massacred, partly in Wizna, partly in Jedwabne, and how he passed for a Pole in order to survive. Listening to him I feel as if he has recorded his recollections on a memory loop, played back to himself hundreds of times, and is now reading back to me a text already fixed in his head. He speaks under such strain that I don't dare interrupt him with questions. Only when he stops do you see how exhausted he is.

Once again Szmulek and I call a bunch of Finkelsztejns. Finally we find Menachem Finkelsztejn's widow. She speaks good Polish. I learn that her husband graduated from the Technion here and was a construction engineer. No, she can't tell me anything about his experiences during the war. When I press her, she cuts me off:

"I know nothing. Do you think I'm stupid? I survived the war in Poland, too, hiding in bunkers, forests; I saw things. We never told each other about it. We never spoke a word of Polish to each other. Neither our son nor our two daughters know anything, because my husband never talked to them about it."

I hear that her sister-in-law Chana, Chaja's youngest daughter, is alive, but the two women aren't in touch.

I tell Szmulek about my Jerusalem encounters with Meir Ronen, how vividly he remembers Jedwabne, though he never visited it after the war, and the Polish language, which he never used after the war.

"I remember Skryhiczyn only too well," says Szmulek. "I'd like to forget it but I can't. I had family there, friends—Polish, Jewish, Ukrainian. I didn't want to go when our cousin Pinio organized a trip in the eighties. Somebody might think I'd come to take his land away. In recent years a lot of Poles have started coming to Israel. They work illegally here, you hear Polish spoken in the street, and I feel close to them somehow, I like to hear them talk, though their Polish is a bit different from the language I knew. When a person lives far from where he was born, he always feels like a branch grafted onto another tree. Even when the graft was successful."

6

If I'd Been in Jedwabne Then

or, The Story of Meir Ronen, Exiled to Kazakhstan

"I, Meir Ronen, born in Jedwabne on February 20, 1926, left the town for good in April 1941. I attended an elementary school named for Adam Mickiewicz, the great Polish poet, who wrote, 'Many played the cymbals / But none dared play before Jankiel.' We had a wooden house on Przytulska Street. Forests all around and the rivers Narew and Biebrza. The landscapes were beautiful, but they were the only good thing . . .

"Our family lived there for generations. I remember a lot of family stories about the time before World War I. Jedwabne had a developed textile industry then, and two of my uncles were smugglers; they'd cross the border at Kolno, smuggling gloves and hats.

"My father, Symcha Grajewski, graduated from the gymnasium before World War I. He had excellent Polish, as well as Russian, Hebrew, German. He was in the Polish Legions, and in the war of 1920 he fought for Polish independence against the Bolsheviks. He had an iron shop and a writing service. He also gave lessons to children in whatever subject they needed. He helped organize the Union of Reservists' parade in Jedwabne and went on picnics in the woods with them. There was dancing, singing, marching exercises, the fire brigade orchestra played, conducted by an organ player who was also the sexton.

"Father wrote letters for people, all kinds of applications to the courts and authorities. Wasilewski, who later became an assistant to Mayor

Elementary school class. Jedwabne, 1933. The school was attended by Polish and Jewish children. Meir Grajewski (later Meir Ronen), first row, third from right; his elder sister Fajga behind him in a polka-dot dress. In the back row, three boys who survived the war in hiding with Antonina and Aleksander Wyrzykowski: second from left, Szmul Wasersztejn; third, Mosze Olszewicz; fourth, Jankiel Kubrzański. Also in the photo: Butcher Nornberg's daughter, in the second row, fourth from left. Meir Stryjakowski, grandson of Jedwabne rabbi Awigdor Białostocki, is standing in the back row second from right. The photo also shows children from the Zajdensztat, Zimny, Jedwabiński, and Kamionowicz families. (Courtesy of Meir Ronen)

Karolak under the Germans, opened an office to compete with him. He hung out a sign: POLISH LETTER-WRITING BUREAU. In Kajetanów, Mierzejewski and Górski were on trial, and Wasilewski wrote to the Stawiski court on their behalf. The defendant and the plaintiff came to court with the same letters. The same ink, the same style, almost the same contents, just the one thing in which they differed—their names—was different. The court rejected them outright and laughed at them. Then they went back to my father. They had spent a lot of money on lawsuits, so Mierzejewski's daughter came to us and asked my father to reconcile them. Father met with Górski and asked him how much he would cede to Mierzejewski. He said, nothing. Then he asked Mierzejewski the same thing. He was told, not a button. They paid my father five zlotys, but who could advise them? The Mierzejewskis lost everything in those court cases, and they owed a lot to Abram Zajdensztadt, who had loaned them money.

"Before the war a lot of Poles owed Jews money and so they made sure they didn't have to pay off their debts.

"In the middle of the marketplace there were the town hall, two wells, and a few chestnut trees. In May we used to go catch mayflies. First the school was on Sadowa Street, then it moved. They built a new school building behind the mill, all modern, with central heating and a parquet floor. People came to Jedwabne in trucks from Warsaw and Königsberg to buy farm produce, and there were also two squares for selling livestock. On Wednesday, market day, it was hard to get through, so many people were out trading.

"On Tuesday toward evening, people started chasing geese and pigs out to the marketplace. A lot of Jews traded grain, selling it all the way to East Prussia. Białystok Jews came for flour. Shoemakers, coopers, wheelwrights were all Jews, but among blacksmiths you had Poles as well.

"We didn't have any Hasids at all. Only the rabbi wore sidelocks, and no one wore a tallit. In that region the Lithuanian Jews were very pious, they wore beards and hats, but I don't remember any of them ever settling in Jedwabne. During Jewish holidays you felt a celebratory atmosphere in town, whole families—at that time six children wasn't a lot—walked across the market square to the synagogue, which was on Szkolna. There was an eternal Babel in the market, Polish and Yiddish mixed together, and on Yom Kippur, it was quiet as the grave. And when the Catholic holidays came, Jews tried not to show themselves in the street, because a lot of people came into town from the villages then, often drunk.

"The state holiday of November 11 was celebrated by both Poles and Jews; there was a special Mass in church and prayers in the synagogue. On the birthday of Marshal Piłsudski, the first chief of state in independent Poland, schoolchildren gathered in the marketplace and Mayor Walenty Grądzki spoke from a podium. We went to temple with little flags to pray for the marshal, and I remember the mayor and police commander Bielecki participating in the synagogue prayers.

"Quite a few Jewish organizations were active in town, but there weren't many Jewish Communists. At night they would hang out red flags, and once on May 1 they released doves painted red. Commander Bielecki, who was friendly with my father, observed who didn't go to synagogue on Shabbat and arrested them for Communist activity. Because what sort of Jew wouldn't go to synagogue on Shabbat?

"Marshal Piłsudski kept a firm hold on the nationalists, because he had a conscience. When he died on May 12, 1935, every Jewish home in Jedwabne hung out a red-and-white flag; so did many Polish homes, but far from all. Later they put a monument to Piłsudski in the New Market, which was then taken away by the Soviets. After the marshal's death, my father's colleagues in the Reservists Union said to him: 'We don't need Jews in our union.' I can still see my father tossing his Legion cap into the stove. He was still friends with some Poles: Dr. Kowalczyk, the butcher Kozłowski, Chodnicki, Białoszewski, and Śleszyński, who later gave his barn to burn the Jews.

"In 1937, a pogrom was being organized in Jedwabne. Rabbi Białostocki and Jona Rotszyld, my uncle, went to see the priest and he promised there wouldn't be any pogrom. My uncle had an iron shop, and they bought everything for the construction of the church in Jedwabne cheap in his shop, and he'd give the church something as an offering sometimes, too. Not long after that he left for Palestine and took my sister with him.

"Our Polish neighbors were the Polkowskis and the Ostrowskis. Ryszard Ostrowski, the policeman's son, used to come over to visit me, and my sister had Polish friends over, most often Śleszyński's daughter. Then there was the driver's son on the Prusowa estate, who had a terrible stutter; in our house he stopped stuttering because we showed him warmth. After school I went to Hebrew school and the driver's son waited at our house for me to come back and help him with his homework. I was five when my parents sent me to the cheder, but the rabbi who taught there had a horse whip and after he whipped me once I didn't go back. Then one of my uncles brought over Alter Wiski, a teacher from Wołkowysk, who set up a private modern school, where we went after Polish school.

"The new school had rows of desks, not a common table like at the cheder, and they taught us to write Hebrew. We Jewish kids didn't go to Polish school on Saturdays, which was not at all to the liking of the teacher, Skupniewski. But what irritated him most was that we always had our homework done on Monday. After Shabbat, Polish kids would come over to our house—they liked being treated to challah—and brought us their notebooks. If I went sledding on a Saturday my uncle would drag me home by the ear.

"I went to school without a cap but there were Jewish kids in Jedwabne who never went anywhere without their heads covered. After Piłsudski's death, people started kicking them out of school for wearing yarmulkes. When we started school, there were thirty to forty Jewish children, and when I finished the sixth grade in 1939, there were only five of us left. When we spoke Yiddish to each other after 1935, the school head Skarżyński would say: 'Get out of this school, you're jabbering in Yiddish.'

"In the beginning we sat together with Polish children at school. I sat in the first row, otherwise I couldn't see the blackboard; nobody in Jedwabne had spectacles at that time. One day a teacher made a fuss about a Jewish boy sitting up front. Then all Jews were told to move to the back of the class. The desks were for two, but we had to sit three at a desk. The teachers addressed us all the same way: 'Moshek to the blackboard.' Once when I didn't get up, the teacher said to me, 'I'm talking to you.' I replied that my name was Meir, not Moshek, and he threw me out of the classroom.

"In the sixth grade, when we sat at the back, teachers didn't correct our homework, and didn't call us to the blackboard, unless it was to chew us out. We were strangers to the class. Polish children didn't talk to us. Teachers would send us home because our ears were dirty or they spotted a flea on one of us. In those times kids had a lot of fleas, Polish kids just as much, but they were never sent home for it.

"After school we had to walk home, and that wasn't always easy. Village boys waited for us, attacked us, beat us. We found a way around, behind the estate where there was a pond, bogs, and meadows. You had to walk fast over a narrow path in order not to fall into the bog. Once, the boys saw us and chased us, but one of them fell into a bog. He began to sink in, but we went back and held out a pole for him. Then they stopped harassing us, because we'd saved the boy from drowning.

"In the spring of 1939 they were putting fresh plaster up in the classroom. While I was standing guard, the youngest Śleszyński girl slammed the door in a nasty sort of way so the plaster fell off. The head, Skupniewski, said: 'Moshek, it's your fault. Go and kneel in the corner.' For me that meant kneeling before the cross that hung there. I said, 'I'm of the Jewish faith and I cannot kneel before the cross.' 'Get out of this school!' he shouted. 'And don't come back!'

"In that last school year of 1938 to '39, not a single Jewish child received a report card.

"When the Germans arrived in September 1939, relations between Poles and Jews were very chilly. Young boys robbed Jews, beat them, ran after Germans, pointed out the *Jude,* but they didn't kill anybody.

"After the Russians came, there began to be shortages of everything: salt, gas, sugar. There were only ration cards. Before the new authorities forbade anyone from having a shop and introduced co-ops, the Russians would barge into Jewish shops and take everything they wanted without paying. Before the war, no matter how bad the Poles were, they still allowed us to go to temple on Shabbat and Jewish shops could close for the day. The Russians ordered us to work and send children to school on Shabbat. They threatened us that if a Jewish child didn't go to school on a Saturday, one of his parents would go to jail. Jews tried to keep a low profile under the Soviets, because they were scared.

"During the Soviet occupation five Jewish louts threw their weight around.

"The first guy, Eli Krawiecki, had a shoemaker's workshop. He would sew pieces of leather together for the shoemaker to make shoes out of them. He was the smartest of them, at least he had a skill. Under the Soviets he had no official function, but he led everything from behind the wings. The Poles later inflicted a cruel death on him: after the Russians had fled, Poles cut his tongue out and left him to die in agony.

"Chaim Kosacki: his father was a butcher, but he was a bum, he didn't do anything. When the Germans arrived, the Poles delivered Kosacki to them and they shot him that same day.

"Abraham Dawid Kubrzański later died in the barn.

"Szajn Binsztejn was in jail for three years before the war for raping a girl. He was a real outlaw. In the synagogue, he was only allowed to stand behind the stove, and only when there was hardly anybody left, when they needed ten to make a minyan, then they'd take him.

"Mechajkał Wajnsztajn was the only one of the five to survive the war. They ruled the town in the first weeks before Soviet authorities established themselves. Their boss was a true Communist, the Pole Krystowczyk. This Pole became council chairman, and Binsztejn police commander.

"Those five guys were virtually illiterate. They wanted my father as their writer. But he told them: 'What are you doing? The war's only just begun; who knows what's going to happen.' Other people told them the same thing: 'What are you doing, we live in Poland, why do you want to sow discord?' It's true that they informed on Poles. But our Polish neighbors blamed all the Jews for what a few no-goodniks did.

"I don't remember other Jews having any links to the Russians. Sometimes someone had been a Communist before the war but he would prefer to keep out of the Russians' way. There was a Jew in Jedwabne, Mosze Lew, arrested for Communism, who left for Palestine later, maybe in 1934. There he was so active as a Communist that the British threw him out and he returned to Jedwabne. He got married in Tykocin and he visited friends in Jedwabne just after the Russians had come, to ask them not to give him away, he was so scared of the Soviets. The Polish Communist party had been dissolved by Stalin in 1937, after all, and the Soviets announced that its members were provocateurs, summoned Communists from Poland to Russia, and shot them there.

"The Soviets began to draw up lists and arrest people. They arrested more Poles. They arrested my father on December 10, 1939. My mother and I had no word of him ever again. After the war I searched for him through the Red Cross. Maybe he was shot in prison, though rumors once reached us that he'd been seen sick in a camp near the White Sea.

"Mother and I were deported to Kazakhstan in March 1940. At that time I was fourteen years old. We traveled with four Polish families for a month and a half in crammed railway cars. Once every few days they let us out and gave us water to drink. They'd be standing with automatic guns ready to fire. In the cars there was a little window high up where you could get a lot of air. When we got in and I took a place near the window, one of the Polish women, Mrs. Białobrzeski, took me by the lapels, sat me down on the floor, and said, 'You can sit down there, Jewboy.' And she put Polish children where I'd been sitting.

"We were taken to Kokshetau, and from there it was sixty kilometers to the kolkhoz in Frunze. This was between Siberia and the Kazakh steppes, on the horizon we could see high dark-blue mountains. The driver threw us out of the car into the street near the kolkhoz offices. We were hungry and dirty. We were so infested with fleas it was hard to bear. Later we all lived together, all of us from the same transport, in one mud hut. There were two huts there, without a kitchen; we lit a fire between them. We had no beds or chairs. There was Granny Grądzka, who was about eighty years old. She didn't like Jews, but she liked listening to their prayers, especially the Kol Nidre. She was the mother of our mayor, who was friendly with Jews. Only Grądzka spoke to us like a human being. She kept saying prayers holding her rosary, and didn't eat much. One day she said to me: 'Mejerczyk, bring me some fresh water.' She drank the water, crossed herself, and died. There was Jadwiga Bronowiczowa and her daughter, Danuta. Bronowicz was the son-in-law of Mayor Grądzki. Bronowiczowa didn't like Jews any more than her husband did: he had a bakery in Jedwabne and when he'd had enough vodka, he went around beating up Jews. There was Mrs. Białobrzeski, the one who wouldn't let me get any air in the train. She was the most contemptuous of us during that time. There was Szymańska with her seven children. They had a dairy in Jedwabne. Four of the children died of hunger. She got along somehow with Jews, you could talk to her.

"There were fifteen Polish families with us in exile—the men in prison, their wives and children here. Only Mama and me were Jewish. We were all sent to the same life of misery, but as for any of the Poles growing closer to us during that whole time, not a chance.

"We'd wash ourselves in the swamp when Kazakh children went swimming. They noticed I was circumcised, whereas the Polish kids weren't, and the little Kazakhs told their parents. One day I was walking through the village and a Kazakh family was sitting on the porch, by a low table with a dish of meat on it, eating with their hands, and they called to me. Not to eat with a Kazakh is the worst possible insult. They asked me where I was from. I said Poland. 'All right, but you're not like the other Polish children. You walk by yourself and they beat you.' I said

I was a *yevrey,* a Jew. 'We want to see what you look like,' they said. I tried to run away but they caught me. I tried to tear myself away. They told the women to go. There I was with my pants down and they raised their hands to the heavens and cried out. They asked me if I ate pork. When I said I didn't, they shouted even louder with relief: 'You're one of us, you're one of us!' They explained to me that my *yevrey* was the same as *musulmanin,* 'Muslim,' in their language.

"From then on the Kazakh boys hit the Polish boys but knew they shouldn't hit me. They helped us, and they always asked for some help from me first so I wouldn't feel insulted, and they'd give me flour, grain, milk for it. The Kazakhs barely spoke Russian, and I quickly learned to speak Kazakh. I'm sure my mother and I would never have survived without the help of the Kazakhs.

"They didn't like the Russians the way Poles didn't like the Jews. In Jedwabne, when a child didn't want to go to sleep, they said to spook him, 'A Jew's going to come and get you.' And there, to spook a child, they said, 'A Russian's coming to get you.'

"The climate was tough, forty degrees Celsius below zero, blizzards. I went to school but I had to stop at the ninth grade—they wouldn't give me board then because my father was an enemy of the people. I worked in Karaganda as a mechanic in an ammunition factory. They didn't send me to the front, just made me repair broken weapons, because they didn't have a lot of arms to go around. Later I worked on Lake Balkhash in a bronze mine. They half-starved us. I left there looking like a skeleton.

"In private the Russians said: 'Russia's our mother, Stalin's our father. I'd rather be an orphan.' But at kolkhoz gatherings everybody got up and said: 'Glory to Stalin.'

"They deported four Jewish families from Jedwabne: us, Sara Kuropatwa, Chana Belbud with her children, and Kubrzańska, whose husband repaired bicycles. I survived with my mother and Sara Kuropatwa. Kubrzańska was sent to Siberia, she went to a mill to grind wheat, a blizzard got going, she lost her way and froze to death. Chana Belbud got a letter from her husband that he'd been let out of prison and he was coming to join them in Kazakhstan. He never made it; on the way he was arrested for speculation and was sentenced again. When she found out she broke down and died of heart failure. Sara Kuropatwa was married. Her husband returned to Poland in 1945, looked for her, didn't find her, and with a new wife he made his way to Palestine in 1947. There he found out Sara was alive and so he had two wives. She never forgave him to the end of her life, and never wanted to speak to him again.

"On the way back from Siberia I met Soviet soldiers who'd been at the front around our region. They told me I wouldn't find anyone I knew because the Germans and Poles had killed all the Jews. I got to Brest-Litovsk on a repatriation train. At the border they didn't meet us with flowers but with stones. It wasn't even all Jews on the train, there were some Poles as well, but from rage at the Jews, they didn't mind beating a few of their own, too. I was advised not to show myself in Jedwabne.

"When I went back to Poland, and heard what happened, I asked, 'Dear God, where were You?' For a moment I stopped believing in God. It's a cruel subject, better not to speak of it. If you didn't have Jewish blood, I would never say this to you.

"I wonder what would have happened to me if I'd been in Jedwabne that tenth of July. Would some Polish pal of mine have hidden me? I doubt it. After all, my Jewish friends all perished, no one hid them. The Poles ceased being friends to us by 1938. Ryś Ostrowski didn't even say hello to me in the street—why would he rescue me? Maybe some friend would have burned me? It was my friends who murdered my friends.

"I knew I wanted to leave Poland as soon as possible. The State Repatriation Office sent us to a suburb of Szczecin. Then came the pogrom in Kielce. I often heard people say, 'How come there are so many Jews left? Didn't Hitler do away with them?' If they saw a lone Jew they'd rough him up. I had trained in Russia to be a metalworker, so I went to state workshops, but there they told me, 'We don't need Jews, go and work for the secret police.' But I didn't want that kind of job.

"I joined the underground group Bricha; we left Poland without any papers. I walked to Czechoslovakia, from there to Austria and onward, almost halfway across Europe on foot. Then the British caught us on the northern coast of Palestine, arrested us, beat us, and sent us to a camp on Cyprus.* I managed to run away from there. Mama had got to Palestine earlier. She got here in 1947. Her two brothers and sister had moved here

---

* The British government ran internment camps on Cyprus from August 1946 to January 1949 for Jews attempting to immigrate to Mandatory Palestine in violation of British policy.

before the war, and my uncles adopted my sister, because we hadn't received permission to emigrate. Here I met my wife. She's from Łomża, her father worked at the town hall before the war. The Soviets arrested him and sent him and his family to Kazakhstan. They got away in 1946, like thousands of Jews after the Kielce pogrom.

"Mechajkał Wajnsztajn, one of those five louts who served the Soviets, was mobilized with the Red Army. He survived the war that way and came to Palestine in 1947. He had the nerve to visit my mother there to tell her it wasn't he who'd denounced us but someone else. A few boys and I were ready to take his head off. I never raised a hand against anyone before then, but I was ready to kill him. My mother talked me out of it and begged me to spare his life. She told me his wife, Nehame Horowitz of Jedwabne, was pregnant and I mustn't make any more Jewish orphans.

"From the ship that brought me to the coast of Palestine I went straight to the front. In the army I did arms maintenance. In 1962, Adenauer gave Ben-Gurion arms and they sent me to an anti-air artillery school in Germany. Ben-Gurion introduced the principle that if you had a state passport it had to have a Hebrew name, so that was when I changed my surname from Grajewski to Ronen. I lived with German soldiers and used to think in Poland that would have been impossible, to treat a Jew that decently.

"I'll never go to Jedwabne; I wouldn't survive it. The church poisoned people so that they turned into beasts. You can count on your ten fingers the Jews who survived from Jedwabne. The priest knew, the Łomża bishop knew, but not a word, lips shut, they didn't say anything to their flock to restrain them. It's painful.

"Look at this photograph from 1938, from the Jewish summer camps my father organized for the CENTOS, the national Jewish organization that helped children in Jedwabne. The photo survived because we sent photographs to my uncle in Palestine and after he died I found it at his children's. First row from the right: he was burned, he was burned, she was burned. That's Jospa Lewin, Józef Lewin's sister, who was tortured by Poles in the marketplace right after the Germans came, and she was burned with the others. In the second row, Motłe Farbowicz, second from the right, emigrated to South America before the war. The rest: he was killed, he was killed, he was killed . . ."

Journal

JUNE 3, 2001

After my return from Israel I go through back issues of the *Gazeta*. Adam Michnik's reply to Leon Wieseltier's piece: "For many years after the war Poles grieved for their murdered compatriots without acknowledging that the fate of their Jewish neighbors was incomparably more tragic— an utterly exceptional tragedy in the history of humanity. On the other hand, there has prevailed among Jews—as Rabbi Klenicki put it—a 'triumphalism of pain' . . . Poles also have a right to the memory of their own pain. And they have a right to expect that Jews will be aware of it as well."

I read about the exhumation. The conclusions are astonishing. Two graves were discovered. In the smaller grave they found charred, crushed fragments of the Lenin monument. This means a first group was driven into the barn, the one carrying the bust of Lenin, and killed inside. The other grave is outside the barn, alongside it.

JUNE 4, 2001

Due to the protests of religious Jews, there will be no more exhumation. Now we will never know how many people perished in the barn in Jedwabne.

In Jedwabne what happened was not a pogrom but a massacre with a genocidal character, the historian Dariusz Stola writes in the newspaper the *Republic*. He cites data from eighteen hundred pogroms in the Ukraine: even when several thousand victims fell in one town, in each case only part of the Jewish community perished. He points to the effective organization and execution of the crime in Jedwabne, the different roles people played: some rounded up Jews, others searched for Jews hiding in attics and cellars, others went on horseback to catch fleeing Jews on the edges of town. Stola also draws attention to the order in which people were killed—first the able-bodied men—and to the division of labor—a group of killers striking with irons and clubs, one who sets fire to the barn, the ones who joined in to help, often visitors from nearby villages, and the ubiquitous onlookers. When the men accused in the 1949 trial withdrew in court the statements they'd made during the investigation, they claimed to have been part of that last category.

A crime on this scale, Stola argues, could not have been committed from a "common impulse" or an uncoordinated explosion of hatred. There was a power structure in what he calls the "Jedwabne state," which had its own hierarchy: Germans on top, then Karolak, Sobuta, Wasilewski, Bardoń, the town authorities in those first days, then the Laudańskis and other helpers of death. People knew that day that the authorities would permit violence against Jews, that violence was expected and would be rewarded with a share of the spoils.

JUNE 5, 2001

Antonina Wyrzykowska, who saved seven Jews and now lives in America, is coming to Poland. I heard the news via a string of acquaintances that leads to Maria Sikorska, with whom Antonina will be staying. Antonina was Maria Sikorska's domestic help for many years. Mrs. Wyrzykowski is about to arrive. I ask Maria Sikorska what Wyrzykowska told her about hiding Jews.

"Nothing. Then one day I went to see a film—in those days they showed you a newsreel beforehand. I look and suddenly I see on the left . . . I recognized her red dress, even though the film was black and white . . . and I cried, 'But that's my Antonina!' They were pinning the medal of the Righteous on her. If I hadn't seen her there, she would never have told me about it herself. Even though I was close to her, supportive of her. She still writes me letters saying she carries my picture with her and prays for me every day. I'm eighty-eight years old, and the sister I take care of is ninety-five; we're probably both kept alive by the force of Antonina's prayers."

I knew Maria Sikorska was one of the four Lew sisters, renowned Jewish beauties before the war, two of whom married well-known Polish poets.

I say, "Mrs. Wyrzykowski, who rescued seven Jews, must have liked the idea that it was you, someone from a Jewish family, who showed her so much kindness."

"Well, you know, one doesn't speak of such things," Ms. Sikorska replies. "Antonina has no idea, when she got back from Jerusalem, she brought me rosary beads."

Wyrzykowska arrives. Well-groomed, pretty, warm, laughing, or rather nervously giggling. She gives brief answers to my questions, and Ms. Sikorska adds to them. It is Sikorska who tells me Wyrzykowska is still cared for by the people she saved.

"Remember when you came back from America and brought a hundred photographs, and on one of them you're lying on a sun bed and Ms. Kubrzańska is handing you a drink on a tray?" says Ms. Sikorska with evident amusement at the reversal of roles in her housekeeper's life.

I ask Mrs. Wyrzykowski why for so many years she didn't even tell Ms. Sikorska that she sheltered Jews.

"Well, you know, one doesn't speak of such things," she says, repeating the exact words I heard from Sikorska only a moment earlier.

The Institute of National Remembrance has released the following sensational news on the results of the aborted exhumation: in the remains of one of the victims they found a cartridge case from a Mauser rifle that shows burn marks, indicating that shots were fired at this person at the entrance to the barn, and a brass part that was melted on the inside.

It all makes sense, except that no one fired any shots. It can't be an accident that in Radziłów witnesses speak of shooting (which doesn't mean Germans were present, because Poles fired shots with guns they got from the Soviet storehouse), whereas in Jedwabne even those who saw nothing but SS uniforms heard no shots. Why is the Institute of National Remembrance creating this farce?

One way or another, we know that a front line ran through Jedwabne at least twice in the twentieth century. First was the front line in World War I, in 1915, then in January 1945, when there was fighting in the immediate vicinity of the town and there were Soviet and German corpses everywhere. I heard about this from several Jedwabne locals, who said, "There were as many corpses as grains of sand on the seashore." So that's why there were so many cartridge cases in the ground.

The Germans didn't shoot anyone, but what was their role? I have no doubt that the massacre of Jews in Jedwabne, and before that in Radziłów, was part of a German operation carried out across a wide stretch of territory. It's hard to imagine Poles supplied with alcohol and guns—as in Radziłów—killing Jews on their own initiative while the police sat quietly by, without any concern that they might soon become targets as well. We know the directive issued by Reinhard Heydrich, then chief of the Reich Main Security Office, on June 29, 1941: "No obstacles should be placed in the way of aspirations toward self-cleansing in anti-Communist or anti-Jewish circles in the newly occupied territories. Rather, such aspirations should be provoked without leaving traces, and if need be they should be intensified and led onto the right track, however in a way that prevents the local 'self-defense groups' from later citing any orders or political assurances given them . . . The aim is to provoke local popular pogroms."

But what happened in Wąsosz, Radziłów, and Jedwabne goes beyond what we are accustomed to calling a pogrom; what's more, that total massacre was committed more effectively and quickly with each new approach. In Wąsosz, the killing was done house by house. At night the locals broke into homes, killed their victims with axes and clubs, then drove the bodies off to a place outside town. In Radziłów, all Jews, young and old, were driven into the barn, many got away, the hunt went on for two more days, the escapees were brought to one place and killed there. Thus the individual killings were an essential supplement to the massacre. In Jedwabne, the ones who could have most easily fled or defended themselves were made to carry the Lenin statue, led out of town, and killed first. The several dozen individual murders were an epilogue, not a prologue to the crime.

The Germans came to Radziłów in two cars on the morning of July 7, and the wagons of the peasants in the area had been on the move since daybreak. That is certain. Stanisław Ramotowski saw them, and the night before he was warned of the pogrom that was under way, otherwise he'd never have managed to hide the Finkelsztejn family. From conversations

I've had with witnesses, it seems that a few Germans appeared in the marketplace on the morning of July 7 and ordered the Poles to kill all the Jews. Does that mean the local population was organizing a pogrom that day and the Germans, hearing about it, came to town to direct their actions, suggesting one collective murder? In accounts from Jedwabne one keeps hearing about the same small group of Germans—one or two cars—who the day before probably had a meeting with Mayor Karolak and the temporary town government. In other words, the Germans urged the town's leadership to carry out a collective murder. But Szmul Wasersztejn remembers that at the meeting, it was the town representatives who were unanimous in saying all Jews had to be destroyed: "When the Germans proposed to spare a Jewish family from each professional group, Bronisław Śleszyński replied, 'We have enough professionals of our own.'" Is it possible that in the case of Jedwabne the Germans only expressed their approval and instructed the Poles on how best to carry out the crime, and then helped the Poles round up the Jews in the market? That version would seem to be supported by the fact that the people who didn't want to take part didn't leave the house that day, or left town to visit relatives or friends in the area. One can only hope prosecutor Ignatiew is able to establish all of this.

JUNE 6, 2001

I drive to Jedwabne, where I've arranged to talk to two schoolteachers. A teacher from the gymnasium told me that in class, when they were working on a nineteenth-century novel that includes the character of a poor Jew, the children said it would be a good idea to stone him. And when a friend of hers once asked them how they imagined other peoples, it was simply shameful what the children wrote about Jews.

"The only accepted life model here is to put money in the tray on Sunday and then drink all week, beat your wife, and moan about the Jews," says a high school teacher. "You should hear the things that are said in the teachers' lounge. The atmosphere is so tense that arguments don't get through to people. And the kids at school are constantly telling Jewish jokes. They even get up in class and ask why there are so many Jews in Poland. Once, I tried to turn the subject around, I said they felt threatened because they didn't know anything about Jews, about their history, their culture, that they need knowledge, because it'll make their lives easier, upon which one pupil got up and said, 'Why should I study if the Jews are in charge anyway.' Where my family comes from I don't hear this constant griping about Jews. And it has always been like this here, even before Gross published his book. Probably because the Poles killed them here and enriched themselves on their Jewish property?"

She herself is not from Jedwabne. When she came here in the sixties, she would hear people say, "The Poles did it," but she only found out what had happened here when she made friends with a colleague, a woman born in Jedwabne. During the war, this woman lived on the little square where the Lenin monument stood. She told her what she saw through the window: Jews falling down carrying big chunks of the smashed Lenin, and Poles finishing them off on the spot. The woman's mother, who hid a Jew in the attic that day, often returned in memory to the crime, even gave details, but was afraid to mention names, apart from one: Kubrzyniecki, who had long since died. Her father told her how one day a local guy who had worked for them for years came to the house. In a new coat, with a signet ring on his finger, he declared he wouldn't be coming to work anymore, because he and his wife were "taken care of." Her father told him, "I don't go around in a dress coat every day, just a worn shirt, but mine doesn't stink."

This woman, Miss Z., still lives in the same house as she did then; I can try to visit her. "But she's probably quite queer in the head by now, she only listens to Radio Maryja and keeps saying she saw a bunch of Germans in navy blue uniforms." I try to protest: "But your mother never mentioned them."

The teacher also tells me about an elderly Miss B., who lived on Cmentarna Street at the time of the massacre.

"She was about to look out the window, because she heard cries and screams, but her mother closed the curtains and shoved her under a quilt. She didn't go out until late in the evening, when she and her friends recognized the charred remains of children they knew in the barn. A neighbor boasted that he'd just gone to get instruments from the houses—he knew which Jews played music, because they were classmates of his and had invited him to play with them. He buried them in the garden because there were rumors going around that the Germans were making people give back what they'd looted. When he later dug up the accordion, it was ruined."

I go right away to see Miss Z., the retired teacher, and Miss B. of Cmentarna Street. Miss Z. doesn't know anything, didn't see anything, she's ill. Miss B. won't talk to me at all.

I look into the church. A bunch of anti-Semitic pamphlets are distributed in the pews, and they all include interviews with Father Orłowski. He is really good at pushing himself into the foreground and dealing with the media. The people around him don't do nearly so well. The Committee to Defend the Good Name of Jedwabne seems to have dissolved after a few meetings, at least I don't hear anything about it anymore. The priest's idea to organize a counter-ceremony on July 10—dedicating a foundation stone for a monument to honor the Poles deported to Siberia after "Jewish denunciations"—was appreciated but did not find anyone prepared to carry it out despite the promises of the Chicago Polish community that they were prepared to finance the whole thing. They even sent the priest a proposal for the inscription: *In honor of Poles who gave their lives to defend Jews, and of those Compatriots who were victims of Jewish collaboration with the Red Army and NKVD as well as the German occupying forces, as a result of which they were deported to Siberia and tortured there or perished in Nazi death camps.*

I learn in town that the dentist Łucja Przystupa, the local negotiator, tells people that bones were brought to the barn before the exhumation, and that the Mossad tried to poison her dog. Among the active deniers are people from the educated town elite: a doctor, a dentist, a teacher.

I go by Przestrzele. It turns out Leon Dziedzic went once to the doctor, once to the neighbors, and heard enough to decide to return to America without waiting for the ceremony of July 10. Ewa and Leszek are sitting as if on hot coals; Ewa keeps going up to the window to check that no one is hanging around the house.

"Our friends have completely dropped us," says Leszek. "No one calls us, as if we were strangers."

"And how are your women friends or acquaintances behaving?" I ask Ewa.

"I have no friends anymore. I lost them all. If my husband weren't a hunter who keeps a gun in the house, I wouldn't get a single night's sleep. I wake up at night and cry. The priest slanders us, saying Leszek isn't a Catholic anymore since he says the things he does. People call us: 'Hello, is that Israel?'; 'Hello, is that the rabbi?' It's awful to walk down the street and hear 'Jewish lackeys.' And in shops my neighbors turn away from me as if I were a leper. In town, wherever I go, whether it's the pharmacy or a store, I feel hostile eyes glaring at me. I go into the teachers' lounge and the silence is deafening. Our children are constantly getting their fingers rapped. Piotrek had his confirmation, and Tomek was sitting in a church pew; the other parents didn't know he was our son and said terrible things about us. We stopped going to church, someone might throw us out of the service. In general, we avoid everything, we try not to go out. I had a friend whose son used to come to see my children, but his classmates told him, 'You hang out with those Jewish lackeys.' He hasn't been back."

The Dziedzices' son Piotrek tells me about school: "A boy in class said Poles had made a mistake; they should have killed all the Jews. The teacher didn't say anything. A boy in my class has written a little ditty on his folder:

> "Where are the Jews of yesteryear?
> They all went up the chimney here.

"Everybody thinks it's funny. And everybody tells stupid jokes about Jews all the time. In Tomek's class the English teacher asked, 'Who likes Jews?' Only Tomek said he did. The teacher asked him why, and Tomek answered, 'Because we all descend from Adam and Eve.' And the class just laughed."

Leszek announces to me, "We've decided to leave for America on June 14. We can't take it any longer. It's hard to make sure the boys don't let anything slip about us going. When they go out we worry."

I ask Piotrek and Tomek, "Do you have friends you're sorry to leave?" They both shake their heads no.

JUNE 7, 2001
An evening at the Godlewskis', a conversation about the exhumation.

"So I'm sitting in the dentist's waiting room," Krzysztof recounts, "and an educated man comes in, college graduate, and he says to me resentfully, 'You're sitting here and they're out there trucking in the bones.'"

They were supposedly trucking bones in so that "as many Jews would have died as Gross wanted there to be." It's unclear whether the priest came up with the idea himself, or repeated it after hearing it from someone else, but it's spread like wildfire that the Jews organized the exhumation in order to remove the fragments of the Lenin monument from the barn and cover up the fact that they died as Communists.

Godlewski tries to convince me that the inscription proposed for the monument is a sensible compromise, that it's a miracle that the council accepted the inscription—after his own efforts and those of Michałowski, along with their visits to the council members' houses in the evenings to collect a sufficient number of votes.

I admire the heroic attempts Godlewski has made to retain faith in people. He once told me about two aunts of a friend who live somewhere near Pisz, who on July 10, 1941, made fritters all day, brought them to the pond behind the manor house—an overgrown, abandoned place, perfectly designed for hiding. They wanted to do something for the Jews who managed to escape the massacre. The fritters disappeared.

"I want to persuade her to get her aunts to tell the story publicly, so it's clear there were people in Jedwabne who felt compassion for Jews."

But there's no way they'll speak of it to journalists.

Until recently, Godlewski said, the council members insisted, "No Jews, no temple, no graves; we'll lay a road right through it." But "something gave at the last session." It turns out that at the last session, on June 4, the council declared that it would "distance itself from the memorial ceremony, and will not agree to the council chairman and the mayor making statements and expressing views on behalf of the town council." It's not enough that the whole effort of organizing the ceremony on the side of the town fell onto his shoulders, but now the council is forbidding him to deal with any of it during work hours.

The town is due to receive guests on July 10, but nothing has been done, because the council members put up resistance to every move. Godlewski managed to get more money from "high up" to restore the marketplace and the roads to the cemetery. (I had a hand in this as I asked Adam Michnik to inform those at the top levels of government that the ceremony might not take place at all because there will be no way to get to the site, and the council won't pay one zloty to build roads "for the Jews.") In the end, there's enough left over for the athletic hall, which has been under construction for about twenty years. But the problems have piled up, and every step of the way it's been like pulling teeth. The land development plan needed to be changed—a formality, but without it no monument could be erected. At the June 4 council session the resolution passed by a miracle, or rather by accident. Sixteen members abstained from the vote; no one voted against. They only realized after the fact that the proposal was passed because one and only one person voted for it—Stanisław Michałowski—and in these circumstances one vote was enough.

The conversation continues until two in the morning. Godlewski sighs as we part, telling me about the next issue on which the council voted: "I'll tell you what the council vote was on organizing a ceremony in Jedwabne. Two to seventeen. The two are me and Michałowski. We lost that vote. We're completely alone. What I'd like most would be to get on a train and go anywhere else. I'm not staying in this town anyway."

JUNE 8, 2001

Jedwabne. I try to meet with Józef, son of Helena Chrzanowska, the one Jewish woman living in Jedwabne with her Polish husband, but Józef's in a state of such terror he's even afraid to talk to me on the phone. When I get to Przestrzele, Leszek Dziedzic tells me he passed Chrzanowski in the marketplace: "One word with me and he was gone. He's being hounded the same way we are, but he can't escape to America and he's afraid that if people see us together they'll give him an even rougher time."

This visit I didn't manage to contact Halina Popiołek either; her niece still won't let her leave the house. But two people burst into tears when they were talking to me, saying they couldn't bear the relentless taunting and the late-night phone calls: "dirty Jew."

I return to Warsaw, just in time to attend the launch of the book *Jedwabne in the Eyes of Witnesses*, published by the Agricultural Chaplaincy (printed "with the permission of the church authorities and edited by Father Eugeniusz Marciniak"). In it I read, "Wasersztejn joined the secret police and wrote pure libel. A Polish family risked their lives for him, and in return we were subjected to a smear campaign."

The event is held in a hall in the All Saints' Church in Warsaw—the same church where recently the penitential service was held. It's here the notorious patriotic bookstore Antyk is situated, where you can get any anti-Semitic publication you want. I had no idea this meant hundreds of books and pamphlets. Waiting for the event to begin, I looked through the book being launched. Janina Biedrzycka offers proof that the Germans were guilty of the crime—otherwise her father would never have given over his barn: "Because if some Pole had come to my father and said, 'Give us your barn,' my father would have got up from his sickbed and said, 'Burn them in your own barn!'"

The hall is packed, there's the excited atmosphere of a rally. The event moderator, Father Eugeniusz Marciniak, introduces the guests, beginning with the priest of Jedwabne: "This is our brave Father Orłowski" (a storm of applause). "Here is Janina Biedrzycka, daughter of the man in whose barn the Jews were burned" (an even greater storm of applause). Father Marciniak: "Wasersztejn was an officer of the secret police in Łomża. Later he fled to Warsaw, where he was head of trade unions until 1956, there are documents to prove it." Guest of honor Father Orłowski: "How can we deepen our ties with Judaism if there are documents like the ones on Szmul Wasersztejn?"

Until recently I thought 1945 was a turning point in the life of the Catholic Church—of course before the war the Church was largely xenophobic, but after the war that faded into the background, and the Church became the bastion defending society against Sovietization. I saw the patriotic bookstore Antyk as pretty anomalous. Of course there was Radio Maryja to consider. But it wasn't until now that the example of the parish of Jedwabne brought home to me how the Church—at least in that area—tirelessly sustains its prewar anti-Semitism.

In 1945, the deaconry in Jedwabne was headed by Father Antoni Roszkowski, who before the war had edited *Common Cause* and then *The Catholic Cause*, which made the battle against Jews their leading theme. Which means that immediately after the atrocity the church sent a priest to Jedwabne whose work was partly responsible for Jews being killed without a pang of conscience. Father Orłowski has held sway in Jedwabne since 1988; before that he was the parish priest of nearby Drozdowo, a hotbed of nationalism, where National Party leader Roman Dmowski spent the last years of his life. As if nothing had changed.

JUNE 11, 2001

I visit Antonina Wyrzykowska at her son's apartment in Milanówek, a Warsaw suburb.

"Do you feel satisfaction now that the truth about the massacre in Jedwabne has been revealed?"

"Why would I, I just feel afraid."

"Will you come to the memorial ceremony in Jedwabne?"

"There's no way. I won't show my face anywhere around here again. My dear, I've really had enough. I used to come to visit from time to time, but afraid, God, I was always afraid."

She hasn't read Gross's book, because she doesn't read books either. She left school after the second grade.

JUNE 12, 2001

I go to Konstancin to take Stanisław Ramotowski back to my house, where he is to be interviewed by prosecutor Ignatiew. In the end I managed to persuade Stanisław to do it, though he's sworn a dozen times that he's "only doing it for me." His health is deteriorating. He has fainting spells, high fever, he coughs up blood. On the way from Konstancin I tell him what I discovered on my excursion to Radziłów with Jan Skrodzki, including the fact of the Mordasiewicz brothers being killers. Stanisław interrupts me.

"Just make sure you write there was a completely different Mordasiewicz family in Radziłów. Stanisław Mordasiewicz is still alive and he's a very fine man."

Similarly, the name Ramotowski is common in the area. In Jedwabne one Ramotowski helped round up Jews in the marketplace, and in Radziłów another Ramotowski lived, no relative of Stanisław's, who participated in the looting of Jewish homes. In Jedwabne I found out that there were two Łojewski families, Poles who took part in the atrocity, and a Jewish blacksmith named Łojewski whose family died in the flames. None of this makes my job any easier. I have to remain vigilant, because the same problem keeps returning: some people killed, others saved, others were Communists, and still others didn't do anything, and they all have the same name.

JUNE 14, 2001

My last conversation with Leszek Dziedzic before the family leaves for the States. If they manage to get the necessary papers, they won't come back. There were three houses in Jedwabne where I could always drop by at any time and be fed: Joanna and Krzysztof Godlewski, Jadwiga and Stanisław Michałowski, Ewa and Leszek Dziedzic. I'm left with two.

7

A Time Will Come
When Even Stones Will Speak

or, The Soliloquies of Leszek Dziedzic

"I read Gross's book as soon as it came out. Once, a friend came by and spent the whole evening reading it. He said, 'I have to know if anyone in my family has blood on his hands.' Some of the names in the documents are misspelled; I want to look into it properly. My father's away, and when I ask my mother she bursts into tears and won't say anything.

"On July 10, a mob killed the Jews. But if at that time the priest had barred the way and said, 'You'll go to hell for this and the devil will settle scores with you,' they would have listened to him and held back, with the possible exception of a few thugs already deep in their cups.

"My father was friends with Szmul Wasersztejn from before the war. Szmul took him along to temple once, although Dad's friends had said when you went in there you had to step on the cross. Dad took him along to church once. I always knew Szmul was hidden with us at first. But I also knew I shouldn't tell anyone about it. One day in the eighties a Fiat 125 drove up in front of our house and there was a stranger on our doorstep. My grandmother Leokadia Dmoch had passed away, and my parents were out. But I remembered Grandmother talking about Szmul's ears sticking out, so I recognized him at once. 'My granny called you Staszek but you are Szmul,' I welcomed him, and I showed him pictures of Grandmother in our family album. He kissed them and cried like I'd never seen any child cry. He said, 'My mother gave me life, but she

Leszek Dziedzic in front of his house in Methuen, Massachusetts, 2012. (Courtesy of Leszek Dziedzic)

couldn't help me save it, and this woman risked her life and the lives of her eight children to save my poor Jewish life.'

"The killing was all about Jewish property, but ever since Gross's book came out I keep hearing people say the Jews had it coming to them, because they denounced Poles. When our neighbors were rounded up for deportation my granny ran out to give them dry rusks for the journey. She didn't see any Jews there. In Przestrzele where we lived it was a Polish woman who betrayed her neighbors to the Soviets, and in the next village it was a Pole. I know the names of five Poles from this area who denounced people. I'm sure some Jew did, too, because there are lowlifes among any people.

"I was crossing the marketplace with my family when a Western TV crew was setting up equipment. My son's friend pointed at the cameraman: 'That tall guy is Jewish.' I asked him, 'How do you know?' 'He's well-dressed and he's got a camera.' He's got stuff, so he must be a Jew. That boy must have heard that at home. When people were going to market and a child was nagging them to take him along, people around here would say, 'I'm not taking you, because children have to kiss the Jewish lady's beard at the entrance.' And when a child wouldn't go to sleep his parents said, 'The Jews will turn you into matzo.' That's how they brought up children, even after the war. How is a kid like that supposed to respect another people? When I read an interview with Rabbi Jacob Baker, I thought, He, whose people we helped to destroy, is able to speak of Poland with such feeling, and how do we speak of Jews?

"I always liked going around with my father and listening to grown-ups talk. Jews were respected in our home. Granny told us about not having money to bury her husband before the war; she had been left with eight children. She went to Father Szumowski, who said, 'If you don't have money, bury him in the cabbage patch.' A Jewish acquaintance lent my grandmother the money without interest or a date by which it had to be returned. Granny managed to pay him back in full before the war broke out. After the war you could get a perpetual lease on land, but my family weren't tempted, because it had all been Jewish land.

"Look at the slogans in the tabloids: 'If you're Polish you're with us'; 'Buy Polish products, remember that buying from Poles means Poles live well.' They were handing them out in front of the church when Bishop

Stefanek was celebrating Mass. Nowadays we're seeing a replay of the same thing we had in the thirties, when the nationalists were sowing hatred. They can't even come up with anything new. A strange way to show your patriotism, destroying and murdering other peoples.

"I don't remember when I realized that Jews had made up half of our town. I'm sure I knew that there was one Jewish woman left in town, she had been baptized, Miss Helena. We used to leave the truck in her court-yard when we drove into Jedwabne. I also knew where the grounds of the Jewish cemetery were, though it wasn't enclosed. Once I was driving past and somebody was driving around on an excavator. I said, 'What are you doing here with an excavator, these are human remains.' He knew it, too, but it evidently didn't bother him.

"On the day of the massacre my grandmother didn't let any of her children go out. She always said a day would come when they'd say who was responsible for Katyń, and who killed the Jews. She didn't live to see either.

"They showed a TV report on Jedwabne where one of the townspeo-ple, Damazy Kiełczewski, was shouting: 'Let them come from Israel and take away their ashes. We'll help them load up.' I heard similar words at a gas station. I'm ashamed for the people of Jedwabne. The Polish Repub-lic was a homeland to many peoples, and a pogrom was an act against the Polish state, it was Poles killing Poles—it was just that some were of the Jewish faith. Jews had their own material and cultural achievements, and they paid taxes like everyone else in Poland. They weren't 'parachut-ists' who appeared during the Soviet occupation, though I heard that version from someone in town recently, too. My great-grandfather set-tled in the Borderlands, and when the revolution came they fled and they had just enough money to buy a house in Przestrzele. We've lived here for eighty years. Many of the Jews killed were from families who had lived here for hundreds of years.

"There were a lot of killings after the war, people were scared of visi-tors at night, afraid they'd come, smash things up, steal things, murder you. Father said you had to have a good sense of who was coming; they came at night and asked, 'Who do you support?' If they were National Armed Forces, and you said you supported the Home Army, they could kill you. The National Armed Forces were fighting, but only to rape women and rob their husbands. It would help not only if Poles apologized to Jews, but if Poles apologized to Poles for everything that was looted in these lands.

"It's a certain kind of people here. Whatever bad happens, it turns out the Jews are to blame. I've been hearing it from the day I was born. Whether it's bad government, or bad weather, or a cow dies, it's always a Jew who's to blame. Dad had money because he was a good provider and he saved, Mama would get up at night to gather strawberries to take them to sell in the morning. When I got home from school I'd go to the neighbors and cut wood for them for a zloty, or pick black currants for them, and the money I made I gave to my dad. It's interesting that they always envied us our money, never our hard work. They said, 'The Dziedzic family have Jewish money.' Anyone who's got money is either a Jew or he got it from a Jew. I got Jewish money, as they say here, once in my life: a hundred dollars from Szmul for my son. People here live on the pensions of their parents who handed on their farms. There's a saying: 'Lord, give me a family with four pensioners and one cow.' Cows take some work, whereas pensions just flow into your pocket.

"For ages I asked my father about the massacre, but he was evasive. He'd say it was better to keep very quiet about all that. Sometimes he would sit on the porch for a bit and cry, and the family would say, 'Papa's remembering the Jews.'

"There's a lot of hate around here now. It seems God has given us all the talk about Jews to try us. There's no other subject of conversation—whether you're in the hospital or in a government office. I went to Łomża to put an ad in the paper, I have silage for sale—Jews is the only thing people wanted to talk about. I heard from one guy, not even the dumbest in town, that the pope is a Jew. I responded, 'It's not for nothing they wear yarmulkes from the bishop upward.' I'm in a store, the owner's mother comes in and says, 'We should kick out all those Jews coming here for interviews.'

"I've been trying to piece together conversations I overheard by chance. My grandmother couldn't forgive her son for marrying into 'a family like that' after the war. I couldn't tell you at what point I realized she called it 'a family like that' because Uncle Klemens's wife's father and brother had a hand in the destruction of Jews.

"When someone tells me the Germans did it, I ask them, 'And when a

Jew was lying by the fence, clubbed to death, was it a German who did that, too?' When they talk about the deportations, I can't even bring myself to say again that Poles denounced people, too. I just ask, 'And what had the children done wrong?'

"I passed a neighbor on the road whose uncle was one of the killers. He recognized my car and said, 'I feel like throwing up.' Then he spat. But I was never afraid of anything. That's why I can talk plainly in Jedwabne about what the Poles did to the Jews.

"There are names that come back all the time. The Laudańskis first, lame Stanisław Sielawa, he was terrible, and then there was Mariak, Genek Kalinowski, who was killed right after the war, Czesław Mierzejewski, Józef Kobrzyniecki, Sobuta, Trzaska, Piechowski, Marian Żyluk, Bolesław Ramotowski the glassmaker, a drunk who beat his horse and his father with the same stick, Władysław Łuba, the one who inherited his blacksmith's tools from the Jews he drowned. It's hard to hide, many people saw them killing. Jews didn't only die in the barn, there were private reckonings with Jews in ponds, in their own courtyards. The killers had learned their trades from them and now they wanted to take over their workshops.

"The truth will never be buried entirely. A time will come when even stones will speak. I often think, It would be enough if in Jedwabne and in every village in the area there were one person with the courage to tell the story to his children. And if the next generation had at least one child who passed it on when it grew up. And so the truth will live.

"If a Pole does something good we praise ourselves to the sky, but when it's bad, he's no longer one of ours. We can't change the fact that we have this legacy from the past. The Germans are partly responsible, but the point is not to lay our own blame on someone else, the Germans have enough on their conscience as it is.

"I can't get my head around the fact that Śleszyński's grandson is haggling over the price he wants on the land for the monument. His grandfather voluntarily gave his barn to burn the Jews and now they're paying his grandson for that land? I wonder if he'll realize on his deathbed what he took money for. That land belongs to the people that lie there. Some partisans were killed on our piece of land. A man came to us asking if he could buy a corner of our land and put up a gravestone for his father-in-law. I told him, 'It's yours, it was sanctified with their blood.'

"I have an ongoing argument with my neighbors. In shops, at the dump, at the gas station, in church, wherever it is, I speak my mind, wherever it gets me. I met a friend in church with whom I sing in the choir. He gave me a flyer saying the Jews brought the Holocaust on themselves, and told me to pass it on. I told him what I thought about it, that his father was a decent man who was in the Home Army and he took no part in the massacre. Another guy told me the government's full of Jews. I said, 'When Jews were reading books, I was playing soccer—and what have you done to get a government job?' 'That's true,' he admitted, 'I didn't get much schooling.'

"A man who has blood on his hands won't tell you what he did. But he'll talk about others killing. The thugs had a problem afterward: how to divvy up the hide they took off the Jews. There were so many feuds and denunciations. In every quarrel neighbors would remind one another: and you killed that Jew, and you stole from that Jew. Before Gross's book it wasn't a secret to anyone who had been the killers, even though no one spoke of it out loud. It was only after the book came out that people kept quiet and it turned out suddenly nobody knew anything.

"I'm trying on my own to reconstruct what happened here in Przestrzele. In two families out of eight there were people who participated in the killing. Later they remembered they happened to have been in Jedwabne that day. Two guys from Przestrzele killed Helena Chrzanowska's uncle and cousin. It was like this: Four Jews were in hiding together, spending the night in a haystack. German police were driving by as one of the Jews was walking in the field, and they saw the grain move. They shot him, and then his father came toward them, he didn't care anymore, he screamed at them to kill him, too. Later they found the other two in the hay. The Germans had the farmers dig a hole, where they threw the bodies, and they told them they could kill the other two with spades and bury them with the others, or bring them in to the police station. The Jews tried to persuade them to let them go, saying, 'You don't think the Germans are going to check how many people are in the hole, do you?' They had let them go when the neighbor came from across the street to tell them they had to catch those Jews, because if the Germans found out they'd burn the whole village down. Two of them, Domitrz and Edek Kotyński, caught up with them on horseback and brought them to the police station.

"'A patriot wouldn't talk that way,' they tell me. I reply that I'm not a murderer's patriot, but a patriot of my country, and I'm not betraying my homeland, only the murderers.

"Once, an acquaintance of my dad's met me with the words, 'You Jewish lackey, if I had a gun I'd shoot people like you. Let your father come back from America, they'll find his head in the Przestrzelak.' And I told him, 'Just make sure you bury it properly, I don't want it to be like the time you killed that Jewish girl and dogs tore her body to pieces.' And I added, 'People like you gave us 1941, and you'd go on doing the same thing.' He disappeared. He knew what I was talking about, because it was his brother-in-law who raped, murdered, and buried a Jewish woman. It was like this: The brother of that killer Mierzejewski was hiding a Jewish woman in his house in Kajetanów. She was supposed to be moved to another place, when two guys from Przestrzele caught her, raped her, killed her, and buried her, not very well, on the bank of the stream. She surfaced in the spring.

"They don't stop short of slander. They ask me, 'How much money did your father get from the Jews for giving an interview?' I said to one, 'What did your father get for killing Jews?' He turned redder than a beet. The blood on the fathers' hands burns the children. I heard from one guy that my father dug around in the ashes for gold teeth, and now what a defender of Jews he is. I came back, 'Right, right, and then he and your dad melted it down in your basement.' Someone was sneering that they hadn't found sixteen hundred bodies when they did the exhumation; he said, 'Now let the Jews tell us where they're buried.' I said, 'They can't tell you because you killed them all.' I can't help but react to that bullshit they go around spouting, but how many times can you swing at them?

"Well, and what if there were fewer than sixteen hundred Jews? They killed the whole people. If there had been three times as many Jews, they would have killed three times as many; apparently there weren't. Does a smaller number make the guilt smaller? No, it's the same. It's hard to imagine this massacre. The burning itself meant terrible pain, and then there was the suffocation. And those people hadn't done anything to anybody. When I think about it I see a father going into the fire with a child. The child trusts his father to save him, but he can't do anything.

"Once, it happened that some vague acquaintance came up to me in the marketplace and shook my hand. And once Stanisław Michałowski congratulated me out loud in a shop. All the decent people in Jedwabne are frightened. Sixty years ago the Jews who lived in Jedwabne and were Polish just like us were robbed of their lives by their own neighbors. And now the killers' descendants harass us for speaking the truth.

"Someone jibed at me once that I don't have a Polish surname because it doesn't end in 'ski.' My uncle Klemens's son called me a rabbi's son, asked me why I don't wear a yarmulke. Apparently he thinks that's an insult. My attitude is that I've never been scared of anyone. At the disco I'd say, 'Don't start up with me or you'll get hurt.' One punch for me was usually enough. But lately my mind has been so affected by all this chatter that I instinctively turn my back to the wall when I go into a store, so no one can hit me from behind. They threaten to burn us. I think they'd be too scared to do anything to us, but I go out to the porch and shoot in front of the house to make a point. My wife and I are most concerned about the children.

"I won't leave any friends here. When I most needed them they turned out to be false friends. What will I say when my American grandson asks me about my memories of my homeland? That Jedwabne was no place to live?"

Journal

I've brought Ramotowski to my house. Today Marek Edelman, who promised to examine him, is coming from Łódź. I give them lunch. Edelman says he finds him in pretty good shape.

"The main thing is for him not to get short of breath," Edelman says.

I press him to tell me the prognosis.

"He could go on like this for a few months, half a year, even longer."

In the *Republic* an interview with Professor Feliks Tych, the director of the Jewish Historical Institute and author of *The Long Shadow of the Holocaust*. Based on a reading of hundreds of diaries (most of them unpublished), he claims that at least 10 percent of Polish society was—sporadically or for a substantial period of time—engaged in activities to help Jews, a majority regarded the Holocaust with indifference, and at least 20 to 30 percent thought the Germans were helping the Poles deal with their Jewish problem. "It's a bitter conclusion, but as a historian I cannot shy away from saying it publicly, even though for many years I didn't even want to say it to myself."

Until recently such an interview would have had no chance of appearing in a mainstream newspaper. I remember the reactions to Jan Błoński's article "Poor Poles Look at the Ghetto" in the *Tygodnik Powszechny* (General Weekly) in 1987, which spoke of the sin of indifference. It provoked a storm of protest, and I'm not talking about nationalist and anti-Semitic circles but liberal Catholics. Gross's book has opened up an entirely new level of discussion.

Tych recalls a truth self-evident elsewhere in the world and difficult to accept in Poland. There was no common fate for Jews and Poles in wartime. Every Jew was sentenced to death, even children. Of those who found themselves under German occupation, 5 to 7 percent of ethnic Poles were killed, as opposed to 98 percent of Polish Jews.

In the evening I summarize the Tych interview for Jacek Kuroń and he tells me of his first day at school in Lvov during the war. His family had just moved, so he knew nobody in the class. The teacher said, "Good thing the Jews are gone." The children in the class responded with laughter, and he didn't dare react.

"My guilt for not speaking up then made me speak up for the rest of my life," says Kuroń.

JUNE 20, 2001

The same unpleasant thing happens to me for the umpteenth time. It surprises me, or I should really say it hurts, when some of my friends and acquaintances say directly or at least suggest to me that I'm "not objective," because of my background. I have the feeling I'm in the hot seat all the time. (I'm repeating the experience of generations of assimilated Jews, though my ancestors already went through this process.) At the same time—if you don't believe the nonsense about the Jedwabne affair being stirred up so Jews can demand billions in compensation from Poland—it's not quite clear to me why I supposedly prefer Poles to have killed Jews in Jedwabne, rather than Germans. The same friends and acquaintances see nothing subjective in the fact that the matter of Polish guilt is being investigated by Poles at the Institute of National Remembrance without questionable blood in their lineage, like Kieres or Ignatiew. (To be clear, I don't accuse them of prejudice, I'm just pointing out a certain lack of balance in the matter.)

JUNE 25, 2001

Białystok. I've come for several days to look at pre- and postwar documents. In the town archive, I run into employees of the local branch of the Institute of National Remembrance, which is right next door. One of them starts to say, "As prosecutor Ignatiew probably told you . . . ," suggesting with insidious hostility that Ignatiew favors one journalist—from the *Gazeta*, to boot—over others.

I'm tempted in these situations to say bluntly, "You want to know to what extent my articles come from leaks by the prosecutor? Here I have to disappoint you, but I work hard enough not to need the prosecutor to establish facts for me, not to mention that Ignatiew is an exemplary official who does not reveal confidential information about an investigation. If anyone is helping anyone here it's I who am helping him, by offering him access to witnesses I've found. On the other hand, the prosecutor is a support to me, something like a therapist."

Because both of us are clearly obsessed with Jedwabne, because we think about it morning, noon, and night. I can always call him, relate to him a recent conversation, and let off steam. I've managed finally to get through Ignatiew's stiffness, his habit of calling me *pani redaktor* ("Miss Editor"), which makes me cringe. We're on first-name terms now, I can even say we're friends. At times I permit myself to exclaim that I can't take it anymore, I've had enough, I'm emigrating. Ignatiew listens and calms me down: "But you know they're not all like that, look how screwed up his life has been because of all this. You were talking to an unhappy, sick person—hatred is a disease."

JUNE 28, 2001
Jedwabne. Stanisław Michałowski called an extraordinary session of the council, because the matter of the memorial ceremony now hangs by a thread. A country road leads to the site of the massacre and the Jewish cemetery across from it, a road that turns to mud when it rains. A construction company was supposed to lay asphalt on the last stretch of it, but Bubel, the anti-Semitic publisher, persuaded "his" council members not to allow the work to be done on the last section of road, which means guests won't be able to get to the monument.

"The town administration stopped bidding for the asphalt paving of the little road leading to the monument," Godlewski tells me. "No one is bothered that firms have already been hired to do all the work. The governor sent a telex saying that they're going to take away our funding, and then we'd have to pay out of our own pockets for the construction that's already been done on the market square. The town would never be able to afford that. The majority reason as follows: 'Give us money; we'll take it and do with it what we like. We'll repair the market square but not the road to the cemetery.' One council member was shouting, 'We won't agree to a road for Jews,' and another, that the town should demand compensation for the ceremony. They wanted at any price to leave the construction undone so that it would be a physical impossibility to get to the monument. I proposed that I would resign in exchange for the completion of the road. I said, 'I think I made a mistake, and I'll offer my resignation, but let's finish what we started, because the town is going to have to pay for it.' And Councilman Dmoch says, 'Resign now, what are you waiting for?' "

The vote on the road work was 7:7. The road will be finished, since in a tie the vote of chairman Stanisław Michałowski counts for two.

"Those seven council members who voted for the continuation of road work," Godlewski continues, "are probably just more sensible than the others; they got scared so much money would have been thrown away. One of the council members signed because he found out I had been invited to a reception at the American Embassy and he wants me to arrange visas for his daughters. But I want to believe that those seven will turn up at the ceremony, and that's almost half the council, so maybe half the townspeople will come, too?"

But the locals read Bubel. Recently he published a conversation with a resident of Jedwabne about how Gross's book was written: "They wrote it in Przestrzele, at the Dziedzices'. Mayor Godlewski was there with some other guys, drinking and writing."

After Bubel wrote that Michałowski's company bypassed the official bidding procedure and got a lucrative commission to replace the windows in the municipal offices, along with a dozen more spurious accusations, the town has been buzzing with gossip about these "scams." Seen from Warsaw, Bubel's little rag isn't very significant, but in Jedwabne it determines people's thinking.

"I can't take it anymore, what he's doing to me," Michałowski explodes. "None of it is true, but people who've known me for years read these idiocies and believe them. Bubel approached me earlier to get me to work with him, he wanted to meet, he called on me, but I showed him the door. He had the nerve to creep into council sessions. He started banging his fist on the table. I warned him. He declared war on me. At every step he undermines me, makes me look like a swindler and a crook, tries to intimidate me. Someone had me followed, probably his people, they even took pictures of my house."

"We laid cobblestones in the courtyard, so people say we did it with Jewish money," Stanisław's wife, Jadwiga, adds. "Crazy things like that. I replied to one guy that, sure, we're going to lay out a Star of David in cobblestones, too."

I arranged with a friend from Jedwabne that at dusk—so no one will see him—he'll get in the car with me and drive me around town. He'll show me which houses are from before the war—I want to re-create prewar Jedwabne house by house. We drive around the grid of streets several times with me scrunched down in the backseat. My guide tells me about the Polish houses as well, and the town fills up with murderers.

"Kubrzyniecki lived here, the one who killed Jews with a knife. Żyluk lived here, not the one who was a big killer, but his brother who also joined in. Bolek Ramotowski lived here. Oh, this is where the man lived who smashed a child's face and made the mother clean his shirt. We're on Przytulska Street, a lot of the thugs were from here—Sielawa, Śliwecki. Przestrzelska Street—the same, a street of killers, Śleszyński, Gościcki . . .

And the next time around: "All of Jedwabne is a cemetery. Here there was a well where two Jews were drowned. Here was a smithy, where Lusiński pulled a Jew out of the line and killed him with an axe. Here . . ."

JULY 2, 2001

President Kwaśniewski in an interview for *Der Spiegel*: "The visit to Jedwabne is the greatest challenge of my presidency."

In Łomża, employees of the Łomżyńska Cotton Works, which went bankrupt two years ago, called a press conference to announce that on July 10 they will blockade the access route to Jedwabne. They stressed this had nothing to do with anti-Semitism, but with their not being paid the salaries owed them for two years.

I call Rabbi Jacob Baker in New York to arrange to meet him in Poland. We have a long and lively conversation in English, even though I only asked him about a possible date to meet. He brands the murderers: "I hear people are talking about how many were killed. It's not good to hear that. They killed as many as they had at hand, and if they'd had more, they'd have killed more." And yet he defends Poland to an extent:

"The murderers acted not only against Jews but against Poland. Your Polish prime minister before the war would never have agreed to that. Sure, a boycott, he called for that, but killing—never."

The rabbi is preparing the address he will give at the ceremony. "I'm assuming the children and grandchildren of the murderers will come to pray. I wouldn't shake the hand of a murderer, because it has blood on it, but if he is sorry for his sins, I'm ready to talk to him. We don't want revenge, only remembrance."

I call Krzysztof Godlewski, as I do regularly, to put my finger on the town's pulse. "It's raining, the construction work has started, nobody is helping us. It's long-term stress, translated into successive packets of cigarettes smoked. And my friends only come to me with propositions I can't refuse: take that day off. Who's coming to the ceremony? I know my mother is. Women have more heart."

JULY 6, 2001

In the morning, Izaak Lewin comes straight from the airport with his grandsons. We're going to the synagogue to say kaddish—according to the Jewish calendar, today is the anniversary of the atrocity. My daughters, Ola and Maniucha, came back from their vacation especially to be here for the prayer ceremony. I've brought Stanisław Ramotowski. Asked to say a few words, he tells—with great panache and feeling—stories about rescuing his wife, and accepts the storm of applause naturally, as if this weren't his first public appearance. How much good he could have done if he'd been invited to schools to tell kids it's worth standing up to the mob and saving a person's life.

In the *Republic*, an interview with the ethnologist Alina Cała titled "Separate Streets, Shared Buildings," about the interweaving of the customs of two communities that lived on the same land for centuries. The Hasids' dress, Alina says, took shape in the eighteenth century under the influence of the Polish nobility's high-collared long jacket, the *żupan*. Paper-cutting, the pride of Polish folk art, probably came from Jewish culture, the round Łowicka paper cuttings are adaptations of *rozejle*, the multicolored cuttings in the shape of little roses that Jews stuck on their windows at Shavuot. Alina describes how powerfully Zionism referred to the Polish Romantic tradition, how Polish Jews frequently joined Zionist organizations under the influence of their schoolteachers' tales about the Polish struggle for independence. She quotes a young man who heard patriotic Polish songs and burst into tears: "Why can't we Jews sing songs in praise of a fatherland?"

I remembered Meir Ronen, who after sixty years of no contact with Poland, was able to reel off to me all the Polish uprisings.

JULY 7, 2001

For the umpteenth time I try to get through to the minister in charge of placing monuments. He is responsible for inviting the families of the murder victims to the ceremony. I had called earlier, right after I got back from Israel, when I read that the Polish government was going to ask them. I wanted to pass along the addresses I had. This didn't seem to be of interest, but I faxed a list of addresses, anyway. Three weeks later, when I called Israel and found out from Jakow Geva's daughter that no one had contacted them, I contacted the minister's office again. I've been bounced from one official to another, treated like a tiresome petitioner.

The same thing happens when I contact other officials from the prime minister's staff who are responsible for the organization of the ceremony. Wherever ill will can be shown, it is. I call the staff office and give them names of people who want to go to the ceremony; I know there are quite a few buses going. At the third name I hear: "And who is this lady? Okay, but she'll have to be the last one."

JULY 8, 2001

Two visits today—a journalist from a Dutch weekly and a journalist from Austrian radio. Lately two foreign journalists a day is the norm. They are preparing articles or broadcasts about July 10. They go to Jedwabne. They try to talk to the locals, who are unwilling; they mostly hear that Jews denounced their neighbors. They meet Father Orłowski, who loves giving interviews. They are confirmed in their idea of Poland as a country of anti-Semites and backward Catholics. They go to the town hall, where they talk to Godlewski. A conversation with him confirms the idea they took away from their visits in the first period of Solidarity, of Poland as a country of brave people unmarked by Communism (often it is I who send them to the mayor, because I want them to encounter that better Poland, too).

Each of them has his or her own perspective, and when I can I always try to learn something of interest. When I pointed out to an American journalist that the main witness to the massacre, Szmul Wasersztejn, died in 2000, the same year that Gross published his book, he presented his "theory of the last witness." When crimes are analyzed in different parts of the world, crimes discovered after being hushed up for years, it often turns out that they were revealed precisely at the moment when the last witnesses were dying. A Japanese TV crew plans to film an hour-long documentary about Jedwabne in connection with the discussion being aired in their country about crimes against the Chinese during World War II. The documentary is meant to show the courage with which Poland is confronting the dark pages of its history.

JULY 9, 2001

At the *Gazeta* we're preparing tomorrow's issue on the sixtieth anniversary of the massacre. I brought photographs Meir Ronen gave me in Israel. I have to write captions for them, but it's hard to see who's who. In the end I figure out that sometimes I have the people on a photograph written down from left to right, and other times from right to left (apparently in Hebrew you tell what's in a picture from right to left, just as you read). I call Ronen. Is he sure Szmul Wasersztejn is the little boy in the last row with the ears that stick out, and is it really Jakub Kubrzański and Mosze Olszewicz on either side of him, the two with whom he survived in hiding, under the Wyrzykowskis' barn? Yes, it's them.

I look at the mock-up of tomorrow's edition. In big print: "A Place That Shrieks," a class picture from a Jedwabne grammar school, an editorial called "Standing with the Truth," and Zbigniew Herbert's poem "Mr. Cogito Seeks Advice":

> So many books dictionaries
> bloated encyclopedias
> but no one to give advice
>
> they studied the sun
> the moon the stars
> they lost me

my soul
refuses the solace
of knowledge

so I wander at night
on our fathers' roads

and here
is the town of Bracław
amid black sunflowers

the place we abandoned
the place that shrieks

it is Shabbas
as always on Shabbas
a New Heaven appears

—I'm looking for you Rebbe

—he's not here—
say the Hasidim
—he is in the world of Sheol
—he had a beautiful death
say the Hasidim
—very beautiful
as if he crossed
from one side
to the other side
he was all black
held in his hand
a flaming Torah

—I'm looking for you Rebbe

—beyond what firmament
did you hide your wise ear

—my heart aches Rebbe
—I have troubles

Rabbi Nachman
might give me advice
but how do I find him
among so many ashes

I draw it to the managing editor's attention that he wanted a picture of Jedwabne's Jews, but he chose for the front page a class picture from 1936, by which time Polish children already formed the majority. But alongside the photo, he runs a handwritten note with the names of the pupils and teachers. The pupils were then fourteen or fifteen. In 1941 they will have been twenty. Three of the Polish boys have the same first and last names as later killers. But are they the same people? I'm inclined to think it's a good choice, a photograph that shows future victims, perpetrators, and witnesses of the massacre sitting side by side, smiling at the photographer.

A friend calls me late in the evening to tell me to listen to the Catholic Radio Maryja. The whole evening's broadcast is devoted to Jedwabne.

"President Kwaśniewski is going to be flagellating the wrong person," I hear, "us, not himself, not a criminal with a Communist background, where Jews played their part; he was raised with all that. Kwaśniewski is exposing Poles to disgrace." They announce that five thousand people have already signed an appeal saying Kwaśniewski's apology in their name harms their personal interests. In less than an hour Radio Maryja mentioned me several times, in the category of "Jews and traitors to the fatherland." I turn it off, because it gets boring—hate speech endlessly repeats the same thing.

JULY 10, 2001

In the double-decker bus I ride with Stanisław Ramotowski, there are about twenty people; there are eight in the bus next to us. Escorted by police cars with revolving lights, in a cavalcade of government buses, partly empty, we speed away to the ceremony in Jedwabne.

Stanisław dozes at the front of the bus, I sit in back near Jakow Geva, the former Jakub Pecynowicz from Jedwabne, and his daughters Rywka, Chaja, and Rachel.

Jakow Geva, smaller than each of his daughters, sits in a tense silence. We come to the place a kilometer outside of Jedwabne where a weekly market is held. We straggle onward on foot through mud and rain.

The zones intended for guests are cordoned off by police. Chopin's *Marche funèbre* sounds in the market square. Behind a blue-and-white flag of the State of Israel, I see Izaak Lewin, his daughters, his son-in-law, and two grandsons. They are dressed in white shirts and white yarmulkes, the Jewish color of mourning. He's here. The family, the flag, and the names of the Jews of Wizna murdered in the Jedwabne barn printed in big letters on a board. I recognize the list dictated to me in Israel by Awigdor Kochaw, which will tonight be shown on television throughout Europe.

A tense Krzysztof Godlewski addresses the families of the murdered: "I have the privilege of speaking to you in the name of the town authorities and residents. I welcome you to the hospitable land of Jedwabne. It moves me deeply that we meet here today to bear witness to the truth."

President Kwaśniewski: "For this crime we should beg the shadows of the dead and their families for forgiveness. Therefore today, as a citizen and as the president of the Polish Republic, I apologize. I apologize in the name of those Poles whose conscience is moved by that crime."

The Israeli ambassador to Poland, Szewach Weiss, speaks in Polish and Hebrew: "The people who lived here side by side and knew each other's names, Rachele, Jankele, Leja, Dejałe, Moszele—and we know each person has a name and these names have meaning—were murdered and burned by their neighbors."

I only regret that no one said anything in Yiddish, the language that sounded in this marketplace for centuries.

Stanisław Ramotowski leans over to me: "The president speaks well. If even one man tells the truth, it's a lot. And so many good people have come, they keep coming up to me to say something cordial and shake my hand. I just hope it doesn't die down. The same thing that happened in Jedwabne happened in Radziłów and Wąsosz and now it's important not to abandon those murdered people."

Behind the barriers for the guests, some people listen attentively to the speeches, but most are just gawkers. They came to see what a Jew looks like, to see the president. There are also those who behave with flagrant hostility, talk loudly, make silly faces, probably displaying their notion of Jewish mannerisms.

We walk in a silent procession to the site of the crime. Rabbi Baker gets up from his wheelchair and leans on a cane: "I stand here as a compatriot of the murdered and the murderers. We are here because of tears wept by Jews and people of other faiths. This has made a great impression in heaven. The president has said that Poland—our Poland—asks forgiveness. Those he asks for forgiveness should bestow it. May these tears, which should enter history as one of Poland's finest moments, cleanse this earth of hatred."

It's bone cold, rain is coming down, and it looks as if the wind is going to blow over the diminutive rabbi. Groups of young men standing on the road leading to the cemetery, who shouted "Yids!" when we walked past, now try to drown out his speech with music blaring from speakers, and make humping motions to the beat.

The climactic moment comes with the psalms, performed by the world-famous New York cantor Joseph Malovany. His song, his cry, are as powerful as if he wanted to gather up the remains of the dead in the cloak of the psalms, whose cry resounded across these same fields sixty years ago.

In the zone for guests there are pitifully few people from political or cultural life, and only three priests. No high-level Church representatives. My friend Róża Woźniakowska-Thun leans over to me: "I'm shocked. I was afraid I wouldn't make it here on time and there would be crowds. There's nobody here. And where are my spiritual guides?"

I complete the list of those who are absent: Antonina Wyrzykowska was too frightened to come. There's no one from the Wasersztejn family. Nor did Awigdor Kochaw come—the only living Jewish witness who was in the market square that day.

8

Your Only Chance Was
to Pass for a Goy

or, The Survival of Awigdor Kochaw

They were being herded down a country road amid fields of rye. They'll kill me anyway, he thought, but I'll try to escape. He bounded out of the crowd, lowered his head, and broke into the rye at full speed. He ran a ways and threw himself down. He lay motionless, holding his breath. He knew the grain would start waving at the slightest movement.

He heard the shouting of boys trampling the grain in search of escapees. Nearby someone shouted, "Damn you, shut up!" Then a whimper or stifled sob. He realized they were raping a girl nearby.

He held his breath again and listened closely. He expected to hear gunshots, maybe even grenades exploding. He thought the Poles were just leading the Jews to the site of execution, where the Germans would be waiting—as they had been before, in Wizna, where he was born. But he didn't see any soldiers. The racket died down, and he went on lying low, nestled into the earth. Suddenly he heard a noise in the distance, like buzzing or air vibrations, and then a column of smoke shot into the sky.

A fire has broken out, he said to himself, and sighed in relief. The houses in town are made of wood, and the fire brigade is all volunteers. They'll rush to put out the fire and leave the Jews in peace.

He lay in the grain and thought comforting thoughts: How many Germans can there be? Not that many, and when the Poles go home the Germans won't be able to handle so many Jews. Or: It's good not to

Jewish Tarbut school in Wizna, fifth grade. Awigdor Nieławicki (later Kochaw) is sitting on the left in the first row. (Courtesy of Izaak Lewin)

Dina and Icchak Nieławicki of Wizna. On July 10, 1941, they were staying with their cousins, a miller's family in Jedwabne, and they were killed by Poles there. Their son Awigdor, who fled from near the barn, survived. (Courtesy of Rabbi Jacob Baker)

hear shooting, maybe there will be no victims. Only, why the stench of burning flesh? But it was possible that someone's cowshed or barn had caught fire with livestock inside.

He wanted to believe this, so he didn't stop to wonder why a shriek had gone up just before he saw the column of smoke. He lay in the grain until the sun set. When everything had quieted down and it had grown dark, he set off to check on the Pecynowiczes, relatives from Jedwabne, where his family had gone after they fled Wizna. On the way there he met a Jew who had been hidden in a Pole's basement during the massacre, and who told him about the burning. He warned him that the farmers had started looting, so it would be a terrible mistake to go to the Pecynowiczes, who were considered wealthy.

Then he knew he had been a witness to the burning of the Jedwabne Jews. He prayed his two sisters, eleven-year-old Cypora Fajga and seven-year-old Chaja Szejna, had not been in the procession from which he had managed to escape. He was fearful about the fate of his parents, whom he had last seen on July 8.

"A few of us found each other, two from Wizna," Kochaw remembered. "We sat in the grain for two days. One of us, a baker, sneaked off to some Polish friends for food. The farmers combed through the fields looking for people hiding, so we decided that each of us would try to get to Łomża on our own. I hoped I would find my parents there, at my uncle's house."

Poles had to have passes, and Jews weren't allowed to travel at all. Awigdor saw Germans checking the traffic on a bridge over the Narew River. He could swim across at night, but he didn't want to move around a strange city in the dark. He noticed that the soldiers weren't stopping carts. Some farmer got off his wagon and crossed the bridge on foot, leading his horse. Awigdor crossed just behind him, pretending to belong with the farmer. That was his debut as a Pole.

Once in Łomża he went straight to his uncle's house, but he didn't find him at home. He realized it was Tisha B'Av, a day of mourning commemorating the destruction of the Temple in Jerusalem. He saw a minyan in a courtyard; his uncle was one of the ten Jews at prayer. No one had heard about the massacre in Jedwabne, as not many people went there and news traveled slowly. They listened to his story as if he were mad.

Awigdor Kochaw, then Awigdor NiełAwicki, the sixteen-year-old eyewitness who escaped from a column of Jews being led to slaughter on July 10, 1941, lived in Israel for over half a century, but he spoke Polish so well that it was only when he asked me for the word for the season between winter and summer that I realized how remote the language was to him.

He showed me a photograph with the caption *Wizna 1937, Fifth Grade of the Tarbut School*—a Zionist organization active in Eastern Europe that prepared youth for life in Palestine. One's gaze is drawn to the smallest boy, looking out rakishly from under a school cap turned sideways. It's him. He is the smallest boy because he skipped a grade. It had grown more and more difficult to be a Jew in Poland, and in one year, four families with children had left Wizna for Uruguay, the United States, and Palestine. They'd had to dissolve the fourth grade, and the weaker students repeated the third grade while the ones who excelled, like Awigdor, jumped straight to the fifth. Hebrew was the language of instruction, but they also taught literature, history, and geography in Polish, because students from the school were allowed to continue their education in Polish schools. Recognition by the Polish educational authorities ensured the school a grant from the government. However, a growing wave of anti-Semitism led to a 1937 decision in the parliament to abolish grants to Jewish schools, and the tuition was high in Wizna—six zlotys a month.

"Of my class, three of us survived," Kochaw recounted. "Dawid Pędziuch, the one in the middle of the bottom row, managed to leave for Palestine; his sister was burned in Jedwabne. The one on the right, Kron, survived the war in Russia. And me. In the picture there's also Zalman Męczkowski, with whom I was supposed to travel to Prussia in 1943, but he didn't turn up at our agreed meeting place. He had family in Palestine, so I don't think he survived, because he would have contacted them after the war. Unless he stayed in Poland, but that's impossible—he was a Zionist."

In the Tarbut School they were taught to recite by heart poems by Chaim Nachman Bialik, "our Hebrew Mickiewicz," as Kochaw calls him. In his most famous poem, the epic "In the City of Slaughter," written after the Kishinev pogrom of 1903, the poet accuses Jews of failing to put up resistance when pogroms took place.

> *Then wilt thou flee to a yard, observe its mound.*
> *Upon the mound lie two, and both are headless—*
> *A Jew and his hound . . .*

The self-same axe struck both, and both were flung
Unto the self-same heap where swine seek dung;
. . . .

Where seven heathen flung a woman down,
The daughter in the presence of her mother,
The mother in the presence of her daughter
. . . .

Do not fail to note,
In that dark corner, and behind that cask
Crouched husbands, bridegrooms, brothers, peering from the cracks,
Watching the sacred bodies struggling underneath
The bestial breath,
Stifled in filth, and swallowing their blood!
. . . .

How did their menfolk bear it, how did they bear this yoke?
They crawled forth from their holes, they fled to the house of the Lord,
They offered thanks to Him, the sweet benedictory word.
. . . .

Come, now, and I will bring thee to their lairs
The privies, jakes and pigpens where the heirs
Of Hasmoneans lay, with trembling knees,
Concealed and cowering,—the sons of the Maccabees!
The seed of saints, the scions of the lions!
Who, crammed by scores in all the sanctuaries of their shame,
So sanctified My name!
It was the flight of mice they fled,
The scurrying of roaches was their flight;
They died like dogs, and they were dead!
. . . .

Your dead were vainly dead; and neither I nor you
Know why you died or wherefore, for whom, nor by what laws;
Your deaths are without reason; your lives are without cause.
What says the Shekinah? In the clouds it hides
In shame, in agony alone abides . . .*

* From *Complete Poetic Works of Hayyim Nahman Bialik*. Israel Efros, ed. New York, 1948.

Many years later Kochaw met one of his teachers in Haifa; she had emigrated to Palestine before the war. Her husband, a senior official in the Histadrut labor union, asked him how he had survived. He replied that he didn't want to earn the scorn that in Bialik's poem even God feels toward the victims.

"That Zionist education," he repeated to me, "gave me strength not to become a sheep led meekly to slaughter." He said, "When I was in the army in Israel, they put pressure on you to change your name to a Hebrew one. After all, if I was in a unit with a Moroccan Jew, he'll never be able to pronouce the name Nieławicki. I had family, so I decided to settle on a name together with them. My cousin, who later died in the Six-Day War in 1967, chose the name Bnaja. I didn't like it and went my own way. I found some relatives of my mother whose name was Stern, or 'star'; in Hebrew, Kochaw. They had become the Kochawi family, because at that time it was a fashion to add a Polish ending. I didn't want the ending."

According to family legend the surname Nieławicki, used by Awigdor's family in Poland, came from his great-great-grandfather's briefly owning land in Nieławice. Those were the days of the Duchy of Warsaw and the Napoleonic Code, which allowed Jews to own land. After the property was sold he moved to Wizna, where he built a large, sturdy house.

"Once, my parents were doing work on the house," he remembered, "and under the paint they found an inscription: *1812, Nieławicki*. I brought my whole class over to show them how long the house had been in our family."

That's where Awigdor was born, and that is where he lived with his parents and his grandfather Meir Hersz Nieławicki for the first years of his life. The grandfather, who did well for himself selling miscellaneous supplies to the tsarist army, bought land in Przestrzele near Jedwabne. Awigdor's father, Icchak Nieławicki, was one of thirteen children; during the war against the Bolsheviks in 1920 he was an infantry soldier and fought to defend Warsaw. His sister Menucha Perel died before her nephew Awigdor was born. One day she encountered some drunken Polish boys. One of them said, "I have to kill a Jew," and stabbed her to death with a knife. The next day they got their draft cards and that's how they avoided the law.

After the 1936 pogrom in Przytyk in central Poland, when Jews trained in self-defense (they even had firearms) put up a fight against the peasants, one of Awigdor's paternal uncles, Joszua, called Szyjek, decided to prepare the Wizna Jews to defend themselves and hoarded knives and axes. He thought they should fight, that pogroms should not be known only for Jewish deaths. Listening to him talk, little Awigdor decided to stop studying Polish, because he was going to Palestine anyway. He didn't do his homework, and refused to answer in Polish at the blackboard. His mother persuaded him that a knowledge of languages can never hurt, and anyway a Hebrew school without Polish wouldn't be recognized.

At home they spoke Yiddish, but his parents also knew Polish, Hebrew, German, and French.

"Mama corrected me when I was speaking Polish to the farmers from the neighborhood: 'Don't wag your hands, that's how Jews talk.' That saved me later when I was pretending to be a Pole," Kochaw remembered.

"In 1929 the parliament passed the agrarian reform requiring Jews to sell their land," he said, "and my grandfather sold his property and lent money to landowners in Janczewo, Krzewo, Bronów, and Bożejewo. They needed funding because with the reform came an order to improve the soil. Soon they started letting their dogs off the chain when my grandfather came to collect his loan payments. Only the landowner Trener, a German from Bożejewo, paid his loan off in regular installments."

All the Jews he knew wanted to go to Palestine. Even his uncle Becalel, who had served with the *uhlans*, or Polish light cavalry, a traditional subject of patriotic songs, and—when his grandfather still had his land—drove a horse-drawn carriage among the farmhands. His father laughed about his brother going to Palestine, joking that there his work would also be driving around in a carriage like a lord.

"Our whole family was waiting to emigrate, but I was the most eager," said Kochaw, who was a woodworking apprentice with a neighbor after he finished the seventh grade. They didn't go, because they couldn't get any money from their debtors. To emigrate to Palestine you had to show you had the sum of a thousand pounds sterling each in the bank and have another thousand for the journey.

Grandfather Stern, owner of a mill, bought a large property for his daughter Dina's dowry, in Chudnie near Nowogród. His son-in-law leased it to a certain Podgórski. "They paid him back in the beginning, but when people started saying the Jews were to blame for all the evil in the world, they stopped," Kochaw remembered. "Father took the matter to court. A lease contract was valid for many years, so we couldn't sell the property before the court ruled on it. Just before the war we won the case in the Supreme Court, but we didn't get our money back anyway."

Of the Soviet occupation, Kochaw remembers most clearly that suddenly everybody became very poor. His father went to see Trener, who as a half German was about to go to the Reich with his wife in accordance with Soviet-German agreements. Trener gave Kochaw's father two cows and had him load up his wagon with food. "If we survive," he said in parting, "we'll meet and figure out how much I still owe you."

Kochaw's birthplace, Wizna, was bombed on the second day of the Stalin-Hitler war. The target of the attack was the floating bridge the Soviets were preparing to throw across the Narew. The market square was burned, but Grandfather Nieławicki's house survived. The residents of the town scattered into the surrounding fields, and Awigdor's father loaded some possessions onto a wagon—they were going to hide in the country for a while.

"We looked around and saw prisoners released from Soviet jail, drunk, looking for Jews to beat up," Kochaw related. "The marauders caught up with us. They beat us with poles, took the horse and wagon. Our relative Fejbusz Lejman was with us, he was old and sick, and died two days later from the beating. We saw a niece of Izrael Meir Dymnicki, the smith, raped in a field. He himself, a sturdy peasant over seventy, had said, when other Jews had fled, 'I'm not afraid, I know everybody in this town,' and stayed put. He was sitting on his porch when the rabble came. 'Get the Jew!' they yelled. When they found a Jew they'd beat him to death."

They went back to Wizna, where Jewish homes were being occupied by residents whose houses had been bombed. The Jews crowded into the few buildings left to them. The Nieławickis hid in Awigdor's grandfather's attic. The town was run by "partisans," as Kochaw calls them, who had been in jail or in hiding during the Soviet occupation. Now they beat Jews in the street and warned Poles not to sell food to Jews or keep them in their homes.

"The Germans used them as helpers," Kochaw continued. "I remember a boy from the National Party, his name was Brzozowiak. He would chase Jews, yelling '*Juden arbeiten!*' (Jews to work!). My grandfather Nieławicki was among the ones he chased. The Germans drove all the

Jews Brzozowiak caught out of town and shot them. The next day the Germans appeared on Srebrowska Street, where many Jews were hiding with the blacksmith Monko. They ordered the men to dig holes in the yard and shot them, too. The Germans didn't touch the women. But when they killed the Goldmans, father and son, the wife and mother begged them: 'Kill me, too.' And they did. It was the same when they shot Kron; his wife, Chana, asked them to kill her, which they did."

When the village head of Wizna declared after the air raid and the fire that there was no room for the Jews in the town, a number of them went to Łomża, others to Białystok, but most went to Jedwabne. Awigdor's parents, Icchak and Dina Nieławicki, and their children took refuge at the house of their relative Eli Pecynowicz, who had a mill just outside Jedwabne, on the road to Radziłów. On Tuesday, July 8, 1941, Icchak decided to go back to Wizna to get some of his belongings from a Polish friend, and his wife decided to go with him. They were to be back in two days. On Wednesday night, a school friend of cousin Dewora Pecynowicz's ran over to warn them: "Tomorrow they're going to finish off the Jews, you've got to run away." A family council was called, but the elders underestimated the threat from the Polish side.

Just in case, Awigdor decided to spend the night in the field, and two of his cousins joined him, Josef Lejb and Beniamin Pecynowicz. The rest of the family slept at home. It was a chilly night, and the mosquitoes were biting so no one got any sleep and the cousins were frantic. It was still dark when the cousins set off for the German police station—they worked there grooming horses and chopping wood for the kitchen stove, and they had to turn up at dawn. Awigdor was awoken early in the morning by the rattling of wagons. This gave him pause, because it wasn't a market day. Then he heard the sound of windows being smashed and women screaming. He knew at once it was a pogrom, and he made for Wizna to warn his parents to stay away. A couple of teenagers started chasing him. Dressed in three pairs of pants and shirts so as not to freeze in his sleep, he couldn't outrun them. They began beating him and one said, "Why take him to the marketplace, let's do him in on the way." But then they passed an older woman, who said, "You caught a Jew, now take him to the others and get rid of them all in one go!"

And so it was that Awigdor Nieławicki found himself in the market square in Jedwabne on July 10, 1941, in a crowd being sent to slaughter.

When he got there the Jews were weeding between the cobblestones, singing, "The war's the fault of us Jews." The Poles had stanchions, poles, clubs, knives. He saw a familiar face—a carter from Wizna, Chonek Kubrzański.

"He refused to carry the statue of Lenin and he was putting up a fight. They hit him with iron bars until he collapsed," Kochaw told me.

They were ordered to line up in fours and march down a road leading out of town; the barn was just on the outskirts of Jedwabne. Awigdor tried to stay on the inside, to avoid getting hit. Because everyone was trying to protect themselves the same way, the procession swelled, filling the whole road.

"We had already left Jedwabne behind," he continued, "when I thought, They'll kill me anyway. But I'll try to escape."

He got away and made it to the Łomża ghetto.

One day a friendly farmer from near Wizna, Pieńkowski, arrived in search of the Niełamicki family. He had brought butter and eggs. Awigdor had urged his family to store their property with him, because it would be safe only with a Pole.

"Pieńkowski had resisted, saying he didn't know when he could return it to us, and he would be ashamed to buy anything, to take advantage of the situation," said Kochaw, to whom it was important to rescue from oblivion the name of one of the few Poles known to him who actually helped Jews. "This was a time when people drove their wagons up to Jewish homes and took everything for a song. When they were setting up the Łomża ghetto there were rumors that you could only bring twenty kilos of luggage with you. The day before we moved into the ghetto I took all our family's things to Pieńkowski. On the way to the ghetto people stood by the side of the road, grabbing bundles and jeering. The Jews comforted themselves: 'We'll have peace in the ghetto, we'll survive somehow.'"

Not until the Łomża ghetto, where the few surviving Jews from Jedwabne found themselves, did it sink in what had really happened. Then Awigdor realized that the noise that had reached him when he was lying in the grain was the sound of a communal prayer said before death, *Shma Israel, Adonai elohenu, Adonai echad* ("Hear O Israel . . ."). Jewish martyrs throughout history had died with this profession of faith on their lips.

Together with his cousins Josef and Beniamin—who had survived because they had spent the day at the police station—Awigdor began to assess the losses in his family. A Pole told them he had seen Eli Pecynowicz and his wife and daughters in the barn. Awigdor understood that this meant he would never see his sisters, Cypora and Chaja, again—they had spent the night at their uncle's. He put out feelers around the area and asked everyone he met about his parents. The family they had in Zambrów had no news of them. Nor had Jews from Piątnica who came to the Łomża ghetto seen Icchak or Dina Nieławicki.

In the beginning, he and his relatives were squeezed into one room with thirty people, but the Germans began selecting people for deportation and soon there were barely ten of them left. The *Judenrat* organized work assignments. They would go out on Monday, work on construction, sleep somewhere side by side, and return to the ghetto at the end of the week. They were not paid anything, and fed only once a day. No one guarded them very closely. The Germans knew that the Jews saw the ghetto as a relatively safe place and that they had very little hope of surviving outside it.

When Kochaw was working between Drozdów and Wizna, he got away briefly to see Pieńkowski, who was moved to tears. He suggested to Awigdor that he come to sleep at their house after work, and promised to ask the police if he himself might not hire the boy to work on the farm. Pieńkowski's wife and son both kept saying, "You don't look like a Jew at all, and you speak Polish just like any of us." It was they who gave him the idea of surviving as a Pole. Pieńkowski seized on the plan right away: "We'll tell everyone you're from Wizna, because I have family there. You can help us harvest potatoes until the war's over." They thought at that time that the Germans would lose and the Russians were about to come back.

He sneaked into the ghetto a few times, because he "needed to talk to Jews," and he also brought food to his family members. Despite threats, there was information being shared among the Jews from the area. In the ghetto he heard that a few Jews were still living in Wizna, and working for the Germans. He heard that his uncle Becalel had survived, the one who liked to play the lord and who had returned from Palestine before the war. He was told that some Pole had seen his parents after the pogrom in Jedwabne and that Rywka Leja, who was in Wizna, knew who this Pole was. This was confirmed by Rywka Kajzer, who had managed to escape from the market square in Jedwabne with her daughter.

One day he risked a trip to Wizna, and Rywka Leja told him how to find the Polish neighbor who said he'd met his parents. He found the man, who confirmed that he had seen Icchak Niełdawicki with his wife and daughters after the killing was over. He described their clothes, said they were on their way to Zambrów and then to Łomża.

For a long time Awigdor refused to abandon hope and did not say kaddish for his parents. When I met him he was still considering various versions of their deaths. The first was that his parents were killed after July 10, somewhere on the way from Zambrów to Łomża. The second was that they died in the fields between Wizna and Jedwabne at the hands of thugs who were prowling the area, intoxicated with killing. And finally, the third possibility, that they were in fact in the crowd driven to the barn, because he thought his mother's face had flashed by him in the marketplace. He suspects his source must have gotten something mixed up, because it's not clear how the daughters were supposed to have turned up at their parents' side; the girls had stayed with the Pecynowiczes.

Another day Awigdor looked in on a house in Wizna where several Jewish families lived. The two brothers Sokołowicz were drivers for the German police; before the war they had had a dairy and produced butter for export. He heard that his uncle Joszua was in hiding with a peasant; in Wizna they were giving out new identity papers, because the municipal building had been burned down and they were trying to re-create the registry of residents. He thought at that point that it was better to have Jewish papers than none at all.

"Rumors were spreading that every Christian who hid a Jew would be executed," Kochaw related, "and Pieńkowski's wife and daughter were terrified: 'We're afraid they'll kill our husband and father; we can help you, but in another way.' I was counting on getting through the winter with them, so I felt as if someone had punched me in the face."

He didn't want to go back to the ghetto, didn't think it was safe, so he decided he would try to pass for Polish. He set off for Wizna across the fields, and went to the authorities, where he found an official who didn't know him. "Name? Wiktor Mielnicki. Father's name? Ignacy. Mother's name? Eugenia." The official automatically filled in under religion: Catholic.

"It was a temporary document, without a photo. At least I was carrying something. I heard there was a farmer near Kramkowo with a large farm whose sons had been sent to Russia, so he was looking for a farmhand. I showed him my papers right away. He promised me food in exchange for labor. I didn't need anything else, but I asked: Maybe you can give me something from time to time to bring to my mother? I always talked about my mother, my grandfather, brothers, because that's what distinguished Poles from Jews, that they had family. He promised me flour and ham once a month."

Someone must have recognized Awigdor, though, because one day the Germans arrived. It was the winter of 1941–1942. He guessed who was coming because he heard the sound of sleigh bells, and Poles were not allowed bells; he hid himself in the hay. He heard his boss explaining: "I have one boy working for me, I don't know anything about him, you'd have to check." They searched the hay above his head with pitchforks but they didn't find the hiding place, which he'd prepared earlier. He ran away as soon as they were gone.

He found his uncle Joszua, who had spent a whole month in a peasant's attic and thought all Jews apart from him had been killed. He complained to his nephew that his host tormented him by wondering out loud if he'd keep him there through the winter.

"It would have been impossible for my uncle to pretend to be Polish, although his looks were more Aryan than mine," Kochaw said, explaining why they didn't go into hiding together. "He was a true Zionist." Awigdor went from village to village. "Praise the Lord," he would start and end every conversation. And he would tell his story: that he was looking for work, because he'd been sent to Prussia to do forced labor and had run away. He was usually given a bed in the stable over the horses, or in a barn, so he could prepare a hiding place and an escape route. Once, he heard the peasants talking about Jews having built a bunker in the marshes and hiding there. When he found his uncle Becalel, he heard from him that their relatives the Zacharewiczes—Awigdor's grandmother, whose maiden name was Zacharewicz, had three brothers, Szaja, Abraham, and Izrael—were hiding in the marshes.

He made it to the other side of the Biebrza river. He found the bunker and inside, thirty young Jews—the elders and children had been killed. They had some money, which they used to buy food from Poles, and two revolvers. They dreamed of joining some partisan group, but in these lands no partisans would accept Jews.

"I didn't want to stay with them because I didn't think they'd survive," said Kochaw. "Too many locals knew that Jews were hiding somewhere in the marshes. Anyway, they didn't invite me to stay because they were already living in terrible poverty."

Szaja Zacharewicz's son Daniel, whom Awigdor knew well because he had lived in their house when he was at school in Wizna, looked a hundred percent Polish and spoke Polish like any peasant. Awigdor said to him, "Come with me, your only chance is to pass for a goy." He refused, but advised Awigdor to find his sister, who had been baptized and married a Pole before the war, and his brother-in-law was a good man. Awigdor went to them, and his brother-in-law found him a job.

"He got a Jew from Tykocin, a leatherworker who was permitted by the Germans to work in the area, to recommend me as a Polish journeyman," Kochaw remembered. "We ate with the Polish peasant family out of one pot, I as a Pole with them at the table, he as a Jew sat to the side and got the leftovers. He never let on that he knew what I was. On Saturday he went back to the ghetto and I stayed with the farmer."

He met a boy who had fled from a German farm near Klaipeda, and who told him all the men were at the front and the farm women needed a helping hand. He told his classmate Zalman Męczkowski, who also looked Aryan and worked at a mill as a Pole, "My papers aren't worth very much, least of all around here, because if I was so close to home, why didn't I get permanent ones? Let's go to Prussia, they haven't seen a Jew there since 1939, they won't remember what one looks like, and the Poles have mostly fled because the work was too strenuous for them." They agreed to leave for Prussia on November 5. But on All Souls' Day 1942, the Germans decided to cleanse the town of all remaining Jews and take them to the Łomża ghetto.

"The day before I was drinking with the boys from the village, by then I'd learned to drink vodka," Kochaw related. "I came back at night so drunk I didn't go into my hiding place, I didn't even pull the ladder up. It was dawn when I heard a voice above me say, 'A Jew, a Jew.' I pretended to be asleep. Someone kicked me: 'Get up, you Jewish piece of shit!' And I went, 'Hell, are you taking me with my noble Polish blood for a Jew?' I turned over on my other side and pretended to sink back into a drunken sleep. My hosts said, 'If he's a Jew, take him.' I understood from what they said that they were supposed to catch all the Jews in the area. They brought me to the village head. I didn't know how my persecutors had found out I was a Jew, but I knew it was a death sentence. There were two older Jews from the Łomża ghetto there who had been hired as laborers. I went over to a bench on the other side of the building, saying, 'I'm not sitting with those Jews.'

"I was left with one guard," he continued. "I say to him, 'They're going to take me to do forced labor, but I just escaped from Prussia. I'm not a Jew.' I started opening my pants. He said, 'It's not me, it's the Germans who'll check.' I told stories about Jews, and asked him: 'How can you, my Polish brother, do this to me?' Nothing helped. I tried another method. I pretended to fall asleep, my head was nodding, and he dozed off as well. My hands and legs were free, I thought I was a dead man anyway, but maybe I could make a run for it. I jumped for the door and ran through the village. He was shouting, 'Catch the Jew!' A boy ran after me, grabbed hold of me; I looked and saw he was one of the boys I'd been drinking with the day before. I say, 'Stanisław, let me go, I'm not a Jew, they just want to send me to Prussia.' He let me go. They started shooting at me. I crossed a yard where there were four dogs, and not one of them barked. I was always good with dogs."

He spent the night in the swamp. In the morning he met a woman he knew from the Łomża ghetto, Farberowicz's daughter from the village Krzewo, whose husband had been shot. She had her two sons with her. She asked him, "Awigdor, I know you pass for Polish, take my little Szmul with you."

"But, you see, miss, I couldn't take him with me. His Polish was very bad." This was the only time while telling his story that Kochaw addressed himself to me directly, as if he was taking me for his judge.

What happened to Raszka Farberowicz later we know from the Yad Vashem testimony of Izrael Lewin of Wizna. Her husband was shot in the ghetto where he lay ill at the time of a liquidation operation. She hid with her children until—as Lewin was told by Poles he knew—she drowned herself in a pond. The Germans killed her children.

Zalman wasn't at the agreed-upon meeting place, so Kochaw decided to make his way to the other side of the Narew River alone. He hid his mother's papers and letters under a stone in a field. He kept only a passport photograph of her, because in it she was wearing a black coral necklace—she was in mourning for her father—and the way the beads fell they looked like a cross.

"I got on the ferry and helped push off, because I knew if I did that no one would ask me about anything. I was a good swimmer, I could ride horses and ski, I could row a boat, all of that helped me. I got work right away, laying stone foundations, two marks a day. I would have worked for free, but I couldn't tell them that. After two weeks the farmer came to say they were looking for Jews who had fled Zambrów, and that they would check papers. I ran away. The banks of the Narew were frozen. I took off my clothes, held my shoes and clothes on my head. There was ice at first but it soon broke and I swam a kilometer or two downstream. I was so frozen I could hardly get my clothes back on."

He looked for work again, saying he had run away from a job with a German farmer. He taught himself to pretend to rummage for something in his pockets, his Polish document from Wizna falling out by accident—a sign he wasn't a Jew. He bought himself handwoven shirts like the ones peasants wore. He went by village farms. He listened to stories of locals who'd been to Prussia, he paid attention so as to remember the names. His own stories about his adventures, which his hosts liked to hear, he embellished with what he'd heard. He learned prayers and carols, in order not to be different from the Poles.

It took him a few months to walk to Prussia; he crossed the border near Kolno.

"There were a lot of German colonies there, but you also met Poles," he related. "There were bogs where you could hide at night. I'd creep up to a house at dawn and if I heard 'Get a fucking move on,' I knew it was a Pole talking to his cow during milking, so I went in to ask for work. I said I'd escaped from Klaipeda, I'd always tell them something interesting about the escape, so they would feed me and I would help on the farm."

He spent a few days here, a few days there. He lived on milk taken from cows in the meadows, and he dug up rutabagas and sugar beets from the fields.

He came to like the people on one farm, and their backwoods house surrounded by an orchard; he began to dream of staying there until the end of the war. He wanted them to believe him, so he told them he was going to let his mother know he had found work, so she wouldn't worry about him. He thought the story about his mother would protect him from any suspicion that he was a Jew. He wandered around the area for ten days, without food, in freezing temperatures.

"I came back frozen through and hungry, but definitely Polish."

His ingenious plan assured him barely a few weeks of relative peace and quiet.

"The farm would have kept me till the war was over, but it turned out they were driving around checking papers. It wasn't even about Jews but escapees of all kinds, and I didn't have the right papers."

He went back to his native parts. Once, he heard from a farmer that "there was some little Jew wandering around here." He spotted the boy in an orchard, he was of Awigdor's age, ragged, unshaven, dirty. Kochaw felt a lump in his throat; it had been a long time since he had seen another Jew. Earlier he had come across a Jew from Russia who had whistled the Zionist hymn (and later national anthem of Israel) "Ha-Tikva." Now Awigdor hummed "Ha-Tikva" and saw immediately that the boy knew the melody. Awigdor said, "Ani Yehudi" (I am a Jew). The boy answered in Yiddish. His name was Lajbel Kadysz and he was from Stawiski. He had been hiding in the woods. His father knew a lot of farmers in the area, so he would get a piece of bread every now and then. Every day he looked for a trace of the partisans so he could join up.

"We heard Soviet cannons and I felt the end of the war was near," he remembered. "The Germans were preparing to withdraw; I told him, 'Be careful, because there's one partisan group here, the National Armed Forces, and they would be happy to kill you.' I helped him get better clothes and told him to pretend to be Polish. We agreed to meet up in Eretz Israel."

Awigdor found a household in the village Biodry where they treated him like a son. One night, it was already March 1944, there was movement in the courtyard, and he heard someone say: "We're the Polish army." The men made the house their base for a month. Once, they asked Awigdor if he could take them to Prussia, because they wanted to get arms there. He didn't believe them. He was sure they'd guessed he was a Jew and wanted to kill him, only not in a Pole's backyard. But he went with them. He had no choice. He showed them a place across the Prussian border where a few laborers, including a Frenchman, a Belorussian, and a Ukrainian, were guarded by just one German. They ambushed them, and freed the laborers. Then they tied up the German and took his gun. It was only then that Awigdor believed the men were real partisans.

"They called themselves the Home Army, and I hadn't heard that name before," he said. "Their aim was to liberate Poland from the Germans and establish an independent non-Communist government. I wanted to join them, but their leader replied that he had intellectuals and students in his unit, the kind of people who had to hide in the woods. 'We prefer to have folks like you in houses as a backup.' 'But I don't have a home,' I said, 'I fled from Prussia, the Germans are looking for me, I want to fight for the fatherland.' And I stayed. Some of them were anti-Semites, but they didn't have the hatred in them that I knew from my part of the country. Only one of them told us he had killed some Jews. The rest just made jokes about Jews and sang anti-Semitic songs."

Awigdor remembered that in the autumn of 1944 when the Warsaw Uprising failed, an order came telling them to break up and bury their guns. Again he was on his own. He found out by accident how Kadysz had died. Peasants had caught him, he'd broken away from them, they chased him, he took a gun from one of them but he didn't know how to use it. The persecutors outnumbered him. They tied him up and killed him.

"We'd promised each other: if you don't survive, I'll try to take revenge for you, and you will do the same for me," he remembered, and added: "I found that village and stayed there for over a month until I had done what I had promised."

I couldn't get more out of him. Only that it was later said in the region that a Jew had taken revenge from the grave.

He was afraid to appear in Wizna, thinking that if anyone recognized him he was a dead man. Instead, he went to Łomża, in search of a fellow Jew, no matter whom. Once, he followed someone because he thought he was Jewish. He understood he'd made a mistake when the man arrived home and two grandchildren ran out to meet him. He knew there were no Jewish families left. He was eighteen years old and completely alone in the world.

Every story of Holocaust survival is made up of hundreds of lucky lightning-fast decisions. Many speak of instinct, intuition, providence. What strikes one in Kochaw's tale is the iron consistency with which he carried out his plan for survival: passing for Polish. He was superb at analyzing risk, faultless at estimating his chances, and he was just an adolescent. He tried to get into the Red Army, knowing that military skills would come in handy in Palestine, but he was rejected. He reported to the Polish army, where he was warmly received, with the words "Poland is Communist now and even a Jew can become a pilot."

"I got on the train with my transfer papers," he said. "And there I met two soldiers who I realized were Jewish. They told me there was just as much anti-Semitism in the new, pro-Soviet Polish army as there was in the underground Home Army. 'We're just waiting for the right moment to leave the country. All Jews are meeting in Białystok. The code word is *Am Cha* [Our People].'"

On May 11, 1945, Kochaw found himself in Białystok. He stood in the city center, said, *"Am Cha,"* and someone came up to him right away and told him where the Jewish Committee was. There he gave testimony about his life during the war. Two others appeared and gave testimony, too: a Jew from Kolno who had pretended to be Russian and a blond, blue-eyed fellow from Szczuczyn who had passed for Polish.

The one who'd pretended to be Russian told him that they could already hear the sound of Soviet cannons when his Home Army unit declared it would cleanse Poland of the Jews and Communists. When someone informed them that there were Jews hiding in the marshes on the eastern side of the Biebrza river, they went there, found the bunker, threw grenades into it, drove everyone out. They made them dig holes, and they shot even the wounded. He remembered what the Jews looked like: a tall blond guy with a mustache, and one who was short and dark. It was him they told to cover the bodies with soil. Then they shot him. From his story Awigdor recognized the bunker he had found in the winter of 1941–1942, and Zajman Zacharewicz, the only dark member of the Zacharewicz family.

At the Jewish Committee, people put up notices, searching for family. Kochaw wrote: "I'm alive. I arrived here on May 19—Awigdor Nieławicki." Nobody responded. However, he saw on the notice board that a Miss Zacharewicz from Styczków, born 1940, was still alive. He searched for the little girl, the only surviving member of his whole large family; he threw lines out all over Poland, but he didn't find her. It was not until

1953 that he tracked her down in Israel, where she lived on a kibbutz near Haifa.

While in Białystok, Awigdor entered what he calls the Zionist underground—the Bricha. He was given a Lithuanian girl to care for, and they took off. Their first stop was in Będzin in Silesia, where they founded a kibbutz—where Jews worked together and prepared for kibbutz life in Palestine—in a former Jewish building. They found a large library with books in Yiddish and Hebrew, many of which were ripped up. They glued and sewed them back together and cataloged them. There were Polish books, too, and it was there that Awigdor first encountered the canon of Polish literature. The next time he took a Polish book in hand was half a century later—Jan Gross's *Neighbors*.

Awigdor, at eighteen, was one of the older kibbutzniks. Guns had been given to them by Jewish deserters from the Red Army. He made a hiding place for the guns behind the stove and organized an armed guard every night.

"I foresaw what later happened in the Kielce pogrom," he said. "When that happened I was already in Palestine and I thought to myself that was exactly what we were prepared for every night. We would have died anyway, but we would have shot first."

They left the country on false passports as Greek Jews. The first point of contact was in Bratislava at the Pod Jeleniem hotel, then in Holland, from where Jewish brigades took them to Marseille. There they were loaded on a ship like herrings in a barrel one night, 750 people in total. Near Haifa they were caught by the British but by a miracle managed to reach land. The British had interned hundreds of Jews on Cyprus.

By March 1946, Awigdor was in Palestine. He joined the Haganah, the underground army, and later as a regular soldier he took part in all the wars Israel fought. First he lived on a kibbutz, but when he married and had a son, he rebelled against the kibbutz law that decreed that children were to be brought up separately, without their parents, and he and his wife started to make their own way. He worked as a mechanic for agricultural machines and as an airplane mechanic for El Al.

Kochaw gave a forty-eight-page testimony to Yad Vashem in 1968. Writing out his testimony, the copyist noted, "His recollections came to him freely, without the aid of questions from me. He spoke for many hours, as if reading a text he had in front of him, one written with precision. He spoke loudly, clearly, and was distressed by what he was relating" (just as he spoke to me, over thirty years later). The copyist went on: "He claimed that the majority of Jews from his village, Wizna, were burned in Jed-. wabne, and that this was done with German permission, but that they died at the hands of Poles." And the copyist added: "I don't understand this part."

Journal

JULY 11, 2001

In the morning I take Antonina Wyrzykowska to early services at the synagogue in Warsaw. Rabbi Michael Schudrich gives thanks to Antonina in a ceremony, handing her a menorah.

"Mrs. Wyrzykowski, who hid seven Jews from Jedwabne, reminds us all how we should live our lives."

"Not at all," Antonina's son whispers in my ear. "A good person has a dog's life."

I drive Antonina and her son to Milanówek.

"You can throw away what they gave you, Mother," says her son. "Just like the people you rescued who went to Florida and invited you to the synagogue only to hand you a bunch of dried flowers. Couldn't they have thrown in a hundred dollars in an envelope?"

I receive from Antonina the menorah she was given in the synagogue, along with a bag of walnuts from her neighbor's garden, three jars of pickled mushrooms—one marked with a sticker that says honey has been added to the vinegar—an icon from Jerusalem, and two prayers to the Lord Jesus. As long as I've known her, Antonina has showered me with presents, to which she likes adding things with Jewish symbols or Hebrew writing. With relief she rids herself of awkward gifts.

In the afternoon, a visit to Rabbi Jacob Baker in a government hotel on

Parkowa Street. I bring a map of Jedwabne; I want him to help me figure out who lived where. But the rabbi's eyesight is very bad and he can't read anything. I try to find out how his meeting with Father Orłowski in Jedwabne went yesterday—it was given a lot of press attention.

"We won't talk about it," says the rabbi's brother-in-law Lester Miller, also a rabbi. "We came here to spread peace and love."

JULY 12, 2001

I go to Jedwabne with the Geva family. We're driven in a little bus belonging to CBS News, which is filming a report for *60 Minutes*.

Jakow Geva (formerly Pecynowicz) tells stories the whole way and his eyes are sparkling. "I feel as if I were twenty years old," he declares. He brings to mind a psychotherapy patient who, after coming to terms with some trauma, finally gains access to his happy memories.

His three daughters, Rywka, Chaja, and Rachel, are all around forty, energetic, warm, talking simultaneously. Rachel tells me her parents' story.

They met in 1947 on Cyprus, where Jews trying to get to Palestine illegally were held in a camp.

"They were both alone, without family, with the feeling they had no one in the world except each other. It was there that Papa found out that Poles burned his family. Mama had lost her husband and little daughter in Russia. She was born in Warsaw, graduated from the university. The family spoke Polish at home. She didn't know Yiddish or Hebrew, their only common language was Polish, but Dad didn't want to speak Polish with her."

"I didn't let even one Polish word slip," adds Jakow.

"Father taught Mother Yiddish and that's what they spoke all their lives," Rachel continues. "Everybody else around them tried to speak Hebrew, but Father insisted on speaking the language he'd spoken at home. They were both tormented by memories. Mama was no longer able to be happy, and it was hard to live in our house. We didn't want to be like our parents or hear about their sufferings. When I was seven years old I would check under the pillow for Nazis. We wanted to feel strong, like everyone else, feel the strength of a new thriving state with its army and kibbutzes. We were ashamed of our house, of the fact our parents spoke Yiddish, that they were too old to be parents and dressed differently from the people on the kibbutzim. We dreamed of having parents born on the kibbutz. In the last years of her life, Mama, who had Alzheimer's, only remembered

Polish. We took a woman from Poland in to care for her. We were afraid of Father's reaction. But Barbara was so nice, she'd kiss Mama, call her 'darling.' So much so that even Papa started speaking Polish with her."

"Now we're proud of Dad for having survived," Rywka chimes in. Her sisters pick up the sentence and repeat it, in English to me and in Yiddish to their father.

When we get to Jedwabne, Jakow Geva acts like a farmer showing us around his land. He wants to chat with neighbors in his street. Not about what happened on July 10 but about his town as it is preserved in his memory. "We kept turkeys, ducks, geese, chickens. We bought a young cow and gave her grain three times a day, and potatoes, hay—and after a month and a half we had lard and sausage for a whole year," he says, finding Polish words without any trouble. "Mama was in the kitchen all the time and whenever someone came by she'd treat them to something. After the grain had been harvested Papa would let a Polish woman from the neighborhood glean the sheaves left in the field. We were among the wealthiest people in Jedwabne. What did it mean to be rich in Jedwabne? It meant you lived like a human being. But not that you had a car. There was only one car in the town back then, it belonged to Kuropatwa and he made money driving people between Jedwabne and Łomża. We had everything we needed at home, and even though around us everybody wanted to escape from here, we had no thought of emigrating."

We're in the Old Market in Jedwabne, walking down Szkolna, the cobblestone street where the synagogue once stood. Today there's a pigsty on the site.

Godlewski receives the Geva family at the town council offices. I get into a conversation with a town official. "There were more guards at the ceremony than guests. They changed at the offices, checked that their holsters weren't sticking out from under their suits. They told us: 'We're here under duress, too.' I don't have an opinion about the event itself, but I think the road work should have been done, because the Jews spent four hours here and left, and the asphalt's still here and it's ours, not the Jews'. I heard Ambassador Weiss in the market, he's a good man, even if he's a Jew. He said he still felt homesick for Poland, that for eight hundred years Jews lived in this country. I don't want to justify anybody, but you also have to understand that eight hundred years is a long time for a visit and not everybody has to like it."

We drive on. At the end of Przytulska Street, where the Gevas'—or rather, the Pecynowiczes'—house and mill stood, there's now a gas station. A young woman leans over the fence of the house next door.

"We had a mill right here," Jakow Geva begins in a chatty way, with a wide shy smile.

"It's we who didn't live here back then that suffer most now," the woman replies.

"The road to the cemetery was there. And this was our private road." Geva points, still smiling.

"Why should our children suffer for it?" she interrupts him angrily.

"The house was all wood. One story, long, and then there was the granary and oil press. I had four brothers and two sisters. There was Josef, Frumka, Mosze, then I came into the world, and then there were Sara and Jenon Chone."

The woman at the fence, now exasperated: "I don't know what happened to the house. We built ourselves a new one."

Most people living in Jedwabne moved here from somewhere else and they don't have the intractability of the native residents, but they do have a feeling of having been wronged, quite understandably for that matter, when blame is cast upon them. What connects both is their refusal or reluctance to sympathize with the suffering of the Jews.

Geva remembers neighbors, the Goszczyckis. We go into the courtyard, knock on the door. A man of about fifty with a handlebar mustache opens the door. Jakow Geva introduces himself by his former surname, Pecynowicz. We hear a cry: "Get out of here, now," and the door slams shut. Geva rings the bell again, thinking it was some kind of misunderstanding. The same middle-aged man opens the door.

"Antek Goszczycki used to live here," Geva explains. "We lived together as the best of neighbors." The man: "He's my father, but he's very ill. Please turn off the cameras! And don't write anything! I'll have to take that notebook away from you, miss! We've had enough of false accusations, the kind we heard from the president's lips. Rabbi Baker was a neighbor of my father's, and now he says the Poles did it. And he's supposed to be a neighbor? Who put Poles on the deportation lists for Siberia? So stop being so arrogant."

We walk toward the marketplace. Geva recognizes the next house, where his cousins the Cynowiczes lived. He knocks before I have time to intervene. It's Wojciech Kubrak's house. I prefer not to imagine what kind of welcome we'll get there. Worse, Kubrak's mother-in-law appears in the doorway. Irena Chrzanowska normally lives in Białystok. I heard from several people about her attacks on Gross during a launch event for *Neighbors* at a Białystok bookstore: "I deny what you say!" she cried. "Jedwabne was swarming with Germans. They went at the Poles with whips!" She said she saw it all through gaps in the high gate of the house. But here's Irena Chrzanowska, an elderly lady sweet as an angel. "Please come in, I have all the papers for the house in order. I will show you."

She got the papers legalizing the transfer of half of the house—one half already belonged to her family before the war—from Cynowicz's heir when he came from Bombay, some time after the war was over. "We arranged for him to make out a document for free, because he came to like us."

Hersz Cynowicz's details can be found on the Internet list of Chiuno Sugihara, the Japanese consul in Kovno. Cynowicz was one of 2,139 Jews whom Sugihara rescued by issuing them transit visas for Japan. That's how Cynowicz made it to Bombay, where he became a leader of the Jewish community.

In the *Jedwabne Book of Memory*, Cynowicz described his postwar visit to Jedwabne. It's a long way from Bombay to Jedwabne, and Cynowicz would probably never have made the trip if it hadn't been for the official visit to India in 1957 of a Polish delegation headed by the Polish prime minister. As the leader of the Jewish community, Cynowicz was invited to a meeting with the prime minister, who was impressed that a Polish Jew occupied such a prominent position and proposed that Cynowicz visit Poland on the fifteenth anniversary of the Warsaw Ghetto Uprising. Not long afterward he was notified by the Polish Embassy that there was a visa waiting for him. After the ceremony, he was given a government car with a driver. "We drove by Maków, Ostrołęka, Łomża. I didn't see Jews anywhere," he recounted. Accompanied by a militia commander he went to visit his parents' house and the place where the mill had stood that belonged to his cousins, the Pecynowiczes. "I went to the cemetery," he remembered, "in the hope of finding at least the graves of my ancestors and the ashes of those who had been burned alive. But the goys had ploughed the place up so no trace of the massacre would remain. I left Jedwabne brokenhearted."

Jakow Geva and Irena Chrzanowska begin a conversation about old times.

"My uncle Cynowicz grew vegetables and had quite a bit of land."

"Just three acres," Chrzanowska counters, "and a horse and a cow."

"Two cows," Geva corrects her.

"A cow and a calf," Chrzanowska specifies.

Jakow is beaming—finally someone is sharing his memories. He doesn't seem to hear how sharply Chrzanowska snaps at me, telling me not to take notes.

Chrzanowska doesn't dwell on the subject of the massacre. They return to prewar recollections, exchange the names of neighbors. She remembers exactly who lived where: "Wasersztejn on the corner of Łomżyńska Street, beyond that Bijonka had a shop, later Atłasowicz, Kubrzańska, the smith Łojewski, then there was a building where seven families lived, including the Nożyks. Konowicz had a shop on the square, and Ibram a haberdashery, and a daughter, Judytka, who was so pretty."

Then she starts telling a story about her family hiding a Jewish woman that day. She mentions some piece of paper she got from the council saying Poles were permitted to have Jews stay in their homes, which she showed when they came to get the woman. Geva, moved, goes up to her and clasps both of her hands. I wonder if she used the same phony story to get Cynowicz to sign his house over to her for nothing when he came on a brief visit from Bombay in 1958.

If you believe these stories, which were also spun by the suspects and witnesses in the 1949 trial, the people of Jedwabne were solely concerned with hiding Jews. What struck me most was how they gave the first and last names of the people they rescued that day. I knew that the people who had really saved Jews were afraid to admit it. It was only when I discovered that the Germans allowed Poles to hire Jews in the Jedwabne and later the Łomża ghetto—they who had survived the pogrom—for unpaid farmwork, that I understood where all those Jews living in Polish homes came from.

I take the Gevas to Łomża to see the exhibition *To Our Neighbors*, organized in the Municipal Cultural Center by two young locals. They collected prewar photographs (I gave them the ones I got from Meir Ronen and Izaak Lewin) and photographs from right after the war, including a photo of the paving stones in the marketplace, taken by a conservationist in 1946. Did he have any idea he was immortalizing a spot that became the first station of a road to Golgotha for Jedwabne Jews on a hot day in July 1941? There's also a photo from after the war of a wild party, a long table, laughing faces. Two of the partying men are killers, accused in the 1949 trial. Perhaps this was a celebration of their return home?

"I'm from Przytuły, not far from Jedwabne," says one of the organizers, Przemysław Karwowski, in response to a question about how the idea for the exhibit came to him. "My grandfather, a police commander, set up a shop when he retired and did business with Jews. When my grandmother went to Jedwabne to buy goods at the market, she went by two Jewish sisters with whom she was friends. They later married, one became Mrs. Konowicz, the other Stolarski, and they had daughters. Grandmother went to market in July 1941 and both sisters were terrified, afraid to leave the house; they begged my gran to save their girls.

"My grandparents lived in a building where some of the neighbors were relatives of Jerzy Tarnacki, who collaborated with the Germans from day one, and was in the German police force. Gran was frightened, but she promised she'd find the girls a safe address at a settlement just outside of Przytuły. She didn't do it in time, and two days later they all perished.

"Przytuły is ten kilometers from Jedwabne, but they smelled the terrible stench all the way there. Gran was in despair. In my family there was always the sad acknowledgment that our Jewish neighbors were gone, but no one ever talked about who burned them. I found that out from Gross's book."

Stanisław Michałowski and his family come to the exhibition to greet the Geva family.

I speak off to one side with his daughter Kasia Czerwińska, a Polish teacher in a Jedwabne school.

"I can't stand it here any longer," she says, telling me about the anti-Semitic jokes that are part of a typical school day, and how unpleasantly she is treated for failing to join in the mockery.

AUGUST 5, 2001

I'm on holiday by a lake 120 kilometers from Jedwabne. In the evening I drive to see Mayor Krzysztof Godlewski. Today there was a council meeting at which people shouted repeatedly that "our Mayor Godlewski and Chairman Michałowski had no right to go to the ceremony. They represented only themselves." The council members accepted Godlewski's resignation.

"After the session that damned anti-Semite Bubel came up to me," the now ex-mayor tells me, "and he says, 'You could have had a hero's glory, and now what? You did for the Jews what they wanted and now they've abandoned you.'"

We sit over a vodka and recall the past year, so difficult for both of us. "Remember when you told me you were Jewish? Well, I'm sure you understand . . . ," says Krzysztof. Before I could tell him no, I don't understand why just because of my Jewish origins he would suspect me of something, Krzysztof has already finished with the words ". . . and then I saw—you're a Polish woman like the best of them! What a great lass! I'm so fond of you, Anna!"

AUGUST 6, 2001

Jedwabne. I hear more details of the council session yesterday. Bubel was sitting sprawled in the front row. Godlewski's resignation was greeted with cheers. When Stanisław Michałowski announced that he, too, would resign at the next session, applause broke out as well.

"Bubel went up to his friends on the council and gave them instructions," Michałowski tells me. "Looking at his smug face I understood who won here."

I arrange to meet Piotr Narewski, a farmer tapped to be the next mayor. "What did the residents of Jedwabne learn from the events of this year?"

"People united in opposition. They behaved splendidly. Their not participating in the ceremony was an expression of that."

In Łomża at the Cytrynowiczes. Jan puts aside for me all references to Jedwabne in the local press. This time there's a rarity: an interview in the local paper with Bishop Stefanek of Łomża—a place where Jews worked together and prepared for kibbutz life in Palestine—who warns that the Poles will put up a fight as long as the Jews don't calm down. Those are his words! He says the massacre in Jedwabne was planned and executed by the Germans, "cleverly involving the local population." He feels for the Poles.

"What was needed was a healing gesture toward those who were drawn into the crime," says the bishop. "Because there have been no such gestures, the wounds have deepened. In the USA many of our compatriots are accused of coming from a genocidal nation. This is a problem that must be dealt with. Otherwise the Poles will defend themselves, and in self-defense you don't measure the blows."

The bishop presents his version of events. They burned only Communists: "It wasn't a total extermination, just a sacrifice, chosen from that part of the Jewish community that remained in town and did not flee with the Red Army." The Germans did it. He speaks of "the tragedy of the Poles who, captive to the occupying forces, watched their neighbors perish . . . and, at the same time, were tempted to lend a hand."

AUGUST 8, 2001

A conversation with Stanisław Ramotowski. He was feeling worse every day and the doctor decided to tell him he has inoperable lung cancer. As is his habit, his response was to rebel.

"How can that be? So I'm lost, I don't get a second longer than the Lord decreed?"

AUGUST 20, 2001

I return to Warsaw from vacation, and drop in to see Ramotowski. It's getting harder and harder for him to breathe; he needs an oxygen tank. "It'll be as much time as God's granted me," he says. "It'll just be hard leaving you on your own like this."

A letter from Leszek Dziedzic in America: "If you have a moment to describe the ceremony, we'd be very grateful. Especially Father, who's on hot coals for the mailman every day, hoping for a letter from you. He's very sorry he wasn't there."

AUGUST 28, 2001

Back in Jedwabne. I hear that "no one talks about the Jews anymore." Or: "They had their Jewish holiday, we had no part in it, and now we have peace and quiet, thank God."

Probably the same peace and quiet that the residents of Jedwabne felt after July 10, 1941: the problem of the Jews had vanished.

I'm trying to find people in Jedwabne who participated in the ceremony of July 10; I know they can be counted on the fingers of one hand. I watch a videotaped television report on the ceremony with Stanisław Michałowski. He picks out a few familiar faces from the crowd: a villager from near Jedwabne, a teacher, a cleaning lady, an office clerk.

I visit each of them in turn. Not one agrees to having his or her name mentioned. The teacher explains: "It's hard enough to live here." Another participant, a man of about forty, tells me: "I thought, Let whatever's going to happen, happen. I hid a knife in my sleeve. When I got back from the cemetery, people taunted me: 'Where are your side-curls?,' 'When are you leaving for Israel?,' 'What the fuck did you go there for?'"

AUGUST 30, 2001

Ramotowski asks me to bring him a pot and pan.

"They feed us well here, but I want to scramble some eggs in the frying pan, and the pot's for some broth. Who's going to make me scrambled eggs on the other side?

He tells me a long story—though talking is painful for him—about a Jewish girl he liked before Marianna.

"She was from Wąsosz. Her family, the Skroblackis, had a cloth shop; I rode my bicycle all the way there to see her. I'd arrange to meet her on a bridge and take her for a little ride, she sat on the crossbar. Once, she took me to the shop and I saw her cut me a length of cloth from a bale, for a suit, because mine had completely threadbare sleeves. Her father, Wolf Skroblacki, was there and didn't protest. It was the summer of 1941 when I saw her again. I was on my bicycle on the way to Szczuczyn, she was walking toward Wąsosz. She told me that while she'd been in Szczuczyn visiting family, Poles had murdered her parents with axes, and she was going home to let them kill her, too. She didn't want to live without her parents. I tried to stop her, I argued with her: 'I'm already hiding one person, I can hide another; together you two will feel more at ease.' She refused, it was 'no no no.' And so we parted ways. I liked my Marianna before the war, but I'd liked that other girl more."

I ask the girl's name.

"That's the worst part. Every day I regret not saving her. At night, I lie awake and can't remember her name."

The next story is about he and his wife keeping kosher and observing Shabbat in the first years of the war.

"There were separate dishes for milk and meat. Marianna explained it to me, and I was happy to go along with it. Friday with us was different than with others. We lit candles and put on good clothes. We didn't work on Saturdays. But later she neglected it, we got a girl in to help with the housework and we couldn't keep it up. Marianna wouldn't have pork in the house, but she made sure no one noticed her refusing it when we were visiting other people."

I saw him about a hundred times this year and it seemed he'd told me everything. Why did he only tell me this story when he knew he was dying?

"Did your wife make you swear you wouldn't tell anybody?" I ask.

Ramotowski smiles and I see that I hit the nail on the head.

SEPTEMBER 11, 2001

I'm in London for a few weeks when I receive the news about the terrorist attacks in America.

In a suburb I visit Rafael Scharf, one of the founders of the Institute of Polish-Jewish Studies at Oxford. He attended the Hebrew Gymnasium in Kraków and left for England before the war. I tell him I'm unable to understand why Rachela Finkelsztejn, by then Marianna Ramotowska, wouldn't leave Poland after the war. She had relatives in America and Palestine. Maybe she felt her Jewish family would never accept her goyish husband, an uneducated man, in the bargain?

"After the war wasn't a good time for mixed marriages," says Scharf, who tells me his story: He dreamed of Palestine. But the war broke out, and he spent it in England. His English wife knew when she married him that as soon as possible, they'd leave for Eretz Israel. After the war she said, "Let's go." But he understood that he couldn't do it to her, that she would always be an alien there, that his friends would lower their voices when she came into the room. They stayed in England. They only visited Israel.

In Poland, Scharf belonged to a student branch of Jabotyński's Zionist-Revisionist party; he was under Jabotyński's spell and so in Israel he directed his first steps to King George Street in Tel Aviv, where the party was based (by this time Jabotyński had died). A moment after he arrived, Menachem Begin came in—a fellow party member from student days, and a friend. But he wouldn't shake Scharf's hand. He said to no one in particular, "Well, look, Felek Scharf is here as a tourist." And then he spat. The old gentleman tells me this with such an expression of pain on his face; it was as if the conversation had taken place yesterday.

"I've lived more than sixty years in London," he says, "and I still feel like a stranger here. Israel is always my point of reference, when I read the paper I start with the news from Israel, that is my world. But I couldn't condemn my wife, who is not Jewish, to that move."

OCTOBER 1, 2001

Back in Warsaw. I go to Konstancin immediately. Ramotowski is feeling lousy. He has no strength to entertain me and asks me to tell him a story he has already heard from me several times, about a Ukrainian boy who was a friend of my aunt's. Every time I tell it I embellish it with new details.

In Skryhiczyn my family lived among Poles and Ukrainians, I tell him, but only one boy, Włodek Kuluk, who played the balalaika, was admitted to the inner circle of my future aunts and uncles. When in the thirties my aunt Ida Merżan sent a story about Skryhiczyn called "My Goat and I" to Janusz Korczak's *Mały Przegląd* (Little Review), Korczak proposed she go to work in the Orphans' Home on Krochmalna Street, and before long she brought Włodek to Warsaw. He worked in an orphanage in Otwock for handicapped children (Aunt Ida, a renowned Korczak scholar after the war, told me that when the children saw a dog, they asked if it was Jewish or Aryan, as they were unable to grasp that the whole world wasn't subject to a dichotomy of race).

Early on September 1, 1939, one of the first bombs dropped on Warsaw hit the Otwock orphanage. Włodek Kuluk brought a large number of the children with him to Warsaw and moved with them into the outbuilding of a friendly guard. It wasn't a great idea to keep a crowd of children who spoke only Yiddish in occupied Warsaw, so Kuluk took them to Białystok, which was already under Soviet occupation (like most of the employees of childrens' homes, and to the vexation of Dr. Korczak, he had Communist sympathies). The children got into a childrens' home and he was conscripted into the army. A tall, handsome blond fellow, he was transferred to Moscow, to an honor guard. One of my aunts, Ita Kowalska, a Communist and before the war a political prisoner, recognized him as he stood guard in front of the office of the newly established Union of

Polish Patriots. After the war my aunt worked to introduce Communism to Poland, and as soon as it was established she brought Kuluk in from the USSR. He in turn, as soon as he got back, set about looking for Jewish children, in the framework of the Bricha—an illegal organization that sought to send Jewish survivors to Palestine. He was to travel with them as their guardian.

Aunt Ita found out three days after the train departed that at the station, when documents were checked, it had been discovered that he was not a Jew, which seemed suspicious, so he was sent to the secret police on Szucha Avenue. She went to intervene on his behalf with some vice minister. "How can it be," she asked, "that when a Jew thinks he's a Pole, he can become a minister, but when a Pole thinks he's a Jew, you arrest him?" They let him go. But that was 1948, and the train he missed was one of the last trains leaving Poland with Jews.

It wasn't until after 1956 that my uncle Pinio Rottenberg brought Kuluk to Israel. Pinio had no doubt that Israel was the only proper place for Jews, and he extended the principle to Kuluk. It entered family legend that Kuluk cofounded the zoo in Tel Aviv. In any case, he worked there. Until the Six-Day War, when two gentlemen from the Mossad turned up at his house and gave him forty-eight hours to leave Israel.

I keep that part of the story from Stanisław, who identifies with Kuluk and hears the tale of his Israeli life as his own alternative and desired fate. The Mossad no doubt suspected a non-Jew who wanted to live in Israel of being a Soviet spy. At least that's what Kuluk told one of my aunts, who bumped into him by accident in the Warsaw Zoo in the seventies, leading a group of schoolchildren on a field trip. After returning to Poland he gave no indication that he was back to anyone in our family, and he never wrote to Pinio, which remained a source of sadness to my uncle twenty years later when he told me about it.

OCTOBER 5, 2001
Conversations with friends about the extent to which the Jedwabne affair had an influence on the parliamentary election results: Unia Wolności (Freedom Union), the only post-Solidarity party that had members present at the Jedwabne ceremony on July 10, did not make it into the parliament; while for the first time two parties whose members openly voice anti-Semitic views—the LPR (League of Polish Families), the party of

Father Rydzyk and Radio Maryja, and the populist Samoobrona (Self-Defense)—did get in. A prominent right-wing politician, when asked about this in the *Gazeta*, replies that the Jedwabne affair had an indirect influence on the League's popularity: "A conviction grew among the masses that strangers—politicians, journalists, historians, and finally forces abroad—had decided to make murderers out of us."

OCTOBER 7, 2001
Jedwabne. I've come to attend the October session of the town council. As Krzysztof Godlewski was forced to resign, a new mayor must be elected. There are two candidates, a farmer and a veterinarian. In the corridors I hear that the farmer has a good chance, because he's supported by the parish priest. But the vet also has a strong position. It is he who puts the "stamp of purity" on milk containers and gives permission for artificial inseminations, so no farmer will vote against him.

I begin to chat with one of the councilwomen.

"Godlewski was a good mayor; you can't say anything against him," she says. "He was the first decent one; before he came in we always had swindlers, abuses, manipulations. It all went wrong for him because of the Jews, because he let them in."

"Should he have kept them out?"

"There was no good solution. I'll tell you, privately, what I think: Jews are human beings, too. And those Polish families shouldn't have joined in when the Germans were out killing. Only please, miss, don't mention my name."

Janusz Żyluk is in the hall. I jotted down a conversation I had with him half a year ago at the residents' meeting with Ignatiew. He came up very close to me and addressed me in such an aggressive tone that I recoiled. "Are you going to write more of your lies?" "I can also write your truth, sir, and have you authorize the statement," I answered politely, but he only snarled back, "I'm not going to talk to you." Leszek Dziedzic, whom I told about the incident, identified him as Janusz Żyluk. He hasn't lived in Jedwabne for years, but he comes back often, and his father took part in the massacre.

He came up to me again at the next council session: "My father was arrested after the war. When he got out of prison, his back was black and blue from beatings, and he died soon after. You visit me in dreams like a bad omen. Why do you hate Poles so much?" And during the next break: "I know Poles took part in it, too. It hurts when people say that everyone murdered, because there were three groups: the ones who wanted to, the ones who were forced to, and the ones who watched." When I told Dziedzic this, he said Janusz Żyluk was one of the few tormented by his conscience; he doesn't know how to handle it, and if anyone covers his head in ashes around here, it's him. When I leave the council meeting, Janusz Żyluk turns to me: "Would you be able to get me a Talmud?"

Stanisław Michałowski is not at the session; he's in the hospital. I visit him in Cardiology. He's badly affected by the witch hunt whipped up by Bubel, or rather the fact that so many people want to believe in Bubel's misdeeds. Michałowski's family lived here for generations, his grandparents had a restaurant on the market square, they were a well-known, respected family. Just as he was: after having built a construction company, he now manages a market ground. Before he got involved with the monument to the massacre he was the most successful and respected citizen in Jedwabne. No one had previously questioned his position.

OCTOBER 9, 2001

I call Janusz Żyluk to tell him there is no Polish translation of the sixty-four volumes of the Talmud, but a friend of mine has four volumes of an English edition and can lend them to him.

"I see. There are some things they don't want others to know," Żyluk replies.

He must have read quite a bit about the Talmud. Those are key words in anti-Semitic publications. In the prewar Catholic press they wrote, "The Hebrew faith is a mere fiction, intended to confuse naive persons of other faiths, while the real Jewish religion is based on the Talmud and other so-called 'holy books' about which prosecutors would doubtless have a great deal more to say than professors."

Żyluk is obviously torn between what he hears around him and reads on anti-Semitic websites, and what gnaws at him and worries him—a consciousness of the crime committed.

"There's no one here," he says to me, "who could look at his own family and say he has nothing on his conscience. Maybe it was because of the toxic air blowing from the marshes, maybe the Church's influence. When they put up a monument in the sixties that said *Place of Execution of*

Jews. Gestapo and Nazi Police Burned 1,600 Jews Alive, people came to hack off *Place of Execution of* from the inscription, for fun, to make it look like it said *Jews' Gestapo*. It's a stupid town. They don't even realize that they're doomed. I don't know any people here anymore, everyone moved away. I went to the cemetery. I said kaddish in my own way, laid a pebble. I asked my mother about the whole thing just once, but she was scared. She's dead now. No one wants to tell me what my father did. You've read the case documents. Is there anything there about my father? If you find anything, please let me know."

OCTOBER 26, 2001

I try to re-create a map of the town before the war; the Jewish accounts I have are contradictory and I know the reconstruction will be impossible without drawing on Polish memory, too. I find Jan Górski, born in 1909, who has lived in Jedwabne since before the war.

"I can mark on your map where the Polish families lived," Górski says politely, "but the Jewish ones? There were plenty of Jews everywhere. Why do you need to know?"

I speak to Antoni Rakowski, born in 1923, one of the young people, like Leon Dziedzic, ordered to bury the charred remains after the massacre.

"I lived in Rostki, two kilometers outside of Jedwabne. In our village we said, 'Pole, Jew, or devil, everyone's a human being.' No one from Rostki had a hand in any of it. When we were burying the bodies, I couldn't look: a Jewish boy, might have been ten years old, who'd clawed at the earth in his agony. I didn't go to the ceremony. I know people laughed at the president kissing Jews."

I don't get very far with the business of re-creating the map: "Give me a break. I remember but I'm not going to tell you." It's a real taboo; easier to get the names of killers. But perhaps it's no wonder, since the priest keeps saying that Gross wrote it all on commission for Jews who want to get their houses back. "The Jews are about to come and take what belongs to them" is a phrase I hear all the time.

OCTOBER 27, 2001

Jedwabne. At the monument I look over the crushed candles, rotting flowers, the ripped-out wires of the lights that were supposed to illuminate the monument at night. I hear that the town's chief of sanitation is afraid to clean up here, because the new mayor could fire him for it, and it's hard to find work in the area.

I phone him. A good sign: the chief doesn't have an allergic reaction to my name. He explains that cleaning up the cemetery isn't part of his official duties; he'd have to have a written order. I ask if he waits for a written order to keep the grounds in front of the Catholic cemetery tidy. "Sometimes we perform those services without an order," he admits.

"When I was a boy," he tells me, "we used to gather walnuts in the 'little graves,' as they were called, which meant in the Jewish cemetery, but the subject of Jews never came up. When people started talking about it, people in Jedwabne were given jobs, they worked on the new pavement, money came from the ministry, there were jobs on the archaeological dig in preparation for the exhumation. A lot of good came of it for the town. You'd have to be blind not to see that. On the other hand, the decision to call an end to the exhumation because the Jews demanded it was a shock to me, that deference of Polish authorities to Jews. It's Jews who rule the world with money."

OCTOBER 28, 2001

Jedwabne. I go by the presbytery. The priest and I speak of the investigation currently under way. The priest says he is in the possession of documents that cast a new light on Ignatiew's inquiry.

"I have documents, but I can't reveal them, because I'm bound by the privacy of the confessional. I can, however, reconstruct the facts. The massacre was carried out by the Gestapo from Ciechanów. Via Białystok, Ostrołęka, and Suwałki, orders were coming from Berlin that Jewish Communists had to be liquidated. The Germans had identified sixty Jewish units fighting arm in arm with the NKVD. It was decided to do battle with them. In the market square in Jedwabne, they read out a decree for the execution of Communists. The *Judenrat* of Białystok passed on to the Gestapo a list of Communists who were to be liquidated in Jedwabne and its environs, twenty-seven towns in total. The *Judenrat* had a bone to pick with the Communists, because they cut off the ears and genitals of *Judenrat* members for collaborating with the Gestapo. Moreover, Wasersztejn in his testimony described precisely the methods used by Jews against Jews, lying about it being the Poles, residents of Jedwabne, who did it to the Jews. You can't say it was about Jews, that's not why they went after them, it was because they had been fighting alongside the NKVD. And the Germans had the idea that you had to destroy the enemy unto the third generation, that's why the families of those Communists were rounded up, too. The proof that they died not as Jews but as Communists is the fact that they were buried with Lenin's head. After all, we know the whole exhumation was carried out in order to remove that symbol, which was a reminder of the reason they were killed. Nothing else was done during the exhumation."

The priest is excellent on military matters.

"Three groups came to Jedwabne: the storm troops, the motorized units, and the air support troops who were near Ciechanów and wore blue uniforms. It was they who brought the cans of airplane fuel from the airport in Przasnysz. And there was a car of civilians from Mazury, who considered themselves Germans but spoke Polish and wore civilian clothes to make it more plausible that they were Poles.

"A journalist from America came to me once and said, 'I'm a Jew,' and I said, 'I thought so.' He asks if the Jews would have survived in Jedwabne if they hadn't joined the Communists. I say that they'd have lived longer, because they wouldn't have been burned as Communists in July 1941. Those are the historical facts. The operation was led by Gestapo commander Captain Marcholl. He was the Suwałki Jew Waldemar Maczpołowski. He betrayed Jewish resistance units, and for being a traitor to his people Himmler promoted him and made him a captain for the whole of Eastern intelligence. The Germans protested that he was circumcised, but Himmler said he would decide who was a Jew and who a friend of the Reich. That's the truth."

Delivering this insane nonsense, the priest radiates well-being and confidence.

"I've had seven operations for intestinal cancer, had twenty-seven centimeters removed, and I'm still alive. It's clearly the work of God. The more curses hung over me, the more I recovered my health. So that the truth be told. The most important thing is that my parishioners behaved well. The lies inflicted painful wounds, but didn't break them. I'm proud of the residents of Jedwabne."

OCTOBER 30, 2001

In the Catholic monthly *Bond,* Izrael Gutman's article "Them and Us" is published, countering the historian Tomasz Strzembosz's thesis about the "collaboration passed over in silence" of Jews and Soviets. Gutman writes from Jerusalem, showing the weakness of the source material on which Strzembosz based his claims. For example, a "Jewish rebellion" in Grodno is supposedly proven by the account of a teacher who on September 17, 1939, saw Jews with red armbands on balconies shooting at people in the street. "How clever of those Jews to have red armbands and rifles ready on September 17, the day the Red Army invaded Poland," Gutman comments. "It's just a little strange they'd be shooting at residents of whom statistically half were Jews."

"Those poor Jews," he continues, "were mostly religious folk for whom firearms were terrifying and spilling human blood unthinkable."

NOVEMBER 9, 2001

Jedwabne. After many attempts I finally managed to arrange a meeting with Jolanta Karwowska, one of the two teachers from Jedwabne who in July of last year participated in a two-week program at the Holocaust Museum in Washington, D.C. For several months there was a hullaballoo at the school about that trip. First the priest expressed his disapproval, and no one came forward, until finally he gave two candidates his stamp of approval.

The door to the big, well-kept house is opened by a nice-looking young woman with a cold eye. I've heard about her before; she participated in the first session of the Committee to Defend the Good Name of Jedwabne. I ask her for her impressions of the Holocaust Museum.

"I wish the Poles could protect their interests in the same way. You can't limit history to the history of the Holocaust."

"Did the trip cause you to reflect on what happened here, in this area?"

"It's not easy to make sense of the confusion in Jedwabne, so many people have become tangled up in it. Poles won independence in 1918 but enjoyed it for only twenty years. They owned the land and they wanted to keep it for themselves. In 1939 it turned out that others, the Russians, the Germans, were lying in wait to destroy that independence. The Poles saw they had to look out for their own interests. What could the poor people do? The Jews were guests here. They felt no tie to the land. And the people they're accusing were ordinary folk, each one had feelings, a heart. We know what would have happened to those who didn't carry out orders, the Germans didn't let anyone meddle with their plans."

"Have you read Gross's book?"

"Excerpts. It was so extreme I'd feel sick if I read the book. I might miss a night's sleep."

"I know you're writing a master's thesis called 'The Catholic Community in Jedwabne, 1939 to 1945.' What will you write about the behavior of the Catholic community on July 10, 1941?"

"July 10 is not within the scope of what I'm writing. Everywhere the rest is passed over, all people talk about is July 10. That's why I want to describe the rest. It's a matter of truthful and objective history."

"Would you have gone to the ceremony if you'd been in the country at the time?"

"Isn't it all about making money from Jedwabne?" she replies. "They talk about compensation the Poles should pay out. Isn't that what it's all about? If it turned out the Poles did it, there would be a basis for financial claims."

"Do you ever hear anti-Semitic remarks from your pupils?"

"The problem of anti-Semitism doesn't exist at our school."

"Will you accept the Institute of National Remembrance verdict?"

"I'll probably still be skeptical. Knowing how clever the Germans were, how can we know there weren't any Germans in disguise among the civilians?"

"Have you touched on the subject with your class?"

"Yes, but we didn't try to settle who was a victim and who a perpetrator."

NOVEMBER 10, 2001

I look in on the Jedwabne Lyceum and am struck by a bulletin board dedicated to Jedwabne history. In a prominent spot, a photograph of the old monument with the inscription saying the Jews were murdered by the Gestapo. I visit a teacher I'm friendly with to find out how this could be. I tell her of my visit to Karwowska.

"It's she who put it this way, we can't change the board until the investigation results are known, and then we'll see. It's a gesture, showing what the school has to say to the children about the affair."

I drop by the church, as I've become accustomed to doing, to pick up the latest anti-Semitic news.

NOVEMBER 11, 2001

Białystok. I phone Jan Sokołowski, who, after *Neighbors* was published, sent a letter to newspaper editors saying that Śleszyński, owner of the barn in which the Jews were burned, had been beaten to death in revenge after the war. Śleszyński's daughter Janina Biedrzycka made him withdraw his statement, because journalists sought her out, asking for details. He sent around a new letter, explaining that he found Gross's insinuations contemptible: "Describing the death of Mr. B. Śleszyński, I was reporting a version of events I'd heard that claimed Jews murdered him for providing the barn for the burning. It turns out this was a rumor. I was trying to defend the honor of the residents and natives of the town of Jedwabne against the 'Jedwabne storm' unleashed in the mass media with the release of the book *Neighbors*. It was written by the Jew Jan Tomasz Gross. It's worth reading to learn how Jews lie."

Sokołowski enthusiastically invites me to visit.

I listen to his crackpot version of history.

"On the morning of July 10 some trucks with Germans arrived. I saw seven of them myself. They were sitting on benches inside the trucks, sticking their heads out, which is how I could see how many of them there were. A group of Jews fled in the direction of the pond, followed by the troops in black uniforms with pistols. A few locals participated as well. Kubrzyniecki, it must be said, was prejudiced against Jews. But I advise you to study this problem—look at dates of birth and it will immediately become clear to you what the real background of the killers was. The cruelest among the killers were born in 1920. Here's how it was at that time. During the Polish-Bolshevik war the Jews didn't go off to fight for Poland's freedom, no Jew from Jedwabne fought, only Poles. These Poles' wives stayed at home, and if they had husbands who had no land themselves but only hired themselves out, they didn't have anything to live on. So they went to work in Jewish households. The Polish women got pregnant from the Jews who worked with them.

"Just you look at old photographs, you can tell right away that the

Tarnackis and Kalinowski are Jewish boys. They weren't recognized by their Jewish fathers because their mothers were Polish. Are you surprised at them having a bad attitude?"

Although I try not to let on how hard it is for me to listen to this kind of idiocy, I probably don't manage to find the right tone, because at one point Sokołowski starts looking me over closely. I realize he must have been expecting someone completely different. I get out in a hurry when he starts yelling at me, just in time to avoid him attacking me physically and ripping up my notes.

NOVEMBER 16, 2001

Stanisław Ramotowski feels so poorly he's unable to get out of bed. He feels he's suffocating, as if he were being held underwater. But he does not utter even a word of complaint. You can tell he's suffering only because he turns his face to the wall and is silent. He has to pretend or his wife, so used to his tender care, would stand by his bedside and cry, "Stanisław, get up, you can't leave me alone."

NOVEMBER 20, 2001

Ramotowski is lying in the hospital with his eyes closed. A doctor comes and speaks of his condition as if he were already a superfluous object. I point out he is a living person. Stanisław, who seemed unconscious, reaches for my hand and kisses it. The whole time he has been ill he has been the model of an English gentleman in his manners, sense of humor, and reticence.

Kazimierz Laudański's next open letter to Adam Michnik was printed in an anti-Semitic rag under the title "If We Share a Fatherland." "Your friends and colleagues treat Poland like a wicked stepmother," he begins, and informs Michnik that Gross, "with his book of lies, is making Poland an abomination in the eyes of the world," and now "the gifted journalist A. Bikont is preparing for print a book with similar content."

In their bitter struggle for survival the Laudański brothers would probably be prepared to write to the devil. At the time of the Soviet occupation they sent letters to Stalin and the NKVD, and after the war, to the minister of security and the Central Committee of the Polish Communist Party. Kazimierz Laudański told me he'd recently written to the Episcopate. Evidently now the Laudańskis think the time has come for letters to the editor in chief of the *Gazeta Wyborcza*.

Inserting this clipping into the correct ring binder—I have twenty-three of them, this one labeled *Jedwabne/Murderers*—I glance at the Laudańskis' previous letters and statements and a shiver runs through me. In one of the local papers I notice a sentence that had escaped my attention until now. Jerzy Laudański says, "Wasersztejn testifies that he saw 75 men chosen for their youth and strength carrying the monument, that those men were ordered to dig a hole, and then killed. In fact it was carried by a dozen or so men, who were later taken to Śleszyński's barn."

The exhumation showed that a group of thirty to forty young Jews carrying the Lenin monument were murdered inside the barn, not outside it. This was an unexpected finding, nobody mentioned it, and most of the accounts spoke of the first group of Jews being driven into the cemetery.

Just as there were many witnesses to the burning of the Jews, because gawkers and petty accomplices to the crime ran behind the crowd being driven to the barn, the only witnesses to the massacre of the first group of Jews inside the barn were the murderers themselves. It's hard not to think that Jerzy Laudański was among those who murdered the first group of Jews.

NOVEMBER 22, 2001
With Marta Kurkowska-Budzan to Łódź to see Marek Edelman.

I contacted Marta because Edelman wished to speak to her. He met her a year ago at a history symposium talking about Gross's book. A girl had come up to him there, saying she was a first-year student at the Jagiellonian University in Kraków, and confided to him, "Because I'm Polish and from Jedwabne, I always had the feeling I carried a terrible secret. I heard about it in the sandbox, and Dad told me, 'Never admit you're from Jedwabne.'"

At least that is how Edelman remembered it. Marta may look like a girl, but she has a doctorate in history. And she doesn't seem like someone tormented by her town's past at all. She boldly faces up to history. Using her access to sources, she recorded conversations about the massacre with Jedwabne residents. When she was in the first or second grade a friend told her a big secret, that the Poles had burned the Jews in Jedwabne and had then gone to the barn to look for jewelry and gold teeth. Marta never forgot this, although the word "Jews" didn't mean anything to her. Many years later she considered writing her doctoral thesis on what happened sixty years before in her town, but the academics she consulted advised against it. She returned to it after her doctorate was completed. She began taping interviews. Then Gross's book came out. Marta is considering a postdoctoral project that would analyze three towns burdened with traumatic memory. She recently organized a trip for schoolchildren from Jedwabne to Kraków. She told me, "Only a couple refused to cross the threshold of the synagogue."

"How resolute she is," Edelman says to me in the kitchen, with a slight reproach in his voice that I brought him someone other than the cowed girl that he remembered who hides the fact that she's from Jedwabne.

In the train Marta and I talk about the myths that have grown up around the massacre. Each of us has heard endless stories about punishments falling on the murderers: one person drank himself to death, someone else fell and was killed on the spot, another person died in a fatal accident or had handicapped children. Stanisław Ramotowski returned to it again and again, that sooner or later the murderers were punished by God. "All of the people active in the massacre," he claimed, "were killed not long after, mostly in accidents. I remember one myself who was crushed by a tree, and another who died of tuberculosis, and a third who went crazy."

Both Marta and I heard a story about how the grass once grew in the shape of a cross between the paving stones of a park in the market square in Jedwabne, and when it was mowed, it grew back in the same shape. That was on a spot where a Jewish woman and her infant were killed in the square (though in the version I heard the woman and her child were killed on that spot by a gang of thugs after the war). Marta also knows a story about criminals who drowned a rich Jew in his fur coat—given that it was a hot summer, it demonstrates how a myth can have little connection to reality—and when they hauled the body out of the water it was naked, the furs and valuables had disappeared. In Marta's eyes all these stories are an attempt to assimilate the traumatic memory of an event that eludes rational explanations.

Marta, to whom the residents react less defensively than they do to me, remembers one local Pole using a Yiddish word, another singing her a Jewish song.

NOVEMBER 23, 2001

I spend the morning in the hospital with Stanisław Ramotowski. I don't know if he's conscious of my presence.

A phone call in the afternoon: Mr. Ramotowski died at 5:45 p.m.

NOVEMBER 24, 2001

I drive to Konstancin to tell Marianna. "What time did it happen?" she asks. "Because I had a strange feeling yesterday just before six."

Stanisław's body will be taken to the area where his family lived. In the evening I phone his niece in Kramarzewo and hear from her that the burial is tomorrow. A burial right away? On a Sunday? It's not at all in the Catholic tradition. It's probably arranged this way so that no one from Warsaw will be able to make it.

NOVEMBER 25, 2001

We set off in three cars, I and some of my friends who met Stanisław through me. We arrive at the cottage. In the kitchen men sit on benches that have been brought in, in the dining room adjacent to the kitchen Stanisław's body is laid out, around him women in black singing.

At the cemetery the priest gives a bland speech from which we are given to understand that Stanisław's only achievement was living here. "You have to say something," a friend of mine urges me. I take the microphone and tell the story of how Stanisław saved a Jewish family while around him other residents of the town were killing Jews or hiding so as not to be a witness to the massacre.

"You seem not to understand the situation," his nephew says to me later. "Stanisław was a respected and liked person here, and then what happened when you took my uncle away and it all became public? People call me 'Jew' now. Please understand me, miss, I don't have anything against the Jewish people, but you have to admit it's unpleasant. And what a hassle it was to get my uncle buried! It's I who lose most in all of this."

NOVEMBER 28, 2001

I try by phone to reach Szmul Wasersztejn's son Izaak, whom I've arranged to meet in Costa Rica, to confirm my arrival. I'm told he's in Boston with his daughter. I phone there and find out that he's in Puerto Rico with his other daughter, who's likely to give birth prematurely, so he'll probably stay there until the baby is born. And I'm about to fly to the States, and I have a ticket from New York to San José, a cheap one, naturally, which can't be changed.

NOVEMBER 29, 2001

Jedwabne has elected its new mayor, the vet. He has all the right views— he doesn't like Jews.

Before my departure to the States I leave my article on Krzysztof Godlewski at the *Gazeta*. I'd like to end it with the new mayoral elections. They certainly close an era in the life of the town, a time when two sides clashed. Now only one side is left standing. But I can't get anyone on the phone, I only get the wives. The election of a new mayor is such a big event that not a single man comes home sober that day.

NOVEMBER 30, 2001

My flight is at 9:00 a.m. From the airport I call Godlewski. His voice is somber. "No one abstained from the vote," he tells me, "which means they all accepted I won't be their mayor anymore." "What do you mean, all?" I ask. "What about Stanisław Michałowski?" Silence. "What do you mean, Stanisław didn't resign in solidarity with you?"

I call Michałowski, who explains that he wanted to resign, but the council removed the item from the agenda, and maybe it's better that way because it'll be easier for him to help Krzysztof find another job. I'm not convinced. We get into such a lively conversation that it only ends when the stewardess signals for me to turn off my cell phone.

9

A Desperate Search for Something Positive

or, The Soliloquies of Krzysztof Godlewski, Ex-Mayor of Jedwabne

"In my office I found a letter from Montevideo, this was a year before Gross's book came out:

"'I, Esther Migdal, born in Jedwabnie. In 1937 I go to Uruguay. I, my sisters *y* brothers *y* my mama. My granny Chana Jenta Wasersztejn stayed there. I'm sorry, because I do not remember much in Polish, is already 62 that I do not speak Polish. I know Poles killed whole city of Jews, who killed my granny her daughters—whole family took the house now he lives in that house. You thugs. You criminals. What says your priest? now you have house it didn't cost anything you can dance. What bad my granny do? Please sir, write how you killed whole city of Jews.'

"My first response was anger. I wanted to throw the letter away, but I hesitated. I wanted to reply, but I didn't know what to say. The letter gave me no peace. When I read *Neighbors* I saw something had to be done.

"I understood that it was an atrocity and hushing it up is contemptible. But I also thought, Others will follow me and we will show the Jews that it was an incident, caused by subversive elements, and that we are a people who love, who feel compassion for others' suffering. Stanisław Michałowski and I went to the monument on July 10, 2000, carrying a banner that said *In memory of the murdered Jewish residents of Jedwabne, and as a warning to others. From the Community.* We did it as representatives of the town authorities, but we paid for the banner with

Krzysztof Godlewski at the site of the monument in Jedwabne, 2001. (Photograph
© Grzegorz Dąbrowski / Agencja Gazeta)

our own money. Somehow we could anticipate that the town council would not agree to that expense. But I believed it was just a matter of time.

"I started to remember conversations I'd overheard as a child, though children were usually sent away when people talked about it. Sometimes it was said of one of the neighbors that 'he was at the barn when the Jews were burned.' But the word 'Jews' was still a complete abstraction to me at the time.

"I see how hard it is for the residents to live with the consciousness that Jedwabne is seen as a town of murderers. I had an idea for turning it around. The city should show that there were a few thugs in Jedwabne, but there were also Poles who saved Jews. I wanted to propose that the school in Jedwabne take the name of Antonina Wyrzykowska. I put the matter forward at a town council meeting. It wasn't received very well.

"Jedwabne needs its people to show their best side, like a fish needs water. One of my friends said to me, 'You're right, your crown won't fall from your head if you say you're sorry,' and it warmed my heart. I'm desperately searching for something positive. I tell people, 'I'm not a public prosecutor. Let's do what can be done and if it turns out the truth is otherwise, it'll only be to the good.' I've said again and again, 'I'm only saying a massacre was committed and we must pay our respects to the victims.' At council meetings I explain, 'All we have to do is what any Christian should do, ensure them a dignified place of rest.' The most important thing is that the families of the victims who are coming to the ceremony should see warmth in our hearts. Then they'll understand that a handful of people were guilty, not the whole community.

"I can already imagine the ceremony. I'd like Rabbi Baker's grandson and a grandson of one of the murderers to shake hands. Or at least I embrace the rabbi. Not a pompous welcome but the kind that might bring a tear to someone's eye, something capable of moving people, bringing them to their knees. I'd like to say, 'Brother Jews, you who were born here, we are deeply moved to have you here as our guests.'

"I confessed my hopes on a local TV program: that newlyweds would sometimes go to the cemetery to lay flowers, as they do in Katyń, where the Soviets killed thousands of Polish officers, and that the monument would become one of the Stations of the Cross. I said in the council that

I'd go to the ceremony out of a heartfelt need. Many residents took that as an insult. I felt people looking at me with resentment. One man stopped me before the ceremony: 'I'm going to fucking shoot anyone who tramples my rye.'

"Most of the residents know Poles took part in it. But they argue, 'We can't admit it, because the Jews want compensation, and it'll be more than our children can afford.' How to convince them otherwise if they get this kind of thing from their priest?

"I tried to create a lobby, but it didn't happen. One of the councilmen told me stories he remembered hearing from family and neighbors about how and where they killed Jews. But after he was refused a visa to the United States, he started saying it was because of the massacre and he changed his tune completely. I keep hearing either that it's not true about the Poles being responsible or that we shouldn't let it drag on because the Jews will take advantage of us and loot all of Poland. They say, 'Krzysztof, be careful. You'll say something you shouldn't. You may get hurt,' but it's not kind advice, it's a threat. The most well-meaning comments I hear are like, 'Why are you doing this? You'll lose a good job.' At a meeting of council members and mayors of the Łomża district someone once answered my 'Good day' with 'Shalom,' and everyone laughed. In stores I hear people call me 'that Jew Godlewski' behind my back. Other acquaintances, people from whom I wouldn't expect it, also try to tell me it's a Jewish conspiracy and it's all for compensation. Lies started circulating about my father, who was in Wronki prison for a few years for being a member of the Home Army; people said that he took part in the killings, that he chopped a Jew's head off, and that my mother-in-law, who lives in the USA, married a rabbi.

"All the time I was looking for the right tone. I tried to justify my fellow Poles by thinking what I had been like ten years ago. I was anti-Semitic. I was given a book about Jews wanting to buy up all of Poland and make us their slaves and I believed it. In school I accepted the propaganda. I believed the Russians were our friends and the Americans imperialists. And though when I was twelve I heard for the first time a conversation with horrifying descriptions of the atrocity, it didn't sink in that it was our neighbors who had done this. It was a time of tough anti-German propaganda, I knew the Germans were bad, the Russians good, so I couldn't get my head around people having collaborated with the Germans. When a classmate told me about the Katyń massacre of Polish officers by the Soviets I didn't want to believe him, either. In time I changed my views, so I believed everybody had that chance. I kept thinking there would be a breakthrough by the time of the ceremony.

"On July 10, a councilwoman, watching the ceremony from behind the curtains of her window on the marketplace, snarled just before I was to speak, 'So welcome them, fucking welcome them, you won't have a job tomorrow.' The next day I went to work and right on the front steps a visitor greeted me with the words 'Still in Poland? Haven't the Jews taken you off to America yet?' I can't cure them. I've had enough. People go on saying we're making money, that the Jews are backing us. They're convinced that Stanisław Michałowski and I are traitors, that we must be getting something out of this.

"For me the debate in Jedwabne can't be reduced to Polish-Jewish relations; it forces us to ask difficult questions of ourselves as Catholics— about honesty, decency, about how many of us helped those in need of our help. Why were there so few Righteous Gentiles? Why are the Jews alleged to be responsible for every bad moment in our history? And so I stood up to the majority of townspeople.

"What hurt most was that when Stanisław Michałowski and I put in our resignations, no one defended us. I'm so depressed I'd take a train anywhere. I didn't mean to insult anyone.

"What I've been doing in the last year has had no connection with my duties as mayor, and I wasn't prepared for that, either spiritually or professionally. You become mayor to build roads, improve the way a health center works, not to teach people to love one another and weep over another's death. For twenty years I planned to leave this town, I thought about how to get away, and now I know why I stayed. I'm glad fate granted me the honor of participating in the ceremony of July 10. After all, one can easily live out one's life without leaving a trace of any kind.

"This year gave me a lot of strength. I thought a lot about suffering, pain, forgiveness. Once, I woke up terrified that I was in a burning barn. Maybe if I hadn't met you, and Gross, I wouldn't be the man I am today. I didn't know I was so stubborn. I didn't know I had so few good friends.

I'm not the same person anymore. I was one of the boys and I estranged myself from them.

"My wounds are probably long-lasting, because—although it's hard to admit—they were inflicted by people dear to me. I think any decent person would have done what I did, and I'm sad that my former friends are suspicious of me. I'd rather lick my wounds in solitude."

Journal

DECEMBER 1, 2001

New York. My daughter Ola and I go downtown with friends to lay a rock at the site of the tragedy of September 11.

DECEMBER 2, 2001

With the *Jedwabne Book of Memory* in a backpack, Ola and I retrace the paths of Jews from Radziłów and Jedwabne who arrived in America in large numbers during the last two centuries. "The Jews from Jedwabne who landed in New York," we read in the book, "were mostly people who had never before slept in a strange house or sat at a stranger's table. They did not go there for fun, but to win bread for themselves and relatives left behind in their native shtetl on the other side of the ocean."

When they saw the horizon with the Statue of Liberty looming up before them after many weeks of ocean travel in a crowded cabin, they still had to pass through the border control point on Ellis Island. The island, now transformed into a museum, was a place where the fates of thousands of refugees from poverty and religious persecution lay in the balance. They waited in queues for many days and even weeks for a decision on whether they would be sent back or accepted into the new world. Those who remained in New York headed for the Lower East Side, then the most densely populated area on earth, where dozens of people slept in one room and the courtyard privy was the only bathroom for an entire building. Gradually they scraped together a living, working over twelve hours a day in sweatshops. There, the emigrants re-created the life of the shtetl. In the old country, Jedwabne and Radziłów were more than sixteen kilometers apart, but ties were close, strengthened by numerous marriages. In New York only one street lay between the synagogues of Jedwabne and Radziłów, and the communities were linked by homesickness for the old country, which led to frequent meetings. When Kalman Lasky from Radziłów arrived in America, he joined the Chebra Par Israel of Yedwabne, and he, a Radziłover, was elected president of the organization for many years.

Rabbi Jacob Baker belongs to the next generation of Jedwabnians who crossed the Atlantic. "When the Polish steamer *Batory* carried me to New York in mid-February 1938," he wrote, "my first wish was—in accordance with the words of Joseph arriving in Sychem (Genesis 37:16): 'I'm looking for my brothers'—to visit the beautiful synagogue built by fellow countrymen from Jedwabne at 216 Henry Street, on the Jewish East Side. Crossing the threshold of this building, I met with many surprises, the first of which was the familiar melody of Jedwabne Yiddish, distinguished most by the characteristic pronunciation of the consonant *ł*."

From the guidebook we learn that there were five hundred synagogues on the Lower East Side at the beginning of the twentieth century. I'd read previously that the magnificent Jedwabne synagogue was built during the nineteenth century. In 1891 the community organized around it registered itself in the state of New York under the name "Chebra Par Israel of Yedwabne, Russia." In turn, the Jews of Radziłów who made a home in New York met at the Radzilover synagogue on Division Street. We find ourselves there first, once we are out of the subway. It's Saturday, and a century ago all the shops on this street would have been closed on this day, and families with children in their best clothing would have been making their way to morning prayers. Now Division Street, like all streets in this neighborhood, has street signs in two languages: English and Chinese. Hundreds of little stores are open, everywhere you hear Chinese disco music. There's no trace of the Radzilover synagogue. Just as we find no trace of the Jedwabne synagogue; there are new school buildings on the site from which hundreds of black kids are spilling out.

DECEMBER 3, 2001

I've arranged to meet Rabbi Baker. I get on the subway in Manhattan and get off on King's Highway in Brooklyn—a completely different world. The languages on the street are Russian and Ukrainian. Bilingual signs on the stores, in Cyrillic (*KANDISHONERY PA NIZKIM TSENAM*) and English (AIR CONDITIONERS ON SALE). I pass many signs for kosher bagels and a stand with Russian Harlequin romances. I count dozens of periodicals in Russian, two in Yiddish, and in English, *The Jewish Press* and *The Jewish Week*; one can also obtain the Polish-American *Nowy Dziennik* (New Daily). I walk quite a long way from the subway station to the slightly more elegant part of King's Highway where Rabbi Baker lives.

The rabbi and I speak English, but every now and then he throws in Polish words: *maliny* (raspberries), *jagody* (blueberries), *grzyby* (mushrooms), *szkoła powszechna* (elementary school), *widły* (pitchfork). HaShem, the unspoken name of God, appears in every other sentence.

"Rabbi Awigdor Białostocki told me when I was little, 'I already envy you for who you will become one day.' In America I went on studying to be a kosher butcher. I spent a large part of my life in Minneapolis, Minnesota. I had fixed hours in the week when I would butcher kosher meat. Later, I had enough to live on in the rabbinate and no longer worked as a *shochet*. I sang as a cantor. I have five children and nineteen grandchildren. America is proud of its Jewish children."

He isn't very firmly rooted in the real world. His sight is bad, he sees only outlines. He doesn't read books or newspapers or watch television. All of this facilitates his communion with the spirits of his ancestors. He lives according to two books: the Torah and the *Jedwabne Book of Memory*. When I ask him about his memories of Jedwabne he tells me about the carter Kuropatwa, who preferred to condemn himself and his family to death in the flames rather than abandon his rabbi; about the lumberjack Neumark, who tore the axe from the hands of one of the cruelest murderers, hacked open the barn door, and got his family out. The rabbi relates these stories as tableaux vivants; his words have color and texture.

It's hard for him to reach back to those memories that are truly his own. He left so long ago; it's been more than sixty years. He left a world that was—despite the growing anti-Semitism—somehow safe, because it was familiar and predictable. He knew every Jew in his town, and knew of many, many others within a radius of twenty kilometers. He would always feel homesick for that world: on the ship taking him to the new country, in the American provinces, in the modest apartment in Brooklyn where he moved in his old age. That homesickness was poured into the *Jedwabne Book of Memory*. "I typed it out with one finger," he wrote. "I had no funds to hire a typist. I thought of the greatness of the martyrs and the pages were wet with my tears."

"How can they say," the rabbi laments, "that Jews collaborated with the Soviets? In Jedwabne not one Jew was a Communist."

I point out to him that there was a small Communist cell in Jedwabne and that Meir Ronen retained bad memories of five of his fellow townsmen, ardent collaborators with Soviet authorities. Baker shakes his head skeptically. When I begin to tell him their names, he informs me at the mention of the very first, Binsztajn, that there was trouble with him even as a child, and later he went to jail for the rape of a handicapped Jewish girl, and that he didn't go to synagogue. In other words, in the rabbi's understanding, he had excluded himself from the Jewish community.

The rabbi is not without his vanity. Remembering the *Jedwabne Book of Memory*, he keeps saying, "I as the author of the first book on Jedwabne," and when he mentions Gross's book, he calls it "that book that came out of my book."

The Baker brothers' book (Julius Baker, who was also a rabbi, died) fits perfectly into the mold of books called in Hebrew *Pinkas zikaron* and in English "Yizkor" books. A book whose aim is to rescue from oblivion a person or a world that has ceased to exist, it derives from the early medieval tradition of reading out during prayers long lists of names of those who perished in pogroms. After the Holocaust these books became such a common thing for compatriots' associations to undertake that in Israel a new profession was born: editor of books of memory.

Each book of memory contains a myth of origins—a story about the first Jewish settlers—the history of a particular community, profiles of worthy persons, like the water carrier or the town eccentric, then there's a description of what happened during the Holocaust, and an account of a ceremony in memory of those who were murdered. As a rule, books of memory, says Olga Goldberg-Mulkiewicz of the Hebrew University in

Jerusalem, do not fulfill the requirements of historical monographs, but they provide invaluable material for the cultural anthropologist by showing the process by which the myth of the happy Jewish shtetl is created. Among the three hundred books of memory studied by Olga Goldberg-Mulkiewicz—including the *Jedwabne Book of Memory*—one hundred contained maps drawn by hand, from memory.

I examine the sketch of the town that opens the *Jedwabne Book of Memory*. It has extraordinary charm: apple trees designate gardens, fir trees the surrounding forests. The street names are in Hebrew; only Nowa Street, where no Jews lived, is also indicated in Polish. The church is much smaller than the synagogue, though in reality it was the other way around. Although the drawing represents prewar Jedwabne, there is also a burning barn.

According to Goldberg-Mulkiewicz, books of memory often reflect the perspective of the particular donors. Thus, we often see some things blown out of porportion, special weight given to certain themes. That's why the Jedwabne book devotes so much attention to kosher butchering—that's what its authors, both Rabbis Baker, spent most of their lives doing.

Rabbi Baker tells me about the butcher Mendel Nornberg, who was his teacher. "It's difficult work. Kosher butchering geese is easier, but chickens and ducks, there's a lot to learn. I heard a knife was found in the barn, I'm curious if it was his. I'd recognize it right away. Nornberg always held his knife between his teeth, so there must have been marks on it."

DECEMBER 4, 2001

I left Poland with the phone numbers of some former Jedwabnian Poles now living in or near Chicago. I called them ahead of time from Warsaw, and was prepared to go there if an eyewitness agreed to talk to me.

"My mother-in-law said no after all," I'm told by a relative of one of them. "She says that the fear never left her. At the time she was a girl of eleven. Her family went into the fields at five in the morning to avoid participating in the killing and she was ordered to stay home and not go out. But she ran off with some girlfriends to see what was going on. She saw boys attack a Jewish boy with a harrow; they caught him when he tried to run away and they jumped him. She heard a young Jew screaming in the fields as he was being stabbed with a knife, begging, 'Kill me.' They

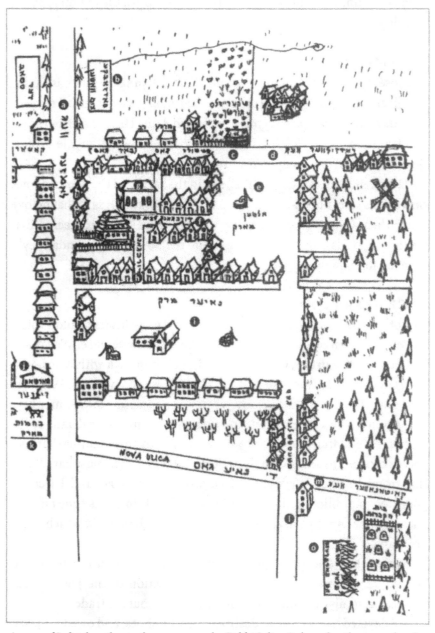

A map of Jedwabne drawn from memory by Rabbi Julius Baker after the war, when he was already living in America. Translation from the Hebrew of places marked by Rabbi Baker: (a) road to Łomża; (b) pond; (c) Przytulska Street; (d) road to Radziłów; (e) Old Market; (f) bank; (g) Beit Midrash; (h) passageway; (i) New Market; (j) sawmill; (k) horse market; (l) Przestrzelska Street; (m) road to Kajetanów; (n) Jewish cemetery; (o) square where the burning took place. (Courtesy of Rabbi Jacob Baker)

didn't kill him,' she said. 'They left him with a drop of life in him to suffer a while longer.' "

DECEMBER 5, 2001

San José, Costa Rica. Happily, Szmul Wasersztejn's son Izaak is home; he's given me the diary his father published at his own expense. I'm reading it day and night, marking passages, which Anna Husarska, a journalist and translator from Poland, has promised to translate for me professionally. She's here for a conference on human rights.

Describing the roundup of the Jews in the marketplace, Szmul quotes the various slurs flung at them by Poles. What's interesting is that no one called them Communists! But they did call them "war profiteers." Evidently the locals still had in their heads the Soviet propaganda they'd been fed for half a year.

DECEMBER 6, 2001

I set off to visit volcanoes in the company of Anna Husarska and Professor Wiktor Osiatyński, who is here for the same conference. We go in a rented car with a driver, Osiatyński in front; I sit in back with Anna, who translates excerpts from Wasersztejn's diary for me viva voce. We crawl across tall hills whose slopes are violet and red with flowers, monkeys dart about here and there, and Anna reads the naturalistic details of the massacre, "children hacked into pieces, dying in their mothers' arms," "heads crushed to a bloody pulp of flesh and bone." "He must have taken that from the Old Testament," Osiatyński tries to joke, and I feel I'm going too far, inflicting this kind of material on him in his time off. So I choose some more pleasant fragments for translation. Of which there are many.

Wasersztejn said that this book was his testament; it is intended to remind subsequent generations of the destruction of the Jews of Jedwabne, but he also included in it many stories about his trade.

He devoted half his life to dealing in selling shoes, and owed his prosperity in Cuba to the profit he made on sneakers. He tells an unverifiable story about some Ukrainian Jew who had two and a half million pairs of army sneakers in storage when the war ended. There was probably not a single person in Cuba whom Szmul didn't urge at one time or another to buy sneakers at a discount. His book is full of practical tips for the footwear merchant. For example, it doesn't pay to sell shoes on credit to persons employed on banana plantations, because they are transient and it's hard to chase them down for the second payment.

I give Anna a section to translate where Szmul tells what he did on the Shabbat after he got to Costa Rica:

"One of our clothing stores was in a neighborhood where prostitutes did business with their drunken clients at night; on Friday nights it had the busiest traffic. It occurred to me I could set up a stand there with women's underwear. As you'd say nowadays, I conducted marketing research. The clientele in the neighborhood favored red and black lingerie. In a fellow countryman's store I bought six pairs of red and black panties and six bras in each color. I put the articles on display on Friday night. At 10:00 p.m. the first woman came by with her man of the moment. Stroking his head, she asked him to make her happy with red panties and a frilly bra. He got out his money and the girl assumed ownership of the items. The news spread like wildfire around San José's red-light district. By 1:00 a.m. when I closed up shop, I only had two pairs of panties and two bras left. We managed to keep that nighttime clientele going for a long time."

This excerpt gives me some hope that the Wasersztejn family will agree to meet me on Shabbat, which begins tomorrow, and will let me take notes, too, which religious Jews usually don't allow on the Sabbath.

It's not easy in the diary to distinguish truth from what is made up or embellished. Did the following cinematic scene really happen? Before Wasersztejn leaves for Cuba in 1946, he has to get out of military service. In Warsaw he somehow gets through security and past the secretary to the most senior general and declares, "You may have had problems in your life, but they were small problems. Mine is enormous. Poles killed my whole family. The earth of Jedwabne is like a sponge saturated with Jewish blood. You can shoot me on the spot, but I'm not joining the Polish army." And he is exempted.

I've arranged to meet his widow in the afternoon. Behind a six-foot fence, the residence where the solitary widow lives is guarded by two small stout security men armed with clubs. In the anteroom is a chaise longue with a cushion in the shape of a Torah scroll. We tread on a carpet so thick and fluffy our shoes vanish into it. In the living room there is an abundance of knickknacks carefully arranged in display cases, ornate mirrors in gold frames, elaborate crystal chandeliers, a porcelain poodle with porcelain puppies, tall statuettes of elegantly dressed Viennese ladies. Next to one of them, coyly pulling back the edge of his robe to reveal a porcelain foot on which two doves have alighted, stands Moses holding the Ten Commandments.

Szmul met Rachela back in Poland, in Bielsk Podlaski, when he was buying a house for the woman who hid him during the war, Antonina Wyrzykowska. He remembered noticing Rachela's attractive figure right away. Rachela tells us, "I fell in love with him immediately. It's easy to fall in love when you're fourteen years old."

After he got to Cuba he found out by accident that Rachela was in New York, and he contacted her at once. "My brother didn't like it," Szmul wrote in his book. "He tried to find me a better match behind my back; he argued that I could daydream of Rachela because it was a beautiful dream, but a Holocaust survivor should act pragmatically. He thought I should marry a Cuban Jewish woman, beautiful, intelligent, and with capital. He gave details about me to Jewish businessmen, who suggested he might introduce me, his younger brother, to their appetizing daughters." But Szmul dug in his heels. He brought Rachela to Cuba and they were soon married.

Rachela belongs to a category of Jews who have a fierce aversion to Poland and no nostalgia whatsoever. She survived the Holocaust in a family of Polish peasants who hid them for money. "Every month we paid them in gold coins to live in a pigsty; the man didn't know where we hid the money, that's how we survived. After the war Poles killed Jews returning home. They killed my mother's brother."

Like many survivors, they never exchanged a word of Polish. They spoke Yiddish and sometimes Spanish. Rachela speaks to me in Spanish, though I know from Wyrzykowska she can get by in Polish. When I ask about a few unclear passages in her husband's diary, she can't help me.

I read about Wasersztejn's Cuban adventures until deep into the night. He describes how in the fifties many Jewish businessmen cautiously began to support Fidel Castro, because they didn't like Batista's repression. Szmul didn't like Batista, either. After the revolution he thought they should sit it out, put all business on hold. He believed a more liberal regime had to come, but things got worse and worse. "Homes and stores were taken over by the government. Fidel hit the middle class. I saw the lines for meat. I began to look around for a way to get out fast. Rachela didn't understand. She fell into a depression, cried a lot. She thought it would all pass."

First they sent a son out of Cuba, the same one I'd talked to on the phone—Izaak, so he "wouldn't be brainwashed." He arrived as an eleven-year-old boy in the care of a Jewish family in Philadelphia.

Many children left Cuba at that time as part of the CIA Operation Peter Pan, whose goal was to protect young minds from Communist indoctrination. These children, now adults who have battled with the trauma of sudden separation from their parents—some for a few years, others for their whole lives—now have books written about them.

DECEMBER 7, 2001

I've arranged to meet Izaak. We talk in a narrow cubbyhole with boxes stacked up to the ceiling: Izaak's firm sells medications. I have a lot of questions concerning various aspects of Szmul's memoir, but he can't answer any of them. His father was constantly telling him about Jedwabne; he remembered the suffering and nothing more.

On the way back I tell the cab driver I came from Poland because there's a lot of controversy at home about a Jew from Costa Rica. He nods proudly, as if we are talking about natural resources: "Oh yes, we have a lot of well-known Jews here: the transport minister, the minister of culture, and a candidate for vice president."

I learn that Jews here are called "Polacos." The verb *polaquair* is also used for traveling salesmen, introduced here by Eastern European Jews.

I find a sentence in Wasersztejn's diary: "In business they called me 'Polacos,' but it wasn't good or bad, because in Costa Rica they really don't care who you are."

DECEMBER 9, 2001

I've been invited to a Hanukkah party at Rachela's. Her sons Izaak and Saul are there, with two grandchildren and Rachela's friend Maria Wiernik. The Colombian servants, two dark women of considerable volume dressed in white lace aprons, bring in food—potato latkes, doughnuts, and blintzes with sour cream, the same things Rachela and Szmul ate in their family homes at Hanukkah—at least the same to look at, because they taste simply horrible. Above all, they're extremely sweet.

I can finally deliver my gift—the photography album to which I wrote the text, *I Still See Their Faces: Photographs of Polish Jews*. Happily this morning, the last day of my stay, my suitcase caught up with me after being unloaded in Nicaragua by mistake.

"He didn't go to synagogue," Wiernik says of Szmul, "but when any repairs were needed, who was the first to pull a check out of his pocket? Szmul. The rabbis, the lawyers, the doctors, all of them knew him well and respected him."

Izaak drives me home. Driving down Avenida Central, San José's main thoroughfare, we pass Szmul's shoe stores, now run by his son. Each of them has a different name: Pompile, Zapatos, Fantasia. No chain, just dozens of small businesses.

"I have one question for you," says Izaak. "How can a Jew live in Poland?"

I try to explain, probably not very well, because Izaak goes on to say: "When I was in Warsaw, I went to the synagogue to ask Jews the same question and none of them could tell me."

I remember my conversation with Ramotowski about the only Jew in Jedwabne, Helena Chrzanowska, living as a Catholic in the middle of town. "How can anyone live like that?" Stanisław wondered. "It's quite different with us, we live on the outskirts, and when I go out I see my little creek, not the faces of killers."

For myself, I am unable to fathom why either Helena Chrzanowska or the Ramotowskis were willing to go on living amid murderers. From Izaak Waszersztejn's point of view there's no difference between Jedwabne, Kramarzewo, and Warsaw—all of Poland is a graveyard.

DECEMBER 12, 2001

Brooklyn. The next meeting at Rabbi Baker's. The conversation moves to Jan Gross. "He's an honest man, a romantic figure," says the rabbi. "But he's no Jew."

For a religious Jew only the mother matters, and Mrs. Gross was a Polish landowner. She was in the Home Army and participated in operations to save Jews. Jan Gross discovered quite by accident after publishing *Neighbors* that the first landowner in the Łomża district, then called Wiska, was his ancestor on the maternal side, Andrzej Wydżga. He said, half-joking: "In Jedwabne my peasants massacred my Jews."

DECEMBER 13, 2001

I travel to New Jersey to meet the rabbi's brother Herschel Baker, born in 1911. We speak English, but from time to time he interjects a perfect Polish sentence. He is kind and gentle, with great charm and a very unusual biography. Before the war he was doing very well in Poland, during the Soviet occupation he went into hiding, and during the German occupation he also hid, but he still managed to engage in trade.

"Older Jews spoke Yiddish among themselves and two languages, Polish and Yiddish, mixed harmoniously in the market," he nostalgically remembers of Jedwabne, which he left in 1931 to move to his wife's hometown. "We had good contacts with our Polish neighbors. I was friendliest with our neighbors' son Franciszek Sielawa. We went to each other's homes, played *palant* [rounders]. After finishing Polish school we studied at the yeshiva, but when Father died—I was sixteen—I started supporting the family and my brothers continued their studies and became rabbis. My children's first language was Polish. We knew they'd go to Polish school, so while they were small we spoke Polish at home, not Yiddish. We knew they were about to learn Yiddish and Hebrew in the cheder, and we wanted them to speak Polish well. Otherwise, how could they live there?"

"Did you feel Poland was your homeland?"

"Of course. I was born there, lived there, had a flourishing business—manufacturing and selling clothes for men and women—and good relations with everybody. I took potatoes and grain in payment from peasants because they had no money. I employed a lot of Poles.

"Toward the end of the thirties there were already too many thugs pestering us, and almost every Jew dreamed of nothing but having a ship's ticket in hand. Not me. Thugs stood watch at the front door of my shop—by 1938 no client would come in by the front door, but they did come in the back, because they'd rather do business with me than with Poles. They could get things cheaper from me and I never overcharged. When people had some money, they'd entrust it to me to invest, so they'd have more. Because I wouldn't leave I lost everything—my wife and our two boys of four and six perished in Treblinka."

He had to hide during the Soviet occupation because he was in danger of being deported as a "bourgeois element." "I lived with peasants I knew. Before the war I'd lent them money and I'd had to visit them many times to get it back, so we already knew each other well. I went home briefly when the Germans arrived and then I had to use those acquaintances again."

When the Germans arrived, the Bakers' (then the Piekarzes') mother lived in Jedwabne with her brothers, the Pecynowiczes. Father Piekarz was dead, and two brothers, now Julius and Jacob Baker, lived in America. The head of the school advised them the day before the massacre to make sure they were out of town the next day. At dawn on July 10, Mrs. Piekarz heard the rumble of wagons rolling into town and later she heard screaming, so she ran to her son in Goniądz. She dressed like a Polish woman and spoke Polish without an accent, which helped her on the road. She ended up in the ghetto with Herschel and his wife and children. Only Herschel managed to hide when the Jews were deported from the ghetto.

"I was in hiding for three years. I'd go see the peasants I knew very early in the morning, at five or six. I'd ask: What do you need most? They'd say: butter, potatoes, cheese, clothes, grain—good grain was expensive! I always tried to find the very best. I had maybe forty households like that in the area that I supplied; they were barter deals."

I ask where he stored his goods.

"They weren't storehouses but hiding places in the fields, in attics, in the gulleys left by potato storage mounds. Late at night, when everyone was asleep, I'd sleep in some barn, so the farmers wouldn't notice. I was up before they were. If I was coming from the north I pretended I'd come from the south. I knew never to say too much, never to say where you're going and where you've come from. Sometimes when I was in someone's barn I heard what they were saying about Jews and I was frightened. But they didn't speak badly of me, they were terrified, but friendly. Sometimes someone would take me in for a while. I lived with a village head and his sister, who was a nun; she took care of me and tried to persuade me to convert to her faith.

"When the war ended I rode a bicycle from Goniądz to Jedwabne. I met Stanisław Sielawa. I didn't know yet he was one of the killers. 'Herszek, you still alive?' he said, and I heard menace in his voice. They were a nice family, poor, with five boys and one girl, they had no regular employment, and they'd work for Jews. There were more people like them, sympathetic enough, but when the opportunity presented itself they turned into murderers. I went to see an old friend of my mother's. She advised me, 'Don't stay here overnight, it's not safe. Don't go back the same way you came, because they might be waiting for you.' I left Jedwabne that night and never set another foot there. Not there or anywhere else in Poland."

He landed in the United States in 1946, worked in the garment industry, dealt in real estate. Before he emigrated he transferred ownership of his house to the brother of the nun who'd sheltered him longest. "Anti-Semites beat him up for having saved a Jew. He had to pack up his wife, his two children, and flee. They settled in Gdynia. I sent him a few dollars every month. When he passed away his children wrote to me, they'd say they wanted black pants with a stripe, for example, and I'd send them."

DECEMBER 14, 2001
A meeting with Jacob Baker, the last before my return to Poland. I decided to speak to the rabbi today about the testimonies on July 10 that have been preserved in the *Jedwabne Book of Memory*, about what is true and what is myth. I study it carefully. Based on texts recorded by a generation now nearing the end of its days, it is a collection of moving, clumsily written accounts of personal experience and stories heard from others; on the one hand they are airbrushed and on the other they are blackened by time. The book serves not only to reconstruct past events and the period of the Holocaust but above all to perpetuate the memory of the shtetl that was left behind and appears in nostalgic recollections as the mythical paradise of childhood.

"First I had to answer one fundamental question," Rabbi Jacob Baker writes, "namely: should I mourn the destruction of my people, praise the beauty and spirituality of childhood memories, or should I gather the scattered remains of my community and help them change their lives, become eternal representatives of our cherished tradition? I came to the conclusion that the basic aim was to immortalize martyrs and resurrect the truth about how they lived so we—and our descendants—could come to know the essence of the moral strength that allowed our ancestors to shape successive generations of proud Jedwabne Jews up to the 15th of Tamuz, July 10, 1941. The killers not only humiliated and slaughtered their victims, they also wanted to wipe out all memory of them. They murdered them twice, first literally grinding them into the dust, and then trying to avoid responsibility for what they'd done. To forget our martyrs would be to become accomplices in their murder."

How, then, to preserve their memory? By presenting them beautifully. The convention of the book of memory is somewhat reminiscent of the magical realism of the Latin American writers I hold dear. Facts are intertwined with fiction. The story is not subject to the rules of logic but aims to reveal the hidden meaning of events. Although good-natured jokes about this or that rabbi are occasionally cited, the picture of the whole is uniform. The town is inhabited by deeply religious Jews living in fear of God, acting in accordance with the Torah commandments, prepared to heroically sacrifice themselves for their community. Subjected to relentless persecution, they show great courage. And when they die, it is joined in prayer with their rabbi.

"The whole Jewish community with Rabbi Białostocki," writes Herschel Baker, "embracing and kissing each other, said the Kaddish and Szmone Esre and perished in the flames." But we know that the rabbi was forced to walk at the head of the group of men carrying fragments of the Lenin monument and was killed along with them, before the burning.

In the *Jedwabne Book of Memory* there is a story about a carter from Jedwabne named Kuropatwa whom Baker referred to in his speech at the July 10 ceremony: "He once saved a Polish pilot from death at the hands of the Russians, so the executioners said he didn't have to go with the others to the barn. He spat in their faces and scorned their mercy. He didn't want a life granted him by those murderers. He cried: 'I go where my rabbi goes!' His wife and daughter tried to persuade him that if he obeyed those people they all might get away with their lives. Kuropatwa declared his decision was final, that he would go with his rabbi, that they could do what they liked. His wife and daughter flung themselves on him with kisses and cried that they would go with him, and they all joined hands, ran up ahead, and jumped in among those designated for burning. All of them began to pray, led by the rabbi. They were seized by a common obsessive conviction that not one accidental thought should sully the purity of their sacrifice."

One of the authors of the book, Itzchok Yankel Newmark (in Poland, Icek Janek Neumark), describes the moment when the Jews were driven into the barn as follows: "Stanisław Sielawa stood at the door with an axe ready to chop off the head of anyone who tried to run away. The sudden force of the hot explosion burst open the door. I saw Sielawa waving his axe, I managed to grab it from him, I caught hold of my sister, her five-year-old daughter, and her son. I saw my father collapsing into the flames."

This heroic scene is a desperate polemic against those who say Jews went like lambs to slaughter. But there are witnesses who remember that the porter Neumark went into hiding earlier and was not in Jedwabne that day.

Neumark also tells of a feat he performed during the Polish-Bolshevik war in 1920, when soliders of the Polish army supposedly organized a provocation: they killed one of their own and dumped the body outside the house of the rabbi of Radziłów. In retribution an order was given to execute ten rabbis and fifty other prominent Jews. The only chance of ensuring their survival was bearing a letter with a plea for intervention to the bishop of Łomża, and this dangerous mission was entrusted to Neumark, who went to the bishop on horseback, evading an ambush, obtained the bishop's favor, and managed with the aid of a letter from him to avert the execution. Due to the blessing of the rabbis who survived— we read in the book—Neumark was later able to escape the burning barn in Jedwabne and survive a concentration camp.

If the array of recollections and accounts in the *Jedwabne Book of Memory* constitute a mixture of fact and imagination, Neumark's story of saving sixty Jews from a martyr's death at the hands of demonic Polish soldiers is a complete fiction. The only part of this tale that may be true is the memory of the violence of Polish troops during the 1920 war. In the *Jedwabne Book of Memory,* his story is given the same status as the other testimonies. Neumark survived Auschwitz and the March of Death. He emigrated to Australia with his wife, whom he met in the camp. It was she who recorded his story for the book. Neumark himself remained illiterate to the end of his life.

In the Auschwitz Museum archive I find the year of his birth: 1910. If he really carried out his first heroic feat in 1920, he would have been a mere ten years old.

The story about Kuropatwa is also most certainly legend. None of the Polish residents of Jedwabne are able to corroborate it.

I have neither the heart nor the courage to talk to the rabbi about his stories being no more than edifying and moralizing fairy tales. So I listen once more to the tales of the carter Kuropatwa's bravery. And the stories I already know so well, of how he himself as a yeshiva student in danger of losing life and passport performed the kosher slaughter of a calf, and did it in the cowshed next to the police station. His eyes sparkle when he asks me, "Have I already told you how I once saved a pious Jew from starving?"

DECEMBER 15, 2001

Right after meeting the rabbi, I set off for Lawrence, Massachusetts, to visit the Dziedzic family. It's been six months since they emigrated to the United States. They are renting a small apartment on the first floor of a house, and seem happy.

"I go to bed," Leszek tells me, "and in my dreams I'm in Jedwabne and I can't get away. When I wake up luckily I'm back in America. But every night I dream of Jedwabne all over again.

"Thanks to God and the Jews we're managing somehow," he declares. "In Jedwabne they say Jews fixed things, and in a way they're right because if you hadn't helped us we wouldn't have been able to leave." (When he was applying for U.S. visas for the whole family I got him recommendations from Jacek Kuroń and Marek Edelman.)

Leszek sits at the computer arguing with online anti-Semites. Piotrek, their son, decided to get straight As at school, to show everyone in Jedwabne the Dziedzices are worth something after all.

DECEMBER 20, 2001

Back in Warsaw.

It becomes clear at yesterday's press conference at the Institute of National Remembrance that there's no evidence that the Jews in the Jedwabne barn were killed by Germans. In the spring they were calling what was found—a bullet from a 9 mm pistol issued with German officers' equipment—proof that the Germans were not only present at the scene of the crime but also fired shots at the victims. After expert analysis it also turned out that most of the shells, until now the crowning proof, are from World War I–era Russian guns. Some of them were fired from rifles used in World War II but not introduced until after the massacre, in 1942. They should have called it "a metal capsule of unknown provenance made of tin melded from an alloy of colored metals"; that's what experts said.

As usual, the sensational material—Germans committed the atrocity at Jedwabne—was on the front pages, whereas this unappealing truth did not receive any particular attention in the media.

DECEMBER 21, 2001

In Łomża visiting the Cytrynowiczes. I reconstruct Jan's life story from my notes, checking the details with him.

It was 1928. He was four years old. A cart drew up in front of his mother's house in Ostrołęka and some people loaded him onto it. The person who ordered the kidnapping was his father, Jakub Cytrynowicz, who had left his Jewish wife for a Polish woman and decided his son should live with them in Wizna and receive a Christian upbringing.

From that time on his name was Jan. Once, some Ostrołęka Jews came to Wizna who had been asked by his mother to take him back from his father, but Jakub called for friends of his, National Party squad members who went around breaking Jews' windows, and they wrested the boy from his mother's envoys.

"His father didn't get along with his first wife, who was Jewish," Jan Cytrynowicz's wife, Pelagia, says, "but he had five children with her. Four of them as a Jew, because he left when she was pregnant, and a fifth, a girl, after he'd become a Catholic and traveled to Ostrołęka on business. That's the kind of man he was."

Jakub Cytrynowicz later abducted two more of his sons. This time he hired a photographer who went from house to house offering to take pictures. Jakub promised him twenty zlotys. He was supposed to grab the older boy and the daughter Sara, whom he'd already somehow managed to have baptized, because Jan remembers they called her Irena in his father's house. But the photographer took two boys, one of them still too young to walk. For that mistake Cytrynowicz deducted ten zlotys from his fee.

I ask Jan Cytrynowicz if he was friends with Jewish children in Wizna.

"It was like this: Jews saw me as a goy, Poles saw me as a convert. Because I'd been baptized, I didn't have Jewish friends. And as long as I got along with my Polish friends, there was no difference, but when we quarreled I would get: 'you Jew,' 'clipped dick,' 'because you come from Jewish stock.' When someone cracked a joke about Jews they'd look to see if I was laughing along."

Jan and his stepmother worked with his father, learning the leather trade. "My stepmother was a kind, noble woman," he remembers. "She was better to us than a mother is to many children. And we were always tormenting her. Father would say, 'Go bother your stepmother.' And we did. She obeyed him, too; she was in love with him and yielded to him. She raised us and she worked all day from dawn to dusk in his workshop in the bargain."

After he turned thirteen his father allowed him to visit his mother in Ostrołęka. He went once, remembered the taste of matzo, but he didn't want to go back. He remembers the baptisms of his brothers, his first communion, and his confirmation. He was an altar boy, and his father played in the church orchestra.

I tell Jan that I spoke about him in Israel with Awigdor Kochaw, who was in the same class as one of his brothers. Kochaw remembered kids calling the Cytrynowicz boys "clipped dick." Wincenty Dobkowski in turn recalled Jan's father walking around the marketplace on Yom Kippur with a pig snout on a stick to spite the Jews.

"Nonsense," says Jan Cytrynowicz.

But Pelagia enters the fray: "Don't you say anything good about your father or I'll get upset."

"My father was what he was, but he didn't let anyone push him around," Cytrynowicz says. "He went along with the nationalists' cries against the Jews, but he never joined the boycott of Jewish trade and services, because he would have lost on it. He had himself shaved by the Jew Froim. He bought veal shanks at a good price from Jewish butchers, because they didn't know how to remove one vein from the shanks and therefore the meat wasn't kosher. He had five workers in his leather workshop, and those shanks made it cheaper for him to keep them."

Pelagia interrupts him: "I'd really like to know when they ate those veal shanks. In the morning they prepared a pot of potatoes and kasha with milk, and that was supposed to last the family and the workers all day. But he ate something better all by himself in his room. I know because my aunt, Jan's stepmother, told me when we lived with her after the war."

"I don't approve of his behavior," Jan confesses, "beginning with his belonging to a nationalist organization, his going around with them and yelling, 'Bully the Jew.' We lived in a two-story house. Downstairs was our apartment and workshop, and the Czapnickis lived upstairs. They traded in saccharine, and their son Chaim was a member of a Zionist organization. They would have meetings and sometimes parties at home. Father was always quarreling with them, and once, when he was drunk, he went upstairs to make a scene; he wanted a fight, but it was he who got a licking. Out of spite he informed on Czapnicki, telling the customs office he illegally exported saccharine across the border to Prussia. For that they gave him five zlotys as a 'border guard associate.'"

This incident took place just before the war broke out. As soon as the Soviets arrived, a provisional government and police force were formed in Wizna. Chaim Czapnicki worked for this provisional authority. Jan Cytrynowicz attributes to this his father's deportation by the Soviets. Czapnicki must have found the receipt for five zlotys among official papers and informed on his father. They caught him smuggling flour to Białystok. He got a five-year sentence as a "dangerous element" and was deported to somewhere near Chelyabinsk.

Jan signed up to move to Wołkowysk (now in Belarus). He worked in a cement factory and went to the technical school attached to the factory. When the Germans arrived they closed the school and he lived in poverty, living now with one, now with another friend. Once, he was on a train and a policeman in the railway guards, a Pole, recognized his Jewish accent. "I should have gone somewhere deeper inside the country, where there were Belorussians, Lithuanians, Tatars, because where there were a lot of different nationalities each one had its own accent and it was harder to pick out a Jew."

He was put on a transport to the Wołkowysk ghetto. It was the winter of 1941 to '42. He was sixteen. He spoke no Yiddish, and was baptized. A Pole among Jews. "Not that they picked on me or reproached me with anything. But you felt it in the air, and no one spoke to me."

He worked in the slaughterhouse, flaying animals. One day there was a commotion during a transport to the ghetto and he escaped. He survived, he says, because he was alone. It wasn't hard for him to run away, but his contemporaries had sisters, mothers, grandmothers in the ghetto, and it wasn't easy to decide to leave their families behind. Jan was hidden by classmates. He saw a notice on the street that anyone who brought a Jew to the police would get a kilo of sugar. Once, he saw a terrified boy with Semitic features yanked along by a man. When it became more and more difficult to find a place to stay with anyone in town, he began wandering in the direction of Wizna. On the road in Grądy he managed to find work chopping wood in a German kitchen. When the Germans knew the end of the war was drawing near, they requisitioned cows and horses, took him as a carter, and told him to herd the animals westward. Toward the end of May or the beginning of June 1944, before the front halted at the Biebrza river, he realized he was near Radziłów, where he used to go before the war, and he ran away. He hid in the area, again working for Germans, in field kitchens.

When the war ended he found his stepmother in Jedwabne. In 1947 his father returned home. He'd been director of a shoemaker's workshop in the Soviet Union and had done some black-market business on the side. He'd done well: he kept gold rubles and gold in the lining of his clothes. "My father soon found himself a new woman, and he persuaded Józek to testify that his stepmother had collaborated with the Germans during the war. That was so she wouldn't get anything in the divorce."

Józek was the youngest brother, the one stolen from his mother before he could walk, and he'd spent the whole war with his stepmother. Their house in Wizna was bombed in the first days of the war and their stepmother had moved to Jedwabne with Józek because it was "easier to find housing there." Someone informed the authorities that Józek was Jewish and the police came for him. They dressed him in thick clothes and used him as a training object for dogs. They would shout *"Jude"* and the dogs would attack him. He wouldn't have survived if his stepmother hadn't bribed the occupation-time mayor with moonshine and pork fat. The mayor declared to the Germans that Józef (or Jósek) Cytrynowicz was a Polish child, Jakub Cytrynowicz had merely given him his name when he married a widow who was pregnant. It worked. They released him and employed him as a stable boy at the police station.

After his father left his stepmother, Jan went on living with her while working with his father at a leather workshop. They quarreled more and more often. "Father only recognized the patriarchy. He wanted me to obey him and I wanted to get married and make a life of my own."

Pelagia: "They fell out over me. When Jan and I got married, he never spoke another word to me. You tell the whole truth now, Jan. Whatever awful things my father-in-law came up with, he'd not hesitate to do them. He liked disputes, he always had to be at odds with someone. Did you tell her how he put his own son in jail?"

After 1989, Jan Cytrynowicz got in touch with the Jewish community and now regularly meets up with two people of Jewish origin who live in Łomża.

"At times I'm not even ashamed I'm a Jew, like when I'm with you," Cytrynowicz remarks with a kind of wonder.

I realize I don't know his Jewish name or the Jewish names of his father and brothers. It is an effort for him to recall them. His father was Szajsa, Tadek was Szmul, and he doesn't remember Józef's original name.

"And you?"

"Jesio."

He seems spooked by the sound of his own Jewish name said aloud.

"I'm telling you things so personal I never told them to anyone. So I'll tell you one more thing. I was so ashamed of my mother before the war that when she came to see us at our father's house, I wouldn't go to her for anything in the world. Because she was Jewish. That's the way it is: a Jew who's reminded he's a Jew feels fear and shame."

I've often encountered the phenomenon of shame for one's Jewishness in Poland. I remember what a problem this was for the prominent Polish writer Marian Brandys, whom I interviewed for the *Gazeta* when he was already in his eighties. I knew his father had been arrested before the war in the witch hunt against Jewish bankers. I asked him about the experience of being Jewish in prewar Poland. The questions were painful for him. Marian once said an extraordinary thing to me: "I'm not ashamed of my background, but it pains me to talk about it." I told him about my daughters, Ola and Maniucha, who went to a Jewish kindergarten and taught me about Jewish customs and holidays. It shocked him that anyone could want to be Jewish of his own free will, and he worried about my possibly harming my children.

I asked him what was most difficult for him in being a Pole of Jewish origin. He replied, "When I was interned in a camp for officers in Woldenberg, and the native Polish officers demanded a separate barracks for the Jewish officers."

There, denouncers identified Jews to the camp leadership. In the

Jewish barracks there were a considerable number of Poles from families who'd been asssimilated for generations, and some of them only found out about their roots at that time. In the Polish barracks a group of officers organized anti-Semitic talks, based on materials supplied by the Germans. Brandys felt he couldn't bear the humiliation of proving his Polishness and decided to formally convert to Judaism. History is for him the foundation of identity, so he asked a friend, a scholar of Hebrew literature, to tell him about the Jewish kings. He went to bed full of good intentions to learn Jewish history, but when he woke up in the morning he realized he didn't remember a thing and till the end of his life, no matter what barracks they put him in, his king would remain the Polish king Łokietek, not King David, and his homeland would be the Polish language.

He devoted one of his books to his time spent in Woldenberg, without once mentioning the Jewish barracks.

DECEMBER 30, 2001
A visit to Antonina Wyrzykowska to wish her Happy New Year.

I ask her about various things I learned from Wasersztejn's book. But Miss Antonina, as usual, doesn't remember. I read her a description of one of the women she hid giving birth and Antonina bringing scissors to cut the umbilical cord. Wyrzykowska would make a good actress. Her eyes widen, she can't believe Szmul would make up something like that. She's so convincing I could almost take that terrifying episode from Szmul's time in hiding as just another one of his fantasies, if it weren't for the fact that Antonina's husband, Aleksander, mentions it in a letter sent to Yad Vashem in the sixties.

10

Only I Knew There Were Seven of Them

or, The Story of Antonina Wyrzykowska

If it hadn't been for her, there's no way he would have survived the war. And if it hadn't been for his testimony, the truth about Jedwabne would never have come to light. Antonina Wyrzykowska and Szmul Wasersztejn met as teenagers. She was sweet, pretty, cheerful; to the end of her life she was a good-looking woman and she giggled like a teenager. He was a homely redhead and a Jew. First fate threw them together unexpectedly and then separated them.

Wyrzykowska never told her children or anyone else what happened in Jedwabne. She didn't want to tell me about it, either. I had to get the truth out of her gradually, building on what I already knew.

"Did you in Janczewko," I asked, "know right away who had killed the Jews in Jedwabne? The Germans or the Poles?"

"Who did it I don't know to this day; after all, I wasn't there."

"Did people mention the names of any of the killers?"

"How would I know things like that?"

"Miss Antonina, you know very well . . ."

"My child, would you like some more tea, or a piece of gingerbread, maybe?"

We spoke many times, and she was always very careful about what she said. She tried to give the impression that she didn't know anything,

Izrael Grądowski (Józef Grądowski after the war). Next to him his wife, Fajga, and their sons: Abram Aaron, Reuwen, and Emanuel. Jedwabne, 1930s. Izrael, one of the Jews saved by Antonina Wyrzykowska, was the only one of the family to survive the war. (Courtesy of Rabbi Jacob Baker)

Jankiel Kubrzański (Jack Kubran after the war), one of the Jews saved by Antonina Wyrzykowska. He is the small boy standing on a stool; his mother, Brosze Kubrzańska, is holding him. Next to them his great-grandmother is holding his sister, Giteł (right), and cousin Judes. His aunt Atłasowicz, Judes's mother, is holding her other daughter, Małka. Jedwabne, 1920s. (Courtesy of Rabbi Jacob Baker)

didn't remember anything. Only occasionally, especially when I wasn't taking notes, she would let something slip.

"You could see smoke and hear screams, and it was five kilometers from Janczewko to Jedwabne. Soon we knew what had happened. I cried, my mother cried, and one of our neighbors did, too. There were a lot of people in Janczewko who didn't cry, because they saw the Jews as enemies. Czesia Wądołowska was rushing back and forth to Jedwabne with sacks. She brought back furs, till she hurt herself with all that lugging and died soon after."

On another occasion she sighed, and said: "Before the war I did the day's work my father owed the church, which was under construction, and I should have felt at home there. But when I saw women come to church after the war in fur coats that had belonged to Jews, I didn't feel at home there anymore."

Another time she confessed: "You feared neighbors more than anyone else. If anyone had guessed we were hiding Jews none of us would be alive today. And there's still fear, because of the men who beat me up after the war for hiding Jews—three are still alive."

"And who were they?"

"How would I remember after all these years?"

She was born in 1916 and lived in Janczewko, a settlement near Jedwabne—not more than a dozen cottages from the road. Her father, Franciszek Karwowski, spent his time working, praying, and helping others. He never swore. He never missed Sunday Mass. When one of his neighbors stole from him he prayed for the Lord to forgive him because he knew not what he did. Antonina's mother, Józefa, scolded him, "You fool, pray louder, so they can take everything we have." Antonina left school after second grade. Her father "bribed" the Jedwabne principal to let his daughter leave school before the mandatory grade, because she was needed to work.

"At least I can sign my name," says Antonina.

At sixteen, she was married off by her parents to a neighbor from the house across the road, Aleksander Wyrzykowski.

There were no Jews in Janczewko. Antonina went to market in Jedwabne and sometimes ran into Szmul there when she brought cloth to his mother, and she sometimes had her bicycle fixed by Jakub Kubrzański, who worked in his father's workshop. Later she saved both of their lives.

"Some time after the Jews were burned in the barn," Wyrzykowska recounted, "my husband saw Szmulek sitting on the steps of his house. He asked him if he wanted to come and work with us; at that time Poles could employ Jews and pay the Germans for the labor. Szmul jumped on the wagon right away and they drove to Janczewko. From that time onward he helped us in the fields."

He was there officially—Antonina's husband managed to arrange with the German-appointed mayor, Marian Karolak, for Szmul not to have to report to the police station in Jedwabne every week. But they didn't let a lot of people know that Szmul was working with them. The Wyrzykowskis and Wasersztejn together, trading with the ghetto, earned what was required to pay the Germans for the right to employ a Jew. They'd go to the ghetto on Sunday, when traffic was heaviest, because Jews who worked on farms during the week would be going back. There were many people then trading with the ghetto, mostly buying up anything of any value at low prices, a loaf of bread for a ring. The Wyrzykowskis and Szmul were exceptions in that regard—they had to make a little money, but mainly they were trying to get food to the hungry.

"I'd be all weighed down carrying bundles of butter, the flat kind, but big chunks," Wyrzykowska told me. "We had a designated hole, and sometimes Szmul arranged for us to be let through the gate with a wagon, and we'd bring in flour and bread. Only you had to put on a badge that said 'Jude' as soon as you came through the gate. I had one and so I could move around the ghetto without risk," she said in a tone implying this was the most ordinary thing in the world.

"The first time I saw Antonina she was handing us potatoes and beets through the barbed wire," said Lea Kubran, formerly Kubrzańska, who survived the war at the Wyrzykowskis', when I met her in the United States. "Once, I ran into her again in the ghetto; she had a yellow badge pinned on. I never heard of any other Pole going around with a badge like that. If they'd caught her, she would have been shot on the spot."

Szmul soon came to be part of the Wyrzykowski family. He slept in the children's room.

"He got used to us calling him Staszek," said Wyrzykowska. "He went with us to May services, I remember. He sang our Polish songs, church songs. With fine, pure pronunciation, even though when he talked he didn't pronounce things as well."

"Franciszek, the finest man under the sun, made it his life's goal to save not only my life but my soul," Szmul Wasersztejn remembered of Antonina's father many years later. "He wept over my being a Jew; Jews didn't go to heaven. Every night he'd lecture me about Jesus." Wasersztejn agreed to be baptized. "I didn't see any particular problem with it, we believed in the same God, and it made Franciszek happy that I was going to be saved."

Wyrzykowska remembers her father sprinkling Szmul with holy water and that no one outside the family attended the christening.

When in the autumn of 1942 the Nazis carried out the liquidation of the ghettos and rounded up Jews living outside them, Wasersztejn managed to avoid the roundup. But the Wyrzykowski house became the least secure place in the area, because the Germans knew he lived and worked there. So the Wyrzykowskis asked Antoni Karwowski, Antonina's brother, to hide him for a few weeks, until they'd made a good hiding place for him at home. Then Mosze Olszewicz and his brother Berek turned up.

"In 1941 my brother and I fled from a pogrom to the Łomża ghetto, and later our parents and sister joined us there," Mosze Olszewicz wrote in 1975 from Buenos Aires in a letter to the Yad Vashem Institute for Holocaust Studies. "We were in the ghetto for a year. At the time of the liquidation the Gestapo surrounded the ghetto and we understood this was the end. We crawled through the barbed-wire fence and wandered around the area in blizzards and bitter cold until we felt we couldn't hold out anymore. Then I remembered a Christian woman. We went to her and asked for a crust of bread. Her husband gave us not only bread but hot milk and more. I can't even begin to describe their goodness. We were there all night and in the morning when we should have taken off, he said, 'Don't go, you're someone's children, too, if we have something to eat so will you. What comes to us will come to you. We can't let you fall into the hands of murderers.' His wife agreed with his every word."

"Olszewicz was the builder of the hideout; he figured it all out as if he had an engineering degree," Wyrzykowska said of him with great respect. "My husband said he was going to the market in Jedwabne and when he came back the Jews had to be hidden so well that he couldn't find them. Then they could stay. My husband came back and couldn't find them; he shouted loudly, on purpose, 'To hell with you, you're not staying here.'"

When the hideout was ready, they moved Szmul in. Then Mosze, with their permission, brought in his fiancée, Elke, as well. Next Srul Grądowski turned up; Szmul had met him after the massacre and given him the Wyrzykowskis' address. The last to come was Jankiel Kubrzański.

"Kubrzański turned up after the Łomża ghetto ended," Wyrzykowska related. "It was cold, and he, poor fellow, was wearing the kind of light coat that's lined with air. 'Mrs. Wyrzykowski, have you seen any of my people?' So I showed him the hideout. 'Hop right in.' I told my husband that Kubrzański had been to the house asking about other Jews. He was interested in what I told him, but I could tell from his face that he didn't want to take in any more Jews. Didn't want to because of food; it wasn't easy to feed five people. They ate nothing apart from what we gave them. So I didn't tell him I'd already moved Jakub Kubrzański into the hideout."

The Wyrzykowskis could have no illusions about what might happen to their family if Jews were found to be living with them. They had two small children; Helenka was seven, Antoś was two.

"Only I knew there were seven of them," said Wyrzykowska, "because those two—Kubrzański moved his fiancée in right away—they were there at my own risk, the whole time. My husband thought we were hiding five. When the hiding was over, Kubrzański turned up at the house immediately, pretending to drop by, because we'd known him before the war. My husband said, 'Why didn't you come to me, I would have hidden you.' I'm sure it's true my husband would have agreed, but why give him more to worry about?"

One day another Jew turned up, a relative of Srul Grądowski's.

"He was a young boy who had escaped from a camp," Antonina remembers. "I gave him better food than I ate myself, and every kind of medicine we had in the house, but he only lived a few days. My husband took him out beyond Kownaty. It was hard to dig a grave in the frozen ground. I don't know what his name was. I didn't know the others' surnames either, only Szmul's and Kubrzański's."

The two couples, the Kubrzańskis and the Olszewiczes, shared a hideout under the pigsty, and Szmul, Grądowski, and Berek were under the chicken house. They could be in contact at night, when they'd go out to get some fresh air; the buildings were connected by a roof. But they rarely did make contact, because it was best for safety reasons that only one person left the shelter at a time.

Wyrzykowska remembers that the greatest problem was feeding seven extra mouths for two and a half years. At that time everything went by ration cards. Each member of the family got a card allowing them to grind twenty kilograms of grain into flour for their own use. This wasn't enough to make bread for everyone, so Wyrzykowska's father ground wheat using two stones.

"One neighbor asked me why we baked so much bread, and Mother explained it was for rusks. The war might get worse and you had to have food stored. Another neighbor asked why we cooked so many potatoes. 'Darn it,' said Mother, 'that's the kind of pigs we've got. They won't eat anything but potatoes, potatoes, and imagine, they have to be peeled.'"

"We were hungry all the time, though Antonina tried so hard," said Lea Kubran. "The Germans took a quota of food, and the family itself didn't have too much to eat. But we never suffered from the cold because the shelter was so small that the steam from a few mouths could heat it."

Two Germans sent from the police station in Jedwabne to guard Janczewko lived in the same courtyard, about a hundred meters from the pigsty.

"We had an indoor cellar that was clean, walled, and the Germans requisitioned it," Wyrzykowska told me. "They slept in one part and had a pantry in the other where they smoked meat and kept stores for the whole police force in Jedwabne. Because of that our Jews couldn't go anywhere, even at night. The pigsty was walled off, with a roof made of boards. They cut a tiny peephole with a knife and when they saw the Germans had gone off somewhere they'd go upstairs. They got some air, stretched their legs, relieved themselves in a can that I'd remove later, and that was the whole adventure. As it was they didn't have enough room for each one to lie down. They spent their time sitting up, and then one person would put his legs over the other's chest. I often looked in on the chicken house, and I brought Szmul, Berek, and Grądowski the same food we ate. Once a day I'd bring potatoes or kasha to the pigsty, pretending it was for the pigs, and then I'd throw in some bread in the evening."

"Antonina couldn't bring us food; she carried a pot for the pigs so no one would see it was for people," Lea Kubran told me. "And she'd have to choose the right moment to hand us the pot. Many evenings we'd say, 'It isn't worth all this trouble,' but a new day would rise."

In the winter of 1942 a rumor went around that the Germans were going to form the Poles into an army to deploy against the Soviets. Wyrzykowski found out he was on the draft list and went into hiding in a neighbor's shed. One day Wyrzykowska's brother ran over to his hideout with the news that the Germans had come to their property with dogs to hunt down Jews. He ran home, feeling he couldn't leave his wife alone in a situation like that.

"One man in the village," said Stanisław Karwowski, Wyrzykowska's nephew, "who went from house to house selling moonshine, they called him Walenty, noticed a Jew at my aunt's house once and told someone whose daughter worked at the police station. She brought the police over immediately. Four of them turned up on horseback with dogs."

"The policemen put me up against the wall, one of them held his gun on me and they told us to hand over the Jews," Wyrzykowski wrote in his Yad Vashem testimony. "They said if I handed them over, nothing would happen to me; they'd only shoot the Jews. I told them there weren't any. I knelt down and cried a lot and prayed God to let me keep my life and save my family and those people."

Wyrzykowski showed great presence of mind. When the Germans saw straw trampled in the barn he explained he slept there because their house was cramped. When they were about to burn the straw to test his words, he begged them not to, because the fire would engulf the whole farm.

"I don't know who told me, because I wasn't smart enough to figure it out on my own," said Wyrzykowska, "but I had sprinkled gas around the pigsty every day. The Germans searched for Jews with dogs, but where there's gas a dog loses its sense of smell. The Lord came to our aid, too, and he's still helping, because four of them are still alive."

"When the police came," Lea Kubran related, "we were all prepared to commit suicide; we had razor blades ready to cut our veins. When they left, we were sure our hosts would tell us to go, because they might not get away with it the next time. Wyrzykowski knocked on the door, embraced my husband, and said, 'My dears, if they didn't find you this time they'll never find you—you stay with us until the war's over.'"

Wyrzykowska saved not just seven Jews but a German in the bargain.

"Once one of the policemen staying across the street from us was left alone. He got sick and I found him lying on the ground writhing in pain. I gave him soda and vinegar, which we always used as a medicine, but it didn't help. I went to my people hiding in the pigsty and asked them how to say in German, 'Your comrade is sick.' I harnessed a wagon, went to the police station, and said, '*Kamrad krank*.'"

Luckily no one at the police station realized Wyrzykowska had spoken to them not so much in broken German as in perfect Yiddish.

"They came for him right away. When he was better and when the other German wasn't looking, or anybody else, he helped me with the threshing. There were other good Germans here, they gave the children candy and when the end of the war was near they said, 'Hitler kaput.'"

When the front moved and they had to evacuate Janczewko, the Wyrzykowskis prepared a hiding place in a potato field, because they were afraid a fire might break out on the front line and burn everyone in the pigsty alive—at night they carried poles and planks out and dug up earth for a hideout. Once the Russians arrived on January 23, 1945, the Jews came out of hiding.

"It was still night when we were liberated from the pigsty," Mosze Olszewicz wrote in his letter to Yad Vashem, "and we came out into the bright world, full of air and light. We were weak, sick, physically and mentally broken. They looked at our pale faces, our emaciated arms and legs, our blinded eyes, and they brought us back to life with warm words, bringing us the best things they had to eat."

"The first day of freedom no one could stand on their own legs," Lea Kubran remembers.

The Kubrzańskis and Olszewiczes soon moved to Łomża. Srul Grądowski had himself baptized and remained in Jedwabne. Szmul went on living with the Wyrzykowskis.

One day Antonina's brother came to Janczewko in despair to warn them he had heard six Poles plotting to kill Wasersztejn. The two men went into hiding right away, leaving Antonina alone with her two children and elderly parents.

"My brother was at the gathering of the plotters," Wyrzykowska said. "He came to our house immediately: 'I decided to tell you, because it would be a pity, they went through so many months of suffering and you suffered so much with them.'"

Leon Dziedzic, whose brother was also at the plotters' meeting, is sure it was a gathering of the local unit of the Home Army.

Wyrzykowski hid in the hope that this was just "guys settling scores" and that as a woman, Antonina would be safe. But the attackers had no pity for women, either.

"At night," Wyrzykowski described, "the partisans came for the Jew; they wanted him to be handed over so they could kill him and then they wouldn't bother us anymore. My wife told them he'd left. They beat her so badly there wasn't any white skin left on her, she was all black and blue."

"She was a devout Christian, I thought they wouldn't harm her," Szmul Wasersztejn recalled. "At midnight six men turned up who had taken part in the pogrom in Jedwabne. They beat old Franciszek and Antonina, threw them on the floor, kicked them, beat them, trying to find out where I was. They stole whatever caught their eye. They forced that brave woman to hitch up the horses and drive them to Jedwabne with the spoils of their looting. She just asked them to leave her sick father in peace. When she got back it was light, she got down from the cart and passed out. She had wounds on her face and the traces of beatings on her back. The children saw it all."

"They ordered me to lie down on the floor and they beat me with clubs," Wyrzykowska recounts. "They beat me so that there wasn't a spot on my body that wasn't black and blue. They screamed, 'You Jewish lackeys, you hid Jews, and they crucified Jesus. Tell us where you're keeping the Jew.' I said, 'The Jew left a long time ago.' They had all left by then, except Szmul was still there, hiding in a hollow in a neighbor's potato field. They mauled my father. They took all our best things. I held out. I even hitched up the horses to drive them home."

Next day the Wyrzykowskis joined the Olszewiczes and Kubrzańskis, who were staying somewhere on the outskirts of Łomża. Wyrzykowska remembers a nocturnal expedition to Janczewko—to get a cow for milk to stave off their constant hunger—as the most harrowing moment in her life. It was a time when many gangs roamed the countryside and they wouldn't have been able to take a cow safely in the daytime; if they met any thugs at night it meant certain death.

Later they moved to Białystok. They slept side by side on the floor. There was nothing to eat.

The incident of Wyrzykowska's beating ended up in court. "On the night of March 13 to 14, 1945, ten armed Home Army terrorists beat up citizen Wyrzykowska, resident of the village Janczewko in the Łomża district, for hiding Jews during the German occupation and presently maintaining good relations with them," one reads in the Białystok security service report, under the heading "Typical Acts of Terror by AKO Gangs in the Report Period." (The AK, or Home Army, in the area had transformed itself by that time into the AKO, or Citizens' Home Army.) The documents show that Antonina Wyrzykowska testified to the security service in Łomża on April 9 that she had been beaten up by a gang. She said, "I can't live here, they'll kill me." She gave names. Most of them belonged to the armed forces based in the forest and didn't answer the summons, but we know that at least one of them, Antoni Wądołowski, was convicted.

Wyrzykowska decided to escape across the "green border"—to leave the country by sneaking across borders—with Szmul and the Kubrzańskis and Olszewiczes. The Olszewiczes found their way via Budapest to Italy. The others found themselves by late spring near Linz, in an Austrian refugee camp. "We walked more than we rode," Lea Kubran told me.

"There were only Jews there, I was the only Pole. I had left my children and whenever I saw a child in the street I felt such pain I couldn't bear it," Wyrzykowska relates. "After a few weeks I went home."

In the first testimony he gave to the Jewish Historical Commission, Szmul claimed that he "had married the woman who saved him." Wyrzykowska doesn't want to talk about that; certainly there was no official wedding.

When did they fall in love? Was it when they drove to the ghetto together, before Szmul was in hiding? Or was it during the period in hiding? Right after? What was the Wyrzykowskis' marriage like after she came back from the refugee camp in Austria? Of Wyrzykowski I only know he was a noble person, a handsome man, and that after the war he became a drunk.

"I talked about it with Szmul many times," I hear from Chaim Sroszko of Jedwabne, who now lives in Israel. He met Szmul in 1945 in Białystok, and was in constant touch with him until his death. "He told me at a certain point he realized he had no right to a woman who had left her children for him. He decided to go back to Poland with Antonina to help ensure her safe return to her family."

The Kubrzańskis lived for almost four more years in a displaced persons camp in Austria before obtaining visas for the United States in 1949.

When Antonina had returned to her husband and children, the family moved to Bielsk Podlaski. Wasersztejn bought them a house and farm there with money sent to him by a brother in Cuba. They knew nothing of what happened to the other Jews they had saved. Before she'd parted from them Antonina had agreed with all of them that they would somehow communicate that they had survived at the first opportunity, but God forbid they should write. She was afraid of getting letters from Jews, and indeed, Stalinist times soon came in Poland, when it was bad to receive any letters from abroad.

It sometimes happened that Wyrzykowska would run into her persecutors in Bielsk, which is not far from Jedwabne. They threatened her, taunted her. She lived in constant fear. Her husband, Aleksander, began to drink, so that in the end nothing was left of the farm Szmul Wasersztejn had bought them. At the start of the 1960s they moved from Bielsk to Milanówek. In this move they were helped by Szymon Datner, as Antonina remembered. From there, Antonina commuted to Warsaw, where she worked as a janitor in Warsaw schools. Aleksander died soon after their move.

Antonina helped her daughter, Helena, and her son, Antoni, financially. Helena started to work in a shop; Antoni found a job with the local government.

"You said your children knew nothing about your hiding Jews. But when they grew up did you talk about it all with them?"

"Why would I? There wasn't any time to tell them about those things. I worked hard, the worst was clearing snow in winter. I took on extra cleaning. Even on the Sabbath I went to people's houses to wash windows."

"Every single day, for years and years, Mama left Milanówek on the 4:05 a.m. train and got home at 10:03 p.m.," said Antoni.

In the seventies Wyrzykowska traveled to America for the first time, invited by the Kubrzański family, who by then went by Kubran. They were waiting for her at the airport in Miami with the Olszewiczes, who had come from Argentina for the occasion (the Kubrans spent the summer months in Florida). They took her to the synagogue, where they had ordered a Service of Thanksgiving for her. Wasersztejn came to visit them there from Costa Rica.

"I hadn't seen Szmulek for a long time. Almost thirty years had passed."

"The first time she came to see us for three months, then a year," Lea Kubran remembers. "There are a lot of Jews and Poles in New London. Antonina has her gossip network here, they take walks by the shore. Our town has a Polish week once a year, when they prepare Polish dishes and play Polish songs. While my husband was alive he spent many an evening dancing polkas with Antonina."

The next time Wyrzykowska spent time in the United States she married a Polish American.

"After the wedding my husband said to me, 'Now we'll go to court and claim that money from the Jews you hid, who ruined your health.' So I told the old coot to go to hell."

She married a third time, again in the States, again an American of Polish origin.

"He was a widower, a stingy, cunning man. He'd buy the fattest chicken in the store, because in America the fatter something is, the cheaper. He was older than me, so once I said to him, 'Staszek, shouldn't you make a will in the event of your death, so your children don't throw me out of the house?' He went with me to a lawyer, they wrote it in English, I was supposed to sign. I once gave it to a friend to read. She read it to me: when I died he would get everything I owned, and my children were disinherited. I packed my bags, went to stay with a granddaughter in Chicago, and sued for divorce. I pray for the Jews they burned in the barn every day and sometimes for my third husband's first wife. I never met her, but when I think she spent twenty-seven years with him!"

Szmul Wasersztejn began to invite her to Costa Rica every winter.

"I liked being there in winter for two or three months, it was wonderfully warm. His sons still invite me, but there's no one to talk to. I don't know their languages."

Wyrzykowska went for the last time in the winter of 1999–2000.

"Szmul was deaf, almost completely," she told me. "He watched television, because he could read lips pretty well, and when I spoke right in his ear he could hear me. We often recalled how good his hearing used to be, he'd hear the creaking of a gate and would be in the hideout before the policeman was at the door. That day his wife, Rachel, had gone to

Miami to see their daughter. She asked whether she should stay, because Szmul felt weak, but he told her to go. Staszek and I—I always called him by his Polish name—watched a tape of my trip to the Holy Land. In the afternoon he told me to go upstairs, because he wanted to take a nap. I was reading my prayer book when I heard a cry. He was sitting in his chair, dead. I saved his life as long as I could, but now I couldn't help him."

Antonina liked spending time at prayer.

"I have a booklet with Saint Anthony's prayers, I say them every day. When a school where I worked as a janitor was haunted, I'd bring my icon of Saint Anthony and some holy water. I'd light a candle and the ghosts would disappear."

She divided her time between Poland and the United States, where her granddaughter lives. She had no room of her own anywhere. When she was in Poland she stayed with her son and daughter-in-law, who gave her their tiny little bedroom and slept in the living room. When I visited her, we sat on the sofa bed—there was no room for a chair—and talked about how the Jews she rescued spoke Polish.

"Lea spoke best, and Mietek Olszewicz knew a lot of Polish jokes," she said, using Mosze's wartime Polish name. Suddenly she made a sign for us to be quiet. Someone had just come to see her son and he might hear what we were talking about.

"I keep my things in the sofa bed and in my suitcase; the closets are full of their things. I hide my photographs. Who would want to look at them?" she said, taking her pictures from America out from under the quilt.

I asked to see the letters she received from Wasersztejn, from the Kubrans, the Olszewiczes.

"I don't have a single one. Once I read them, I rip them up. Mietek Olszewicz wrote me that there were Polish clubs in Buenos Aires, that they played soccer, but he didn't go in for it because he couldn't stand the sight of Poles anymore." She appreciated that Mosze Olszewicz took care that no one would suspect her of having Jewish contacts: "He never wrote 'Mosze' on the back of the envelope, always 'Mieczysław.'"

I drove Antonina and her son home after she was honored in the synagogue with a menorah. The whole way I listened to her son's diatribes.

"The Jews get money from the Germans for having survived. But I ask you, miss, who helped them survive? Wasn't it my mother, who risked her own life and her children's? They get five hundred dollars a month, that's two thousand zlotys, right in your face, you just multiply that by seven people and twelve months. It adds up to a pretty penny, right? And I have a twenty-year-old Fiat that's all fucked up. You can't deny my mother saved those people, it's a fact. I'm happy with my mother. But my sister thinks it's better not to admit it, because we'll all get our throats cut. I have to say my sister has a negative attitude. In the city office where I worked they fired the oldest workers because they knew too much. They fired me, too, and I would never have said anything, it's not my style. I just turn my back and don't see anything. I always say to my mother, 'Don't be afraid, you aren't giving any names, and you didn't see what happened because you weren't there at the barn.' Here a Yid bought a grocery store in Milanówek. I was talking about it with my friends. They're worried that Jews are going to move into our little town. And I tell them, 'That Yid gets up at dawn and does everything that needs to be done, and they even help each other. And what do Poles do? Do they help? Make an effort? They get drunk and envy others. In the end Yids will own half of Milanówek,' I tell them, 'and we will clean their shoes.'

"My sister is an anti-Semite. I don't have anything against Jews. If she found out my mother had been in a synagogue she'd raise hell. You can hardly blame her. She's sick, she can't afford to buy medicine, and she knows how much the Yids owe Mama."

I turned to Antonina. "They invited you many times, surely they help?"

Her son: "But none of them has ever thought to hand over the cash directly."

Antonina protested gently: "When I needed medicine, Szmul gave me money."

Another time when I visited Antonina she was worried she'd catch hell from her daughter again.

"I don't know where Helenka read that I went to visit the president. 'What the hell did you go there for?' she yelled, and hung up on me. I can't be too surprised, the whole thing makes trouble for my children. When my son's wife goes to the office they say, 'What? You're still working here? You must have plenty of money if your mother-in-law hid seven Jews!' "

I asked Wyrzykowska how many people she had told in the course of her life that she had hidden Jews.

"I could have told people I trusted, but generally you didn't boast about it because you were scared. The guys who beat me up aren't scared. I had the pleasure of saving Jewish lives. But people look at you askance for it. Maybe if I'd hid blacks they'd see it differently. You know the country you live in, so you tell me how many people would be happy to hear I hid Jews? One in ten, and that's giving them the benefit of the doubt. Honestly, if you have a Jew for a friend, the Poles are your enemies. Why that is, I don't know. When I got the distinction, that Righteous Among the Nations medal, my Helenka threw it right in the trash. And it's better that way, because who would I show it to anyway? I told a priest in Chicago I had rescued Jews and that I prayed for them every day. He didn't tell me that was wrong, so apparently it's not a sin. I would never tell a priest in Poland things like that. No, not for the world."

11

I, Szmul Wasersztejn, Warn You

or, The Road from Jedwabne to Costa Rica

Wasersztejn told his children, born in the other hemisphere, that he had to rescue from oblivion the atrocity committed in his native country as a warning to future generations. Toward the end of his life he hired a local journalist and told him the story of his life. His hearing and sight were already quite poor, and he wasn't able to read what he dictated. He wanted to commemorate the victims and brand the killers, but the Spanish-speaking journalist got the Jewish and Polish names so mangled that there's no way of figuring out who was whom. Only a knowledge of Szmul's life makes it possible to guess that the "Viashilikowski" family were Antonina and Aleksander Wyrzykowski. Szmul remembered the landscape of his childhood with nostalgia, and the journalist who was his audience threw in orange groves on top of fields of rye. The result was a book of more than four hundred pages, *La Denuncia: 10 de Julio de 1941* (Denunciation: July 10, 1941), which Szmul's son Izaak published at his own expense in 2000, after his father's death.

The same year saw the publication of Jan Gross's *Neighbors*, which drew on Wasersztejn's testimony. And so it was that his testimony, stored in the archives of the Jewish Historical Institute in Warsaw, began to circulate publicly. His words prompted horror and disbelief. But he died before his testimony set into motion a veritable avalanche of events,

Szmul Wasersztejn and
Antonina Wyrzykowska,
1945. (Author's private
collection)

From left, seated: Antonina
Wyrzykowska, Szmul
Wasersztejn, Lea Kubrzańska.
Standing in back: Jankiel
Kubrzański and Mosze Lasko,
also from Jedwabne. The
Kubrzańskis, Szmul, and
Antonina had met Lasko by
accident. Displaced persons
camp, Linz, Austria, 1945.
(Courtesy of Jose Gutstein,
www.radzilow.com)

provoking a wave of denials and anti-Semitic attacks on the one hand, and on the other a courageous reckoning with the truth.

What we read in Wasersztejn's diary bears a closer resemblance to the apocalyptic visions of Hieronymus Bosch than to the actual crime. In the marketplace Wasersztejn sees "old Jewish women, their faces smeared with blood," "naked women trying to hide their shame with scraps of cloth, their thighs slashed with razors. Blood, curses, death." On Cmentarna Street he sees a "heap of corpses," "two young women, their bellies ripped open by a knife, their intestines hanging out," "a beautiful six-year old girl, whose throat had been slit with a razor." This whole cacophony of rape, killing, screaming must have grown and got jumbled up in his head.

In the book, which is completely unedited, horrifying descriptions of the atrocity sit side by side with lofty reflections on the nature of the universe and exaggerated accounts of Wasersztejn's own exploits. I find it appalling, and only after a while do I realize the absurdity of my own expectations of Wasersztejn: that he be a wise and noble figure. The more I immerse myself in his story, the more moved I am by the reminiscences of Szmul, who was never meant to be a tragic hero.

"The hot summer of 1941 fell on Poland like a plague," Szmul begins his recollections. "Jedwabne was raging like a furnace. The earth was arid, the plants had withered, the ponds were dry, it was all like kindling—it only took a spark and a gust of wind for a fire to break out and start a conflagration."

Then he moves back in time, describes his birth and his mother's labor in childbirth: "Was the fever that burned her temples not an anticipation of the flames of the pyre on which she was burned, murdered by Christian Poles of Jedwabne? Was the hand she saw in her delirium trying to wrest me from her arms not the same hand of death that tried to wipe me from the face of the earth? The cat that leaped at the window with its claws out, shattering the window as my mother was giving birth to me—was it not a foreshadowing of the moment when the project of revenge leaped up in my mind, a revenge that would smash to pieces the Church and the pious Pharisees who praised God after killing my mother, brother, and other Jews of the town?"

The whole story is written in this style. Florid descriptions sit next to reflections full of pathos (shocked by the denial of the Holocaust and the desecration of Jewish cemeteries, he writes, "I, Szmul Wasersztejn, bear witness from Costa Rica and warn you: there is a worldwide conspiracy against Jews"), from which only a tenacious reader may fish out any meaningful details of the Jedwabne tragedy and compare them with the account Szmul gave after the war.

In 1945 he testified that on June 25, 1941, Poles had stoned Jakub Kac to death with bricks and stabbed Eliasz Krawiecki with knives—"they put out his eyes, cut out his tongue, he suffered agonizing pain for twelve hours before giving up the ghost"—and two young women, Chaja Kubrzańska and Basia Binsztejn went to a pond, "choosing to drown themselves with their children rather than fall into the hands of thugs." After drowning the children, "Basia Binsztejn jumped, going right to the bottom, while Chaja Kubrzańska struggled for several hours. The thugs who had gathered round made a spectacle of it.

"I saw it with my own eyes," he said. But in his recollections of half a century later it looks slightly different. On July 2 he saw a group of thugs torturing Jakub Kac: "They shoved him, abused him, struck his face, kicked him. One guy hit him on the head with a thick pole. The brain of the old man, who'd been a friend of my parents, spattered onto the pavement." The thugs went on to the house where Kubrzańska and Binsztejn lived. "They resisted, but their children were taken away from them. No one cared that they were herding women stripped of their clothes, because they were all cowards and just stood there looking without seeing, listening without hearing. The women were taken to a place out in the country where there were clay pits that filled with water in the rainy season. They ordered the women to drown their own children. They refused. Then they took the children and stuck their heads into the stinking swamp. The earth swallowed them up. Now it was the turn of the beaten and crazed women. One of the thugs brought heavy rocks, which they tied to the girls' necks. They buckled down, the mud rose up to their lips, to their nostrils, and they drowned."

The stoning of Kac, Krawiecki being tortured to death, the drowning of two mothers and their babies for the entertainment of assembled company—these facts are confirmed by other witnesses (a woman from Jedwabne told me, "My mother's sister saw two Jewish women being forced to drown themselves and their children. She came home in tears"). Chaja Kubrzańska and Basia Binsztejn were sisters whose husbands collaborated with the Soviets. The summer of 1941 was indeed dry and hot, and there was more mud than water in the ponds along the Łomża road to Jedwabne, so they couldn't drown themselves quickly.

When I began to talk to witnesses, most of the facts Wasersztejn reported in his 1945 testimony, later archived at the Jewish Historical Institute, were corroborated. But only after reading his diary, where the description of events is more detailed, did I realize that he couldn't have been an eyewitness to everything he described. It's only natural: a witness, especially one conscious of being one of very few survivors, will want to tell everything he knows about the events, whether he saw them himself or heard of them later from others.

Let's take the scene of the women being drowned. Wasersztejn wouldn't have remembered it one way and told it another way many years later. It's more likely that he tried to piece together events from fragments of information—somebody saw both women with their children at the clay pits with local thugs standing around, somebody found their bloated remains. In 1945 he said it happened on June 25, but in his book he said it was July 2. The point is not the difference in the dates, because he might easily make a mistake after so many years. From the accounts of witnesses, it emerges that the scenes of torture and killing occured over the course of many days. On the other hand, it's because of Szmul's account that Jakub Kac ceased to be for me an anonymous pogrom victim and instead became a leatherworker who made horses' harnesses by hand, putting his entire being into each piece of work.

But for Wasersztejn's testimony, brought to light many years later by Jan Gross, the atrocity in Jedwabne might never have been exposed. It's a paradox that the path to truth was cleared by a witness account that raises certain doubts. But one can imagine another scenario. Say Wasersztejn was questioned competently back in 1945, and the document left in the archives clearly distinguished what the witness saw himself from what he heard secondhand. The question is, would his account have sufficient power to provoke Gross to write a book on Jedwabne, a book that led to an investigation conducted by the Institute of National Remembrance?

Facts can be pried out of Wasersztejn's descriptions when they are compared with the accounts of other witnesses; his testimony also evokes the atmosphere of those days. The first days after the Soviets withdrew must have been much as Szmul described them in his diary:

"The municipality issued a decree that Jews had to clean the streets in town, whether cobbled streets or dirt roads full of mud. Each family was assigned a section of road to clean. They had to sweep the walkways, remove horse manure, keep the gutters clean, clean public buildings, remove garbage. If they refused they were whipped. Jews were forced to close their shops. People stopped buying shirts from my mother. Food reserves went fast. A potato was a treasure. Under cover of night, gangs of thugs threw rocks through windows, yelling 'Go to Palestine.' Many merchants were beaten for not closing up shop. Drunken gangs ruled the town. Anti-Semitism had created an atmosphere in which that scum could call themselves 'defenders of the community.' Pogroms occurred in several places. Killings, robberies, rapes, destruction of Jewish property. We were like flitting shadows." In his 1945 testimony, he mentioned that one gang that went from house to house beating and robbing Jews included the brothers Wacław and Mieczysław Borowski, who "played the accordion and clarinet to drown out the screams of women and children."

Then comes the moment on July 10 when neighbors become party to the atrocity: "We had played with their children when we were children. We'd done them favors, given them potato peelings for their hogs. Now their voices sounded implacably: 'All Jewish residents are to gather in the marketplace without delay.' From the moment the Germans arrived in town we became garbage to them. Mama looked for our Torah. A neighbor, grabbing her roughly by the arm, threw her out of the house, yelling: 'Don't you play with me, miss, or I'll run out of patience.' We tried to go with some dignity, but some of them poked our backs with sharp poles, herded us on, cursed us: 'Jewish dog,' 'Son of a bitch,' 'Profiteer,' 'Damn Christ-killers.'"

Many of these scenes cannot be confirmed or denied, as they probably had no witnesses—apart from the victims and their persecutors, many of whom have talked later about what happened. "On Sadowa Street two girls, almost completely naked, were raped by gangs. Sara, Sosnowski's daughter, was separated from her son and raped by five men in a granary. They crushed her pale, smooth body. Knowing she worked in a bank, they tortured her so she would tell them where the money was." Is that really the way his neighbor Sara, daughter of Hana and Zundel Sosnowski, died?

Szmul remembers saving himself by proposing a deal to a classmate called "Mushałko" (in fact he did go to school with Tadeusz Musiałek): If he got him out of the marketplace, Szmul would give him a few kilos of tobacco he had hidden near his house. When they got away from the marketplace Wasersztejn supposedly told him there was no tobacco, but that he had to survive because there had to be a witness who would reveal to the world the insanity of the atrocity taking place (it's hard to believe that Szmul, who had such a strong instinct for self-preservation, would have used such an argument, which would very likely have provoked the man to kill him). After a brief scuffle, he said, he escaped and hid in the Jewish cemetery in an open grave, covering himself with grass.

In his 1945 testimony it goes like this: "He agreed to get me out, but not my brother, who was in the group led by the lame 'Diewicszi.' I begged him, but he said there was no fooling with the lame guy. He drew a finger across my throat: 'Shut up, all Jews are going to be killed at 4:00 p.m.' My heart contracted. They were all doomed to an unworthy death: my mother, my little brother. Someone had to remain alive, perhaps the God of Israel would help me stop the injustice. Mushałko was trembling with rage, his eyes were full of hatred. Two burning circles. He spat on me, hurled insults at me, came at me to take my head off. He ran for reinforcements, I fled to the cemetery. Twenty meters from my father's grave I saw an open grave."

Only the cemetery is not in the direction of the Wasersztejn house, and there's no reason Musiałek would have led him that way.

If Szmul really hid in the cemetery, which was not yet (as it is now) covered with a grove of hazel trees and was one of the most dangerous places in town, where many killings took place that day, he had to have hidden himself very well in the grave—how much could he have seen from there?

However, he claimed he saw the first group of Jews being led to the vicinity of the barn. The murderer with a prosthetic leg must have been the lame Stanisław Sielawa (the Costa Rican journalist calls him "Diewicszi"), who is said to have cut off the heads of victims with an axe; his helpers stabbed them with knives, and then they piled the murdered and dying into a pit dug in advance. But Wasersztejn couldn't have seen Sielawa killing Jews, because—as transpires from the exhumation—the first group of Jews, the ones forced to carry the statue of Lenin, were killed inside the barn. On the other hand, the Jews in that first group were killed in the fashion described—gathered in one place and killed with an axe and knives. There must have been tales told about it in town and Szmul must have heard them after the massacre, from Poles.

In the first, brief testimony taken from Szmul Wasersztejn by the Jewish Historical Commission, we read, "The subject was in the bushes. He heard screams where 128 men, the strongest ones, were all killed in one location." He must have heard the screams without realizing they were coming from the barn. Immediately after the war, he told his friend Chaim Sroszko he had hidden in the cemetery. He told a Jew he met in Białystok, and who gave testimony to the Jewish Historical Commission in 1947 about what Szmul had told him, that he not only heard but also "hid between the graves and saw everything." He must have persuaded himself of the truth of his story.

He described events that immediately followed the burning of the Jews: "Women and children went out looting, one house after another. The men killed and the women and children robbed." When he visited Poland in the eighties, he heard from an old acquaintance, "Szmulke, I know who took your mother's things." He didn't want to know who it was.

At dawn on July 11 he heard the voices of two young Jews who had survived as he had. Together they made it to the house of a friend, then to another. There the people gave them food and drink, shed tears with them over the dead, but were afraid to keep them. The head of the household found out that the Germans had forbidden further killing of Jews. Szmul returned to the house on Przestrzelska Street in the hope of finding his mother or brother there. The house had been plundered, the sewing machine and the stores of food were gone. He sat on the threshold and burst into tears.

A passing German took him to the police station. There were already sixteen escaped Jews there, and later, as he describes it, the Germans refused to hand the Jews over to the Poles. "We need them"—they supposedly said—"for cleaning our horses and shoes." The Jews moved into one of the post-Jewish homes and reported for work in the morning. Once, one of them came back with a torn rectum after being raped by drunken policemen. Szmul didn't go to work the next day. He went back to his plundered home and wept.

It was there that Aleksander Wyrzykowski saw him and took him to work on his farm in Janczewko. Szmul writes that the killers of July 10 looked for him there. He hid in the basements and granaries when they came to the farm in Janczewko to sniff around. He succeeded in escaping because he was better at finding hideouts than they were.

In the autumn of 1942, when the Germans ordered the Jews working on farms to be rounded up, and police patrolled the area picking up runaways, Wasersztejn managed to avoid the hunt and hide in a barn belonging to the Dziedzic family, who brought him back to the Wyrzykowskis' a few days later.

Szmul remembers that it began to snow and Wyrzykowski saw tracks leading up to the stable. There he found Jakub Kubrzański and Mietek Olszewicz with his brother Berek, two girls they'd met in the ghetto, Lea and Elke, and the older Srul Grądowski. In his book he writes, "Wyrzykowski was terrified, but he hid it from them, he embraced them. He ran to his wife, 'We have six more Jews.' They brought them bread and water. The Jews had already forgotten that such kindness was possible, they ate the bread in tears. Wyrzykowski said there were too many of us, that he and his family would be shot for it. I realized I should thank them, leave without resentment, and look for another solution. I said I was leaving to share the fate of my brothers. We were thinking of going to Belorussia through the swamps."

The next day Wyrzykowski appeared: "As a Christian I cannot send you off to your deaths, but I can't send my own family off to die for you, either. First I was tired and I thought I had no choice—you had to leave the farm. But then I thought of a fairer solution. My wife and I are going to the market in Jedwabne. We'll be gone for many hours. Szmulek, you know I'm familiar with every inch of this property. If you can find a place where we can't discover you, I promise to feed you until the day that God ensures your survival. But if I find your shelter, this will be your last night here. I'll give you water and food for four days, clothing, and a hunting knife. Szmulek, is that clear?"

They all wandered around the farm, unable to find a good hiding place. In the end, Szmul wearily sat down on the edge of the pigsty. Then he teetered and fell into a heap of manure. He got up in a rage and kicked the ground. "How mysterious are the ways of God," he wrote. "*And there was light.* What I saw on the toe of my shoe was a chunk of sticky red clay." He came up with the idea of digging a tunnel and a subterranean shelter.

"I called the others. I said: 'We'll be living on two square meters, breathing the excrement of pigs and the urine of sheep. We need dry grass, manure, and fresh animal shit.' At five p.m. everything was completed. The girls found great stuff for covering our catacomb: two pieces of cardboard, seven planks in good condition, dry grain, half a sack of chicken feathers, and an old lamp—we took all those treasures down underground with us. We swept away all the outside tracks, we felt like worms living in the earth.

"We covered ourselves up with a pig's trough. We heard Aleksander and Antonina going from the house to the barn, from the barn to the pigsty. They looked for us in the privy, the chimney, the chicken coop, the granaries, in the fields, in the garden. They got to the toolshed, threw all the tools out, banged on the wall, looked under the piles of sheep's wool. Weeping, they asked God for forgiveness for having made the Jews flee to Belorussia on snowbound roads so that they might never get there. The first night we were underground wasn't easy. It's hard to describe the stench of pig shit. Piss is acidic, and then the decaying manure giving off hydrogen sulfide—that natural process choked our breath."

Wasersztejn describes how at eight in the morning he theatrically strode into the Wyrzykowskis' house. He said their hideout would stand up to the Gestapo and the pogroms, and Aleksander responded, "I'll keep my word. You'll get one meal a day. There has to be someone on guard day and night, and when it's quiet two people can come out of the stables. Only Szmul can come to the house under cover of darkness. Szmulek, now you should say goodbye to our kids, tell them you're leaving. I'll bring you water for a bath twice a week. I'll give you a jar for relieving yourselves. Antonina will talk to the women about what to do when they have their periods. From now on your lives depend on us and our lives depend on you. We will launder your clothes, iron them, mend them, trim your nails and give you an Old Testament, because my father-in-law told me for Szmul that's the Jewish Bible."

In fact, Wyrzykowski proposed to Mosze Olszewicz that he build a hiding place and Olszewicz built it. Szmul wasn't there at the time, he was hiding with Antonina's brother. "When Szmul came it was all ready," Lea Kubran remembered in conversation with me. Wasersztejn must have heard the story about building the hideout many times, in detail, from Olszewicz and become so familiar with it that it felt like his own story.

"The first days were a nightmare," Szmul wrote. "I remember Elke screaming hysterically when she discovered roundworms five centimeters long. Srul gagged when a worm called a cheese worm, white with a brown head, fell straight into his mouth. We suffered terribly, we threw up, but with time we became adjusted to the environment. We got used to watching the world through cracks. Our sense of smell grew more acute. The smell of baking bread reached us through the stench. We ceased to be Szmulek, Lejka, Elke, Mosze, Berek, Srul, Jankiel. We were the brotherhood of the pigsty. Just like Alexandre Dumas: all for one and one for all. Amidst the worms and dirt we were a metazoan, a subterranean monster with fourteen hands, ears, eyes, and nostrils, seven heads, mouths, and asses, five penises, two vaginas, and just one need: to survive. We had to surrender totally to each other where feelings were concerned, utterly resigning our own personalities. And share everything but the women. Elke and Lejka loved two of the men. And though we others also had our sexual needs and aching members, we should thank God we had the strength to control our sexual appetites."

Wasersztejn describes how one day Germans came to Janczewko looking for a place to encamp. They chose the Wyrzykowski farm. They had two trucks, they pitched a tent, set up a kitchen under the tent, and took the barn for living quarters.

"When the Germans were staying in the barn above us, one of the women was ready to give birth," he wrote. "Antonina brought a sheet, scissors, alcohol. She explained how the woman should push, breathe. Right after that the Germans turned up with dogs. They were laughing so much we knew they were drunk. They began to snore. In the night the woman went into labor. She had a rag in her mouth to keep herself from screaming. I told my friend that bringing a child into the world when the Germans were so close would get Antonina killed and I left it to his conscience. I saw an urgent question in his eyes. He spoke softly with his woman. The underground mother was contorted with pain, she bit the rag so hard blood flowed from her mouth. The child began to come out, and as soon as its little head appeared the father put a hand on its mouth to stop it from crying. He held it there till it turned blue; the mother lost consciousness. He held it until it was still. We cut the navel. When the mother came to she prayed in Hebrew, stroked the dead child, and cried herself to sleep. The father kissed the child's forehead. When the Germans left to go on patrol he took the remains and went out and buried them under a heap of shit. How many more months were we to go on crouching there, amid the stench? And now we were tormented by the memory of the child whose life we'd sacrificed so that we could live."

This testimony has the sincerity of passion and despair. But Szmul could not have been an immediate witness to the child's birth and death—in fact, there were two shelters and Szmul was hiding in the other one. Nor was there an additional German unit bedding down in the barn over their heads.

He spent more than two years underground. "One morning," Szmul wrote, "Antonina came to us: 'The Germans have gone, you can come out. I hope you remember what it feels like to be vertical.' A person doesn't need sun, light, food, freedom as much as he needs to move. We started dancing, jumping, stretching, raising our arms to the sky. The Red Army soldiers, with their coarse faces, stinking of vodka, prodded us, laughed, gave us vodka, but also kept us in their sights. We cried at the sight of the blue sky—we weren't moles anymore."

Wasersztejn set off for Jedwabne. The roads were—as he wrote—stained with blood. There were corpses of German soldiers all over the place. The Poles had torn from them everything of value. First that seemed horrible to him, but then he looked at his own ragged shirt, pants, and leaky shoes tied up with string, and decided he had the right to look for something better. He managed to gather together a cap with ear muffs, officer's boots, gloves, and a military coat made of leather. He and Izrael Grądowski happened upon a Soviet unit. "Good news," said the officer, "we're executing Germans today. I'm sure you'll enjoy that." They quickly moved on.

Wasersztejn knew he'd leave Poland, but he wanted to ensure the Wyrzykowski family's material security. "Their house was built in a time of poverty. I thought I had the right to choose some house that had belonged to well-off Jews and move it to Janczewko. There was a nice wooden building occupied by a Pole. I went in and told him to get out because it was my house. He was going to put up a fight, but Soviet trucks happened to be passing by and I greeted an officer. The Pole got scared and ran out the back way."

He didn't manage to move the house. The same evening he was warned thugs wanted to kill them and he escaped, finding his way first to

Łomża, and then to Białystok. He and the Wyrzykowskis moved into a
suburb, sleeping side by side on the floor. He started trading. He'd buy
cloth and thread in Łódź and sell them in Białystok. To avoid the squads
searching the trains for Jews, he hid near the tracks and jumped on at the
last minute when the train started moving. "I remembered," he wrote,
"someone talking about how great trade was in cloth from Łódź. I got
money for a ticket, two bales of cloth, and I'd have half a zloty left for
something to eat. A railway official who didn't hate Jews told me about
four places where Polish fascists were killing Jews by the railway tracks."

In Szmul's detailed account there isn't a word about him taking
Antonina Wyrzykowska with him to Austria, tearing her away from
her husband and children. But we know one way or another that when
Wyrzykowska decided to go back to her family, he brought her back to
Poland.

He stayed another brief period in Poland, and returned to trade.
Through the Joint Distribution Committee he found his eldest brother,
Mojżesz, in Cuba, where he had been since 1938. Szmul's mother, Chaja
Sara, had worried ceaselessly about their future in Poland from the time
her neighbor Hana Sosnowska had been killed in the pogrom in Radziłów
in 1933, and so the family had shelled out the money for Mojżesz's passage at the price of many privations.

Mojżesz cabled: "Szmulke, don't go anywhere, wait for my letter."
Szmul wrote back that the farmers who had hid him had lost their farm
and everything they owned because of it, and he swore not to leave Poland before he had ensured their security. His brother sent him enough
money to buy the Wyrzykowskis a house in Bielsk Podlaski, a horse, a
mare with two foals, two cows, a radio, and some furniture.

Szmul left the country by plane via Stockholm ("God of Israel, I never
saw so much food, such elegant women, such beautiful clothes"). From
Göteborg he sailed on a ship to the island of Aruba in the Antilles ("I saw
a black man for the first time. On the pier people stood with signs in Polish, Hebrew, and Yiddish: 'If there are any Jews on this ship, come to us.'
And there were Aruba Jews who took care of us.") On November 15, 1946,
he landed at the airport in Havana. He saw no one whom he recognized
as his brother, so he said loudly, "I am Szmul Wasersztejn," and found himself in the arms of a man crying and saying, "Szmulke, Szmulke." Of the
whole family only the two of them had survived. But he saw uncertainty

in his brother's eyes as to whether it was really him. "I asked him: 'Remember, Mosze, the little black cow with white patches that gave us more milk than the light one? Remember the shirt Mother made for it? Remember we had four hectares of grain? And those short pants you passed on to me when you left for Cuba? And our charcoal iron? And remember the brick missing in our bread oven?' When I said that he knew for sure it was me."

He started out in business right away. His brother gave him six dozen hides for riding breeches, and he set off with them into the interior. "I told a countryman in the town of Cienfuegos how I'd survived and about the murder of the Jews. He felt sorry for me and bought three dozen hides, and gave me the addresses of eight other Jewish merchants. Every time I had to tell them the story of the massacre and every time they put in orders for shoes. That's how I began."

Szmul soon realized this was a great marketing strategy. "Like an old broken record on a hand-cranked gramophone I told the story again of the events of 1941 to '45 and closed a 700-dollar deal," he wrote with disarming frankness. "Not many Cubans have traveled across Cuba as much as I have. Havana was alive with music and singing, couples embraced on the coast boulevard washed with the foam off the sea waves, and I went on selling, day and night. At the end of 1947 I had 25,000 dollars."

In 1948 he married Rachela Goldwaser, whom he'd met in Poland. His business kept growing and his wife worked alongside him, day after day, from dawn to dusk. They started a factory for tennis shoes, and saved a lot. By the beginning of the sixties they were wealthy Cuban citizens.

When Fidel Castro came in, the Wasersztejn family managed to leave the island. They lost their whole fortune. They found themselves in Philadelphia, not knowing the language or having any idea what to live on. The money they'd illegally sent to the United States disappeared. The children went hungry, Rachela wept. One day Szmul read a description of Costa Rica in a back issue of the local Jewish newspaper: magnificent volcanoes, a large middle class dominated by Jews, a democratic government, and beautiful women. It sounded enticing, so he found Costa Rica on a map. Then he found the Costa Rican consul in Philadelphia, who turned out to be Jewish, which seemed to him a good omen. He noted that he spent a dollar on an umbrella, because the consul had warned him that it rained a lot in Costa Rica.

"He arrived on Sunday, and by Monday he had his own shop," I was told by Maria Wiernik, a friend of Rachela's in Costa Rica.

Wasersztejn described his first steps, when he was still alone. In the morning he went for a walk in the commercial quarter of San José and saw a sign that said: BUSINESS FOR SALE. "It was a small business but packed with shoes, exactly the thing I knew." Although he didn't manage to convince the owner he would pay for the shop with his earnings, he did convince the next one along the street. He called his wife: "I have 30 pairs of shoes, you can come." Soon, this time in the landscape of Costa Rica, he resumed the customs of the prewar shtetl. He journeyed on rutted roads, looked for ways to ford rivers, and went from door to door. He knocked, and offered his wares: shoes on credit.

"I became a respected man. Every day I'd go to the Soda Palace for a coffee," Szmul wrote of himself when he had won a place among the financial elite of Costa Rica. On the 1997 video recording his trip to Poland, he declares proudly when he steps onto the plane, "We're traveling first class!"

After school, the children helped him sell shoes. But he took care to give them a good education. Izaak is a doctor of pharmacology, the owner and director of a laboratory that produces medications. Saul is a medical doctor, and Szmul's daughter, Rebecca, went to law school.

"He pushed us to study and work," Saul told me. "He'd always say that God gave Jews a head for business so they could give work to others. There were twelve hundred people working in his shoe factory. It filled him with pride that thanks to him, so many people could support their family. For him, to be a good person meant working hard, giving work to others, supporting charitable causes."

While other boys were playing soccer, going to the beach, or visiting New York, the Wasersztejn boys were working to help their father. They didn't know him outside of work. They went to bed before their parents got home at night, and when the children woke up they'd already left. Saul wasn't even tall enough to reach the tabletop before his father told him, "You're different from other children: they have uncles, grandfathers, and you don't. They were killed by their Polish neighbors. You were named after your uncle whose head was split open with an axe when he was twelve years old."

"My father associated any news of atrocities committed in the world with Jedwabne," the elder brother, Izaak, said. "He thought he should warn the world, because if the world knew about Jedwabne the evil wouldn't happen again. He wanted the people he loved to know about it. It was his obsession. I had to listen to him talk about the massacre hundreds of times. A child, to become a happy person, has to grow up trusting other people. Hearing again and again about the killing of the Jews by their Polish friends, I lost that trust. To go on living I had to block those memories in myself. They come back to me in depressions. My brother Saul suffers from the same thing, but somehow we manage to live and work. Our brother Gerardo is schizophrenic. There used to be no mental illness in our family. We are marked by Jedwabne."

They often wondered why their father was unable to show tenderness, never hugged them, never kissed them, never took them out for ice cream, to the races, to the movies. Maybe he tried to be tough outwardly because he was sentimental by nature? Maybe all his feeling was burned away in the barn that day and he no longer had any tenderness in him?

Szmul taught his sons to respect the State of Israel. "People respect us because we have our own state," he said. "They didn't respect us before." He subscribed to Israeli newspapers—*Yehuod Hamot*, the *Jerusalem News*. He'd start his day with them. He didn't go to synagogue—just once a year, on Yom Kippur. That was the only day in the year he didn't work, but at sunset, when the Day of Atonement had ended, he ran over to open his store.

"I wanted to be different from my father," Saul told me, "show that there were other ways to be good. That's why I became a doctor. But when my father started to have health problems I got involved in running the business with him."

Wasersztejn had shops that sold *schmattas*, or clothes and shoes, and a shoe factory. When the market flooded with Chinese products the factory started to lose money. Saul finally managed to persuade his father to shut it down and limit himself to shoe stores. They ran the business together for twenty years. A friend of the family told me they fought so badly they sometimes came to blows.

"We had fierce arguments, mostly about him wanting to invest in land; I knew it didn't pay," Saul said. "Jews wanted to educate their children and own land, that was supposed to give them a feeling of security, and they couldn't buy land in prewar Poland. When my father died I realized I'm really not so different from him. I don't work on Saturday, but only because my wife forbids me to. I take a two-week holiday, because my wife insists. But still, I run the business from dawn to dusk. I own seventy-one shoe stores all over the country. And you know what? Lately I've been investing in land."

The video of the Polish trip shows Wasersztejn kneeling down, crying, kissing the earth near the site of the murder. He shows his sons: "That's the road I escaped by. Here's the rock I hid behind. Here's where they drowned the girls in the pond." And, "For hundreds of years they lived alongside us as neighbors, and then they dragged us out of our houses and killed us in Śleszyński's barn, at three o'clock in the afternoon." He says kaddish. "Dear mother, dear brother, how hard it's been without you all these years. I think of you every day."

Earlier in Jedwabne, I'd heard about that visit. How Wasersztejn had come, wanting to give everybody one hundred dollars because he was ashamed of the lies he'd told. How he went to Janczewko on the outskirts of Jedwabne, where he'd been in hiding, and cried, and when someone came down the street he took out a ten-dollar bill. Stanisław Karwowski, Antonina Wyrzykowska's nephew who lives in Jedwabne, told me, "I'm ashamed to say what he gave me when he came back all those years later: forty dollars. But the neighbors told everyone it was three thousand."

"Every spot in Jedwabne was marked by his memories. Here a child had fallen, there he'd heard screams, here the priest had locked the church door," Izaak says.

In the marketplace in Jedwabne they were told, "Don't ask any questions, just get out of here." They'd planned to stay longer, but they left at once.

When Jan Gross visited Szmul in Costa Rica, there was no longer any getting through to him, Szmul was absorbed in his illness. I was in San José just after his death, which occurred in February 2000.

He could barely hear a thing in the last months of his life. He told his sons he heard his mother—she was in the barn crying out to him, begging him for help.

By the time he became the target of attacks and insinuations, he was already gone, and it may have been better that he was spared all that. He became the whipping boy for all those who denied Poles did the killing in Jedwabne. Right after Gross's book appeared, people in the town started claiming that Wasersztejn had been on a truck with a gun when Poles were deported to Siberia.

"He was a young boy on whom fell the burden of supporting his mother and younger brother, because their father had died before the war," Rachela remembered from her husband's stories. "He went from village to village buying meat and selling it on the black market. He was trying to survive. He didn't know a word of Russian and he gave the Soviets a wide berth."

Rachela's words fit with what I heard from Meir Ronen in Israel: "I knew Szmul from school, we called him 'Pietruszka' [Rooster] because he was a redhead. During the Soviet occupation he didn't spend time with any of the idiots who supported the new order." In 1939, when the Soviets arrived, he wasn't yet seventeen. Friends a year younger were indoctrinated by Soviet schooling, and the ones who were a year older, subject to the Soviet army draft, were sent to classes in Russian and Marxism-Leninism. He narrowly avoided both.

Leon Dziedzic of Przestrzele remembered him from that time: "I saw him often during the Soviet occupation because he traded in meat, and in our barn—it was quiet in Przestrzele—he would slaughter and flay the animals. Sometimes he slaughtered a pig, too, but he did that secretly, not only from the Soviets but from other Jews, because for them it was a sin."

At the public meeting of Jedwabne residents with prosecutor Ignatiew, the barn owner Śleszyński's daughter, Janina Biedrzycka, asked, "Why does that Jew sign himself Wasersztejn, when his name was Całka? I have a name and I don't change it. Would he have changed his name if he hadn't collaborated?" In fact Wasersztejn was called Wasersztejn both before the war and till the day he died. During the Soviet occupation, when all residents of Jedwabne were forced to take Soviet passports, which gave each person a patronymic, he probably wrote "Całkowicz" down as his patronymic. His father's name was Becale, or Całka—and that's why the Wyrzykowskis called him Staszek Całka when he worked for them; in those days it sounded a hell of a lot better than Szmul Wasersztejn.

In the winter of 2001, Professor Tomasz Strzembosz gave wide currency to the news that, as he maintained, "confirmed on all sides that Całko or Całka was Wasersztejn and that he was an agent of the security services in Łomża after the war." The Catholic Information Agency picked up on this.

"I wrote that I was witness to the fact that Wasersztejn left Poland right after the war," I hear from his friend from Jedwabne, Chaim Sroszko. "I demanded they publish a correction. No response."

In the right-wing press and in several books on Jedwabne, the same phrases are repeated, with Professor Strzembosz cited as an authority: "the agent Wasersztejn," "Jewish thug," "secret service hood," "it's not the first time, nor will it be the last, that Jewish secret service agents lecture their victims on morality." People in Jedwabne who eagerly read the anti-Semitic press soon started to repeat these phrases.

"Wasersztejn tortured my father at the secret police prison, that's the truth about Jedwabne," one of the residents shouted at me. I asked when that was. It had supposedly taken place in the fifties. Of course by then Szmul had long since left Poland.

I asked Szmul's sons if they ever tell anyone about their father's experiences. "A person living on the Pacific would never understand it," said Izaak. "Once, I told a prominent intellectual here what my father was dictating a book about, and he thought it was a work of fiction."

Szmul wrote to remember and warn others, and also, in spite of everything, to inspire. That's why his book offers descriptions of people facing death with dignity.

"A pious Jew, who looked like he had stepped out of one of the books of the Prophets, wrapped himself in a prayer shawl, enveloped a 500-year-old Torah with his body, raised a prayer book to the heavens, and, proclaiming the power of God in Hebrew, stepped into the flames. A moment of silence fell. The monsters were paralyzed for a moment by the strength of his Jewish faith and they silently watched his prayer shawl, which was throwing off giant tongues of fire.

"One dragged out a beautiful Jewish girl by her hair, her name was Telca. He walked to the edge of the cemetery where I was hiding and made her lie down, saying he was going to have her. She kept resisting, until finally she said: 'Stop this slaughter and I'll give myself to you.' The man shuddered as if someone had hit him on the head. He struck the girl with a savage cry. From that mouth that men dreamed of as an oasis in the desert, no sound came. He lifted her up and threw her into the burning barn."

He also describes finding out from a Pole who "hadn't killed anyone with his own hands but whose silence and passivity made him a criminal" how his twelve-year-old brother had died. He had been in the group of young Jews who were killed with axes near the barn. "He was strong and handsome. The Jews were taken to the lame man, who killed them with an axe and shoved them into a grave with his crutch. They left my brother almost until last. He tried to defend himself with a spade. They tried to beat him to death with clubs. It would have killed any other man, but Saul wasn't like any other man. He fell, bleeding, but got up again. They beat him on his head, and he got up. The lame man came at him with the axe. Saul got up a third time, though his head was coming off his torso, took a few steps toward the butcher, and that guy took out a World War I bayonet, stabbed him three times, and cast him into the grave."

In conversations with survivors in the Łomża ghetto, with his fellow captives in hiding at the Wyrzykowskis', and finally with Polish witnesses, Wasersztejn must have fixed every detail of the massacre in his mind. Later all the facts, woven together and multiplied, tormented him day and night, forming what he himself called an "orgy of blood." He told the story hundreds of times, until it had been transformed into myth.

He must have seen himself as the last repository of the truth about the Jedwabne massacre. For decades, reports of it failed to penetrate human consciousness. Hence his book, written in blood. He started dictating it in 1995 and finished in December 1999. Can he have hoped that someone would hear the tale one day? No more than a castaway on an uninhabited island who throws a bottle into the ocean in the hope that someone will find it and take his fate to heart.

Journal

In Łódź at Marek Edelman's birthday party. I talk to his daughter-in-law, the painter Zofia Lipecka, about her installation on Jedwabne. The Warsaw Center for Contemporary Art at Zamek Ujazdowski was to have shown it, everything was on track, when something went wrong. Her e-mails remained unanswered, and in the end, it turned out there was no money for the installation.

Marek Edelman was active in the Bund, a party that said the place for Jews was in Poland and that they should fight for social justice for all, not emigrate to Palestine in search of the Promised Land. He has remained faithful to that view his whole life. (After the war, the Bundists would go to train stations to try to halt the flood of Jews fleeing Poland.) But when in 1968 anti-Semitism received government endorsement and his children, Ania and Aleksander, would come home from school in tears, he thought it best for them to emigrate to France with their mother. Alina Margolis-Edelman invited a school friend of Ania's, Zofia Lipecka, over for Easter, and Zofia stayed with them and finished school in France. Alina, a pediatrician, now travels with the humanitarian missions of Doctors Without Borders. She was in Vietnam to help the boat people fleeing a Communist hell, in El Salvador, Chad, Bosnia. Ania became a chemist, Aleksander a biophysicist, and Zofia Lipecka a painter and Aleksander's wife.

Zofia's installation shows close-ups on several monitors of the faces of people listening to Szmul Wasersztejn's testimony. There are public figures like Jan Gross, friends, acquaintances, and also completely random people, seventy-five of them in all. "Some of them are listening intently, others weeping," says Zofia, who read to them and recorded their reactions. "I cried over it like a baby many times," Zofia tells me. "There are Poles, Jews, French people, as well as a Chinese woman, an Algerian woman, a Vietnamese woman who was reminded of the Vietnam War by the descriptions of the cruelty inflicted, or the black cleaning lady in the cultural center where I work, who later tried to console me by saying as a Pole I really don't have to feel so guilty."

JANUARY 3, 2002

I extend my leave from the *Gazeta*, because I'm only half done with my book.

I'm trying to reconstruct the life of Józef, formerly Izrael or Srul, Grądowski, one of the seven Jews rescued by Antonina Wyrzykowska. I saw a prewar photo of him in the *Jedwabne Book of Memory*. An elegant man in pince-nez with his handsome wife, Fajga, in a low-cut dress and with three robust boys, Abram Aaron, Reuwen, and the youngest, Emanuel. A bucolic scene, photographed in the open air, a rarity in those times. I found out about him in Jedwabne; I'd read about him in trial documents and in Wasersztejn's diary. I talked about him a lot in America with the brothers Jacob and Herschel Baker and with Lea Kubran, in Israel with Jakow Geva, and recently with Antonina Wyrzykowska.

I'm able to reconstruct what happened to him on July 10, 1941. In the morning three Poles armed with clubs forced their way into his home; he knew them—Feliks Żyluk, who lived in the same building, best of all. They dragged the whole family out to the market square. They were led away from the square by a Pole from Szczuczyn, where Fajga came from. Grądowski never revealed his name.

He and his wife and two of their sons moved into the provisional ghetto in Jedwabne. When in the fall of 1942 the Germans ordered all Jews to report to the police station, Grądowski was worried that they hadn't been told to bring any tools. He thought they weren't being summoned for work and they should run away. He managed to get to the Wyrzy-kowskis in Janczewko, where he hid until the end of the war.

What happened to the rest of his family is unknown. Grądowski said his wife and children were caught by policemen and taken to the ghetto in Zambrów. However, Leon Dziedzic claims two of Grądowski's sons were killed in Przestrzele near Jedwabne. They were hiding in a haystack in a field belonging to a neighbor of the Dziedzices. It was November, it was freezing, and before they had time to look around for a better shelter the woman saw them and reported them to the village head. He passed it on to the police, who came for them and shot them on the spot.

After the war was over Srul Grądowski went to Szczuczyn in the hope that someone in the family had survived there. Szmul Wasersztejn accompanied him; the roads were perilous and it seemed safer for the two of them to navigate them together. They found no one. Srul, who was nearly sixty, almost two generations older than the other six saved by Wyrzykowska, didn't have the strength to go with them to try to sneak across the border. He found his old home in Jedwabne. He had himself baptized. He married a Polish woman who had worked in their household before the war. He wanted to melt into the surroundings, and so he changed his name to a Polish one. He didn't seek contact with surviving Jews, didn't report to the District Jewish Historical Commission to give any testimony. He was some kind of middleman in takeovers of formerly Jewish houses, giving false testimony about alleged relatives.

Rabbi Baker, then Jakub Piekarz, a student at the Łomża yeshiva, knew Izaak from before the war. He'd taught Grądowski's sons Hebrew, which paid for a pair of shoes that lasted him the whole school year. "At that time he was one of the nicest people in Jedwabne," Baker recalled. "But later Izrael became Józef and they granted him his life on the condition he give up the lives of others. That can't be forgiven."

The rabbi relied on the account of Rywka Fogiel in the *Jedwabne Book of Memory*: "At that time of misfortune Izrael Grądowski profaned the name of God. On the day the Jews were burned he and his family ran to the church, fell at the priest's feet, and asked him to baptize him. In this way he saved his own life. It was that man who turned against his own brothers. About 125 Jews managed to go into hiding and escape the burning. The newly converted Christian betrayed their hiding places to the Poles."

I know this isn't true. Grądowski was baptized in August 1945 (this is confirmed by an entry in the Jedwabne parish record book). There wasn't even anyone for him to betray the surviving Jews to. They themselves had left their hiding places to move into the ghetto, which seemed to them the safest place—after what the Polish population had done— because it was guarded by the Germans.

On the other hand, what Jakow Geva told me is true: after the war Grądowski tried to trick Jedwabne families who'd emigrated to the States and Palestine, telling them their relatives had survived and attempting to get money out of them.

Lea Kubran remembered that Grądowski wrote to them after the war—she was then with her husband in a displaced persons camp in Austria—asking them to send him a Jewish calendar. Later they found out that he wrote in letters to Jedwabne Jews on the other side of the ocean that he still felt himself to be a Jew, witness the Jewish calendar on his wall. Then he would ask them for money.

Herschel Baker also told me about this. Right after the war he'd visited Grądowski. "His wife opened the door and said, 'He's not talking to any Jews.' I said, 'Please call him.' She slammed the door in my face. He was at home and must have heard us talking, because I recognized his voice when he asked her, 'Who was that?' When I left Poland I made contact with my brothers by mail from a transit camp. They wrote that Mama and other Jedwabne Jews had survived, they'd heard about it from Izrael Grądowski, and they'd sent money for him to pass on to them. But I already knew very well they were dead. He wasn't an honest man."

As if that sin of taking money for people he knew to be dead weren't enough, the *Jedwabne Book of Memory* adds a much more terrible one to it, that of betraying his fellow Jews. So as to exclude him once and for all from the community of pious Jews.

In 1947, Całka Migdał from Uruguay mentioned him in a letter to the Central Committee of Jews in Poland (the letter that sparked the Jedwabne trial): "The one man who remained alive was Srul Grądowski. We don't want to ask him too much, because he is alone among so many non-Jews that he may be afraid of speaking the truth. Please find out if Srul Grądowski is worthy of our aid. He used to be our neighbor. We cannot understand how a single Jew could have survived among so many who helped to destroy all the Jews of the town, how he can look them in the face."

In fact, he managed to live there because, like Marianna and Stanisław Ramotowski of Radziłów, he testified on behalf of the murderers. Called as a witness, he kept saying the Germans carried out the massacre, and he declared the accused men innocent.

Of Józef Żyluk, who herded him and his family out to the market: "I owe my life to Żyluk."

Of Aleksander Janowski: "I doubt he participated in the burning of the Jews because he's an honest man with an excellent reputation."

Of Roman Górski: "He came to us when we were in the marketplace, wanting to hide my family, but his daughter called him because his wife had taken ill."

Of Władysław Miciura: "That day I was taken to the police station, and Miciura and I did some carpentry work there . . . I never saw Miciura leave the police station."

The court wasn't interested in the fact that these testimonies were mutually contradictory, because according to the needs of the accused men, Grądowski was either in the market square, in the magistrate's office, or at the police station.

Józef Grądowski signed letters along with other townspeople stating that the convicted men were upstanding citizens. In his request for an appeal of the trial, Zygmunt Laudański referred to Grądowski as someone who could testify to his innocence.

The time came, however, when he decided to tell the truth. "At the time the Jews were rounded up I was a Jew," he declared in the trial of Józef Sobuta on December 11, 1953, in the courtroom of the District Courthouse in Białystok. "I knew Sobuta and saw him in the market square when he chased Jews with a club in his hand." But at the next trial against Sobuta in 1954 he said, "He shouldn't be condemned because it won't bring back those people who died. I didn't speak of Sobuta's part in the massacre during the investigation because I was afraid, knowing the police wouldn't protect me in Jedwabne, but at the trial I am saying what happened, because I've made a pledge to tell the truth, come what may."

Grądowski told the court: "During the burning of the Jews a Jewish child squirmed out of a shed and a Pole saw the child, caught him, and threw him onto the fire; he was a bad man. I took a Polish orphan in instead and I'm raising him as my own without regard for the harm done me by Poles."

The court ruled that his testimony was unreliable. However, it did listen to the testimony of Sobuta's wife about Grądowski having demanded two hundred zlotys to testify on his behalf and not getting the money. In an investigation launched in 1967, Grądowski was interrogated again, and told what really happened, but then retracted it.

"About eight in the morning Feliks Żyluk, Antoni Surowiecki, and [Antoni] Grzymała came to me . . . They were carrying iron and wooden cudgels." He held to his story in a confrontation with Antoni Grzymała, but six months later, at a subsequent interrogation, he reversed his position and said that these three hid him and his family in Żyluk's house, and that the Jews were driven into the market by "men I didn't know, dressed in civilian clothes, wearing masks, who spoke to us in Polish."

Grądowski died in 1971 at the age of eighty-two. More than a decade later, the Łomża periodical *Contacts* interviewed his wife, and she agreed to talk under the condition no names were used, neither hers nor anyone else's. But it's easy to decipher who she was talking about. After the war Feliks Żyluk was once again Grądowski's neighbor: "My husband never reproached him with taking part in the pogrom and dragging him from the house to the square by force . . . My husband was very pious and it's probably only for that reason that he bore various insults."

It seems that he became less submissive toward the end of his life. Leszek Dziedzic remembered that when someone started speaking ill of Jews or harassing him, Grądowski had a saying: "So why do you kiss that Jew's feet in church?"

Mrs. Grądowski continues: "Feliks Ż. built his children a house in Ełk. During some visit to his native parts he heard of the death of my husband. He came to me indignant that I hadn't let him know of the burial. I couldn't hold it back then: 'My husband would turn in his grave if I had invited you.' And now Feliks is in the graveyard as well, and my time is coming, and no one will remember the old injustices and hardships."

His wife survived him by a quarter of a century, dying in 1996. In Jedwabne I heard the same story several times, how Grądowski took in a boy to raise him, but God punished him for an insincere conversion and his adopted son, Jerzy, turned into a bum and finally drank himself to death. Jerzy's widow told me these are slanderous stories—he died of a grave illness, she said.

Antonina Wyrzykowska still cherished fond memories of Srul, later Józef Grądowski. When she moved from Janczewko, she seldom went home, but when she did she always went to see him.

"He had a funeral parlor," she tells me. "There was another undertaker in Jedwabne, and when the owner heard of anyone's death he'd go to the family to say, 'I hope you're not going to the Jew?' But what kind of Jew was Grądowski, since he'd converted a long time ago and had a Catholic wife? When they took in the boy, he wasn't a Jew at all and still people would pester him about being Jewish. Józek kept his Yiddish accent until the end of his life and when he saw me he'd say, 'Mrs. Wyrzykowski, I haven't forgotten what you did for me. When your father dies I'll give him a coffin for free.' Grądowski died, and my father lived another ten years, to his ninety-fifth birthday."

JANUARY 5, 2002

Whenever I have a free moment, I go to see my aunt Hania Lanota in the countryside. She's translating for me the memoir of Chaja Finkelsztejn of Radziłów. It is written in Yiddish, with fragments in Hebrew and occasionally a sentence in German. It makes no difference to Hania. She translates aloud as fluently as if she were reading me a book written in Polish.

JANUARY 27, 2002

I spend another day with my aunt, translating Chaja Finkelsztejn's memoir. Her description of the massacre is a masterpiece of reportage. Chaja is observant, penetrating, with great feeling for narrative, tone, use of detail.

And so on the morning of July 7 she saw a Gestapo officer and the council secretary Stanisław Grzymkowski looking through the broken windows into the Beit Midrasz. After the Radziłów Jews had been burned, Chaja realized that she'd witnessed the search for a place of execution, and that they'd probably rejected the synagogue in the center of town out of fear that the fire would spread to buildings nearby. It was probably Grzymkowski who had suggested the unused barn standing at a safe distance from town; in Chaja's version its owner had left for Argentina, so he couldn't protest.

The problem is the absence of names; Chaja either doesn't give them at all or gives only first names. Her account is so solid and precise, it would be good to fit the right surnames to the acts she describes.

FEBRUARY 9, 2002
Professor Strzembosz, who lent credence to all those who denied the guilt of the Poles, has been named Person of the Year 2001 by the *Tygodnik Solidarność* (Solidarity Weekly): "While the liberal left seeks 'a terrible knowledge about the grandfathers and fathers of contemporary Poles' in order to buttress their smug theories about the moral impoverishment of 'this nation,' while certain media outlets endlessly seek to outdo each other in spitting on Poland and abusing her, Tomasz Strzembosz seeks the truth about her."

FEBRUARY 10, 2002
Jedwabne. A meeting of residents in the religious education hall. The priest gives the lecture I already know so well on the Jews killing themselves and each other on their own initiative. Many older people, some of whom must have been witnesses to the events of that time, nod along with the priest when he speaks of the integrated German forces.

I ask the priest to comment on the Institute of National Remembrance's statement that the bullets that came from the cartridges found in the barn were not fired in 1941, and so there is no evidence for the Germans having been present. "The truth will come out," he answers calmly. "The townspeople have other cartridges they keep in their houses."

FEBRUARY 19, 2002
Hania Lanota translates a further section of Chaja's memoirs for me.

When Jews could still live outside the ghetto, with farmers who paid the Germans for Jewish labor, the Finkelsztejns lived in a village near Radziłów. "Father bundled straw for the first time in his life," Chaja says sadly. "My niece and I ploughed the fields and Menachem, who only knew how to carry a bag of books, had bleeding hands from the farmwork."

Hania comments sharply that this part of the martyrology could have happened to any city dweller unused to village life. She herself was raised in Warsaw, but spent a lot of time before the war in Skryhiczyn with our family, working in the fields. And those Jews who worked the land, among them many of my aunts and uncles, turned out to be fantastic workers later on the kibbutzim in Israel. Evidently Hania doesn't like Chaja much, she finds her too severe. It's true her judgments of people are razor-sharp. But in her defense I must say she is often equally tough on Jews.

In the fall of 1942, when the Germans demanded that Jews return to the ghetto, the Finkelsztejns went into hiding. Hania Lanota, who herself escaped from the Warsaw Ghetto and hid on the Aryan side, reading to me how the murderers come to the village demanding that Chaja's family be handed over, keeps saying, "It's monstrous! In Warsaw people feared blackmailers but I could walk down the street, I had friends from before the war whose houses I visited. This woman lived in a kind of zoo where wild animals had been let out of their cages."

The family who hid Chaja told her that in front of the Łomża ghetto wagons had stopped that were supposed to take Jews on their last journey, and peasant women had grabbed bundles from the Jewish women and stripped them down to their underwear. Did anything like that happen in Skryhiczyn, the village from which my family was transported to the ghetto? One day the Skryhiczyn peasants were ordered to drive their wagons to the ghetto and drop the Jews off at the train, which transported them straight to a death camp. They were driven by peasants they'd known for years. How did those forced helpers of death behave? Did they talk to them? Were they silent? Did they say goodbye? Maybe they took their belongings because "they wouldn't need them anymore"?

FEBRUARY 20, 2002

Every child in Jedwabne "knows" that it was Jews who did the interrogating, convicting, and sentencing in the Jedwabne trial. At the same time, as becomes clear from the legal documents from 1949—which the Institute of National Remembrance is analyzing—the investigation was conducted by an ethnic Pole, and the interrogations of the accused men were conducted by eight ethnic Poles and three Belorussians (just as in the 1953 trial, a Pole conducted the investigation, and interrogations were led by four Poles and one Belorussian).

I try to find the prosecutors of that time.

Paweł Tarasewicz, who in 1950 rose to become the head of the secret police in Ełk, now lives in Białystok: "I don't know, I didn't see anything, I wasn't in charge at that time, I don't remember the case."

Włodzimierz Wołkowycki, a young clerk at the time, now lives in Bielsk Podlaski: "I went to Jedwabne many times, interviewed a lot of people, I'd like to help you but I don't remember anything."

Stefan Kulik, who now lives in Warsaw, claims from the start that it's a mistake. When I read him his personal data from the court papers, he remembers something, but when I ask a further question on beatings during the investigation he once again remembers nothing. "I have inner ear trouble, I was in the hospital for it, and that makes it harder to remember things."

FEBRUARY 24, 2002
I read the documents of court cases conducted after the war concerning crimes committed against Jews by locals in towns in the vicinity of Jedwabne and Radziłów.

The employees of the Institute of National Remembrance are now tracing them, and there were quite a few. In virtually every town there were instances of Jews being killed. There are a few cases that tell us of massacres committed after the great wave of pogroms in late June and early July 1941, killings from late summer or autumn 1941, when the Jews were in ghettos and only left them occasionally when they were hired by the Germans to do unpaid labor for Polish farmers.

Stanisław Zalewski pleaded guilty to murders committed in August 1941 (he was sentenced to death in 1950). The victims were twenty Jewish women, fifteen to thirty years old, hired from the Szczuczyn ghetto for garden work on the Bzura estate, not far from Szczuczyn. "We rode there on bikes," Zalewski said. "Earlier we'd gone to the estate smithy and fit the ends of poles with steel to make them better for killing. An hour later two hay carts arrived from the Bzura estate, one of them driven by Krygiel, and the other by Henryk Modzelewski. When the carts drove up to the house we chased the Jewish girls from the cellar and told them to get on the carts. We drove them to the Boczkowski forest, where a pit had been dug. There we ordered the Jewish girls to strip down to their slips and panties, only two young Jewish girls who had old clothes were not forced to undress. We began leading them one at a time to the pit and beating them to death with poles. Tkacz killed four Jewish girls. Before they killed one of the girls five men raped her. After raping the girl I took Tkacz's wooden pole and personally killed her, hitting her three times on the head with the pole, and she fell into the pit. I took slippers and a dress from the murdered Jewish women. Three days later the German police came to the village head and on their command I showed them the site of the massacre. One policeman asked me what we'd used to kill them, and I said poles. When I spoke these words I was struck with a truncheon by a German policeman, who said: 'Why didn't you bring them back to the ghetto?' Then they told me to bury them better."

One of the witnesses said of the participants in the massacre, "We were all in the National Party."

Not much later a Jew named Magik was tortured in the environs of Szczuczyn. "In the autumn of 1941," one of the witnesses testified, "my mother Kazimiera and I were returning on the road from the village Skaje to Szczuczyn where we'd harvested potatoes, and I saw clearly how Konopko Franciszek, holding a birch stick as broad as a hand, with Domiziak Aleksander of Szczuczyn, who was holding the same kind of birch stick, drove the Jew Magik, whom I knew and who manufactured candy in Szczuczyn up to 1939, toward the Jewish graves. When the above-mentioned men chasing the Jew reached us I heard Magik plead with Domiziak, 'Let me go, Olek. I fed your children, I gave you so much candy for free, I have a gold watch I'll give to you.' I saw Konopko kick the Jew Magik from behind with the tip of his shoe and say: 'Go to hell, you motherfucking Jew.'"

FEBRUARY 25, 2002
I'm reading court documents from the Radziłów trials and Chaja Finkelsztejn's memoir by turns, trying to reconstruct the atmosphere in the town after the July massacre.

Apparently, life took on a certain glow. People enjoyed their new cottage, their new down quilt, their new bucket. They bustled around repairing the newly won houses, and since most of them had been looted earlier, windows were put in, stoves were fixed, walls were whitewashed. Although we learn from Chaja's memoir the satisfaction was perhaps not as strong as the envy felt toward those who'd gotten their hands on more loot.

The 1949 and 1953 testimonies of Helena Klimaszewska cast light on the skirmishes over the houses claimed. Klimaszewska was mother-in-law to Józef Ekstowicz (called Klimas or Klimaszewski, after his grandmother), the youth who set the barn on fire in Radziłów. In August 1941 she came from Goniądz to Radziłów with his grandmother, as she'd heard that "there were empty houses there after the liquidation of the Jews" and that "Godlewski was in charge of the formerly Jewish homes." She asked him "to release one formerly Jewish home."

"Don't you dare," said Feliks Godlewski, standing on the threshold of the house he'd taken from the murdered Zandler.

Klimaszewska pointed out to him that he already disposed of four houses himself.

"A shitload that's got to do with you. My brother's coming from Russia, where the Soviets sent him, and he's got to have a house."

Klimaszewska persisted in asking about a house.

"When we had to liquidate the Jews, none of you were to be seen, and now you want houses," Godlewski said angrily, and he sent his children to the police nearby to get Henryk Dziekoński (one of the leaders of the massacre who went to work for the Germans), so that he, as a representative of the authorities, could talk sense into the woman.

"If the gentleman won't give it to you, you'd better leave," instructed Dziekoński.

Helena Klimaszewska also remembered that when she was talking to Godlewski, Józef Ekstowicz's grandmother kept babbling to him about her grandson being sent out to set the barn on fire when they needed him, and now they wouldn't even give him a house.

In Radziłów the market still took place on Thursdays, only there were no Jewish stalls, and the trade was mostly barter. Since the ruble had lost its value, no one trusted the deutsche mark, either. The Jews who'd survived the pogrom lived crammed into one room near the synagogue. There were about thirty of them, including two refugee families from Kolno. Chaja Finkelsztejn's nephew was there, too. He told her the police had taken them under its protection, so they no longer needed to fear death at the hands of Poles, but they had to do pointless hard labor for the Germans, like removing stones from the river, and they were guarded by a Pole who made sure they didn't take a moment's rest.

Thanks to Chaja's memoir I can reconstruct the course the massacre in Radziłów took much more fully than I did in the *Gazeta*. At this point, I think I could describe the events hour by hour.

The theme of stolen things returns again and again in the memoir. We read of women rushing to plunder her house while the men escort the Jews to the barn. Chaja describes being in hiding and looking through gaps in the sheathing of a barn on Sundays at farmers' children going to church dressed in clothes stolen from her own children. Moving from one household to another, everywhere they found Jewish clothing or furniture, because even those who didn't pillage were given such things in payment for butter or honey. What Chaja describes in her memoir I already read once in the form of a poem by Sara Ginsburg, known by her pen name, Zuzanna Ginczanka:

> Non omnis moriar—*my proud possessions,*
> *tablecloth meadows, staunch fortress shelves,*
> *my billowing sheets and precious bedclothes,*
> *my dresses, my bright dresses will outlive me.*
> *I leave no heirs behind when I depart,*
> *so may your hand dig out all Jewish things,*
> *Chominowa of Lvov, brave snitch's wife,*
> *prompt informer, Volksdeutscher's mother.*
> *May they serve you and yours, for why*
> *should they serve strangers. My neighbors—*
> *what I leave is neither lute nor empty name.*
> *I remember you, as you, the Schupo near,*
> *remembered me. Reminded them of me.*
> *May my friends sit and raise their glasses,*
> *drink to my grave and to their own gains:*
> *carpets and tapestries, china, candlesticks—*
> *may they drink all night and at dawn*
> *start the search for gems and gold*
> *under sofas, mattresses, quilts, and rugs.*
> *O how the work will burn in their hands,*
> *the tangles of horsehair and tufts of wool,*
> *blizzards of burst pillows, clouds of eiderdown*
> *stick to their hands and turn them into wings;*

my blood will glue oakum and fresh feathers
transforming birds of prey into sudden angels.

Ginczanka was in hiding on the Aryan side, first in Lvov, then in Kraków. She wasn't as lucky as the Finkelsztejns. Someone denounced her. We don't even know when and in what circumstances she died. And by what miracle the sheet of paper survived with the prophetic poem, an adaptation of Słowacki's famous "Testament," which she wrote just before her death.

12

They Had Vodka, Guns, and Hatred

or, July 7, 1941, in Radziłów

The massacre in Radziłów is exceptionally well documented, thanks in large part to the testimonies of the Finkelsztejn family. They are extraordinary witnesses: both parents and children were in the marketplace that day, and when they hid in dozens of places after the massacre they heard stories from the people who hid them and on that basis reconstructed the course of events day by day, hour by hour, in the belief that the day would come when they would bear witness. The eldest son, Menachem Finkelsztejn, gave testimony in 1945 to the District Jewish Historical Commission in Białystok. The father, Izrael Finkelsztejn, testified in 1945 in the first investigation into the participation of Poles in the massacre. The mother, Chaja Finkelsztejn, gave a detailed account of the killings and the events that preceded them in the memoir she wrote in 1946. In April 2002, in Kansas City, I talked to the youngest daughter and the only living Jewish witness of the massacre. In 1941, she was seven years old.

Much information is provided by the testimonies from the trials that were held between 1945 and 1958. The men accused of participation in the murder of Jews were: Henryk Dziekoński, Józef Ekstowicz, Feliks Godlewski, Antoni Kosmaczewski, Leon Kosmaczewski, Ludwik Kosmaczewski, Henryk Statkiewicz, and Zygmunt Skrodzki.

I spoke to several dozen eyewitnesses to the massacre—and some of

Sara, daughter of Pesza and Izrael Gutsztejn, and her husband, Jakob Zimnowicz. Radziłów. They were killed by Poles on July 7, 1941, together with their eight-year-old daughter, Szulamit. (Courtesy of Jose Gutstein, www.radzilow.com)

Pesza Gutsztejn of Radziłów. She was seventy-one years old when she was killed by Poles on July 7, 1941. Her great-grandson Jose Gutstein in Miami created the virtual Radziłów shtetl: www.radzilow.com. (Courtesy of Jose Gutstein, www.radzilow.com)

them, I have to assume, were not only witnesses but, as underage boys, also minor accomplices to the killing.

1.

When the Russians fled Radziłów on the night of June 22–23, many Jews left their homes to wait out the first days of the German invasion elsewhere. The Polish inhabitants of the town—whether a majority or only a segment of them is hard to establish now—watched the arrival of the Germans with relief; after the hated Soviet occupation any change seemed to them for the better. A few Poles joined forces to prepare a triumphal gate; someone dragged from the attic a dusty portrait of the Führer that had been displayed at city hall for a few days in September of 1939.

Menachem Finkelsztejn described the deafening cannon fire that woke the residents of Radziłów in the early-morning hours of June 22. "The eight hundred Jewish inhabitants of the town understood the gravity of the situation right away." Some decided to flee to the east, but on the roads they met "well-armed Polish Fascist gangs" who stopped Jewish refugees and robbed and beat them. They tried to hide in the surrounding villages, in the fields, to avoid the moment when the army would enter the town. But the peasants didn't allow them into their yards. "Having no alternative, they all began to return to their homes. The Poles in the area watched the terrified Jews with scorn and pointed to their own throats, saying: 'Now it's going to be—*cut the Jew's throat.*'"

Chaja Finkelsztejn saw young people putting up the triumphal gate, cleaning it, festooning it with greenery and flowers. Menachem testified that they hung a swastika on it, with a portrait of Hitler and a banner with a Polish slogan, *Long live those who freed us from the Jewish Communists!* The subjects I interviewed remembered the same thing. Franciszek Ekstowicz saw poles being driven into the ground, entwined with flowers, and some banner hung between them. Andrzej R. is prepared to swear that the inscription was short: *Welcome* and another word he doesn't remember, and that green branches were woven around the poles.

The army came in on tanks. Eugenia K., then seven years old, watched the townspeople throw flowers on the tanks, which passed through Radziłów and continued on. Chaja Finkelsztejn, who was standing at the gate dressed as a Polish peasant woman, remembered what some people were saying: "The Christians welcomed them with enthusiasm, shouts of 'You are our saviors! You've saved us from the Soviets!' 'Look how handsome they are, how the smell of perfume wafts around them,' one Christian woman gushed." Chaja was moved by the sight of wounded Russian prisoners of war led through the town, while the locals threw stones at them.

A few daredevils jumped up on the tanks to help track down Red Army marauders. "The Russians were fleeing across the Biebrza river," a witness told me, "and there were Poles sitting on the tanks showing them where to cross to catch the Russians." A temporary authority was made up of Polish residents. Henryk Dziekoński, who was part of it, testified at his own trial: "With friends I started to organize a municipal authority to keep the order," and he gave the names of the other eight members of this self-appointed authority. Of nine of them I heard from witnesses that they participated in the massacre. They paraded around with rifles left by the Soviets and with red-and-white armbands.

Chaja Finkelsztejn described the town in those first days as follows: "Christians sat on benches in front of their homes, in holiday dress and a festive mood. They were all people we knew. Seeing how happy they were I had no desire to greet them. Very small Christian children pointed out Jews in the street to the Germans, crying: *Jude, Jude.*' They set their dogs on Jews, shouting: 'Get the Jew!'"

Scores were settled with Communists and traitors—as several people told me, those are the rules of war. That part of history is not covered over in silence.

Halina Zalewska told me, "Just before the Germans came there was a big deportation, the women and children had already been sent away, and the men were kept for interrogation and then freed by the Germans when they disarmed the old Osowiec fortress the Soviets had been using as a base. So those farmers came home enraged and ready for a brawl."

Andrzej R. told me, "The deportation just before the Germans arrived was later called Black Thursday. They not only deported people but told the remaining relatives to come to a meeting, where it was explained to them why the deportations were right. A local Jew came out and said, 'All you ravens who squawk are going to Siberia.' Poles found that guy right after the Russkies left. That was the afternoon of June 23. First they tortured him in the marketplace. They tied a big flat stone to his neck with string and made him look into the sun. When he closed his eyes they beat his head with a stick. There were two men standing next to him, one smacking him on the head with a stanchion from one side, the other from the other side. Meanwhile, the Poles were asking him where the Kapelański family was. Kapelański was an organist who had been deported with his family. They led him down Łomżynska Road to the bridge and threw him off. The water was shallow. I watched what they were doing to him until it was over."

Halina Zalewska remembers the victim was blinded by the sun before he died.

Chaja Finkelsztejn met a Jewish girl, a school friend of her son's, who had spoken warmly of the Soviets at a ceremony at the gymnasium. "Her lips were black and blue, she'd been beaten up by Polish friends overnight."

On the same day the Russians left, the locals flung themselves at the military store in the temple on Gęsia Street that stocked clothes, food supplies, and rifles. They started with Soviet stores, but bands of locals also broke into Jewish homes—many Jews had left town for those first few days and were hiding with people they knew in the countryside or sleeping in the nearby fields.

Radziłów was on a drunk. That was because of the distillery that was taken over.

Czesław C. told me, "As soon as the Russkies left, our boys went to the Słucz distillery. It was full to the brim. Poles were thirsty for vodka, and some of them held a grudge against the Jews, and that grudge was well-founded."

Mieczysław Kulęgowski told me, "They brought buckets of vodka back from the Słucz distillery, and some of them died in the process because a storehouse caught fire. They had vodka, guns, and hatred."

The German tanks were followed by the arrival of a group of Wehrmacht soldiers in Radziłów. They savaged Jews, and were keen for Poles to participate. They cut off old men's beards, mutilating them with scissors and beating them. On June 25 they put on a display of what Poles were allowed to do to Jews. That some of the locals happily participated in this, we know from both Jewish and Polish witnesses.

Menachem Finkelsztejn described the Germans ordering Jewish men to gather at the synagogue, and the Poles standing guard at the exit roads and turning people on their way out of town back by force. Germans ordered Jews to take their holy books from the synagogue and burn them.

Later "they harnessed Jews to wagons, got on the wagons themselves and whipped them with terrible force, driving down every street." Jews were driven to the muddy river, told to undress completely and go into the water. Andrzej R. has a detailed memory of this scene. "They harnessed Jews, drove them on with a whip. There was a barrel on the wagon and the Germans sat on the barrel in their swimming trunks, because that June was hot. We stood and watched. Kids were laughing; after all, no one knew how it would end, so in those first days there was a lot of laughter."

Chaja Finkelsztejn: "The peasants wouldn't sell any food to Jews and took their cows away from them. Those who rented rooms to Jews told them to move out, because they were having their windows broken."

On June 27, the German command left Radziłów, but the violence only grew. The spontaneously formed city authority was in charge, but groups of Germans would come by the town every now and then. From Chaja Finkelsztejn's testimony it emerges that on the same day the Wehrmacht left town, a large group arrived late in the evening—they are described as "Hitler's dogs"—in khaki clothing, on wagons with camouflage tarpaulins drawn by four horses. They forced their way into her home, beating everyone there badly, including the children, and ransacking the house. There were locals around, and the previously mentioned Henryk Dziekoński "showed them around" the house. The next day the peasants took the Jews' cows, herded them into the marketplace, and when the Germans came by again—with trucks this time—they were taken away. A sign that even if there was no German unit stationed in town, there must have been a post somewhere nearby. Because Jews could no longer buy food, the removal of their cows meant condemning them to starvation.

The scenes of homes being invaded, residents being beaten, dwellings being destroyed and looted took place every night. Numerous accounts allow us to reconstruct who belonged to those gangs.*

---

* Members of the gangs that went by Jewish homes from June 23 to July 7, beating and robbing, were: the brothers Jan and Henryk Dziekoński; the brothers Aleksander, Feliks, and Stanisław Godlewski; the brothers Leon and Antoni Kosmaczewski; Ludwik Kosmaczewski, Paulin's son (so called to distinguish him from another Ludwik Kosmaczewski); Jan Kowalewski; Stanisław Leszczewski; Zygmunt Mazurek; Bronisław and Leszek Michałowski; the brothers Jan, Antoni, and Feliks Mordasiewicz; Aleksander Nitkiewicz; Józef Paszkowski; Wincenty Piotrowski; Aleksander Polkowski; the brothers Andrzej, Ignacy, and Józef Ramotowski; Zygmunt Skrodzki; Mieczysław Strzelecki and his sister Eugenia; and Józef Sulewski, a.k.a. Nieczykowski.

Antoni Olszewski told me, "Thugs tied Jews to the bottom of Czesio Bagiński's wagon and hitched up his horses. He told me this himself once when I brought a sick horse to him. He said no one asked Bagiński for permission, he was a young man, they just pushed him off the wagon and did as they liked with the Jews. There wasn't a lot of water, just a muddy pool, but it was enough to drown them. I never heard of any German being there."

Chaja Finkelsztejn wrote, "The nights were terrible. Poles young and old were running around. They dragged clothes, linen, quilts, pillows out of our neighbors' homes. They took sheepskins from our neighbor, a furrier, and we heard the smashing of windows and wild cries. Every night we heard terrible screams and pleas for help. Jews hid in attic hideouts and in cellars, in rooms where you could move a wardrobe and hide a door. From many houses they took the fathers, beat them until they lost consciousness, brought them round and beat them again, dropping them off back home covered in blood. When women wept to see their husbands beaten like that, they said: 'Shut up or we'll do the same to you.' That torture went on for two weeks."

Halina Zalewska told me, "There was something going on every night. My mother said to the thugs, 'Get it over now, one way or the other, I can't sleep with all this screaming and howling all the time.'"

Menachem and his father, Izrael Finkelsztejn, testified that the pillaging was frequently accompanied by rape. When Jan Skrodzki quoted an excerpt from Menachem's testimony about Jewish women being raped to his cousin Halina Zalewska, she protested vigorously, without noticing that she was actually confirming the testimony: "Those Jewish cows. What man would want them. Only the Kosmaczewski brothers raped, Leon and Antoni, and the Mordasiewicz from the other side of the garden plots. Kaziuk Mordasiewicz took Estera, the tailor Szymon's wife who did our laundry, and did with her what he liked. He led her into the muddy bank of the Matlak river, took her behind the weir and made her roll around. She begged us to intervene on her behalf. My father was even going to, but the thugs banged on the door and shouted: 'If you speak up for Jews you'll be the first to be burned.' Well, they burned Estera with the rest of them."

On Sunday, July 6, the horrifying news came that Poles had killed all the Jews in nearby Wąsosz. At noon, as described by Menachem

Finkelsztejn, a lot of Poles from Wąsosz came to Radziłów. The locals didn't let them in, but they also didn't allow the Jews out.

"There were a lot of peasants, men and women, at all the roads leading out of town, watching every move made by the Jews," Chaja Finkelsztejn wrote. "We heard peasants shout that they were trampling the grain so no wretch could hide in it." Chaja's brother went to Father Dołęgowski to ask him to intercede: "My brother pleaded and wept and the priest did nothing but chide and scold."

2.

On July 7 trucks drove into Radziłów from early morning carrying men from the surrounding villages armed with poles.

Stanisław Ramotowski: "It was still dark, in the night of July 6 to 7, when they started coming into Radziłów on trucks to crack down on the Jews."

At about 7:00 a.m. two or three cars appeared in the marketplace. This was surely a group of officials from the security police and the security service led by Hermann Schaper, one of the small German units that aided in the "pacification" of these areas, and that were involved in (among other things) the local populations' "cleansing themselves" of Jews. Schaper was a Gestapo officer from Ciechanów. The Institute of National Remembrance managed to find the ninety-one-year-old Schaper, and prosecutor Ignatiew tried to interrogate him in April 2002. But he wouldn't say anything, offering his poor health as an excuse.

When was the murder of the Radziłów Jews planned? And who planned it? That they were gearing up for a pogrom that day was known beforehand. We can assume that the arrangements were made the day before between Schaper and the temporary authorities in Radziłów, though none of the witnesses remembers any meeting or earlier visit from the Germans. Of course, it's possible that no one remembered a visit of one or two Germans in a private car. We don't know how the deals were made. Did Schaper order the killing of the Jews, did he encourage it, or did he merely express his consent?

At dawn, when the peasants were heading for the pogrom, individual murders were already taking place. Mojżesz Perkal was beaten to death. One of Perkal's daughters, sixteen, half-alive, squatted down beside her dead father's body. The peasants dug a grave and threw her into it along with her father. Chaja Finkelsztejn heard about it at 7:00 a.m. from their former driver. "He was very upset," she said. "He cursed the murderers: 'Sons of bitches! To bury a girl alive!'"

Andrzej R. told me, "Three Germans arrived in an open car. I was standing nearby. They said, 'It stinks of Jews here. When we come back in a few days make sure it doesn't smell like this.' They pointed to Feliks Mordasiewicz, who was standing nearby—it was his responsibility. 'How am I supposed to do that?' he asked. Then they got five rifles out of the car, the long ones with a single shot."

Halina Zalewska told me, "Four Germans arrived in the marketplace in two Jeeps, they wore caps with skulls on them, they'd brought rifles to be handed out. The young people especially went to listen to the Germans. The Germans told them, 'You have Jews here whose fault it is that your families are freezing to death in Russia. Gather them all in the marketplace under the pretext of weeding the pavement.'"

Antoni K. told me, "There were five Germans and a driver. White caps, white gloves. A lot of people gathered there, I was there, too. A German got out and said, 'Take all the Jews first to weed the grass in the marketplace. We're going to the market in Jedwabne, then we'll come back to see what you've done. If you don't you're finished.'"

Antoni K., when asked how the people gathered there knew what the German was saying, answered after a pause that he'd spoken Polish. That may be right—we know Schaper knew Polish. The herding of Jews into the marketplace—an action probably coordinated by the self-appointed authorities according to the instructions of the visiting Gestapo—was well organized. All adults and youth were rounded up. A part of the Polish population was tasked with guarding the roads so the Jews didn't escape. Stanisław Ramotowski saw a German on a balcony over the marketplace, taking photographs of the roundup of Jews.

Halina Zalewska told me, "They went by the cottages saying, 'Jews, our Polish marketplace is very overgrown, go and weed it.' Oy, oy, they went happily, the Jews, they brought scrapers, it could have been worse. And in the market our people selected the worst Communists. When someone had a grudge against anyone, he found his man in the market and settled scores with him. The Jews were hiding in the chimneys, and the Poles pulled them out. One, a Communist, was so scared of dying that he cut his own throat with tailor's scissors."

Henryk Dziekoński (1953 interrogation): "We began to drive all the Jews residing in the Radziłów municipal area into the marketplace regardless of sex and age, and I took active part in this. One of the Gestapo officers appointed me the head of a group that was tasked with liquidating Jews and specified that we were allowed to cut Jews up with knives and do them in them with axes. One of our group who also took part in the slaughter of Jews said that this would lead to a reciprocal shedding of blood, and then one of the Gestapo officers told Aleksander Godlewski (who is now in prison): 'You've got a barn, you can burn them all.' After the Gestapo officers had spoken the aforementioned words, I started to gather the Jews into groups of four with all my friends. When we'd formed them into ranks I stood at the head of the column and led them from the market toward the barn."

It took several hours to round up all the Jews. They were beaten into singing the Soviet song "My Moscow."

Chaja Finkelsztejn describes how Jan Walewski, nicknamed "the American" (because he'd returned from America after many years), beat a Jew standing near her son until he collapsed with blood pouring from his throat and ears. She saw a woman friend of hers holding a three-month-old infant naked in her arms—someone had torn away the blanket it had been wrapped in. The Gestapo took wine and snacks from their cars. After enjoying a meal in view of the rounded-up crowd they set about beating Jews. A German tied a stone around one Jew's neck, beat him with a stick, and made him run around in a circle. At some point the Gestapo left. Then the Poles ordered the Jews to move down Piękna Street. By the time they were driven to the barn there were no Germans around.

Andrzej R. told me, "I ran home to tell my mother something was going on. I fed the rabbits, ate lunch, and when I got back to the marketplace the Jews were forming a column. I saw friends from school playing in the courtyard."

Halina Zalewska told me, "They were driven down Piękna Street, past our windows, and a Jewish woman who was our neighbor said, 'Mr. Zalewski, you are such a respected, decent person, please take our things and save us.' But the young people had switchblades in their hands. The Jewish woman was carrying her little son, another was hanging on to her legs, and one of the Poles—he must have come in from another town because I never saw him before or after—drove her on, lashed her with a stick, and the child's head was split open. Daddy just watched from behind the curtains and cried."

Henryk Dziekoński (1949 interrogation): "The Jews didn't try to escape, at least I didn't see them try. They went like sheep. One Jew started to run away. Feliks Mordasiewicz caught up with him, hit him on the head with a pole he had in his hand, hard enough to draw blood, and the Jew turned back toward the barn."

3.

The walls were made of stone, the doors of wood. To keep the Jews from escaping, poles were propped against the doors and boulders were dragged up to the barn to hold them shut.

Janina Staniurska, Jan Skrodzki's cousin, who lives in Gdynia: "I was twelve years old at that time. A few people were hiding in the grain and vicious thugs were searching the fields with sticks. I was coming back from the meadows on the other side of the Matlak, I'd brought food to a boy who was grazing our cow there. It was late afternoon. I looked and saw a man running toward me with a stick, yelling, 'You're a Jewess.' He took me to the barn. And there, O Lord, they were burning people alive, they were trying to escape, climbing onto the roof, jumping. Two neighbors who lived near us stuck up for me: 'She's not Jewish. What do you want from the chauffeur's girl?' They called me that because my father was a driver. Then they explained that peasants had come in from Wąsosz, that's why they didn't know us. After that I was always afraid of passing by that place."

We know beyond any doubt who set fire to the barn: Józef Ekstowicz (or Klimas or Klimaszewski). Many witnesses remember it. Tin canisters of gas were most certainly used. Those who tried to escape were shot at.

Halina Zalewska told me, "Józef Klimas was fat, short, so his friends had to give him a leg up."

Andrzej R. told me, "I saw with my own eyes how Józef poured gas on the barn. Then he chased a girl who'd managed to jump out of the barn. He caught her and killed her."

Józef Ekstowicz, a.k.a. Klimaszewski (1948 interrogation): "The initiators and main executors of the atrocity were: Dziekoński, Godlewski, and the Kosmaczewski brothers. They were armed with rifles and made me pour gas on the barn. They gave us a leg up—the other arsonist was a boy who'd come in from the nearby village of Karwowo—we climbed onto the roof and we poured the gas all over the roof."

Henryk Dziekoński (1949 interrogation): "It is not true that Klimaszewski, then a minor, was forced to set fire to the barn, as he did it of his own free will. When gas had been poured on the roof and lit with a match the roof caught fire like a lightning flash. A moment later some man fell out from under the burning thatch with his clothes on fire. Mieczysław Strzelecki, who was standing near me, shot at him with his rifle. When the shots were fired the man threw himself down or jumped, in convulsions."

There were many people at the barn—killers and gawkers.

Bolesław Ciszewski told me, "I saw them being herded there, I saw the fire being lit. What a wail! Most of them were small children and old people. The babies were thrown on top."

"Why did you go there?"

"I was curious. A whole lot of people came from curiosity, mostly young people, some women. Some of them had weapons, poles and sticks they were. One Jew-boy ran away across the peat bog. One guy, drunk as a skunk, who had a Mauser, aimed at him and you won't believe it, miss, drunk as he was, he got him."

Halina Zalewska told me, "I snuck out of the house and saw them being burned. I heard about Rachela Wasersztejn—she was the most beautiful girl in the village next to my sister Zosia—that her baby was thrown in over the top. I'd seen her a minute before. She had recently given birth, and they took her and her baby from the bed where she had given birth. She passed by our windows. She was walking along with her baby and crying."

Rachela's husband, Berek Wasersztejn of Radziłów, who was not in Radziłów that day, got to Białystok and managed to survive until the end of the war, joining a group of Soviet partisans. He testified at the trial that a Polish woman he knew had told him about the death of his wife, Rachela: "My wife was hiding. When they found her, they took her to the barn. Leon Kosmaczewski told her to go in with her child and because the flames were so high they set a ladder up for her. My wife began to beg them to at least take the baby, who was ten days old. Kosmaczewski took the child by its legs and threw it over the roof and he stabbed my wife with a bayonet and threw her in as well."

Wolf Szlapak, who had been beaten up, lay at home, unable to move, with his small son and sick mother.

Halina Zalewska told me, "Mieczysław Strzelecki first took all of Szlapak's jewelry from him, and then shot him in his own bed."

Chaja Finkelsztejn wrote, "Szlapak and his seven-year-old son were murdered in their beds by Mieczysław Strzelecki, who worked for Szlapak as a driver."

Finkelsztejn heard about a number of cases of old people who hadn't been able to make it to the marketplace—one of them had returned from America in his old age because he wanted to be buried in the country of his birth—being killed in their beds. Also about neighbors who agreed to hide a family but who, after having robbed them, gave them up to the killers or even killed them themselves.

Those who escaped from the column and hid in the grain were hunted down.

Andrzej R. told me, "By nightfall there wasn't a single Jewish house unoccupied. So much running around there was, so many quarrels about who would take what. There wasn't so much stuff in the houses anymore because the Jews had given their goods to neighbors they trusted, for safekeeping. Sawicki, the butcher, who had a cheap slaughterhouse on Kościelna Street, had loaded all his most valuable things on a hay cart in June and removed them, and later I saw him driven to the barn with his wife and eldest daughter."

Halina Zalewska told me, "The Germans came at sunset, bringing more ammunition, and ordered them to check if the most important sheep had been taken. They meant the rabbi."

Other witnesses did not remember the German commando unit coming that same day. Chaja Finkelsztejn claims they only appeared three days later.

4.

Many Jews hid in cellars and attics when they heard about the roundup in the marketplace. Thugs dragged them out and killed them on the spot or took them to the ice pit. This was an elongated pit on the way to the barn, a few meters deep, where ice chopped from the river in winter was kept. There they shot them, felled them with axes, or threw them alive into the pit, which was filled with corpses. They drove in barrels of lime and sprinkled it on each layer of victims.

The hunt for survivors and the act of killing them on the spot or at the ice pit went on for the next three days, till July 10. Both Jewish and Polish witness accounts confirm this.

Izrael Finkelsztejn (1945 trial witness): "The manhunt went on after that and whoever was caught was killed. When they ran out of rifle ammunition they started to kill them with spades and things like that."

Halina Zalewska told me, "Those they didn't burn they killed and threw into pits for butter and cream cheese near the dairy and covered them with lime. I went there once at twilight, the earth was moving, half-dead people were crawling out, reviving, but the lime finished them off."

Andrzej R. told me, "I saw the Drozdowskis and both Dziekoński brothers, Jan and Henryk, and Władysław Dudziński, shooting Jews at the ice pit. There were lots of people around eager to shoot. When they ran out of bullets they threw them into the pit alive. The earth went on moving for three days. I saw Antoni Kosmaczewski and Heniek Dziekoński taking a whole family to the ice pit—the owner of a coal and ironworks, his wife and two children, who had sat out the burning in a hideout in their own attic."

Chaja Finkelsztejn wrote, "The Gestapo gave the Poles a free hand for three days. They searched every nook and cranny, every place where a Jew might hide. When on the third day the Gestapo drove up to the pit where those Jews who hid had been killed, an eight-year-old boy emerged from among the corpses. They wouldn't allow him to be killed and he lived on till the liquidation of the rest of the Jews. Then his terrible suffering ended."

In the testimony of Menachem Finkelsztejn, in the testimonies of the accused and witnesses of former trials, in the conversations I conducted, the same names of the main culprits in the massacre are confirmed: the brothers Jan and Henryk Dziekoński; the brothers Aleksander and Feliks Godlewski; Edmund Korsak; Antoni, Józef, and Leon Kosmaczewski; Mieczysław Strzelecki.

Andrzej R. says that one Jew who hid in a house on the outskirts of town was found by thugs and brought to Radziłów from near Racibór. They tied him to a wagon plank and cut off his head with a tree saw. "I didn't see the act of sawing myself," he says, "but I saw the headless body in a ditch."

Antoni Olszewski was three and a half years old at the time. He claims that he has fixed in his memory like a photograph an image of himself stamping on earth covering the body of a Jewish boy not much older than himself, murdered by neighbors. "Some time after the burning I saw a bloody cap in our cabbage patch. They had dragged out a child who was hiding nearby and beaten him to death. Mama screamed at them to bury him deep, otherwise our pigs would pull him out. The elders covered him with earth and I and Józek Szymonów stamped on it to make it firmer. I remember that stamping to this day, I could show you where it was."

Halina Zalewska told me, "The stench and the fatty smoke—it was human fat—hung in the house for weeks."

Andrzej R. told me, "Jan Ekstowicz, a World War I veteran who'd lost both his arms, took two children in, he had them baptized right away. But soon someone denounced him and the police took the kids away."*

5.

How many Jews were burned in the barn in Radziłów? Menachem Finkelsztejn gave a figure of seventeen hundred Jews driven into the marketplace, and another time he said one thousand. But Jewish testimonies usually give an exaggerated number of victims. In the files on the trials the number most often given is six hundred. How many were murdered in the ice pit or wherever they were caught in town is even harder to say; the number three hundred is repeated, but given the fact that Radziłów probably had no more than six hundred Jews, this number must be too high. It seems plausible that about five hundred people were burned in the barn and about a hundred, maybe two hundred, fell victim to individual murders.

How many killers were there? Chaja Finkelsztejn wrote that "almost all the Christian townspeople" gathered at the marketplace, forming a dense mass. "If one of the Jews, realizing what was coming, tried to

---

* The parish record book has an entry saying that Jan Ekstowicz, thirty-five years of age, a farmer from Radziłów, came at 8:00 a.m. on July 30, 1941, and two ten-year-olds were baptized: Jan Gryngras, son of Szmul and Rejza Bursztyn, and Stanisław Wierzba, son of Szymek and Ryfka (Herszek's daughter).

escape and was lucky enough to get through the crowd," wrote Menachem Finkelsztejn, "Polish women and children standing around as if at some kind of show stopped him and sent him back." "All of Radziłów took part in the roundup of Jews and there were also people watching," Józef Ekstowicz testified (as a witness in 1951). "Almost the whole population participated in rounding up Jews. There were men, women, and children," testified Henryk Dziekoński (in his 1949 interrogation).

"Can you say how many of us Poles of Radziłów took part in it?" Jan Skrodzki asked Jan R.

"Ask me who wasn't there, it would be easier to count. But people took part in different ways. Some were active, others semiactive, others just gawked. I remember one woman following behind the Jews, weeping."

Journal

FEBRUARY 27, 2002
New York. I'm here to spend two months working on my book. It's all thanks to Lawrence Weschler, who has taken over the New York Institute for the Humanities at NYU and managed to find an office in the building for his charges. I am taking a little break from the role I've assumed of my own free will: social worker and shrink to a few decent people from Jedwabne and its surroundings.

FEBRUARY 28, 2002
I'm describing the history of the Finkelsztejn family on the basis of Chaja's memoir and I dream of finding her daughter, Chana, of whom I know only that she lives in America. I haven't managed to get her contact information from Menachem's widow. I phone Uncle Szmul in Tel Aviv to ask him to try again. If she doesn't have her sister-in-law's address, maybe she knows someone who does? Szmulek calls me back to tell me he got the following reply: "She's somewhere in Kansas, I don't know the address, we're not in touch, and besides, Chana has a memory disorder so nothing can come out of a meeting with her."

Since I now know it's Kansas, and I'm in the States, I'll try to find her there, nonetheless.

MARCH 1, 2002

On the *Gazeta* website I read accounts of the parliamentary sessions at which Institute of National Remembrance director Leon Kieres gave a report on the institute's activities. MPs from the party League of Polish Families attacked him like a fight squad. "Because of your manipulations, silences, acquiescences, Director Kieres," one MP shrieked, "World Jewry and President Kwaśniewski said kaddish in a display of chutzpah in Jedwabne in July 2001. When may we expect your resignation as the president of the institute so that a Pole can be elected to the post who cares about the truth of Polish history and who loves the Polish people?" Other MPs attacked the institute, saying that it is "harnessed to a battle against Polishness." One of the MPs declared that what President Kwaśniewski said was the "culmination of the stoning of the Polish people" and that Kieres threw the first stone. These performances were rewarded with applause. Neither the parliament vice marshal who chaired the session nor any of the MPs replied. Kieres explained that he undertook the investigation as a Polish patriot, and that he comes from a Polish family. Read: he's not a Jew.

MARCH 15, 2002

Today is my last day to buy the ticket to Buenos Aires that I reserved. I'm traveling there to meet Mosze Olszewicz, the man who hid under the Wyrzykowskis' pigsty with his fiancée, Elke. With Awigdor Kochaw, he is the last living witness of the Jedwabne massacre. I've written to him, but in vain, and so I've decided to appeal to Antonina Wyrzykowska for help. She wrote the Olszewiczes a letter, and on the day before I flew to New York, I went by to say goodbye and to ask her to call Mosze from my cell phone just in case.

"Anna is my friend and she's done a lot for me," I hear Antonina say to Elke Olszewicz. "I haven't asked you for anything and I never will. Just receive Anna."

I want to make sure the Olszewiczes will meet me, so I phone to confirm the date. I hear Elke's impatient voice: "Why dig it all up after so many years, who needs that? Please don't call again." And the receiver is slammed down.

MARCH 30, 2002

I manage to get through to Eliasz Grądowski, for whom I've left innumerable messages on his machine. He is eighty years old and still has a bicycle repair shop in Brooklyn. In 1941 he stole a record player from the cultural center in Jedwabne and that saved him—he was deported to Siberia. Although he wasn't in Jedwabne at the time of the massacre, he appeared before the court in the 1949 trial as an eyewitness. He was one of the main figures in the bogus legalization of Polish takeovers of post-Jewish property. He invokes Antonina Wyrzykowska, who's been a friend of his ever since he met her by accident in Brooklyn.

"What are you doing here?" he asked her.

"I'm waiting for the bus. And what are *you* doing here?"

"I'm waiting for the bus, too."

His response to me now is angry: "You've exploited Antonina quite enough by now. In America you would pay thousands of dollars for the kind of interview she gives you. She should have a villa, but instead it's journalists who make fortunes from it. How much are you getting for this?" The argument is the same as in Jedwabne—that the Jedwabne affair is all about money. And the sound of the phone being hung up is the same, too.

A conversation with Leszek Dziedzic. For some reason he's less enthusiastic about his life in America. It's hard to get out of him what's the matter.

"I worked for my brother because I don't have my papers yet, but his wife and I can't see eye to eye about the Jews, we quarreled and now I'm out of work."

APRIL 4, 2002

Ty Rogers tells me that as the attorney for the families of the Jedwabne victims, he presented to the Polish consul in New York in advance a list of people who should be invited to the ceremony of July 10, 2001. He was told the Wasersztejns could not be invited. "You know, you understand"; "It's a delicate topic in Warsaw"; "We know what Wasersztejn was." Unused to such conversations, he went on asking what the problem was until someone finally said, well, Wasersztejn was employed by the secret police, wasn't he?

I phone the Polish consulate to hear from the other side about Ty Rogers's conversation with the consul regarding Wasersztejn's alleged links to the secret police. What am I talking about, they say, there was no such conversation. When I press the consul, saying it's unlikely an American lawyer would invent something like that, I learn that "in fact some such suggestion may have come from Poland and apparently reached Mr. Rogers."

Everything is based on insinuation. Wasersztejn did not work for the secret police after the war. But what if he had? Would that have diminished the horror of his mother's burning in the barn?

APRIL 12, 2002

A phone conversation with Giselle, Chana Finkelsztejn's daughter. Chana is alive, she remembers everything and will talk to me. She's happy someone has taken an interest in her story after sixty years. What a relief! My obsessive inquiries, dozens of phone calls, compulsive Internet searches have paid off.

I reserve an airplane ticket to Kansas City. I'll be interested to find out if Chana is aware of her mother's diary.

APRIL 18, 2002

Lunch with Irena Grudzińska Gross and Jonathan Schell. Like me, Schell is completely absorbed in writing a book. I tell him about the ghosts of the past, he tells me about the ghosts of the future—he's writing about the threat of atomic energy—and we understand each other perfectly.

An afternoon flight to Kansas City. Giselle Widman picks me up at the airport. The city counts four million inhabitants. The suburb we drive to at first glance looks like all the others, except that there's a mezuzah over every door. On the street where Giselle lives, real estate prices depend on the distance to the synagogue. The synagogue is Orthodox, so no one is allowed to drive on Shabbat.

APRIL 19, 2002

Giselle brings her mother from the nursing home where she lives. A lovely, delicate, elegantly dressed lady in golden slippers. We speak English. I've prepared fifty-six questions. Unfortunately, Chana, now Ann Walters, has serious memory problems, just as her Israeli sister-in-law said.

She's every inch a lady, even in the face of illness.

"I'm so sorry, I see the image before me, but when I want to describe it, it dissolves. Please stop me if I repeat myself," she says, telling me the last happy memory of her childhood for the tenth time. It was during the Soviet occupation, and because the Soviets took care of talented children she was singled out and taken to Jedwabne to perform. She played a little fish caught on a line and begging for its freedom by dancing and singing for the fisherman.

These must have been the same performances of which a woman from Jedwabne told me: "On the occasion of the October Revolution the former Catholic House, which had been turned into a club, organized a theater competition for the schools in the area. I was in a choir that sang Russian songs. First place went to the Radziłów school, which had a lot of Jewish girls."

Chaja mentioned little Chana's performances in her memoir. She didn't want to let her daughter go to Soviet events, but the Polish teacher persuaded her to give her consent. However, she didn't go to see her daughter perform.

Chana, or Chanełe, as she used to be called, remembers shards of the events.

How her brother Szlomke came home bloodied before the war because children had thrown stones at him, shouting, "Jew!" and how Polish girls from the neighborhood came to play with her and then stopped coming because other children were making fun of them.

How before the massacre, just after the Russians left town, Polish houses had crosses chalked on them in the morning, so the Germans could see right away which houses were Christian and which Jewish.

How on July 7, 1941, she saw her Jewish girlfriend with curly blond hair—she can't remember her name—being hit by someone and blood running down her cheek.

How the priest said at the religious instruction classes she had to attend after July 7 in order to be baptized that the sweet baby Jesus was cruelly killed by the Jews, for which a curse had fallen upon them and that was why so much ill befell them.

How her godparents promised her after her baptism that they would take the whole family—if they survived the war—to Częstochowa to thank the Virgin Mary for converting them to the true faith. But she knew from her mother that they'd only become pretend Catholics.

How during the time they were in hiding, her mother woke her at night because she was speaking Yiddish in her sleep.

Ann speaks in a low voice: "This murmuring stayed with all four of us after being in hiding."

In the afternoon Giselle takes me to pick up her son from his Jewish school. She tells me indignantly about the animosities at play here. The German Jews treat the East European Jews as inferior. The descendants of those who managed to flee Germany before the war call themselves "Holocaust Kristallnacht Survivors," and don't consider her mother a survivor because she wasn't in a concentration camp.

The school is situated in an enormous Jewish Community Center with conference halls, a café, shops, and in the middle a glass-walled library, where Holocaust literature predominates. It also holds the memorial book of "survivors," in which Ann does not figure. I am introduced to the library director and the director of the center. I'm supposed to give an interview to the local paper. My visit is supposed to strengthen Giselle's position in this community.

A hefty young man in a yarmulke and oversize army pants comes up to us. So this is Ann's grandson, who owes his existence to his great-grandmother's heroism.

A Shabbat dinner in the company of a large group of invited guests. The talk is in English. An older gentleman leans over to me and points out an elderly couple, whispering in Polish, "They're a great couple, who would have thought she's from Hungary? Because everyone else here is from Poland."

APRIL 20, 2002

Ann is glad to have me listen to her stories. She makes mistakes, she repeats herself, but she also keeps retrieving crumbs from the recesses of her memory. She always remembered a peasant woman who took her in toward the end of the war, when she was dirty, flea-ridden, and sick, and treated her like her own child, bathing her and carrying her outside, because she wasn't strong enough to stand on her own legs. "I can't remember her name, and I so want to remember." I promise her that I'll go to the place where they were hidden and try to find out.

After the liberation she went to a Polish school for two years. "I had no friends there, I just focused on hiding what I'd been through.

Emotionally we had already been in Palestine for many years, but when we finally got there, I felt just as alien as in my Polish school. I watched the children playing and tried to imitate them, so no one would notice I was different. I was closest to my mother and my sister Yaffa (in Poland she was called Szejna), but we never talked about what we'd been through, we didn't want to hurt each other. I may have gone too far in not talking or thinking about it, and for that reason when I search for memories I see a white sheet in my head."

She married, went to Kansas to be with her husband, helped him in his jewelry business, which never interested her. When ten years ago he demanded a divorce, it was a relief to her. She couldn't talk to her husband about what she'd been through.

"He was in a concentration camp, his family died in the gas chambers. It was as if he went around with a sign: 'My parents died in the camps, I went through hell.' He made it clear to me I didn't have it so bad, because he'd had it much worse. To survive the camps you had to be clever. He managed. He wasn't warm, he wasn't compassionate, he was aggressive."

We phone Haifa to check in with Szlomid, Chaja Finkelsztejn's granddaughter. She's the daughter of Yaffa, Chaja's daughter who is no longer alive. "Mama never told us what she'd suffered," Szlomid tells me. "It's probably part of Polish culture to shut your mouth and not tell people about what hurts? Maybe that's why so much suffering came out of her when she was dying. At the end of her life she could only speak Polish, and the last months she was shaking as if in fear, repeating the same Polish words, which none of us understood."

APRIL 21, 2002
At the local Jewish Community Center, Ann and I watch a video made years ago of her telling the story of being in hiding. Then and now, in her conversations with me, Ann often refers to miracles.

"It was a miracle that when the squad came to beat us, Mama hid me under the bed and I got away." "A miracle occurred when we were walking on the road after the burning of the Jews in Radziłów: a peasant who knew us shouted to us to hide in the rye—I remember the feeling of wanting to be deeper down in the earth—and no one found us." "It's a miracle, after all, that when we were driven out of our hiding place because the man hiding us got scared, and we were going through the village in the night, dogs barked but nobody looked out the window. And the second time was the same kind of miracle—two German policemen came into the yard and the man we were hiding with told us to get out immediately by the back door; everything gave us away, most of all the color of our skin, it was summer and we were pale as ghosts, but we got away." Then about her brother: "It's a true miracle Menachem didn't die, even though he had a blood infection and was fainting with fever. The cat must have stolen a piece of pork fat from the housewife and was startled and didn't finish it, and Mama put that fat on his arm and alternated it with cold compresses." "It's a miracle we managed to pass for Christian converts. They themselves said that by converting us and then saving us, they were opening a road for themselves to heaven." "A miracle happened in the barn where we were hiding; we had a gas lamp there, gas spilled, and a fire broke out, but Daddy put it out. So many miracles happened to save us. God was good to us. And a few Christians were, too. Many Poles were hostile to us, but not all."

Chaja Finkelsztejn's memoir is the story of a woman who defends her family like a lioness in the face of a historical cataclysm. "I was hard as steel and cold as iron"—she repeats that phrase many times. After these few days spent with Ann I realized how high the wall was that Chaja built to shield her children from the threat of the outside world.

First Chaja died of Alzheimer's. Then the same happened to Ann's brother Menachem, and finally to her sister Yaffa. It must really be a miracle that it is thanks to this family, so deeply marked by an illness that degrades memory, that the memory of the Radziłów Holocaust survived.

APRIL 22, 2002
Today I left for New London to meet Lea Kubran, who was hidden by Antonina Wyrzykowska.

Her husband, Jack Kubran—Jankiel Kubrzański in Poland—survived because on July 10, 1941, he was taken on to work at the German police station, which was the safest place in Jedwabne that day. Lea lived with her parents in nearby Szczuczyn. She survived because she happened to be at her friend Elke's house across the street. Her cousin, who managed to jump out of the window, told her how their neighbors, peasants with whom they were friendly—her father used to lend his bicycle to them—had burst into their home. They murdered everyone with axes. Lea had six brothers and four sisters.

When she was little her mother read her a prophecy that there would be a war and only one person would survive from each family. Lea responded, "I want to be that person." "I survived, because that was my destiny," she says. "And I suffered and risked so much."

After the pogrom in Szczuczyn she and Elke made their way to Łomża to Elke's family. The Olszewiczes, Elke's future in-laws, were already camping out there, having decided in time to move to a larger city in fear of a pogrom. Soon the next refugees arrived from Jedwabne: Mosze, the Olszewiczes' son, and his friend Jankiel Kubrzański. They told terrible stories, which no one wanted to believe, about all Jews having been burned there.

Lea knows that Poles came for her future husband when he was working at the German police station on July 10, 1941, but the police wouldn't let them take him. The Germans said, "You have enough Jews." In the evening they told the Jews to go: "Go—we're not going to protect you anymore."

In the Jedwabne trial Karol Bardoń, one of the perpetrators, testified: "A few people went into the yard at the police station and tried to take away three Jews chopping wood. Then the station commandant came out to them: 'Was eight hours to deal with the Jews not enough for you?'" Kubrzański must have been one of those three.

Before long everyone had to leave the house, because it was situated outside the borders of the ghetto being formed. But they stayed together for now. Lea fled the ghetto with Jankiel the day before it was liquidated. They hid with a peasant, but someone informed on them.

"The farmer came rushing into the pigsty shouting, 'Run, the police are coming for you,'" Lea Kubran relates. "We started running, it was the autumn of 1942, but there was already heavy snow. They caught us, took us to the village head. They beat me, I still have a scar on my forehead. The Germans got drunk with the village head to celebrate having found Jews, and told the farmer they were supposed to drive us to the station in town on a wagon. The farmer took us on his cart. The farmer tied Jankiel's hand to mine, two policemen sat in back, the farmer in front. They were taking us to our deaths. The policemen were so drunk they fell asleep in the cold, and the Pole said to us, 'Run away, they're asleep. I'll wake them when you're far away.'"

Lea breaks off to give us dinner. When she speaks English she has a heavy Yiddish accent, but her Polish is pure Jedwabne. She says *"Bogu dzięka"* (Thanks God) as often as Wyrzykowska does ("Thanks God my daughter got a good education").

"We'd run a good distance," she continues her tale, "when the Pole shouted loudly so we could hear him, 'They're gone! They're gone!' They beat and kicked the Pole and chased him away. We found a barn and burrowed into the hay, our hands still tied together. Jankiel dropped by Antonina's on the way to find shelter. We knew Szmul Wasersztejn worked there and that we could count on Antonina. She told Jankiel the Olszewiczes were already with her. He stayed a night. I hid with a farmer I knew on the Narew River who'd told Jankiel he wouldn't let me stay," Lea goes on, "but I hid in his barn without him knowing it. My parents came to me in my sleep, telling me what to do, and then I felt as if my father had offered me his hand so I could pull myself up to the very top of the barn. Jankiel had promised to look for a place for both of us, and if it turned out we had to part, we'd find each other after the war—if we survived. Eleven days went by, maybe twelve. I thought, I'll wait one more day for Jankiel and then I'll drown myself. I cried myself to sleep, and the next day I heard voices. He hadn't found another place so he'd gone back to Antonina, and she'd told him to bring me, too."

When they came out of hiding after the war, they lived in the family house of the Kubrzańskis. Briefly.

"Poles were living there," Lea continues her story, "but we reassured them that we only wanted to spend a few nights and leave, so they behaved well. One night partisans came. Olszewicz wasn't there, he was looking for a place to live in Łomża, because we already knew it wasn't safe in Jedwabne. Within a second Jankiel had stood on the sofa and pulled himself up, there was a trapdoor over the sofa, and angels must have guided his movements for him to have made it. I said there weren't any men at home, and one of them slapped my face, saying I was lying. They went outside, and I heard them saying to their leader, 'No men, just two women, what do we do with them?' But they didn't do anything to us, and the same night we fled to Łomża by foot."

After the Kubrzańskis arrived in the United States they settled in Connecticut. Lea, after raising three children, worked as a cook at a Jewish school, twice winning first prize in a local contest for her chocolate cake. Jankiel, by then called Jack, began as a night watchman in a dairy, then a dairy worker, eventually rising to foreman.

The Olszewiczes settled in Argentina. "Elke and Mosze ran a business," Lea tells me. "They sewed bags made of leather and plastic, the kind you use for shopping, not for going out to the theater; it was a good trade because there hadn't been bags like that in Buenos Aires before. Mosze had such a good head for business he could have been minister of trade. In the ghetto he did anything to avoid doing forced labor. He sold and bought, going back and forth between the ghetto and the Aryan side. He used to say, 'Where you have two people, you have a business.'"

Lea lived with Jankiel for more than fifty years, as did Elke with Mosze. It is only when I talked to Lea that I realized she and Elke were only about fifteen when they went into hiding, Berek Olszewicz the same; the others weren't even eighteen yet.

APRIL 24, 2002

I'm scarcely on the ground at the airport in Warsaw when my cell phone rings. I am told Marianna Ramotowska is in the hospital. I go to see her straight from the airport. The first call I make is to Ignatiew. These are the times that make me fully aware of the extent of my obsession with Jedwabne.

MAY 3, 2002

Jedwabne. Dozens of photocopies are circulating around town of the letter sent last spring by the mayor and the town council chairman to the government authorities with a request for aid in preparation for the July 10 ceremony. Supposedly the new mayor found the letter in his predecessor's desk and decided to make it public. "That disgraceful letter," the town's residents call it. Father Orłowski's beloved anti-Semitic rag printed it under the headline "Proof of Betrayal," taking the opportunity to accuse council chairman Michałowski of informing the "kosher crowd" about the mood of the townspeople: "Recently—discreetly, at home, not in his office—he talked for several hours to the chief Jewish slanderer Bikont of the *Gazeta Wyborcza*. This journalistic hyena has already frequently made her mark in the pages of the *Gazeta Wyborcza* with lying polonivorous articles. May the Poles of Jedwabne know who is informing on them."

I try to joke about it with Michałowski, but I realize he's not in a laughing mood.

I visit an older lady, Miss Szmidtowa, who lives in a secluded little house with a multitude of cats and dogs but without running water or gas.

On a video recording made by Szmul Wasersztejn I watch the welcome in Jedwabne: "Stasiulek!" she cried—using the fond diminutive they used for him during the war. "Stasiulek, come in." In Szmul's memoir I found a description of how he had turned up on the steps of her family home many years before—it was July 11, 1941—and she greeted him with the same astonishment and joy: "Szmulke, but I thought you were dead." She and her mother wept when he told them that his mother and brother had been burned. They were afraid to keep him, but her father drove to Jedwabne and learned that Jews could safely return home, because the Germans had forbidden any further killing.

Leszek Dziedzic had tried in vain to persuade Miss Szmidtowa to talk to me when he was still in Poland.

"You see, she lives on her own in the middle of nowhere," he said, attempting to explain her refusal to me. "Someone could come and throw a stone through her window and nobody would even notice."

It's not the first time I've dropped by her house, trying to get her to feel comfortable with me, drinking tea from filthy glasses. She enjoys my visits. But I haven't gotten her to budge an inch.

"I didn't round anybody up, I'd sooner give them bread. And I don't know who did the rounding up. I didn't want to remember, so it didn't stick in my mind. I only know I've seen some bad times in my life."

She denies ever hearing of Szmul Wasersztejn.

MAY 4, 2002

Jedwabne. I drive up to the house of Franciszek, Antonina Wyrzykowska's nephew, with whom I've spoken once before.

He clearly doesn't recognize me and thinks Father Orłowski sent me. The priest sends journalists to him as his expert on Wasersztejn. After all, Wasersztejn hid with his father in Janczewko for several weeks in November 1942. The son, however, keeps saying with pleasure that Szmul Wasersztejn is a lousy bum who slanders Poland. He probably doesn't realize what he's really telling me.

"Why did Wyrzykowska hide people?" Janina Biedrzycka once asked me. I said to her, "Why did you let them get away? If you hadn't, there wouldn't have been anyone to hide."

MAY 8, 2002

Milanówek. A visit to Antonina Wyrzykowska. I ask her about her nephew, Franciszek.

"Franciszek wrote me that his son bought a broken tractor and I was supposed to get it repaired by President Kwaśniewski, because Franciszek can't afford the spare parts. Someone else in the family asked me who I knew in TV, because I must have some good connections. I wrote back I know people who clean the streets and run the school cloakroom and if that's any use to him, I could give him some contacts."

"It was just any old life, mine was, my angel," Antonina sums it all up in parting.

MAY 9, 2002

I phone Krzysztof Godlewski, who left for the United States a month ago.

"Jedwabne is nothing compared to Chicago," he complains. "The local Polonia paper is printing a series called 'Jedwabne—the Lie of the Millennium.' I'm constantly hearing jokes about Jews and crematoria. *The Protocols of the Elders of Zion* is basic reading. I don't admit that I'm *that* Godlewski, the mayor of Jedwabne."

MAY 29, 2002

The foundation of the president's wife, Jolanta Kwaśniewska, has invited me to Jedwabne for a meeting she's having with high school students. Twenty gymnasium high school students are traveling to America on a trip organized by an American organization, the Jan Karski Educational Foundation, with the support of Kwaśniewska's foundation. I had heard about this trip before. Already in the fall the school was buzzing with talk about whose child would get to go to America. The main attraction is a trip to Disneyland. Early registration was conducted by Jolanta Karwowska, the teacher who went on the trip to the Holocaust Memorial Museum in Washington, D.C.

"The children worship her like an icon and accept everything she says," a teacher friend told me. "And she says she's going to America to sound out the Jews. But also that she won't be taken in by them. She goes around the school with a photo of the lady she met on her trip to the Holocaust Museum, whose foundation has now invited her to come to America with the children. She shows it around: 'This is Miss Kaya, there's a piano in the background and over it the Virgin Mary. She's a Catholic. I wouldn't go on a Jew's invitation.'"

I intervened with the president's office to prevent them from sending the children to America in the care of the school's chief anti-Semite. Whether it's a result of that intervention or independent of it, it's a relief that she's not the one going.

On the road to Jedwabne I talk to women working for Kwaśniewska's foundation. They gave the students selected for the trip some homework assignments that we will now see. The students had to prepare projects on some religion or nationality present in the region. I ask how a school where anti-Semitic remarks are the order of the day deals with the Jewish people. Yes, it was a problem. The themes of Jews and Judaism were taken up only after several interventions by the foundation.

I share my skepticism with the ladies of the foundation. They tell me they have the task of rooting out racial prejudice. "To root out anti-Semitism would take considerable systematic work with the children," I say. "Shouldn't they be given some more doable task, like re-creating prewar Jewish Jedwabne with the children, or cleaning up the cemetery? Maybe then it might make sense to reward them with a trip to Disneyland?" But the ladies from the foundation argue that they are proposing an excellent educational program: building a bridge of understanding has been shown to work in childrens' camps in the former Yugoslavia.

We arrive at the school, the auditorium has been decorated, the students are dressed up. Kasia Czerwińska (council chairman Stanisław Michałowski's daughter) and Joanna Godlewska (Krzysztof Godlewski's wife) greet me with kisses on the cheek. I'm aware this has a heroic dimension here. The third teacher I know says to me in passing, "Of course we have to pretend we don't know each other."

The young people are supposed to tell us about their projects. About the Lithuanians we learn how deeply rooted they were in this area, about the Tatars that they live in Gdańsk, and you can see their mosque there. The Jews sound like creatures from another planet.

There are tables set up: "Jedwabne yesterday" (two historical projects by students on their town, one of which doesn't even mention the word "Jew," even though at the end of the nineteenth century Jews accounted for over 80 percent of the town's population, and after that, a still considerable part of it; the other has a photo of the old monument and of "Jedwabne today." There is a color photograph of all the most important events in Jedwabne in recent years, like the bishop blessing the school, and one black-and-white photo downloaded from the Internet. It shows President Kwaśniewski laying a wreath at the monument. The shot was taken from above, so that the yarmulke he's wearing is in the foreground. (Mayor Godlewski told me after the ceremony, "The president wore a yarmulke, and I knew I should wear a yarmulke because it was a religious ceremony, but I admit I chickened out—I was afraid they'd burn my house down.") The yarmulke is a symbol of what the residents think of the ceremony of July 10: that it was a Jewish holiday. I go up to the little girl sitting at the table and ask her if she knows what happened in Jedwabne on July 10, 1941.

"A crime was committed," she recites quickly. "We don't know who did it but we don't feel any aversion to Jews, either."

"What does that Jewish cow want from our kids?" I hear one teacher say to another.

I learn that the school organized a meeting with the parish priest for the children going on the American trip and their parents. He told them that the Jews were trying to get to the young. He talked about Jews denouncing Poles to the NKVD, about Jews wanting to cast guilt on the Poles to demand compensation, whereas on July 10, 1941, hundreds of Germans and 2,500 Mazurites came to town. The school's history teacher sat next to the priest and said nothing. The school head assured people the trip was for purposes of tourism and "had nothing to do with any ceremony or Jews." Now every parent parrots this when attacked by those whose children weren't lucky enough to be selected for the trip: "Our child is going for purposes of tourism."

JUNE 3, 2002

A phone conversation with the school head in Jedwabne, Krzysztof Moenke, who is accompanying the children to America. I ask about the meeting with the priest.

"The father didn't want the young people to go unprepared. And it's going to be a tourist trip."

I ask why no one ever thought of inviting Antonina Wyrzykowska, the heroine of Jedwabne, who saved seven Jews, to the school.

"Before the affair flared up I'd never heard Wyrzykowska's name," the principal replies, somewhat off point. He has lived in Jedwabne since his birth and his parents were here during the war.

"But once you *had* heard of her?"

"I wouldn't want to drag children into that subject. Jedwabne lived in peace. And what is Israel getting up to with the Palestinians?"

JUNE 14, 2002

I'm going to Radziłów with Jan and Bożena Skrodzki. I was invited along with them to the wedding of the grandson of a farmer from Trzaski who hid Jan during the Soviet occupation. I've just given Jan the documents from another trial discovered by the Institute of National Remembrance. The accused is Antoni Kosmaczewski, Leon Kosmaczewski's brother. He testified that he killed seventeen-year-old Dora Dorogoj in revenge for her collaboration with the NKVD, and that he did it together with Zygmunt Skrodzki. They committed the crime in June 1941 in broad daylight, a hundred and fifty meters from inhabited buildings.

"I felt hatred toward Dora Dorogoj," Kosmaczewski stated during his interrogation, and explained why. On April 13, 1940, she was on the NKVD truck that came to his house to take him away. He was released after four days in jail.

"When the German forces entered our region in 1941," Kosmaczewski continued, "and the Red Army retreated, I started looking for Dora Dorogoj to take revenge on her. I found out she sometimes came to the Kopańczyks at their settlement in Słucz . . . I then asked Kopańczyk: 'Don't take pity on her, but when she comes to you, send someone to let me know—me, Antoni Kosmaczewski, that is—that she's with you.' About two days later a messenger from Kopańczyk came to me in Radziłów, I don't know his name, to tell me Dora Dorogoj was in their house. At that time I went straight to Zygmunt Skrodzki, the tailor who lived in Radziłów, who had also been looking for Dora Dorogoj. We set off for the Kopańczyks, where Dora Dorogoj was peeling potatoes. When we went into the house, Dora Dorogoj recognized us and was very frightened.

Skrodzki told her to collect her things and come out into the yard. When we went out into the yard Skrodzki gave her a beating with a stick right there in the yard because she was stubborn and refused to go. Skrodzki found a shovel in the yard and gave it to Dora to carry. She began to beg and say: 'I know where I'm going.' Skrodzki replied: 'You should know.' We walked a hundred and fifty meters from the Kopańczyks' buildings—I think it was one of the Kopańczyks' fields—and Skrodzki and I ordered her to dig a hole. When she had dug a hole about 60 centimeters deep, 80 by 50, we started to beat Dora Dorogoj. Zygmunt Skrodzki beat her with a stick, like the swipple on a flail. I, Antoni Kosmaczewski, struck her with a rock I held in my hand. And so we both beat her until she was dead and we buried her in that hole right after we killed her."

No search of the area was conducted for the remains of the murdered girl. When Kosmaczewski retracted his testimony at the same trial and Skrodzki never admitted guilt, the court exonerated them for lack of evidence.

"They killed her in the swamp and cut off her head," Halina Zalewska told me. Menachem Finkelsztejn testified: "The killers concluded a girl wasn't worth the bullet, that's why they cut off her head."

A few days after Dora was killed, the Dorogoj family was burned in the barn in Radziłów. Her father, Mosze, and one son, Akiwa, escaped. Chaja Finkelsztejn remembers in her memoir that after July 7, 1941, the Germans let them live in their own home, where Dorogoj had his workshop, because they needed a shoemaker. "They asked the priest to baptize them," she wrote, "but the priest refused."

When the Germans deported the remaining Jews from Radziłów, the Dorogoj father and son fled.

"I knew the Dorogojs from before the war," Stanisław Ramotowski had told me. "They lived in a redbrick house on Nadstawna Street. He was a shoemaker, but one of the poorest. I knew they were in hiding, because the elder Dorogoj once crept out to my mother's house, trying to find me, but by then I was already in hiding myself. They hid, but a few people knew about them."

They managed to take the basic shoemaker's tools with them and supported themselves by making shoes, which someone from the village collected and sold.

"I had a look at the cellar where they survived the war," Andrzej R. told me. "It was a bunker dug out of the ground, covered with rocks that the farmer had cleared from the field and thrown into a heap. In the spring of 1945 there was still a pile of scraps from a shoemaker's workshop there."

In the same trial Antoni Kosmaczewski confessed to killing both Dorogojs after the war. Every older inhabitant of Radziłów knows the brothers Kosmaczewski took part in that crime.

In Kosmaczewski's account, in February 1945 he supposedly heard from farmers in Słucz that the Dorogojs had come out of hiding, moved to a farm there, and were threatening that when the Red Army arrived and the hour of retribution with it, they were going to shoot Kosmaczewski with their seven-shooter number 9. Kosmaczewski testified how he killed them: "The evening of the next day I took a wagon of my brother's, Józef Gabriel Kosmaczewski, and Józef and I drove to Walewski. I told him that the Russians were coming close and the Jew Dorogoj was threatening to kill me and Zygmunt Skrodzki in revenge for the death of his daughter, Dora Dorogoj, whom we had killed together. I hinted to Walewski that I had a liter of vodka in my pocket and I was going to apologize to those Jews in order to be reconciled with them and ask their forgiveness for killing the daughter. Walewski listened and believed me when I said I had vodka and was really going to apologize. He went to Samołki, where the Jews were, and brought them back to his own yard . . . I was standing in the hallway with an axe, hidden behind the curtain . . . The old Dorogoj on entering the hallway was struck by me on the head with the blunt end of the axe and he fell without even a squeak. Seeing this the younger Dorogoj began to run away screaming. I caught up with him and tripped him so he landed on the ground, and in a second I hit him on the head twice with the axe, the blunt side, and killed him dead . . . After killing those Jews I called my brother Józef, who was about 10 meters away, and Feliks Mordasiewicz, resident of Radziłów, but present in Słucz at that time. When they arrived we loaded the Jews onto a sled and drove them into the forest at Słucz and threw them down on the snow, leaving them aboveground. There I searched them for arms, but found none."

JUNE 15, 2002

Trzaski. The mood at the bridegroom's house is festive, but Jan Skrodzki announces, "I want you as my friends to know why Anna and I are going to Radziłów and what I found out about my father." And disregarding the excitement of the wedding he reads them the description I just handed to him: "Zygmunt Skrodzki beat her with a stick, like the swipple on a flail . . ." He only stops reading when the ceremony of leading the bridegroom to his wedding begins.

We drive to the church in a cavalcade of cars, and afterward attend the wedding feast in a Jedwabne restaurant. I briefly drop in on friends. They can't get over the fact that someone from the area had the courage to invite me to such an event: "In Jedwabne everyone would be scared he'd get his cottage burned down."

JUNE 16, 2002

With the Skrodzkis I go to see Franciszek Ekstowicz, the man who was once a journeyman with Skrodzki. Jan reads him Kosmaczewski's testimonies.

"That was not your father who did the killing," Ekstowicz protests. "I swear to you. Kosmaczewski had a falling-out with your father and that's why he pointed the finger at him."

"I know he's not telling the truth," Jan says to me after we leave.

I ask his wife, Bożena, how Jan, given the chance to accept the "easier truth," doesn't take advantage of it.

"You saw yourself how Franciszek wasn't really paying attention, he was moving around the kitchen, but when the name Dorogoj was dropped he froze. He knows it is the truth and Jan knows it. In some sense Jan always knew, but it's only now that he's engaged in this research that he has finally admitted it to himself. His mother once said to his father in anger, 'What kind of life have I had, I was alone—you went to jail for killing a Jewish girl.' And why did his father cut himself off from the family toward the end of his life? And before that never wanted to meet anyone from Radziłów, even a former journeyman, who lived in Otwock, not far away? He was running away from his own memory."

JUNE 17, 2002

More people I've heard of before are turning up in the pages of Chaja Finkelsztejn's memoir.

There's Lejzor Zandler, who bossed everyone around under the Soviets as the manager of the Finkelsztejns' nationalized mill, and gave propaganda speeches against the former owners, or "vampires." I know the rest of his story from Ramotowski, who met him during the German occupation, when he was intending to find his way to the Soviet Union and join the Communist partisans there.

There's the medic Mazurek, described by Chaja as one of the most important people in the village after the Germans arrived, next to the priest and the village head: he is the same older gentleman who was a friend of Ramotowski's mother. It was at his urging that Rachela got herself baptized, and Mazurek himself became her godfather and a witness at her church wedding to Stanisław Ramotowski.

There's Marian Kozikowski of Konopki, who took part in the atrocity but also got the Finkelsztejns out of the market square. His name appears several times in the trials of the Radziłów killers. Józef Ekstowicz testified that Marian Kozikowski was in the auxiliary police and gave him the order to set the barn on fire. If Kozikowski was in the auxiliary police, the Finkelsztejns could have left the market square with his permission. He was lord and master in town that day. He must have saved the Finkelsztejns for money.

There's Wolf Szlapak, a family friend of the Finkelsztejns and a Zionist activist who traveled around Poland collecting money to buy land in Palestine. He was supposed to go to America, but he didn't make it before the war broke out. Stanisław Ramotowski remembered Szlapak from before the war, when he used to see him in his iron shop on the market: "Tall, handsome, he looked as distinguished as if he were some kind of leader."

Chaja describes how before the war the Zionists invited emissaries from Eretz Israel to the town. They spoke about Palestine in a crowded synagogue. The Communists tried to break up the meeting and Wolf Szlapak called the police. Chaja emphasizes that he didn't mention that the people disturbing the peace were Communists.

That must have been the same gathering I read about in the Interior Ministry reports: "On May 2, 1932, at the Municipal Court in Szczuczyn, the trial took place against Abram Strzałka and 12 other Jews, Communist members of the Perec Jewish Library Association in Radziłów, accused of disturbing the public peace in the town synagogue. The court sentenced each of the accused men to pay a fine of thirty zlotys or go to jail for seven days."

Wolf Szlapak was murdered on July 7 before his fellow Jews perished in the barn. Halina Zalewska told me about it: "Mieczysław Strzelecki first took Szlapak's valuables and then shot him in his own bed."

When I was in Radziłów with Jan Skrodzki this time, we looked over Szlapak's old house on the Radziłów marketplace. Made of logs, it stands unaltered to this day, slightly sagging, and not so grand for a wealthy merchant.

It is occupied by Stanisław Mordasiewicz. This is the man whom Stanisław Ramotowski kept telling me I shouldn't confuse with the family of the killers Mordasiewicz, because he's such a decent guy. He must have distinguished himself among the local population before the war, because when Wolf Szlapak's brother turned up in town after 1945 (he survived because he had been deported to the Soviet Union) he offered Mordasiewicz the purchase of Wolf's house at a knockdown price.

Stanisław Mordasiewicz knew Szlapak's killers had buried him in his own yard. He dug up the remains. He wrapped them in a sheet, laid them on his wagon, and buried them in the Jewish cemetery. He told no one about it, because he wouldn't have survived in the town.

13

The Dreams of Chaja Finkelsztejn

or, The Survival of a Radziłów Miller's Family

The Polish residents of Radziłów and the Germans are rounding up the Jews, forming them into a double column that stretches the entire length of the street from the Beit Midrasz to the church. They beat them with poles and the butts of rifles. The Finkelsztejn family—Chaja; her husband, Izrael; and their children, Menaszka, Szlomko, Szejne, and Chana—quietly leave their house to hide from their persecutors. They slip away as if they were invisible. But they see the Germans and Poles yanking out the beards of Jews, laughing till their sides split. The family steals past walls of houses plastered with caricatures of Jews from *Der Stürmer.* But the houses end and the fleeing family can no longer take refuge behind walls. They stand by the fence of the churchyard. In desperation they decide to hide there. Chaja unlatches the iron gate and . . . wakes up.

This is the first of the prophetic dreams that would accompany Chaja Finkelsztejn until the end of the war, guiding her steps, giving her strength and raising her spirits.

The Finkelsztejns were among the wealthiest families in town. Chaja's husband was a miller. They knew the local peasants, who brought them their grain for milling. They took care to maintain neighborly relations; Izrael added flour to the scale, threw in little presents for the peasants' children.

Wedding photograph
of Chaja and Izrael
Finkelsztejn.
Radziłów, 1921.
(Courtesy of Jose
Gutstein,
www.radzilow.com)

Chana, the fourth and
youngest child of Chaja and
Izrael Finkelsztejn. Radziłów,
1937 or 1938. (Courtesy of Jose
Gutstein, www.radzilow.com)

Their mill stood by the road leading out of Radziłów toward Jedwabne. When the Soviets arrived, they requisitioned the mill and shortly after they threw the owners out. "A compassionate Christian," as Chaja recalled in the memoir she wrote right after the war, rented them a place to live. With heavy hearts they burned their archive of Zionist activity, dating from 1917. The Soviets took repressive action against Chaja and Izrael on two counts: because they were seen as "bourgeois elements" and as Zionists. Izrael was repeatedly brought in for interrogation. Every night they trembled in fear of deportation. Chaja prepared for that eventuality, buying reams of cloth in the knowledge that money might lose its value from one day to the next, but cloth would always be ready currency. They managed to avoid deportation thanks to Chaja's efficiency in bribing Soviet officials. They got their house back, albeit with a policeman as a lodger. They watched through the windows how the new managers of the mill settled in, among them the tailor Lejzor Zandler, a Communist sympathizer before the war, and the Pole Malinowicz.

When Chaja proposed that a Jewish refugee from Krynki tutor her children, the man exclaimed, "Am I dreaming? So there are still Jews who feel the need to learn Hebrew and the Talmud?" They studied in secret, with the shutters closed.

On Yom Kippur 1940 her husband, employed as a manual laborer at what used to be his own mill, moved the hands of the clock forward two hours and in that way made it to evening prayers. The Jews prayed in the Beit Midrasz, because the Soviets had turned the synagogue into a storehouse. In January 1941, on the anniversary of the mill's nationalization, it held a celebration called "A Year Without Property Owners." "After that a few old Christian workers of ours came to us," Chaja wrote. "They told us it had started with long speeches about what happiness the Communists had brought the workers by getting rid of the proprietors, who were drinking their blood. They had cursed us. Lejzor Zandler had spouted all kinds of slander and filth about us. Someone from our own family had joined in. We'd brought him up, taught him his trade, and he chose a new path following false prophets. I pointed out to him once that he should remember his past, that he had been an instructor preparing Jews for departure to Palestine, and that he was wrong about Communism, that Communism wasn't going to liberate the Jews, that as soon as the wind turned the Russians themselves, our old *pogromchiks*, would spill Jewish blood. 'A state of Israel is our only hope,' I explained to him. And he joked, 'Maybe you want a blue-and-white flag with a star on it? If you don't shut up, you'll end up in the Gulag in Arkhangelsk.'"

In June 1941 they were warned that a deportation was imminent and that they were on the list. But that very night the Russian-German war broke out.

Franciszek Rogowski, a wealthy peasant from Trzaski, four kilometers from Radziłów, came to see them immediately. "He belonged to the gentry, his brother a doctor, another a priest, the three others were still students. He managed the farm with his father and one of his brothers. He wanted to show his sympathy. We asked him to hide our belongings. First he was scared, then he agreed. He suggested he could take our cow, too. If the need arose, we could hide with him. But he'd only hide our family, and he'd only do it in such a way that none of the neighbors saw us arrive."

They transported to Trzaski the baskets and suitcases they'd already packed, which took up an entire shed at the farm. But when they went to the Rogowskis after the German invasion to sit out the first days of the German occupation, they were not welcome: "We read from their faces that they were more interested in our belongings. Their eldest son, with feigned kindness, invited us to sit down and told his mother to give us bread and milk. That woman, who once had been as friendly to us as the rest of the family, had changed her attitude. She hardly said anything. She frostily invited us to the table. We were not overwhelmed by the honor. I told the children to eat something. But they felt the chill, too. Our little boy fell asleep, exhausted, and when he woke up he started to cry for us to leave because they were going to kill us. He saw in them a readiness to kill in order to have our things."

The next day Chaja decided to go home, because she was worried about the ducks and geese left on the farm. She put on her shoes, tied a scarf around her head, and, pretending to be a village woman, set off for the town. She stood amid the crowd of onlookers when the inhabitants of Radziłów enthusiastically greeted the invading Germans. "I remembered how they'd entered Radziłów in 1915," she later wrote. "The same pride, the same heads held high. But how did they look in 1918 as prisoners of war? They were beaten by peasants armed with poles. I prayed for the day when they would be on the run again. I was sure it would come, but would we live to see it?"

When she was reunited with her family, it turned out her worried husband had gone looking for her. He returned shaken. He had barely escaped a peasant who had come at him with a knife crying, "It's because of you Jews they're going to send me to Siberia." He owed his escape to a ruse: he had intentionally dropped his jacket, knowing the peasant would stop to pick it up to see if there was any money in it . . .

They heard the Poles had given the order that no goods were to be sold to Jews, and no one was to give them shelter. And that everything had calmed down in town, so the Finkelsztejns could go home. Their house was already occupied by German officers, but the Germans gave back part of the house. In *Der Stürmer*, the German rag they found lying about the house, they read that Britain had proposed to create two states in the territory of Palestine: Israel for the Jews, and Arabia for the Arabs. For a moment they felt happy.

On June 27, the Germans stationed at the Finkelsztejns' left Radziłów along with the rest of the troops. Chaja writes: "I realized that it was almost Shabbat and I needed to get something ready for Saturday. I had a goose hidden away, the rest of the poultry had been stolen. I brought it to the *shokhet* through the back lanes. He was sick in bed, he hadn't recovered from the profanation of the holy books from the temple. His own place had been looted and trashed by Christians he knew. His daughter, who was a friend of mine, told me in tears that she'd tried to resist them but they'd hit her, yelling: 'Stupid Jewish cow, what's the difference, who's going to keep it safe for you?'"

That was the second day in a row that the Poles of Radziłów and the German soldiers had preyed on the Jews, beating them up, making them burn holy Torah scrolls. Four-horse carts draped with camouflage nets drew up right by the Finkelsztejns' house. From the window Chaja saw some Germans in camouflage jumping off them. "The peasants and their wives, young and old, ran out to greet the Germans, happy they were driving the Soviets out. The Poles pointed out to the Germans which houses in town belonged to Jews."

Dozens of them burst in, both Germans and Poles. Henryk Dziekoński led the way. "I called out to him by name," wrote Chaja. "I knew

him, he'd been at our house many times. His father was a policeman be-
fore the war, and he himself worked at the post office at the time of the
Soviet occupation. I asked him what he had against us. He replied that all
Jews were the same: 'No one took pity on us when we were deported to
Siberia, and nobody's going to pity you, either.'"

They threw everything from the shelves and sideboards on the floor,
trampled things with their boots, broke china, poured food out and sprinkled gasoline on it, broke windows. "In a sadistic frenzy they smashed
the chandelier with rubber clubs. They ran around the house, searching
the rooms. They carried out the loot to the mob of peasants standing in
front of the house. Their wild cries of 'Jude' were deafening," we learn
from reading Chaja, who threw herself at the attackers to help her husband get away. She heard them shoot at him, and she didn't know if he'd
been hit, if he'd made it through alive.

They beat the children, and Chaja defended them like a lioness, kicking and biting the attackers, taking most of the blows herself. She broke
through to the cellar, where one of the intruders was trying to rape her
daughter Szejna, and tore her from his grasp. By the time midnight
struck, the house had emptied out, but Chaja, the most heavily wounded
of the family, was covered in blood. She stood at the window, waiting for
dawn to go look for her husband. She fell asleep on her feet and it was
then that she had the dream about all the Radziłów Jews being herded
into one place.

"I understood that this was a sign and that we had to find a place to
hide," she wrote. "My body was black and blue all over, my head was covered with open wounds, but my brain worked coldly, trying to find a solution. I had no faith in the priest's human feelings. Yet, perhaps in spite of
everything, we should look for help there, at the source of all the poison
and the most bitter venom?" Izrael returned unhurt at dawn, and with
her energy renewed, Chaja, ignoring her wounds, went around, trying to
find some guarantee of safety for her family amid a hostile community.

Chaja decided to take the bull by the horns and go straight to those
responsible for the pogrom. She wanted to ask them: "Why?" Ask them
to restrain the locals from tormenting Jews, ask them not to help the
Germans. She started with Mordasiewicz, both of whose sons had been
taking part in the harassment of Jews. He told her they only did what
they were ordered to do from higher up, and that he couldn't help her.

"If that's the case, Mr. Mordasiewicz," Chaja replied, "please advise me who I should see." He mentioned the prewar village head Stanisław Grzymkowski. Chaja went to see him immediately. "He covered over his scowl at seeing me with a polite smile," she related. "He was pacing the room. Every time he passed the sideboard he'd cut a little slice of bread, put slabs of pork fat on it, and calmly eat it. He listened to my story without out a shadow of compassion. He must have known about the attack, maybe he'd even given the order. I asked him: 'Why was this done to us? Can anyone reproach us with being friends of the Communists? Do you know how we have suffered at their hands, more than our Polish neighbors?'"

After hearing that remark he softened a bit and sent her to the medic Mazurek, because—as he claimed—"his rank is higher, his word has more weight."

Mazurek, whose son was one of those attacking Jews at night, complained about all the work he had dressing the wounds of Jews. He couldn't see any way to help, and suggested she go to the priest. So she went where her dream told her to go.

In the presbytery she saw the copper pots Jews used for laundry, which must have arrived there as loot. She showed the priest her head injuries, her swollen face, the bruises showing from under her neckline, and said her whole body looked like that. She explained, "As their spiritual father, you should tell them from the pulpit that they shouldn't help the Germans because it besmirches the good name of Poles, and the Germans alone do plenty of harm to the Jews." The priest responded nervously that he wouldn't say a good word about the Jews: "Though I'm a big man"—he was tall and fat—"I would become small to my congregation. I'm not sure they wouldn't kill me on the spot. They might regret it later, but in the heat of the moment they could kill me, that's how great their hatred is of the Jews. Every Jew between twelve and sixty years old is a Communist." Chaja tried to explain that those among the Jews who were rotten had run away with the Red Army and the Jews who had stayed behind were innocent, but the priest insisted that all Jews were Communists.

Chaja had an extraordinary instinct for negotiation and great intuition about people. "You may not accept my guarantee for all the Jewish people, but you have to accept it for my family," she told the priest. "I'm positive there aren't any Communists with us." And the priest admitted the Finkelsztejns were decent people and praised their children for refusing to wear Communist red scarves in school. He advised her to sit out the worst of what was to come in the countryside. He promised, "I can't help you directly, but I will help indirectly." Her memoir tells us that the priest's promise did in fact ensure them a few days of safety.

Chaja also goes to see a friendly Zionist, Wolf Szlapak. "Szlapak was in touch with the leader of the local group of nationalists, who assured us we didn't have to worry about our house or belongings. He didn't know we'd been attacked the night before. He was surprised I'd gone to the priest for help. 'He's an anti-Semite. We think he was leading the killers.' 'That's why I went there,' I replied."

The idea came up that Szlapak might try to negotiate in the name of the whole Jewish community and organize a collection of money and valuables to buy their security.

That Saturday the woman housekeeper who worked at the Finkelsztejns' didn't turn up for work, and for the first time in her life, Chaja broke the Sabbath and lit the fire herself to warm up soup for her children's Shabbat dinner. She went to see her sister-in-law to get a meal to warm up. "When she found out I'd lit the fire myself, her jaw dropped. She began accusing me of being one of those who brought all these misfortunes on the Jews. I replied that a threat to one's life supercedes the sanctity of the Sabbath. And that if I had to I'd light the fire in the kitchen every Saturday. I still see her face, full of anger. She couldn't forgive me. But the children were pleased to have had a hot meal. I was sure I'd acted for the best."

In the evening she sent her son Menachem to Szlapak. It turned out the thugs had got into his house, too, had dragged out the women who were hiding there and beat them, and warned Szlapak that only he and his family were under protection. The Jews nevertheless decided to continue gathering money and jewelry. "It wasn't easy, because it was dangerous even to cross the street," Chaja commented. "But the news that we'd talked to the gang leaders got around fast and people believed it offered some hope."

When Chaja had put her children to bed at night, she sat by the window with her husband to watch for any thugs approaching. There was no point in bolting the door, as the windows had already been broken. All night they heard screams from the neighboring houses. In the morning Dziekoński turned up. "He'd come to apologize. He said he'd been drunk.

We could see someone had sent him to humble himself before us." The following night, when they sat listening to the screaming again, some thug came up to the window and shouted, "Go to bed! Nothing bad will happen to you!"

Meanwhile, people carried household equipment, bedclothes, clothing, silver, and china over to Szlapak's house, and the room designated for the ransom was almost completely full. Then thugs broke in, stole everything, and beat up Szlapak. "His wife said he was bleeding, his lungs were injured. She asked me to look at him. I didn't feel I had it in me but I couldn't refuse. I pulled myself together and went in to see a man who'd believed the killers would respect him enough to make a deal with him. I went through the dining room where his children and the children of refugees and neighbors were sitting, all of them sweet as flowers and so sad. Szlapak lay all bandaged up, his blackened face looking out from under the compresses. I left in silence, for I could find no words of solace."

Days and nights passed, and the thugs went from house to house beating, looting, raping, but they stayed away from the Finkelsztejns' house. Chaja and her husband fought off sleep, keeping vigil by the beds of their sleeping children.

One time Chaja dozed off for a minute and dreamed that the killers had burst into the house and stolen everything. In her dream she was angry she hadn't poured out the bottle of cognac, she'd only buried it, and now it might fall into the hands of the murderers. "I ran to the cellar, and there was a broken bottle, and forget-me-nots, blue with yellow hearts, had sprung up in the place where the cognac had spilled." Chaja told a Jewish neighbor about the dream and heard from her that flowers were a good omen. On the other hand, it wasn't good that the flowers were all growing in the same spot. She decided to be vigilant and prepared to flee the town.

On Sunday, July 6, the Polish caretaker who had looked after their mill before the war came to see them. She informed them that a lot of peasants had come from Wąsosz to help the Radziłówians kill their Jews. She wanted to take the Finkelsztejns' belongings before others turned up ("It's better if I have them than if others do," she explained). A moment later the wife of a Jewish accountant from Wąsosz who'd worked for them before the war burst in with a small child. "Her face was wild. She asked for a piece of bread. The killers had told her that her whole family in Wąsosz had been slaughtered like calves. They mentioned the names of her murdered sisters and brothers. In a wild voice she cried: 'Run! Run away!'"

Chaja dressed the children, and they sneaked off to the Rogowskis in Trzaski, who were afraid to let them in the house. They allowed them to sleep in their field. At dawn the Finkelsztejns returned home. But soon the news reached them that the Gestapo had arrived and ordered the Jews to weed the marketplace, and the Finkelsztejns were driven from their home by their Polish neighbors. It was the morning of July 7, 1941.

The order didn't include children but some zealots rounded up whole families. Chaja's memoir allows us not only to reconstruct in detail the course of the atrocity, but also to see it through her eyes.

They stood in the heat of the sun, surrounded by a thick wall of neighbors who were making sure no one escaped. Some Jews were beaten and bleeding: the ones who wouldn't go to the marketplace voluntarily. Mothers stood holding their children, others worried what would happen to the little ones they had left at home. All were worn out by two weeks of nightmares and hunger, for the boycott was effective and they were unable to buy anything from Poles, while the food they'd stored up was looted by the gangs rampaging in the night. The Gestapo and Poles beat whomever they pleased, they tortured people, tore out the beards of old Jews. Many Jews quietly prayed—one heard the soft murmur of the prayer *Sh'ma Israel*.

"What's going to happen now, Chaja?" a woman friend asked her.

"Death is certain," she answered. "Only how will it come?"

And suddenly, unexpectedly, hope returned. The Gestapo got into their cars and drove off.

A minute later a peasant whom the Finkelsztejns had hired as a thresher before the war led the family out of the marketplace, where they were weeding along with the other Jews, and let them get away. Chaja doesn't mention how it came to be that he saved them and protected them from the other Poles. The priest's safe conduct was certainly not enough; she must have paid the peasant off. On the way they were stopped by the living wall of people, but it parted when someone shouted, "Let them through. They go free."

They saw Jewish children wandering around in search of their parents.

The two youngest children they'd left at home, Szejna and Chana, were soothing other weeping kids. Szejna's schoolmates ran up to the window, shouting, "Do you know what's happening with the Jews? They're going to burn them in a barn." Szejna burst into tears, but her parents wouldn't believe it. They were just barricading themselves inside the house when a gang of boys burst in, led by their laundress's son. The boys led them out of the house, and when Chaja wanted to lock the door, they tried to get the keys from her, because "she wouldn't need them anymore." She explained that they'd been set free, but they wouldn't listen. But when they saw the smoke, the attackers told them they were lucky and could go back home.

Their return startled the neighbors, who were already carrying their belongings out of the house. Chaja told them to take what they wanted and the whole family, including Chaja's niece, left town. They met a group of peasant women who burst into tears and wrung their hands over their misfortune. Suddenly a peasant they knew and had hired once to dig peat shouted, "Into the wheat! Hide!" A man on horseback was coming down the road. They heard him say that all the Jews had been burned and only the miller had escaped with his family; he was looking for them. He asked the peasant if he'd seen them and the man said he hadn't. The smell of burned hair and clothing and charred bodies was just reaching them.

In the village of Konopki, far from the main roads, Izrael saw a peasant woman he knew and called her name. She was terrified, because she'd heard that no Jew had survived, and since she believed the souls of Jews were damned, she thought the miller's soul had turned up at her doorstep. They went to find the village head Bolesław Zawadzki, who was happy to see them. "I felt so sorry for you," he said to Izrael. "I was a *predsiedatel* [chairman] under the Soviets and I'm in a difficult situation, but if you converted to our faith, maybe we could manage to persuade somebody." He sent for his brother-in-law and neighbors. As they were wondering about how to hide the family, a peasant woman from Radziłów who'd married in Konopki, a sister of the killer Mieczysław Strzelecki, came by. She had been a school friend of Chaja's niece and Chaja's brother had given his things to her parents for safekeeping. "Something evil flared up in her eyes," wrote Chaja. "My niece understood at once, and said: 'Zosia, I don't need those things, I won't take them from you.' And the woman said: 'Yes, why bother? They'll find you and kill you anyway.'"

The village head's brother told them that Jews who had hidden were being dragged out of various shelters, doused with gasoline, and set afire or shot near the barn. He had gone to Radziłów with his cart to salvage something of their belongings, but the townspeople wouldn't let him in. "As it later turned out he was a good man," Chaja wrote. "But the hatred of Jews was so great that nothing surprised him. He told us the story matter-of-factly."

Marian Kozikowski, who had pulled them out of the marketplace, turned up at the village head's house. He was furious when he saw Chaja's niece there. He shouted that only Chaja's immediate family had the "right" to be saved. "You could see from the fury in his eyes what terrible acts he'd performed," she wrote. He bragged that he'd cut the throats of thirty Jews and started sharpening a knife in the kitchen, screaming, "I'll have to cut her throat, too." Only the village head's resistance and the women weeping put him off the idea.

Chaja found out from Poles she knew what had happened to the Szlapak family. The brutalized Wolf Szlapak didn't go to the marketplace. "Mieczysław Strzelecki, who'd worked for Szlapak as a driver, murdered him and his seven-year-old son in bed. He buried their bodies in a pit by the garbage dump behind their house. His sick mother was dragged out of bed, thrown on a cart, and the horse driven into a gallop. She couldn't hold on, fell under the wheels, her nightdress got snagged on something, and she was dragged over the paving stones until there was nothing left of her but bloody stumps of legs."

On July 10 the Finkelsztejns saw the glow of a fire on the horizon. It was the burning barn in Jedwabne filled with Jews. Later they heard that there was killing going on all over the area, in Grajewo, Stawiski, Łomża, Kolno, Szczuczyn, and anywhere there was a Jew to be found.

The villagers rushed to see who had been killed. Then they reported who they'd recognized, who had been burned, who had suffocated, and who had only singed hair. They said that small children were untouched by the fire, because their mothers had shielded them with their own bodies. You could find out about almost every Jew killed in town. How he had behaved in the face of death, whether he'd begged for mercy or only prayed. They said the butcher's wife had been killed, even though she tried to convince the killers that she understood that the Jewish God had forsaken them and that she would run to the church to ask the priest to baptize her. A bricklayer who'd worked for the Finkelsztejns before the war and who after completing the work had raised a toast to the Jews who gave Poles work, told them that he had witnessed the death of Chaja's brother. He explained, "One word from me and he would have been spared, but I thought: His whole family was killed, why would he want to live?"

Peasants from Trzaski went to the priest in Radziłów and told him the Finkelsztejn family wanted to become Catholics. "The priest told us to send our children to religious instruction with the Polish children. After the first class they came home. They'd recognized Jewish clothes on their classmates. When the priest praised their progress, even people who'd been our enemies before began to visit us in the village. The conversations were always about the same thing: who looted how much and how rich the Jews were. They said Szlapak had a whole room full of all kinds of goods, that they took a box of silver cutlery from there for the priest along with other things his housekeeper could use. The killers boasted of their heroism, describing how the Jews screamed, how they'd tormented the girls, they imitated the grimaces of the victims," Chaja wrote, summarizing the tales she was subjected to in the village.

Chaja recognized her own belongings, too, but she never let on. One peasant woman from Trzaski complained to her that the Radziłówians wouldn't give the peasants Jewish clothes because they hadn't been there during the killing, trying to draw her into an argument about who should receive the victims' property. The woman said, "I see it differently. We didn't kill, so we should get what belonged to the Jews. We deserve it more."

They lived in Konopki and worked in the fields. "Our hosts talked to us all the time about how wonderful it was that we were converting to Catholicism. Because of it we could go to heaven, unlike the other Jews who would turn to dust. And we would see the light that Jews couldn't see. They told us about a Jew named Dawid who constantly asked the time, though he was looking at the sun. 'Because the Jews crucified Christ and that's why darkness fell on them and why they saw darkness at midday.' We felt we were choking on those words."

It shows in the Radziłów parish records that a baptism took place on the morning of July 21. The Finkelsztejns came to town with a large entourage. Chaja received the name Anna; Izrael—Bolesław. Menachem became Józek; Szejna—Marysia; Szlomo—Janek; and Chana—Jadzia. The same morning the fifty-year-old Bolesław was married to the forty-seven-year-old Anna in accordance with Catholic rites.

An anti-Semitic booklet distributed to villages fell into their hands. In it they read the story of a monk who heard a child weeping in church every Friday. One day he hid behind the pulpit and saw the priest with the host in one hand and a needle in the other. He was pricking the host, blood was spouting from the host, and a child's sobbing was heard. The priest was arrested and turned out to be of Jewish origin. "We understood that the point of that booklet being distributed in the village was to prevent those fanatically pious and primitive villagers from helping us," wrote Chaja. "But they went on taking care of us. They probably thought we had great riches."

They lived in Konopki until the autumn of 1942. Chaja doesn't mention it, but until that point they must have been officially hired from the Germans by their host (the Germans "rented out" Jews for unpaid farm labor to the Poles), and they actually met the payments themselves. In November 1942, when the ghetto was liquidated, the village head informed them they should pack their things, because they were to be delivered to the military police station. They persuaded him to let them go into hiding. Later they heard stories about the peasants being told to bring their wagons to transport the Jews to the Bogusze estate—the last stop for the Jews of Radziłów before Treblinka.

One peasant woman told them she couldn't watch what people were doing to the Jews, how women took bundles and warm clothes away from the Jewish women and even ripped their dresses. She confessed that she herself had taken a Torah and other holy books from the rabbi's house after the burning of the Jews, because she'd heard there were dollars hidden in them, but she hadn't found anything.

The Finkelsztejns hid in the village of Dusze, where they were found by Radziłów thugs, herded onto a wagon, and taken to the police. They managed to leave the eight-year-old Chana with the family that had sheltered them. Money was effective in dealing with the Germans, and the priest's intervention took care of the thugs. When the Finkelsztejns got back, their things had already been divided up and their little daughter had been handed over to a murderer with whom the host family had had a quarrel about the fact that they were keeping Jews. They found their daughter, but their things were gone. From then on they were on the run, moving between neighboring villages: Trzaski, Konopki, Dusze, and Kubra.

They changed hiding places frequently, never telling anyone whose house they had come from or whose they were going to, so that the people who hid them didn't know about one another. They were afraid because they thought they were the only surviving witnesses to the massacre. Many of the farmers distilled vodka, and when the villages celebrated, the family trembled in fear of some drunk betraying them. And it did happen that the tipsy village head quarreled with their host about having kept them too long. The village head said the war was going to be over soon and because of the Jews the farmer would get excessively rich. He yelled that the Finkelsztejns had to go, otherwise he'd give them up to the Germans. When he'd sobered up he came by to apologize.

There were a few Jews in the area—sometimes they'd come to the window and ask for bread. Some Poles threw stones at them, then captured them and handed them over to the police for a kilo of sugar. One of the farmers who hid the Finkelsztejns told them—without comment—that one village head gave a Jew up to the police, who sat him on the hot stove and asked who had hidden him, and later let their dogs loose on him. But the Finkelsztejns themselves were always told that the priest asked after them and reminded people to help the miller's baptized family.

Once, they heard one man who hid them asking a farmhand to leave him his hammer: "You took so much from the Jews, you didn't have anything in your workshop before, and now you, your father, your brother, have all this equipment." And the man replied, "The priest told us that it's for our work, our blood that the Jews sucked." At another house, Chaja listened to a farmer's mother saying, "It's right that this came down on the Jews, because they killed Christ. They've made ghettos for Jews in America by now, too." The Finkelsztejns couldn't react.

One night Chaja dreamed she was walking down the street in Radziłów and met an acquaintance, Wiśka Dubin, running from the street where everyone was burned, and saying, "Chaja, we have our revenge." Two days later they read in the newspaper that the Germans had been defeated at Stalingrad. By night Chaja dreamed of the Germans' defeat, by day she dreamed of Palestine.

People were saying with increasing frequency that the war was almost over, but policemen also came to villages more and more often to do house searches at night. "Many young men hid," Chaja wrote, "but they only hid when the police came near. Otherwise they were marching around the village, singing drunken songs about the fall of Warsaw."

It was increasingly difficult to find a place to hide. "The farmers said they didn't want to die at the end of the war because of us." They had to split up because no one wanted to risk hiding such a large family. "We decided to hide our two youngest daughters in a good place far away from us, because we might not survive together. I taught them the history of the Jews. I talked to them about the Spanish Inquisition, the Marranos, Spinoza, the places where there had been pogroms: Pińsk, Kishinev, Białystok, Przytyk, Radziłów, and the history of Zionism. I kept telling them: 'When you're safe, don't believe what the murderers say, that there are no Jews left on earth. There are sure to be Jews somewhere, and you should find them and ask them to send you to Palestine.' "

In the spring of 1944 they heard Franciszek Rogowski had died. He was the man with whom they'd kept their things and where they'd gone to retrieve them one by one. "Such a disaster. He was a decent man, but his wife was a real lowlife and their children were under her influence. While he was alive, she couldn't do anything." Izrael went there with one of the children when the Finkelsztejns no longer had anything to live on. "They said that there had been a search for our things, that they'd had to bury them, that they were spied on because of us. My husband left with empty hands. Not a minute went by before Rogowski's eldest son came out to watch where he was going. None of us went back there again."

Chaja goes on to remember Franciszek Rogowski's wife bumping into them later in Dusze, at the Karwowskis': "She took our hostess aside. Karwowska came back pale. But I told her: 'Mrs. Karwowski, you knew where we lived, everything we had, the divans, velvet curtains, clothes, the things we had stored up for bad times, we gave all of it to them for safekeeping, and when her husband died, they wouldn't give it back to us. They would have flung us into the arms of death in order to keep it all.' I began to cry and she wept with me." It was a real relief for the Finkelsztejns to stay with the Karwowskis at Christmas 1943. They could stay as long as the farmhand had off. "The head of the household received us warmly, like an old friend. He gave us a place to sleep in the granary. In the morning he brought us hot milk. With tears in his eyes, he assured us the war was almost over. He talked about the horrible things done in the surrounding villages by people he never would have thought capable of such things. There was another wealthy man in Dusze, his wife and Mrs. Karwowski spent time with us, comforting us. That week gave us strength to keep going."

They changed their hiding place more than fifty times. They lived in filth, in stifling spaces, in fear. From time to time at night Chaja would sneak into a cottage to boil their clothes in a pot. The children told one another riddles in Hebrew and dreamed of a deck of cards. Chaja's son Menachem found cards they used to make a deck. They played Sixty-six, Clobyosh, Thousand. "That village had a group of partisans," Chaja wrote, "they got underground newspapers but not one of them could read, so the village Home Army commander who knew where we were hiding came to us, stood by the trough, and Menachem read the news to him."

One day Chaja dreamed that she was wandering in the fields looking for a hiding place. She spotted someone on a bicycle. She recognized Marian Kozikowski, the killer who had led her and her family out of the marketplace. He said, "Come to me, I have a good place for you." She woke up and realized Kozikowski was far from home, doing labor in Germany. No one in the family objected when she proposed they set out for Konopki, to Kozikowski's wife.

After much pleading and the promise of payment, Kozikowska agreed to give them a spot in the attic of her barn. But only for two people: Chaja and Menachem. They brought Chana in secretly and managed there for five months. Izrael visited them in despair with their daughter Szejna; they didn't know what to do with themselves, they had hidden in so many places in the course of a few days, and they hadn't eaten for several days. But Chaja and the two children had nothing, either. She saw her husband looking like an old man of eighty, wrinkled, with dull eyes. Szejna, then fifteen, consoled everyone, saying they'd find another shelter, they'd live out their lives among Jews in clean beds.

"Our hostess Marianka made sure we had nothing to protect us from the cold. She wanted it to look as if we'd just arrived and she'd known nothing about it. She told us it wasn't worth the sweat, that we wouldn't survive anyway; she heard the peasants talking and knew that as soon as we came out of hiding, they'd kill us. And we went on saying that we'd reward those who helped us. Marianka's mother-in-law bemoaned the fact that her son had been taken by the Germans. She said: 'I don't know if I'll ever see him again, he has grave sins on his conscience, he killed Jews, but only after the whole village urged him on.' To console her, I told her that he had saved our family from the flames and that that would be in his favor, and that he would survive. And he did."

When the family could find no shelter in the winter of 1944 they went to the Rogowskis'. "They led us to the hiding place. They already had one prepared because they were hiding food from the Germans. It was very cold there. At night there was a blizzard and snow came through the cracks. They brought us hot food. Once we went to their kitchen, the women were spinning, they had compassion for us. It was the first time in three years we were in a room. The son said it was terrible what had been done to the Jews. But the mother said since we'd been there she hadn't been able to sleep. The village head knew about us and wanted us to leave the village. He told people at meetings they shouldn't hide Jews, because they could get killed. We stayed with them until they told us to leave."

By now, the first Soviet planes could be seen in the sky. They counted the days to the German defeat. Chaja's next dream gave them new psychic strength: a Zionist meeting, everyone is leaving, and the family wants to leave, too, but the doors are locked. Then Wolf Szlapak comes to tell them to wait quietly until he brings them the keys. They considered it an omen that their family friend Szlapak had come from the other world to help them.

Meanwhile, the next cataclysm was at hand. The inhabitants of Radziłów and its environs were given the order to evacuate, because the front line was moving in their direction. The Finkelsztejns remained behind in the abandoned village, in a cramped shelter under the threshing floor, which was filling with water. There Chaja suffered bouts of claustrophobia, feeling as if they'd been buried alive. Their host had left them two half-baked loaves of bread and a rusty water pot and told them where the rutabagas were kept. They ate moldy bread, nibbled on frozen rutabagas, and drank water red with rust. Chana cried with hunger; Menachem said he wanted only to live long enough to eat his belly full. All of them asked, "Will we ever sit in a warm room watching rain and snow fall outside?" Chaja told them they would survive and make it to Eretz Israel.

When Menachem got a hand infection and fainted from fever, she dreamed the war was over and her son was chosen as a delegate to a

Zionist congress. Hope returned to her. She saved her son by putting a tourniquet above the elbow and applying cold compresses day and night for several days.

When the front line moved, the Finkelsztejns made their way to the Karwowskis' in Konopki, where they'd spent Christmas the year before. "I won't throw you out," Karwowska promised. They encountered kindness more rarely than a hunger for profit. "We found a human heart, that was rare. Before that it was as if I had been turned to stone." When it got too dangerous they moved on, but they left the emaciated Chana at the Karwowskis'.

In January 1945 they found their next and last shelter with the Klimaszewski family. Zosia, the sixteen-year-old daughter, who showed them much compassion, was ill with typhus. Chaja describes how Zosia's mother refused to take her to the hospital despite her pleas, because it would have meant giving up her own down blanket. And she was worried that since she hadn't yet buried any of her children they didn't have an angel in heaven to wait for her. She greeted her daughter's death with relief.

They came out of hiding as soon as the Soviets appeared on January 22, 1945. The Konopki village head warned them to stay in hiding, telling them that the previous day father and son Dorogoj had been murdered. But the Finkelsztejns set off for Knyszyn, and from there to Białystok. "The few Jews who survived were attacked," Chaja wrote. "There was a count of seventy Jews from the area killed on the roads and in villages. In Białystok it was dangerous, too, you couldn't go out at night. A gang attacked a house near us where Jewish bakers lived. They beat them and told them to stop baking or they would be killed. A Jewish woman was shot in broad daylight in front of the door of the shop she was opening. We were sitting on hot coals." Once, when someone knocked on their door at night, they barricaded themselves in. In the morning it turned out it had been the militia. They were furious, shouting, "Pity Hitler didn't finish you off. We're going to rip you to shreds, we're not protecting you."

The children went to school in Białystok. When Széjna first said her surname, the whole class burst out laughing. The teacher hushed the kids and spoke about equality. Chaja found her children a Hebrew teacher. They left for Łódź, where Menachem became director of a school preparing Jews for life on a kibbutz. The dream of Palestine was about to be fulfilled.

They left Poland with Greek repatriation papers. They traveled the road covered by many Jews trying to reach the Promised Land after the Holocaust: false papers, an expedition crossing borders illegally, moving between transit camps, their ship arrested when they could already see the lights of Haifa, internment in a camp on Cyprus. By 1947 they were all in Palestine. Szlomo was eager to join the army, though he wasn't yet sixteen. He said, "Mama, remember how many times we dreamed of fighting the enemy? And now you tell me to wait until they call me up. Do you want someone else to die in my place?"

Izaak Lewin of Wizna, who survived the war in hiding with his parents in a village halfway between Wizna and Radziłów and met Szlomo in a camp in the Italian town of Selvino, told me about him: "Szlomo was more of a hero than I was. He lived on ideals. I stuck with the other boys from our camp, but he took off to join the Palmach, the elite unit of the underground Jewish army, right away. They did the most fighting and lost the most men."

"Szlomke came to see us," wrote Chaja. "He had no permit to leave the barracks, but he crawled through the barbed wire because we were nearby. He wanted to see if he'd grown, he compared the marks on the door, and it turned out he had grown by several centimeters. He was hoping he'd get the day off at Passover, it would have been our first Seder together since 1941. But he had to leave at 5 a.m. I called to him 'Szlomke' as he was going..."

This is how Chaja Finkelsztejn concludes her memoir.

Szlomo Finkelsztejn was killed in 1948 near Kiryat Anavim on the way to Jerusalem.

"After our arrival in Palestine," I was told by Chana, now Ann Walters, "our parents became young again for a brief time, they sang Halutz songs after dinner, but after Szlomke died the house was never cheerful again."

Chaja managed to guide her whole family through the hell of the Shoah not just because they were wealthy, and not even because they managed to play the part (as she described it) of pious Christians. They survived thanks to her extraordinary strength of spirit. She managed to inspire her children with that hope, and instilled in them love for a distant country. She later paid the highest price for having succeeded: the death of a son in the name of a country that she had taught him to love.

In 1966 a woman from Yad Vashem came to Chaja in Haifa to record her testimony. "She accused the Poles of having burned the Jews alive," the woman noted. "She was so upset that it was difficult to understand what she was saying. She said she had three hundred sixty pages of memoirs and had waited for years for the chance to publish them."

Not only were Chaja's memoirs never published, but it seems no one even read them during her lifetime.

Journal

It's the third day I take Bożena and Jan Skrodzki along with me on a search for the places where the Finkelsztejns were in hiding. Chaja couldn't have had much hope that anyone from Poland would ever study her memoir. Still, most often she didn't give either the surnames of the killers or the helpers, nor did she mention the names of the villages, so that even a meticulous analysis of the text offers little chance of re-creating their itinerary. But we know that among the villages where the Finkelsztejns hid was Trzaski, where the Borawskis now live.

In Trzaski we manage to find the house of Rogowski, who came to the Finkelsztejns to offer help as soon as the Soviets arrived. Without Chaja's information that one brother was a doctor, another a priest, and three were students we would never have found them, because—as we heard at the Borawskis'—"you can throw a stone at any house here and find yourself face-to-face with a Rogowski."

We talk to the grandson, Leopold, who's about fifty. He lives more in New York than here. He knows his grandfather helped the family of a Radziłów miller. I tell him Chaja described his family in her memoir and mourned the death of his grandfather (it all fits: Franciszek Rogowski died in March 1944). She writes most admiringly of the grandfather, less so of the rest of the family. I suggest I read him only what she says about his grandfather. "No, no, please, read it all," his grandson says. So I also read the excerpts about Franciszek's wife not wanting to return the Finkelsztejns' things to them after her husband died, how she went by the neighbors' to urge them not to store anything for the Finkelsztejns: "They would have flung us into the arms of death in order to keep it all." I feel awkward reading these things, but when I glance at our host I see Chaja's words aren't making too much of an impression on him. When I finish, he asks, "Do you have any Jews in your family? I worked for a Jew in America; he was a decent man. Maybe you can help me find work in New York?"

He tells various stories he's heard about the war without much emotion. "My uncle told me a Jew had warned him he was going to be deported, and later when my uncle went to the barn when it was all over, he saw that Jew, partially burned."

"Just between us Poles," Jan Skrodzki draws him out, "tell me, are you an anti-Semite?"

"I don't like Jews."

"And why is that?"

"They live near me in New York, the kind with curls, religious Jews, and I just don't like the sight of them."

The theme I know so well of God's punishment runs through our conversations. And so there was a shoemaker who was a landlord, and one Pole chased him and helped burn him. The Pole moved into the shoemaker's house, but when he fell asleep in his Jewish featherbed, he didn't wake up the next day. Or the story about the Jewish family Cherubin, whom the Poles dragged out at night, killed, robbed, whose blacksmith workshop they took over, and how they later had abnormal children.

JUNE 17, 2002

We move onward following the route described by Chaja. Far from the highways, we travel along village roads to scattered cottages. Every time I talk to witnesses of the events of sixty years ago it turns out they can confirm almost every detail she mentions. But it isn't until I get to the places where they were in hiding that the memoir written in Yiddish acquires a palpable reality.

Nowadays you don't meet many descendants of the former residents here. In Konopki, where nineteen families lived, only a few of them remain, and many houses are boarded up. Dusze has virtually emptied out. But all who remain remember the miller's family. They don't know their surname or their Jewish names, but they remember Chaja's children Józek, Janek, Marysia, and Jadzia (or, respectively, Menachem, Szlomo, Szejna, and Chana).

Previously when I visited various households where Jews were hidden, the people were nervous and asked how I found them, asked me not to mention their names. In Trzaski, Konopki, and Dusze, hiding Jews became a normal thing during the war, accepted by virtually the whole community, and people now speak of it without fear. Almost everyone we talk to remembers his father, grandfather, or uncle hiding a Jew—as well as the Finkelsztejns, two families hid in these villages, and like the Finkelsztejns, they would spend short periods of time with various host families. Only one of those we talk to brings out *Gross's Lies*, the pamphlet from the series "Know Your Jews," a standard text in nearly every Jedwabne home.

"They converted and lived among us," Franciszek Mroczkowski says. "We had a gramophone in our house, and Marysia came to dance. The Jew tailored a bit, he made me a cap, and he complained it wasn't quite right, the shape, but it suited me. I gave him butter and salt pork for it. And so those Jews were saved. They thought they'd be equal to Poles when they were baptized, but Hitler ordered them to be destroyed and they had to hide in a bunker."

Franciszek Grądzki, the oldest of the residents of Trzaski ("I'm afraid to tell you what year I was born because death is listening in"), remembers Józek or Menachem Finkelsztejn warmly: "He was eighteen. The Jewish boy used to graze a cow with us. A good boy. We gave him a religious pendant and he wore it, but he refused a rosary."

This doesn't mean the sympathy felt toward the family extended to Jews in general. Mroczkowski speaks with pride of his brother, who participated in a pogrom in Radziłów in 1933: "My brother was with the National Party, it was a decent, good organization, close to the church. He joined in the hullaballoo in Radziłów, when a Jew shot at a Pole from a balcony and the Polish police attacked. It was mandatory to turn up on those occasions. They harassed Jews," he says, laughing.

"Were they right to harass them?" I ask.

"Poles weren't doing well. Nowadays a worker will rebel and go on strike. I think right is on the side of the people who aren't doing well, what do you think?"

No one knows what happened to the Radziłów miller's family later. Describing their time in hiding, people access their own memories, but describing their later history they draw deep from anti-Semitic stereotypes: of their riches, their working for the secret police, being part of a conspiracy.

I promised Ann Walters, formerly Chana Finkelsztejn, that I'd find the name of the woman who took her in as her own child and nursed her back to life. From Chaja's memoir I've deduced this woman must have lived in Dusze. I find the house. It's a pretty redbrick structure, unoccupied. The neighbors tell me that during the war Zofia Karwowska lived here. They don't know whether or where any of her descendants are living.

JUNE 25, 2002

In the Dominican church in Służewiec, Father Ryszard Bosakowski meets with students who are going to Jedwabne to clean up the Jewish cemetery. I find the whole group in distress. They had hoped to involve the local youth. Father Bosakowski had had a promising conversation with the lyceum director, but later he couldn't get hold of her. The secretary repeatedly told him that the director was out, until she finally told him to direct all calls to the parish priest. And hung up.

I phone an acquaintance in Jedwabne to ask how it's possible that a school director would refuse a call from a priest. "I know, I know," he replies with an obvious sneer, "you'd like her to become involved in the cleanup of the cemetery, but she'd lose her job within the month."

I hear that Tadeusz Ś., the man with whom Adam Michnik and I first spoke, tells people he had an encounter with "that Jewish bitch Bikont" and that he's learning Hebrew because "you have to know the language of your enemies."

JUNE 29, 2002

Trip to Zabrze. After the publication of one of my articles in the *Gazeta*, I received a letter from Grzegorz Karwowski (another Karwowski, no relation to the others appearing in this book) about how his family, who lived in the Radziłów area, had hidden Jews during the war. When I realized after an exchange of e-mails that one of them must have been

Helena Chrzanowska, then called Sara Fajga Kuberska, now the one baptized Jewish survivor in Jedwabne, I persuaded him to take me along
when he next visited his father, who now lives in Silesia.

We take the train. On the way I tell Karwowski that I meet with such
intense anti-Semitism in his native region that it feels to me almost like
physical aggression. Reflecting on the causes of all the hatred unleashed
by the "Jedwabne affair," I came to the conclusion that the forgotten
atrocity somehow weighs upon the current residents, even on those who
had nothing to do with it, or didn't even live there at the time. Karwowski
has a different hypothesis. He thinks the residents of that poor region of
Poland who travel to America to earn money, most often in the Chicago
area, encounter the rabid anti-Semitism of the Polish community there
and bring it back with them to implant it at home. Perhaps he has a point.
The anti-Semitic leaflets from across the ocean and the words of support
from the Polish community in America were in any case a factor in de-
termining how the town behaved in the period when it became a focus
of media attention.

When we get there I learn that Grzegorz's grandparents hid not only
the future Helena Chrzanowska and her mother, but just before the
Red Army arrived they also gave shelter to "one of the daughters of the
Radziłów miller." Antoni, Grzegorz's father, was nine by then and remembered Chana Finkelsztejn: "She sat by the stove, very polite, without
saying a word." As if he were talking about the Chana I met in Kansas.

Antoni doesn't like all the fuss over Gross's book. From his point of
view, that of a man whose family sheltered Jews, it's harmful to Poland.
Although when we start talking about specifics, he has no doubt about
what happened: "The Germans arrived. Jews entrusted their belongings
to the wealthier farmers, because a Jew would be afraid to trust a poor
man with anything. And that's the worst disgrace, that the farmers who
were entrusted with things by Jews weren't concerned whether or not
those Jews survived. There was terrible looting going on. When they were
burning the Jews, one of my neighbors, Polakowska, went to a Jewish
house and came back with bedclothes. But her husband refused to make
use of them, he told her to throw them all into the road and burn them."

"Helena Chrzanowska's family," he tells me, "hid with us, but also
with Onufry Kosmaczewski and the Klimaszewskis. But you shouldn't
think every family that hid Jews did it for humanitarian reasons. My

parents didn't take advantage as it happens, but right after the war you could tell who had hidden people for money. Dusze, Trzaski, Konopki—all those villages enriched themselves greatly during the war."

I've been trying to reconstruct Helena Chrzanowska's family history for a long time. I knew her parents, the Kuberskis, lived in Kubra before the war—nearer to Radziłów than to Jedwabne. I talked to Janina Karwowska, a retired schoolteacher who lives there and got to know Helena better during the Soviet occupation.

"We got to be friends when we were in the same class," she tells me. "I visited them at home, she had me over for matzo. How clean it was there! Helena's mother had married a smith from Kubra, but she came from Jedwabne. They lived in the village surrounded by Poles. They were well-liked and respected people, who readily helped others."

I know that peasants came for her father on July 7, and took him to the marketplace in Radziłów. Sara, then fifteen, witnessed it. This I heard from Leon Dziedzic. He didn't know where she'd gone into hiding.

Chaja Finkelsztejn's memoir helped me trace what happened to her during the war.

On July 7, 1941, the family with whom the Finkelsztejns were hiding told them that "they caught the smith Ezra from Radziłów and he's dead." The Kuberski family, the mother and four children, survived just as the Finkelsztejns had, and even in the same villages. They were baptized and for as long as possible were hired out to work in Polish households, for which the Germans were paid. Chaja Finkelsztejn met them once at a farmer's she knew. She wrote about them without warmth: "The smith's wife and her two sons and daughter converted to Catholicism, and the priest took them into his protection. Unlike us, they took it seriously, they believed in their new God. The smith's wife would lie awake at night, praying with her rosary. When we saw that it pained our hearts." She explained to Helena's mother that the war wouldn't last forever, that they were Jews, that after the war they could go to America or Palestine. She urged her not to pay attention to her daughter's Christian suitors, because after the war the girl could marry a Jew. Chaja described the future Helena Chrzanowska: "She didn't greet us. She was trying to show that they were real goys, that they were in a better position, even though we used to be rich once. Angrily, she asked her mother whether she'd fed the pigs. Then she repeated to the peasants what I'd said to her mother."

From October 1942, when the Kuberskis got a summons to report to the police station, they had to go into hiding. Helena's mother changed hiding places often with Helena and her younger brother, Icek, moving around the Radziłów area. They were in Chrzanów, Kubra, Doliwy, Trzaski.

Helena's elder brothers got by on their own. "The smith's sons stayed with Poles who were also in hiding from the Germans," Chaja Finkel-sztejn wrote. "I knew they would be betrayed. And sure enough, one of those brothers was sitting in a peasant's cottage when the police passed by. They threw him out of the house. The policemen saw him and shot him, and they picked up the Christian family." Chaja knew about it because news of this spread throughout the area immediately, and the farmer she was hiding with got scared and told her to leave the shelter.

When Jan Skrodzki and I were in Trzaski, we found traces of the blacksmith's family from Kubra. We kept hearing a story about farmers taken to the police station for having hidden Jewish boys. Their neighbors put all their salt pork and sausage together, and after a week they bought off the police, who released the farmers.

"Helena never told me how she survived the war, and I never asked her about it," Janina Karwowska tells me. "As soon as the occupation ended I remember her mother going to church with her and her brother Icek, where they prayed loudly and wept."

Immediately after the war her mother recovered her grandfather Abram Kruk's house, right on the marketplace in Jedwabne, and she moved into it with Icek.

Icek was killed right after the war. I first heard the story from Leszek Dziedzic: "Icek grazed cows in a field near ours, those were fields left by his grandfather Kruk. Friends who were grazing animals with him killed him when they were playing."

Later I heard it again from several of the people I talked to, but without any names.

"They were playing tag and throwing pebbles. He was younger than them but better at it. He won. They started throwing stones at him. He only just managed to get home. Those boys killed him because they'd lost to a Jew. They beat his chest so badly while he lay on his back that the boy lay dying for two days. He was a Catholic and when he felt he was dying in that field he asked them to give him a crucifix that he could kiss. They handed it to him upside down, and he was just conscious enough to turn it over and kiss it. He only just made it home. The mother of one of those young murderers went to the priest to say a Jew couldn't be given a Catholic burial."

I ask Karwowska what she knows about Icek's death.

She was at their house at the time. "He was lying there half-conscious, dying, crying and crying until he passed away. Helena told me one of her brother's pals had hit him on the temple by accident while they were playing."

I tell her Icek was stoned to death by boys from his village and that I've collected several witness statements that confirm it.

"I remember," Janina Karwowska says in astonishment, "Helena said they had no pity, the boys were throwing pebbles and it was all from a little stone like that. Her mother died shortly after that, I think it was the same year."

I recall what Antonina Wyrzykowska told me once. She knew Helena Chrzanowska well, they used to visit each other. Helena wrote to her in America: "If I'd known what kind of a life I'd have, it would have seemed a shame to save it."

Now I ask Antoni Karwowski if he knows how Helena's brother Icek died. Not until I quote what other witnesses have said is he prepared to talk to me about it. He names the boys who grazed cows with Icek when he was beaten to death: Zygmunt, Genek, Władek. The first to throw stones at Icek was said to be Genek. He doesn't want to give me the boys' surnames, and I have no way of finding out.

I always ask everyone about Helena Chrzanowska. I know so much about her by now, including her life after the war and that of her sons. I thought of devoting a chapter of this book to her, but I realize that too much of what I know is shrouded in secrecy.

JULY 1, 2002

I take part in a funeral ceremony in Kraków for Jan Kott, one of the greatest theater critics of the twentieth century and father of my friend

Michał. Jan Kott died in December 2001 in Santa Monica, California, and in accordance with his wishes, his ashes are to be buried in Kraków.

He came from an assimilated Jewish family—his father had him baptized so he would be rooted in Poland and Polishness. In an article written not long before he died, he said that after the Jedwabne affair the memory of his father came back to him.

His parents did not wear armbands during the war, they lived in Kraków on the "Aryan side." His father was picked up in a café where he was the middleman in some transaction, and held under arrest. In jail, when he took a shower with his fellow prisoners and they saw he was circumcised, they informed on him. That was the day he was to be released. His wife was already waiting for him at the prison.

Jedwabne stirs memory, conscience. The editor of the Catholic monthly *Bond* at some meeting or other cited the story of a village priest who had peasants coming to him after sixty years to confess their betrayal of certain Jews to the Germans.

JULY 10, 2002

Prosecutor Ignatiew announced the initial results of his investigation yesterday: "The perpetrators of the crime, strictly speaking, were the Polish inhabitants of Jedwabne and its surroundings."

Just before dark I drive into Jedwabne to lay a rock on the monument. On the last two anniversaries Mayor Godlewski and council chairman Michałowski each laid wreaths there. Not this year. The former mayor has left the country; the chairman didn't turn up.

JULY 16, 2002

I'm working on my book on a farm near Sejny in eastern Poland, far from the world, in a landscape filled with lakes, hills, and berries. An acquaintance calls from Jedwabne to tell me someone has hanged a cat in the Jewish cemetery and asking what office to inform. I call Ignatiew with that question, and in passing I also tell him about the lakes and hills.

"Landscape patriotism, that's good, too," says a pleased Ignatiew, whom I use as a kind of vehicle for discharging my anger at my countrymen. He bears it bravely, but it must be hard for him.

JULY 19, 2002

I return from Sejny via Jedwabne. When Leszek Dziedzic and Krzysztof Godlewski left Poland I no longer had houses where I could drop by without flitting around in the dusk, trying not to be seen. I know I can always go by Stanisław Michałowski's, but I also know a visit from me is not really what he needs. I understand, after all, he's left here on his own.

I look in on Henryk Bagiński, who drives up to the monument regularly in his little Fiat with a rake, plastic bags, and sometimes a scythe. He cleans up, gathers broken vigil lights, cuts the grass around the monument. He recounts to me an exchange he had with a neighbor on the street:

"We'll have to pay sixty billion after the president went and admitted it."

"No, we won't, the whole of Poland isn't worth that much."

"Your granny was fathered by a Jew, she was!"

JULY 20, 2002

Jedwabne. A conversation with Stanisław Michałowski. "Did the papers really have to write about this?" He's talking about the Jan Karski Prize awarded to Krzysztof Godlewski and presented to him at a Brooklyn synagogue. "You have no idea what's going on in town. People take this as clear proof it was all set up, that Godlewski was manipulating the town council from the start, taking Jewish money."

At first I thought of Jedwabne as a shabby little town whose destiny it was to bear the heavy burden of an inconvenient truth. To most of the residents the burden was undeserved—they neither took part in the atrocity, nor do they come from here. In time I became accustomed to thinking of it as an evil realm, like Tolkien's Mordor. I keep telling myself that as I search for testimony on the massacre, I only come into contact with a small part of the souls of the people I talk to, with the darkness in them. The principal who allows children to be educated in the spirit of racial hatred is, after all, an enthusiastic organizer of kayaking trips. The young woman who made abusive phone calls to a friend late at night just because she'd gone to the monument (she distorted her voice, but it came out when the police put a tap on the phone) may be a caring mother. And maybe the mailman who found a summons from the prosecutor addressed to a witness and called the witness up to threaten him always was, is, and will be á reliable deliverer of mail. Maybe. But for a while now I've returned from each trip to Jedwabne sick (and I'm not talking about sick at heart, but with the flu, angina, bronchitis) and I've told myself it was my last trip.

JULY 22, 2002

A conversation with Marek Edelman. While I was away from Warsaw he left a message on my answering machine to say he absolutely had to talk to me about the article on Szmul Wasersztejn I published in the *Gazeta*.

"How could you write that a witness didn't see what he says he saw?" he asks. "You can never be sure about things like that. How many witnesses do I know who saw things they never could have seen, but they really saw them? Because they ran up and for a split second peeked into a train compartment through a crack in a plank, or the moon suddenly lit up a patch of a field. On the third day of the Warsaw Ghetto Uprising, through a hole ripped in the wall somewhere around the fourth floor of a house at 24 Franciszkańska Street, I saw the carousel wheel on the Aryan side turning, and red and blue dresses of the girls blowing in the wind. I really saw that, though it's not at all obvious I would have."

I drop by the editorial offices of the *Gazeta* to read letters that arrived while I was away.

"I have been writing this letter in my mind for the last twenty-five years. Your article on Szmul Wasersztejn made me feel I have to share my reflections. Mama told me that in the village she came from there was a humpbacked woman named Józia, a Jewish orphan who was a fantastic seamstress. One Polish family wanted to shelter her, but other neighbors first got money out of her and then killed her. And so, dear countrymen, should we not ask forgiveness for Józia or for Jedwabne? And as a sidenote: not too long ago I worked at one of the ministries. I hung a nice poster of Janusz Korczak over my desk. The next day the poster was torn and I was warned I shouldn't 'hang Jews on the wall.' Maria Chrzą-stowska, Warsaw."

The letters I receive at the *Gazeta* fall into three categories. Those with insults or stories of Jews torturing Polish patriots at the secret police (or both) form the majority. Those with the names of Poles who hid Jews, with the plea that we write about them. And letters like the one from Ms. Chrząstowska, saying that in such and such a place—on the road, in the woods, in a shelter, after the liberation—a Jew, or a Jewish family, a Jewish child, was killed by a next-door neighbor, someone who lived across the street, in the next village. Sometimes they even give the name of the town and the names of the perpetrators.

AUGUST 25, 2002

When I get back from Bavaria, where I worked on my book in the home of my friends Nawojka and Nicolas Lobkowicz, a letter from Professor Strzembosz in response to my Wasersztejn article is waiting for me at the *Gazeta*. Strzembosz admits that it looks as if Wasersztejn never actually worked for the secret police. On the other hand—he writes—"it has been confirmed that of the Jewish survivors of pogroms there were two who—without any doubt—worked for the secret police." Just to play it safe this time, he doesn't give their names.

The professor seems not to have noticed that he has thrown his scholarly authority into the scales by repeating gossip as if it were source material. The whole right-wing press has been citing Strzembosz's revelations as authoritative. The professor should write them a letter correcting the calumnies he cast on Wasersztejn.

For him, Wasersztejn is not an individual, he's a Jew—a general, collective concept, and in that sense it makes no difference if it was Wasersztejn who was in the secret police or someone else. Any Jew will do. I wonder how Strzembosz would feel if I wrote that he worked for the secret police and then sent a letter to explain it wasn't him but some other Pole whose surname starts with *S*.

A conversation with Adam Michnik in the office; I show him Strzembosz's letter. I complain about my country, as is my wont of late. Adam tells me to look around and see what a discussion of the past looks like in Lithuania or Ukraine, how difficult it has been for knowledge about collaboration to get out in France, even though the government and the better part of the population took part in it.

SEPTEMBER 1, 2002

I read the press from the summer. I find attacks on Ignatiew not only in marginal, openly anti-Semitic papers, but also in the widely read Catholic weekly *Sunday*. They are instigated by Bishop Stefanek: "Even such authorities as the Institute of National Remembrance have joined the laboratory of hatred. There was no investigation into Jedwabne but a celebration of all kinds of lies. Feigned investigation activities, feigned exhumation procedures. The most difficult thing for me to accept is that the Institute of National Remembrance involved itself in a political program to deceive society."

I talk to Ignatiew. "I'm not dreaming of the murdered in the barn anymore," he says. "I sense that I fulfilled my obligation toward them well."

SEPTEMBER 10, 2002

Back in Jedwabne. I keep telling Stanisław Michałowski that I'm surprised at his decision to stay on as council chairman after publicly announcing that he would resign together with Godlewski. He explains to me that I judge Jedwabne too harshly, that part of the population thinks differently than I seem to realize, and he feels he is their representative. He's running in the October municipal elections, and that will be a test of how many people think like he does.

I listen to the gossip going around town: the Dziedzices have settled in Israel; Godlewski, who worked with Gross from the first on the writing of his book, sneaked out of the country to receive a payment of a hundred thousand dollars for selling out Jedwabne; Michałowski also received money from Jews, only in secret.

I hear details about the trip organized under the patronage of the president's wife, Jolanta Kwaśniewska. The kids of Jedwabne had a ball in Disneyland in Florida. On the other hand—after protests from parents—they did not visit the Holocaust Museum or meet with students at a Jewish school, which had been envisaged in the initial plans.

I drive to see a farmer near Radziłów of whom I heard he "killed and robbed Jews in Radziłów, and when there weren't any more left, he killed and robbed Poles, for which he now receives a fat pension as a National Armed Forces combatant."

He's eager to talk. In his version, there wasn't a single Pole in the marketplace in Radziłów or on any street nearby on July 7, 1941, because that day the Germans had forbidden Poles to leave their houses. Swaggeringly, he tells me about the postwar partisans, about his part in retaking Grajewo from the Soviets in 1945. Tortured by the secret police, he gave up nothing. He spent a few years in jail and got out, while those who'd confessed got the death penalty. I quickly say my goodbyes. No point in fooling myself into thinking that I'll get anything out of him.

SEPTEMBER 13, 2002

New York. My friends here have invited me to stay so that I can get some distance from Jedwabne and write my book. I'm spending two months in Manhattan. My daughter Ola, who goes to an American school during this time with Sara, the daughter of Joanna and Ren Weschler, tells me she said "See you Monday" to a friend after class. "Monday?" the girl, of Irish origins, said, amazed. "On Yom Kippur? Here we have that day off from school."

I think, sadly, that in Poland it wouldn't occur to anyone even to remember the Jews on the Day of Atonement, a holiday that the Jews observed for centuries on Polish territory.

SEPTEMBER 20, 2002

I phone Krzysztof Godlewski in Chicago. Prosecutor Ignatiew's finding that it was Poles who were the direct perpetrators of the crime came as a shock to him. "I have to accept it," he says, "because I met Ignatiew and I have no doubt as to his thoroughness. But up until now I believed the investigation would show the Germans did it and that some of the worst locals joined in, and that we were apologizing for them."

I phone Leszek Dziedzic in Lawrence, Massachusetts, and fill him in on the gossip from Jedwabne.

"I don't have anybody to tell me what's going on there," he says bitterly. "I was born and raised in Jedwabne, I spent forty years there, half my life if God gives me a long life, and I don't have anyone I can call to tell me the latest."

His father feels so homesick here that he declares every day that he's going back to Poland because he wants to die at home. "I explain to him, 'Daddy, the priest won't even bury you, you know.'"

OCTOBER 20, 2002

New York. Leszek Dziedzic has come to meet Rabbi Baker, and I go along as his interpreter.

Dziedzic declares, "You, Rabbi Baker, and I, Leszek Dziedzic, are both from Jedwabne. I came here to meet a neighbor. I don't ask forgiveness for the murderers, they are alien to me. But I ask your forgiveness, Rabbi, on behalf of those who lacked the courage back then to help Jews."

"They think, 'The Jews want to take away our homes,'" says the rabbi. "But we want the murderers to regret their guilt, not their homes."

"July 10 was a great opportunity for reconciliation," Leszek argues, "but in Jedwabne the priest wouldn't allow it. Tell me, Rebbe, why is that? We have one God, we took your faith, we pray to a Jewish Mother of God. How can Father Orłowski not be afraid to stand before God one day?"

The rabbi: "I thought of asking him that, but he wouldn't have an answer."

OCTOBER 28, 2002

I call Stanisław Michałowski in Jedwabne to find out how the municipal elections turned out. He was not elected.

"It's a failure but not a disaster," he says. "One hundred and twenty-eight people voted for me."

"How many votes did you get before?"

"I lost two hundred and fifty-two since the last election. People said, 'So why did you have to choose the wrong side?' It's payback for my contribution to the preparations for the ceremony in Jedwabne. The priest has a lot to do with it."

I try not to sound as if I'm saying "I told you so" (he should have resigned with Godlewski). Apparently I don't succeed very well, because Stanisław adds, "I wanted to hide from you how people think here. I was ashamed. But it is the way it is."

OCTOBER 29, 2002

In a Japanese restaurant in Manhattan. A couple of friends from Poland have brought a friend, a girl who's studying here.

"Is your book for or against Gross?" she asks.

I bristle. Did this, one of the questions I get most often in random conversations in Poland, have to find me in Manhattan? There is only one supposedly correct answer to a question put like that: my book will be against Gross. I prefer to write this book in New York, imposing on my friends' hospitality, precisely so as not to hear questions like that. The girl hasn't read Gross's book, by the way, but she has an opinion.

NOVEMBER 24, 2002

Back in Poland. A visit to Marianna Ramotowska, who is more and more closed off in her own world. This time she doesn't recognize me. When the present becomes increasingly foggy, the past takes on color. So I ask her caregiver, who spends twenty-four hours a day with her, whether Marianna ever recalls her childhood. No. Evidently she has locked away under seven seals her memories of the time when she was still Rachela.

NOVEMBER 29, 2002

I spend another day studying the two fat volumes of the Institute of National Remembrance's *About Jedwabne*, edited by Paweł Machcewicz and Krzysztof Persak. Over fifteen hundred pages, most of them documents—440 of them in all—found in archives in Białystok, Warsaw, Ełk, Jerusalem, Minsk, Grodno, Ludwigsburg. The Institute of National Remembrance book offers at least approximate answers to most of the questions filling the newspaper headlines in the course of the sharpest debate of the past few years. It's Gross's great achievement that he provoked more than a dozen scholars to turn their attention to materials no one had touched before.

How many active participants were there in the crime in Jedwabne? Krzysztof Persak, who made a penetrating analysis of trial materials from 1949 and 1953, excluding ambiguous testimony, counted eighty-five persons mentioned by name and surname. The number of residents of Jedwabne and nearby villages who took part in the atrocity in some form he estimated at well over a hundred.

Can the determinations of the 1949 trial be accepted? Law professor Andrzej Rzepliński showed in a devastating critique that the crime was minimized, and the investigation conducted with extraordinary inefficiency: it can't be ruled out that some of the secret police officials and prosecutors shared the anti-Semitic prejudices of the accused men. "It is beyond doubt," we read, "that the case was conducted in such a way as to reveal the least amount of evidence possible that might incriminate the accused and other Polish residents." Rzepliński puts his faith in the testimonies of witnesses who pointed to murderers during the investigation but who withdrew their statements at the trial. And so, analyzing the testimony of Bronisława Kalinowska ("Jerzy Laudański was hurtling down the street saying he had already killed two or three Jews"), he states,

"Her brave testimony during the inqury was 'corrected' in court, because this older woman, I have no doubt, was more afraid of the members of the Laudański family who remained at large and of the family of the other accused men than she was of the secret police."

Can we believe prosecutor Waldemar Monkiewicz, who claimed that 232 Germans carried out the massacre? No, says the historian Krzysztof Persak, who analyzed the case documents from 1967. For the documents do not even offer a trace of evidence that might lead one to that conclusion. "The conduct of the prosecutor at that time," we read, "can only be judged as a manipulation of evidence and a falsification of the results of the investigation."

How many victims were there? Marcin Urynowicz, attempting to determine this on the basis of various contradictory reports, thought that in 1939 the Jewish community in Jedwabne numbered roughly a thousand people. We don't know how many Jews lived in Jedwabne in 1941, but no more than that. In the barn, he claims, considerably fewer than a thousand people must have perished—it's known that some were killed individually, with clubs, axes, and some managed to hide from the killers that day." (But he doesn't take into account how many refugees had come to town from Radziłów, Wizna, Stawiski, and other smaller Jewish settlements in the area.)

Did the Germans plan the massacre in Jedwabne or merely give permission for it? Professor Edmund Dmitrów carried out a meticulous search in German archives. He found no documents that would enable us to ascertain what role the Germans played.

DECEMBER 1, 2002

I was planning to reconstruct the course of events in Jedwabne, Radziłów, and Wąsosz, the three places where Poles murdered all their Jewish neighbors.

At the Institute of National Remembrance in Białystok I read accounts of the atrocity in Wąsosz, where in one night, July 5, 1941, all the Jewish residents were killed with spades, pitchforks, axes. How many Jews perished is hard to say, probably 250. The July nights were short, so that when the bodies of murdered people were carried off on wagons it was already getting light and everybody could watch what was going on from behind their curtains. It happened on Saturday night, so people going to Sunday Mass saw pools of blood in the streets. There was a trial in 1951, but no one was convicted.

I put off Wąsosz, and now I realize I don't have the strength to confront another nightmare.

I start editing my book.

14

Decent Polish Kids and Hooligans

or, On the Murderers of Jedwabne,
Radziłów, Wąsosz, and the Surrounding Areas

1.

Reading a book on the Polish underground in the Łomża district I found a mention of one Maksym Jonkajtys of Szczuczyn, "head master of a grammar school, selfless patriot, one of the first partisans during both the Soviet and German occupation, shot in 1943." However, I didn't immediately realize this must have been the same school head Jonkajtys who, according to the testimony of Basia Kacper from Szczuczyn, led the pogrom in his native town.

I had read Kacper's testimony at the Jewish Historical Institute at the very beginning of the road that led me to write this book. I remember being struck even then by the phrase she used: the pogroms were organized by "decent Polish kids and hooligans." But a long time passed before I became fully aware of the horror of this phrase, and, at the same time, its precision. I had to go through the testimonies of Holocaust survivors a second time to realize that I'd had the knowledge underlying Kacper's formulation at hand the whole time.

The local teacher, postmaster, policeman, medic—the testimonies at the Jewish Historical Institute from Stawiski, Jasionówka, and other places in the Łomża area where Jews were killed show that the representatives of these professions, prestigious in the prewar Polish provinces, not only incited people to the atrocities but took part in them themselves.

(Photograph © Krzysztof Miller / Agencja Gazeta)

The role of the local political elites in the ominous events of the summer of 1941 is even more obvious.

2.

As a rule the town elites in this part of Poland were made up of prewar National Party members. Many of them were in prison during the Soviet occupation, or went into hiding for fear of being arrested, taking part in the anti-Soviet partisan movement.

After the Soviets left and the Germans invaded, it was these people who tended to set the tone in the towns, organized civilian guards, and were in theory there to preserve the peace but in practice carried out acts of revenge, in the first place against Communists, both Jewish and Polish, but immediately afterward, against their Jewish neighbors. These makeshift civilian guards and police squads—units that had existed for just a few weeks (until the German authorities had installed themselves—and the Germans employed some of their members in the auxiliary police, or *Hilfspolizei*)—led the majority of pogroms and massacres.

In Radziłów people remembered Henryk Dziekoński and Feliks Godlewski committing their atrocities wearing the white-and-red armbands of the civilian guard. After the war Henryk Dziekoński tried to convince the court that the killing of Jews had been prompted by ideas; he stubbornly repeated during the investigation and at the trial that he had called upon the locals to refrain from looting, and simply to burn Jewish property. He didn't want anything to sully this act of patriotism.

Only after the political elite of Radziłów had become active did the lowlifes and criminals of the town join in.

In Jedwabne, National Party members included Bronisław Śleszyński, who gave his barn for the burning of the Jews, and Czesław Laudański, father of the brothers Jerzy and Kazimierz, convicted for their part in the crime.

In many towns, particularly smaller ones, the auxiliary police formed on the basis of the civilian guards was the only force representing the German occupation. (However, many of those Poles participating in the atrocity, who were at one with the Germans on the Jews, quickly ceased to collaborate with them, and some of them went to the partisans; other Poles remaining in the auxiliary police assisted the partisan underground.)

Of the eight men accused of taking part in the murder of Jews in Radziłów—and I know from witnesses that all of them in fact played a leading role in it—six were in the resistance during the Soviet occupation and joined the Home Army during the German occupation, and some of the eight were active in the Polish underground after the war. One of the killers, Feliks Godlewski, is described as follows in a book dedicated to local Home Army heroes: "In the underground resistance from 1939. In Kedyw (Special Forces) from 1944. Fought with 3rd squadron 9th mounted rifles in Grzędy. Determined and courageous. Condemned to many years in prison after the war."

The only thing is, Godlewski was convicted in the trial on the murder of Jews in Radziłów. But in local memory this sentence is just another item in his heroic biography (in the course of the investigation he was additionally charged with beating individuals collaborating with the Soviet authorities).

It is also known of other participants in the Radziłów atrocity that they fought with the Home Army. And so we read in Chaja Finkelsztejn's diary the following remark about Zygmunt Mazurek: "He was among those killing Jews, but he was one of the more intelligent murderers." The Mazurek family belonged to the local intelligentsia; Zygmunt's father, Jan, a medic, was a decent man who looked after Jews who'd been beaten up. "The son makes sure his father has enough to keep him busy," Chaja commented. Zygmunt Mazurek, code name "Kuba," who worked as a teacher (he became a doctor after the war), was the person in Radziłów with the highest rank in the Home Army. After the war he was the legendary deputy leader of the regional hero "Bruzda" in the most famous underground operation in the region—the taking of the secret police, militia, and Soviet command buildings in Grajewo in May 1945.

Several of the men accused in the 1949 trial of killing Jews in Jedwabne were later active in the underground. Bolesław Ramotowski, Roman Górski, and Franciszek Łojewski were Home Army soldiers (they left the underground in 1947). After the war, National Armed Forces meetings took place in the house of one of the leaders of the massacre, Józef Sobuta (who had taken part in demolishing Jewish shops before the war).

However, in Jedwabne, in contrast to Radziłów, murderers taking part in the partisan movement and underground operations was more the exception than the rule. Karol Bardoń played an important role in the town council in Jedwabne: he had come to the area from Silesia in the thirties (he worked as a mechanic, first in Radziłów, in Chaja Finkelsztejn's mill, then in Jedwabne, in Hirsz Zdrojewicz's mill). In Soviet times he had a post in the Soviet administration and was head of the Jedwabne municipal supplies department. Maybe he was a German agent and he was dealt with as a representative of the Germans? In late June, early July of 1941, the town was under the rule of mayor Marian Karolak. And it was he who led the operation to round up Jews. Why did everyone submit to him? Was it because, as the son-in-law of the long-serving prewar mayor Walenty Grądzki, he had the support of the town elite?

The Wąsosz massacre was headed up by nine men, as was established in the 1951 investigation. All nine murderers were prewar members of the National Party. Marian Rydzewski, the leader, was in the National Party, in the Home Army during the war, and after the war, in one of the armed underground organizations. Townspeople remembered him years later in an article in the local weekly *Kontakty*: "The worst animal was one guy who later joined the Home Army. People remember that he marked each victim on his rifle with notches."

3.

Bielsk Podlaski, Choroszcz, Czyżew, Goniądz, Grajewo, Jasionówka, Jedwabne, Kleszczele, Knyszyn, Kolno, Kuźnica, Narewka, Piątnica, Radziłów, Rajgród, Sokoły, Stawiski, Suchowola, Szczuczyn, Trzciane, Tykocin, Wasilków, Wąsosz, Wizna: the postwar court documents record acts committed against Jewish neighbors in several dozen towns in the area. In many of them the Germans were the initiators and executors and the Poles joined in, helping them to drive the Jews into market squares, beat them and humiliate them, and sometimes kill them. Elsewhere, Poles were the immediate culprits, and Germans served as instigators and co-organizers. But in Kolno, Rutki, Grajewo, and Szczuczyn it seems that the anti-Jewish incidents were not provoked by the Germans at all, but had the character of grassroots initiatives provoked by the Polish population, according to the Institute of National Remembrance. Why in this region did pogroms and killings reach a level unequaled in other parts of Poland? And how is it possible that people whose hands are stained with the blood of innocent victims quickly appear—as members of the Home Army—in the guise of national heroes? From a certain point onward these questions accompanied me in my writing of this book. I returned to them again and again in the course of my various conversations.

Professor Adam Dobroński, a historian from Białystok and a specialist in the history of the region, had no intention of replying to such awkward questions. He diverted me as best he could by lecturing me on the region's history, which was in itself a kind of indirect response.

"Jedwabne, historically it belonged to the Łomża *gubernia*. A nursery of Polish national identity and Catholicism; that's how the area was described in the nineteenth century. It was a realm of petty nobles. If we're talking about participation in popular uprisings, the Łomża area was in the forefront." These lands stood out for their systematic supply of nationalist MPs. In 1905, at a time when the territories belonged to the Russian partition, the National Party won all the mandates in the elections for the Russian parliament. "The petty aristocracy absorbed nationalist ideology like a sponge," Dobroński continues. "It was felt that this was a patriotic Catholic area with an alien element, the Jews. Add to that the shifting of the borders after World War One, which resulted in the Łomża district becoming a periphery, and the economic crisis of the thirties, which deepened the stagnation in life here. These were towns without a future, without any impulse to progress. The local population suffered a cultural degradation, it was characterized by primitivism, and the war exacerbated that state of affairs, at the same time preserving the memory of forebears who had fought to defend faith and fatherland."

Listening to his disquisition, I was not yet aware—nor was he, in all probability—that his arguments go to the very heart of the problem that torments me. Even when you have all the information in hand, it's hard to grasp that a readiness to commit atrocities and a readiness to give one's life for the fatherland could flow from the same source—but a source that was poisoned somewhere along the way.

4.

On my very first visit to Jedwabne I came across the name of Jerzy Tarnacki, a man who participated in the killing of the Jedwabne Jews on July 10. Many of the witnesses I talked to had a vivid memory of him: as a member of the prewar nationalist squads ("He bullied and provoked young Jews, and when there was a wedding in the synagogue he caused as much disruption as he could"); as a common looter ("Even before they started killing Jews, he was already looting Szmul Wasersztejn's property"); as the man who drove Jews into the market square and who, with Józef Sobuta, made them destroy the Lenin statue ("He beat Jews and made them sing"); and, finally, as a *schutzmann*, a policeman under the Germans ("He was worse than many of the Germans, and when it was clear the Germans would lose, he went into the forest").

He is accused in witness statements from the 1949 trial ("I saw with my own eyes how Jerzy Tarnacki took part in the killing of Jews. He was forcing a Jew into the market square and he had a stick in his hand; what he did to that man I don't know, I just saw him leading the aforementioned Jew in the direction of the fire").

It is evident from the trial documents that he was not arrested and he did not stand trial, because he'd gone into hiding. He was sought by the militia.

We know that Tarnacki was part of the partisan group in the Kobielno wilds, and was active in the anti-Communist underground after the war.

The historian Tomasz Strzembosz refers to his correspondence with Tarnacki in articles describing the nefarious role of Jews during the Soviet occupation, and the selflessness of the Polish patriots whose partisan hideout was in the Kobielno wilderness. Of the Kobielno partisans, among them Jerzy Tarnacki, who is mentioned by name, Strzembosz wrote, "Those whom I managed to find, they are the 'Last of the Mohicans,' the remainder of a battered generation of Fighting Poland. I bow my head low before these people."

At the office of the Białystok branch of the Institute of National Remembrance I studied a microfilm with a security service docket dated 1952, written (with many mistakes) in the hand of Jerzy Tarnacki. In it he promises "to execute all tasks entrusted to him conscientiously, not hiding any actions hostile to People's Poland," "not to speak of his collaboration with anyone, even the nearest of kin," and also "to arrive punctually at the arranged meetings." He makes it clear that he will only collaborate with those employees who recruited him and under no circumstance ask them to visit his house. He selects the alias "Above Board."

The Jerzy Tarnacki who murdered Jews and went to work for the German police as a *schutzmann*, the Jerzy Tarnacki who joined the partisans in Kobielno and was active in the Home Army and the anti-Soviet underground, and, finally, the Jerzy Tarnacki who collaborated with the Communist secret police—they are all the same man.

5.

So, taking part in the murder of Jews didn't disqualify a person from being accepted into the ranks of the Home Army. Unfortunately there is absolutely no doubt about this—murderers could become soldiers in the Polish underground army, even if they had committed their crimes in broad daylight, in the center of town, in front of many witnesses.

In this area, every underground organization would have tolerated people in its ranks who were guilty of killing Jews. The difference was that with the National Armed Forces, having saved or helped Jews definitely disqualified you, while the Home Army opened its ranks to both killers of Jews and protectors of Jews. The same Zygmunt Mazurek who belonged to a gang that tormented Jews, proposed that the Home Army accept Stanisław Ramotowski, who he knew had saved a Jewish family, married a Jewish woman, and been in hiding with her.

6.

In the autumn of 1943, Józef Przybyszewski, who represented the National Party in the Polish government-in-exile based in London, became the regional delegate of the émigré government in the Białystok district. I decided to check to see if the similarity of surnames with the editor in chief of *Camp for a Greater Poland Youth*, the periodical of the anti-Semitic extreme right wing of the National Party, was coincidental. Przybyszewski was convicted by a prewar court and charged with being "morally responsible for the Radziłów pogrom" in 1933. I find out that they are one and the same man.

In my notes on the prewar period I find quotes from Przybyszewski's programmatic article "Our Position on the Jewish Question": "The Greater Poland movement will endure so long as there are Poles in Poland who sell their country into Jewish hands, consider giving Lvov to the Ukrainians or Vilnius to the Lithuanians. Poland must be nationalist, and Jews are a race unsuited to assimilation." And also notes from Interior Ministry reports: "On December 13, 1932, a meeting took place in Radziłów of members and sympathizers of the National Party numbering about 60 persons. The National Party secretary from Łomża, Józef Przybyszewski, gave a speech arguing that Jews are the most privileged people in Poland, crowding all Polish schools, growing so arrogant that they go so far as to murder Polish fellow students. He called on those gathered to boycott Jewish merchants and to organize themselves under the flag of the National Party, which, as he put it, would soon take power in the country after the fall of the current government."

Why did the Polish government in London choose a rabid anti-Semite as their representative in the region? They knew the local population had joined with the Germans in persecuting and killing Jews. Not only did the underground authorities refuse to support this, they warned people loud and clear not to succumb to German propaganda. However, they evidently thought—surely with some grounds—that one could build networks of resistance in this region only on the nationalist movement, with its powerful anti-Semitic coloring. Chaja Finkelsztejn, who heard singing from her hiding place, wrote, "The youth marched through the village singing of the fall of Warsaw. They sang with such pain, those same people who had bathed in the blood of innocents."

Jan Gross in his book wrote that the murderers were "just like anybody else, quite ordinary people," using a phrase from Christopher Browning. In the discussion about the book it was often said that it was the underclass who took part in the killing. A prominent sociologist, Antoni Sułek, wrote, "The most active participants in the atrocity were not 'ordinary people' but people from the margins of society, from the lower rungs of the social hierarchy, unsettled, unfettered by bonds of family. Not the kind of people who had their own houses but the kind who hoped to get housing and property from Jews; not farmers thinking of the approaching harvest but idle village 'youth,' not fathers but overgrown boys and loners."

In fact, Jews were killed both by "quite ordinary people" (in Tykocin, as Menachem Turek testified, "the lives of Jews were put in the hands of a former shepherd, Antek Jakubiak, who became the commander of the newly minted police force") and by "people from the margins" (like Józef Kubrzyniecki of Jedwabne, known before the war as a local hood who stole for a living).

Jews were killed by people ready to serve any power, like the brothers Jerzy and Zygmunt Laudański in Jedwabne or Władysław Grodzki, the teacher from Jasionówka. Grodzki was in the National Party before the war, worked for the NKVD during the Soviet occupation, and, as soon as the Germans entered, began killing and robbing Jews, then joined the auxiliary police force (he was condemned to death after the war).

"Quite ordinary people," including people with stable lives, spouses, and numerous offspring, killed Jews—this emerges unambiguously from the investigation papers.

Unfortunately, there was also a whole other category, the local patriotic elite, raised in a nationalist and extremely anti-Semitic spirit by the local organs of the National Party and by their own priests.

7.

I heard stories more than once about meetings of the Home Army after the war where plans were made to kill surviving Jews.

The best-known case in the region involves the Dorogojs, Mordechaj and his son Akiwa (called Icek). They came out of hiding on January 23, 1945, right after the Soviets turned up. By January 28 they were dead. The open secret among the locals was that they had been killed by Antoni Kosmaczewski, who earlier had murdered Mordechaj's daughter, Dora.

At his trial, Kosmaczewski claimed that he had received permission from his Home Army superiors to kill the Dorogojs, who—as he testified—had threatened to kill him in revenge for his killing Dora. "So I was terrified and I went to my company leader, since I belonged to the illegal Home Army, to ask them what to do about those Jews . . . My leader told me that 'if you have witnesses to it, get rid of them.' The leader's name was Bujnarowski; he was from Radziłów, but now he's dead."

What to think of an accused man explaining that his Home Army leader was responsible for his killing of Jews after the war?

My first impulse is not to believe that the Home Army could have had anything to do with it. But here the Institute of National Remembrance finds a document.

LIQUIDATION REPORT, FEBRUARY 1945

Date of liquidation: January 28, 1945
Who carried out the liquidation and how: Home Army patrol

Surname and first name of liquidated person and place of residence: Dorogoj Mordechaj, Radziłów

Reason for liquidation and who suffered from his hostile activity:
Soviet snoop, threatened the entirety of the organization's work

Make press announcement (Yes/No): No

A second identical report concerns Dorogoj, Icek.

The documents are signed by Lieutenant Franciszek Warzyński
"Wawer" and Major Jan Tabortowski "Bruzda." Both are legendary heroes in these parts.

8.

"The priest stood at the gate. Jews came to be baptized but the priest
stood there and said nothing." This is the scene described by Janina Biedrzycka, daughter of the owner of the barn in Jedwabne, who saw the
priest's behavior with her own eyes in Jedwabne on July 10, 1941.

Before the war, priests in the Łomża district often headed boycotts,
and the vicar of Radziłów, Władysław Kamiński, smashed the windows
of Jewish shops together with nationalist squads. There are no reports of
priests taking part in the pogroms and murders of 1941, but we know
that most of them took a passive stance, and sometimes even a permis-
sive one. Many testimonies relate that a pogrom started after Mass
("On a bright Sunday Poles prepared sticks spiked with sharp thorns,
bound with rope and barbed wire," Mendel Mielnicki of Wasilków
testified. "Coming back from church, all of them headed for the Jewish
quarter and Jewish homes, and a pogrom began, with beatings and
looting").

There were, however, some exceptions. Father Aleksander Pęza of Grajewo called on his parishioners to come to their senses, appealing to
them not to collaborate with the Germans or to succumb to anti-Jewish
provocations (testimony of Nachman Rapp, recorded in 1948).

A priest from Rutki, together with the local school head, tried to restrain a group of men who'd been in hiding under the Soviet occupation
and came out of the forest to settle scores with the Jews (testimony from
Rutki, from the Ghetto Underground Archive).

Father Cyprian Łozowski of Jasionówka beat with a stick those of his
parishioners who plundered Jewish homes and threatened them with

damnation (testimony of Jehoszua Bernard, recorded in a Budapest refugee shelter in 1945).

We know of one documented case of local elites who defended Jews. In Knyszyn, after the German invasion, "Doctor Nowakowski, pharmacist Rzeźnicki, and the local priest intervened with the authorities, who stopped the persecution. The Jews went on living where they always had." The Knyszyn priest and the local elite intervened a second time when the pogrom was being planned: "In July 1941 criminal elements in the Polish population got together. They were headed by the policeman Stach Bibiński, among others. They marked Jewish houses with a Star of David and Polish ones with a cross. The Jews lived in terror that night. The next day it was quiet, and that was thanks to the local intelligentsia, who had restrained the mob. The priest himself chased away a boy who was about to break windows. The same priest told the faithful in his weekly sermons not to persecute Jews but to help them, because no one knew what time would bring" (testimony of Samuel Suraski for the Białystok Institute of National Remembrance, 1948).

Was any authority capable of restraining the pogrom fever among the local population as June turned to July in 1941? It is difficult to know. The fact remains that few tried. They deserve all the more praise for having done so.

Journal

JANUARY 10, 2003

I listen to a cassette tape sold outside a Białystok church: it has a talk on it given in Częstochowa, at Jasna Góra, the most sacred place for Polish Catholics.

"I would like to share with my fellow chaplains and my bishop some reflections on the Catholic-Jewish dialogue. For today we are dealing with Talmudic Judaism, which has nothing in common with Biblical Judaism. Jewish thinking, Jewish attitudes come from there, from the Talmud. We find it in *The Painted Bird*, in the stories of Isaac Bashevis Singer, in the recent reports on Jedwabne. It's all made-up."

The name of the speaker is never mentioned, but I recognize the voice of the priest and professor Waldemar Chrostowski, vice president of the Catholic University in Warsaw.

"Why is there talk of the number sixteen hundred, despite the exhumation?" I listen on. "We Christians wish to reconstruct the facts. For the Jews, the facts have no significance. We express sympathy, but their answer comes down to this: how much can we get out of this? Germany paid a hundred billion marks to Israel. When that source dried up, they started to look elsewhere. We didn't know about a lot of these accusations, they were turned into moral categories, but then they were translated into sixty-five billion in financial compensation. They tried to do it through Auschwitz, through the business of the cross built in Warsaw. When that didn't work, they switched to Jedwabne, preparing three years for it. We warned the offices of the president and prime minister that they should not allow the government to apologize to the Jews. Because after that money would have to follow."

Father Chrostowski, the former vice president of the Council of Christians and Jews, is the primate's expert on the Christian-Jewish dialogue.

APRIL 4, 2003

In the *Republic*, Father Stanisław Musiał, with the same vigor with which he denounced anti-Semitism in the Church, takes on the war in Iraq. He writes of crime and lies, and attacks Catholic bishops in the United States who supported sending U.S. soldiers to Iraq. I don't like this war either, I'm proud of my daughter Ola, who goes to antiwar demonstrations in New York after school. It only exacerbates my feeling of alienation, because the majority of the people I know in Poland are in favor of the war, and my newspaper is, too.

APRIL 29, 2003

The funeral of Father Orłowski, who played a crucial role in the denial of Poles' responsibility for the massacre. Two bishops went all the way to Jedwabne for it.

MAY 1, 2003

A conversation with the sociologist Ireneusz Krzemiński, who has just finished a study of anti-Semitic attitudes. He repeated the same questions he posed ten years ago, in 1992.

Only 14 percent of Poles think that in Auschwitz, where 90 percent of the victims were Jews, they killed mostly Jews. The fact that the Jews suffered more than Poles during the war is accepted by fewer Poles than before—barely 38 percent.

"The results leave no room for doubt," he says. "After the Jedwabne affair flared up, the number of anti-Semites in Poland increased significantly. Why? Jedwabne sharpened our sense of competitive suffering."

MAY 4, 2003

I'm preparing captions for photographs from Jedwabne.

The experience of wresting information from oblivion is familiar to me from my work on the album *I Still See Their Faces*. I remember the moment when I saw hundreds of pictures of Jews on the floor and at once realized I didn't want to write the text I'd been commissioned to write on former Jewish shtetls. Instead, I should write captions for these photos, resurrect as much as possible of a lost world, reconstruct not just the fate of those in the photographs but the wanderings of the photos themselves.

From the beginning it seemed to me that most of the photographs sent in to the contest were caught up in others' lives, hanging on for dear life in the family albums of Polish neighbors, in the chests of drawers of distant acquaintances. It happened that someone had kept for half a century a photo found next to the railway tracks leading to the camp in Brzezinka, even though the people in the picture were strangers to the finder. But sometimes it seemed that this strangeness had been strictly self-imposed. In the third, fifth, tenth meeting or phone conversation, people would reveal to me that those were in fact family photos. Their Jewish relatives.

And so it was that a woman who told me various details from the biography of a man in a Polish Army uniform—that he'd been in the Polish Socialist Party, that he'd been murdered at Katyń—burst into tears and admitted he was her father. "From the time our neighbors betrayed us during the war and we survived only by a miracle," she explained, "my mother and I decided not to admit we were Jewish." Her children know nothing of their origins. The next time I saw her she once again referred to the man in the photo as "that gentleman."

Similarly, a professor at the Warsaw University of Technology who comes from a prominent Jewish family gave me priceless information about her ancestors. She knew virtually everything about them, and felt deeply connected to the Jewish community. However, she never mentioned her background to anyone: "For obvious reasons it would be inappropriate."

JUNE 15, 2003

According to the results of the recently conducted national census, Poland now has eleven hundred Jews.

I remember last year's visit from the census taker. The census had a question on nationality. But to indicate another nationality you first had to answer no when asked if your nationality was Polish. So I have no right to feel both Polish and Jewish! In any case the Polish language itself forces me to define myself in a certain way. The language has no expression that would allow me to call myself equally a Pole and a Jew.

We had a discussion at home. Maniuszka said she feels Jewish, at least one-quarter, after her grandmother, but on the other hand she doesn't really understand what it means to be Jewish if you're not religious. So she chooses the Polish nationality. Ola has no doubt that it is wrong to put her in a position where she has to make an exclusive choice, and so if she has to, she would choose the Jewish nationality. Me, too.

The census taker filled in the checks in the appropriate sections without batting an eye. On her way out at the door she said casually, "I did a two-week course to get this job. They taught us not to be surprised at anything."

JUNE 24, 2003

I interview Imre Kertész for the *Gazeta*. The fact that this long-awaited Nobel for Hungarian literature had to fall to a writer not very well-known in his own country, who made the Holocaust the chief subject of his prose, prompted mixed emotions in Hungary. The Holocaust is a dark and painful topic that has been consigned to oblivion because of the participation of the Hungarians in the destruction of their Jews.

Besides his subject, the fact that Kertész is a Jew does not sit well with many Hungarians. I tell him about the late, great Polish writer and essayist Gustaw Herling-Grudziński, whom I tried to get to talk about his Jewish origins in an interview I once did for the *Gazeta*. He was furious that I touched on the subject at all, and had me cut it out altogether when he authorized the interview before publication. He behaved as if having Jewish ancestors was something odious excluding him from the company of Polish writers. The saddest thing is that there's something to that. Herling-Grudziński is not an isolated case; I know other Polish writers who passed over their Jewish origins in silence, sometimes even to the extent of lying about their childhood in autobiographical writings. This is a terrible testimony to present-day Polish anti-Semitism. It wouldn't occur to a writer with French ancestors to hide them from anyone, and no one would look upon such a writer with suspicion, as if he were some kind of frog eater, not one of us Poles.

One of the most devastating stories related to this subject was told by Alina Margolis-Edelman, Marek Edelman's wife, who was in hiding during the war with a patriotic family of renowned Warsaw architects (they were told she was the daughter of a murdered Polish officer). When the ghetto was in flames in April 1943, her host said, "Pity Tuwimer isn't frying in there with them." It was offensive to a Polish patriot that a great Polish poet, Julian Tuwim, was also a Jew.

Before Jedwabne it seemed to me this pretense of "racial purity" was connected to the trauma of the war. However, from the time I experienced alienation due to my own background, I think those writers or poets didn't have the strength to confront the suspicion of their readers, to undergo manifestations of hostility and exclusion just because they had a bit of "foreign blood."

I tell Kertész how comforting I found his *Guardian* essay "The Language of Exile," in which he explained why he, a Hungarian and a Jew living a large part of the year in Berlin and feeling at home there, feels in Hungary as if he were just visiting, a bit of an interloper. I tell him that it was only in the course of writing this book that I realized that to many of my fellow Poles I'm a "stranger." And that I return to Poland from my increasingly frequent trips to New York concerned about what I'll hear next. His essay helped me understand the obvious: that the sense of alienation doesn't bother you when you're abroad, because there's no reason you would feel you belonged. It only hurts in your own country.

"It's best to be somewhere in between, somewhere on the road," Kertész advises.

JULY 10, 2003
Jedwabne. My daughter Maniucha and I lay rocks on the monument.

AUGUST 7, 2003
Jedwabne. I'm trying to get authorizations for statements for my book. Henryk Bagiński agrees to reveal it is he who systematically cleans up the Jewish cemetery. On the other hand, there's a person in my diary I feel close to who asks to remain anonymous, even on statements made publicly.

JANUARY 19, 2004

With complete self-sacrifice, Jacek Kuroń has struggled through the first version of my manuscript between dialysis sessions and intensive sessions in the hospital.

"I don't know how many people will read this," he worries. "Theoretically I was prepared for the whole thing, you'd already told me so much about it, but even so I had to stop reading every several dozen pages, so hard did I find it."

I also sent my manuscript to a close friend in Paris, whose family was driven from Poland by the anti-Semitic campaign of 1968. "I'm afraid," she wrote me, "not many people will like your book. Quite apart from anti-Semites and other 'patriots,' a book like this will make decent and honest people feel bad, and no one likes that. I think my father will lose the little faith he still has in Poles and in being seen as Polish by anyone but himself (though he will certainly value the book). So the hardest is still to come, but I'm sure you know that."

APRIL 9, 2004

Marek Edelman, reading the manuscript of my book, keeps putting it aside, moaning, "Who's going to read this? Who's going to be able to read it?" And that the reading inflicts an almost physical pain on him. "For me the hardest thing to bear is not that Jews were massacred in Jedwabne and the area," he says, "but that it was done with such cruelty and that the killing gave so much joy." After reading the first twenty or thirty pages, Edelman lets me know that he has been drawn into the book.

APRIL 29, 2004

Marianna Ramotowska has died.

This occasion has brought home to me the meaning of the word "expired." Stanisław suffered and struggled with his illness, but Marianna left the world quietly, gently. With every visit her bed seemed larger to me—she was always small and thin, but she got smaller and thinner, and her skin was like parchment.

The doctor assures me she didn't suffer.

APRIL 30, 2004

The historian Dariusz Stola, whom I asked to read my book, has given me an array of comments beyond factual ones. He says I react neurotically when someone approaches the matter differently from me, that I, too, often take an accusatory tone, that it's clear there's too much bitterness in me. He also draws to my attention how much of what is happening now in Jedwabne is being played out in the theater of the imagination.

"The people you talk to live in constant fear that someone's going to burn their house down, kidnap their children, knock them down in a dark alley. But no one has been physically hurt, right?" he asks to make sure.

Fair enough. Apart from one older lady who was beaten by family members, people annoyed by nocturnal phone calls, isolated incidents of bullying like pushing someone in a shop so they drop their groceries, idle threats—not one of my interlocutors has been hurt. It's just that here are respected members of the community who had relatives, friends, acquaintances, a position, and who suddenly felt cast out of the circle as they were surrounded by hostility and condemned to ostracism, often by their own families. Is that so trivial? I spend the night reading through my book and deleting sentences written bitterly, neurotically, in an accusatory tone.

JUNE 15, 2004

I've been poring over the map of prewar Jedwabne based on postwar aerial maps, and two local surveys. I add the information I've gathered, giving specific people specific addresses.

The *List of Post-German and Post-Jewish Real Estate Abandoned in the Town of Jedwabne*, which I found in the Łomża City Archive, is an inestimable help to me. It is from 1946, but it includes the surnames and addresses of prewar owners of some houses and properties. Luckily the list also contains data on the size of the houses. That makes it easier to reconstruct which family might have lived in which of the little blocks drawn on the map. I have at my disposal a list drawn up by Tzipora Rothchild (who emigrated to Palestine before the war) for the *Jedwabne Book of Memory* in the seventies. I have information from so-called notification reports of people who perished in the Holocaust, from Yad Vashem. Unfortunately, they contain dozens of ambiguities that derive from the fact that they are filled in and sent to the institute not only by the families of victims but also by their friends and acquaintances, so the same person may figure in several places and then the birth dates, names, or number of children typically do not correspond.

The greatest help to me is the extraordinarily precise memory of Meir Ronen. When I met him in May 2001 in Jerusalem, he told me—street by street, house by house, neighbor by neighbor—about people alive only in his memory. He gave their names, often their addresses as well, and I took it all down, so that the abstract space of prewar Jedwabne began to fill with details.

In the work of deciphering the addresses, family connections, and assets of the inhabitants of Jedwabne I am also helped by Chaim Sroszko from Holon near Tel Aviv, with whom I'm in constant phone contact. Years ago, just for himself, Sroszko reconstucted over two hundred names and all the shops in Jedwabne, but sadly he can't find the papers. It turns out he is the one who dictated the list to Tzipora Rothchild that appeared in the *Jedwabne Book of Memory*. Now he labors for the third time, for me. Adding his remarks and corrections, I see not everything adds up. Sometimes I have to choose between his memory and Meir Ronen's. I have the sense there's no way of avoiding some errors, that some doubts cannot be resolved, that in many cases question marks will remain.

I also have individual names and addresses of Jedwabne Jews that I jotted down from various documents, such as the case documents on transfers of post-Jewish houses to new owners, "1939 data on fire insurance," and an excerpt from a directory published in 1929 by the International Advertising Association, in which there may be no addresses but the owners of shops and businesses are given.

A different problem I struggle with is the spelling of names and surnames. Most of them were translated from Yiddish to Hebrew, from Hebrew to English, and then I translated them into Polish (in Hebrew there were already various versions of some of them). The word "guess" is sometimes more appropriate than "reconstruct." On Tzipora Rothchild's list there's the surname Skocznadel. It seemed so implausible to me that I didn't know whether to put it in, when a friend of friend made me realize that the name literally means "leap-needle," and so this was probably a tailor's family.

JULY 1, 2004

I read the prosecutor's findings. I now have the opportunity to compare what the same witnesses told me and what they told the prosecutor.

We come to similar conclusions, but here and there mine go further, because I'm not inhibited by the rigors of a legal investigation. Ignatiew's findings are a shock to me for reasons I didn't anticipate: they show how universal the tendency to lie is in this case.

Ignatiew must have disqualified many eyewitnesses as unreliable. I'm not talking about inaccuracies related to some, even essential, details—even a person with an excellent memory can make a mistake—but fabrication, lies.

My anti-Semitic interlocutors did a lot of shouting about kosher newspapers and Jews denouncing Poles to the NKVD, but seldom did they bother to tell clearly fabricated stories. In the testimonies for the prosecution about July 10, 1941, in Jedwabne, they tell bald-faced lies. In these stories, the streets of Jedwabne were seething with Germans.

According to Halina Czarzasta of Kajetanów there was talk before July 10 of a petition that the Jews made to the police requesting guns so they could settle scores with the Poles. On the day of the massacre she herself set off for Jedwabne, where she saw a group of Jews carrying the bust of Lenin on the road to the cemetery, followed by a dark green military car escorted by German soldiers on foot and a few Polish civilians to the side, one with a stick. She heard many single shots.

According to Stefan Boczkowski from near Jedwabne (who told the same story in many interviews), when the Jews were herded to the barn two or three military trucks filled with uniformed Germans pulled up. They unloaded metal containers from the trucks and set the barn on fire.

According to Teodor Lusiński of Jedwabne (who also put on a good show for the press) a jeep drove into town at 4:00 a.m. along with eight trucks covered with tarpaulins, each carrying uniformed Germans with guns. At 4:00 p.m. this witness heard orders given in German through a megaphone that the Jews were to stand in rows of four. He saw men carrying the Lenin bust enter the cemetery, where at a German command the Jews lay down side by side, lifted their top garments to bare their chests, and proceeded to kill one another using bayonets that were handed to them. At night he heard a sequence of shots. Later he learned that the surviving Jews had tried to pray at the burnt barn and the German guard fired at them.

According to Jadwiga Kordas from near Jedwabne, two trucks drove slowly across the marketplace at about noon with armed policemen from a special unit—a "death squad." The Germans shot at Jews fleeing the market and later from the burning barn. The next day when the witness returned to Jedwabne, it was already being said that only Jews who had collaborated with the Soviets and their families had been killed. The Jewish doctor who treated the witness declared that the burned Jewish Communists deserved what they got because under the Soviet occupation they'd used the Jewish temple as a toilet.

Tadeusz Święszkowski from Grądy Małe saw two military trucks with tarps coming. He wasn't at the barn. In the afternoon he went to Kajetanów to visit his uncle, so he only saw the smoke from a distance. Later he heard that three hundred Jews had been rounded up in the marketplace of whom half escaped, thanks to the help of Poles among others.

Tadeusz Święszkowski is my Tadeusz Ś., the retired Warsaw doctor whom Adam Michnik and I met in August 2000 and who refused to have his name printed. In the version he gave us, he saw two Gestapo officers on motorcycles coming into town. He himself followed behind the Jews and saw three Germans driving about a thousand Jews into the barn.

Ignatiew summarizes the reliability of witnesses in a few sentences. He counts among the unreliable witnesses those referred to by Strzembosz, including Tadeusz Święszkowski.

I read a list of objects retrieved from the ashes during the exhumation: keys, hundreds of kopeck coins used under the Soviet occupation, silver coins and gold coins, one with Piłsudski's profile, dental bridges and crowns, seventeen gold wedding bands, three seals, earrings, medallions, brooches, plastic and metal buttons, rings, a bracelet, necklaces, watches, a gold-colored pendant in the shape of an open book with Hebrew writing, a tallit pin, bent spoons (used to weed grass in the marketplace), metal shoe caps and rubber soles, cape hooks, a zipper tab, a safety pin, trouser buckles and suspender clasps, snaps, eyeglasses, a metal box with shoemaker's nails, a sewing machine drum, a thimble.

JULY 10, 2004

I lay a rock on the monument to the murdered. A bus came from the Jewish community in Warsaw and kaddish was said. I don't think anyone from Jedwabne came.

15

Strictly Speaking, Poles Did It

or, A Conversation with
Prosecutor Radosław Ignatiew

You wrote in your ruling, summing up the results of the investigation into the crime of July 10, 1941: "At dawn inhabitants of the surrounding villages began to arrive in Jedwabne with the intention of carrying out the plan made earlier to kill the Jewish inhabitants . . ." That first sentence is really enough, you could leave it there. I don't think I'd dare to formulate it so categorically. What is it that makes you so sure?

At the time of the exhumation many valuable objects were found in the graves: watches, jewelry, gold rubles. It would have been no problem to take them from the Jews standing in the market square and leave town. In Jedwabne the looting didn't start until the barn was set on fire. That's why I assume people came to town to kill.

You say, "The perpetrators of the crime, strictly speaking, were the Polish inhabitants of Jedwabne and its surroundings—a group of at least forty men . . . They actively participated in committing the crime, armed with sticks, crow bars, and other tools." Let us try to trace how you came to the description you gave of the atrocity in your final findings. You read Gross's book . . .

It was the very beginning of our tenure at the prosecutor's office of the Białystok Institute of National Remembrance. I was the prosecutor, clerk, storekeeper, chauffeur, and even the cleaner; I went around dusting after hours so that the two rooms we'd been assigned would look decent.

Anna Bikont and the prosecutor Radosław Ignatiew of the Institute of National Remembrance. In front of Stanisław Ramotowski's house in Dziewięcin, near Radziłów, 2001. (Photograph © Krzysztof Miller / Agencja Gazeta)

It was my first case at the Institute of National Remembrance. Gross's book did not make for easy reading, it aroused opposition, denial. I was raised in a patriotic tradition. I'd heard of the wartime blackmailers of Jews, *szmalcowniks*, but I felt an inner resistance to believing that Poles had murdered Jews. Yet it didn't take me long to realize that a prosecutor is above all an investigative officer who should rely on the established evidence, setting aside his own convictions.

When did you first realize that the story Gross told had really happened?

That wasn't the goal of my investigation. I wasn't concerned with whether Gross's book was good or bad, true or false, though I was often asked questions like that.

All right. Professor Strzembosz read the trial documents from 1949 and saw in them a manipulated Stalinist investigation in the course of which many innocent people were convicted. And you, did you see something different?

It was immediately clear to me that the proceedings of 1949 were conducted improperly.

But the conclusions you drew were different from those of Strzembosz.

They hadn't even tried to determine the personal details and number of victims, the precise course of events. Witnesses gave the names of many of the perpetrators, but the court wasn't interested. In that trial, twenty-two locals were accused of having participated in bringing Jews to the marketplace and then leading them in a procession to the barn, on the Germans' initiative. That was it. Despite the fact that it was obvious from witness statements that some of the perpetrators had participated directly in acts of murder. It was terrifying, what you could learn from the trial evidence—how carefully the crime was organized: one group drove the victims from their homes, others blocked off the roads leading out of town, a third group guarded those gathered in the market square.

Those were Stalinist times, young Home Army soldiers were being condemned to death, and here were obvious killers being cleared. You can't tell from the case documents why some were convicted and others were released. Do you think they released the ones who agreed to collaborate with the secret police?

More people were arrested than were later charged in the trial. In the monitoring and investigative documents of the Łomża secret police, you can find information about a person being charged, and then that person is not mentioned in the accusation either as a defendant or as a witness. In the case of one of the men suspected of participating in the atrocity, we found evidence of his having signed an agreement to collaborate with the secret police.

Historians and journalists liked to refer to prosecutor Monkiewicz's findings from the 1970s.

I don't want to comment on that investigation. It makes me uncomfortable.

Please try, it's very important. Monkiewicz stated that a unit of 232 Germans led by Wolfgang Birkner arrived in Jedwabne on trucks on July 10, 1941.

There is no indication that the operational group led by Birkner, which was then near Białystok, retreated eighty kilometers. Especially in a situation when the Germans had so many unsecured areas in front of them. It's a supposition produced out of thin air, without the support of any data. The prosecutor assumed the perpetrators of the crime were Germans. But if it was the Germans, which Germans? Apart from Birkner's command, there were local policemen there, of course. In the conclusion, he indicated the surnames of policemen from Jedwabne remembered by witnesses. That conclusion about Birkner and the policemen was passed on to the German authorities for criminal prosecution, to help them find the culprits. What Monkiewicz sent to the German investigators returned to Poland like a boomerang: people here could say the Germans did it, because it's in the German files.

Monkiewicz himself now speaks about the guidelines he'd received from the Main Commission for the Investigation of Nazi Crimes, that he was to prosecute only German criminals. Was the investigation set in motion with the express purpose of erasing traces of Polish participation in the crime?

What I can say for sure is that the investigation was badly conducted. The 1949 trial fulfilled the basic principle of an honest trial, because no one was convicted who wasn't guilty, though not all the men accused of participating had charges brought against them.

The second investigation led by Monkiewicz took almost eight years, from 1967 to 1974. In all that time nothing was done beyond the interrogation of sixteen witnesses. They didn't re-create the course of events, there are no indications at all that any use was made of the criminal trials of 1949 and 1953.

At the same time, Monkiewicz conducted a parallel investigation into the crimes committed by the police in Jedwabne. During those proceedings someone gave testimony that on the day that people were burned one of the residents of the village Korytki was very active in herding the Jewish population into the Jedwabne market square. The man accused was summoned and interrogated as a witness. But they only asked him about the circumstances of the killing of members of his family in 1943 by the Germans!

Reading those documents I thought that as an official in the employ of the Polish state and in view of the memory of those murdered I would do everything within my power to conduct the next investigation properly. Unfortunately, we didn't manage to determine if there were living perpetrators of the crime who had not yet stood trial. That meant criminal proceedings were dismissed. But Institute of National Remembrance prosecution investigations also have the goal of revealing the fullest possible truth about the circumstances of the crimes being studied. I really put enormous effort into finding as much information about the crime committed in Jedwabne as possible. It was important to me to determine the names of the murder victims, so that they wouldn't remain anonymous. Sadly, I only managed to find some of those names.

During the time you were conducting the case, there were several false alarms sounded in the press—ammunition shells being found in the barn, so the Germans had done it . . .

After the press had been told that shells had been found near the site of the crime, witnesses started testifying that they'd heard shots. Before that I'd only found one such statement.

In March 2001 you launched the next investigation, into Radziłów. I knew from interviews with witnesses that after the war there had also been trials "for the Jews" there. I gave you the names of the defendants, the only way to find the cases and the place where the trials took place—Ełk. Before that no one suspected there had been trials anywhere but Jedwabne.

A portion of the documents from the postwar trial survived thanks to the director of the state archive in Ełk, a born archivist. He told me that in the early sixties an order was conveyed to him to lose, which is to say destroy, all archival documents on cases related to the August decree ("on the punishments of Fascist and Nazi criminals . . . and traitors to the Polish Nation"), leaving only a select few. The man described how he'd gone to the prosecutors he knew, saying to them, "I'll give you a stamp to confirm you destroyed them, and you put away those documents on some high shelf." He phoned people outside of Ełk, but they didn't know him or trust him, and they destroyed the documents. A few years later a new decision gave them permission to preserve those documents. We don't know what percentage of documents relating to criminal cases was destroyed. Questions of the culpability of certain persons were switched to separate proceedings, but we didn't find the documents for those cases. Trial procedure dictates that we give the suspects the benefit of the doubt, and so we had to assume that although we were unable to find the documents, the people who were charged at the time had been tried.

The witnesses, Father Orłowski among them, speak of German units, motorcycles, trucks, shooting. This is openly mocking the murdered, isn't it? What do you feel, when you listen to that kind of nonsense?

I never assume that witnesses are mocking or consciously giving false testimony.

Sure, because then you'd have to call a whole lot of witnesses to account for giving false testimony. Father Orłowski above all.

I don't think Father Orłowski or other interviewees consciously gave false testimony. If witnesses, having heard something about cartridge cases being found, tell me about shooting, that may mean that they put together new information from the media with the foggy image of the events that took place sixty years ago, and they're truly convinced they heard that shooting.

Every testimony, even from a person who has preserved a distorted image of the events, contributes something, especially if you follow up with questions about concrete details. For example, it may help us to exclude certain scenarios. I questioned the interviewees about how the Germans they saw on the day of the crime looked. Black service uniforms and saddle-shaped caps, khaki field uniforms with helmets, SA uniforms, air force uniforms, pistols in holsters or the aimed barrels of machine guns—I got a cross section of every army unit, including ones seen in movies. I heard about single shots, multiple shots, barrages from machine guns. Some saw uniformed Germans at the barn and only them, not a single Pole, because they were all hiding in terror. Or they saw Germans jumping off trucks. I heard that people were only killed in those Jewish families whose family members were accused of actively supporting the Communist system, and that the German commander who refused to burn Poles, Jews, and Russians together in the barn was shot by the SS. Others saw only Poles committing crimes.

I rely on the existing knowledge but also, to a great extent, on intuition. I pay attention to unconscious digressions, in other contexts, which often say more than a whole long conversation about a particular subject. How do you eliminate unreliable witnesses?

I ask a lot of questions that may seem to have no connection with the case or to be off subject. They best allow one to judge the reliability of a witness, at least whether he really was where he says he was and could have seen everything he testified to seeing. One of the witnesses, when asked about how the Jews were killed, stated that he was hiding by the market square and heard German soldiers shooting. In a neutral context I asked him about any sounds he might have heard that day. He hadn't heard any. I also checked what texts about Jedwabne the interviewees had read. In a sixty-year-old case, that sort of pollution of memory by reading is very significant. It was evident that some of the witness accounts dealt in information derived from the media, which presented various views on the subject of the course of the crime and the culprits. For example, a witness tells me he saw seventy-five Jews carrying the Lenin monument. I ask him how he knows there were seventy-five. Because he heard them being counted one by one. But that's a number Gross cited from Wasersztejn, and no one confirms it. I felt it was manna from heaven whenever I met a witness who hadn't read Gross's book or any other publication.

The witness accounts are so different from one another that there was no way of verifying one account only with the aid of other accounts. I also verified them by relying on so-called material evidence, that is, facts determined by exhumations, documents and materials from archives, examination of the terrain, study of cartridge cases. Material evidence doesn't lie, so if a witness's claims are contradicted by it, I had to assume the person didn't remember or was mistaken.

And what about the reliability of Jewish witness accounts? What do you think of Szmul Wasersztejn's testimony?

Wasersztejn reconstructed the course of events of the atrocity, but in some places his testimony is also unreliable. I think some of the scenes described in Jewish memoirs, both Wasersztejn's and in the *Jedwabne Book of Memory*—killers using saws, casting children into the fire with forks, using a girl's head as a football—did not actually take place. Maybe someone kicked a head, I can't exclude that possibility, but the scene of a soccer match with a victim's head doesn't seem plausible to me. These events were so terrible that their description by the victims' families often takes on a mythologized form.

So let's reconstruct what can be known.

From the early hours of the morning, Jews were driven from their homes out into the market square. They were ordered to pull up the grass from between the paving stones. The residents of Jedwabne and its surroundings were armed with sticks, crow bars, and other weapons. A large group of men was forced to smash the Lenin monument, which was in a little square off the market. Around noon they were ordered to carry a piece of the smashed monument to the market square, and then to the barn a few hundred meters away. They carried it on two wooden poles. The rabbi was among them. Victims were killed and their bodies were thrown into a grave dug inside the barn. Pieces of the Lenin monument were flung on top of the corpses. The grave was probably not covered, because at the time of the exhumation they found burn marks on some of the pieces of the monument. The second, larger group of Jews was brought out to the market square later. It included women, children, old people. They were led to the thatched wooden barn. The building had gas poured on it, probably gas from the former Soviet storehouse in Jedwabne. In the case documents from 1949, Antoni Niebrzydowski stated that he gave out eight liters of gas from that storehouse. That quantity was enough to set the barn on fire.

Does that mean that the people in the second group saw the massacred bodies of their fathers, brothers, and sons before meeting their own deaths?

It's possible.

Did you ascertain what the last walk of the Jews of Jedwabne was like? Did they know they were going to their deaths?

Quotidian objects were found with the remains, like a box with shoemaker's nails, tailor's thimbles, spoons, gold coins, and a surprising number of keys: to gates, houses, padlocks, cabinets. As if they had the illusory hope that they were setting off on a path from which they'd return one day.

How many Jews were killed on July 10, 1941, in Jedwabne? You write that not fewer than 340 people were murdered. Didn't more than that die?

Not more than a few hundred. The number of sixteen hundred victims or something near that appears improbable. I asked all the witnesses about it and one of them had a convincing answer: "After the war I served in a unit, we had a roll call of about five or six hundred soldiers—and I associate that visually with the number of Jews I saw when they were led out of the market." There were forty or fifty in the group carrying fragments of the Lenin monument; in the second group—several hundred, we can say no fewer than three hundred. That is the approximate number of victims found in the two open graves. But no work has been done at the Jewish cemetery. There are reasons to believe there might be another grave there. If someone killed a man in his basement or garden, he wouldn't have buried him in his own backyard, by his own well. Rather, as there was a Jewish cemetery, they had to have organized transportation of the bodies and have buried them there. I can't exclude the possibility that there are single graves somewhere. We probably didn't find all the places where victims were buried. But even with earlier killings in other places, it's hard to imagine there were more people killed separately than there were burned later in the barn.

There's also no way to accurately estimate the number of victims, because on the day of the atrocity there were Jews from surrounding villages—Wizna, Kolno—hiding in Jedwabne. Some Jews, perhaps several dozen, survived. The majority of them later lived in the ghetto in Jedwabne, a place separated off from the Old Market. From there they went to the Łomża ghetto, but not all of them. One of the witnesses said he'd seen a group of Jews from Jedwabne passing by Jerziorko, outside Łomża, after the atrocity. That witness's father, a farmer, had a Jewish intermediary in the grain trade, in Jedwabne. And that man turned up at the witness's house with his twelve-year-old daughter to ask him to hide them. The girl said Christian prayers to prove she could pass for Polish. The witness's family had to refuse for fear of being denounced by a neighbor.

In Jedwabne and its surroundings I looked for an example of a Pole punished by the Germans for not having taken part in the killing—it would be proof that some had acted under duress. I didn't find any.

I don't know of any such example, either.

So can you speak of an order, if there was no sanction for not carrying it out?

There was no need for any sanction, because there were people who eagerly set about hunting Jews. It could have been a vague order, that you're to do something with the Jews, which is not an order as I understand it. Such orders might have been given in accordance with SS general and Nazi police chief Reinhard Heydrich's directive as formulated in two documents toward the end of June and the beginning of July 1941. In an appendix added at the end of June 1941, Heydrich stated that anti-Communist and anti-Jewish actions should be provoked on newly occupied lands, but in a way that would leave no trace of German involvement. On the other hand, an order given to the leaders of operational groups on July 1, 1941, concerned the principles for carrying out "cleansing actions" meant to "pacify" the areas occupied by the Germans. It speaks of not including Polish groups with an anti-Communist or anti-Jewish bent in those actions. Or not to harm them, because they could be used to harm others in the future.

In other words, the Germans' role was to egg on the local population?

What does egging on mean? If there hadn't been conditions for the perpetration of a crime like that, no amount of egging on would have had any effect. We know of German reports from areas farther north expressing dissatisfaction that the local population couldn't be incited to anti-Jewish excesses. It's undeniable that there had been actions against Jews in the Łomża district before the war, and it seems to me that the Germans took advantage of the strong anti-Semitic feeling that already existed there.

But can we determine whether the Germans put forward the idea "to clean up the Jews like they did in Radziłów," or merely accepted and supported the tendencies of the locals, expressed by the town authorities?

I wasn't able to determine that. As a prosecutor I'm not going to enter into the realm of speculation. I have too little information, and for that reason some circumstances were never clarified. The crime in Jedwabne was committed at the instigation of the Germans. It's not possible that an action on that scale happened without German acceptance. You have to keep in mind that Jedwabne was just behind the front line, in an area under German military administration. In the event of unexpected sui generis unrest in the town, the occupation forces would have reacted immediately. The presence, even passive, of German policemen from the station in Jedwabne, as well as other uniformed Germans—if we accept they were there—is in the eye of the law equivalent to permission to commit the crime. So the Germans should be ascribed criminal responsibility in the broader sense.

Many witnesses say the locals who drove Jews into the square were accompanied by some uniformed Germans, apart from those from the police station. It was certainly a small group, not a powerful unit. The Germans had too many towns to guard, locations where they wanted to "clean up the Jews." We have German reports of that time that express alarm: 'We don't have anyone to man the posts.' Suddenly, the police in nearby Szczuczyn, five men, were supposed to keep order in seventy-four towns. The rapid advance into the Soviet Union meant that units of Einsatzgruppe B in the zone of army unit "Środek" were operating farther and farther east. They left behind them lands where they hadn't used the opportunity to "clean up." To take care of this, the Germans organized a few small operational groups toward the end of June and beginning of July to take over the tasks of Einsatzgruppe B in the area of former Soviet borderlands.

I can state that the perpetrators of the atrocity were Polish residents of Jedwabne and its surroundings, at least forty men. There is no proof that the townspeople in general were the perpetrators. To claim that there was a company of Germans in Jedwabne is as implausible as maintaining the whole town went crazy. Most people behaved passively. I can't judge where that passivity came from. Maybe some people felt compassion for the victims but were terrified by the brutality of the killers. Others, though they may have had anti-Semitic views, were not people quick to take an active part in actions of this kind.

A few hundred burned in the barn, forty killers—that's a lot fewer than Gross wrote.

Those are our findings. The number of victims and culprits indicated emerges from analysis of the evidence. We were unable to come to a fuller count; in the trial documents from 1949, for example, there are the names of a significantly larger number of people connected to the committing of the crime. Only that information was not checked at the time. Now, after so much time has passed, it was impossible for my team to verify it.

You were born in Białystok; you live not far from there in Łapy. Jewish life used to flourish in the towns in your area. Did you know about that before you got involved in the Jedwabne case?

No, I was never interested.

Jews were like aborigines to you?

The concept was just as remote. From the time I worked on the investigation into Jedwabne I read a lot of material, books on the history and relations of Poles and Jews. But even so I don't always know how to behave. I met Rabbi Schudrich and another rabbi from London at the Jewish cemetery in Jedwabne. When they said kaddish for the dead, I was going to say the Catholic prayer Eternal Rest, but on reflection I just said goodbye.

Before I began working on Jedwabne, I had the feeling anti-Semitism was a marginal phenomenon. Since I've been involved with Jedwabne, I meet it every day. You, too?

I believe— I'm convinced it's not a universal sentiment. But I have to say in the course of the investigation I encountered blatant expressions of anti-Semitism.

What was for you the most difficult moment in the investigation?

When I saw the tooth buds of infants during the exhumations and imagined for a moment what I would feel if someone from my family had died that way, if those had been my children.

Acknowledgments

I thank the heroes of my book, who agreed to return to their darkest memories.

ı I thank all those who helped me, by taking me in as I wandered in search of witnesses and documents, by reading my manuscript, and simply by offering support at the difficult time in my life when I was working on this book.

Special thanks are due to Joanna Szczęsna, who edited the book at each successive stage of its composition.

I would also like to mention my friends in America. I didn't take it very well when well-meaning acquaintances (and less well-meaning strangers) discouraged me from writing a book on the crime in Jedwabne, and that is why the first version was written in cafés in Manhattan, and—thanks to the benevolence of Lawrence Weschler—in a guest room at the New York Institute for the Humanities at NYU and in the office of Professor Marta Petrusewicz at CUNY. During that time I was hosted by Ann Snitow and Daniel Goode, Joanna and Lawrence Weschler, Anna Husarska, Sławomir Grunberg, Irena Grudzińska-Gross, and Ewa Zadrzyńska.

I will cherish in grateful memory the creator of the website www.radzilow.com, Jose Gutstein of Miami, who agreed to the publication of prewar photographs of the people of Radziłów, and also the late Rabbi Jacob Baker of Brooklyn, who gave his consent for the publication of photographs and maps of prewar Jedwabne.

I lack words to thank my American translator, Alissa Valles, for her brilliant work. I also express my gratitude and admiration for my editor at Farrar, Straus and Giroux, Ileene Smith. I'm deeply honored by the amount of time, heart, and skill Alissa and Ileene invested in my book. Working with FSG, in every department I dealt with, was a happy adventure all the way. I remain in grateful debt to all of these people.

Index

Page numbers in *italics* refer to illustrations.

A Note About the Author

Anna Bikont is a journalist for the *Gazeta Wyborcza*, Poland's main newspaper, which she helped found in 1989. For her articles on the crimes in Jedwabne and nearby Radziłów, she was honored with several awards, including the Press Prize for reportage in 2001 and the Polityka Prize for historical writing. In 2011 she received the European Book Prize for the French edition of *The Crime and the Silence*. In 2008–2009, Bikont was a fellow at the Cullman Center of the New York Public Library.

A Note About the Translator

Alissa Valles is the author of *Orphan Fire* and the editor and cotranslator of Zbigniew Herbert's *Collected Poems: 1956–1998* and *The Collected Prose: 1948–1998*.

Printed in the USA
CPSIA information can be obtained
at www.ICGtesting.com
LVHW040729150724
785511LV00002B/221